CAPTAINS' LOGS

THE UNAUTHORIZED COMPLETE TREK VOYAGES

Edward Gross and Mark A. Altman

LITTLE, BROWN AND COMPANY
Boston New York Toronto London

• • • •

Acknowledgements

For taking the time to be interviewed over the years for this book, we'd like to thank the following people in their "order of appearance": Robert Justman, Joseph Stefano, Jerry Sohl, James Burns, Dorothy Fontana, Oscar Katz, Leonard Nimoy, Robert Butler, Stephen Kandel, William Shatner, James Goldstone, Samuel Peeples, James Doohan, George Takei, DeForest Kelley, Nichelle Nichols, John D.F. Black, Joseph Pevney, Marc Daniels, Harve Bennett, Glen Larson, David Gerrold, Steven Carabatsos, George Clayton Johnson, Gary Lockwood, Adrian Spies, Vincent McEveety, Joseph Sargent, Paul Schneider, Oliver Crawford, Michael O'Herlihy, Carey Wilbur, Ricardo Montalban, Ralph Senensky, Lester Colodny, Walter Koenig, Norman Spinrad, William Campbell, John Meredyth Lucas, Jackie Fernandez, Gilbert Ralston, Jerome Bixby, David P. Harmon, Art Wallace, Margaret Armen, James Komack, Fred Freiberger, Judy Burns, Arthur Heinemann, Richard Colla, Jon Povill, Allan Scott, Robert Goodwin, Harold Livingston, Joseph Jennings, Bob Collins, David Gautreaux, Larry Alexander, Worley Thorne, Robert Wise, Alan Dean Foster, Dennis Clark, Robert Sallin, Mike Minor, Jack Sowards, Nicholas Meyer, Robin Curtis, Steve Meerson, Peter Krikes, David Loughery, Ralph Winter, Mark Rosenthal, Dennis Martin Flinn, Cliff Eidelman, Steven Charles Jaffe, Kim Cattrall, Rick Berman, Michael Dorn, Bob Lewin, Herman Zimmerman, Jonathan Frakes, Herb Wright, Corey Allen, Paul Lynch, Maurice Hurley, Katharyn Powers, Michael Baron, Richard Krzemien, Michael Reaves, Rob Bowman, Cliff Bole, Patrick Stewart, Tracy Torme, Joseph Scanlan, Hannah Louise Shearer, Gates McFadden, Marina Sirtis, Melinda Snodgrass, Dennis Russell Bailey, Winrich Kolbe, Robert Scheerer, Robert Iscove, David Livingston, Les Landau, Michael Piller, Ira Steven Behr, Ron Moore, Peter Alan Fields, David Carson, Timothy Bond, Chip Chalmers, Jennifer Hetrick, Lisa Wilke, David Bischoff, Susan Sackett, Elizabeth Dennehy, Jeri Taylor, Larry Carroll, David Carren, Marc Scott Zicree, Rob Legato, Andreas Katsulas, Colm Meaney, Brannon Braga, Marvin Rush, Brent Spiner, Michelle Forbes, Grant Rosenberg, Patti Yatskue, Avery Brooks, Rene Auberjonois, Siddig El Fadil, Terry Farrell, Armin Shimerman, Nana Visitor, Bob Blackman, Malcolm McDowell, Bernie Williams, Kate Mulgrew, Tim Russ, Robert Beltran, Robert Duncan McNeill, Garrett Wang, Robert Picardo, Roxann Biggs-Dawson, Jennifer Lien and Ethan Phillips. Special thanks to Mark Chimsky and Andy Ward, and our agents Linda Chester and Lori Fox.

• • • •

Book design by Paul Nicosia

• • • •

First Little, Brown Edition

This publication has not been prepared, approved or licensed by any entity that creates or approves STAR TREK, nor is it affiliated with Paramount Pictures. This is a scholarly work intended to explore the evolution of STAR TREK over the last 30 years.

Parts of this book have been previously published under the titles CAPTAIN'S LOGS and CAPTAIN'S LOGS SUPPLEMENTAL.

10 9 8 7 6 5 4 3 2 1

Published simultaneously in Canada by Little, Brown & Company (Canada) Limited

Printed in the United States of America

••CONTENTS••

• • • •

CAPTAINS' LOGS: AN INTRODUCTION

*C*aptains' Logs is the definitive chronicling of the voyages of the Starship Enterprise and in many ways this tome is written as much for us as the many readers who will hopefully keep dog-eared copies on their shelves for many years to come.

The fact is there never has been a book like *Captains' Logs*, nor has anything approximating a compendium of this sort ever been assembled. Books have dealt with the *Star Trek* mythos in their separate component parts: *Trek '66* (or *Trek Classic*, as it's fondly, if not reverently, referred to), the so-called *Lost Years, Star Trek: Animated*, the Movies and, of course, *The Next Generation*.

Our feeling, though, was that *Star Trek* is a single universe with continuity stretching from the original series through its latest incarnation, *Voyager*. So why hasn't anyone ever conceived of a book that would trace every mission of the Enterprise and beyond? Quite frankly, it was a book we were dying to read and since no one else had done it, we decided it was up to us to do so. We've compiled many years worth of research, covering every episode of every *Star Trek* series. Although you won't find any of the comics or novels here, this book does feature the animated series, which have stirred debate among *Trek* scholars concerning its relevancy as part of the official canon. We have decided to allow our readers to make that determination. While we don't go into depth regarding the animated series, we nonetheless provide a complete list of credits and episode summaries.

We have compiled reams of interview transcripts and research done over the course of a decade regarding the *Star Trek* phenomena, and both authors have been frustrated by their material turning up edited, abridged or plagiarized in other volumes and magazines dealing with the subject. Rather than paraphrase or read attributed copy, you will find the creators and cast of *Trek* speaking in their own words as taken directly from the authors' taped transcripts, about every trek through the 23rd and 24th centuries. Brief synopses are provided, but what lies at the heart of this book are the candid behind-the-scenes anecdotes and recollections of the makers of *Trek*. It's not only a glimpse into the hallowed halls of the creation of *Trek*, but an insightful look into the creative mind and the business of producing for both mediums as well as an exploration of what may very well be the most important products of 20th century pop culture.

Together, the authors have assembled the ultimate *Trek* guidebook, following the missions of Kirk & Company for three years on NBC, through the most recent adventures of Captain Kathryn Janeway and the crew of the starship Voyager. We hope you enjoy reading this book as much as we enjoyed writing it.

Happy voyages!

Mark A. Altman
Edward Gross
September 1995

••••

CHAPTER ONE
The Trek Begins

It's been nearly three decades since the premiere of *Star Trek* on NBC and this show continues to fascinate us today. While many proponents of *The Next Generation* have decried the original show as "hokey" and "irrelevant", they fail to acknowledge that the series has entrenched itself as part of our cultural mythology and that without it there would be *no Star Trek: The Next Generation..*

Kirk, Spock and McCoy are as familiar to most Americans as Washington, Jefferson and Benjamin Franklin. And while the American manned space program has grown mired in entropy and most of today's school-children couldn't name the three astronauts who first set down on the lunar surface, these three fictional pioneers of the cosmos are revered not only by dedicated *Trek* fans, but by casual media watchers as well. *Star Trek* trivia can be found everywhere, ranging from Trivial Pursuit to *Jeopardy*, and more stand-up comedians have tried their hand at parodying William Shatner's gesticulating, staccato recitations of galactic law as Captain Kirk than they have most Presidents.

In fact, *Star Trek* lingo has popped up almost everywhere. The first Space Shuttle was renamed after the show's starship, the Enterprise; William Shatner spoofed his heroic Hornblower image in *Airplane II: The Sequel* and on *Saturday Night Live*; and such terms as "Beam Me Up, Scotty" and "energize" have appeared on T-shirts and become a part of the drug subculture often associated with crack-cocaine. Just say "He's Dead, Jim".

Since the original show's five year mission was abruptly canceled after three seasons on NBC, *Star Trek* has risen like the proverbial phoenix from the ashes throughout the subsequent decades, leaving those reports of its death, like those of its literary antecedent Samuel Clemens, to be greatly exaggerated. Fans' devoted ardor has built upon the foundation of the first 79 cherished episodes, spawning a diverse array of products, ranging from homemade uniforms and costumes to homoerotic literature featuring liaisons between the original series' Captain Kirk and its alien Vulcan science officer, Mr. Spock.

In fact, although *Star Trek* is slowly disappearing from the airwaves to be replaced by its progeny, *The Next Generation*, in syndication, the show holds up remarkably well today. While some of the special effects and sets may look primitive, the stories are just as relevant and the characters no less compelling than they were in 1966.

Despite the vastly larger budgets of TNG, *Deep Space Nine* and the *Star Trek* features, the original *Star Trek* still plays extraordinarily well today because of the passion that is inherent in the show as instilled by its writers, producers and actors. Remarkably, the successors to the original show have carried on the tradition established by *Star Trek*'s original three year run and expanded upon many of the characters and storylines conveyed in such episodes as "Space Seed" (Khan in *Star Trek II*), "The Doomsday Machine" (Will Decker in *Star Trek: The Motion Picture* was the son of Commodore Matt Decker), "Journey To Babel" (Sarek returned as an aging diplomat in TNG'S "Sarek"), "The Naked Time" (remade as TNG's "Naked Now") "Amok Time" (*STIII* reflected the seven year Vulcan mating cycle established here) and "Mirror, Mirror" (sequelized on DS9's "Crossover"). Other mediums have also continued the voyages with novels from Pocket sequelizing "All Our Yesterdays" and "City on the Edge Of Forever" and DC Comics presenting remarkable follow-ups to "Mirror, Mirror" and "The Savage Curtain" / "Errand of Mercy."

For those who would quibble over whether the original show, TNG, *Deep Space Nine* or *Voyager* is better, they're missing the point. All three shows are a triumph for televised science-fiction, proving that intelligent, thought provoking, character driven speculative fiction can be brought to the screen without catering to the so-called lowest common denominator.

Few, if any, science-fiction shows have reached the level of critical or popular recognition that *Star Trek* achieved and when one reflects back on the first five year voyage of the Starship Enterprise, it's hard not to understand why today we refer to those three years of maiden missions as *Trek Classic*.

Yet despite the phenomenal success of *Star Trek*, science-fiction has been unable to find a home on network television, with such rare exceptions as *Beauty and the Beast* and *Quantum Leap*. Things do seem to be on the verge of changing, however, as witnessed by the debut of the Sci-Fi Channel on cable television systems around the country, such current genre fare as *Highlander*, William Shatner's *TekWar*, Steven Spielberg's *SeaQuest* and *The X-Files*. Not to mention, naturally, *Deep Space Nine* or *Voyager*.

A distinct possibility for the failure of SF-TV in the past could very well be that the network executives couldn't understand the basic essence of a particular genre show, or they deemed it to be above the heads of the average television viewer.

"Too cerebral, and that's a direct quote," explains veteran producer Robert Justman, regarding the original *Star Trek*'s first—and rejected—pilot, "The Cage." Such a statement seems indicative of network opposition to the genre in those days as well as the present. "NBC's reasoning was that the show seemed to be 'too intellectual' and they wanted something that was more akin to action/adventure."

This hardly seems surprising when considering the time frame being discussed: the early 1960s. Up until that point, and with few exceptions, science fiction on television had consisted primarily of such programming as *Captain Video*, *Sky King* and *Rocky Jones*; entertaining series devoid of intellectual substance. Essentially they were *safe* shows, and that was alright with—indeed, preferred by—the networks. Certainly there were more innovative writer-producers out there who recognized all that the medium could be if given the opportunity to truly create. The executives, however, seemed to believe that those rare individuals could be held down and beaten back, their creativity suppressed. For the most part, they were right, but amidst

••••

Rod Serling's The Twilight Zone *was an early forerunner of* Star Trek: *using allegory to comment on the world of the day.*

genre mediocrity arose such visionaries as Rod Serling, Leslie Stevens, Joseph Stefano and Gene Roddenberry.

A highly acclaimed writer in television's golden age, Serling had grown frustrated with network censors who would not allow him to deal with the ideas and themes he felt necessary to explore. To counter this opposition, he created *The Twilight Zone*, an anthology with a twist. By couching his stories in a science fiction, horror or fantasy setting, he was able to cover dramatic ground that no one else had been able to.

In the introduction to *The Twilight Zone Companion*, author Marc Scott Zicree writes, "When *The Twilight Zone* debuted in 1959, it was a flower blooming in a television desert, made vacant by an endless number of situation comedies, westerns, and cop shows. To its faithful viewers, *The Twilight Zone* offered far more than empty laughs or a lesson in urban or frontier justice. Instead, at its best, it lived up to the promise of its opening narration, revealing a vista of realities not weighed down by the merely probable. At a time when the rest of television was hammering home the unstated but nonetheless apparent message that the realities and expectations of life were bracketed within very narrow borders, *The Twilight Zone* presented a universe of possibilities and options."

Another series that attempted to

present psychological challenges to the audience was Leslie Stevens and Joseph Stefano's *The Outer Limits*, which was, in a sense, the antithesis of *The Twilight Zone*.

"My approach," explains producer/writer Joseph Stefano, "was to do drama and Gothic horror, with some kind of science fiction element, because I was not a science fiction fan. There wasn't much science fiction that I had seen or read that I liked very much. In a way, I was creating a different form. If you look at *my* science fiction as opposed to what other writers did on the show, you'll see the difference.

"They were really much more Gothic horror tales, and much more scary than the others. After *Psycho*, it was expected of me. But I had certain moralistic rules—if you did any damage to the universe, you had to put it back together again by the conclusion because we were on early and we had children watching. I didn't want to overly scare young people, so we always put the world back together with the control voice at the end."

As he explains it, dealing with the television networks is like dealing with "a two-headed monster. On one hand, they want high ratings, and on the other, there are people who want to safeguard the hearts and minds of viewers and they come from the same source. So, one half of the network is telling you to cut this or that out, and the other half tells you to give them more. I don't think it's as big a problem as it was, because they've determined a time when sex and violence should be on TV. We had very little sex in *The Outer Limits*, and very little violence except in the scary sense, not violence as in shooting eight people. I see no reason to do a cop show."

Robert Justman, who worked on the series as assistant director and had also performed the same function on *The Adventures of Superman*, adds, "In doing *The Outer Limits*, what the network wanted was not necessarily an intelligent science fiction show. What they wanted was a science fiction show that would return a lot of numbers. Their theory was that to do that you had to have a monster in every show. If you're

an intelligent person and you like monsters, no, it wasn't a problem keeping science fiction on the air. But if you're an intelligent person and you don't think it should be monsters to do an intelligent show, yes, it was difficult.

"Somewhat of the same attitude was found in the early days of *Star Trek*," he continues, "when the network suggested what they wanted to open the first season with, 'Man Trap.' It had a monster. We felt that it wasn't a very good show compared to some of the others we had already made. We lost the battle, they won the battle and 'Man Trap' aired first."

Veteran science fiction author Jerry Sohl, whose teleplay credits include *Twilight Zone, Alfred Hitchcock Presents* and *Star Trek*, says of *Outer Limits*, "The thing that I disliked about it is that you had to see the monster of the week right away, and my feeling was that they should have had some shows where you never knew who the monster was or what it was until near the very end. They don't show the murderer in a crime story right off the bat. You have to figure out who it is and that's half the fun. My story was called 'The Yellow Sand,' and it was in *Imaginative Tales* in 1956. It was a story in which they kept sending spaceships to Mars and they never came back. They would have communications from there, but that would eventually stop. In my story they land and one by one the people disappear and there's nothing there but sand. Where did they go? Obviously, you walk on the sand, and these sharks would come along and eat the people. In the episode, right away, as soon as they land, we see these monstrous sharks. That's just dumb. You should have had these people go out to the other spaceships, like they did in *Alien*. What do you do for suspense?"

From that point of view, Stefano offers no apologies. "In all honesty," he explains, "I cannot say that I was unable to do what I wanted with the show. I pretty much had the exact series that I wanted. There were times when the ABC Standards and Practices Department would ask me to delete something, or, in one case, they pointed to a show which was disturbing to them. There was nothing we could do about it—it was just very disturbing."

Unlike other genre shows, *The Outer Limits* was a hit right from the beginning, but ABC proved that it didn't understand what it had on its hands, as they moved the series to Saturday nights, positioning it directly against the formidable *Jackie Gleason Show*. Needless to say, Gleason ran until 1970. *The Outer Limits* didn't, and it was another nail in the coffin of SF-TV, making it that much more difficult for the next show of its type to come along.

"I left at the first season's end because of the schedule change," Stefano admits. "I said to ABC, 'If you move it like that, the show is *dead*. I will not spend 20-hour days producing and writing a show that's going to be killed because of a pointless schedule change.' The series they put in our slot, *Voyage to the Bottom of the Sea*, ran for four years. If they had left *Outer Limits* where it was, it would have gone on for four or five years. I was in such firm disagreement that I *refused* to be involved with a show that was going down the drain, and that's exactly what happened to it. It went half a season and they canceled it." (Interestingly, history would repeat itself several years later when Gene Roddenberry refused to line produce *Star Trek*'s third—and ultimately final—season, citing a similar schedule change.

Jerry Sohl, feeling frustrated, wanted to do something about the lack of true science-fiction on television.

"Theodore Sturgeon, Richard Matheson, George Clayton Johnson and myself got together and formed what we called The Green Hand," he relates, "and we were really going to know television dead by doing really *responsible* science-fiction. Certainly, the medium could stand better material. We wanted script and quality control. We wanted to breathe something new into the shows; bring the medium up to date and in step with what was happening in SF at the time. We thought that at least half of primetime should be devoted to SF and fantasy."

Their initial attempt at fulfilling this dream upon incorporating met with great success in that Herbert F. Solow, in

"My approach was to do drama, Gothic Horror and some kind of science-fiction element," says Joseph Stefano of The Outer Limits.

charge of television production at Paramount when *Star Trek* was produced, believed in them. Then working at MGM, he gave the group an office on the lot and special parking spaces.

"We had *all* the privileges," Sohl smiles, "including eating in the MGM executives' dining room. To top it off, we had our own refrigerator right there in the office, and our own secretary. It was our opinion that science-fiction had come of age, and we immediately met with the executives at CBS, NBC and ABC, and they seemed genuinely impressed. But we learned it wasn't because we were formidable or heavy with talent and experience, or even angry young men with axes to grind. It was simply because they had *never* seen four science-fiction writers all at once, and four writers in such apparent agreement."

During these meetings, The Green Hand pitched a variety of ideas for TV series, including Richard Matheson's *Hunter*, about a cop who, through an accident, develops ESP which he uses to solve crimes; and Theodore Sturgeon's *E.T.*, which dealt with an extraterrestrial trapped on Earth who has difficulties understanding and adjusting to what he finds on this planet.

"Does he fall in love?" asks Sohl rhetorically. "What kind of super powers does he have? How would people adjust to him when they found out that he was an alien? We had a million storylines ready, but the networks rejected both ideas, believing the average viewer wouldn't understand concepts like ESP and extraterrestrials."

Next offered was *Gestalt Team*, a concept which had three astronauts of the future whose special talents have been blended and meshed, and who are trouble-shooters on the rim worlds, battling aliens and the human floatsam and jetsam who try to survive out there by criminal means.

"The network loved it," says Sohl with a laugh. "Positively loved it! But loving it didn't mean underwriting the two-hour feature production at MGM or saving a slot on the fall primetime schedule. They just loved it. That's all. Period. And that was the end of it."

Gestalt Team was followed by *A Touch of Strange*, which would have been a *Twilight Zone*-like anthology telling only pure fantasy stories; and a series idea about an android.

"He was a male android who

Gene Roddenberry, seen here on the set of Genesis II, *saw* Star Trek *as the only means of expressing his honest point of view on television.*

escaped from a secret army base where he was made and was being tracked down by assorted government agencies and forces," Sohl explains. "He was always on the run. He didn't want to return to the factory where he was 'born.' As he moves about the country, he learns something about himself and experiences things like emotions, not the least of which is love. Since he can't harm humans, he is always in a predicament, for people want to kill that which they don't understand, since they're afraid of it. A thousand stories came to our minds, but the networks balked. They felt that people would never buy a million dollar man.

"In the end, they didn't buy *any* of the series we offered. It was too bad for the networks, too bad for The Green Hand and too bad for the viewing public. The corporation was dissolved and the four of us went our separate ways. But the ironic thing is that *all* of our series premises eventually became TV shows in one form or another."

Most notably the android series which not only could be linked to *The Six Million Dollar Man* but more directly to *The Questor Tapes*, a TV pilot co-written and produced by a fellow by the name of Gene Roddenberry.

By 1963, Gene Roddenberry, a former police officer and pilot, had proven his writing abilities on such television series as *Dr. Kildare, Naked City, Mr. District Attorney* and *Highway Patrol*, before heading the writing staff of *Have Gun, Will Travel*. He also began to investigate the possibility of creating his own series by writing such original pilots as *333 Montgomery* (starring DeForest Kelley), a World War II adventure entitled APO-923 and a remake of the Kelley pilot called *Defiance Country*. None of them went to series, though they certainly whet Roddenberry's appetite in terms of becoming a producer.

"These pilots were produced by other people," Roddenberry explained, "and none of them sold. I began to see that to create a program idea and write a script simply wasn't enough. The story is not 'told' until it's on celluloid. Telling that final story involved sound, music, casting, costumes, sets and all the things that a producer is responsible for. Therefore it became apparent to me that if you want the film to reflect accurately what you felt when you wrote the script, then you have to produce it, too. This is why television writers tend to become producers.

"Producing in television is like storytelling," he said. "The choice of the actor, picking the right costumes, getting the right flavor, the right pace—these are as much a part of storytelling as writing out that same description of a character in a novel. Although the director plays an important role in this, the director in television comes on a show to prepare for a week, shoots for a week, and then goes on to another show. Unlike the producer, he is neither there at the beginning of the script, nor rarely there for long after you end up with some 25,000 feet of film which now has to be cut and pasted into something unified. There is immense creative challenge and pleasure in taking all of these things and putting them together into something that works."

"Writing for the television audience," he explained in 1988, "does the same thing as the great sculptors and painters and composers also do. What you do is say to the world, 'Hey, these are things as I see it! These are my comments. This is how I see the world.' And you do this with utter selfishness, which is what an artist should always do. All writers should be selfish and say, 'This is the way that I see it,' and under the voice should say, 'Screw you! If you want yours, you can do it too.'"

It was with this attitude that Roddenberry approached his first television producing assignment: 1963's *The Lieutenant*, which starred Gary Lockwood, who would, incidentally, go on to guest star in *Star Trek*'s second pilot, "Where No Man Has Gone Before." In the series, Lockwood portrayed Lt. William Rice, and the essential thrust was an emphasis on the life of a newly commissioned officer in the Marine Corps during peacetime.

The Lieutenant only lasted 29 episodes, but it was significant for several reasons. First off, it created a working relationship between Roddenberry and a great many people who would eventually work on *Star Trek*, including Leonard Nimoy, Nichelle Nichols, director Marc Daniels, Lockwood, Walter Koenig and director Robert Butler. Additionally, it was during the production of this series that he developed his initial concepts for what would eventually become *Star Trek*.

Roddenberry's interest in science fiction can be traced back to his childhood.

"I was 11 years old," he recalled, "and there was a boy in my class who life had treated badly. He limped, he wheezed, I don't know all the things that were wrong with him, but he was a charming, lovely, intelligent person. He, because of being unable to get on the athletic field and do many of the things that others were able to do, had sort of gone into his own world of fantasy and science fiction. He had been collecting the old *Amazing* and *Astounding* magazines from those great old days and he introduced me to science fiction. I started to read them and then discovered, in our neighborhood, living above a garage was an ex-con who had come into science fiction when he was in prison. He introduced me to John Carter and those wonderful Burroughs things. By the time I was 12 or 13, I had been very much into the whole science fiction field."

Which is not to say that when he got into writing, he saw science fiction as the primary creative vehicle to express himself.

"Although I suppose you could have called me a science fiction fan, this certainly was not the Alpha-Omega of my reading," related Roddenberry, whose first script in the genre was *The Secret Defense of 117*, starring Ricardo Montalban. "I think all writers are omnivorous in their reading. I know few writers that I respect that read only science fiction. Isaac Asimov, for example, I know reads broadly on history, economics, sociology, everything. As a result, when I decided to become a writer, I decided to become a *writer*, not just a science fiction writer."

Like Rod Serling before him, Roddenberry did see science fiction (with *Star Trek* as the particular mode of communication), as an opportunity to explore some of life's "larger" themes, while continuing a tradition of literary creativity begun centuries earlier.

"I had been a freelance writer for about a dozen years and was chafing increasingly at the commercial censorship on television, which was very strong in those days," he's said. "You really couldn't talk about anything you cared to

talk about [and] I decided I was going to leave TV unless I could find some way to write what I wanted to. A writer is an artist who's very job is about opening his mind to things. I recalled that when Jonathan Swift was writing *Gulliver's Travels*, he wanted to write satire on his time and went to Lilliput in his story to do just that, [and] then he could talk about insane prime ministers and crooked kings and all of that. It was sort of this wonderful thing. Children could read it as a fairy tale, an adventure, and as they got older they'd recognize it for what it really is. It seemed to me that perhaps if I wanted to talk about sex, religion, politics, make some comments against Vietnam and so on, that if I had similar situations involving these subjects happening on other planets to little green people, indeed it might get by and it did.

"I apparently went right over the censors' heads, but all the fourteen year olds in our audience knew exactly what we were talking about. Also, I had watched science fiction. I was not a science fiction writer, though. I had written all sorts of things. I had said, 'Gee, too much of science fiction is about gadgetry and not about people. And drama is people. If I ever get the chance to write science fiction, I'm going to try to make it scientifically accurate as possible and write them the way we wrote the old *Playhouse 90s*.' And it worked.I thought that [*Star Trek*] might be a way I could infiltrate my ideas, and that's what it's been all the time. It's difficult for people to understand that even in the barren vineyards of television you might do these things. Actually, you can do them better there because you reach more people with more impact. You don't do it by each of your episodes being a fine *Hallmark Hall of Fame*, or those great shows that are meaningful and deep and advertised as such. The power you have is in a show like *Star Trek*, which is considered by many people to be a frothy little action-adventure; unimportant, unbelievable and yet watched by a lot of people. You just slip ideas into it."

Roddenberry's initial ideas for *Star Trek* concerned a starship of the Federation of Planets whose mission would be to—if you'll pardon the cliche—"explore strange new worlds,

seek out new lives and new civilizations...to boldy go where no man has gone before." Interestingly, many people have expressed their feeling that the concept was heavily influenced by the classic science fiction film, *Forbidden Planet*.

"Definitely not," differed Roddenberry to reporter James Burns in the 1970s. "The only time I ever thought of *Forbidden Planet* specifically when I was laying *Star Trek* out was when I said to myself that here were some mistakes they made in the film that I did not want to repeat. I think one of the obvious mistakes, and one that amazed me when I saw the show, although I generally liked [it], was the fact that you had a ship capable of interstellar travel and you had a cook aboard who scrubbed pots and pans by hand, and I said, 'Hey, come on, it just doesn't fit.' At least they would have had a radar range oven or something if they had interstellar capacity! But, no, I cannot remember a single time during the planning of *Star Trek* that I looked at another show and said, 'I will borrow this.' On the other hand, of course, you have this marvelous thing called a brain that all of your life is storing away information and sometimes you pull it out and say, 'This is Heinlein in such and such.' Or even probably what happens more often is your brain, being the marvelous thing it will, will take bits and pieces from three or four things and then meld them together in something you need for a particular show. Most writers who are good writers, or at least *care*, very seldom borrow things specifically. *Hacks* do that. On the other hand, most good writers do write things where people can go to them and say, 'Ah, this is a bit of this from this and this a bit of that from that,' but they don't write it that way."

Wagon Train To The Stars....

In 1991 the world celebrated *Star Trek*'s 25th Anniversary, but in 1963 its basic premise was unlike anything that had been seen on television before. As stated previously, Gene Roddenberry had developed his initial thoughts for the series while producing *The Lieutenant*. His secretary at the time was Dorothy (D.C.) Fontana, who had aspirations to be a professional writer and would eventually play an important role in the *Star Trek* mythos. As Roddenberry's right hand, she was among the first to see the original series premise.

"He asked me to read it in early 1964," she recalls. "This was the very first *Star Trek* proposal; the series presentation. I read it and said, 'I have only one question, who's going to play Mr. Spock?' He pushed a picture of Leonard Nimoy across the table and I, of course, knew Leonard because he had appeared in my first [sale], *The Tall Man*. I thought the proposal had a lot of possibilities and was certainly exciting. Of course you could never tell if it would sell and if somebody else would believe in it, but I certainly did. The captain at the time was Robert April, who eventually became Christopher Pike and the ship was the Yorktown. Mr. Spock was pretty much like the Mr. Spock that appeared in 'The Cage,' and the doctor was Dr. Boyce. The other characters weren't as settled. Nobody was doing anything like it on television."

Roddenberry's original series presentation, dated March 11, 1964, described *Star Trek* as "a one-hour dramatic television series; action-adventure-science fiction; the first such concept with strong central lead characters plus other continuing regulars...; and while maintaining a familiar central location and regular cast, explores an anthology-like range of exciting human experience."

He went on to describe the series premise as one akin to the then enormously popular *Wagon Train*, with regular characters travelling to distant worlds which bore some similarity to ours. Once there, they would encounter whatever circumstances would lead to action, adventure and drama. Their method of travel would be a "cruiser" named the U.S.S. Yorktown, a vessel enroute on a "well-defined and long-range Exploration-Science-Security mission which helps create our format." The time period is described as being some point in the future, which could mean either 1995, 2995 or some other date.

"In other words," Roddenberry wrote, "close enough to our own time for our continuing characters to be fully identifiable as people like us, but far enough

into the future for galaxy travel to be thoroughly established (happily eliminating the need to encumber our stories with tiresome scientific explanation)."

The key to the series, he added, was the concept of the Yorktown encountering numerous parallel worlds. In other words, planets whose conditions, both atmospheric and in terms of lifeforms, would mirror that of Earth. Said Roddenberry, "The 'Parallel Worlds' concept makes production practical by permitting action-adventure science fiction at a practical budget figure via the use of available 'earth' casting, sets, locations and so on. As important (and perhaps even more so in many ways), the 'Parallel Worlds' concept tends to keep even the most imaginative stories within the general audience's frame of reference through such recognizable and identifiable casting, sets and costuming."

There is little doubt that Gene Roddenberry had, at times, wanted to put his head through a wall with frustration as he tried to sell the premise of *Star Trek*. In the past he has discussed at length the long battle it was to convince *anyone* that this show could work. Initially, MGM, the studio behind *The Lieutenant*, had expressed interest in the project, but ultimately declined. Finally, he found someone who would listen: Oscar Katz of Desilu (the company created by Desi Arnaz and Lucille Ball).

By the time Roddenberry and Desilu came to a creative understanding, Lucille Ball was running the studio, having bought out ex-husband Desi Arnaz's share of the business. Oscar Katz, a former CBS executive was brought over as Vice President at Desilu in Charge of Production, and it was his job to develop product for the studio.

"The studio made money two ways," Katz explains. "One, by shows which they owned, such as *I Love Lucy* and *The Untouchables*. The second way was as a rental studio. For instance, Bing Crosby Productions shot all their stuff there as did Danny Thomas and Sheldon Leonard. Desilu owned three lots, and the studio probably made money just by having real estate which was going up in value while they were sitting there.

"The number of shows they owned was declining," he continues.

"Desi, in a sense, was a ballsy guy who at one time had seven or eight series on the air that Desilu owned. But now it had declined and they were down to practically Lucy's show and 14 or 15 rentals."

To change the situation, Desilu signed with talent agent Ted Ashley, proposing that they be represented for sales purposes by his agency. Ashley in turn brought in Oscar Katz who—somewhat reluctantly at first—was brought in as a studio executive.

"I started working for Desilu in April of '64 and began to develop programs," Katz details. "April is a late date to begin developing pilots for the fall, so I had a tough time. I think the first year I did three or four pilots, which means that I might have had 15 or 20 projects in earlier stages of development from which the four were selected. They had to be sold to a network in order to get financing. I think all four sailed, but it was hard to attract creative people. Desilu had a reputation for heavy overhead charges, etc. The second year, I did five pilots and of the five three got sold, which is a pretty good batting average."

While one of the pilots ultimately became "unsold," the other two went into production. The first was a show called *Mission: Impossible* and the other was this little science-fiction thing, *Star Trek*.

Says Katz, "If I had to pick the three people who had the most to do with getting *Star Trek* into a reality, they would be Gene Roddenberry, myself and an agent at Ashley named Augman Schwimmer, who today is a lawyer. I had problems signing creative people, getting them to pitch projects. Schwimmer said, 'Let's get a couple of guys in the long form and the short form, let's make overall deals with them. Let's not say, 'I like this property, I don't like this property.' Let's approach them and say, 'We'd like you to come to Desilu and would like you to make Desilu your home. The way we'd like to do it, don't tell us your properties. We'll make a deal for three properties to be determined.' In the long form, Roddenberry is the guy he recommended. I knew Roddenberry from previous contacts and we made the same sort of deal with one or two guys in the comedy field."

••••

Star Trek was the first project that Katz and Roddenberry decided to collaborate on, and this led to a meeting with CBS.

During that meeting, as Stephen E. Whitfield reported in *The Making of Star Trek*, "Gene talked for almost two hours, outlining his ideas for the series, explaining ways in which a science-fiction series could be made on budget, and ways it could be made to appeal to a mass audience....They were particularly interested in his ideas on spaceship design, the types of stories to do, how to cut costs, and other technical aspects that Gene had developed. At the end of the two hours, and after having been questioned closely by most of those present, he thought he had sold them. Then they said, 'Thank you very much. We have one of our own that we like better. But we do appreciate your coming in.'"

In the same book, Roddenberry said, "My attitude was, 'You S.O.B.'s, why didn't you tell me that after the first ten minutes? If you want technical advice and help, hire me and pay me for it!' It's like calling a doctor and having him analyze you for two hours and then telling him, 'Thank you very much for pinpointing what's wrong, and I've decided to go to another doctor for the treatment.'"

Elaborates Oscar Katz, "We were in a dining room with six or seven executives, one of whom questioned us rather closely about what we were going to do on this show. We answered his questions and it turned out that his interest was due to the fact that they were developing a science-fiction show of their own."

That series was *Lost in Space*, which CBS would debut in the 1965 season. In the meantime, Roddenberry and Katz continued to push forward and finally convinced NBC to take the risk and finance the pilot. In the sales pitch to NBC, Katz explains, the network executives were told that there are four kinds of stories that would represent the *Star Trek* concept.

"'You have to remember that the space ship is five stories high,'" Katz remembers explaining, "'it has 500 people on it. One of the girls, who's a female yeoman in the crew, it turns out has signed on because she's having trouble back at home in Boston with either a boyfriend or her parents. She's getting away from them and she has an emotional relationship problem. Our two leads, unspecified, are the catalytic agents who help her face her problem and solve it. You never see her again because she's just one of the crew people.' And I said, 'In that respect, what you have is *Wagon Train*. *Wagon Train* had two leads, the Wagon Train traveled through the west— although it never got where it was going— and a guest star who was in wagon number 23 had an emotional problem which the two leads had to help solve.

"'The second kind of story is you have to remember that they're out for five years at a clip. They get a message from earth that a planet on which there are earth people doing mining there is claim jumping. They have to go to the planet and do a police action. In that respect, it's *Gunsmoke*. The third thing that happens is they go to a planet where everything is pretty much like earth, the atmosphere, etc., and subsequently the people on this planet look and have developed very much like us, except that their Chicago, their Al Capone, is in the future, or their Civil War is about to break out. They're either ahead of us or behind us. So it's people that look like us that are going through what we went through or what we will go through. The fourth type is where they go to a planet where the atmospheric conditions are different than on earth. Everything is different. The people don't look like us, they don't behave like us. They're fierce looking animals or whatever.'

"So I said, 'Those are the four types. What we've got is *Gunsmoke*, *Wagon Train* and two outer planet type shows. What would you like?' Well, they picked type four and the reason they picked type four was it was the hardest to do. With the Desilu reputation, they wanted to make it as hard as possible so we could prove ourselves. I tried to talk them out of it, because I knew it was going to be expensive and, even more, I felt that it might not be representative of the series. But they couldn't be talked out of it. That's how the first pilot, 'The Cage,' came into being."

"The Cage" was expanded into a teleplay, simultaneously renaming

Prior to commanding the starship Enterprise, actor Jeffrey Hunter portrayed Jesus Christ in King of Kings.

Captain Robert April-Christopher Pike, and the Yorktown the Enterprise. What Roddenberry ended up with was a teleplay in which the United Space Ship Enterprise arrives at the planet Talos IV to answer a distress signal. Pike is taken prisoner by the telepathic Talosians who want him to mate with another human being named Vina, so that they can repopulate their nearly lifeless world. To accomplish this goal, they use their abilities to plunge Pike from one fantasy into another, attempting to blur his hold on reality and creating a false sense of security. Number One, Mr. Spock and other crewmembers work together to free him and, together, they end the Talosian plan.

Jeffrey Hunter, who had recently played Jesus Christ in *King of Kings* and co-starred with John Wayne in *The Searchers*, was cast as Captain Pike, though other actors had been considered.

"I remember Lloyd Bridges was very much under consideration," Roddenberry recalled, "except when I approached him with it, he said, 'Gene, I like you, I've worked with you before in the past, but I've seen science fiction and I don't want to be within a hundred miles of it....' I understood what he meant then, because science fiction was usually the monster of the week, the ink blot that gobbled up Tokyo. I tried to convince him that I could do it differently, but at the time I wasn't sure that I would treat it dif-

Leonard Nimoy seen here in his first science-fiction film, Zombies of the Stratosphere.

ferently. I wasn't sure I could manage it."

Majel Barrett, who would go on to marry Roddenberry and portray Nurse Christine Chapel in the ensuing television series, was cast as Number One, with John Hoyt as Dr. Boyce. One of the most integral roles to fill was that of Mr. Spock. After considering Martin (*Mission: Impossible*) Landau and Michael (*The Wild, Wild West*) Dunn, Roddenberry decided to go with Leonard Nimoy, whose credits included *Zombies of the Stratosphere* and two episodes of *The Outer Limits*.

Roddenberry reflected on working with Nimoy during an episode of *The Lieutenant*, noting, "He had played a Hollywood producer, of all things, in an episode with a gum-chewing, wise-cracking secretary who later became my wife. I looked at him during those days and I thought that if I ever did this science fiction series, I'd use him because of his Slavic face and his high cheekbones. And so I just cast it with a phone call by asking him to come over."

Elsewhere, Leonard Nimoy recalled the experience. "The first time I heard about *Star Trek*," he mused, "was in 1964. Gene Roddenberry was producing a television series called *The Lieutenant* [and] I was playing a flamboyant Hollywood [producer] who wanted to do a movie about the Marine Corps. When the job was finished, Gene called my agent, my agent called me and they asked for a meeting. I went in to see

Gene at what was then Desilu Studios and he told me that he was preparing a pilot for a science fiction series to be called *Star Trek*, that he had in mind for me to play an alien character. As the talk continued, Gene showed me around the studio, he showed me the sets that were being developed and the wardrobe that had been designed, the prop department and so forth. I began to realize that he was selling me on the idea of being in this series, unusual for an actor. I figured all I had to do was keep my mouth shut and I might end up with a good job here.

"Gene told me that he was determined to have at least one extra-terrestrial prominent on his starship," added Nimoy. "He'd like to have more, but making human actors into other life forms was too expensive for television in those days. Pointed ears, skin color, plus some changes in eyebrows and hair style were all he felt he could afford, but he was certain that his Mr. Spock idea, properly handled and properly acted, could establish that we were in the 23rd Century and that interplanetary travel was an established fact. And with this, our ship would not be the United States Ship Enterprise, it would be the United Space Ship Enterprise, put out there in space by a federation of planets and the crew would be interplanetary in nature. In Spock, we would have a character who reminded us of that constantly.

"The first pilot of *Star Trek* was filmed at Desilu Studios in Hollywood in 1965. It was the most expensive television pilot ever produced up to that time....That first pilot had some great production values and it had some wonderful ideas, but NBC decided that it was too cerebral and it wouldn't sell."

"The Cage" was directed by Robert Butler who had also worked with Roddenberry on *The Lieutenant* and has since gone on to become the "King of the Pilots," having helmed the initial episodes of *Batman, Moonlighting, Remington Steele, Hill Street Blues, Midnight Caller, Lois & Clark* and others.

"Gene had finished writing 'The Cage,' and he asked me to read it, which I did," recalls Butler. "I remember thinking it was a terrific yarn, but that it was somewhat obscured because it was such a

showcase script. 'The Cage' showcased such solid, good and fascinating science fiction disciplines, examples and events, that it was, I thought, a little obscure. The story was somewhat remote, and I discussed whether or not people would get it. I could tell at that point that Gene was so consumed with it that he couldn't have heard any objections."

Butler goes on to explain that one of his suggestions was to change the show's name from *Trek* to *Track*, for the simple reason that the former sounded a bit too "tedious."

"It's such old news now, that it sounds totally odd," says the director, "but at that time, without the brainwash of the show becoming a massive hit, I remember *Star Trek* sounded kind of inert and boring to me, whereas *Star Track*, I thought, had a bigger vista to it, but in that discussion, and others regarding the obscurity of the story, Gene was not in the mood to receive any such input.

"Subsequently," he elaborates, "after doing the pilot and executing it in the way we thought it should be done, I'd heard that NBC had said, 'We believe this. We think there's a show here, but we don't understand it. Do it again.' Apparently the network, at its level, was feeling exactly as I did.

"Good ideas were being examined," Butler emphasizes. "Underneath all this I sensed a very honorable and well intentioned group of ideas. By the same token, I also remember that it was somewhat stiff. A street show is very loose in terms of language and characters, but in a science fiction show, or a show where you're creating a new reality, you have to adhere to and honor that new reality. You invent a set of circumstances which translates to a kind of rigidity. After all, they're in the equivalent of an army, and in any kind of service your behavior is more prescribed. Ideally, I don't like that because it's just another constraint. That kind of came with the territory, and wasn't good or bad. But I'm more comfortable with looser behavior."

NBC turned down 'The Cage' as being too cerebral for the television audience. Surprisingly, Roddenberry agreed with them to a certain degree.

At a *Star Trek* 20th Anniversary convention in 1986, Roddenberry discussed what happened with "The Cage," as well as the network's motive for rejecting the pilot.

"The reasons were these: too cerebral, not enough action and adventure," he said. "'The Cage' didn't end with a chase and a right cross to the jaw, the way all manly films were supposed to end. There were no female leads then—women in those days were just set dressing. So, another thing they felt was wrong with our film was that we had Majel as a female second-in-command of the vessel. It's nice now, I'm sure, for the ladies to say, 'Well, the men did it,' but in the test reports, the women in the audience were saying, 'Who does she think she is?' They hated her. It is hard to believe that in 20 years, we have gone from a totally sexist society to where we are today—where all intelligent people certainly accept sexual equality. We've made progress.

"We also had what they called a 'childish concept'—an alien with pointy ears from another planet," he added. "People in those days were not talking about life forms on other worlds. It was generally assumed by most sensible people that this is the place where life occurred and probably nowhere else. It would have been all right if this alien with pointy ears, this 'silly creature,' had the biggest zap gun in existence, or the strength of 100 men, *that* could be exciting. But his only difference from the others was he had an alien perspective on emotion and logic. And that didn't make television executives jump up and yell, 'Yippee!'

"At that time, space travel was considered nonsense. It wasn't until we were off the air three months that man landed on the Moon and minds were changed all over. The Talosian planet's 'ridiculous' premise of mind control annoyed a great many people and the objection, of course, overlooks the fact that the most serious threat we face today in our world is mind control—such as not too long ago exercised by Hitler, and what's now exercised by fanatical religions all over the world and even here in our own country. Mind control is a dangerous subject for TV to discuss, because the yuppies may wake up someday and be discussing it and say, 'Well, wait a minute, television may be the most powerful mind control force of all,' and may begin taking a very close look at television. And so most executives would like to avoid that *possibility.*

"Looking back," he added elsewhere, "they probably felt that I had broken my word. In the series format I had promised to deliver a 'Wagon Train to the Stars'...action/adventure, science-fiction style. But, instead, ['The Cage'] was a beautiful story, in the opinion of many the best science fiction film ever made up to that time. But it wasn't action/adventure. It wasn't what I had promised it would be. Clearly the problem with the first pilot was easily traced back to me. I got too close to it and lost perspective. I had known the only way to tell *Star Trek* was with an action/adventure plot. But I forgot my plan and tried for something proud."

Explains Oscar Katz, "I asked NBC, 'Why are you turning it down?' and I was told, 'We can't sell it from this show, it's too atypical.' I said, 'But you guys picked this one, I gave you four choices.' He said, 'I know we did and because of that, right now we're going to give you an order for a second pilot next season.'"

Where No Man...

Although okaying a second pilot, NBC did make several "suggestions," including the removal of Mr. Spock because, according to Oscar Katz, "they thought Spock's ears would be scary."

"They rejected most of the cast and asked that Spock be dropped too," Roddenberry concurred. "In fact, they particularly asked that Spock be dropped. This is one of those cases where you go home at night and pound your head against a wall and say, 'How come I am the only one in the world that believes in it?' But I said I would not do a second pilot without Spock because I felt we had to have him for many reasons. I felt we couldn't do a space show without at least one person on board who constantly reminded you that you were out in space and in a world of the future. NBC finally agreed to do the second pilot with Spock in it, saying, 'Well, kind of keep him in the background.'"

This was particularly ironic when one considers that Spock would eventually go on to become one of the most popular characters on the show. In fact, the constant struggle between logic and emotion that waged through the half-Vulcan/half-human touched a generation searching for direction.

Adding to the scenario, Nimoy explained, "The network eliminated one character entirely, the role of Number One...They told Gene to also get rid of the guy with the ears, insisting that the audience couldn't identify with an extraterrestrial character. Gene battled this but was finally forced into a compromise. He felt the format badly needed the alien Spock, even if the price was the acceptance of 1960s style sexual inequality. A new pilot was written and Mr. Spock was in Number One's place as second-in-command as well as having some of the woman's computer mind qualities. Vulcan unemotionalism and logic came into being."

In terms of how that second pilot came into being, Stephen Kandel, who would go on to write the popular Harry Mudd episodes of the weekly series, explains that NBC was "of two minds: to forget it and to abandon it. So, after much argument and discussion, Gene got the money to write three additional pilot scripts. 'The Cage' had been a sample of what the series would be like and that frightened the network. They thought the audience wouldn't understand it."

While work began on the three scripts, Roddenberry learned that two key players of "The Cage" did not want to be involved the second time around: director Robert Butler and actor Jeffrey Hunter.

Says Butler, "I told Gene I had been there and done it already, and didn't wish to repeat myself. Another reason I didn't wish to do it is that science fiction, directorially, is a bit of a chore, because you have to share the reigns with graphics, special visual effects and all the other people who supply the tricks. It's very much direction by committee, and I was a little impatient with that. I like working on pilots because you're in on the formulation, and you're handed fewer givens so, equitably, you

William Shatner in his days before assuming the role of Captain James T. Kirk, seen here in The Defenders.

direct more. The more control and freedom I have to direct, the more I enjoy it. I will say that we were all praying and doing our best [on 'The Cage']. The phenomenon was bigger than I expected, not that I really measured it at the time. That wasn't in the equation. You just roll up your sleeves and decide what the hell it is you're trying to do. Then you jump in and never look back."

Of Jeffrey Hunter's departure, Roddenberry said, "I thought highly of him and he would have made a grand captain, except his family convinced him, or his wife or someone, that science fiction was really beneath him."

Adds Oscar Katz, "When you make a pilot deal with an actor, you can't tie him up forever. You usually have a hold on him for approximately six months, but you *don't* have the right to do another pilot with him for the following season, so we had no hold on Jeffrey Hunter. And either he or his wife didn't like 'The Cage' and he didn't want to do the second pilot. I already had the set built—I think it was the largest set in the history of Hollywood, that planet in 'The Cage'—we had the interior of the space ship, the miniature of the outside of the space ship, etc. We had everything and all we had to do was write a new script. But we didn't have a leading man. Business affairs negotiated with Jeffrey Hunter, and we all thought it was the usual actor/network situation. They don't

want to do it for reason XYZ, and it's a device for getting the price up. We kept increasing the price and he kept saying no. One day I said, 'What's with Jeffrey Hunter?' and I was told he just won't do it at any price. Finally I said, 'Tell Jeffrey Hunter to get lost. Tell him we're going to do the pilot without him.' And that's how Shatner got into it, because Hunter wouldn't do it."

Taking over the center seat would be Canadian-born actor William Shatner, whose career had included highly acclaimed roles on stage (*The World of Suzie Wong, A Short in the Dark*T), screen (*The Brothers Karamazov*) and television (*Twilight Zone, The OUter Limits, For the People* and the pilot for an unsold series, *Alexander, the Great*).

"I was offered the part in a rather peculiar fashion," Shatner related to the English press in the 1970s. "They had made a pilot of *Star Trek* with an actor who is now deceased, Jeffrey Hunter, and NBC did not like the pilot but they liked the idea. They said change the cast, change the story but give us another pilot for *Star Trek* and we'll pay a certain amount of money. So they showed me the first pilot and said, 'Would you like to play the part and here are some of the storylines that we plan to go with; you can see the kind of production we have in mind. Would you care to play it?' And I thought it was an interesting gamble for myself as an actor to take, because I've always been fascinated by science fiction. I liked the production; I liked the people involved with the production, and so I decided to do it. But it was under these peculiar circumstances of having a first pilot made that I did it.

"I then talked at great length with Gene Roddenberry about the objectives we hoped to achieve, and one of those objectives was serious drama as well as science fiction. His reputation and ability, which I knew first-hand, was such that I did not think he would do *Lost in Space*. And I was too expensive an actor, with what special or particular abilities I have, to warrant being put in something that somebody else could walk through. So I felt confident that *Star Trek* would keep those serious objectives for the most part, and it did."

Bob Justman, who would go from assistant director on "The Cage" to Associate Producer on "Where No Man's Gone Before," explains, "Gene was very happy that he was able to get Bill Shatner, who was highly thought of in the industry. I had worked with Bill on *Outer Limits* and he had a good reputation in the television and entertainment industries even at that time, well before the second pilot of *Star Trek*. He was someone to be reckoned with and we certainly understood that he was a more accomplished actor than Jeff Hunter was, and he gave us more dimension. The network seemed to feel that Jeff Hunter was rather wooden. He was a nice person, everyone liked him, but he didn't run the gamut of emotions that Bill Shatner could do. Shatner was classically trained. He had enormous technical abilities to do different things and he gave the captain a terrific personality. He embodied what Gene had in mind, which was the flawed hero. Or the hero who considers himself to be flawed. Captain Horatio Hornblower. That was who he was modeled on."

Enthused Leonard Nimoy, "Bill Shatner's broader acting style created a new chemistry between the captain and Spock, and now it was quite different from that of the first pilot."

And the relationship between the two characters and actors—despite whatever ego problems would arise later—positively sparked. David Gerrold, famed science fiction writer, *Star Trek* scholar and author of the episode "The Trouble With Tribbles," notes, "All of the movies and all of the episodes hold together because Shatner holds it together. Spock is only good when he has someone to play off of. The scenes where Spock doesn't have Shatner to play off of are not interesting. If you look at Spock with his mom or dad, it's very ponderous. But Spock working with Kirk has the magic and it plays very well, and people give all of the credit to Nimoy not to Shatner."

Surprisingly, Nimoy himself agrees with this observation. "During the series," he says, "we had a failure-I experienced it as a failure—in an episode called 'The Galileo Seven.' The Spock character had been so successful that somebody said, 'Let's do a show where

Spock takes command of a vessel.' We had this shuttlecraft mission where Spock was in charge. I had a tough time with it. I really appreciated the loss of the Kirk character for me to play against, to comment on. The Bill Shatner Kirk performance was the energetic, driving performance, and Spock could kind of slipstream along and make comments and offer advice, give another point of view. Put into the position of being the driving force, the central character, was very tough for me and I perceived it as a failure."

While Shatner was hired, the three NBC-requested scripts were finished. Roddenberry wrote "The Omega Glory," dealing with a crisis on an Earth-like planet involving Federation colonists; Stephen Kandel wrote "Mudd's Women," which, he says, began with the premise "'What if we start with a character that's not alien or highly technological, but rather somebody whom the audience would identify with easily?' What we came up with was a roofing salesman; a con man."; and Samuel A. Peeples wrote "Where No Man Has Gone Before," which chronicled the metamorphosis of Enterprise crewmember Gary Mitchell into a God-like being.

"My vague memory is that there had been several problems with 'The Cage,'" reflects James Goldstone, who had been signed to direct *Star Trek*'s second pilot. "One of them was that it cost so much money and the other was that it took so long to shoot. NBC was skeptical that a series could be manufactured, so to speak, on a weekly basis. One of the requisites put on the second pilot was to shoot it in, as I recall, eight days, which would then prove to them that a weekly series could be done in six or seven days. We needed the extra day because we were doing the prototype. The other requisite, I would *guess*, it being television, is that NBC very much wanted something that could be 'commercial' against the police shows and all the other action things that were then on television. Things have not changed, I guess. They always want something that will hook the audience and keep them."

In terms of the intention for the second pilot to be faster paced than the original, he says, "I really can't tell you whose idea that was, whether it was

mine or Gene's or the network's. There's also a difference between a two-hour show in an embryonic conceptual form, and something that is going to be a part of a weekly series. The concept of our show was not so much a pilot as it was an example of how we could go on a weekly level."

From the outset, he was enthused about working on the show. "Gene's whole concept," Goldstone details, "was of doing the sort of classic storytelling form in which you can tell the same kind of stories that were told in the Elizabethan Theatre, told in the 19th Century, that were told in classic novels. The convention with westerns is that if you take it out of today, and put it into a western setting, people accept these conventions. We would create conventions which people would accept, and you could therefore tell dramatic stories which people would accept because it was not on the streets they lived on, but were projected forward a little. On the same level, the characters and the dramatic conflicts, albeit space fiction, were really human conflicts. Now I don't know if that applies to all the episodes, and in fact I don't know if that applied to any of the episodes except the one I did,

because I don't know anything about all the other episodes. It would have been miraculous if they could have kept in nonmechanistic.

"A combination of NBC, Gene, perhaps other executives at Desilu and I, read all three [scripts], discussed them in length, decided on what became 'Where No Man Has Gone Before,' and then embarked on a great deal of polishing and rewriting on a conceptual and physical level, so that we could make it in eight days. This one just seemed to have the potential to establish those characters on a human level. The only gimmick is the mutation forward, the silvering of Gary Mitchell's eyes, and it works because it's simple, as opposed to the growing of horns or something. Ours was a human science fiction concept, perhaps cerebral and certainly emotional."

Samuel Peeples, who has written more segments episodic television than anyone could ever keep track of, had actually had some connection with Gene Roddenberry and *Star Trek* prior to "Where No Man Has Gone Before."

"Gene Roddenberry and I had known each other from writing *Have Gun, Will Travel*," Peeples recalls. "He was trying to start a science fiction series

Director James Goldstone took audiences "Where No Man Has Gone Before" with the second Star Trek *pilot.*

and he knew that I had one of the largest science fiction collections in the world. He was researching his show and asked if he could go through my magazines and get some ideas for the Enterprise. Gene went through all the covers, and that's really how the Enterprise was born.

"In the beginning," he continues, "Mr. Spock as we know him now, didn't exist. He was a red-tailed Devil who didn't eat. He absorbed energy through a red plate in his stomach. This is the way he was laid out in the original concept. I argued with Gene that it should be a humanized character because I was adamant that it should be straight science fiction without fantasy. The first pilot he did for NBC, 'The Cage,' was more fantasy than science fiction. NBC was apparently unhappy with it, so they told him they would commission a second pilot, and they wanted a story. Gene asked me to do it, and I did, guessing it would be more of a challenge to me because it's easy to open up your mouth and criticize somebody else's concept. Then if somebody says, 'Okay, let's see you do it your way,' you've got to prove that you know what you're talking about."

In Peeples' script, the starship Enterprise comes across a charred metallic "black box" (similar to what is used today on airplanes) from a long-lost space vessel. Captain James R. Kirk (the middle initial eventually changed to T. once the pilot led to series) has the device beamed aboard. In the meantime strong ties are established between the captain, Lieutenant Gary Mitchell, and first officer Mr. Spock. The Enterprise approaches an energy barrier at the edge of the galaxy and attempts to make its way through, resulting in the ship nearly being destroyed and metamorphosizing Mitchell's natural ESP abilities. Those powers grow to the point where he becomes a god-like being, manipulating everything around him.

Spock listens to the black box and learns that the captain of that vessel was desperate to learn anything he could about ESP, and shortly thereafter ordered that his ship be set for self-destruction. Now Kirk is faced with one decision: kill Mitchell before the Enterprise is crushed by the man's ever-

increasing power.

"We were intrigued with the corruption of power theme manifesting over the ordinary individual," says Peeples. "That was the basic premise, and we had to put in extrapolations of known scientific principles. At that time, the radiation belt had been discovered around the Earth, and my premise was that galaxies themselves might be separated by this type of barrier.

"Gene and I were trying to avoid the space cadet cliche," he elaborates. "We were both very concerned about it being an adult show. One thing, as later episodes proved, was the problem which never should have existed: the bug eyed monsters. We both discouraged the idea, believing that we should keep things as realistic as possible. If a person was different physically, then explain the reason for that difference. In a particular atmosphere, he might have a larger lung. If it was a planet with an extraordinarily bright sun, he would have different eyes. We were actually trying to project reality against an unfamiliar background. In other words, we would deal with reality according to the environmental background we encountered."

"Where No Man Has Gone Before" went into production soon thereafter. Joining Shatner, Nimoy and Gary Lockwood was Paul Fix as Dr. Mark Piper, George Takei as Physicist Sulu, James Doohan as Chief Engineer Montgomery Scott, Lloyd Haynes as Communications Officer Alden and Andrea Dromm as Yeoman Smith, with Sally Kellerman "guest starring" as Dr. Elizabeth Dehner. As fans of the show recognize, the final STAR TREK cast was slowly taking shape.

Doohan was actually brought into *Star Trek* by James Goldstone, with whom he had worked before.

"All he wanted to hear were different accents," related the actor in *The Star Trek Interview Book*, "and that's what he heard. He called my agent and said, 'I want Jimmy down here,' and when I got to the set he asked, 'Well, what sort of an accent shall we do today?' That was kind of fun....I did a bunch of accents, they handed me the pages of the script, I did the accents and they asked, 'Which do you like?' So I told

them. I said I preferred the Scottish, because I think it's traditional that Scotsmen are famous as engineers. They said, 'Well, we rather like that, too,' so I immediately just came right out and named him Montgomery Scott, after my maternal grandfather."

George Takei, who had made a name for himself dubbing Japanese monster films like *Rodan*, and made guest appearances on *Playhouse 90, Hawaiian Eye* and *77 Sunset Strip*, found himself intrigued with the notion of appearing on *Star Trek*, though he thought the show might be a little *too* different.

"Since the pilot was so unlike anything that we had ever seen on television, even under the guise of science fiction," he muses, "I wondered whether or not it would sell. As professional actors, the cast all had worries about the saleability of 'Where No Man Has Gone Before.' We were hoping and praying that it would go, so it was a pleasant surprise when NBC did buy *Star Trek*."

NBC viewed the pilot in early 1966, and gave Roddenberry the green light for his series, much to the delight of everyone, as they were proud of what they had achieved.

"I was very happy with it," enthuses James Goldstone. "From a director's point of view—or this director's point of view—you have certain targets and certain problems which have to be overcome in any picture, whether it's a $20 million feature or a television show. A director measures his success in two ways. Obviously, like everybody else, you measure it by whether or not it's a critical and commercial success, but you also measure it in terms of overcoming obstacles. The obstacles were temporal, budgetary, but they were also conceptual. I was very proud of the work we were able to do. When I say we, I don't mean it in a generous sense. I mean that it was a very collaborative effort, as are all pilots. We, being Gene, especially, Bobby Justman and the main actors who later became the main stars. Everything was planned in detail, and Bobby and I knew if we didn't move from one set to another or one scene to another by a certain hour, we were in trouble."

At a convention appearance, Roddenberry offered, "The second pilot seemed to have great concepts: humans turning into gods. But they were nice safe gods, gods who go 'Zap! You're punished.' Kind of like the guys you see on those Sunday morning shows...The biggest factor in selling the second pilot was that it ended up in a hell of a fist fight with the villain suffering a painful death. Then, once we got *Star Trek* on the air, we began infiltrating a few of our ideas, the ideas you folks have all celebrated. *Star Trek* fans are people who are ready for the 23rd century dreams now. And I wish to God our leaders could catch up with them."

Elsewhere, he expressed his satisfaction over having been given the opportunity to do a second pilot. "Science fiction pilots are difficult things to do," he said. "You know, if you are going to do a pilot on a police show, let's say mid-town robbery squad, the network can reasonably expect you to get 95% of everything right and it's easy to do because you know what cops wear, you know how to catch a taxi, how to use a telephone and how to work a .38. When you get into SF you're very lucky if 75% of your pilot is believable because you're creating, in space science fiction, everything new. It was very helpful to be able to do one pilot, stand off, take a look at it and then do a second. The second pilot was really better in many ways because we had a chance to look at the costume work, how the gadgets worked and all that."

Oscar Katz left Desilu immediately after *Star Trek* was picked up as a series, but he believes he knows why the show has gone on for nearly three decades in one form or another.

"I think the secret of *Star Trek*'s success was its attention to details," opines Katz. "Up until that point, the science-fiction movies on television were all Irwin Allen-type shows, whereas Gene's concept was science-fiction in the true sense of those words. It was like what things might be about in the future, not only in the size of the concept and the ship and they problems they face, but in the smallest details. And Gene was a stickler for details. For instance, do you know why nobody salutes on the ship? That's because Gene decided—after consulting with military people in

Washington—that on a ship that's on duty with several hundred people in a limited space for five years, they are not going to salute each other. Take the scene in sickbay with the instruments on the wall. Y'know, you stick a thermometer in somebody's ass and you read the temperature on the wall. Gene had a meeting with NASA about what that was going to look like. The same thing with the uniforms. I think what made *Star Trek* was its 'truth', its science-fiction truth not only in the big things that were spoken about, but also in the smallest details. I think the fans appreciated that and that's what made them go wild. It's interesting, but I think *Star Trek* is probably the most valuable property ever developed in the history of television. You've got four series, seven movies and merchandising you can't believe. It's amazing." And for *Star Trek*, it was only the beginning.

Space...The Final Frontier

The public's first view of *Star Trek* came at the Cleveland, Ohio Tricon on Labor Day weekend in 1966. There, 20th Century Fox screened their upcoming special effects extravaganza, *Fantastic Voyage*, Irwin Allen, the man behind such series as *Lost in Space* and *Voyage to the Bottom of the Sea*, presented the pilot episode of his latest effort, *The Time Tunnel*; and Gene Roddenberry unspooled "Where No Man's Gone Before," later adding "The Cage" due to public demand.

Roddenberry reflected, "I was nervous [at Tricon], particularly when I saw them watching other films that were shown before, and booing, and stomping, and laughing at things. I walked out there thinking, 'They're finally going to show this one.' There was a rather loud gentleman surrounded by other people discussing something at the time my show was starting, and upset already, I turned on him: 'For Christ's sake, could you be quiet? My show is on now.' And Isaac Asimov said, 'Yes, you're perfectly right. We will tone it down.' And someone said, 'You're dead, you just insulted Isaac Asimov.' Well, it turned out that I had not, and over the years we became fast friends. He understood. Then I watched how they accepted this show. I

said to myself, 'Yes, there *are* people, if we go this way and try these things, who are going to appreciate them.' I realized then that we would have fans of some sort and, of course, where that went is insanity."

Also in attendance was author Jerry Sohl, who explains, "There was what felt like 3,000 people watching a new Irwin Allen show, and as soon as they saw his name they started booing. They just booed his name. Then when Gene Roddenberry showed *Star Trek*, they really loved that. I was really surprised. Then when Gene Roddenberry and I sat up at the podium answering questions, I was introduced as the 'head writer of *Star Trek*.' Which I wasn't. I just went along with it because I thought it would be good politics. And it was. It was fun."

While not the head writer, Sohl was one of the first people that Roddenberry had contacted to pen scripts for the forthcoming series.

"Gene Roddenberry knew that I was a science fiction writer from people evidently telling him I was," says Sohl. "So he called me up one day and asked me if I would like to go down to the studio. I met him there in like 1965, and he said, 'I have this idea for a science fiction TV show which I think the networks are going to buy, and I wanted to talk to you about the possibilities of stories. Would you be available? I'm meeting with other science fiction writers like A.E. Van Goght, Ray Bradbury, Frederic Brown.' He would meet with them down there and really sort of drained them by one lunch of any ideas. We all did the best that we could, suggesting what to do. We hoped that it wouldn't be like Truman Bradley's *Science Fiction Theatre*. We wanted something more than that. He told us that it would be a good thing, but nobody believed that it would be. I spoke to some writers afterwards and they said, 'Well, what did he do? Gene Roddenberry has only done *The Lieutenant* series and he was a police officer. What the hell does he know about science fiction? It's just going to be a pile of shit.' So we all agreed that, yes, it would be a pile of shit, but we would all work for it anyway. But it didn't turn out to be that way and we wound up being very friendly with him."

As scripts were being written and the series concept honed, Roddenberry turned his attention to casting. William Shatner, Leonard Nimoy, James Doohan and George Takei (with Sulu promoted from physicist to helmsman) would remain, while Paul Fix was out as the ship's doctor and Lloyd Hanes vacated the communications console. In their respective positions were DeForest Kelley as Dr. Leonard "Bones" McCoy and Nichelle Nichols as Lieutenant Uhura, representing one of the first times that a black actress was a network series regular.

Kelley had established himself as a highly qualified actor, usually playing the heavy in any number of television westerns.

"Roddenberry pulled me out of the westerns category," Kelley recalled in the 1970s. "I made a pilot for him in 1960 called *333 Montgomery*, in which I portrayed a famous criminal attorney in San Francisco named Jake Early. This series was before *The Defenders* and it was controversial in nature and ahead of its time. Roddenberry wrote it and produced it, and I starred in it. Unfortunately, it did not sell, but that was really the first pull out of westerns for me, and then later, of course, Gene did *Star Trek*."

The Lieutenant had represented one of Nichelle Nichols' first dramatic roles, and she was thrilled that Roddenberry had contacted her regarding *Star Trek*. In particular, she loved the character devised for her, Uhura.

"I tried to put into Uhura the qualities that I admire and demand of myself," she told *The Official Star Trek Fan Club Magazine*. "Then I tried to develop the kind of person who would be entrusted with that kind of responsibility. She's head of all communications on that ship, so she's not just there pushing buttons. Those buttons are talking to people down in the bowels of the ship. She's responsible for maybe a hundred people. For her or anyone to be entrusted with that kind of responsibility, I felt she had to have a strength and a dignity and a command of authority very much like Spock has."

Of all the characters, it quickly became obvious that the three most prominent would be Kirk, Spock and McCoy. As Roddenberry explained it, deliberately so.

"The three star billing were the ones that you would see a lot of," he said. "Plus science fiction wasn't 'in' in those days and we were going to do a lot of things we knew people might not understand and I wouldn't have stream of consciousness. In novels, stream of consciousness goes inside the hero's head and you can read what he's thinking. You don't have that in television and so I thought that if I took a perfect person and divided him into three parts, I could have the administrative, courageous part that would be the Captain; the logical part who is the Science Officer and the humanistic part with the doctor. Then, when something comes up, the Captain could say, 'I don't know, fellas. We must do it,' and Spock would say, 'However, the logical thing is...', and the doctor would say, 'Yes, but the humanity of it,' and I could have them talk about it without having stream of consciousness, and it worked!"

A large part of that success was due to the abilities of, and chemistry between, Shatner, Nimoy and Kelley, who managed to sustain a relationship beyond the words written on the printed page.

"They all added to their characters," points out Robert Justman. "For example, as Nimoy added to the character of Mr. Spock, we saw certain things in the portrayal that Gene thought could be taken advantage of and expanded, which we did. You have to learn in making film to deal with the film and not necessarily with what the original conception was. Film has a life of its own and if you try to bend it toward what you originally intended and it didn't turn out that way, it's going to turn out to be quite awkward. You have to learn to take advantage of what's there, to perhaps give it a new shape. It's an interesting problem. You have to have a good concept for a character to begin with to enable the actors to do something with it. Gene has in the past, and with the new show, developed some very interesting characters. Brent Spiner's character [on *The Next Generation*], Data, is basically Pinnochio, but he's learning all the time. He's someone who wants to be human,

not wooden. He wants to be like everyone else, to be better than he thinks he is, not knowing that he's pretty good as he is. We all want to do better, so we can relate to that and the character."

With the proper cast in place, Roddenberry turned his attention back to the show's scripts. He knew that theirs was going to be one of television's first intelligent science fiction series, with realistic characters and extrapolations on today's technology. In other words, every aspect of the Enterprise would be based on items being developed in the present. For example, the diagnostic beds in sickbay, as advanced as they seemed, were studied by one of the U.S. armed forces, who told Roddenberry that they had been developing something along similar lines. Even the weapon system known as phasers was only one step removed from the laser beam.

"We realized that lasers might very well become commonplace by the time the show got on the air," he said, "or at least within the next couple of years. Rather than run the risk of being outdated, we decided to say 'phaser' instead. The reason we picked phaser is the 'phasing' principles in physics by which power can be increased. It was logical and it sounded good, so we used it. We didn't want people saying to us three years from now, 'Oh, come on now, lasers can't do that."

The scripts for *Star Trek* had to have a special quality to them, with the original game plan being that top science fiction and television writers would be supplying the show's stories. To ensure this thematic integrity, Gene Roddenberry hired John D.F. Black to serve as associate producer and story editor.

"What *Star Trek* always strived to do, from my perspective, is to take things people can relate to now because it's real in our own lives, and *move* them," explains Black. "What happens if somebody burns down your building? It's the same thing as a monster showing up in your building. So, they used the monster. The parallel was clean."

As Black speaks, he creates the immediate impression he is a man of integrity, caring deeply about his craft and the world around him. It was this integrity that he brought to the original

Star Trek TV series.

"I came on about two months before we shot anything," says Black. "I can't remember specifically which writers were on line, but I went in with an ultimate respect for writers. I insisted, as any credible writer would, that I get the opportunity to give shots to young writers who had a great story. I was also talking with Theodore Sturgeon, Ray Bradbury, George Clayton Johnson, Jerry Sohl—that kind of literary heavyweight. It was an awesome thing to confront."

As Black explains it, the *Star Trek* offices at the Desilu Studio were directly below those of *Mission: Impossible*, which was gearing up for production at the same time.

"At the end of the day," he laughs, "we would gather together and talk. Everybody was going crazy. You know, how the hell do you do a science-fiction series? How the hell do you do *Mission: Impossible*? We would bat the day's story problems back and forth, so there's no way to tell who came up with what about what at what time. It was all madness. It was a great deal of work; more work than I had ever done in so compacted a time. It was 12 to 18 hours a day. I can remember many nights wandering around the sets at midnight, trying to figure out story logistics.

"The way television was, there was a hell of a lot that you *couldn't* do, but there was also a hell of a lot that you *could* do then, but nobody was noticing. So, when a show like *Star Trek* came along, it was a marvelous advantage. There was no writer I knew who didn't want to work on that show. We were looking for the most acute science-fiction minds it was possible to acquire, because we were doing something new. But our dilemma was, first of all, that every plant that we showed had to be made. Every weapon or device had to be invented. What the hell did a plant look like on Rigel 9? Dilithium Crystals were a rock which one of my kids brought home. It had a beautiful crystal-like shine, and I really fell in love with the look of it and took it into the office. Somebody asked me what it was and I said, 'It's a Dilithium Crystal.' I didn't know what the hell it was, but it became the power source of the Enterprise. We were creat-

ing *everything*. Conceiving an idea was one thing, getting it on film was another. Cost is relative in doing any series.

"I wasn't that familiar with science fiction," Black admits. "I had read a great deal of it, but science fiction is playing tennis without a net. You could do anything you wanted, and if you look at the one segment I wrote, 'The Naked Time,' you'll see that what I did, purely and simply, was take drunkenness and remove the slurs and staggers from it."

Adding to Black's pleasure was that the realistic qualities of the characters made the series that much more enjoyable to write.

"There was such a natural balance between William Shatner and Leonard Nimoy," Black observes. "There was no way to tell, really, whether they got along or not because they had an easy relationship off camera, and on camera there was an absolute difference that was writeable. You had the advantage in any scene between Shatner and Nimoy where Shatner could take one side and be correct, and Nimoy could take the purely logical side of the situation and also be correct. The scene carried out the conflict which could spark anything along the lines of what was upcoming. I don't mean to sound like a professor of a screenplay class discussing a script's structure, but that's the reality. We know that conflict is the heart of any scene, and the more conflict you have between the characters, the better it is. And it was just built in.

"Uhura was a little more difficult to deal with. Nichelle was breathtakingly gorgeous, a skilled actress and limited to, 'I'm hailing them, Captain.' We could open it up a little, but not much. George Takei, when he came in and became the helmsman, had that marvelous Centurian deep voice that very few people are even aware that he has, although they heard it over and over again. That voice really gave strength to that chair, so that when the captain said whatever to George, and he said, 'Aye, Captain,' the audience knew he was going to do his best and that it was going to be enough. Scotty...if he got an awful lot of repetition because the engines had to go out a number of times, Jimmy

Doohan never lost that characterization that he walked in with on the first day. The dialect stayed in place, as did the amount of smile he permitted. He was a very gifted actor. If we go to our friend Bones, DeForest Kelley, he was as experienced an actor as you could ask for. He had gone from juvenile to character juvenile, to young leading man to leading man and there he was on *Star Trek* with an enormous amount of background and an enormous amount of training. He had his character in hand, although it changed *slightly* during the first five or six episodes where he became a tad more earnest. The conflict built in between he and Spock was electric....Even the extras who would run in and out with their little zap guns were into their characters and into the show. I think that was relevant to the audience. It triggered their emotional responses.

"The show was meaningful for many people. Billy Shatner had just done *Alexander, the Great*. He was good, but it was not a hit. On that night of the first shoot, I left the office and found Bill leaning against my car, and he had a look of enormous innocence on his face. I said, 'How's it going, Billy?' And he said, 'Fine.' I figured there was something going on. And he just looked at me and said, 'It's just so damned important to us.' And I said, 'Yeah, we've got a hit.' That's what you say to everybody when it's in the fan and you don't know what's going to happen next, particularly to actors who are so vulnerable. And he said, 'I hope so,' and walked away. The sense I had was that we were all doing the best we could, and we were giving it everything we had."

"There was a very good team feeling," Dorothy Fontana concurs. "Gene had put together an extremely good team, between the cast, crew and staff, who were united in the feeling that this is a good show, we're doing a fine show and let's keep it up. In fact, I don't think I've ever encountered such a great team spirit on any other show I've ever worked on, although I've had good working relationships with other crews. But that whole unity of everybody, from the top to the least important production person, was right there."

Joseph Pevney, who would play

an extremely important directorial role in the history of *Star Trek*, was as equally enthused about the series. He had begun his career in features, but was eventually convinced to try television where the "real money" was. He began with an episode of *Wagon Train* and moved to other shows, before joining the crew of *Star Trek*. While he directed several episodes of the first season, he would alternate with Marc Daniels during the second.

"I met with Roddenberry," he reflects, "and, wow, what an amazing genius of a man. We had lunch together one day and he told me his background. A very interesting human being. I think he's a half a touch removed from genius. Some of the stuff he did on *Star Trek* is unbelievable. NASA used to come down to the sets to say, 'How did you know about this medical thing...?' They were working on principles he had already thought of. We went down to NASA and watched the development of the 'X' models. Well, we were very big with NASA and all the sci-fi buffs, who dug it the most.

"I'm a high-tech fellow myself," he adds. "I'm very interested in radio, computers, but what I was really interested in was the very creative treatment of the stories. The stories were solid, very well done and the imagination ran rampant. Everything was possible. There was no fantasy in *Star Trek*; it was very real. The people were real, the situations were real, even the episode with the Tribbles was real. It was hi-fi science treated very realistically, socially conscious, good anti-fascist democratic background. All of that stuff was very pleasing to me.

"I also loved the characters. Gene was constantly trying to give it a universal aspect, because that's what's going to be in the theory regarding the future when we go to other worlds. There will be all kinds of things out there. Some will not be completely humanoid, but that was okay. He was quite convincing about that. So he wanted some more nationalities in the show. He had an oriental, a black, eventually a Russian....The '60s were boiling with this out here. At that time we had all kinds of college things going on. The beginnings of the ERA and so on. Civil Rights were tumbling all over the place. Gene was saying, 'Let's put a Russian in there.' Wow, what a shockeroo that was."

The late Marc Daniels, who helped pioneer the situation comedy by helming the early episodes of *I Love Lucy* utilizing three cameras and a live studio audience, concurred with the assessment of the characters. "Right from the beginning, it was easy to see that the characters were extremely well drawn. There was some trial and error with the peripheral characters, but the main ones—Kirk, Spock and McCoy—were excellent. With that many characters, it was difficult to give each of them their due. There was a very good contrast between them because you didn't have the same thing going on between any two of them."

While the creative behind the scenes atmosphere was extremely upbeat, things weren't made easier by such obstacles as a weekly budget and directives from the network.

Says Robert Justman, "NBC wanted as many 'planet' shows that they could get. Of course that was very difficult for us to achieve. They, as anybody does, wanted more for their buck. The more things you could cram in a show, the more action you could cram into a show, the happier they were. Their need was to achieve good numbers. In a way, I guess that was our need, too, but we were more concerned with the content of the shows. The network was concerned with content too, but it was their kind of content and the kind that would, in their mind, attract viewers.

"But we were doing the show we were doing. It was all we could do just to do the show. Forget about worrying about anything else. It was a new show, and because of that the network programming department was understandably nervous about what we could show and what we couldn't show, and what subjects we could deal with. Luckily the fact that the show was allegorical in nature, sometimes the content escaped the network's notice. They took the content of the show for what the content *purported* to be. Allegory oftentimes is not about what's there, but what's *not* there. You see, when you're doing a show for a network, you not only have to deal with programming departments and development, but also with what in NBC's case was called the Broadcast Standards Department, which was the censors. Programming might accept a story that Broadcast Standards might find objectionable. It was quite difficult to satisfy three masters, two of them being the network and one of them being ourselves."

While reflecting on those early days, Justman points out that he cannot describe the process of bringing an episode of *Star Trek* to the screen.

"I don't think we have enough time," he smiles. "Just imagine the most incredibly difficult process you can imagine and double it. The gestation is very, very difficult. We had to satisfy many masters. I can't begin to tell you. Add to that the time constraint; you never had enough time to write the episodes properly much less produce them properly. The world of series television is an arcane sort of world; an arcane art. In essence, you really can't do anything in a way that's true. You can only do the best that you can do. You have a finite amount of time and you need to sleep at least a few hours every night, so you accomplish what you can accomplish within those constraints. That's it. It's not easy. The reward every now and then is perhaps turning out a show that affects people, causes them to think and perhaps changes their lives....There was a feeling that we were all together, doing something that was different. Not only different, but worthwhile. *That* was the feeling."

Star Trek premiered on September 8, 1966 and, as Justman states, it quickly proved itself to indeed be different and worthwhile, though the critical reactions were not all that positive. Neither were the show's ratings.

In the early weeks of *Star Trek*'s run, audiences were treated to episodes that were completely unlike anything they had seen. "The Man Trap" pit Captain Kirk and company against a "salt vampire" who drained the human body of all its natural salt; "Charlie X" was an adolescent alien with telekinetic abilities who could bend the laws of nature to suit his immature needs; "The Enemy Within" split Kirk in two, resulting in a battle between the good and evil of a man's soul; "Balance of Terror" was a submarine war drama in space between the Enterprise and a war vessel from their enemy, the Romulans; "The Menagerie" was a two-part episode that ingeniously incorporated "The Cage" in a tale of Mr. Spock's apparent mutiny of the Enterprise, forcing it to go to Talos IV, a world deemed off limits by the Federation; and so on. The characters were extremely realistic and the stories plausible no matter what the conflict. Science fiction on television had finally come of age.

"Gene Roddenberry did a good thing in having little moral lessons in most of the shows, and it seemed to be that pointed kids in the right direction," opines writer Jerry Sohl. "Not only that, it made the show entertaining. I don't think it was sugar-coated particularly, because some of those episodes had some pretty racy things in them. On a whole, I think it was, in its time, about the best thing that existed as far as science fiction on screen was concerned. Just the idea of going where no man has gone before is very good."

Behind the scenes, however, in terms of the writing of the scripts themselves, things didn't seem to be going too smoothly after a while, at least as far as John Black was concerned. He was doing whatever he could to bring in top science fiction writers, but they weren't being treated with the respect that he felt they deserved.

Said Roddenberry, "It seems that way, but it wasn't true. I didn't want only science fiction writers, because many of the science fiction writers available to me then talked about objects, about science rather than about people. Over half of them are just good regular writers because I wanted my show to be about people, not objects, and if you think back, the things you remember are the characters. During the first year, I wrote or rewrote everybody, even my best friends, because I had this idea in my mind of something that hadn't been done and I wanted to be really there. Once we had enough episodes, then the writers could see where we were going, but it was really building people to write the way I wanted them to write. I lost a lot of friends, writer friends, because writers don't like to be re-written, but the whole thing was in my head, and I [couldn't] say, 'Mr. Spock, write him like you would

write so-and-so,' because there'd never been anyone like that around. So I rewrote them and lost friendships."

Robert Justman agrees with Roddenberry's feelings. "When we were doing the original show," he explains, "the well known science fiction writers came up with all kinds of marvelous concepts, marvelous premises. Just because you have marvelous premises when you deliver a teleplay, doesn't mean that you've written a proper drama. We had that problem with a number of them, where their premises or concepts were terrific, but they didn't write a drama. They didn't write anything that could actually be photographed or made. The characters didn't necessarily behave in a logical fashion. If you create a character, a character has to be believable and do believable things. If your character doesn't do believable things, your audience is going to get turned off. Whereas you might accept it in the world of prose, you're not necessarily going to accept it in TV drama."

"I guess I'm prejudiced," he says. "I think Gene Roddenberry is a genius. He's an original thinker. Not only in creating *Star Trek*. I *know* him and have known him for years when he has said and done some amazing things," Justman continues. "He's an original thinker. His background was very humble, but he's a man who educated himself and he's found that his mind is fertile ground. It's an astonishing mind. You don't jump into a pool and swim without making waves.

"When you're beginning a series and you have a series premise and you have the methodology and you have a series that has a certain life and logic, your scripts must adhere to that concept. You can't expect a writer to come in and write one episode who is not heavily involved in the series or hasn't been since its inception, and be able to achieve the kind of reality that you the creator have envisioned for the show. Therefore, the show needs rewriting for various reasons. Not only for its content, but for technical reasons and reasons of format. I've done *Star Trek*, I've done a bunch of other series and I've never yet produced a show where the scripts from the writers didn't need revisions in order

to make them as close as possible to what your concept of the show is. It's seldom happened that I've ever shot a show that hasn't been rewritten. Only a few times that I can think of. Generally they're scripts that were turned out by the creator of the show. That's his or her concept, and if the creator happens to be a very good writer, generally there won't be too much need for revisions. Minor revisions, but they're not important."

It's pointed out that the list of complainants over the years have included a variety of highly respected writers, such as George Clayton Johnson, David Gerrold, Dorothy Fontana, Alan Dean Foster, Harold Livingston and Harlan Ellison.

"Bruised ego," Justman says simply. "I can't say I blame them. Nobody wants to be rewritten, because you put a lot of thought and emotion into what you're writing. You believe it's correct or you wouldn't have written it that way. Harry Truman used to say, 'If you can't take the heat, stay out of the kitchen.' No use determining that you're going to work in a certain medium if you're not willing to accept the rules that go with it; the restrictions that apply. This may surprise you, but people don't like to rewrite because it's hard work. You'd much rather get in a script that you can put right to work, but that's not necessarily the way things happen.

"I think Dorothy Fontana knows how to construct a proper drama. So does David Gerrold. You learn this after a while. But people have opinions and sometimes opinions diverge and the guy with the power is the one who prevails. If Dorothy had created a show, she would be doing something very much in the way that Gene has done. Same thing with David. *You* know what your show is supposed to be, and you're going to make it come out that way because that's what you're there for."

John Black offers his view, from the vantage point of *Star Trek*'s story editor and the one dealing directly with the writers.

"Gene was working from the position that he had created the show," says Black, "so it was *his*. G.R.'s approach was that he was in control of the show and he approached the scripts in that way. My deal going in was that if I was going to get really good heavyweight writers, I know that they don't want anybody to screw with their material. They want it to be their concept. The only reason they're going to take television money, which is short, and it was shorter than short story money at that time, and the only way that I will talk to them about it, is if they can rewrite their own material without interference. We could give them all the input we want, but we can't put pencil to paper on their material. Gene said okay, and the head of the studio said yes and that's the way I took the deal.

"This is the reality," he elaborates. "When stories came in on Thursday or Friday, I would read it, make my notes, copies would be made and G.R. would take them home on the weekend. And instead of notes, he would come in on Monday with a rewrite. He would have rewritten everything. God knows how much. And it would never, in my judgement, have been that much for the better. In some cases he got closer to the pattern that the show was becoming, because it was evolving while I was there. But G.R. has never been the writer that Harlan Ellison, Jerry Sohl or Teddy Sturgeon were. He isn't it. That's no knock. Very few people are up to that standing, but Gene couldn't keep his hands off a script. God knows what he would have done with 'To be or not to be, that is the question,' but there's one thing that's absolutely certain: what would have been in the script and what was shot would not have been 'to be or not to be, that is the question.' But it *was* his show. At first it was difficult and then it became impossible. And there was no way to know what would come in the next morning.

"When I did 'The Naked Time,' I delivered my first draft and gave a copy to G.R. I figured, 'Here I am, I'm working on the show and if anybody knows the show it's me, besides G.R. And G.R. brought back a rewritten script. I couldn't cope with it. That was not something I could suck up. The question in my mind, and I put it to G.R., was what the hell am I doing here if I don't know the show? And I asked him what his problem was with it. He told me and I said, 'Okay, I

will rewrite it.' And I rewrote it from my original, then he rewrote my second draft. So nobody got their show on the air...

"You know, you labor over a line...I'll give you an example. This is not an example from 'Naked Time,' but this is the kind of change. If I needed the essence of a cliche someplace, or where the cliche would have been perfect just as it is but it would have been a cliche, as a writer I say, 'How can I state this, where the cliche is clear but it isn't a cliche?' This is the hypothetical line that I would write: 'It's a gift horse. Leave its mouth alone.' Now that's an artfully written line. G.R.'s change would be, 'Don't look a gift horse in the mouth.' There could have been a lot more art in *Star Trek* if G.R. kept his hands off the scripts.

"After Gene would do his rewriting, I'd get the script back, try to satisfy him and get it back to as close a shape to the writer's work as I possibly could. The writer would come in, we would have a story conference, we would discuss changes, the writer would go away and, generally, I would get the writer to do the polish...if there was time. The dilemma with *Star Trek* was that what seemed to a writer to be something that could be done easily inside the context of the starship, became impossible. So alterations were made in a lot of things. They were slight, but necessary. The writers, I think, deserve credit for everything good in everything they did...while I was there, anyway. Any faults you could find in any material can be blamed on me and G.R. The stuff we got was, by and large, brilliant. I cannot remember one instance where I sat across a table from a writer and said, 'Why is this happening?' and they couldn't explain it to me. There was always a reasoning. *Star Trek* was an experience that I'm very glad I had. Talk about a love story. This sounds like a real love story."

Black left *Star Trek* after the first 13 episodes, feeling that he could not compromise himself any longer. "It's always mattered to me that my word was good," he says, "and if I told somebody that they would be permitted to rewrite their own work, that nobody would touch it, and then I would get it back already diddled with, that was not going

to move us into a very happy state of mind. I was there because I could talk to those writers. Those writers respected me and I respected them. Integrity mattered, and I couldn't bear to see quality work changed to the point where the dialogue did not have the sharp edge that it had, and G.R. would use the word 'fast' at least once a page as in, 'We've got to get there...fast.' I was watching too much good material getting screwed up and I couldn't take it. I confronted an executive at the studio and I said, 'I can't really continue if my word does not remain good,' and he said, 'It's G.R.'s show.' So I said, 'Would you like my resignation, or would you like to fire me?' And he said it could be one or the other. There was *no* alternative, so I left the show.

"Please understand, though, it was an experience I wouldn't trade for almost anything. I had never known pressures like the ones on that show, just by its nature. The beautiful demands that the writers made were wonderful. Man, to be sitting across from Ted Sturgeon and talking about a story that was so deeply important to him, and trying to perceive it and become aware...It was the kind of thing where you wanted to exclaim, 'My God, that's incredible!' It was sometimes scary, sometimes emotionally scathing, sometimes great fun, but you had to be there. You had to be present all the time, or you would have missed it. One never knew, particularly with *Star Trek*, what was important. The imagination ran wild. The energy level was just astounding. Looking back at it, I think I'd like to do it again. I can't be certain, but in remembering, I think I would."

While this was going on, both Roddenberry and Justman were working 16 to 20 hour days in an attempt to maintain the show's quality.

"Gene was very fatigued and so was I," says Justman. "We both nearly didn't make it through the first season because of overwork. We were at our wit's end. I was so tired that first season that I came unglued one night at home. My wife called Gene and said, 'That's it, I'm taking him away.' You try working for about six months, seven days a week and averaging three or four hours of sleep a night, with enormous pressure. Eventually something's going to give. It

• • • •

happened to be me that night and Gene was next. We were both basket cases. As a result of that, I think that's how Gene Coon came to be on the show. Gene Roddenberry just couldn't do it by himself. He was excellent, Gene Roddenberry wrote wonderful scenes, but it took its toll."

When Gene L. Coon joined the *Star Trek* staff as line producer, Roddenberry became executive producer.

"I had no choice," said Roddenberry. "The only way I could get people like Gene Coon to come in and produce—and I needed a producer, more helping hands—was to become executive producer, actually a supervising producer. Today, it would be different. No one would object to a very complex show having two, three or even four line producers with a supervising producer over them. In those days, it was unheard of, but I just had to get some extra people in any way I could. I had found myself working 12 or 14 hours a day and I could no longer do it. Everyone on our staff was in the hospital at least once during those three years just from total exhaustion. We were doing a half a science-fiction movie every week. Imagine what a burden that is. Science-fiction movies usually take 20 weeks to do. We were doing one every week!"

Gene Coon is generally considered to be one of *Star Trek*'s greatest strengths, having a natural feel for the kind of story that would be appropriate for the series. Under his sure creative hand came such episodes as "Arena," based on the Frederic Brown story of the same name, which pit Captain Kirk against the lizard-like Gorn creature, and resulted in the crew of the Enterprise being spared by an alien race because Kirk showed the advanced trait of mercy; "A Taste of Armageddon," a powerful Vietnam analogy in which two planets waged a bloodless war via computer, with people living in designated areas voluntarily walking into disintegration chambers; "Space Seed," which introduced Ricardo Montalban as Eugenics superman Khan Noonian Singh and gave the audience a taste of what Earth's future would be like; "The Devil in the Dark," an episode revealing that a creature known as the Horta who was killing Starfleet miners was actually a mother

protecting her young; and "Errand of Mercy," which introduced the Klingons.

"He shaped a lot of the individual shows," says Bob Justman regarding Coon, who passed away in the early 1970s. "But he didn't shape the concept. It was Gene's concept and it was never changed. Gene Coon rewrote the episodes while he was there. He wrote some originals and he was a workaholic. He would push himself to the limit and was marvelous. But the concept of the show had been established early in the first season. It was always Gene's concept. He shaped the show the way he wanted it to be. Then Gene Coon did his best—and his best was really very high—to make the show live up to that concept. Gene Coon was almost totally involved with story and script. He did some casting, but he had nothing really to do with the editing of the show or the scoring. I did all of that, as well as the props, the set dressing and all the other garbage.

"Honestly speaking," he continues, "Gene Roddenberry would have died if he didn't have Gene Coon or someone to do this. Gene Coon was a brilliant find; you couldn't find anyone better. The problem is that we wore him out, which is why he ultimately left in the middle of the second season."

Generally, Gene L. Coon may very well have been the one to define *Star Trek* for future generations. Indeed, his contributions to the series were important enough for William Shatner to mention him at the commemoration of the Gene Roddenberry Building on the Paramount lot several months before Roddenberry's passing.

"In my opinion," offers Shatner, "Gene Coon had more to do with the infusion of life into *Star Trek* than any other single person. Gene Roddenberry's instincts for creating the original package is unparalleled. You can't even discuss it. He put it together, hired the people and the concept was his and set in motion by him. But after 13 shows, other people took over. Gene Coon spent a year and set the tenor of the show. Gene [Roddenberry] was more in the background as other people actively took over."

For producer Harve Bennett, who steered the *Star Trek* feature film series for nearly 10 years, Coon was an

inspiration. "Gene Roddenberry was the Douglas MacArthur of this particular campaign, the George Patton," says Bennett. "And guys like Gene Coon were the Omar Bradleys."

Veteran writer/producer Glen A. Larson, whose credits include *Quincy, Knightrider* and *Battlestar: Galactica*, had worked with Coon while the two of them were on the staff of *It Takes a Thief*. During their tenure together, Larson came to look upon Coon as a mentor.

"I used to figuratively sit at his feet and listen to him talk about the business a great deal," reflects Larson. "That was really my whole introduction to television, through Gene. I think Gene Coon was the spirit and soul of the show. I don't think the show would have gone in the direction that it did nor had its enormous credibility of not for Coon. From what I could tell, Gene Coon *was Star Trek*. When he was no longer there, I think the show quickly denegrated to monster of the week, which was always the danger of science fiction in television, because you generally don't have the people around with the intellectual capacity to really explore important themes without making them so obscure that there's no hope of holding an audience. Gene had a good sense of drama in addition to strong concepts."

Gene L. Coon was born in Beatrice, Nebraska and educated within the public school system in both Nebraska and California. Following high school, he attended Glendale College. In 1942 he enlisted in the United States Marine Corp, where he spent four years. From there he wrote scripts for a variety of television series, including *Wagon Train, Bonanza, Have Gun, Will Travel, Rawhide, Alcoa Premier, Riverboat, Suspense, General Electric Theatre, Mr. Lucky, Peter Gunn, The Rebel* and *Maverick*. In the early '60s, Coon went to work at Universal Pictures where he co-created *McHale's Navy* and *The Munsters*, the latter of which was originally intended to be a hip satire of *The Donna Reed Show*. From 1964-67, Coon wrote several produced screenplays and penned two novels, *Meanwhile, Back at the Front* and *The Short End of the Stick*. But he seemed to find his true niche in *Star Trek*.

Examining the chronology of *Star Trek*, it becomes obvious that many of the show's more memorable aspects went into effect during Coon's reign.

"If you look at the episodes that Roddenberry was responsible for in the beginning," notes David Gerrold, "which was pretty much like the first 10 episodes, there's not a lot of that noble purpose there. There's a bumbling around trying to find out what the show is about, yet at the same time they did some great episodes. Because no one knew what *Star Trek* was, they were continually inventing it. You see stuff like 'Charlie X,' 'The Enemy Within,' and they also did a lot of rip-offs—'The Galileo Seven' was *Flight of the Phoenix*, 'Balance of Terror' was *The Enemy Below*—and so they didn't really know what they could do with the show yet. When Gene L. Coon first came on board in the second half of the first season, you start getting things like the Prime Directive and a lot of the stuff that was later identified as the noble parts of *Star Trek*. Gene L. Coon created the noble image that everyone gives Roddenberry the most credit for."

Continues Gerrold, "When Gene L. Coon came in, one of the things that happened is that by then they knew what they could do, and he would concentrate on those areas. The episodes he did were more sure of themselves, but they weren't as adventurous in the same way. The characters by then were more established, so Coon let the characters have the relationships with each other. The advantages were that when Gene L. Coon took over, the characters locked into place very tightly and crisply. And it became Kirk, Spock and McCoy. Before that time, there was a vagueness because Roddenberry didn't know who or what the show was about. After Gene Coon took over, he decided it was about Kirk, Spock and McCoy, and the other characters were ancillary. That became kind of the formula, which was successful."

Coon's scripts contained thinly-veiled social commentary, which became a staple of the series and something that is generally credited to Gene Roddenberry.

"We never sat around talking about that kind of thing," says Dorothy

Fontana. "I think that's just the kind of writing that Gene Coon did. It influenced the writers who came in, who were structuring their stories. You could see this kind of flow happening. Another thing that happened is that the humor between the characters began to become more and more developed, particularly the Spock and McCoy relationship became a lot more fun. It evolved into what it ultimately became, which was a basic friendship. It was a friendship conducted with little insults and jabs, but it was always fun. The verbal fencing matches. It was fun to create those conversations once we started getting into them. I think Gene Coon led the way on that."

Notes David Gerrold, "Roddenberry always took the show too seriously and everybody preached. I think Roddenberry wanted to be a preacher and couldn't make it or something. Everybody preached and Gene said, 'No, in the future our people work together,' but what he would write would be sermons. In Gene L. Coon's scripts, people interacted with each other in a whole different way and didn't preach, although it was mandatory to do a little preaching at the end of the script where the captain explains—the captain being the father figure. Gene L. Coon's characters joked with each other. I think that's why the fans loved the show so much. While our people were having an adventure, they were never too busy to snipe at each other, which was the way they showed their affection. I think there was never a question of how much Spock and McCoy loved each other, and that was shown by how vicious they would get when they would start sniping at each other. I think a lot of that was Gene L. Coon."

While Coon "replaced" Roddenberry as the show's hands-on producer, story editor John D.F. Black's role was taken over by a young writer named Steven Carabatsos, who considers himself one of the few people involved in *Star Trek* who has *not* come up with an explanation for the show's enduring success.

"It beats the hell out of me why the show has gone on the way it has," he laughs. "In retrospect, I suppose anyone who talks about the program wants to invest *every* moment with great significance. The honest fact is that when it was

first on, to me, at least, and I'm sure to many other people, it was just another show, 79 episodes of employment for most of them. Granted that because of all the famous science fiction writers involved, there was a sense of more going on, but you have to understand, nobody knew what we had there. *Nobody* had any idea. Even when the show came on, it didn't light up the stars."

Carabatsos, not a science fiction fan, was asked by his agent if he would be interested in meeting with the two Genes about the possibility of taking on the position of script consultant. That meeting went well, and Carabatsos entered the realm of the 23rd century.

"The show hadn't been on the air yet," he says. "By the time I came on, there were about six episodes in the can. I'm sure today it's even more frantic because the stakes are higher, but at that time, on the shakedown year of a show, everyone was trying new things and was concerned about it being a success, as well as being the kind of show they wanted it to be. In something as new as *Star Trek*, Roddenberry wanted to do a *legitimate* science fiction program. Not the silly stuff that had been on previously that allegedly passed for science fiction.

"Gene Roddenberry worked very hard. I've got to give the man a lot of credit, he busted his butt. But he had taken on executive producer responsibilities and the line producer was Gene L. Coon, who was actually making sure the scripts got into the right form for shooting and physically produced the show. He's the one I reported to once I came to work.

"In those days, most of the writing was done by freelancers as opposed to today where you've got all these people on staff with commitments for three to six episodes or more. Some of the scripts could have the rough edges rounded off and could be put before the cameras quickly, while others required substantial rewriting, which Gene Coon and I handled. It was an exciting time for me, because I was really just a kid, and this was a big opportunity. I also remember being impressed by the fact that Roddenberry was enlisting a writing corp of experienced science fiction writers. All of them came to their assignments with great enthusiasm and a sense of excitement to do *their* kinds of stories done in the way they wanted them done. My problem is that I didn't share that background; I didn't quite feel that I had the same preparation for it."

He remained with the show for approximately 15 weeks before moving on to other areas. To this day, however, he remains amazed that people are so impressed when they learn he worked on *Star Trek*.

"It was early in the days of one-hour dramatic TV programs," he muses, "and everyone was happy to have a show that lasted more than a year. As it turned out, *much* longer than a year."

When Carabatsos departed, Dorothy Fontana slipped into the position of script consultant, a role she essayed until the end of the second season. Having proved herself to Roddenberry and company, she was a welcome addition to the staff.

"I had dealt with the scripts all the time," Fontana explains, "and had my own opinions about them. I just never put them down on paper, although I spoke to Gene and Gene Coon secretly about the shows they were doing. I got involved with the show first as a writer, so I had my own story conferences with them about it. I felt I could do that same job [of script consultant] and so did Gene, so he let me have it."

Despite an ever changing cre-

ative staff, *Star Trek* did manage to maintain its high level of quality. Unfortunately there was another battle being fought, and that was the battle of the Nielsons: once on the air, it became obvious that *Star Trek* was losing the ratings war. In fact, NBC began indicating that the series might be cancelled at the midpoint of the first season. Amazingly, however, as word of this got out, science fiction author Harlan Ellison spear-headed a letter writing campaign to keep the series on the air.

This effort was a success, resulting in a tremendous response that proved there was indeed an audience out there watching *Star Trek* each week and waiting for further adventures aboard the starship Enterprise. The series not only lasted the full season, but was renewed for a second year.

Star Trek had survived a rejected pilot, network opposition and near-cancellation. Unfortunately, this only represented the first round of an interstellar boxing match that would continue over the next two years.

William Shatner and Pat Breslin in the "Nick of Time" episode of The Twilight Zone.

• • • •

CHAPTER TWO
Season 1 Episode Guide

"The Man Trap"

"Charlie X"

"Where No Man Has Gone Before"

"The Naked Time"

"The Enemy Within"

"Mudd's Women"

"What Are Little Girls Made Of?"

"Miri"

"Dagger of the Mind"

"The Corbomite Maneuver"

"The Menagerie" (Pts 1 and 2)

"The Conscience of the King"

"Balance of Terror"

"Shore Leave"

"The Galileo Seven"

"The Squire of Gothos"

"Arena"

"Tomorrow is Yesterday"

"Court Martial"

"The Return of the Archons"

"Space Seed"

"A Taste of Armageddon"

"This Side of Paradise"

"The Devil in the Dark"

"Errand of Mercy"

"The Alternative Factor"

"City on the Edge of Forever"

"Operation Annihilate"

Before becoming the humanist Dr. Leonard "Bones" McCoy, DeForest Kelly had forged a career of playing Western heavies.

Episode #1:
"The Man Trap"
Original Airdate: 9/8/66
Written by George Clayton Johnson
Directed by Marc Daniels
Guest Starring: Jeanny Bal (Nancy Carter), Francine Pyne (Salt Creature), Alfred Ryder (Professor Carter), Michael Zaslow (Darnell)

The Enterprise is assigned the task of proceeding to planet M-113 in order to deliver medical supplies to the planet's only two inhabitants, Doctors Robert and Nancy Crater, the latter of whom had been romantically involved with Dr. McCoy. Rather, he had been involved with *a* Nancy Crater. This one turns out to be a shape-changing salt "vampire" who seduces its victims by appearing as someone they know and then attacking, draining their bodies of natural salt content. The creature gets aboard the Enterprise and must be destroyed, despite the fact it is the last of a species.

••••

Writer George Clayton Johnson explains that his original title for "The Man Trap" was "Damsel With a Dulcimer," but that Gene Roddenberry changed the title as well as some its structure, which the author felt lessened the impact of the episode.

"I'll give you just an example,"

Johnson reflects. "The initial scene of 'The Man Trap' as initially conceived was that Leonard McCoy and Captain Kirk are entering the transporter on the ship for the purpose of being beamed down to the planet surface to begin the story. We've seen a fly-through of the ship, because that's standard format and we've heard the song and we know what show we're watching now, and we cut to the beginning of the first act and we're not on the bridge, we're approaching this transporter room, walking through hallways, talking and coming into this transporter room.

"Now the character that I wrote for the character of Dr. McCoy, who was a very undefined character, I'd only seen one show of it and was expected as a professional writer to visualize all the surrounding tiles, each tile together would form this huge, colossal thing we know as *Star Trek*. But we just had one of the few of the tiles, one or two or three of the tiles in place, and I had only seen one of them, so on the basis of that one I was expected to dream up *my* version of *Star Trek*. So I had Captain Kirk saying something to Leonard McCoy about, 'What's wrong, Bones?' and Bones saying, 'Look, I just don't like the whole idea of the transporter. I don't care how tight any beam is, there's some scatter and I don't like the idea of atoms of myself being left all over the damn universe. I just don't like that idea. And this thing gives me the creeps.' And that sort of dialogue, whereupon Captain Kirk says, 'Nonsense,' and they show up on the planet surface, whereupon we get some of the underground. In place of that comes a scene written to replace it where McCoy and the Captain are getting into the transporter; they are talking about some flowers that are being carried to give this girl whom McCoy is going to be meeting, who is his old girlfriend, whom he knows is going to be on this planet, this so-called Nancy Crater.

"Now the business about the flowers, for me, is kind of in a certain way very subjectively soft, whereas the business about the transporter is for me very objectively hard, and it also makes a promise of future episodes. It says that one of these days we may see a story about a transporter malfunction. It lets

you know that there are limitations on the universe. But it was taken out, so that later on when we see the first transporter malfunction story, we are not prepared for it; if we are regular viewers, it comes out of the blue to us. Now I felt that was damaging to the entire concept. That little mini-story implanted in just a few lines of dialogue, setting the scene, is superior dramaturgy to the business about, 'Oh, I see you need to take along some [flowers] to get girls to like you. Is that your thing?' [It's just] a little bit of familiarity between two pals."

"The idea of the shape changer," he says."I received the go ahead from Gene on the idea, then I went home and worked hard for about 30 days and I came back with a script with which I was very dissatisfied with, and I was reluctant to show the story editor. I told the story editor, John D.F. Black, what my feelings were, and he asked me then what I was doing, and I started telling him and at a certain point he said, 'Oh, you see a problem is that you don't get the creature aboard the ship fast enough. The danger is once the creature gets aboard the ship.' The minute he said that, I could see where my thinking had been wrong, the initial concept of the structure, the very shape which the story took, which suddenly collapsed it into my mind, and I went home and in a matter of just a few days completely rewrote it with his blessing, brought it back and he liked it immediately."

Recalling the experience of George Clayton Johnson, John D.F. Black states, "George Johnson is the best 'soap opera writer' that ever functioned in nighttime melodramatic television....Please, God, don't make it sound like I'm saying anything negative, because it isn't. It's a very unique way and it may be George's natural style to write. It's very real, but at the same time there's that kind of theatricalism which is maybe a touch more than what [Richard] Matheson or I would do. It's just a touch more....I say soap opera for wont of another phrase. George worked harder on story with more conscientiousness and more dedication than anybody, because George, of all the writers involved with the show, really wanted *Star Trek* to be a smash. He really wanted science fiction out there, on the tube for people to see. He was dedicated to the media, he was dedicated to the show and there was nothing he wouldn't do. If we had asked him to sneak into the lot at night to build sets, he would have done that."

Shortly before his death, director Marc Daniels opined, "From the point the series began, it was very touchy in terms of how we should deal with these monsters. Did you go for cheap thrills or take the more intelligent approach? What we came up with was the idea that in order to get the audience involved in a very realistic way, you had to treat everything as though it were real."

Episode #2:
"Charlie X"
Original Airdate: 9/15/66
Written by Dorothy Fontana
Story by Gene Roddenberry
Directed by Lawrence Dobkin
Guest Starring: Robert Walker Jr. (Charlie), Abraham Sofaer (Thalasian), Patricia McNulty (Tina Lawton), Charles J. Stewart (Captain Remart), Dallas Mitchell (Tom Nellis)

Shortly after the captain of the Federation ship Antares drops off adolescent Charlie Evans on board the Enterprise, the Antares is mysteriously destroyed. Following other unexplained incidents, the blame falls on Charlie who reveals himself to have incredible telekinetic abilities to alter matter and cause people to "go away," i.e. vanish. Charlie, whose immaturity governs his actions, becomes an even more dangerous threat when he falls in love with Yeoman Janice Rand and will stop at nothing to get her to return his feelings.

••••

This episode features a startling moment when Charlie closes in on Janice and the camera fades to black. One gets the impression that he is forcing himself upon her sexually, though this is left entirely to the imagination.

"'Charlie X' was a story that was in the original series presentation," explains Dorothy Fontana, "and I told Gene that if no one else wanted to do it, I would like to do the teleplay. That's precisely what happened. I was in Europe when they shot it, but I did like the way it turned out, and I thought Robert Walker, Jr. was an especially good choice for Charlie."

Several years ago Walker recalled his experience on the episode, particularly the fact that star William Shatner was "very, very helpful. I had only been an actor for about five years and he had always been kind of an idol of mine. I had always thought that he was a terrific actor. I had watched him on different programs for years before I did 'Charlie X.' But he was very helpful and very friendly and the same with Leonard Nimoy. They took the time and were patient with this new, reluctant budding actor.

"That was an interesting, awkward period of my life," he added. "I almost felt like Charlie X. I was 26 when I did the episode but I was a late developer. It was a very difficult time. I didn't have much self-confidence as an actor or as a person. I felt awkward and ineffectual and really kind of lost. I felt at loose ends really. It was a very vulnerable time for me but also a very exciting time for me. You know, at that time, I was very much like Charlie X. We had a lot of similarities."

In the pages of Pocket's *The Star Trek Interview Book*, director Lawrence Dobkin recalled, "Probably my best memory of *Star Trek* is all those people, that young in the series: they did not yet have approval of the crowd. They hadn't any support for what was clearly an attempt to bring the humanities into another time zone, to graph today's relationships in some fashion onto a different time frame, and keep the simplicities and the realities and the human interaction going. My God, what a talented bunch. Wow! It was a very fruitful period in so many ways, fruitful for all of us. It was a fortunate time, and people took chances, people took grave risks....I had played with science fiction in one form or another, and it's very difficult to empathize with something quite strange, quite out of the way. It's difficult for an audience to come to terms with even as human a creature as Captain Nemo in the Jules Verne science fiction...But here, Roddenberry's thrust made very real people and very concerned relationships."

Episode #3:
"Where No Man Has Gone Before"
Original Airdate: 9/22/66
Written by Samuel A. Peeples

Actress Sally Kellerman portrayed Dr. Elizabeth Dehner in "Where No Man Has Gone Before."

Directed by James Goldstone
Guest Starring: Gary Lockwood (Gary Mitchell), Sally Kellerman (Elizabeth Dehner), Paul Carr (Kelso), Paul Fix (Dr. Piper), Andrea Dromm (Yeoman Smith), Lloyd Haynes (Alden)

As the Enterprise attempts to broach an energy barrier at the edge of the galaxy, crewman Gary Mitchell—a close personal friend of Kirk's—is transformed into a god-like being who must be killed before he can inflict his power on the universe.

••••

Actor Gary Lockwood, who portrayed Gary Mitchell and who would later go on to portray astronaut Frank Poole in Stanley Kubrick's *2001*, recalls working on *Star Trek*'s second pilot.

"To tell you the truth," he smiles, "I thought it was a little bizarre and I thought it was kind of embarrassing and I hoped it worked out because everybody was excited about it. It was a very hard job to do. You couldn't see the other actors. I'd rehearse and get everything all ready, but I couldn't see the actors because of the contact lenses that changed my eyes. They didn't blind me for the first few days, but after a few days the eyes swelled up and got sore. Then to have them on for just two or three minutes was agonizing. Scenes were rehearsed without them. The other thing about it, people always thought I was kind of egotistical so when I got to play that part, a lot of people laughed and said, 'He's finally found his niche.' That's been a joke among my friends.

"That character was tough to reach, because there's no prototype character to look at. So you create a mental image and try to fill that slot. All I tried to do was downplay the mechanics and not be too dramatic. It's the same thing I did in *2001*. Try to play the part very quietly and very realistically, and later on people don't think you're pushing. That's the way to sustain it. There was a natural progression to the character. In order to do that, you have to think it out. Let me say one thing to you that I can say about American actors I don't like and who don't like me. You have to apply a certain amount of intelligence to your role first, and then you can apply the emotion after you've made an intellectual decision. Too many young kids I work with are all trying to figure out how to make the line comfortable. You work in Europe, they're trying to bend to the line. Here they're trying to bend the line to them. It's a different approach. With Gary Mitchell, the idea was trying to go to the character and not make the character comfortable to me. I'm *not* Gary Mitchell."

"I guess 'Where No Man Has Gone Before' is effective because it sold the series. You've got to keep in mind that the *Star Trek* pilot was made in those days on a very, very tight budget. I think there was a big fight between the network and Roddenberry over making the second pilot, so there was a lot of pressure on him. They came up with this idea of two characters getting ESP, which I liked. I think they made up for not having an opportunity to do a lot of effects by just creating a couple of interesting characters, and that helped sell the show. It was a good creative decision on the part of Roddenberry."

Director James Goldstone points out that he most definitely contributed to the creative process of the episode, as emphasized by the notes he wrote on one of his scripts for "Where No Man Has Gone Before."

"A major point," Goldstone wrote, "which applies all the way through the script, and to which there might be specific reference below, concerns the character of Mitchell and the evolution of his mutation toward god status. The purpose is dramatic, to create a subtext. My proposal is that from the time Gary suffers the first realization of what is happening....once he begins to give in to it, to

enjoy it, even, he moves from his human status toward the status of a god within all and any of the criteria we place on such dieties in our Christian-Judaic culture. Specifically, I propose that he become oracular, in the sense of Moses or even Cotton Mather. I propose he do this in his stature, his way of using his hands and arms and eyes, silver or normal, his attitude at it applies to the script, aside from those specific stage directions, perhaps physical actions that pertain to the dialogue. I don't mean to suggest that it become so stylized as to become a symbol rather than a human being. I suggest it happen on a more symbolic level. This can be done by starting him more on the flip, swinging level of articulation so that we don't even notice at one moment that this drops, but it does, on its way to becoming more formal, then more laden with import, more self-declarative, and finally downright miraculous."

Despite this type of contribution, Goldstone emphasizes that he does not believe in the auteur theory. "The director is the person who actually implements the work, but if he doesn't work with the writer, and if he doesn't work with the producer, the technicans in the preparation, then he's being cut off at the knees and so is the film. Television, especially, has just become a producer's medium. People would probably rather not have me, because I'm a pain in the ass. I want to do the things that directors, as I understand it, are supposed to do."

Episode #4:
"The Naked Time"
Original Airdate: 9/29/66
Written by John D.F. Black
Directed by Marc Daniels
Guest Starring:
Bruce Hyde (Riley), Stewart Moss (Tormolen), John Bellah (Dr. Harrison)
While attempting to remove a group of scientists from the doomed planet Psi 2000, an Enterprise landing party is infected with a disease which they bring back aboard the starship and quickly spread. The result is that the crew's inhibitions are stripped away, as though by alcohol, and they start living out their fantasies or confronting their darkest demons. Lieutenant Riley, who establishes himself

as "captain," tampers with the engines and the Enterprise is threatened with destruction as it moves closer to the planet's atmosphere. Dr. McCoy labors to find a cure before it's too late.

••••

In John D.F. Black's opinion, "The Naked Time" was a perfect example of just how limitless the *Star Trek* format was.

"There was *no* limit," he enthuses. "We could have villains that you could see and villains you couldn't see, as in my 'The Naked Time.' You could have any character do a complete turnaround simply because there was a difference in oxygen somewhere. We jumped right in there without one single solitary thing in terms of theatricalism that we couldn't do. We could have done Oedipus or anything, although the censors wouldn't allow us to do the Oedipus story. Nor would they allow it anytime you got into those overtly sexually driven stories at that point in time. Except for 'Mudd's Women,' which was basically prostitution at large, which was in the papers every day. We were not promoting it or coming out against it. All we were saying is that it happens here and it happens in outer space, and the censors let it go. We had a lot of support from the censors at NBC. We had some static, but, by and large, they went *with* the show, and that doesn't happen often."

Added director Marc Daniels, "That was the one where I had very little preparation, although I think it turned out all right. The characters were falling into place and we began to get into the workings of Kirk's mind, Spock's powers and things like that. In one of the early episodes, Spock got hurt and bled green blood. I think Gene thought that idea was going too far, but they kept it in later episodes. The green blood was my idea, because if Spock was going to have a yellow complexion, he ought to have green blood. Anyway, in 'The Naked Time' George Takei went a little out of control. We had sharp swords there and he was getting a bit carried away. We had to 'shut him off' so that he wouldn't accidentally hurt anybody."

George Takei recalled, "When I learned that I'd have to fence for 'The Naked Time,' I became panic stricken. I didn't know how to use a sword! I started taking fencing lessons only three weeks before the episode shot."

Interestingly, this show would serve as the springboard for the second episode of *Star Trek: The Next Generation*, "The Naked Now." Unfortunately, it was not as interesting, because the script was more concerned with sexual hijinks among the crew than characterization.

Episode #5:
"The Enemy Within"
Original Airdate: 10/6/66
Written by Richard Matheson
Directed by Leo Penn
Guest Starring: Jim Goodwin (John Farrell), Edward Madden and Garland Thompson (Technicians)

A transporter malfunction splits Kirk into two beings: one pure evil and the other good. What follows is a battle between the two as each battles for supremacy at the expense of the other, though it becomes obvious that they need each other. Spock and Chief Engineer Scott attempt to devise a method of combining the two Kirks into one. Meanwhile, a landing team is trapped on the surface of Alpha 177 and sub-zero temperatures. The Enterprise cannot beam them aboard for fear that what happened to Kirk would happen to them as well.

••••

"Dick Matheson and I knew each other, not well but we had crossed over each other for a long time before I was ever on *Trek*," says John D.F. Black. "In his case what I had to do with the script was miniscule, because he really wanted to make his own fight with G.R., and could do it. He was a professional. I know he had had a conference with G.R. at some point that I was not at, and then we had a talk about the final draft in G.R.'s office and I was there. He understood what the show was. He did not think it was a disguised comedy, he did not think it was the last man on the moon. He knew what we were doing. He tuned in immediately, as he had done on *Twilight Zone* before, so it was difficult for G.R. to make any kind of real arguments about structure. He had some bitches about where the story turned here and where it turned there, but by and large that was one of the easy ones."

In the pages of *Starlog* magazine, director Leo Penn admitted, "It was a challenging show to do. We had to hire a photo double, and it was particularly tough in the scenes where they [the two Kirks] had physical contact. You had to resort to shooting over the double's shoulder, switching them around and so on. It took time, but the results were worth it."

In that same interview with journalist Pat Jankiewicz, Penn noted, "Within certain aspects of American Indian culture, they surmise that evil possesses more energy than good, and Indians believe if they could get to the evil one and comb the snakes out of his hair, he would be cleansed and be able to use that energy for good. One is constantly interested in the struggle between good and evil....In every human being there's good and bad. Hopefully the good is reachable. There are some leaders who bring out the best in people, and Captain Kirk was certainly such a person."

Episode #6:
"Mudd's Women"
Original Airdate 10/13/66
Written by Stephen Kandel
Story by Gene Roddenberry
Directed by Harvey Hart
Guest Starring: Roger C. Carmel (Harry Mudd), Karen Steele (Eve), Susan Denberg (Magda), Maggie Three (Ruth), Gene Dynarski (Ben Childress), Jim Goodwin (Farrell), Jon Kowal (Gossett), Seamon Glass (Benton)

The Enterprise beams aboard interstellar conman Harry Mudd and the three incredibly beautiful women he has along with him as cargo. Kirk regrets saving them from their doomed vessel when he cripples the Enterprise in the process, and the only way for the ship to continue on its way is to make it to a mining world to replenish their dilithium crystal supplies. Harry manages to contact the miners first and manipulates them with the women, thus hoping to achieve his freedom from the authorities. As time goes on, it becomes obvious that the women's beauty has been achieved artificially.

••••

"Gene had the idea of using a personal enhancer-allure drug," says writer Stephen Kandel of the script's origins, "and I provided the idea of the character of Harry Mudd. We spent an afternoon talking about it and out of the conversation evolved the story idea and then, of course, I wrote the story. Gene went over it in great and meticulous and obsessive detail, and then I wrote the script.

"I thought Harry was a marvelous character of the highly recognizable human quality set against the alien in time or alien in space activity that evolved," he enthuses. "That's what made it amusing, and it's also hard to do because you had stern-jawed Kirk who would meet an eight foot intelligent reptile and deal with him as any astronaut would. Then the reptile would meet Harry Mudd, whose first impulse would be to run and hide, and second impulse would be to sell it scale enhancer."

John D.F. Black says, "The basic problem we had with 'Mudd's Women' was not the script so much as the wardrobe as designed and getting it past the censors. It was a very overtly sex oriented piece."

Episode #7:
"What Are Little Girls Made Of?"
Original Airdate: 10/20/66
Written by Robert Bloch
Directed by James Goldstone
Guest Starring: Michael Strong (Dr. Korby), Sherry Jackson (Andrea), Ted Cassidy (Ruk), Harry Basch (Brown), Vince Deadrick (Matthews), Budd Albright (Rayburn)

Nurse Christine Chapel is to be reunited with her fiance, Dr. Roger Korby, who is on the planet Exo III. When she and Kirk beam down to the planet's surface, they learn that Korby has discovered an ancient technology that allows him to create androids which are an exact duplicate of people. He uses this technology to make an android of Kirk, with the intention of using the Enterprise to spread this new race throughout the galaxy.

••••

"Robert Bloch is one of those venerables," opines John D.F. Black. "He's a writer with a phenomenal and enormous stature among science fiction writers. I respected him and when he

The late Ted Cassidy, forever known as The Addam's Family's Lurch, *portrayed Ruk in "What Are Little Girls Made Of?"*

came in the story was already on line; the deal had already been made when I signed on to the show. It was a story that I wanted to see what the hell he would do with in the translation from story to teleplay. I don't think I would have touched it. G.R. did. I don't know what went wrong with it. I think it was one of those things that on paper was one thing, and translating it through actors and through a director was another. But the script, by and large, worked as I perceived it. I know that there was a long stretch between the first draft and the second, and I can't remember if it was because it was difficult to execute what had been told to Bloch or whether in fact he had some hang-up and he was pissed at the comments. You've got to remember that stories were affected by cost factors all over the place. I think there was a cost factor involved in the Bloch piece, but I'm not sure."

Director James Goldstone is more succinct with his memories. "There were problems," he says simply. "I got a panic call from Bobby Justman that whatever plans they had for the episode had turned into a big problem. Would I please help them out? I happened to be free that week. Largely out of affection for Gene and other people involved, I read the script. It was not like anything else I'd done, and it was not like the pilot in any way. My memory of it is that I was not at all emotionally involved, nor did I think it was the kind of story we had

originally conceived of. It was done as a favor to Gene and others, rather than something I wanted to do."

Episode #8:
"Miri"
Original Airdate: 10/27/66
Written by Adrian Spies
Directed by Vincent McEveety
Guest Starring: Kim Darby (Miri), Michael J. Pollard (Jahn), Jim Goodwin (Farrell)

Upon Enterprise discovering an Earth-like planet , a landing team that includes Kirk, Spock, McCoy and Rand beams down and discovers a group of 300 year old children. They learn that a disease prolongs youth, but upon reaching adolescence—no matter how long it takes—it triggers madness and then death. Infected, the landing party is trapped there unless McCoy can devise a cure. In the meantime, a young woman named Miri develops a strong crush on Kirk, and is extremely jealous of the captain's affection for Rand.

••••

"I had no idea *Star Trek* was going to be such a big deal. I wrote 'Miri' to the best of my ability and it was a good script, I thought, but it was *just another script*," admits writer Adrian Spies. "I had already won big awards, including the Edgar [the Mystery Writers of America award], and had been nomi-

nated for an Emmy. I didn't think this was going to fit into that kind of category for me. *Star Trek* just didn't sound like my schtick. But to this day, people say, 'Oh my God, you wrote "Miri!"', and I get chagrined. In those days, Gene told the writers he called that this was 'really an anthology. This is a chance to write about anything you want.' I didn't know what he was talking about. But we were two professionals and we worked out the story together. He had good ideas and good contributions. In the final analysis, it was a good experience. I just wasn't into very much science fiction at that point.

"I have a feeling that [with 'Miri'] I was trying to develop an idea for a film," he adds, "and when I went to see Gene I offered him the idea of a bunch of kids in this place where they are permanently young, but are really very old. If he was to tell you that he came up with the idea, I wouldn't say no, but it's not my memory. I do remember that he said, 'You have to develop a language for these people.' I said, 'What the hell are you talking about?' He said, 'The kids would talk differently.' In that conversation, he made up the word 'grups' for grownups. I immediately liked it. That's an example of a creative producer at work."

"The idea of 'Miri' was absolutely intriguing and fascinating, and it felt wonderful right from the get go," smiles John D.F. Black. "The stresses that

"Miri" stars Kim Darby and William Shatner were reunited in ABC's 1972 TV movie, The People.

••••

were built in had a natural energy in the concept. It was there from the first draft and Adrian kept it there throughout. He was easy to work with because he was a consummate professional and experienced at the time. What it would take you 10 minutes to say to somebody else, you could say to him in 30 seconds and he would have a clamp on it and know exactly what you meant. We were lucky to have him."

Director Vincent McEveety had gotten his big break on *The Untouchables* and had moved on to Gene Roddenberry's *The Lieutenant* before helming six episodes of *Star Trek*.

"'Miri' was a great love story with beautiful performances," he continues, "and it's definitely my favorite episode. I think if we have one obligation as so-called 'creative people' in this business in the function of writing, producing and directing, it's to entertain. By entertaining, I mean moving the audience. If you can move somebody, change somebody, give somebody a change of heart, have them look at something different than they may have in the past, provide some kind of introspection to themselves and have them walk away saying, 'Wow,' then I think you've done what you set out to do. If you're just putting out some joke or a kaleidoscope of scenes, that might be enough for Saturday morning, but it isn't enough for a show with the caliber of *Star Trek*. I think 'Miri' fit in perfectly."

Episode #9:
"Dagger of the Mind"
Original Airdate: 11/3/66
Written by Shimon Wincelberg
Directed by Vincent McEveety
Guest Starring: James Gregory (Dr. Tristan Adams), Morgan Woodward (Dr. Van Gelder), Marianna Hill (Dr. Helen Noel), Suzanne Wilson (Lethe)

While delivering supplies to penal colony Tantalus Five, Kirk happens upon the madness of Dr. Tristan Adams, who is using a revolutionary neural neutralizer to control and manipulate his patients. Fearful of exposure, he uses the device on the captain.

••••

John D.F. Black smiles sheepishly at the memories of working with writer Shimon Wincelberg. "When I did story notes, I never did the first draft for the writer. My notes were expressions of what I thought, i.e. 'What is this piece of shit?' and things like that. Well, I wrote scathing notes about Shimon's story: 'It doesn't look like something he's written, it looks like he's taken it out of his trunk...an ancient piece that really doesn't deserve to see the light of day,' and so on. In my notes to myself, from which I would write courteous notes in which I would offer proper criticisms, I pulled no punches. Then, I wasn't in my office and Shimon showed up for his story conference. G.R. sent Dorothy Fontana into my office to pick up my notes. She xeroxed my notes and gave them to Shimon, and then he came into my office later on and thanked me for being that frank and that honest. He told me I was right and went home to rewrite the story. Now that's not only a gentleman, but that's an honest and dedicated writer. I thought his title was one of the more artful and the concept was absolutely clean. If you think about it, it's really an intelligent concept and I wasn't even sure if it would work as *Trek*. But it got a little more 'commercial' as it went from first to second draft and finally to filmed episode."

Episode #10:
"The Corbomite Maneuver"
Original Airdate: 11/10/66
Written by Jerry Sohl
Directed by Joseph Sargent
Guest Starring: Anthony Hall (Dave Bailey), Clint Howard (Balok)

The Enterprise destroys a dangerous alien probe while exploring an uncharted region in space. Moments later, they are locked in the tractor beam of a ship identifying itself as the Fesarius, which has threatened them with destruction. All attempts at escape fail, and Kirk develops an ingenious plan to trick his opponent. What's even more ingenious is the episode's denouement, in which the *true* identity of the Fesarius' captain is revealed.

••••

Writer Jerry Sohl explains, "I was thinking suppose you ran across a cube in space. A cube is so damn finitive and so square and so unlike nature, and so un-asteroidish, that you know right away that it represents intelligent life, unless of course it could be some salt cubes or something like that. Anyway, a thing like that in space, whirling around all by itself, has to be a great mystery. Immediately I thought, 'What is it doing there?' Then I thought, 'It's like an electronic warning system at the frontier, and Kirk and his group are so arrogant that they just destroy it,' which, of course, is the point where this ship appears and says, 'Okay, you guys stepped too far and it's tough shit.' That's where my thinking went.

"You go in with a half a dozen ideas," he adds, "and that was one of them and they liked it. I had it entirely different in my mind to begin with, but in talking it out they knew what they wanted. I wanted Kirk to be on a mission wherein he was being observed by a person from the Federation who is sitting there watching and making a report on him. They occasionally have people who go on airplanes and sit with the pilot or co-pilot, and make a report on them. Why shouldn't they do that on space ships? But the truth of the matter is that they thought, and rightly so, that that would clutter up the story. I went through it, and it would have been too much to get into one hour. I thought it turned out very well with considerable drama and incident. How the hell were they going to get out of this one? And then they added the fellow at the end, which was so much like the end of many of my novels, where a little kid is behind the whole thing. That tickled Gene Roddenberry, and Robert Justman was quite taken by the whole thing. It worked out very well, and I was highly pleased with it. It was probably the best *Star Trek* that I did anyway."

John D.F. Black notes, "The thing about 'The Corbomite Maneuver' is that it was such a simple story. When you think about it, structurally, in terms of most science fiction, and I can think of three or four others that we had that would be the exact antithesis; that were so much more complicated naturally that it was something to watch. Here the situation was to watch that the story was not expressed as simply as it really was. Television and any entertainment medium is magic. We are all in the magic business. Well, here it was like close-up magic, which is what Jerry was doing. It was like he has five cards in his hand and he wipes his hand and he's got four, he wipes it again and he's got three, and you're only a foot and a half away and you don't know what he did with them."

Director Joseph Sargent, whose other foray into the world of science fiction was the 1970 cult classic, *Colossus: The Forbin Project*, recalls, "They chose mine to open up the series [though it aired as the tenth episode]. The comforting thing is that I had a hand in shaping the characters. For instance, they had an Asian, a Scotsman and an alien. I suggested that they have a black communications officer. Gene Roddenberry instantly jumped on the idea because it provided an interesting balance."

Sargent, however, had a differing view of that logical "alien," Mr. Spock.

"Leonard Nimoy was unhappy because his character was without emotion," Sargent laughs. "He said, 'How can I play a character *without* emotion? I don't know how to do that. I'm going to be on one note throughout the entire series.' I agreed with him and we worked like hell to give him some emotional context, but Gene said, 'No way, the very nature of this character's contribution is that he isn't an earthling. As a Vulcan, he is intellect over emotion.' Leonard was ready to quit because he didn't know how he was going to do it. Humorously enough, after I saw *Star Trek IV*, I called him and we discussed the ironies of life. If he had quit, he wouldn't be anywhere near where he is now. Not only is he a household symbol, but he's also a very high-priced director."

Despite only directing one episode, Sargent's feelings about *Star Trek* and what it was trying to do are very succinct.

"I'm *not* a science-fiction fan because after a while, it gets into a sameness," he states. "But *Star Trek* was filled with imagination and substance. Each episode had that distinctive added dimension to it. It's science fiction with something to say, along the lines of Ray Bradbury, who I think was a big influence on Gene Roddenberry in terms of making the stories say something as well as provide entertainment. That's why *Star*

Trek has been so enduring. It's not just because the characters are fun and appealing, which they are, and not just because somebody's beaming somebody else up, but also because they're beaming up something a little more important than action and adventure."

Episode #11:
"The Menagerie"
Original Airdates: 11/17 and 11/24/66
Written by Gene Roddenberry
Directed by Marc Daniels
Guest Starring: Jeffrey Hunter (Captain Pike), Susan Oliver (Vina), Malachi Throne (Jose Mendez), Julie Parrish (Miss Piper), Hagan Beggs (Lt. Hanson), Peter Duryea (Tyler), Meg Wylie (The Keeper), John Hoyt (Dr. Boyce), Majel Barrett (Number One)

When a crippled and paralyzed Christopher Pike is beamed aboard the Enterprise, Spock commandeers the vessel to Talos IV, a world deemed off-limits by the Federation. As a result, the Vulcan is placed on court martial for mutiny, and during the trial the ship's viewscreen flashes back to footage from "The Cage," which details Pike's connection with the Talosians. It is Spock's hope that Pike will find some happiness amongst the illusionary abilities of that alien race.

••••

This two-part episode represented one of the most ingenious uses of old footage ever devised, effortlessly maintaining the audience's attention while utilizing *Star Trek*'s rejected pilot. The concept was Gene Roddenberry's, and it was a brilliant stroke on his part.

"'The Menagerie' presented a difficult technical problem," observed Marc Daniels. "I had to work around what was there. The script did it, of course, and it was certainly an interesting episode to do. Most of it took place in this room where they watched the flashbacks. We handled the unavailability of Jeffrey Hunter by taking another actor, Sean Kenney, [and] putting disfiguring make-up on him in a wheelchair, which was a neat way out of it. It took a considerable amount of preparation and work to get it done properly, but we were all satisfied by the results."

Robert Butler, who had shot "The Cage" several years earlier, recalls

that he would have liked a different look for the Enterprise and her crew than the one audiences eventually would see. "I remember to some extent begging Gene and company not to do a new show, a new world, a new bunch of costumes, a new craft. I begged him to do a timeworn craft that had been up there for twenty years, a captain who had been out there for seven, etc., and it all fell on deaf ears. I really like that much, much better. Not long ago, I got into heavy discussions with Harve Bennett about doing the second feature. The first movie was very expensive, and was run through the feature department at Paramount. Then Harve was hired to run the subsequent movies through the television department with greater economy applied. And though Harve didn't offer me the job, we talked about my doing the thing, and I've known him forever, so it was easy to say, 'Harve, let's save time for both of us and don't hire me if you want to do it clean, because I want to do it dirty. I wanted to do weathered uniforms and all the rest of it.' And he said, 'Well, it's good we're having this conversation because in my view the fans are going to expect what they've seen, which is to say a clean show,' and I said, 'Well, it doesn't sound like I'm your best guy.' So we just agreed to have dessert and forget it. But I still like that idea, and it was certainly proven in *Star Wars*. It brings a great reality and a great frailty and humanity to what is potentially sterile stuff. Anyway, I'm satisfied that I was right and they were wrong at that point, but it didn't have much to do with the success of the show."

Episode #12:
"The Conscience of the King"
Original Airdate: 12/8/66
Written by Barry Trivers
Directed by Gerd Oswald
Guest Starring: Arnold Moss (Anton Karidian), Barbara Anderson (Lenore), Bruce Hyde (Kevin Riley), Eddie Paskey (Lt. Leslie)

A travelling Shakespearean troupe led by Anton Karidian is being transported to their next performance by the Enterprise. Prior to this, Kirk has been contacted by Dr. Thomas Leighton, who tells him that Karidian is actually Kodos the Executioner, former governor of

Arnold Moss (Anton Karidian in "Conscience of the King") portrayed an alien in The 27th Day.

Tarsus IV who masterminded the deaths of many of his people when it seemed that they were threatened with starvation. No sooner had these deaths (which included members of both Kirk and Leighton's families) been carried out than the Federation supply ships arrived. Kodos disappeared and Karidian's career began at roughly the same time. The captain has agreed to provide transportation for the actors on the sheer *chance* that Karidian and Kordos are one and the same. The noose tightens around the man's neck when a series of deaths begin to occur on the Enterprise.

••••

In the pages of *Starlog* magazine, guest star Arnold Moss explained to journalist Diane Butler, "They tell me ['Conscience of the King'] was one of the three best episodes they ever did. The character was called Anton Karidian or Kodos, either one or the other. You never knew which because he was either a man from some other planet who had killed 8,000 people or an actor—a Shakespearean actor who traveled from planet to planet to entertain....My episode was well-written, it was beautifully directed. Then, it was credible, and

in a thing like *Star Trek,* where the whole premise is incredible, you must have something that's believable. Everything there was quite believable."

Episode #13:
"Balance of Terror"
Original Airdate: 12/13/66
Written by Paul Schneider
Directed by Vincent McEveety
Guest Starring: Mark Lenard (Romulan Commander), Paul Comi (Andrew Stiles), Lawrence Montaigne (Decius), John Warburton (Centurion), Stephen Mines (Robert Tomlinson), Barbara Baldwin (Angela Martine), Gary Walberg (Hanson)

In a game of interstellar cat and mouse, the Enterprise comes up against a flagship of their unseen enemy, the Romulans, which has the ability to cloak itself. The episode takes on the feel of a submarine war film as the two commanders try to outthink each other and achieve victory.

••••

"Balance of Terror" finally introduces us to an enemy of the Federation, and a longtime one at that. It's established that it's been 75 years since the last military contact between the Federation and the Romulans, and that neither race has ever seen the other. What they do know is that the Romulans are an off-shoot of the Vulcan race, which provides some wonderful moments as Lieutenant Andrew Stiles, who lost family members in the Federation's last battle with the Romulans, turns his prejudice on Spock, accusing him of being a spy.

Writer Paul Schneider admits that it was he who created the Romulans. "It was a matter of developing a good Romanesque set of admirable antagonists that were worthy of Kirk. I came up with the concept of the Romulans which was an extension of the Roman civilization to the point of space travel, and it turned out quite well. It holds up remarkably well.

"I had the concept of this battle in space and this battle over a neutral zone," he continues, "and I sat there with Gene and developed it with him. Gene said, 'Take it this way, that way,' I added my bit and a story came out of it. I've forgotten how many times I revised the

story, but I think a couple of times before it went into teleplay."

Director Vincent McEveety recalls, "They were very heroic characters pitted one against the other, and it dealt with the length to which people would go for their honor. It was a morality fantasy play, but terribly gripping. I thought that Mark Lenard's performance was brilliant, as was Bill Shatner's. It was a two-people show that I felt was real strong. I had, incidentally, seen *The Enemy Below,* but I didn't notice the similarity until later, when somebody told me about it. Obviously it's the same story."

"I remember that that one was tough," says John D.F. Black, "but I can't remember why or what steps we took. I can presume why. We were dealing with the Romulans and the Spock relationship to them, and that was something that needed very special handling, as was the case any time Spock met with aliens. It was important not to blow the Spock character and not to equate him to somebody who sucks salt out of somebody else's body. We had to keep him Spock. Then it became a habit and subsequently when I saw the episodes I wasn't involved with, Leonard, by the time I was gone, already had a lock on what he wanted to play as Spock and he was right. He made Spock his own character and so he survived that way. I don't think he ever said an out of character line on the show. At the very beginning it was because of care on our side, and then it became Leonard protecting the character. If you notice the takeoffs, the comics are never able to pull off a spoof of him. They can use what became the cliches of the character, but they can't catch Spock. Leonard had him, and the character just somehow survived from script to script."

Episode #14:
"Shore Leave"
Original Airdate: 12/29/66
Written by Theodore Sturgeon
Directed by Robert Sparr
Guest Starring: Emily Banks (Tonia), Oliver McGowan (Caretaker), Perry Lopez (Rodriguez), Bruce Mars (Finnegan), James Gruzaf (Don Juan), Shirley Bonne (Ruth), Sebastian Tom (Samurai)

Captain Kirk grants shore leave

for the crew on an idyllic Earth-like planet, and it turns out to be one of the most incredible leaves anyone has ever had. Those Enterprise people who are among the first are amazed to discover that their every wish is coming true; they are meeting people from their past and living out fantasies. Things turn dangerous, however, when these apparitions turn deadly.

••••

Writer Theodore Sturgeon enthused, "Gene believes—'In the beginning was the word.' One reason *Star Trek* worked is that it was a writer-oriented show. I was all over that lot. Wherever I wanted to go, I was free to go. I studied the actors. I wrote Kirk just exactly the way Bill spoke. Leonard spoke Leonard's own language. There was a fiendish design in my doing that. My lines weren't changed very often."

As to the character of Kirk he added, "I didn't see a tremendous originality in the *concept* of Kirk. I don't mean that we had done this before, but that kind of protagonist, as conceived, had been around before. But then Shatner did it as well as it could possibly be done. He was just right for it. He was awfully good at what he did. And *then* he began to put more into it. There were things like the emotional quality, and the humor, and the relationship with Spock, the protectiveness of each other, say. *That* came out of Bill's character."

Episode #15:
"The Galileo Seven"
Original Airdate: 1/5/67
Written by Oliver Crawford and S. Bar David
Directed by Robert Gist
Guest Starring: Don Marshall (Boma), Peter Marko (Gaetano), Rees Vaughn (Latimer), Grant Woods (Kelowitz), Phyllis Douglas (Mears), John Crawford (Commissioner Ferris)

While enroute to deliver medical supplies to Makus III, the Enterprise pauses to examine a quasar formation. Kirk tries to quell the objections of Galactic High Commissioner Ferris by pointing out that such examinations are as much a part of the starship's mission as delivering medical supplies are, and that the delay will be a short one. Disaster strikes, however, when Spock

leads a team aboard the shuttle Galileo and crashes on the surface of Taurus II. The quasar phenomenon disrupts Enterprise sensors so they are unable to locate the shuttle or the survivors.

Meanwhile, on the planet's surface, Spock uses his purely logical mind to deal with their situation in a hostile environment, and comes across as a cold-blooded monster. With McCoy's encouragement he is ultimately forced to take a very human chance to ensure that they survive and are found by the Enterprise.

••••

Writer Oliver Crawford details, "I did the story and teleplay for that one, and then, as often happens, someone else was called in. They probably felt that I had run dry on the idea and came as far as I could, and they got Shimon Wincelberg [a.k.a. S. Bar David] to do a polish, just as I had done for other *Star Trek*s and other shows. Most of my approach as a writer had been to look to old movies and say, 'Gee, this would make a good *Star Trek* or a good western or a good detective story.' The foundation for 'The Galileo Seven' was actually an old [1939] motion picture called *Five Came Back.* That was about a plane crash in the Andes and the survivors who have to deal with headhunters over the next hill. I remembered it because it was such a dramatic gimmick, a very tight one."

Episode #16:
"The Squire of Gothos"
Original Airdate: 1/12/67
Written by Paul Schneider
Directed by Don McDougall
Guest Starring: William Campbell (Trelane), Richard Carlyle (Jaeger), Michael Barrier (De Salle), Venita Wolf (Ross)

The Enterprise is captured by an alien being named Trelene who is equipped with a wide variety of powers that enable him to manipulate the world around him. Having grown bored with loneliness, he has chosen Kirk and his crew to stay on his world to provide him with entertainment. Coming across as an impudent child (and turning out to be just that), Trelene grows furious when Kirk disrupts his plans, and he puts

humanity on trial.

••••

Trelene and "The Squire of Gothos" would be reincarnated some twenty years later as the premiere episode of *Star Trek: The Next Generation*, "Encounter at Farpoint," in which the new Enterprise encounters the all-powerful (and very Trelene-like) Q, who forces Captain Picard to stand trial on charges against humanity.

Says Paul Schneider, "'The Squire of Gothos' flowed through the process with less changes than 'Balance of Terror.' It just worked very well. I do remember that I was very excited that they built a whole special set for it; a totally round set which was then kind of a new concept in itself. If you look at the episode, you'll see that the camera goes all the way around.

"My inspiration was an anti-war message," Schneider continues. "The fierce toy soldier loving child insisting on getting humanity involved in further warfare. The biggest problem was coming up with a climax. How do you end something like that? So we used the climax of *The Most Dangerous Game.*"

Guest star William Campbell's strongest memory of working on this episode was meeting producer Gene L. Coon.

"Gene Coon and I became very dear friends," he says. "I found him to be a guy you could not dislike. He was awfully fair. I remember there was much ado when I was getting the wig for 'Squire', and I was building my part around the particular wig that I was going to wear. On the day we were supposed to do that scene, the wig was wrong. I looked like Shirley Temple, and we went through a long thing. Remember, you don't give a television script historic intent. When you do a series, after a while you're doing it by rote and you want to finish your day and get back to normal. When I held up the production by saying I refused to use that wig, Bill Shatner was disturbed. He said, 'Bill, what the hell difference does it make? Who's going to notice that?' I said, 'I know it, don't you understand?' The next thing you know, there was a call for the director, who did not want to get in to the debate, although I had the feeling the director was on my side. We called Gene Coon and Gene didn't take two seconds to say, 'Campbell's right. Get another wig. Go to another sequence.' Which is exactly what we did, and it didn't hold up anything. That's the kind of guy he was. He was very sensitive about the quality of the show, how it was done."

Episode #17:
"Arena"
Original Airdate: 1/19/67
Written by Gene L. Coon
From a Story by Fredric Brown
Directed by Joseph Pevney
Guest Starring: Carole Shelyne (The Metron), Jerry Ayers (O'Herlihy), Grant Woods (Kelowitz), Tom Troupe (Lt. Harold), James Farley (Lang), Sean Kenney (DePaul)

When a Federation starbase is destroyed, the Enterprise sets off in pursuit of the attackers. Enroute they enter an uncharted sector of space where Kirk and the commander of the other vessel, the lizard-like Gorn, are transported to a planet's surface where they are forced to carry out their barbarism against each other in a battle to the death, with the loser's ship and all those aboard being destroyed. What follows is a savage struggle, with Kirk's ultimate humanity sparing both him and the Enterprise.

• • • •

"A tough show to do for the actor in the Gorn suit," says director Joseph Pevney. "It was designed by a fellow who has since died, and the suit was very hot. The guy I found for that was a fellow named Gary Cooms, a stuntman, and he worked out just fine. I talked Roddenberry into using a stuntman, because the Gorn was a heavy rubber suit. An actor would have been worn out in nothing flat, and I would not have been able to get enough footage without building a fan into the suit. I said, 'We'd better get a guy accustomed to roughing it out there,' somebody who would be able to go for that length of time in order to get enough footage or we'd be stopping all the time to allow someone to put the suit on and take it off again and again. They didn't realize that stunt people are very talented. Now they're beginning to realize it because all of TV is stunts."

According to the on-air credits, the script for "Arena" was based on the Frederic Brown short story of the same name. "What happened," says Dorothy Fontana, "is that Gene Coon wrote the story as an original. When it was read by research, they said, 'Oh, this is very much like the Frederic Brown story.' Gene said, 'Yes, you're right. I must have read it and didn't realize it.' So he instantly gave credit to Frederic Brown and Mr. Brown was properly paid. The way the development came about, the relationship between the antagonists—Kirk and the Gorn—had a lot of nice stuff to it. It could have been just a brute contest, but it wasn't. It turned out not to be that way."

Episode #18:
"Tomorrow is Yesterday"
Original Airdate: 1/26/67
Written by D.C. Fontana
Directed by Michael O'Herlihy
Guest Starring: Roger Perry (Captain Christopher), Ed Peck (Colonel Fellini), Hal Lynch (Police Sergeant), Richard Merrifield (Technician Webb), John Winston (Transporter Chief Kyle)

After an encounter with a black hole (here referred to as a black star), the Enterprise is hurled backwards in time to the 20th Century and in Earth orbit. There they are photographed by the Air Force's Captain Christopher, who is flying by in his jet when the starship enters the atmosphere momentarily. Kirk has the craft placed in the ship's tractor beam, but it proves too frail and breaks up. Christopher is brought aboard before the fatal moment, and is the world's first man to see the future. Kirk's dilemma: how to return Christopher without threatening the course of history.

• • • •

"'Tomorrow is Yesterday' was kicked off by 'The Naked Time,' which ended with the Enterprise spinning off of a collapsed star," says Dorothy Fontana. "Originally, it was supposed to be a two-parter, but John D.F. Black had a movie deal and couldn't be involved with the second part. I said that I would develop the idea of being thrown back into space. They were going back in time at the end of 'The Naked Time,' so I took the idea and played with it.

"Then, I had everything Kirk does, though it's the right thing to do, land him deeper and deeper into trouble. Once he begins to get his footing in this strange and different time, he starts putting his feet right again. The human interest aspect is the pilot who wanted to go into space and didn't make the cut, as it were. But the irony of history is that his son, who wasn't born yet, gets to make a space flight which is vital to the space program's development. All of that, I felt, made for a fun and an interestingly human show. The sequel idea was dropped, and we actually wound up putting a new front end on it so that it would sit alone without being linked to 'The Naked Time.'"

Episode director Michael O'Herlihy, who had a long directorial history with the Walt Disney Company, notes, "I rather liked the script. The one thing I did like about *Star Trek* is that Gene Roddenberry went into the realm of science fiction, but he didn't go too far too often. Take the one I did, which was rather nice with the time warp thing. I'm not a science fiction fan, but even I could relate to it and understand it. I wasn't interested in funny things with ears coming out of them. But playing around with psychic forces and time, I understood. I enjoyed it very much."

And despite his modern-day sensibilities, he didn't find it difficult to deal with *Star Trek*'s future reality.

"I can only speak as a director and a storyteller," he explains. "You have the story to tell and you must tell it with as much honesty as you possibly can, that this *did* in fact happen. You can't say, 'This only happened because we're making science fiction.' This is the story, fellows, so it has to be told to the best of our abilities. That has always been my attitude on every show I've done. Once you begin to edit the veracity of the reality or unreality, you're wrong. Then, you're turning into a preacher instead of a director. I've always tried to do my best from that point-of-view.

"On *Star Trek* you can suspend your disbelief and just tell the story as if people at this time and at this space are dressed in these funny clothes, although you must not consider them funny clothes. You must consider that this is the way people live. It's like going back to the 12th Century. We know that has happened, so we can just tell the story. In this other material dealing with the future, we don't know whether it would happen or if it could, but I don't think people are going to change anyway.

In studying the *Star Trek* phenomenon, O'Herlihy is quick to point out that he has *not* devised his own theory as to why the show has remained so popular.

"I know very well that in retrospect we can all come up with something we did to make the show a success," he confides, "but it was just an accident that became a fashion."

The method of time travel as established in "The Naked Time" and "Tomorrow is Yesterday" was utilized again to great effect in the 1986 feature film, *Star Trek IV: The Voyage Home.*

Episode #19:
"Court Martial"
Original Airdate: 2/2/67
Written by Don M. Mankiewicz and Stephen Carabatsos
Directed by Marc Daniels
Guest Starring: Percy Rodriguez (Commodore Stone), Joan Marshall (Areel Shaw), Elisha Cook, Jr. (Samuel Cogley), Richard Webb (Finney), Alice Rawlings (Jamie Finney), Hagan Beggs (Hanson), Winston DeLugo (Timothy)

A computer malfunction implicates Kirk in the death of crewman Ben Finney, and he stands trial for negligence. It is up to Spock and Kirk's lawyer, Samuel Cogley, to prove his innocence as well as the truth about Finney.

••••

"I thought that wasn't a very good one," said Marc Daniels. "I didn't like it because the actor who was playing the prosecutor, Elisha Cook, Jr., wasn't very good with his lines. When you're on a six-day schedule, trying to make time, and you've got to keep stopping and going back, it drives everyone absolutely crazy. You've got a courtroom scene and you're shooting him a line at a time because he can't remember two. When you put it in the editing room, you don't see that because you cut to someone else and then come back to him. Cook is a fine actor, but he had a terrible time with that....See, these

are the kind of things I remember."

Episode #20:
"The Return of the Archons"
Original Airdate: 2/9/67
Written by Boris Sobelman
Story by Gene Roddenberry
Directed by Joseph Pevney
Guest Starring: Harry Townes (Reger), Torin Thatcher (Marplon), Charles McCauley (Landru), Christopher Heid (Lindstrom), Brioni Farrell (Tula), Sid Haig (First Lawgiver), Jon Lormer (Tamar), Morgan Farley (Hacom), Ralph Maurer (Bilar), Eddie Paskey (Leslie), David L. Ross (Guard)

While checking up on the crew of the Archon, who transported down to Beta III, the Enterprise learns that the people there are being controlled by a computer named Landru who takes over their minds to make them all a part of the body. Kirk takes it upon himself to destroy the mechanism and bring freedom back to that world's people.

Episode #21
"Space Seed"
Original Airdate: 2/16/67
Written by Gene L. Coon and Carey Wilbur
Directed by Marc Daniels
Guest Starring: Richard Montalban (Khan), Madlyn Rhue (Marla McGivers), Blasidell Makee (Spinelli), Mark Tobin (Joaqin)

The Enterprise comes across a derelict "sleeper ship" named the Botony Bay, which contains a crew of approximately 70 men and women in suspended animation. Led by Khan Noonian Singh, these people turn out to be the result of genetic experimentation on Earth in the 1990s. Basically a race of supermen, with strength and intelligence nearly ten times that of an average person, they had attempted to take over the Earth and triggered World War III, the Eugenics War. They managed to flee in the Botony Bay, and are now revived in the 23rd Century.

Khan seizes the moment and, using historian Marla McGivers, nearly takes over the Enterprise. Kirk and company manage to gain the upper hand (barely) and sentence Khan and his people to the somewhat savage Ceti Alpha V. At least it will give Khan, McGivers

and the others a chance to tame a world, rather than waste their lives in a Federation penal colony.

••••

Surprisingly, Khan Noonian Singh may never have come into existence at all if it hadn't been for Captain Video.

"Hell," laughs writer Carey Wilbur, "the plot for 'Space Seed' came from an old *Captain Video* I did some 30-odd years ago. Of course we did some very far out things on that show, including the popular idea of people being transported in space while in suspended animation."

Allan Asherman's *The Star Trek Compendium* states that "Carey Wilbur began his outline for 'Space Seed' by explaining how out of place in today's world a man from Renaissance times would be."

"That sounds a little grand to me," Wilbur smiles. "I was just thinking of an adventure story, although there was some of that element there. I had this idea, which I revived from Captain Video because I thought it was time to do it again. It was a crazy story where we did the legend of men being turned into beasts, and our villainess had been transported from the days of Greek mythology to the future. So in doing 'Space Seed,' we took away the mythological powers and replaced them with a genetically altered human being.

"To be honest, I don't remember a heck of a lot about Khan. He was a

Ricardo Montalban, the quintessential Khan, seen here in the TV movie version of **The Mark of Zoro**

criminal who had been deported in a seed ship who tried to take over the Enterprise after he was more or less accidentally revived."

As a writer for hire, Wilbur had been asked to supply a script for the show, which eventually became "Space Seed." Gene Coon did a rewrite on it and the author had no further contact with *Star Trek* as he went off to other assignments.

"I had no qualms about Gene rewriting me," he points out. "He was an excellent writer and certainly knew the show better than just about anyone. I'm sure he rewrote the script to conform to the series, but I've never seen it. I think I've only seen three or four things I've written, for the simple reason that I know what's in them. The only exception has been *Lost in Space*, which I wrote numerous scripts for. We were doing fairy tales and I used to watch them all the time. Hell, I used to watch other people's episodes as well, simply because it was such a fun show.

"People want to believe that there's going to be that glorious period of space flight. We want to believe that there's something out there. *Star Trek* offered the human race a future, and God knows we need the promise of the future."

Stated director Marc Daniels, "There's not much I remember about the episode except that we used those capsules which carried people in suspended animation. Ricardo Montalban was a very capable and good actor, and the episode, of course, led to *Star Trek II: The Wrath of Khan*. Part of the problem in 'Space Seed' was trying to visualize Khan's tremendous power—where he could turn out a finger and turn somebody upside down. That was difficult, but we got away with it thanks to stunt people and judicious editing."

Recalls actor Ricardo Montalban, who had previously starred in Gene Roddenberry's *The Secret Defense of 117*, "I thought the character of Khan was wonderful. I thought it was well-written, it had an interesting concept and I was delighted it was offered to me. I still get fan mail from it. Not just from the United States, but from other countries. People remembered this Khan character whenever I talk about having done a *Star Trek*."

Episode #22:
"A Taste of Armageddon"
Original Airdate: 2/23/67
Written by Robert Hamner
and Gene L. Coon
Directed by Joseph Pevney
Guest Starring: Gene Lyons (Ambassador Fox), David Opatoshu (Anan 879), Robert Sampson (Sar 627), Barbara Babcock (Mea 349), Miko Mayama (Tamura)

Ambassador Robert Fox is on board the Enterprise to negotiate a peace treaty with the planet Eminiar VII, despite that world's obvious lack of interest in such a treaty. Kirk himself points out, "It *is* their planet, Mr. Ambassador," but Fox arrogantly forces the starship forward. It is a short matter of time before they find themselves immersed in an interplanetary war between Eminiar and Vendikar which is being fought by computers. Said computers pinpoint the location of theoretical bombings, and people living in those areas voluntarily march into disintegration chambers so that their respective societies will live on.

Enterprise unwittingly becomes a target and Eminiar's leader, Anan 7, expects Kirk to have his crew enter the disintegration chambers to keep the peace. Kirk, naturally, has his own ideas and sets about carrying them out.

••••

Perhaps the reason "A Taste of Armageddon" is so powerful is that it seems a perfect allegory to the soldiers in Vietnam at the time, and the body counts of those killed in action which were revealed over nightly newscasts. As those numbers grew, it seems that they, too, were walking into disintegration chambers of a sort.

"The original story was by Robert Hamner," recalls Dorothy Fontana. "Gene did a rewrite on that. I think some of the things he added really had a lot to do with the character of Kirk. To the best of my recollection, it was Gene Coon who wrote the speech at the end that man has a reputation as a killer, but you get up every morning and say, 'I'm not going to kill today.' It seems to me that Gene Coon added that speech in particular. It was one of those things that began to identify Kirk far more solidly than we had before."

"The final speech from Bill," muses Joseph Pevney, "the demand for peace and not giving up human lives to a computer, was rewritten several times until we got it the way we wanted. Gene Coon rewrote the script and it was quite powerful."

Episode #23:
"This Side of Paradise"
Original Airdate: 3/2/67
Written by D.C. Fontana
Story by Nathan Butler and D.C. Fontana
Directed by Ralph Senensky
Guest Starring: Jill Ireland (Leila), Frank Overton (Sandoval), Grant Woods (Kelowitz), Dick Scotter (Painter)

The Enterprise investigates the status of a group of Federation colonists on Omicron Ceti III, who are presumed dead after being exposed to the deadly radiation of Berthold rays over the past three years. Instead, what they find are the colonists in absolutely perfect health, and in a peaceful bliss. Both are chalked up to spores on the planet which strip away the more negative feelings, resulting in an idyllic state of mind.

Kirk's problems begin quickly as the influence of the spores spreads through the ship, with everyone wanting to remain on the planet. Even Spock is affected, as he lets down his veneer of logic and expresses the love he feels for colonist Leila Kalomi, with whom he had had a relationship. Kirk, who is alone on the Enterprise, must snap his first officer out of the state he's in, before the starship burns up in the planet's atmosphere.

••••

The script for "This Side of Paradise" was begun by Jerry Sohl, but rewritten by story editor Dorothy Fontana to the point where Sohl decided to put his pen-name on it.

"I have a whole draw full of ideas," says Sohl on the story's genesis, "and I had the idea that spores, as you know, are inanimate up until the point when they are mixed with water or with anything else, then they come alive. Like yeast. So I had the idea that these things could be consumed by someone and as a result the whole character chemistry of that person could change to a nice, peaceful and loving person. In other

As Leila, the late Jill Ireland allowed audiences a glimpse into the past of Mr. Spock in "This Side of Paradise."

words, it was a psychedelic kind of thing. A lot of that was going on at the time. The premise of the thing was that everyone on the Enterprise takes LSD. What would happen? In effect, that's what this was. They go down to the planet and they all get the spores in them and turn into different people. That was the basis of the whole thing, and I thought it was an interesting premise. It was the only time that Spock was allowed to be a loving, caring, cherishing human being. That was my idea. Worked out just swell, I think. I've forgotten what the payoff was. I think they had to be made angry. The adrenaline going into your system is what defeats the spores."

Dorothy Fontana adds, "That was actually the rewrite that got me the job of story editor. Originally that story and script featured Sulu as the love interest, and the spores were contained in a cave, so, therefore, they weren't much of a threat unless you went into the cave. My idea, that I stressed to Gene, was that it could be made a better story if we have the spores all over the place, so that you can't avoid them, and that Spock is the love interest. Everybody kind of said, 'Spock?' And I said, 'Trust me.' And Gene did. It was an enjoyable episode to write, because there are so many things you can get into which, under normal circumstances, you wouldn't dare,

because it would not work. But under these circumstances, it did. It also had wonderful actors. Leonard's always good, but Jill Ireland was exquisite. Bill was good also. We always played Bill, at least back then, as the man whose real love affair was with his ship. He was a dedicated officer and a man who really did want to go down to the sea in ships. In this case it was a sea of stars. That ship was truly his love."

In tracing his involvement with the series, director Ralph Senensky admits, "I don't even know how it happened. There's an agency that books you and I guess I must have been pitched. All of a sudden the agent called and said, 'Do you want to do *Star Trek*?' They sent me the script for 'The Devil in the Dark,' and I was kind of excited about it. I was not a science fiction buff, so I went out and bought a lot of Arthur Clarke and read practically everything I could. I took the script back to Iowa, where I was visiting my family, and while I was there another script arrived in the mail with another note saying that they had switched and I would be doing 'This Side of Paradise.' I was kind of disappointed, because I liked 'Devil in the Dark' better. But 'This Side of Paradise' was a very good show and it's developed its own reputation.

"I didn't know it at the time, but it's probably because it was such a major personal story for Spock. He did things in that story that he never got to do, like hang from a tree. As a freelance director in television, you just bounce from show to show and that was one of the bounces. As you bounce around, you find little niches, places where it's comfortable. You like them, they like you and you stay on. *Star Trek* was such a place."

Episode #24:
"The Devil in the Dark"
Original Airdate: 3/9/67
Written by Gene L. Coon
Directed by Joseph Pevney
Guest Starring: Ken Lynch (Vandenberg), Barry Russo (Giotto), Brad Weston (Appel), Biff Elliot (Schmitter), Janos Prohaska (Horta)

When miners on Janus VI are being murdered by a creature that can move through solid rock, chief engineer Vanderberg contacts the Enterprise and

asks for assistance in hunting it down and putting an end to the threat. The starship arrives with Kirk and Spock leading a landing party to investigate the situation. What they discover is that this so-called creature is actually an intelligent being known as the Horta and that it has only killed to protect its young, which are encased in silicone shells that the miners mistook for worthless rocks.

••••

In *The Making of Star Trek*, Gene Roddenberry explained, "What's been wrong with science fiction in television and in motion pictures for years is that whenever the monster was used, the tendency was to say, 'Ah, ha! Let's have a big one that comes out, attacks and kills everyone.' Nobody ever asked, 'Why?' In any other story, if something attacks (a bear, a man or whatever), the author is expected to explain, 'Here is why it is the way it is, here are the things that led it to do this, here is what it wants.'

"A classic example of doing this right was one of our most popular episodes, written by Gene Coon, entitled 'The Devil in the Dark.' The 'Horta' was an underground creature which attacked a group of miners. In the end they find out that it attacked because—surprise—it was a mother! It was protecting its eggs because the miners were destroying them in the belief that they were just strange-looking mineral formations. With this understood, the Horta suddenly became understandable, too. It wasn't just a monster—it was *someone*. And the audience could put themselves in the place of the Horta...identify....feel! That's what drama is all about. And that's its importance, too....If you can learn to feel for a Horta, you may also be learning to understand and feel for other humans of different colors, ways and beliefs."

"From my point of view," says Joseph Pevney, "the primary problem was photographing the Horta. We had to put glisten on them, a kind of sheen to make them stand away from the walls because everything was the same color. We then exaggerated the motion of the way it moved so we would be sure to see them.

"It was a tough show to do, because William Shatner's father died during the filming of it. They were very close, but he managed....He was very shaken then and Leonard was very good to him. They were together all the time and Leonard was able to provide him with a great deal of comfort."

David Gerrold opines, "I would have to point to 'Devil in the Dark' as being the best episode Gene L. Coon ever wrote, because it really gets to the heart of what *Star Trek* was. Here you had this menace, but once you understood what the creature is and why it's doing what it's doing, it's not really a menace at all. We end up learning more about appropriate behavior for ourselves out of learning to be compassionate, tolerant, understanding. To me, in many ways Gene L. Coon was the heart and soul of *Star Trek*. He was the guy who had to roll up his sleeves and make it work. He was the guy who would do a rewrite if a script needed a rewrite and try to stay true to the original concept. He actually, of all the people who worked there at the time, had the clearest story sense, both in terms of story structure and dialogue. I think that shows in the scripts that he did. 'Devil in the Dark' he wrote over a weekend."

Laughs Coon's friend Lester Colodny, "Not only did he write it in a weekend, but he probably read two books, made dinner for 14, redid the entire front lawn, helped me with 30 pages of my book, rewrote four other pieces for the studio, went to visit two friends....he was incredible."

In terms of the development of the script idea, Dorothy Fontana recalls, "The costume guy who did a lot of creatures for us came to the studio and said, 'I have to show you this new creature,' and it was this kind of lumpy thing that was orange and misshapen and it was real low to the ground. He put a rubber chicken out in front of the thing. He climbed inside this suit and on his hands and knees he brought this creature over the chicken and the chicken disappeared. After he passed over it, some bones appeared out the back. Gene said, 'I've got to find a way to use that,' and he came up with the Horta. Of course it's a wonderful story, because it's really all about mother love. It was a great story."

John Colicos, the Klingon Kor in "Errand of Mercy," seen here as Baltar in Battlestar: Galactica.

Episode #25:
"Errand of Mercy"
Original Airdate: 3/23/67
Written by Gene L. Coon
Directed by John Newland
Guest Starring: John Abbott (Ayleborne), John Colicos (Kor), Peter Brocco (Claymare), Victor Lundin (Lingon), David Hillary Huge (Trefayne)

Tensions between the Federation and one of their arch enemies, the Klingon Empire, are growing more intense, and Kirk is told to secure an alliance with the people of the strategically located Organia. No sooner have Kirk and Spock beamed down than the Klingons arrive, with their military commander, Kor, commandeering the world as the latest possession of the Empire.

Kirk is frustrated by the absolute complacency of the Organians, and his frustration turns to anger when he learns that things have grown worse between the Federation and the Klingons. It appears that an intergalactic war is about to begin, when the Organians reveal themselves to be something far removed from human, with the power to stop both sides from warring....permanently (though this fact was later forgotten in the *Star Trek* feature films).

••••

A highlight of "Errand of Mercy" is when the Organians stops the conflict between the Federation and the Klingons, and Kirk protests their interference. "You have no right to interfere," snaps Kirk. We have the right...."

"To wage war, Captain?" asks an Organian.

As David Gerrold notes in his book *The World of Star Trek*, "And then [Kirk] realizes that the whole purpose of his mission was to *prevent* a war."

"Gene Coon came up with the Klingons though we never liked the name," explains Dorothy Fontana. "We said, 'Gene, can't you come up with a different name than Klingon? We hate it.' But we never come up with anything better, so we left it. Then the Klingons kind of became a stock villain, because they were easier to do in make-up than the Romulans. We wound up doing the Klingons quite a bit and they became a very good adversary, because once you established them, you had to find out ways to explore them."

Actor John Colicos, in reflecting on his role as Kor, told *Starlog* magazine that when he got the role, make-up maestro Fred Phillips said, "'What do *you* want to look like?' I saw the script as a futuristic Russia and America at loggerheads over this peaceful little planet, so I said, 'Let's go back in the past and think of Genghis Khan, because Kor is a military commander, ready to take over the entire universe with his hordes.' My hair happened to be very short and combed forward, so I said, 'Spray my hair black, kink it up a bit and give me a vaguely Asian, Tartar appearance. Let's go for a brown-green makeup so I'm slightly not of this world,' and within two hours, this thing emerged and that was it."

••••

Episode #26
"The Alternative Factor"
Original Airdate: 3/30/67
Written by Don Ingalls
Directed by Gerd Oswald
Guest Starring: Robert Brown (Lazarus),
Janet MacLachlen (Charlene Masters),
Richard Derr (Barstow),
Eddie Paskey (Lt. Leslie)

Easily one of Star Trek's most convoluted and least appealing episodes, "The Alternative Factor" was the 20th episode shot but was held up to air as the 26th. The Enterprise encounters two versions of a man named Lazarus, one of them seeming perfectly rationale and the other a snarling madman from an anti-matter universe. The latter is planning on opening a rift between the two dimensions, damning both to a form of Armageddon. It is up to Kirk and the rational Lazarus to set things straight before its too late.

••••

"I had in mind parallel universes, in which there are positive and negative forces," writer Don Ingalls relayed to Lee Goldberg, "and you have to keep the two universes separate, because if they're drawn together, you have annihilation. You have the bright side, the positive world we know and the negative world, where everyone's a villain. My idea was that one person from the negative world tries to break through—and if he succeeds, he destroys everything."

Episode #27:
"City on the Edge of Forever"
Original Airdate: 4/6/67
Written by Harlan Ellison
Directed by Joseph Pevney
Guest Starring: Joan Collins (Edith Keeler), John Harmon (Rodent), Bartell LaRue (Voice of the Guardian)

The Enterprise is in the midst of studying time disturbances in the area of a particular world, when McCoy accidentally injects himself with an overdose of cordrazine. As a result, he becomes a paranoid madman and beams down to the planet's surface to avoid everyone's attempts to sedate him.

Kirk and Spock lead a landing party in pursuit, and there they find an ancient stone structure which identifies itself as the Guardian of Forever, a time portal into the past. When the moment presents itself, McCoy leaps through its center and does something in the past that causes history to be changed: the Enterprise is no longer in orbit. To try and counter this, Kirk and Spock pursue him to Earth in the year 1930, where they meet the focal point in time: Edith Keeler, social worker.

Keeler, we learn, was meant to die in a traffic accident but something McCoy does alters that. As a result, all of history is changed and in the altered history she leads a pacifist movement that delays America's entry into the second world war, thus giving Nazi Germany the chance to capture the world. Kirk's decision is simple: he must allow Edith Keeler to die as she was intended to. The one thing he had not counted on, however, was falling in love with her.

••••

"City on the Edge of Forever" is generally considered the best episode of Star Trek ever produced. At the same time, it is perhaps the most controversial due to the fact that Gene Roddenberry supposedly rewrote Harlan Ellison's original teleplay and Ellison was not happy about the rewrite.

"How can I do this without be a creep?" Ellison rhetorically asked a journalist. "Gene Roddenberry and I had a falling out in terms of creativity, about what would be done with my show. I thought that the rewrite that was expected of me, and that I did several times, and the couple [of] other writers [put] on to follow me up, cut the guts out of my show. I thought that, at the time, Gene had lied to me, and I will not work with anyone who lies to me. Life is too short. So Gene and I didn't talk for many years as a result of it, and it was strictly on an artistic basis. Gene has always been a very kind and decent man, but I think he was under pressure from the network at that time as the budget was being cut, and I think he wanted to satisfy the network so he did things to my show which I was not happy about and which he had promised me would not be done to my show. Subsequently, Gene and I buried the hatchet as it were, we reached reproachment, and he has done a number of very kind things for me and so I'd kind of like to not bad mouth him at this point because this is many years later.

"There's two ways of looking at it," he continued. "First of all, the one that won the Writer's Guild award was my original version of the script, it was not what was shot. The Writer's Guild awards are the most honest awards in this industry, not like the Oscars which are Mickey Mouse. They're nothing but popularity awards. The Writer's Guild awards are given on the basis of the written material. And so it was in fact my original script that won the award. The one that won the Hugo was the televised version and of course I would like to be arrogant enough to think that the script was just so damn good that even butchering it couldn't hurt it, but in comparison to most of the other segments that were on Star Trek, which I wasn't wildly enthusiastic about, it was a pretty good show. But having done the show myself, having written it, and I know how good the quality of the script was, I can only say that what people see was one twentieth of what was there originally."

At a 1988 presentation at the Museum of Broadcasting, Roddenberry was asked if Star Trek: The Next Generation would use writers like Harlan Ellison.

"Most of those I wouldn't want in the same room with me," he replied. "I've given all of them a chance. Harlan got a chance on the first show and wrote a $350,000 estimated budget show when I only had, in those days, $186,000. And when I told him to cut the budget, he sent me back the script, saying in parenthesis to do it with special effects. He then submitted it to the Writer's Guild, which gave him the Writer's Guild prize which he deserved for the script, except that many people would get prizes if they wrote scripts that budgeted out to three times the show's cost. I rewrote that script for Harlan and it won the Nebula Award, which he rushed up on stage and took credit for, too!"

For over two decades fans have accepted the fact that Roddenberry did the rewrite of Ellison's script, however Glen Larson disputes this point, stating that it was actually Gene L. Coon who was responsible. This startling revelation came to Larson's attention during a Writer's Guild Award ceremony in which the script was a

••••

nominated entry.

"That night," Larson reflects, "I knew that something was troubling Gene and I asked him what was wrong. And he said, 'There are two scripts up tonight for the Writer's Guild Award, and I wrote them both.' One of them was by Harlan Ellison ['City on the Edge of Forever'], and he said, 'If Harlan wins, I'm going to die.' Harlan was just an amazingly stubborn person. That night he also told me a story about Harlan. Harlan would write a script that said, 'Five thousand people accosted him on the city streets.' Gene said, 'Harlan, why do you bother writing this into a script that you know is for television? You know we can't have 5,000 extras.' So Harlan would go home, do the rewrite and say, 'Four thousand extras.' And that was his rewrite. Gene would have to sit down and make a television show out of it. Obviously he kept all of the theoretical things, but he would have to write a script that was a script that could be shot on the stage with a rock.

"But Gene made his contributions in an unheralded way," continues Larson. "His name wasn't on the Ellison script. It is unique in the business these days, it wasn't so much then, for someone to do the kind of work he did and not submit for an arbitration or a credit. It's that simple. An awful lot of guys today will put their name on it and let the Guild fight it. Coon had a great respect for writers. Therefore, even if he had to do a massive amount of work, he would not take away the guy's credit, which, by the way, is linked to residuals. Nevertheless, if you knew a guy was going to stand up and accept an award for what you did, that was more painful than the money. The mere fact that somebody was going to get credit for his thoughts and actual words, because they were so important to him, was almost too much to bear. He shared that with me. He didn't make that a public announcement, but he was feeling great pain. Harlan would stand up and bow from the floor."

As far as Roddenberry's taking credit for the rewrite, Larson offers, "Gene [Coon] was there. Gene made the show work. Gene was the guy and later on, when *Star Trek* gained prominence, I was always surprised at what I heard

Roddenberry say, because there are people who create something who don't know how to make it work on a week to week basis, a show to show basis. I suspect that's kind of the way Roddenberry was. I'm not an expert on that. I'm giving you this directly from the horse's mouth, because [Gene Coon and I] used to sit there and talk about things every day."

Director Joseph Pevney is someone who doesn't agree with Ellison's view of his own script.. "This was the end of the first season," he says. "Harlan was very happy to get his story on *Star Trek*. He was down on the set thanking me. It's great that Gene rewrote it, though, because Harlan had no sense of theatre. He had a great sense of truth, which was very nicely placed in there, all of the 1930's stuff was well documented. It was a well conceived and written show. But in the original script's dramatic moments, it missed badly.

"It was a motion picture," he continues. "I treated it as a movie, as I did all television. It was a very honest episode and the doctor was so good for the first time. I think he's kind of dull, but he came to life magnificently. It was a pleasure working with the actors. They realized their full potential in that one."

It's noted that Captain Kirk's final line, "Let's get the hell out of here," probably represented one of the first times that the word "hell" had been used on television.

"That was a problem," he points out. "Bill said it and there were objections from the network. Roddenberry had a meeting with them and said, 'There's no word that has the same connotation as hell in this particular moment.' Of course Bill fought for it too. We all wanted it, because it sounded so great. I think finally the network said, 'What the hell, who's watching the show anyway? Leave it in.'"

Although "City" aired at the end of the season, its development had begun at the beginning and John D.F. Black has strong memories of working with Harlan Ellison.

"Harlan always had 40 things going," Black smiles. "He was doing a book and he had this short story he had to get in, or whatever. Now Harlan didn't

*Joan Collins, Kirk's love interest in "City on the Edge of Forever," seen here in less bitchy, pre-*Dynasty *days.*

know anything about the production side. He knew half of what I knew, and I didn't know anything. I knew what a travelling matte was, and I think Harlan knew that too, and we knew what the difference between a fade and a dissolve was, and those kinds of things. But production...can you build a 40-foot tall pyramid on a stage? We didn't know what height you could build it. That's technical and certainly outside our expertise.

"At one point," he elaborates, the memories washing over him, "Harlan was supposed to deliver, was supposed to deliver, was supposed to deliver...and he was ill or he was this or he was that. The story just wasn't finished. We all lie. After a while it came down to, 'For Christ's sake, Harlan, when are we going to get the story?' And Harlan said, 'Maybe it would just be better if I came in and had an office on the lot.' Which, at that juncture, was terrific because we wanted the story. And I loved Harlan, although I don't know what G.R.'s feeling for him was. So Harlan shows up with a phonograph, his typewriter and about 12 records of the Rolling Stones, among other things. We put him in an office at the very end of the corridor. At first Harlan would be there with this rock and roll playing very loud, with the casting people trying to have readings and saying, 'Turn it down, Harlan.' Or I couldn't hear people in my office on the telephone and I'd tell him to turn it down. At one point, I guess the second or third day that he was there, I walked down the hall because the Stones were playing very loud, knocked on the door and there wasn't any answer. I opened the door and Harlan wasn't there. The machine was just playing.

"I had to go over to the set. I had to go there three or four times a day, and there he was sitting there talking to Leonard and Billy, having his picture taken. I said, 'Harlan, you're supposed to be writing. What are you doing over here?' He said, 'I came over here for lunch with the comapny.' 'Harlan, it's 3:30 in the afternoon. The company has lunch at 2.' 'Well, I wanted to see what they were doing.' I said, 'Harlan, please go back to the office and finish the story.' So Harlan walked back with me, went into his office and the record goes on again, because I had taken the arm off earlier, and I figured that I would leave my office door open so that I could see him if he went down the hall. And I never saw him.

"When I went down the hall in the middle of the next day to see how he was doing. I got there, the record was playing and Harlan wasn't in his office again. What he had done was gone out the window, and Bobby Justman was of the mind that we should nail the door and the window shut. In any case, Harlan ultimately finished the story. I read it, made my notes and gave it to G.R. and he made his notes on it. If I recall correctly, and this I'm not certain of at all, Harlan did not continue to occupy that office. He either went home to continue the teleplay or he had some other thing that he had to finish first, and the story stayed on the shelf until Harlan got back to it. I remember conferences on the story with Harlan, and it was enormously interesting. I thought it was a little corny conceptually. I didn't think it was the best thing that Harlan could have done.

"I remember the hassles about the expense inherent in it, and what had to be adjusted. Sequences that had to come out because they were impossible to do, and things like that. I remember he had come in with a script in which all of the *Star Trek* people were on a merry-go-round which came out of the side of a

mountain. Justman said, 'My God, that effect would cost us a half a million dollars just to try it. There's no guarantee it would work. Where the hell would we get a merry-go-round that moves from inside a mountain to outside a mountain?' And Harlan was explaining how we could do this out of cardboard, and got so pissed at Bobby because he couldn't budget it."

Episode #28:
"Operation Annihilate"
Original Airdate: 4/13/67
Written by Stephen W. Carabatsos
Directed by Herschel Daugherty
Guest Starring: Dave Armstrong (Kartan), Craig Hundley (Peter Kirk), Joan Swift (Aurelan), Maurishka Taliferro (Yeoman Zara Jamal)

Responding to a report of mass insanity on Deneva, the Enterprise arrives and Kirk is stunned to learn that his brother, George, is dead as a result of the disease. Further investigation leads them to amoeba-like creatures about the size of large rodents, which become one with a "host's" nervous system. Our heroes must discover a way to rid Deneva of this, and the answer comes from their apparent sensitivity to intense light. McCoy begins experimenting and Spock volunteers as a test subject, but things backfire when the Vulcan is blinded in the tests. Bones is devastated to later learn that the creatures can be destroyed by ultra-violet light, so Spock was blinded for no reason.

Needless to say, Spock's blindness is temporary, as he was protected by an additional eyelid that all Vulcans have to cope with the sunlight of their home world.

••••

"'Operation Annihilate' was not really my original idea," admits Steven Carabatsos. "Somebody gave me the idea—Roddenberry, I believe. He had wanted to do an episode involving Captain Kirk's brother. Kind of a family connection. More than that, I don't know what he suggested. We were just looking for basic jeopardy, character involvement and the uniqueness of the arena. Each planet was an opportunity to create a brand new world, a brand new society. As we approached each episode, that was one of the things that we had to address. I do know that it was eventually revised, which is normal for TV."

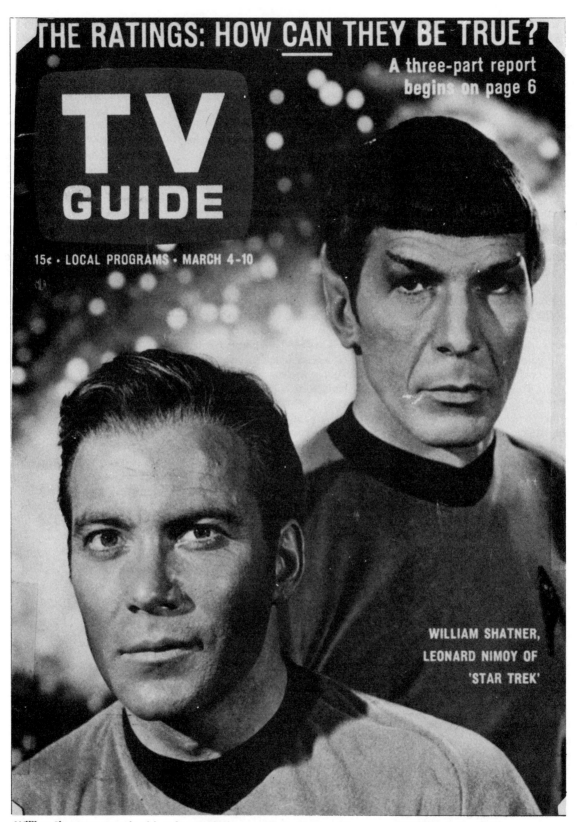

THE RATINGS: HOW CAN THEY BE TRUE?

A three-part report
begins on page 6

TV GUIDE

15¢ · LOCAL PROGRAMS · MARCH 4-10

WILLIAM SHATNER,
LEONARD NIMOY OF
'STAR TREK'

William Shatner as Captain Kirk and Leonard Nimoy as Mr. Spock graced the cover of TV Guide in the 1960s.

CHAPTER THREE
Trekking to Season 2

Star Trek's second season introduced several changes to the series, among them the addition of actor Walter Koenig as Russian navigator Pavel Chekov. This character made the bridge of the Enterprise a true United Nations-like ensemble in space.

"The Russians were responsible," said Gene Roddenberry. "They put on the Pravda youth paper that, 'Ah, the ugly Americans are at it again. They do a space show, and they forget to include the people who were in space first.' And I said, 'My God, they're right.' Walter Koenig and I had worked together on a show I did earlier, and he's great and I brought him in. And then I wrote the Russians and told them, 'I'm sorry we did it, and here's the information.' I never heard back from them. But not 'cause they're bad guys. The Air Force announced they had succeeded in phasing a thing and they were gonna call it a 'phaser.' And I wrote them and I said, 'I hope you use it with the respect for life as we did.' They didn't answer that either."

Both director Joseph Pevney and Walter Koenig himself remember the actor's hiring somewhat differently.

"When Roddenberry said he wanted to put a Russian on the show," recalls Pevney, "I said, 'I just used a kid in a television show at Universal named Walter Koenig, who I think I heard do a little Russian. Why don't we have him in and have him read?' Gene saw him and fell in love with him. He looks Russian; his face has a Slavic look to it. He looked right and was not a typical Russian cliche."

Added Walter Koenig in the pages of *The Star Trek Interview Book*, "Well, the facts are that they were looking for somebody who would appeal to the bubble gum set. They had somebody in mind like Davey Jones of *The Monkees*, and originally it was supposed to be an English character to kind of break off that segment of the audience;

however, in acknowledgement of the Russians' contribution to space they made the decision to go that way. All that stuff about *Pravda*—you know, the complaining—that's all nonsense. That was all just publicity. But it was a very practical decision. They wanted somebody who would appeal to eight-to-fourteen year olds and they decided to make him Russian."

"On the other hand," says Koenig today, "I had no idea how momentous this casting was in my career. I was told that the character might recur, but there was no guarantee. It was a matter that one of the things that happened, fortuitously, was that George Takei was shooting *The Green Berets* and was late reporting for the second season. They brought me back mainly to fill that seat for some sense of continuity, because at that point we had not had an audiece reaction. I guess I was lucky that George was unavailable."

By the time *Star Trek* had entered its second season, there was also a shift in attitude, both creatively and behind the scenes. In terms of the scripts, there had been a gradual shift toward featuring Kirk and Spock, and, to a somewhat lesser degree, McCoy as the primary focus of the stories, while Sulu, Scotty, Uhura and, now, Chekov, were delegated to background duty and such lines as "Hailing frequencies open, Captain," "The engines canna take any more, Captain," "Warp factor three, Captain," and "Aye, Captain."

In 1990, Nichelle Nichols related to *Starlog* magazine, "Initially, *Star Trek* the series and *Star Trek* the films were designed for an *ensemble* of stars who would each be given equal time. But at some point, the decision was made to separate Bill and Leonard Nimoy from the rest of us. And I'm not happy with that situation. I don't mind Bill and Leonard being the stars. But, in light of the fact that we were totally typecast through *Star Trek*, I felt the least they could have done was not totally defuse our characters."

The other actors (James Doohan, Walter Koenig, George Takei) have expressed similar concerns over the years, highlighted each time a new *Star Trek* feature film is being produced and

the press chronicles their efforts to get their characters more to do.

Director Joseph Pevney most definitely felt the change in attitude during the second year, and he *didn't* like it.

"In the beginning, there was the word and the word was cooperation," he states emphatically. "But then they started reading the fan mail. This was the first year and they were on tenter hooks. Everytime the phone would ring it was like, 'Are we cancelled? Are we cancelled?'

"Everybody was lovely in the beginning," he continues. "The relationships were exciting and good and then Gene Roddenberry let things get out of hand. I have to blame the producer on this, because the director is a lover and a father image and all that, and he's in love with his people and must treat them very carefully so as not to offend or hurt. But the producer's function is to be the stern father who punishes for misbehavior and so on. Gene could never play that role. Gene Coon could a little, but they didn't pay too much attention to him because Roddenberry was the top boss. So they would give lip service to Gene Coon, and then Roddenberry would come down and love everything he saw.

"Right after the pick up, things started to occur. The actors wanted to make a bigger contribution in the writing, so they wanted a rehearsal table thrown on the stage. The motivator of all this was, I think, Bill Shatner. Leonard could make his contributions in a quiet way by going into the office and talking to Coon or Roddenberry, and they were all very receptive. But all of a sudden things started to move away from the producer and director and to the actors. So, like a producer himself, Bill would arrange the table and seats and he would talk to the property man to move the thing over to the side. Well, when you're doing television in five or six days, or whatever the schedule was back then, there's no time for this constant rehearsal, a reading rehearsal, off-stage, with pencils in hand and making changes. Because once you start making changes on the set, they have to be approved by the producer."

Robert Justman adds, "Bill *was* the instigator of the rehearsal table. He wanted to be able to rehearse and I said,

'Okay, I'll tell you what. In between takes we'll set up a table, we'll grab everyone and go over the next scene.' Bill had wanted to do that and we made it possible. It was useful. It certainly helped an awful lot."

"It's time consuming," Pevney differs. "It destroys the most important thing of all, the disciplinary control of the director on the set. It's a very critical and tentative thing, which the television industry has gone away from completely. The director on a television set is nothing anymore. He doesn't mean a god-damned thing. He's an errand boy, which is one of the reasons I don't work anymore. I'm an angry guy when it comes to this kind of shit. I come from a disciplined school where everything is in the script. Nothing else counts. What is the story? And *that* is your function. Your responsibility is to tell the story as the writer intended it. That is my definition of a director. Once that's interfered with, he loses all control. So, anyway, everytime you would have a 'Cut. Print,' you'd have these guys rushing over under Bill's command to the table to work on the next scene."

Robert Justman responds, "I don't think Leonard or Bill ever gave up wanting to make the show better. Especially Leonard. He always wanted to make it better, make his character more believable and not take the easy way out. The problem is, of course, that the actors get the script a few days before they start the shooting, and then it's a little late to try and effect changes. We did try to accommodate them as much as we possibly could, even though it made our lives hell. There wasn't any time."

It's pointed out to him that Pevney believed that the directors were losing control of the series. Justman considers this for a moment.

"I initiated a policy in the second season that may have had something to do with that feeling," he admits. "We alternated directors rather than in the first season where we had scatter-gunned. [For the most part] we had Marc Daniels and Joe Pevney alternate, because they knew the show, they seemed to know what to do with the show first season very well and the film was generally

very, very good. So I said, speaking from a cost factor, we'd be able to get as many shows as we could possibly get with the time and money we had to spend. These two guys were very, very good, but at the same time we found out—I found out—familiarity breeds contempt. I shouldn't say that. It tends to relax a little bit too much when it's the same guy every time and you lose a little bit of that excitement you wanted to maintain. You should understand that Joe was extremely well liked on the set. The cast really liked him, the crew really liked him. He was very likable and motivated. Marc on the other hand was a different kettle of fish.

"Marc, in my opinion, turned out better shows, but he was a more difficult personality. He was truly well-versed in all forms of drama and comedy. His experience was unlimited, because he had been a successful movie director, stage director, television director and he had a good eye for compositions. He was a very all around kind of director, but he was more demanding than most. He ran a tougher set."

Pevney particularly noticed the problems when he and Marc Daniels would go off to do other shows and directors such as Ralph Senensky and Vincent McEveety would step in to helm episodes.

"While Marc and I went off to other shows, they brought in new directors and the new directors had ideas," he explains. "But the actors were already ingrained in behavior patterns which did not permit new inventiveness which was, as they felt, opposed to their character. That was the real beginning of the problem. Bill would not do certain things because Kirk wouldn't do that. Leonard certainly felt that way, very strongly, because his character was so deeply ingrained that he knew precisely how Spock would behave in a certain setting.

"It was right in certain respects," he allows, "with the actors protecting themselves, and it was wrong in the fact that their minds were closed to new inventiveness. There were good and bad things involved, but then when we would come back, there would be a whole different attitude by the actor. Now the actor had become co-producer, co-director and co-writer. A whole different attitude toward

me, Joe Pevney, or toward Marc Daniels. Now my attitude toward that is a very strong one. I don't bend with that kind of stuff. The director is the director. You want to be a director, God bless you. Go and be a director. But when I'm the director, I'm the director and you are the actor and you make the greatest contributions that you can, and I make the choices."

To a certain extent, director Vincent McEveety agrees with Pevney's observations.

"I think it's true of many series," he states. "Look at how locked in *Gunsmoke* was. Take Jim Arness, for example. How much did he vary from his basic portrayal? Any time there was a stretch, they'd pull back. The traditional words on *Star Trek* were, 'Well, Spock wouldn't do this, Kirk wouldn't do that.' All of a sudden, they're entities in and of themselves, when they were nothing two years prior when no one knew what they would do in a situation. By saying this, I'm not necessarily being critical, but, as Joe Pevney said, it is extremely limiting and that's all. I have worked on too many series where the attitude from the actor has been similar, if not more vocal, and they've been extremely successful.

"They call it protecting the character," elaborates McEveety. "The character first, before story, before stretch, before anything, because they claim in their vision that that is the key to the success of the series, and I think in many instances they're right. What you have to do is write *for* the character. Sometimes writers get very lazy and just write a script, but these actors are very concerned about being put in a weak position. That's okay in acting class, but they're depreciating their character. If anything was lacking in the later years on the show, even more than not accepting growth of the characters or even more conflict, it was lack of writing. I think it became more cliche writing, if you will. They came up with a story, went in there and put the actors in that story. They bring in writers that aren't terribly familiar with the series who say, 'Wouldn't it be fun if Spock did this?' Then you get on the stage and find out that Spock just doesn't do those kinds of things, so it isn't much fun. It's not writing with total intelligence."

Director Ralph Senensky remains philosophical about the whole situation. "Doing episodic television is like jumping on a freight train that's in movement," he says. "As a director, what you have to do is jump on it and not break your legs. Once you've boarded it, you have to climb on top of the train, run across and get in the engine and take over running it. What happens is that before you can bring anything personal to the story, you have to get acquainted with who the people are. Not in terms of who you want them to be, but in terms of who they really are already. These are already-established characters. You do that, and *then* you can start to find the warts and things to do, outlets to extend and expand. As a result, what would happen is that you have to kind of rely on the cast to help you out. You'd say, 'Would your character do this?'

"I just accepted it," he continues. "A major area where they would get into that tact with was not so much in the acting, but in the scripting. The script might not fulfill their character or would go off on tangents. Sometimes actors come in the first season and get a job that they're thrilled to get, but by the second season they know more about writing, directing, producing...whatever else, than anyone. There is a taking advantage of that position too. There's a very fine line that I certainly appreciate, because actors do help. Through the years I've found myself many times using the actor as a way to get a script changed when we've both agreed that it should be. I would go through the actor, because the producer will be more apt to relent if the actor goes to him than if a new director comes in and says, 'I don't like your script.'

"I remember on the third season episode 'Is There in Truth No Beauty?', it was the first day of shooting and the cast literally refused to shoot it. Gene Roddenberry, who wasn't very involved in the third year, came down, they had a meeting and we lost half a day. We literally sat around talking and then I went off to shoot something with the guest stars. I shot a scene with them in the afternoon, while Gene was rewriting the other sequence to try and mollify the objections. That's not only *Star Trek*, that's an ongoing battle. That doesn't mean that

I'm more lenient about it than Joe or Marc, but I've had it in so many other places too, that people shouldn't think that it only happened on *Star Trek*."

Star Feud...?

The rumors of behind the scenes conflicts between lead actors on a weekly series have probably been around for as long as the medium has existed. As is the case in most rumors there is one side, the other side and the truth. Did Jack Klugman and Tony Randall love each other on *The Odd Couple*? Yes, there's no doubt. Just look to the recent slew of Eagle Snack commercials featuring the two actors as proof that their friendship has spanned over two decades. Did Penny Marshall and Cindy Williams have difficulties on the set of *Laverne & Shirley*? Considering the fact that the last season featured Laverne (Marshall) without Shirley, one can assume that they did.

And what of William Shatner and Leonard Nimoy on *Star Trek*? Since the days of the series to the making of the feature films, there have been reports of a strained relationship, due mostly to the whirlwind they found themselves caught up in and, some say, the unleashing of their egos. To an extent this is understandable. When you've got millions of fans elevating you to a level above humanity, it has got to have an effect. Still, both actors have stated over the years that there was never a feud.

"I really love Leonard," Shatner explained in the 1970s. "I really care for him a great deal. He's a very fine human being. He stands behind what he says with his total character. When he says something, he really means it. You can take him at his word. He is slyly humorous and very affectionate in his own way, which is remarkable. And to address myself to the elements of friction on the stage, I would put it in a way that two children [from] the same family might squabble over something. Loving each other, but squabbling. Any member of a family would know what I mean, and that means all of us. You can say, 'No, I don't think that's right' in that quarrelous tone and be angry at the moment, and

The classic trio: Dr Leonard "Bones" McCoy, Captain James T. Kirk and Mr. Spock. (Photo copyright © Globe Photos)

then forget it the following moment because you care about that person."

In *The World of Star Trek*, Nimoy said, "Bill and I are both very committed to and concerned with the work that we do, and we both tend to have strong personalities...and we both have strong feelings about what's right and what's wrong. So, yes, there were times when we had differences of opinion about how a thing should be done or whether it should be done at all. But, we are very good friends, we're very close."

World of Star Trek and "Trouble With Tribbles" author David Gerrold relates, "During the first season, *Saturday Review* did this article about *Trek* that Spock was much more interesting than Kirk, and that Spock should be captain. Well, *nobody* was near Shatner for days. He was furious. You've got to look at it from his point of view. He had been hired to be the star of the show. It was 'Starring William Shatner, *with* DeForest Kelley and Leonard Nimoy.' All of a sudden, all the writers are writing all this great stuff for Spock, and Spock, who's supposed to be a subordinate character, suddenly starts becoming the equal of Kirk. The show that started out about Kirk is now about Kirk and Spock. Bill definitely feels that he was lessened by that. On the other hand, Leonard is a very shrewd businessman, a very smart actor, and recognized that this Spock business was a way to be more important than an 'also ran,' and he pushed."

Science fiction author Norman

Spinrad wrote season two's "The Doomsday Machine." In that episode, the Enterprise encounters a device that has the capability of wiping out entire star systems. Guest starring is Commodore Decker (William Windom), who commanded a starship recently destroyed by the weapon. Spinrad was surprised by some of the ways that he *had* to approach the characters and his on-set observations.

"I had had a long unpublished novella that took place entirely on a space ship which was kind of a variation on *Moby Dick*, so that became 'The Doomsday Machine,'" reflects Spinrad. "I was also told to write a part for Robert Ryan, who they wanted to give a good role to. So I developed the idea of Robert Ryan playing an Ahab-type character. And then when they didn't get Ryan and they got William Windom, things had to be adjusted. I had to make him a little softer, and I think it might have taken some of the edge off of the story.

"In the original version, Commodore Decker was much stronger," he continues. "They don't find him slumped over in the ruined ship. Instead, they find him staring out the viewscreen and in a *very* bad mood. There was also the feeling that a guest star with that kind of presence would overshadow Captain Kirk, and therefore his character had to be toned down and his lines reduced. Also, some of Spock's lines had to be given to Kirk.

"Yes, he [Shatner] counted lines. I was on the set during the making of that episode. Marc Daniels was directing and they couldn't get it to work. The reason for this is that it was a dialogue sequence set up as Kirk, Spock, Kirk, but the intervening Spock line had been taken out in the line count, so there was no reaction line for the next line to work. I took Marc aside and said, 'Have him grunt or something,' and I explained that there was a missing line there. But things like that did happen. Observing it depended on how close you were to the production. Here I was watching the director struggle. But not too many people were able to hang around the set. The point is that they have to give their lead characters prominence."

Spinrad notes that he was impressed with the series itself, and to a degree could understand the difficulties between the actors.

"I thought that it was a genius thing that Roddenberry did," he muses. "The anthology series was dead on television as a doornail, and he devised a format in which you could do a self-contained anthology story every week. All you had were these people on a spaceship who could go to any damned planet they felt like. It was a genius concept because it literally left them open to do anything at all. As far as the characters, Spock was a really interesting and good character. The rest were fairly typical 'type' characters, without strong or weird characteristics.

"That was always Bill Shatner's problem. He just wasn't given as interesting a character to play as Nimoy was. He was the lead character—supposedly the most important—but he couldn't be most interesting. It was not a reflection on him as an actor, because I remember him as a very good actor before that, but he didn't have the part even though the contract said he did. That led to all the line stealing and all that kind of crazy lunatic stuff in any number of scripts where the captain went crazy because somebody was trying to take away his ship. In a funny kind of way, this gave the character of Kirk more depth. It gave Kirk a little edge somewhere that was really Shatner, which is a good way to use it. Another thing to consider is that if this cast has been together for this long, then the actors have got to become a part of the character which can give them more depth...if people know what they're doing."

Joseph Pevney considers the notion of the feud, and nods his head in understanding.

"If there are rumors about a rivalry," he begins, "they're probably true. Now Leonard and Bill are both good actors. They enjoy working with each other. If the script is equally as good to both characters, there's no problem. It's when one became a straight man for the other that you have rivalry. That they resent and probably for good reason. Sometimes, storywise, it's impossible to have both people answer the question, but a good writer can solve that in two seconds. All he's got to have is a straight man who's a third character, and let both of the heroes be heroes. It's not *too* difficult to do. Roddenberry was always conscious of it, but he lost control of the show because of Bill and Leonard. I'm sure of that.

"I left the show long before it folded, because I couldn't enjoy working with those two anymore. The whole character of the show had changed for me. The quality of the writing deteriorated, I think primarily because they were scared that whatever they submitted would be torn to shreds by Bill and Leonard. There was loss of confidence from the top in the material, and if you do that, you're shaking up something awful. If I had come in with the script for 'The Trouble With Tribbles' during the third season, I would have been laughed off the set. They'd say, 'You can't do this piece of shit,' and that would be the end of it. The hero of the show was a little fuzzy animal, and they don't want that. They want to constantly be the heroes and this is the mark of a spoiled actor. This is a guy who reads his mail and is no longer aware of the need for teamwork.

"When we started the show, teamwork was the key word. Nobody was more important than anybody else. The captain was the captain of the ship, but the actor was no more important than anybody. When Gene Coon left the show, a lot of the discipline had gone out of it. From the time I made 'Arena' to the time I did my last show, there was a hell of a difference. If you run both of them, there was a difference in performance quality, changes which give you a sense of the overbearing captain and Spock. And a kind of challenging between the two of them on screen, which is okay in life and rehearsal, but shouldn't be there on screen. Then Leonard would say, 'I'm the second in command, when can I do a story where I'm commanding the ship?' Well, those stories came to be and, after a while, Bill would say, 'Wait a second, I'm the captain!' There you've got problems, originating from, I would say, actor to producer, because when they were through with their shows, Leonard, primarily, and Bill would be up in Gene's fanny, making suggestions as to how the show should go, some good and some

• • • •

48

horrible. All of them, I think, very selfishly instigated. Now I wasn't witness to this, I only heard it from Gene Coon and Gene Roddenberry, who was coming to the studio less and less. The whole atmosphere, the feeling of teamwork and whole *Star Trek* quality disintegrated."

The Changing Season

Despite whatever controversies were brewing behind the scenes, *Star Trek*'s second season presented some of the show's finest episodes.

"Metamorphosis" was a different kind of love story, between an energy being and the human it rescued a century earlier; "Who Mourns For Adonais?" actually pit Kirk and company against the Greek god Apollo, and managed to pull it off believably; "Amok Time" delved into the nature of the Vulcan mating cycle; "Mirror, Mirror" was a fascinating look at the dark side of the universe as Kirk, McCoy, Scotty and Uhura are transported to a mirror dimension in which the Federation serves the place held by the Klingon Empire in "our" universe, and members of the crew move up in rank through assassination; "The Deadly Years," in which Kirk, Spock, McCoy and Scotty are victims of advanced aging; "The Trouble With Tribbles," *Star Trek*'s first comedy about a fuzzy critter that multiplies like crazy and actually threatens everyone aboard the Enterprise and the space station K-7; "Journey to Babel," which had the Enterprise serve as transport for various races enroute to a peace conference, and a show that introduced us to Spock's parents, Sarek and Amanda; "The Ultimate Computer," in which the Enterprise becomes the toy of the M-5 and is used in war games exercises that become a horrifying reality; and "Assignment: Earth," a pilot for a series that never happened in which the Enterprise travels back in time to Earth in the 1960s, where they encounter a man from the future who has been trained to help mankind save itself from the threat of nuclear destruction. All of these were examples of *Star Trek* at its best.

Story Editor Dorothy Fontana reflects, "In the first and second season I think we went from strength to strength, because, basically, we knew our direction by the sixth show in terms of the actors who filled out the characters. We had begun to know them as the characters and began writing for their strengths. I think the stories just got better, although you always have a klinker or two. On the whole, I think our batting average was awfully good during the first two seasons."

While there was great success in terms of the stories utilized on the show, there was also a disturbing sense of repetition in the use of the "parallel worlds" theory. Season one had used Earth-like settings three times, one of them ("Miri") being an alien world, while both "Tomorrow is Yesterday" and "The City on the Edge of Forever" took place on Earth in the past (respectively the 1960s and 1930s). During season two, however, "Bread and Circuses" gave us a modernized twist on Old Rome; "A Piece of the Action" was a light-hearted variation of Chicago in the Roaring 20s; "Patterns of Force" represented a world being run by a Nazi regime; "The Omega Glory," was a frontier story involving a Federation captain who "infected" an alien society, resulting in the development of a Constitution quite similar to America's; "A Private Little War," another frontier tale this time serving as a Vietnam analogy in which the Federation and the Klingons each arm different sides of an alien world to maintain a balance of power; and the aforementioned "Assignment: Earth."

Although some of these shows were quite good, it nonetheless seemed to point to *Star Trek* losing a bit of its edge.

"Once you solve the mystery in anything, the thrill is gone," says Robert Justman. "The thing that's motivated me in working in the television business was getting the challenge of a new show and finding out if you could do it. My feeling was once you knew you could do it, I wanted to try something new. So, yes, the original magic, the original excitement, tends to pass on once you solve the mysteries of it. But there was still the comraderie.

"We had another problem in the second season that was highly intensified during the third," he adds. "In the second season we were cut down on how much we could spend per show by a sizeable amount of money. Despite the fact that there had been cast escalations, so our cast costs were higher. This in turn had an effect on the kind of shows we could do. It was even worse the third season when we got cut down again despite even more cast escalations."

Corroborates director Ralph Senensky, "There wasn't any money. If you saw the soundstage we shot on, you'd be amazed. One of them was the starship interiors, which filled the entire stage and it wasn't that big a stage to begin with. The other one was the stage where we built everything else we needed. For example, in 'Metamorphosis' we had the Enterprise shuttle, the Galileo, on the sound stage. We were supposed to have a spacecraft and sell the idea of a huge, huge planet. I don't know if you remember the wide shots we did, but the spacecraft looks so small that you would think it was a model. This was achieved by our cinematographer, Jerry Finnerman. We literally had the spacecraft at one end of the stage and the camera as far back as it could go on the other end of the stage. Jerry shot it with a 9mm lense just to give it that scope. You see it today, I think it's marvelous. But you couldn't use the 9mm with actors because it distorts. That's an example of the budgetary limitations. Rather than fight it, you try and find a way to use the imagination and rise above it."

For Senensky, a major change in atmosphere came when Paramount Pictures took over Desilu.

"Desilu was like a family," he smiles. "Herb Solow, who was the head of the studio, used to come down and talk with you on the sound stage. He didn't seem like the other studio heads who never seemed to talk to you. Herb went out of his way to help you. Can you imagine a studio working like that?

"I think when Paramount bought the company, it had a lot to do with the demise of the series. Gene Coon had told me that the shows were originally scheduled for six day shoots, though they averaged six and a half days or seven. It was pretty remarkable when you consider the kind of quality they were delivering. When Paramount bought it, a kind of corporate mentality took over. In a way I think that's why I resent Paramount having such a hit in *Star Trek*, because if they had their way, they would have killed it off. It survived in spite of them and now they have this bonanza making all of this money. With them there was a six-day schedule, *period*. They would not allow for any overruns at all. You would have a 7:30 crew call in the morning, you'd start shooting at 8:00 and you'd go until about 7:00, 7:30 at night. We're talking a six-day schedule and you had to absolutely pull the plug at midnight on the sixth day. In terms of actual hours, it really pulled us down to about a five and a half day schedule. It was a big cut. The other schedule hadn't given you that much grace, but all of a sudden you felt like you were shooting schlock because you were shooting so quickly."

As noted, Gene Coon decided to leave *Star Trek* in the middle of the second season due to the fact that he had simply burned himself out. Twelve to 16 hour days for months at a time had proved too much, and he departed.

Glen Larson, based on conversations he had with Coon, believes that the producer had simply had enough of *Star Trek*, and could not work on the series any longer.

"Gene had two scripts on his desk in front of him which he had to rewrite," Larson relates. "He suddenly put his pencil down and finally said, 'This is it,' and he got up and walked out. It had been an around the clock, very draining experience."

Part of the problem, according to actor William Campbell (who had portrayed Trelene in season one's "Squire of Gothos"), was that high-quality writers were no longer attempting to write for the show. Opines the actor, "I think it was starting to become a tremendous chore to come up with anything new. Don't forget, they were using writers from the outside and it was becoming more difficult to get them. You've got to remember that we're talking about a period when the great writers no longer were doing anything. When television was making its first inroads, you had some of these great people doing television shows."

Coon left and eventually went to work for Universal Pictures and *It Takes a Thief*, though he nonetheless continued to write for *Star Trek* under the

pen name Lee Cronin. This, according to Glen Larson, was not by choice.

"At first, Gene Roddenberry wouldn't let him leave because he had a contract," Larson offers. "The only way they'd let Gene out is if he continued to write for the show, and he continued under a psuedonym. He would be in there typing away while were were supposed to be doing *It Takes a Thief*, but that was great because more and more of it fell on me and I became an instant producer. Roddenberry knew they needed Gene, and didn't feel they could function without him, so he had to promise to make script commitments."

To replace Coon, Gene Roddenberry chose writer/director/producer John Meredyth Lucas.

"I was on the lot shooting *Mannix*," recalls Lucas, "and I wrote a script for Gene Coon. Gene was going to retire and suggested that I take over because I had produced *Ben Casey*. He asked if we could get together, I went over his house, we talked for a while and that was it. At that time, Bob Justman was handling the production end of things. When I came in, I got into production too, and was also directing. Gene had said, 'When they hired me, they knew I was writing and that was it.' That was *not* the way that I produced.

"When I joined the show, they had a very complex system of memoranda to everybody. Everyone involved would send incredibly long memorandums, almost equivalent to the old Hollywood technique. I abandoned that pretty quickly because it took so much goddamned time. I also remember that there was a great deal of tension with the actors. Not civil war but a great deal of tension among the cast and the company. As a matter of fact, Gene took me out to location to introduce me as producer. We came up to the company. When they'd gotten a particular shot, we walked over and Shatner walked away from us. He would not speak to Gene or to me. They were feuding over something, though I've no idea what the problem was.

"There was tension among Shatner and Nimoy and Gene. Just a great deal of tension that had built up. In happens on every show, but it was particular-

ly noticeable on *Star Trek* when I first came in. I won't say I solved it, but I simply ignored it, went on and was on the set a great deal. I tend to be hands-on with everything. It was just a different kind of approach. Whatever had caused the tension, I'm not quite sure. Actors tend to feel that if you're not there all the time and petting them a little bit, or at least there to hear their screams of anguish, that they're abandoned. Eventually we all became very friendly. That doesn't mean there weren't complaints about someone's part not being meaningful, but we developed a mechanism to talk them out."

Actor William Campbell offers this view: "I don't know anything about the relationship with the two guys, but I can tell you this. What happens to actors when they've acquired a position on a television show, after a short period of time—they can't help it—they become precious. And recognize that in some ways they can tell producers off, can make their presence felt. They all have ideas.

"I don't remember a situation where Gene Coon would tell either of those actors how to act, nor did he suggest that he was a director, but he did have an inner sense and he might have held the line on certain things that they would have changed. Or areas where they would have liked another direction be taken, and Gene Coon perhaps debated them on occasion and they didn't like it. But I never heard him say word one bad against anybody."

Jackie Fernandez, the woman who married Coon shortly after his tenure on *Star Trek*, recalls, "Basically Gene wasn't crazy about actors. They were just too needful and too egocentric. He wasn't. He didn't get along with Robert Wagner either when he went over to *It Takes a Thief*. I would take his feelings about these actors he didn't get along with with a grain of salt, because he didn't care for actors in general."

When John Meredyth Lucas took over the writing reigns, he was determined to get back to what he felt *Star Trek* had been in its original concept.

"If there was one element that I brought back to the show when I was producer, because it had been a little bit lost, it was Gene Roddenberry's inspiration for the series: Horatio Hornblower. *That's* the thing that I kept trying to bring back. The constant warfare—frontier warfare—to make Kirk Captain Hornblower again. A lot of that stuff had gotten lost into the areas of fantasy, which is fine. But as the season progressed, there'd been less and less of the Hornblower elements, which appealed to me as exemplified in 'The Ultimate Computer' and things like that.

"A creative problem on the show was that we loved doing pieces which had some kind of concept. That's a terrible word to use when you're talking to the network. You would think that high concept would mean a lofty purpose, but to them it simply means something you can tell in one word. The network tended to want green space monsters that ate the ship each week, and we tended to want to do shows which had,

what seemed to us, some kind of concept, saying something and being different. But God knows we did our share of the green monsters eating the ship."

In between all of these elements being worked out, and while the show continued to touch its primary audience—the youth of America—NBC made the announcement: STAR TREK would be cancelled at the end of the season. Fortunately, a second letter-writing campaign kept the show alive. Barely.

• • • •

CHAPTER FOUR
Season 2 Episode Guide

"Amok Time"

"Who Mourns For Adonais?"

"The Changeling"

"Mirror, Mirror"

"The Apple"

"The Doomsday Machine"

"Catspaw"

"I, Mudd"

"Metamorphosis"

"Journey to Babel"

"Friday's Child"

"The Deadly Years"

"Obsession"

"Wolf in the Fold"

"The Trouble With Tribbles"

"The Gamesters of Triskellion"

"A Piece of the Action"

"The Immunity Syndrome"

"A Private Little War"

"Return to Tomorrow"

"Patterns of Force"

"By Any Other Name"

"The Omega Glory"

"The Ultimate Computer"

"Bread and Circuses"

"Assignment Earth"

"Amok Time" co-stars Leonard Nimoy and Arlene Martel reunited at an early Star Trek convention.

Episode #29:
"Amok Time"
Original Airdate: 9/15/67
Written by Theodore Sturgeon
Directed by Joseph Pevney
Guest Starring: Arlene Martel (T'Pring),
Celia Lovsky (T'Pau),
Lawrence Montaigne (Stonn),
Byron Morrow (Komack)

Spock begins to lose control of himself as he is overtaken by pon farr, the Vulcan mating cycle that occurs every seven years in which the affected male must return to the homeworld to mate or die. It's a cycle much like the salmon on Earth, which must return to its birthplace to spawn eggs or die trying.

As Enterprise is in the midst of a mission, Kirk—who believes that Spock merely needs shore leave—is unable to divert to Vulcan for several days. Spock, in the midst of his madness, countermands the captain's orders and has a course laid in for his homeworld. Eventually Kirk comes to understand what is going on and disobeys Starfleet orders to go to Vulcan.

There, the madness takes its full control on Spock and through the manipulations of his of his supposed betrothed, he is pitted against Kirk in a battle to the death.

••••

Then Story Editor Dorothy Fontana recalls the conferences regarding the specifics of Vulcan mating.

"I don't remember whether it was Gene Roddenberry, Gene Coon or Ted [who came up with the Vulcan seven-year mating cycle], but the way we have established it, most people don't stop and understand this," says Fontana. "Vulcans mate normally anytime they want to. However, every seven years you do the ritual, the ceremony, the whole thing. The biological urge. You must, but any other time is any other emotion—humanoid emotion—when you're in love. When you want to, you know, when the sex urge is there, you do it. This every seven years business was taken too literally by too many people who aren't stopping and understanding. We didn't mean *only* every seven years. I mean, every seven years would be a little bad, and it would not explain the Vulcans of many different ages which are not seven years apart."

The late writer Theodore Sturgeon once recalled, "Do you know that [the actors] got so far into their characters that they would *speak their own lines*? In 'Amok Time', for example, in the last scene where the doctor was so pleased to see the sudden flash of humanity in Spock, where Spock suddenly came up with this brilliant smile and said, 'Jim!' when he saw Kirk alive and had thought he was dead—and then was still denying having any emotional reaction, at all, and Dr. McCoy said, 'In a pig's eye!'—that was De. That wasn't me. De put that in his very own self. They all did that from time to time. Bill certainly did. And when it worked, they let it stand, because that was one of the things the show had going for it."

Adds director Joseph Pevney, "'Amok Time' was a good one. I brought in the actress who played T'Pau. The fight was absolutely excellent, and one of the most exciting we ever did. What made it dramatically interesting is that it took place between Kirk and Spock. During this episode, Leonard Nimoy and I worked out the Vulcan salute and the 'Live long and prosper' together. He dis-cussed this finally in an interview and he never mentioned my name. He said the director, but never me by name. Well, Leonard is now a big director, and I hope he doesn't change as a human being. He was a nice Yiddish boy with a nice mastery of the language. I just hope he doesn't believe all the bullshit, because it's so easy to believe. I don't care who you are, you can get captured by it."

Elsewhere, Leonard Nimoy recalled, "We arrived on the planet, the three key figures—Captain Kirk, Mr. Spock and Dr. McCoy—were greeted by a procession coming out from the city. When the procession arrived, we discover that Vulcan is a matriarchy, the head of the planet being brought out, carried in a sedan chair by some bearers. The character was named T'Pau, played by Cecilia Lovsky, a wonderful actress, and she was to be seated and I was to approach her and we were to say some nice things to each other. I thought, 'Here's a special opportunity to create something special in the way of a Vulcan greeting; some kind of signal that they have between each other.

"And I said to the director, 'Humans shake hands when they meet and military people salute each other.' He asked me what I had in mind. I was raised in an orthodox Jewish family, and during the high holidays I'd go to the temple with my parents and sit with my father and my brother, and at a particular point in the service, the kohanim, who are the priests of the Hebrew tribes, would bless the congregation with a blessing that is familiar to all of us from the old and new testament, 'May the Lord bless you and keep you,' and so forth. When that time comes during this ritual, the congregation turned their back and does not look at these men. I'm not sure of the reason for that, but in any case, children are taught not to look at the kohanim while they are performing this blessing. My father would say, 'Don't look, turn away.' Of course, I being a curious eight or nine year old child, I peeked. What I saw was....." Nimoy demonstrated the gesture. "...These gentlemen were holding their hands in this position while they were giving this benediction to the congregation...I was fascinated. I thought I've got to learn how to do that, and I worked long and hard to accomplish it."

••••

Carolyn Palamas, impregnated by Apollo in an early draft of "Who Mourns for Adonais?", was played by Leslie Parrish, seen here in The Wild Wild West.

Episode #30:
"Who Mourns For Adonais?"
Original Airdate: 9/22/67
Written by Gilbert Ralston and
Gene L. Coon
Story by Gilbert Ralston
Directed by Marc Daniels
Guest Starring: Michael Forest (Apollo),
Leslie Parrish (Carolyn Palamas),
John Winston (Kyle)

The Enterprise is literally snared by the hand of the Greek god Apollo, who has decided that the time has come for mankind to worship him again. Kirk must use the force of the starship as well as crew woman Carolyn Palamas, who is in love with Apollo, to combat his awesome powers and gain their freedom. Finally realizing that the species cannot be forced to worship anything, Apollo moves to a spiritual plane, joining the other gods who had long ago realized that their time had come and gone.

• • • •

There is a startling moment in this episode where Carolyn Palamas rejects Apollo's love (despite her feelings to do otherwise) and she is ravaged by a storm of Apollo's making. If you watch this scene, you can't help but get the feeling that he is raping her. Indeed, an earlier draft of the teleplay had her pregnant with his child.

Of this script, Dorothy Fontana notes, "I think Gene Coon basically enhanced the relationships, the fact that

the god wanted this woman to not only be his consort, but his foremost among his worshippers. And then the antagonistic relationship between Kirk and Adonais. Kirk wasn't going to fall on his knees and worship a god. No way. Again, it was a matter of character development."

"Immodestly," writer Gilbert Ralston begins, "I'm an expert in Grecian history, and I got interested in some of the characters tucked away in my various textbooks. Using Apollo just seemed like a good idea, and Gene Coon liked it very much.

"I liked *Star Trek* because of Gene and some of the people who originally worked on it. Their conception was highly intellectual and very sophisticated, and it was fun to write because they were apparently very demanding in so far as literary quality was concerned. Shows like that were always a pleasure. It was a *people* show, without an emphasis on stunts and special effects. It was about people, and the fact that one had funny ears didn't make any difference. They were not afraid to emotionalize what they did and, in its own peculiar way, it had a kind of reality which I think was very important. I think *Star Trek* will continue as a kind of quasi-classic for a long time to come."

Episode #31:
"The Changeling"
Original Airdate: 9/29/67
Written by John Meredyth Lucas
Directed by Marc Daniels
Guest Starring: Blaisdell Makee (Singh),
Arnold Lessing (Lt. Carlisle),
Vic Perrin (The Voice of Nomad)

Over four billion people are obliterated in the Malurian star system, and the perpetrator is a combination probe and computer identifying itself as Nomad, which has more power than the Enterprise or the entire fleet.

Nomad is brought aboard the Enterprise. Mistakenly it believes that Captain Kirk is actually its creator, Jackson Roykirk, and for that reason, he obeys Kirk's commands. In a Vulcan mind-meld, Spock learns that the machine was actually an Earth probe lost in space centuries earlier. Captured by a machine planet, it was given intelligence and the ability to purify all things impure.

Kirk must trick the machine into destroying itself.

• • • •

Writer/producer John Meredyth Lucas says, "I was always fascinated by the concept of the machine as God. That was really the spark for it; the selling point. Although 'The Changeling' does comment on worshipping the machine, I was not trying to make any particular statement. It was simply a fascinating concept that a machine could become—in a very real sense—alive. In the story it was accidental, but it became a very real, judgmental being and a threat."

It's pointed out that *Star Trek: The Motion Picture* was quite similar to this episode. "If anything," he replies, "it's a little hard to sustain that plot for a full movie. God knows the effects and everything else that had been done are effects which were pretty damn good in their day, but are primitive today. The plot, of course, I recognized."

"'The Changeling' required a great deal of ingenuity," recalled Marc Daniels. "We had to have three different Nomads mounted in three different ways. One on a wire, to hover in a room; one on a dolly, to be moved through corridors and onto the bridge; and one on the floor. You just couldn't take one on a wire through the door, hence the dolly system. If you wanted to see Nomad in all its authority, you would put it on a wire."

Episode #32:
"Mirror, Mirror"
Original Airdate: 10/6/67
Written by Jerome Bixby
Directed by Marc Daniels
Guest Starring: Barbara Luna (Marlena),
Vic Perrin (Tharn)

During an ion storm, Kirk, McCoy, Scotty and Uhura are transported to a parallel dimension on an alternate, savage Enterprise. In this universe, the Federation is as feared as the Klingons and crewmen move up in rank by assassination. Spock (with a beard!) is still first officer, but his logic is coupled with a shocking ruthlessness.

Kirk and company try to fit in until they figure out a way home, barely avoiding discovery by those around them. Simultaneously, Kirk tries to convince Spock to see the logic in changing the order; that the Federation will ultimately be defeated by rebel forces and he, Spock, can be the man who can lead the revolution.

Scotty ultimately devises a plan by which they will attempt the conditions present during the ion storm and transport to their own universe, but if they miss the window of opportunity they will be trapped there forever.

••••

Veteran science fiction author Jerome Bixby, whose script credits include Rod Serling's *The Twilight Zone* and 20th Century Fox's motion picture *Fantastic Voyage* was a real coup to the series.

"Mirror, Mirror" came about because "I wanted to do a parallel universe story. I had already done a fiction story called 'One Way Street' which was a parallel universe story, and I thought that would make a good *Star Trek*. The universe I created was a very savage counterpart, virtually a pirate ship, into which I could transpose a landing party. I submitted the outline, they loved it and I did the script."

"That was a good one," commented Marc Daniels. "I'm not sure if it was 'Mirror, Mirror,' but I remember a big fight scene which resulted in several bodies lying on the floor for quite some time. After a while there was a considerable amount of snoring from these people who were supposed to be unconscious. I also remember that Nichelle Nichols was furious because I used a stunt woman in the fight. She said, 'I want to do that. That woman doesn't look anything like me!' I said, 'You've got to be out of your mind. This is a complicated stunt. You could get badly hurt unless you know what you're doing, and the production couldn't afford to have you knocked out.'"

Episode #33:
"The Apple"
Original Airdate: 10/13/67
Written by Max Ehrlich and Gene L. Coon
Story by Max Ehrlich
Directed by Joseph Pevney
Guest Starring: Keith Andes (Akuta), Celeste Yarnall (Martha Landon), Jay Jones (Mallory), Shari Nims (Sayana), David Soul (Makora)
Captain Kirk does the computer

shuffle again as the Enterprise goes to a world run by Vaal, an ancient computer that controls the laws of nature as well as the inhabitants.

While this is an idyllic world, the people are exactly like children. No cares and no concerns, allowing Vaal to take care of them and, in turn, making offerings to "him" in appeasement. Kirk and company must make them see that this is wrong; that they have a right to govern themselves.

••••

Actor and Gene Coon friend William Campbell points out, "Gene recognized some of the shortcomings of *Star Trek*. He saw the cult atmosphere and felt that no American would go along with that concept—being policeman of the universe. It was a little L. Ron Hubbardish. Here you've got a leader who's omnipotent, this rocketship is a city traveling around spanking people who are getting out of line. You don't tell Captain Kirk what to do, because he's boss. There's no sitting down and saying, 'We're having a meeting of the council to find out if we're going to let you do this.' He knew the impossible parts of it, but he said, 'We can take young people—because they're going to be the leaders of the future—and show them that right should be right, because today we don't know who the good guy is.'"

Episode #34:
"The Doomsday Machine"
Original Airdate: 10/20/67
Written by Norman Spinrad
Directed by Marc Daniels
Guest Starring: William Windom (Commodore Decker), Elizabeth Rogers (Lt. Palmer), John Copage (Elliot), Richard Compton (Washburn), John Winston (Sgt. Kyle), Tim Burns (Russ)
After several star systems have been destroyed, the Enterprise investigates the situation and discovers what's left of the U.S.S. Constellation, with her commander, Commodore Matt Decker, the only person on board. He relates a terrifying tale, detailing how a virtual tunnel in space emitted energy waves that sliced up whole planets which it devoured. He beamed his crew down to one of the local worlds in the hopes of protecting them, but that particular

Veteran character actor William Windom played Commodore Matt Decker, commander of ruined starship, in "The Doomsday Machine."

planet was the next target.

Kirk and Spock come to the conclusion that this thing is actually a doomsday machine—an ultimate weapon—created by a long dead race, that has been destroying planets for centuries. Now the hope is that the Enterprise and whatever can be salvaged of the Constellation will be able to defeat it before it continues on its way.

••••

"The Doomsday Machine" was famed science fiction author Norman Spinrad's first television script.

"I had seen both *Star Trek* pilots at conventions, met Gene Roddenberry a couple of times and wrote a review of *2001* in *Cinema* magazine, in which I mentioned *Star Trek* favorably," Spinrad recalls. "Gene asked me to come in and pitch something. Then he said, 'These things are really expensive. We're over budget on a lot of them, so can you think of anything that takes place entirely on the ship in terms of sets?' I had had a long unpublished novella that took place entirely on a space ship which was kind of a variation on *Moby Dick*. So that became 'The Doomsday Machine,' which is how it came to be known.

"I just rewatched the episode again for the first time in a long time," he elaborates, "and I was more pleased with it than I remember being, especially in comparison to the crap that has been on television since. I didn't think it was all that hot when I first saw it, because what I saw was the unaltered version that was in my head, and I thought it could have been done a lot better. And that godawful Doomsday Machine itself! Originally Gene Roddenberry asked me to design the thing. The concept was actually made less complex because there was a limit to what they could do. In my original concept, it is neither a machine nor an organism. It's a combination of both; a tailored weapon/organism."

Episode #35:
"Catspaw"
Original Airdate: 10/27/67
Written by Robert Bloch and
D.C. Fontana
Directed by Joseph Pevney
Guest Starring: Antoinette Bowers (Sylvia), Theo Marcus (Korob), Michael Barrier (DeSalle), Jimmy Jones (Jackson)

Star Trek does Halloween! Beaming down to Pyris VII, Kirk, Spock and McCoy confront Sulu and Scotty, who have been transformed into zombies. At the same time, they battle aliens who are out to conquer the universe and go about it through some traditional all hallows eve methods, right down to black cats and witches.

••••

Robert Bloch told *Starlog* magazine, "They wanted a Halloween story. I wanted to do something that would involve changes in appearances. So I decided that instead of having the usual Jekyll and Hyde transformation, I'll have a female who was capable of chameleon-like adaptations, and the rest just fell into place. I do have quibbles about the way in which things were done. It wasn't their fault, but they just didn't have the budget. 'Catspaw' cried out for the use of opticals in post-production effects. Shooting a cat's face in tight close-up is not exactly any substitute for having a giant cat. Running down a few feet of cardboard corridor isn't the same thing as having your characters trapped in a labyrinth of frightening proportions! Otherwise, 'Catspaw' was shot pretty much as I had written it."

Director Joseph Pevney dismisses the episode with, "That's not a very

good one. I hated the actors in that one."

Episode #36:
"I, Mudd"
Original Airdate: 11/3/67
Written by Stephen Kandel
Directed by Marc Daniels
Guest Starring: Roger C. Carmel (Harry Mudd), Richard Tatro (Norman), Mike Howden (St. Rowe), Michael Zaslow (Ensign Jordan), Kay Elliot (The "Stella" series), Rhae and Alyce Andrece (The "Alice" series), Tom and Ted LeGarde (The "Herman" series)

The Enterprise is forced to an uncharted planet by an android minion of Harry Mudd. Harry, it seems, has been elevated to the level of Emperor by the population of androids existing on a world he accidentally crashed on. Desperate for human company, he has brought the starship there. Unfortunately, the androids have another idea in mind. They are determined to stop mankind from destroying itself and, to do so, wish to spread their kind throughout the race as sort of intergalactic watchdogs. Captain James T. Kirk—licensed machine killer—does his stuff again.

••••

Marc Daniels noted, "Probably the biggest problem had completely to do with all the twins we had to present. It required a lot of trick photography, and it was necessary for us to be absolutely precise or else the story wouldn't have worked."

"Roger C. Carmel was wonderful as Harry," exclaims writer Stephen Kandel. "He inhabited the character and expanded it. He developed the character physically as an actor."

Gene Coon had given "I, Mudd" to David Gerrold, who performed an uncredited rewrite on the teleplay. "Gene Coon," Gerrold says, "could recognize a doable story and had a good sense of how to translate it to television. He asked me to do a rewrite of 'I, Mudd.' He said, 'We want to get to the planet faster at the end of act one, and Kandel gets us there at the end of act two.' I read the first draft Stephen Kandel script, and it was good. I thought it was shootable. But I understood it when Gene Coon said, 'Structurally we want to do this instead.' I understood exactly what he

Intergalactic con-man Harry Mudd was portrayed by Roger C. Carmel in the episodes "Mudds Women" and "I, Mudd."

wanted. First of all, he was testing me to see if I could rewrite, I'm sure of that, but secondly, much more important, he was teaching me something about story structure. When you're going to a planet with an interesting problem, you want to get there quickly. He said, 'How can you cut two acts down to one, and how can you fill the extra act?' He gave me some suggestions and instructions and let me go home. I bought it back over the weekend and he said, 'That's it, you've got it.' I put in the idea that there are 500 girl robots, and he said, 'That's a funny idea, let's go with it.' My feeling is that Coon's strengths were that he was receptive, he listened, he understood what would make a good television story, he had a great sense of structure and great sense of dialogue. I think he was just an all around good producer."

"I thought Harry Mudd was a good character," the late Roger C. Carmel told *The Official Star Trek Fan Club Magazine*, "but when the show developed such an emotional attachment with a large audience then I certainly thought that the character I played would also persist. I think it was very well written. When I did the shows, I never thought it would evolve into this. I don't think any of us thought of it in terms of the immortality it seems to have achieved."

Episode #37:
"Metamorphosis"
Original Airdate: 11/10/67
Written by Gene L. Coon
Directed by Ralph Senensky
Guest Starring: Glenn Corbett (Zephram Cochrane), Elinor Donahue (Nancy Hedford)

Kirk, Spock and McCoy are transporting Federation Commissioner Nancy Hedford to the Enterprise via the Galileo, when they are captured by an energy cloud that brings them to Gamma Canaris N. There, they meet Zefram Cochrane, a famous scientist who disappeared over a century earlier.

Cochrane, it's revealed, told the energy cloud—an intelligent creature he refers to as "The Companion"—that he was lonely; that he needed companionship. Instead of freeing him, the Companion brought the Galileo there.

Ultimately, this turns into a cosmic love story between Cochrane, the Companion and Nancy Hedford and, as such, becomes one of *Star Trek*'s most touching episodes.

••••

"We had the problem to cope with of the Companion," relates director Ralph Senensky. "We didn't know what it was going to look like, and they didn't know what it was going to look like. What they wanted me to do was shoot it in such a way so that they wouldn't have to do any travelling mattes. In other words, in the scene where you see the Companion and Cochrane in a long shot and then his point of view of Kirk and Spock watching, and then when the Companion engulfs him...if I had just shot a wide shot with Cochrane to the right of the frame and blank space at the left of the frame for the Companion, and just stayed with that shot so that they would have had to move whatever the optical was across the screen, that becomes very expensive. I worked it out where I would move the camera. They would just be able to do the optical in the middle of the shot and the camera would carry it where they wanted it to go."

"This was a very delicate and touching love story," enthuses Dorothy Fontana. "The idea that a man could accept a relationship with this alien, and

the young woman, to save her life, accepted the alien into her body. It was really a lovely story and a very touching one. I think Gene Coon did it with great deftness and delicacy."

Episode #38:
"Journey to Babel"
Original Airdate: 11/17/67
Written by D.C. Fontana
Directed by Joseph Pevney
Guest Starring: Jane Wyatt (Amanda), Mark Lenard (Sarek), William O'Connell (Thelev), Reggie Nalder (Sharas), John Wheeler (Gav), James X. Mitchell (Josephs)

The Enterprise serves as a transport for various alien races who are enroute to the planet Babel and the signing of an important peace treaty. Murder and intrigue ensue, as well as a glimpse into the relationship between Spock and his parents, Sarek and Amanda.

••••

"'Journey to Babel' came about because of the mention a couple of times of Spock's parents," explains Dorothy Fontana. "I said to Gene, 'We've talked about them, let's show them.' He told me to go and do it and I came up with 'Journey to Babel.'

"John D.F. Black had mentioned Spock's mother without being specific in 'The Naked Time,' and I mentioned the mother and the father, without giving them names, in 'This Side of Paradise.' I sat down then and created two characters, especially the relationship with Sarek and the rift between he and Spock, and Amanda positioned in the middle. She was a thoroughly human woman with an all Vulcan husband and a half-cast son, which is bound to create a lot of character problems. It was wonderful casting."

Interestingly, more money could be spent on the show's makeup effects due to the fact that it took place entirely on board the Enterprise.

"You always did trade-offs in that sense," she says. "If you went on location, you had to give away your costume and makeup. If you stayed on the ship you could do more. I did ship shows so we would have more money to go on location and make more elaborate planet sets."

Joseph Pevney elaborates, "That

was a good show in certain areas. I thought the greatest contributor to it was the makeup artist. He did a fabulous job of bringing alien humanoids on board. Remember *Star Wars*? The entire sequence in the bar looks like it came from this episode."

Episode #39:
"Friday's Child"
Original Airdate: 12/1/67
Written by D.C. Fontana
Directed by Joseph Pevney
Guest Starring: Tige Andrews (Kras), Michael Dante (Maab), Julie Newmar (Eleen), Cal Bolder (Keel), Kirk Raymone (Duur), Ben Gage (Teer Akaar), Robert Bralver (Grant)

Both the Federation and the Klingons vie for an alliance with the people of Capella IV, which is no easy task for Kirk and the Enterprise as the Klingon commander, Kras, backstabs them and attempts to manipulate the Capellans at every turn.

Added into the mix is the pregnant Eleen, wife of a former ruler who becomes a pawn in the negotiations and nearly costs Kirk and McCoy their lives when the latter delivers her child.

••••

"Basically an adventure," Dorothy Fontana relates, "but I felt the story that a woman was a pawn, and that she and her baby were the most important pawns in the game, was an interesting story. What happened was that they learned that they were no longer pawns.

Julie Newmar, decked out here as Catwoman, portrayed Eleen in "Friday's Child."

••••

She felt that she was no longer a pawn, that she had the power to make decisions for herself. In a way it was sort of a women's lib story, but I didn't mean it that way. I just meant it as a character development kind of thing in the sense of a person finding themself."

"This was the first time that I had been given the opportunity to wear a costume in a film role," recalls Tige Andrews, who portrayed Kras, "and I was very much into the role. I particularly remember feeling more like 'someone else' during the filmmaking. It was a fun part."

Episode #40:
"The Deadly Years"
Original Airdate: 12/8/67
Written by David P. Harmon
Directed by Joseph Pevney
Guest Starring: Charles Drake (Commodore Stocker), Sarah Marshall (Janet Wallace), Beverly Washburn (Arlene Galway), Felix Locker (Johnson), Carolyn Nelson (Atkins), Laura Wood (Mrs. Johnson)

While on the surface of Gamma Hydra IV, Kirk, Spock, McCoy and Scotty are infected with a disease that causes premature aging. Chekov, who is also there but separated from the others for a short time, is not affected.

As the landing party beams back aboard the Enterprise, the aging becomes more pronounced, threatening their lives. McCoy labors to find a cure, using Chekov as his guinea pig. In the meantime, Kirk's memory is starting to slip, and Commodore Stocker, who was being transported by the vessel, eventually realizes that he's got to take command. He orders the Enterprise to proceed to Starbase 10, which lies in the midst of the Neutral Zone. This is all the provocation that the Romulans need to launch an attack.

••••

Details writer David P. Harmon, "I was inspired to write the script by examining the American syndrome versus the Oriental reverence of old age. The concept of youth and beauty is such a shallow one, simply because it doesn't last very long. That's the inch of truth I was looking for. How important is it in the overall scheme of things in a person's life, if at all? But *we*

make it important."

For Joseph Pevney, "The Deadly Years" was a show filled with behind the scenes conflict. "I had a run in with DeForest Kelley during the making of this episode when he thought he was fantastic. We had quite a thing on the stage after the makeup was applied when he said, 'Bill can't do that, that should be me.' I tried to explain to him the situation. He was playing this old man and doing it quite well, incidentally, and Bill, I think, was maybe copying some of the things DeForest did to give him an aged look, because Bill was not very good as the old man. DeForest was beautiful in the role. The big problem there, of course, was time and two or three hours later I would get my first take. It was just ridiculous. It was just a gimmick on the show. Who in the hell cared if the wig wasn't precisely wrinkled in the right place? Nobody's going to know. Alright, if you're in motion pictures, spend a day. But you can't do that in television. But the actors no longer cared about schedules. I never shot a show off schedule, but I *heard* about them going over schedule and, after a while, the show became too costly."

Episode #41:
"Obsession"
Original Airdate: 12/15/67
Written by Art Wallace
Directed by Ralph Senensky
Guest Starring: Stephen Brooks (Garrovick), Jerry Ayres (Rizzo)

Kirk becomes obsessed when he has the opportunity to battle a gaseous creature that feeds on human blood cells, and one which he faced as a lieutenant. Half the crew of the USS Farragut perished during that earlier battle, and Kirk has blamed himself ever since because he had hesitated in firing his phaser at the creature.

••••

"Gene Roddenberry and I were having dinner one night," writer Art Wallace explains, "and then it came to me that it wouldn't be a bad idea to do a version of *Moby Dick*, which became 'Obsession.' I just substituted the cloud for the great white whale."

Jack the Ripper reincarnated himself in the persona of actor John Fiedler in Robert Bloch's "Wolf in the Fold."

Episode #42:
"Wolf in the Fold"
Original Airdate: 12/22/67
Written by Robert Bloch
Directed by Joseph Pevney
Guest Starring: John Fiedler (Hengist), Charles Macauley (Janis), Peter Seurat (Sybo), Joseph Bernard (Tark), Charles Dierkop (Morla), Judy McConnell (Tankris), Virginia Ladridge (Karen Tracy), Judy Sherven (Nurse), Tania Lemani (Kara)

Kirk, McCoy and Scotty are visiting Argelius Two for shore leave, following an accident in which Scotty injured his head. No sooner have they arrived then a serial murderer strikes, and all evidence points to the chief engineer.

A mystery follows, in which the crew of the Enterprise discovers that an alien force of pure evil that had appeared on Earth in the form of Jack the Ripper, has unleashed itself on Argelius.

••••

Doing a variation of Jack the Ripper was suggested to Robert Bloch by the *Star Trek* production team. "They wanted me to do a Jack the Ripper story in the future," he once explained. "So, I said, 'All right, let's put him into a computer or something instead of having him skulking around with a knife on shipboard.' There were a number of changes made to that script because I knew very little about computers. I still do."

••••

Episode #43:
"The Trouble With Tribbles"
Original Airdate: 12/29/67
Written by David Gerrold
Directed by Joseph Pevney
Guest Starring: William Schallert (Nilz Barris), William Campbell (Koloth), Stanley Adams (Cyrano Jones), Whit Bissell (Lurry), Michael Pataki (Korax), Charlie Brill (Arne Darvin), Ed Reiners (Fitzpatrick), Guy Raymond (Trader), Paul Bradley (Freeman), David Ross (Guard)

An emergency distress signal brings the Enterprise to space station K-7. There, the Undersecretary of Agricultural Affairs, Nilz Barris, is panicking because the Klingons are in the quadrant and he wants the grain (quadrotriticale) in the station's storage compartments protected, due to the fact that it is the only grain that will take root on Sherman's Planet.

Kirk is *not* amused, believing that Barris misused the emergency signal and he can barely be bothered to post two guards near the storage compartments. Things get out of hand, however, when Uhura is given a furry tribble by space trader Cyrano Jones, and the creature multiplies like crazy. In a short matter of time, they are all over the station and the Enterprise. Add into the mix a Klingon conspiracy and you've got a real roller coaster ride of an episode.

••••

"The Trouble With Tribbles" was significant in *Star Trek*'s history because it proved that the show could do comedy with the characters remaining true to themselves. This episode more than any other probably influenced the decision to go with the lighter tone of the feature film *Star Trek IV: The Voyage Home*; and it was the show that the writers and producers kept returning to in terms of best using the characters in a humorous situation.

And how does it feel for David Gerrold to have written one of *Star Trek*'s most popular episodes?

"I have to be real honest here," he says. "It feels great. I remember when I wrote 'The Trouble With Tribbles,' I looked at it as an honor and a responsibility, and I set out to write the very best *Star Trek* episode ever made."

"A delightful show from begin-

ning to end," enthuses Joseph Pevney. "I had a lot of fun with it, went out and shopped for the tribbles, and made some contributions to that show. It was the first effort of a writer named David Gerrold and I thought he made a hell of a contribution to the show. My biggest contribution was getting the show produced, because there was a feeling amongst the people involved that we shouldn't do it. It was a comedy and we had no business doing outright comedy. I certainly wanted to treat it as such, because that's the way it was intended. It was a lovely, warm show and I put Stanley Adams in it. 'Tribbles' was a highly successful episode in terms of audience appeal, and the network was happy with it. It turned out fine, with Bill doing bits he loved to do. The premise was humorous as hell."

Episode #44:
"The Gamesters of Triskelion"
Original Airdate: 1/5/68
Written by Margaret Armen
Directed by Gene Nelson
Guest Starring: John Ruskin (Galt), Angelique Pettyjohn (Shana), Steve Sandor (Lars), James Ross (Tamoon), Victoria George (Jana), Mickey Horton (Kloog)

Kirk, Chekov and Uhura are spacenapped by the beings of Triskelion, and forced to partake in gladiator games they have designed to amuse themselves. Kirk turns the tables by making a wager which will either provide many more participants in the "sport," or the aliens will have to free those already in slavery. One guess as to who wins the bet.

••••

"The idea for 'Gamesters' was a science fiction premise I'd had in mind for a long time, before there was ever a *Star Trek*," explains writer Margaret Armen. "I thought that one of these days I might do it as a science fiction short story or a story about a planet where people are used as gaming animals. So when *Star Trek* came on the air, I thought, 'Oh, wouldn't I love to do this story as a television show.' It was there, jotted down among a couple of other ideas I had to present to Gene if and when I got in to see him. *Star Trek* seemed the perfect vehicle for the nucleus of this story, and when I went in to Gene with it, it was

very roughly developed since I had never written for the show before. But Gene immediately saw the potential in it, and talked it through with me until it had been tailored to the *Star Trek* format.

"I was happy with the results," she continues. "I wasn't completely happy with some of the fight action toward the end, but it was very effective. I don't know if the fight action that I had suggested would have been more effective or not. I felt it would have been more unique, but you never know because the writer is never on the set or anything. There may have been some reason why they had to use the old net that was used during Roman games."

Episode #45:
"A Piece of the Action"
Original Airdate: 1/12/68
Written by David P. Harmon
Directed by James Komack
Guest Starring: Anthony Caruso (Oxmyx), Vic Tayback (Krako), Lee Delano (Kalo), John Harmon (Tepo), Steve Arnold (Zabo), Sheldon Collins (Boy), Dyanne Thorne, Sharyn Hillyer (Girls)

A century after the crew of the USS Horizon visited Iotia, the Enterprise arrives to examine the level of "contamination." What they find is a society based entirely on a book detailing the mob wars of Chicago in the 1920s. After initially approaching the inhabitants—mob bosses and all—on an intellectual level, Kirk realizes that he's got to do as the Romans do and it's only a short matter of time before he and Spock come on like mobsters, slang and all.

••••

"A Piece of the Action" was obviously influenced by "The Trouble With Tribbles," and while the results are quite humorous, this episode is a little more uneven.

Writer David P. Harmon believes that the very best episodes of *Star Trek*, and indeed all drama, featured what he calls "an inch of truth."

"As long as you had that, you could easily put it into a science-fiction setting," he explains. "Gene Roddenberry and Gene Coon didn't want a '20s or '30s type pulp. They wanted an inch of truth and from there you could expand.

••••

They knew exactly what they were looking for, and although it was hard work, you didn't mind rewriting until it was exactly right.

"I had read an article in *The New Yorker*," Harmon says of the episode's origins, "not about *Star Trek*, but about an idea. I pitched it as a possible show. Again, the story had what they were looking for, which was that honesty. I felt that our western civilization is based on a Judeo-Christian ethic, so what I did in 'A Piece of the Action' was say that suppose a ship crashed, and the people on the planet salvaged a book called *The Life of Al Capone*, which they treated as their version of *The Bible*, and from which they built their own society."

Although uncredited, Gene Coon had done a rewrite on this particular teleplay. Points out Dorothy Fontana, "I think one of the main things Gene added was Kirk and Spock really getting into the gangster stuff, and the whole business with Kirk trying to drive the car. That was certainly Gene Coon, which added so much to their characters. Again, you get another look at the relationship between these two men, and also the fact that they had a sense of humor."

James Komack, a journeyman director in television whose credits include episodes of *77 Sunset Strip, Dr. Kildare, Hennesey, My Favorite Martian* and *The Dick Van Dyke Show*, was approached to helm an episode of *Star Trek* by Gene Roddenberry, because the show's creator wanted to take on a humorous episode.

"I was a natural contender," says Komack, "because I had done long forms and was a comedy director. He called me in, I loved the show, read the script, made some adjustments and said, 'I would love to do this,' and I found myself on the starship Enterprise.

"Usually when you're a director working on episodic television, the actors mostly know their part, who they are and what they do and all you're doing is trying to find new ways for them to move around. The acting was already locked in because they'd done it. This was fun because it was [one of the first times] they did a comedy and Bill Shatner loves to do comedy. Leonard Nimoy I knew

from *Combat,* and I populated it with funny comedy gangsters and then set about doing it."

One interesting dramatic dilemma was sustaining the reality of the future while combining it with the past.

"Absolutely," Komack concurs. "That was tough, remembering that these guys were from another time and we're trying to make a picture about the '20s. You constantly have to say that it's got to be the '20s from everyone else's point of view, but it's got to be future-time for Leonard Nimoy and Bill Shatner, and that gets a little bizarre. The joke going on around them was that they had never seen a machine gun before, they never saw pool tables or cars. We'd have to work out the jokes right then and there. You'd say, 'Wait a minute, you've never seen that before. I've got to shoot something that shows you've never seen this before.' Spock and Kirk came down with this great intellect and great intelligence that they possess, and they were dealing with monkeys. These guys had an I.Q. of about room temperature, and it was funny to watch Kirk and Spock stare at them, because they were just ludicrous. They had a book, they were mobs, they were taking over cities. Their brains just weren't working that well. That was great fun."

But did he have to handle attitudes made up of, "Well, Kirk wouldn't do this and Spock wouldn't do that?"

"That's where they formulate their own characters," he replies. "When you come on a show they say, 'I've been doing this show for three years. I would never say that.' You can't argue with the guy. But in this episode I could say, 'Hold it. You're down in the 20th Century, pal. You're dealing with morons. You've never done this before, so therefore you could say this.' And they would buy it that way. But not in the spaceship. In the Enterprise they had it down."

Episode #46:
"The Immunity Syndrome"
Original Airdate: 1/19/68
Written by Robert Sabaroff
Directed by Joseph Pevney
Guest Starring: None

A giant, one-celled amoeba-like creature has destroyed the Gamma 7A

star system as well as the USS Intrepid, a starship with a full complement of Vulcans. The Enterprise computers determine that the cell is about to reproduce, and a plan is devised in which the starship itself will be used as an "anti-body" that will infect it before reproduction can take place.

••••

Interestingly, there is a moment in this episode that would be repeated almost verbatim in George Lucas' *Star Wars*. When the Intrepid is destroyed, Spock jerks his head up, feeling the pain of all those lost souls. In *Star Wars*, Obi Wan Kenobi has a similar reaction when a planet is destroyed by Darth Vader's Death Star.

Episode #47:
"A Private Little War"
Original Airdate: 2/2/68
Written by Gene Roddenberry
Story by Judd Crucis
Directed by Marc Daniels
Guest Starring: Nancy Kovack (Nona), Michael Witney (Tyree), Booker Marshak (Mbenga), Arthur Bernard (Apella), Joe Romeo (Krell)

Put simply, this analogy of the Vietnam War deals with a balance of power established on a frontier planet between the Klingons, first, and then the Federation. As the Klingons have interfered with the natural progression of the inhabitants, one part of the race is more advanced than the other. Kirk sees no choice but to bring the other part up to speed so that there will be a level of equality.

"A balance of power," Kirk says. "The oldest, dirtiest trick in the book but the only one that preserves both sides."

••••

"I like the science fiction aspects of *Star Trek*," said Marc Daniels, "but I also like the fact that in the first two seasons there was some genuine dramatic appeal and social feeling about them, and they weren't gimmicky in terms of just being space operas. 'A Private Little War' is an example. I remember that episode also provided a problem in terms of wardrobe. The people on this planet were supposed to be dressed in prehistoric clothing, and we

••••

discovered that costuming them would cost a fortune. Bill Theiss, who was always adept at handling such crises, bought a bunch of cheap sheepskin jackets, cut off the sleeves and turned them inside out. We were always trying to work around things like that because of budgetary limitations."

Writer Don Ingalls, who used the pen name Judd Crucis, wrote the first draft of the teleplay. As he explained to *Starlog*, "Mine was more of an adventure in a vacuum; Gene's [Roddenberry] was more a political statement. His story was more tilted to parallel Vietnam than I did."

Offers Walter Koenig, "That was the one episode that I thought digressed from a rather liberal, political posture. I had a very strong feeling about it. I thought that in maintaining this balance of power we were justifying the building of armaments. It was just like the Cold War to a point."

Episode #48:
"Return to Tomorrow"
Original 2/9/68
Written by John Kingsbridge
Directed by Ralph Senensky
Guest Starring: Diana Muldaur (Ann Mulhall)

Three aliens who have been without bodies for centuries—having lived in a purely mental state—ask Kirk, Spock and McCoy to "loan" them their bodies so that the trio can construct androids that will house their minds. After some reluctance they agree to do so, although the being that takes over Spock decides that he likes being flesh and blood, and he will stop at nothing to keep his host, even at the expense of his two companions or the crew of the Enterprise.

••••

Guest star Diana Muldaur, as most *Star Trek* fans know, would go on to portray Dr. Kate Pulaski in the second season of *Star Trek: The Next Generation*.

"It's funny, but when we get into 'Obsession,' 'Bread and Circuses' and 'Return to Tomorrow,'" says Ralph Senensky, "which were all shot on that crazy, fast schedule, it's like I shot them on fast forward and my primary memory of them is just trying to get them done; done by midnight on the sixth day. The

pressure was there to try and give the actor the chance to give a performance, which wasn't always easy."

Episode #49:
"Patterns of Force"
Original Airdate: 2/16/88
Written by John Meredyth Lucas
Directed by Vincent McEveety
Guest Starring: David Brian (John Gill), Skip Homier (Melakon), Richard Evans (Isak), Valora Norand (Daras), William Wintersole (Abrom), Patrick Horgan (Eneg), Bart LaRue (Newscaster), Ralph Mauer (SS Lieutenant)

Parallel Earth time again, as the Enterprise goes to Ekos, a planet controlled by a Nazi movement. The Nazis are led by Federation historian John Gill, who believed that the efficiency of Hitler's regime, if handled with a conscience, would theoretically work. Unfortunately, history merely repeats itself and it is into this nightmare that Kirk and Spock find themselves thrust.

••••

"The totalitarian, particularly the Nazi, society had always fascinated me," explains John Meredyth Lucas. "How could this come about? I know the history, but how in the minds of people could this come about? I started off with the premise that I would try to explain it. The explanation is that it was a system that worked because it was told to work. I have a story that I'm playing with; a story—a true story—that takes place in China and deals with the eradication of disease in an area, and American doctors visiting can't find any cases of disease. It's wonderful, but when you have the resources of a nation totally and completely behind you, and you're given to do such and such which you cannot do in a democratic society, you can accomplish an end like that. I was trying to explain in my head, which is not to say that I was looking for a true explanation, how this could happen, and the premise was that it was an efficient society for accomplishing specific ends. But I wanted to explore how it could have come about and how an entire country could get swept up in it. It's still difficult to comprehend. Thankfully there was very little problems in terms of covering such dramatic material. Gene tended to do no censorship on that basis. He would come in and, if

anything, would encourage wilder statements. He was a very adventurous guy, so there was no opposition in terms of 'My God, what are you writing about?'"

"That was the most forgettable one I've done," counters director Vincent McEveety. "It's so forgettable that I can't remember anything, except where I shot it. As you know, you get 'em in every series and you can't say, 'Look, I'm sorry, but I don't want to do this one.' They say, 'Tough, buddy. It's yours.' The story seemed awfully forced and hokey to me. I can't put it any other way."

Episode #50:
"By Any Other Name"
Original Airdate: 2/23/68
Written by D.C. Fontana and Jerome Bixby
Story by Jerome Bixby
Directed by Marc Daniels
Guest Starring: Warren Stevens (Rojan), Barbara Bouchet (Kelinda), Stewart Moss (Hanar), Robert Fortier (Tomar), Carol Byrd (Lt. Shea), Leslie Dalton (Drea), Julie Cobb (Thompson)

Members of the Kelvan race take human form and assume control of the Enterprise by turning the majority of the crew into tetrahedron blocks. The goal is to report to their people that Federation territory is ripe for colonization. Kirk, Spock, McCoy and Scotty come up with a plan to use the Kelvans' newly acquired human emotions against them.

••••

"I made the mistake of not paying attention to the format, the poop sheet saying 'this is what we want, this is what we don't want, avoid these, these are the staples,'" admits Jerome Bixby. "'New writers tend to be, particularly when writing stories about the cosmos at large, overwhelmed by the immensity of it all, and don't fall into this trap.' Well, I fell into it head over heels. I was doing a story about the Enterprise being hijacked to the Andromeda Nebula. At best—at hyper-c velocities—a 300 year voyage, so Kirk and the others are facing the end of their existence as they had known it. They are totally the prisoners of these great, powerful entities. Creatures from Andromeda want to take over our galaxy, because radiation levels there are making existence impossible for them. And I went off into a, I guess,

60 page essay on how lonely it is to be in that boat. I was told that it was very good, but it wouldn't make a *Star Trek*. And so I didn't know how far I was off the beam until I began to see revised pages. I didn't work with Dorothy; she rewrote my script. Primarily, she interjected the humor and the conflict into the episode."

Dorothy Fontana says, "I don't even recall what my contribution to it was, but it was enough to get me a split credit. I seem to recall that it was an effort to involve the characters—the *Star Trek* characters—more. The initial concept was good, but there wasn't enough involvement of our people. The one thing I definitely put in was Scotty's drinking contest. I love that. It's one of my favorite scenes that I've written."

Episode #51:
"The Omega Glory"
Original Airdate: 3/1/68
Written by Gene Roddenberry
Directed by Vincent McEveety
Guest Starring: Morgan Woodward (Captain Tracey), Roy Jensen (Cloud William), Irene Kelley (Sirah), David L. Ross (Galloway), Eddie Paskey (Leslie), Ed McReady (Carter), Lloyd Kino (Wu), Morgan Farley (Scholar)

Yet another renegade Federation captain, this time Ronald Tracey, interferes with a frontier society and alters its progression. When Enterprise arrives, Kirk, Spock and McCoy discover that Tracey has sided with the Kohms, utilizing advanced technology against the Yangs. Our heroes must set things right, with Kirk using a somewhat parallel version of the U.S. Constitution to convince both sides that they must be united as one.

••••

"I know it was a way out show," laughs Vincent McEveety, "but I thought Bill brought it off tremendously well. In lesser hands, and I'm talking about acting, it could have been terrible. He made it extremely powerful. I had empathy for the character and, as an audience, realized the importance of that particular document to me as an American citizen; seeing what they were faced with in a rather primitive state. I thought it was extremely powerful in making a statement."

William Marshall, Dr. Daystrom in "The Ultimate Computer," seen here as Blacula in the film of the same name.

Morgan Woodward (Captain Tracey) told *The Official Star Trek Fan Club Magazine*, "'Omega Glory' was simply a good man gone bad, perhaps because of some ego-induced insanity. Captain Tracey didn't become a starship captain by being a jerk or a bad guy. It was just a good man gone bad. That's the way I tried to play him."

Episode #52:
"The Ultimate Computer"
Original Airdate: 3/8/68
Written by D.C. Fontana
Story by Lawrence N. Wolfe
Directed by John Meredyth Lucas
Guest Starring: William Marshall (Daystrom), Barney Russo (Wesley), Sean Morgan (Harper)

Dr. Richard Daystrom is given permission by the Federation to hook his state-of-the-art computer, the M-5, to the Enterprise to prove that a starship can be run more efficiently by a machine than by humans.

For a time, things go perfectly and Kirk begins to feel useless, but eventually the M-5, whose memory patterns are based on Daystrom's, acts without logic, destroying another starship for no reason. Kirk, rising to the occasion, talks a machine to death.....again.

••••

Dorothy Fontana details, "The other writer involved was Lawrence Wolfe. Unfortunately this was a script that didn't want to work, or the writer didn't want to make the changes that we recommended and they were rather strong changes. As I recall, and I may not be right on this, it was because the *Star Trek* characters were not deeply involved in this story about the M-5 and Dr. Daystrom. *Star Trek* isn't about technology. *Star Trek* is about the characters. And how this machine acts on them, or how they act on it, is the story. The writer just did not want to make the changes. He kept bringing back the same script, until finally there was a rewrite that Gene assigned to me, and I did the best I could with it."

Episode #53:
"Bread and Circuses"
Original Airdate: 3/15/68
Written by Gene Roddenberry and Gene L. Coon
Story by John Kneubuhl
Directed by Ralph Senensky
Guest Starring: William Smithers (Merik), Logan Ramsey (Claudius Marcus), Ian Wolfe (Septimus), Rhodes Reason (Flavius Maximus), Lois Jewell (Drusilla), Bart LaRue (Announcer), Jack Perkins (Master of Game)

••••

On planet 892 IV, the Enterprise discovers a society that resembles Earth in the 20th Century, though there is an ancient Rome slant to it in that gladiator battles are televised as a sport for the public. Captain Merik, Kirk and his boys learn, had some time earlier gotten sucked into the politics surrounding "the game," eventually having his crew beamed down one by one so that they, too, could participate.

Mixed in with this is the struggle of what everyone assumes are "sun" worshippers, but who turn out to be servants of the "son" of God, Jesus Christ.

••••

"Certainly there was a nice philosophy going on there with the worshipping of the son," says Dorothy Fontana, "and then the indication that it was the son of God; that Jesus or the concept had appeared on other planets. I thought that was a nice touch. There have been other stories written with the same theme as the main point, but just adding it at the end really seems quite nice."

Director Ralph Senensky notes, "Gene Roddenberry is a very creative man. When we did 'Bread and Circuses,' I remember having a meeting with Gene about it and he was going to do some writing. I went there the next morning at 6:00 to get the new material, because there were things about that script which weren't working. Both Gene Roddenberry and Gene Coon were writing on that show as we were shooting. I don't remember what the problem was, except that we were doing the Roman arena in modern times with television. I do remember that my concern was that the whole thing about the 'sun,' which they talked about from early on, might not be a mystery when we got to the end. We didn't want to tip that we were doing a Christ story from the word go. That

took some doing because it wasn't really in the script, but they did it. They were sealing up the loose ends, because originally when they were talking about the sun you knew right away that they were talking about the son of God."

Episode #54:
"Assignment Earth"
Original Airdate: 3/29/68
Written by Art Wallace
Story by Gene Roddenberry and
Art Wallace
Directed by Marc Daniels
Guest Starring: Robert Lansing (Gary Seven), Terri Garr (Roberta Lincoln), Jim Keefer (Cromwell), Morgan Jones (Nesvig), Lincoln Demyan (Rawlings)

In this pilot for a separate series, the Enterprise is doing some Earth research in the 20th Century, when they encounter Gary Seven, a man who had been captured by alien beings and trained to save mankind from destroying itself.

Seven teams up with secretary Roberta Lincoln and tries to carry out his assignment. Kirk's dilemma is that he isn't sure of Seven's true intentions: will he help mankind or destroy it?

••••

"'Assignment Earth' is interesting in a sense," points out writer Art Wallace, "because I had gone to Paramount and pitched a series idea to them. They had said that Gene Roddenberry had come up with a very similar idea. So I saw Gene and we decided to pool the idea, which was about a man from tomorrow who takes care of the present on Earth. That was intended to be the pilot, although it was never made into a series. It was a very good pilot and it's a shame, because I think if they had done it as a series with just Gary Seven, it would have been a very successful show. I believe Gene and I split the credit on that one."

"Assignment Earth" was a pilot for a proposed series which would have starred Robert Lansing.

Guest star Robert Lansing told *Starlog* magazine, "What Gene had done was go to futurists and scientists and ask them what advanced societies out in space might do towards more primitive societies like ours. One of the futurists said that they would probably kidnap children from various planets, take them to their superior civilization, raise them, teach and enlighten them and then put them back as adults to lead their worlds in more peaceful ways. That was the idea behind Gary Seven."

"It was interesting trying to balance the episode between the regular crew and Robert Lansing," said Marc Daniels. "It was also difficult because we came back to the present and it's always a dangerous idea to take the *Star Trek* characters into the present. Suddenly you're in a very tangible situation. The show's reality becomes that much harder to sustain."

••••

••••
CHAPTER FIVE
Voyages Interruptus

"As you know, we had a good fight," Gene Roddenberry told a gathered Berkeley audience in 1968 regarding the letter writing campaign to save *Star Trek*. "NBC was certain I was behind every fan, paying them off. And there was a group from MIT picketing the building and a group in New York and...bless MIT, bless Cal Tech, bless them all. They [the network] had a coterie of junior executives down there buttonholing all of the people saying, 'Listen, did Gene Roddenberry send you?' And they finally call me up. They say, 'Listen, we know you're behind it.' And I said, 'That's very flattering, because if I could start demonstrations around the country from this desk, I'd get the hell out of science fiction and into politics.' From what I've seen of politics lately, they could use a few good science fiction fans.

"At any rate," he continued, "you all know we won the fight and at that time I told them that if they would put us on the air as they were promising—on a weeknight at a decent timeslot, 7:30 or 8:00, I would commit myself to produce *Star Trek* for the third year. Personally produce the show as I had done at the beginning. This was my effort to use what muscle I had. In fighting a network, you must use what muscle you have. They are monolithic, multibillion dollar corporations whose interests are not necessarily in the quality of the drama. Basically, the hard facts of life in television and the one you must understand is that a show is bought or sold on how much toothpaste or underarm deodorant will that show sell. Basically, that is why a show is bought and why and how it is kept on the air.

"But at any rate, about ten days to two weeks later I received a phone call at breakfast and the network executive said, 'Hello, Gene Baby...' Well, I knew I was in trouble right then. Said, 'We have had a group of statistical experts researching your audience, researching youth and youth-oriented people, and we don't want you on a weeknight at an early time. We have picked the *best* youth spot that there is. All of our research confirms this and it's great for the kids and that time is 10:00 on Friday nights.' I said, 'No doubt this is why you had the great kiddie show, *The Bell Telephone Hour* on there last year.'

"Well, I want you to understand some of the politicking, some of the pressures they dropped on me. The only gun I then had was to stand by my original commitment, that I would not personally produce the show unless they returned us to the weeknight time they promised. As a matter of fact, I threatened for a time to walk with the whole show because this was the only possible muscle to say—I don't own any General Motors or anything like that, so I had to threaten them with the one thing I do on the show, which is what I might be able to bring to the show on a line producership level. I wasn't particularly anxious to put in a third year of 14 hours a day, six days a week, but *Star Trek* was my baby and I was willing to risk it if I could have a reasonable shot at a reasonable time. And we talked it over and held fast. We almost swayed them and ultimately they said, 'No, we will not do it.' And then I had no option, I could not then say, 'Well, I'll produce it anyway,' because from then on with the network any threat or promise or anything I made, once you back down you become the coward and your muscle from then on in any subsequent projects will never mean anything.

"So I had no option but to then drop back and become executive producer of the show, and I did find a producer, Fred Freiberger, who has produced *Slattery's People* and *Ben Casey*, and has impeccable credits and an honest love of science fiction since boyhood. He is backed up, of course, by our regular staff of Bob Justman and the directors, the cameramen, Bill Theiss, costumer; Matt Jeffries, art; so backed up by the regular staff they are now producing *Star Trek* while my function in it is judiciary, is policy administration. I limit myself to reading the scripts, commenting on them and the runs. I forsee a good season if we have a lucky break on the weekend, the shows that come before us, and with your help we ought to be able to maintain our audience and go for a successful year and then to others.

"But I felt I owed it to the fans who did so much for the show to give them the inside story of what happened from the time we won the campaign till I received the 'Gene Baby' call."

Despite his attempts to provide a proper explanation for why he stepped away from the series, there is a widely-held feeling that his doing so was a veritable slap in the face to the people who labored to keep *Star Trek* on the air. In a sense, it was as though their efforts meant nothing.

Actor George Takei has noted, "Gene was aware that even if he had stayed with *Star Trek*, NBC intended to cancel the show after its third year. From another vantage point, maybe it should have been a matter of personal integrity on Roddenberry's part. *Star Trek* was Gene's creation and the third season would be identified with him whether he liked it or not. If the quality of the show was in some way to erode, it couldn't help but reflect on Roddenberry. Inevitably, it would be Gene's reputation that was at stake. Now, Gene Roddenberry's a human being, so I can certainly understand his position. At the same time, giving myself distance and perspective, I can't help but wish that Gene had looked at the entire picture and realized how *Star Trek*'s third season might finally affect his professionalism and artistic integrity."

Over the years, Roddenberry added to the comments he had made at Berkeley, stating, "I think there was a little rationalization in [my decision]. I think also what was affecting me at that time was enormous fatigue; I think maybe I was looking for an excuse to get out from under the fight that I had not just been having for two years, but really for four....I think the fatigue just caught up with me....I think I would come back and produce it the third year myself if I had it to do over. I'm not taking a back-handed slap at the people who did produce it the third year, line produced it. Obviously when you bring a producer in and you're going to let him produce it, you've got to let him do it his way. I think his way, or their way, was somewhat different than our way the first two, so it did look different....As long as the original creator stays with the show, it gives it a certain unity. When other minds become involved, it's not that they are lesser minds or not as clever writers, but you lose the unity of that one driving force."

There is a feeling amongst some people that *Star Trek* was on a downward cycle anyway due to the departure of Gene L. Coon.

"I'm going to tell you a blasphemy," says one writer, who doesn't wish to give his name. "The real brain behind *Star Trek* was not Gene Roddenberry. It was Gene Coon. Everybody who has ever worked on that show knows that. And let me give you a prime example. Gene Coon left during the second season, and everybody has always said that the reason the show went downhill in the middle of the second season is because they lowered the budget on them in order to keep it on the air. That *is* a factor. The main factor is that the guy with the writing talent was no longer there."

"I'll say it and I won't even threaten you if you attribute it to me," adds David Gerrold. "Gene L. Coon came in early in the first season and pulled it together, and he stayed there until more than halfway through the second season. If you look at the episodes in sequence, you can see that the best episodes are the ones where Gene Coon's hands were at the tiller. Gene Coon made the show work, very, very strongly. What I think you see happening is that in the first 13 with Roddenberry, there's a bumbling around trying to find out what the show is about, yet at the same time they did some great episodes.

"Where the show really lost its creativity was third season, in which it became Kirk, Spock and McCoy have an adventure and everything works alright in the end. The stories were bad science and bad fiction. It was pure television crap. It was the worst stuff of the '60s when we point to it and say, 'Television is not doing drama, it's just doing television.' It's automated daydreaming. There's nothing there for the mind to fasten on to."

There's no denying that *Star Trek* had its share of creative problems as the third season approached. John

Meredyth Lucas moved on to *The Fugitive* when word came down that *Trek* had been cancelled and before the letter writing campaign proved fruitful; director Joseph Pevney had departed the fold and Dorothy Fontana, who had been there before there actually was a *Star Trek*, was ready to move on.

"I felt that I was becoming perhaps too associated with *Star Trek*," she explains, "and wanted to prove that I was able to write other shows. In fact, when I left I did several westerns, dramatic contemporary shows and so on. I had to prove to other producers that *Star Trek* wasn't all I could do."

To make matters worse, the budget for the series was lowered yet again, as it had been at the outset of season two, while cast salaries increased.

"The third season we were reduced to what I call a radio show," reflects Robert Justman. "We couldn't go on location any longer because we couldn't afford it. We had to do shows that we could afford to do. It was quite difficult and that did affect what the concept was. Certain concepts just couldn't be handled. We didn't have the money. Forget about what the actual numbers are, but in those days, in the first season, each show cost $193,500. That was good money for those days. The second season was $187,500. The third season was $178,500. So that was an enormous drop. The studio had deficit financing situations and every time you shot a show you lost more money. In those days, they didn't think they had a chance of syndication, especially since everybody knew that third season was it. They just cut it down to the bone to cut their losses.

"It was very simple," he continues. "When you get moved in a timeslot to a night when your audience isn't home, you know that the handwriting is on the wall. Remember, they tried to cancel us at the end of the second season. By the time the third season rolled along, it was no longer Thursdays at 8:00. It wasn't Fridays at 8:00. It was Friday at 10:00. If your audience is high school kids and college-age people and young married people, they're not home Friday nights. They're out, and the old folks weren't watching. So our audience was gone."

This was the less than auspicious conditions that greeted Fred Freiberger as he assumed the reigns of *Star Trek*'s producer.

Freiberger Steps In

Fred Freiberger's long list of credits include co-writing *The Beast From 20,000 Fathoms* and *The Beginning of the End*, as well as producing stints on *The Wild Wild West*, *Ben Casey*, *Space: 1999*, *Superboy* and, of course, *Star Trek*.

"I was familiar with *Star Trek* only in that I had seen the first pilot they had done," says Freiberger. "I had seen Gene Roddenberry at the beginning to talk to him about producing the show at the start, but I was going to Europe on a vacation that I had planned. I mentioned to Gene—not that it was offered to me, but I was up there as one of the candidates—that the pilot was terrific, and if the job was still available when I got back, I was interested. I thought the pilot was pure science fiction and very intriguing. By the time I came back, he had gotten Gene Coon and I was off doing other shows. Then, when third season came along, my agent brought me into Gene's office and he said he would like me to produce the show. Gene Coon had done the first season, John Meredyth Lucas did the second and I assumed he wanted to change producers every year."

Obviously *Star Trek* had changed quite a bit between "The Cage" and the third season, and one must question whether a new producer coming in felt the series to be a daunting challenge.

"It wasn't a question of daunting," replies Freiberger, "it was a question of going in on a show that was being successfully produced with a lot of people involved who were very loyal to the show. You can walk into *Family Affair* and it can be daunting for you. You get into a situation where everybody knows each other and they've been together for some time. I was more concerned with improving the ratings, because the show had about a 20 or 24 share. Today that would be a hit. In those days, even if you had a 30 share, you were very iffy. It was the loyalty of the fans that kept it on when NBC threatened to cancel it. They did keep it on, and it was impressive that

NBC succumbed to the campaign. But in all three years, the ratings remained the same no matter what went on. It kept the same fans. Our hope was to improve the ratings, and we tried different kinds of stories. But the ratings always stayed the same....always.

"The cutting of the budget hurt us badly," he adds. "Then the salaries of the actors were raised and we were hit with a lot of restrictions. We had to do at least four of the shows completely on the Enterprise. There were a lot of restrictions, but that's no excuse if the stories aren't very good or aren't executed properly. It's a question of judgement and you have to go with what you think. That's the way television works. I think, on balance, we did some pretty nice stories and some that didn't come out so good. Some shows you're happy with, some you're disappointed with and others you're ashamed of. That's the way it goes, but if you're a pro, you accept those things, you understand them and all you can do is make sure that everybody does their best."

Unfortunately, a great many of the creative people involved with the third season were disappointed with the direction the show took. Marc Daniels—who had played so integral a role in the course of the series—directed "Spock's Brain," and decided that one episode under the new regime was enough.

"Fred Freiberger and I didn't agree on what the director's role was," Daniels said. "There are many writer/producers who don't consider the director a partner. They consider him, shall we say, an employee. This is particularly true in episodic TV. They just want you to do the work, get the shots and forget the rest of it. I didn't particularly care for that kind of thinking."

Margaret Armen, who had written for both Gene Roddenberry and Fred Freiberger, explains, "I suppose they were looking for two different types of stories. Fred was looking for all action pieces. That's why he wasn't crazy about 'The Paradise Syndrome.' He didn't think that there was enough violent and terrifying action in it. He didn't realize that the suspense would come from the characters, their relationships and so forth. There was some action in it, but there was no monsters and that sort of thing.

So Fred was looking primarily for action pieces, whereas Gene was looking for that subtlety that is *Star Trek*. Action, but with people carrying the story."

Writer David Gerrold, who has had "sparring" matches with Freiberger in the press before, admits, "I understand Freddy Freiberger's problems a lot better today than I did 24 years ago. Oddly enough, I have a respect for the man that I don't think he realizes. He's able to do something that not a lot of people can do: he can bring in a show on time, under budget. He can do the job. There are people who crumble under that kind of pressure....As a producer, I'm sure his opinions are correct for what he's doing. As a writer, I think his biggest weakness is that he doesn't have a sense of humor. He doesn't allow the show he's working on to have fun."

A major blow was the departure—about two thirds through the season—of Robert Justman, who had been involved with *Star Trek* since production of "The Cage."

"I felt I was in prison and I had to get out," he exclaims. "I just didn't want to take it anymore, because I was so unhappy with what was happening with the show. We couldn't make the kind of shows that we wanted to make because we couldn't afford them, and I felt that the content of the shows was going downhill. I finally asked for my release and left. I left a lot of bruised feelings behind at Paramount. They pleaded with me not to go, and I said, 'Fine, I won't go. Just take me off the show and I won't take any other jobs and I'll come back to you on anything else you want me to do in the spring.' They didn't want that and I said, 'I'm leaving. I just don't want to stay anymore.' I went to work at MGM.

"It was my feeling that the show wasn't what it ought to be. There was also the feeling of disappointment over the fact that I was made co-producer instead of producer. I know that doesn't mean anything to people not in the industry, but in effect I had been line producing the show since the beginning, even though my title was associate producer. When the third season came around, instead of producing the show, Freddy was brought in with the title of producer and I was made co-pro-

ducer to him. The studio felt, as all studios do and I can't blame them, that they wanted a writer to be there to do the work of story and script. On the other hand, I felt that I could produce the show with someone there to do the writing.

"Of course there's a lot of ego in that. I was much, much younger and ambitious. I can't blame the studio, but in the meantime I was unhappy about that and I didn't like the way the scripts were turning out. There was no excitement, or there wasn't enough excitement. And when they had good concepts, they kind of got whittled down and weren't as magical as they ought to be."

Strangely enough, he found that the atmosphere behind the scenes remained fairly positive.

"As far as I could see, the atmosphere was still much the same," Justman reflects. "I got on fine with everyone, as always. I got on fine with Freddy Freiberger, as always. He was a nice man. I think he did what he did as best he could do it. I never had any harsh words. I don't think I ever had an argument the whole three seasons with anyone. I would disagree with Gene Roddenberry at times and fight him on certain things that I thought we ought to do or should not be doing, but in the end if Gene said it was yes, it was yes. If he said no, it was no. Whether I felt he was right or wrong, if that's what he wanted to do, that's what I would do. After all, it was his show. I had wonderful feelings working with those people. It just wasn't the same without Gene in a hands-on position that third season."

Freiberger believes that the morale on *Star Trek* was fine until the last few shows when the end was approaching. "When they cut the budget down, you know that's not a good sign. The last couple of shows the morale went down a little, but prior to that I hadn't noticed. Despite that, if you're a pro, you do the best that you can right up until the last minute. Listen, three years for a show—any show—isn't bad, especially when the ratings are so low.

"Our problem was to broaden the viewer base. To do a science fiction show but get enough additional viewers to keep the series on the air. I decided to do what I would hope was a broad canvas of shows, but I tried to make them more dramatic and to do stories that had a more conventional storyline within the science fiction frame."

While it's true that that the third season lagged seriously behind the first two in terms of production and script value, it nonetheless produced a number of effective episodes. "Spectre of the Gun" was a surrealistic western written by Gene Coon; "The Tholian Web" dealt with the disappearance of Captain Kirk and provided some wonderful moments of characterization between Bones and Spock; "The Day of the Dove" pit Enterprise crewmen and Klingons against each other in armed combat; "Plato's Stepchildren" featured the first interracial kiss on television and examined the abuse of power; "Let That Be Your Last Battlefield," while heavy-handed, demonstrated the idiocy behind prejudice; and "All Our Yesterdays" was a time-travel adventure that further developed the McCoy-Spock relationship, while allowing Spock to do things no one had ever seen him do before.

While Freiberger currently lives in semi-retirement, it would seem that the accomplishment he will always be remembered for is producing *Star Trek*. Sometimes, though, that particular credit isn't always what it's cracked up to be.

"I've been the target of vicious and unfair attacks even to this day," Freiberger points out. "The fact that at the end of the second season *Star Trek*'s ratings had slipped, it was losing adult fans and was in disarray, carries no weight with the attackers. The dumping was all done on me and the third season. It seemed it was now *Star Trek* law to lay everything on Freiberger. Every disgruntled actor, writer and director also found an easy dumping ground on which to blame their own shortcomings. Whenever one of my episodes was men-

tioned favorably, Gene Roddenberry's name was attached to it. When one of my episodes was attacked, Roddenberry's name mysteriously disappeared, and only then did the name Freiberger surface. As an example, I read an article in the *L.A. Times*, praising 'Plato's Stepchildren' as the first television show to allow an interracial kiss. A breakthrough. Roddenberry was lauded for this, when in fact Roddenberry wasn't within a hundred miles of that episode.

"I have no quarrel to make with the right of critics, self-styled or otherwise," he adds, "to dislike my episodes and to state that dislike. What angers me is when they choose to attack my character, sometimes labeling me as indifferent or uncaring. None of that could be further from the truth, and I'm thankful that on occasion people like Bob Justman have gone out of their way to publicly and vociferously stand up for me.

"I have read that the fans didn't like any of my episodes. If true that hurts me, but there is another truth. In my travels throughout the United States, Canada and Europe, I have run into many *Star Trek* fans, and not one of them has ever treated me with anything less than courtesy and respect. For that, I thank them."

Interestingly, speaking of his tenure on *Star Trek* reminds Freiberger of his World War II experiences.

"I thought the worst experience of my life when I was shot down over Nazi Germany," he reflects. "A Jewish boy from the Bronx parachuted in to the middle of 80 million Nazis. Then I joined *Star Trek*. I was only in prison camp for two years, but my travail with *Star Trek* has lasted 25 years and still counting."

And thus, at the end of its third season, *Star Trek* was cancelled by NBC with no hope of a reprieve. Cliched as it may be, however, nearly twenty seven years later we realize that the end was merely the beginning.

••••

CHAPTER SIX
Season 3 Episode Guide

"Spock's Brain"

"The Enterprise Incident"

"The Paradise Syndrome"

"And the Children Shall Lead"

"Is There No Truth in Beauty"

"Spectre of the Gun"

"Day of the Dove"

"For the World is Hollow,
And I Have Touched the Sky"

"The Tholian Web"

"Plato's Stepchildren"

"Wink of an Eye"

"The Empath"

"Elaan of Troyius"

"Whom Gods Destroy"

"Let That Be Your Last Battlefield"

"The Mark of Gideon"

"That Which Survives"

"The Lights of Zetar"

"Requiem for Methuslah"

"The Way to Eden"

"The Cloud Minder"

"The Savage Curtain"

"All Our Yesterdays"

"Turnabout Intruder"

Episode #55
"Spock's Brain"
Original Airdate: 9/20/68
Written by Lee Cronin
Directed by Marc Daniels
Guest Starring: Marj Dusay (Kara),
Sheila Leighton (Luma),
James Daris (Primitive Man)

The Eymorgs steal Spock's brain to use as a power source on their planet, and the race is on for the Enterprise to retrieve it before his body dies. The less said about this one the better, though it's surprising that Gene Coon, under the name Lee Cronin, is credited with the teleplay.

• • • •

"In the original version of the script," recalled Marc Daniels, "Spock didn't go along, staying, instead, on the Enterprise. I thought that was dull, so I decided to bring him along. Then the concern was whether or not he would look like a zombie walking around. Thankfully Leonard was able to pull it off."

Producer Fred Freiberger says, "A hell of a concept, but how do you get drama into it? We had a lot of problems making that work."

"I suspect," muses David Gerrold, "that 'Spock's Brain' was Gene L. Coon's way of thumbing his nose at Roddenberry or something. If not Roddenberry, he was thumbing his nose at how seriously the show was taking itself. I suspect what had happened is that they were a little panic-stricken because there weren't a lot of scripts to shoot. The history of *Star Trek* is management by crisis. I think somebody called up Gene L. Con and said, 'We need a script in a hurry, can you do it?' And he did it under a pen name, and I don't think he deliberately set out to write that show seriously. I don't think there's any way you can take that episode seriously. You've got to take it as a joke. What's the stupidest science fiction idea to do? What if somebody stole Spock's brain? I think Gene L. Coon had that kind of sense of humor to do that kind of impish stuff. He had an irreverent sense of humor, and I think he wanted to poke *Star Trek* because someone was taking it too seriously. Maybe it was his way of not buying into it."

Episode #56
"The Enterprise Incident"
Original Airdate: 9/27/68
Written by D.C. Fontana
Directed by John Meredyth Lucas
Guest Starring: Joanne Linville (Commander), Jac Donner (Tal)

Star Trek meets *Mission: Impossible* as the Enterprise is sent on a secret mission to penetrate the Romulan Neutral Zone and steal a cloaking device from one of their vessels. Enroute, there is a romantic relationship between Spock and the Romulan commander and Kirk is given the opportunity to put on the pointed ears as he has himself surgically altered to resemble a Romulan.

• • • •

"There were errors in that episode that I protested against, and I believe David Gerrold's *The World of Star Trek* covers those in a memo I wrote in regards to my protests about it," details Dorothy Fontana. "Overall it was not a bad episode, but I did have a lot of complaints about it and things that weren't approached or handled right. It was really based on the Pueblo Incident, in the sense that here's this ship caught spying and they have to find a justification for their being there. Kirk's sanity is put on the line in terms of why they're there. Then, of course, they have to get out safely, preferably with the information they came for. Now that's not what happened with the Pueblo, but the Pueblo Incident kicked off this line of thinking in my mind.

"[But] let's face it, the romantic scene between the Romulan Commander and Spock was totally out of context. Any Romulan worth her salt would have instantly suspected Spock because they are related races. That was wrong. Kirk's attitudes were wrong. A simple thing— the cloaking device was supposed to be a very small thing, about the size of a watch, for instance, and it could be easily hidden. Here's Kirk running around with this thing that looks like a lamp. You know, highly visible. This is stupidity as well as illogical thinking. Visually it was stupid, conceptually it was very bad. There were a lot of things, little things, that were changed, but my biggest objection is the scene between Spock and the woman, because I really did not believe

it. And I did not believe that the Romulan did not suspect Spock of something underhanded. She does know enough about Vulcan and Vulcans to know that something's afoot."

Episode #57
"The Paradise Syndrome"
Original Airdate: 10/4/68
Written by Margaret Armen
Directed by Jud Taylor
Guest Starring: Sabrina Scharf (Miramanee), Rudy Lolari (Salish), Richard Hale (Goro)

When a planet is threatened by an asteroid, a landing party beams down to try and evacuate the population. An accident gives Kirk amnesia and he is eventually found by a tribe of Indians, who look upon him as a god. Referring to himself as Kirok, he takes a bride in Miramanee and is ultimately the victim of the changing mood of the crowd, who realize that he is actually human and not someone to be revered. This episode is marked by a particularly tragic ending in which Miramanee is killed, along with her and Kirk's unborn child.

• • • •

"My thinking," says writer Margaret Armen, "is that these people on a space ship for years and years have to get awfully sour, and have a special longing for their home planet and the simplicity of an Earth-type nature. So I wondered what would happen if they were just hungry for R&R on an Earth-like planet, and they suddenly and unexpectedly came upon a planet which has a primitive Earth sort of idyllic civilization. Kind of like the Garden of Eden, with primitive and friendly natives and so on. From there I worked out the story as it was shown on the screen. It's supposed to be an uninhabited planet, but when they beam down it turns out to be a primitive Indian civilization, and Kirk, who is extremely strung out and tired at the time....we had to cut some of the build-up to that because of time....was really taken by this idyllic situation.

"There just wasn't enough time to show it," Armen elaborates. "One of the reasons he is at the obelisk alone is that he wandered away from the group, enjoying the flora and the fauna. I liked 'The Paradise Syndrome,' but I thought it

• • • •

was too bad that we couldn't get a little bit of Kirk's longing for, well, the paradise syndrome, before he beamed down. But Freddy wanted more action and less *approach* to action. There again, some of the action which he wanted....I would have preferred action which I had suggested, and I wouldn't have made such a big thing of it. I think action is inherent in it, as well as danger and suspense. I had a little bit more character building in the situation."

"Quite frankly, I wasn't happy with that show," concurs Fred Freiberger. "It didn't come out as well as I had expected. To me, it lacked a certain element. That was one of the shows I was disappointed with. The good thing was that we shot it on location, which was very rare indeed in the third season. That's probably one of the reasons I wanted to do it; I wanted to get away from a bare planet set."

Episode #58
"And the Children Shall Lead"
Original Airdate: 10/11/68
Written by Edward J. Lasko
Directed by Marvin Chomsky
Guest Starring: Melvin Belli (Gorgon), James Wellman (Professor Starnes), Craig Hundley (Tommy), Pamela Ferdin (Mary), Mark Robert Brown (Don), Brian Tochi (Ray), Caesar Belli (Steve)
The Enterprise retrieves a group of orphaned children on Triacus. A short matter of time later, it becomes obvious that they are being manipulated by "Gorgon, the Friendly Angel," who turns out to be something far more sinister. Kirk and company must make the children see him for what he truly is.

●●●●

"To boost the ratings," explains Fred Freiberger, "we tried to get something unusual in there and in this case unusual in terms of casting. So we brought in attorney Melvin Belli. It could have been a better show. I thought the idea was good, but it just wasn't as strong as it could have been. Besides, I don't think it boosted the ratings."

Melvin Belli told *Starlog*'s Eric Niderost, "I enjoyed myelf *immensely*, and I was struck by the professionalism of William Shatner and Leonard Nimoy and all the rest. They were very profes-

sional—yet imbued with a great sense of fun. The most fun for me personally was my 'melting' death scene. Even though they had taken casts of my face much earlier, the makeup required for the scene still took the better part of the morning. They would shoot for a time, pause, then take me back to makeup to make me look more hideous. I remember they built up my nose with putty and made my jowls sag with each successive stage. Then it was back to the soundstage to shoot some more."

Walter Koenig admits that he was not comfortable with the casting of Belli. "Freiberger had a reputation as someone who comes in and takes an ailing show and forces it into the ground. I don't know if that's true or not, but that's the reputation that he had. I think it [*Star Trek*] really requires someone with a knowledge or background in science-fiction, in the genre itself because the stories start to be extrapolations, a more prosaic kind of storytelling. To me, the most heinous violation he [Freiberger] perpetrated was casting Melvin Belli in 'And the Children Shall Lead.' That infuriated me because Marvin was a friend of his, evidently, and it's one thing to cast friends who are actors, and another to cast friends who are not actors. Not only did it dilute the impact, whatever there was to begin with, but it took an acting job away from an actor. I was really upset about that. It was very unfair."

Episode #59
"Is There in Truth No Beauty?"
Original Airdate: 10/18/68
Written by Jean Lisette Aroeste
Directed by Ralph Senensky
Guest Starring: Diana Muldaur (Miranda), David Frankham (Marvick)
The Medusans are a race of energy patterns deemed so horrifying to look at that they have a tendency to drive humans insane. One of their kind is taken aboard the Enterprise by Dr. Miranda Jones for transport, and amidst insanity and attempted murders, we learn that all things are not as they are initially perceived.

●●●●

"We did a lot of morality shows, and I thought this was a hell of an example of one," enthuses Fred

Diana Muldaur, later to portray Dr. Pulaski on Star Trek: The Next Generation, *appeared in two classic* Star Trek *adventures.*

Freiberger. "The basic concept is that on the outside what is reputed to be ugly and horrible, is really something lovely and beautiful. Hopefully it will teach the viewer to be more tolerant."

Director Ralph Sensensky states, "My problem with the episode is that it felt like they were trying to turn it into a monster movie. All of those shots which kept cutting back to the box and those light effects.....they kept trying to build menace in an artificial manner. To me those kinds of cuts were insulting to an audience, like it was telling them that it was time to be nervous. It just curtailed the imagination. An audience is smarter than that. It was just a different mentality, treating it as a monster show rather than a subtle picture."

Episode #60
"Spectre of the Gun"
Original Airdate: 10/25/68
Written by Lee Cronin
Directed by Vincent McEveety
Guest Starring: Ron Soble (Wyatt Earp), Rex Holman (Morgan Earp), Bonnie Beecher (Sylvia), Charles Maxwell (Virgil Earp), Sam Gilman (Doc Holiday), Bill Zuckert (Sheriff Behan), Ed McReady (Barber), Abraham Sofaer (Melkotian Voice), James Doohan (Voice of Melkotian buoy)
Upon ignoring warnings not to proceed into Melkotian space, Kirk, Spock, McCoy and Chekov find them-

●●●●

selves on a world surrealistically mirroring the old west, where they are to take part in the famous gunfight at O.K. Corral. They are the Clantons, and if history proceeds the way it's supposed to, they will be killed by the Earps.

••••

"When Gene Coon wrote the original script, it was set in an actual western town," states Fred Freiberger. "Bobby Justman and I thought about how we could help it some and therefore we did this surrealistic kind of town to try and give it an other-worldly approach. Vincent McEveety was a hell of a creative director. I thought he did some wonderful things with it. I thought the show came out well, and that was satisfying considering that was my first episode on *Star Trek*, though it aired later in the season. "

Recalls Walter Koenig, "One day during the second season I asked Gene Roddenberry to have a meeting between seasons when it looked like we were going to be on 8:00 Mondays. I asked him about how my character would evolve based on its popularity. I went to his house and he proceeded to show me some memos he had written, and memos from Schlosser and Werner, the guys at NBC, through Paramount. All the memos were very positive, saying let's involve Chekov more, he has appeal. Let's bring him down to the planets more, involve him with members of the opposite sex. And it looked enormously promising. 'Spectre of the Gun' was the first episode written with that in mind for third season, and it reflected what my participation was going to be. Immediately thereafter we were switched and everybody sort of threw up their hands and gave up on the show. They brought in Freiberger who had no particular style as far as I could tell, or empathy for the character. I don't think he had any antipathy either. I just don't think he saw it as being important."

"That was an episode which was fun, a comic strip and certainly not significant," Vincent McEveety muses. "I thought it was reaching a bit, and not one of my favorites. Even though it was hokey, it was more enjoyable to me than 'Patterns of Force,' because I thought it was far more stylized. It was saying,

'Okay, we're going to do a fantasy, and here we are.' There was too much realism in the Nazi story. I didn't like the treatment of it or anything about it. I don't know if they were running out of material or if they thought it would be wonderful to put these guys in a Nazi occupied city, or put them back in the West or Old Rome. Some of it worked, some of it didn't.

"Even though 'Spectre of the Gun' is not one of my favorites by a long shot, the effects, the wind, the stylized sets—the fragmented sets—all make it feel like a stage play. It was the kind of thing that takes a lot of imagination to relate to. You may have ended up empty from it all, but it was certainly an arresting story. Whereas at the end you're not saying, 'What a brilliant piece of work; a great show,' you might say, 'Hey, that was interesting.' If even that. However, it's interesting that what little fanmail I get in my life usually pertains to that show. People love it, which I can't believe, because I don't."

Episode #61
"Day of the Dove"
Original Airdate: 11/1/68
Written by Jerome Bixby
Directed by Marvin Chomsky
Guest Starring: Michael Ansara (Kang), Susan Howard (Mara)

An energy force that feeds on anger, hatred and hostility arms both the Klingons and Kirk's people with swords and sets them at each other's throats on board the Enterprise. Kirk and his opponent, Kang, must come to grips with what exactly is putting them through this, and combat it before both sides are slaughtered.

••••

"'Day of the Dove' was kind of my response to the Vietnam thing at that time," says Jerome Bixby. "Throw down the swords. I wanted to write a peace story. My original story was very late sixties, and I ended it with a peace march which, thank God, also came out."

In the pages of *The Star Trek Interview Book* he added, "I originally wrote 'Day of the Dove' for Kor, the Klingon from 'Errand of Mercy,' but John Colicos was unavailable. He was abroad doing a film, and he said that when he first read the script he wept and threw

"Day of the Dove" featured actor Michael Ansara in the role of the Klingon named Kang.

himself at walls and nearly jumped off a balcony because he wanted to play the part so bad, but he was committed to that other production and he couldn't play Kor. So they changed it to Kang. They were looking around for a Klingon and they almost hit on Joe Campanella, but they didn't think he could draw quite enough fire. So they hit on Michael Ansara, who just ate up the part."

"A shipboard show," Fred Freiberger points out. "Considering our restrictions, I thought it came out well. It was more of a derring-do kind of show, and Michael Ansara was wonderful."

"What a *magnificent* character to play!" Michael Ansara enthused to journalist Mark Phillips. "Immediately, just from reading the script, I knew how special the role was and how rare it was to find a character like this in either television or film. Kang had nobility and that's a quality that I have always been fascinated by."

Episode #62
"For the World is Hollow, And I Have Touched the Sky
Original Airdate: 11/8/68
Written by Rik Vollaerts
Directed by Tony Leader
Guest Starring: Kate Woodville (Natira), Byron Morrow (Admiral Westervelt), John Lormer (Old Man)

What appears to be an asteroid is actually a cleverly disguised vessel that is on a direct course for a Federation planet. Kirk and Spock must unlock the secrets of the ship's computers to alter its course and save countless lives. In the meantime, McCoy discovers that he has an incurable disease and, as he falls in love with one of the ship's inhabitants (Yonada), he elects to stay with her until the end. Naturally, they find a cure.

••••

"That was a love affair for Doctor McCoy," reflects Fred Freiberger. "I was trying to spread the material to the other actors, and I wanted to give DeForest Kelley something because he was always just kind of hanging around without a lot to do. I wanted him to have something a little more solid, and I liked the idea of the planet being a spaceship in transit. I thought it was an okay show."

He does admit that it was somewhat difficult to service the entire cast.

"They wouldn't be actors if they didn't want more to do," laughs Freiberger. "You're doing an ensemble show and what's selling the show, hopefully, is the personality of the stars and the relationship between the three most prominent ones, Shatner, Nimoy and Kelley. You would try to give all the others something, but it's very difficult because you have so many format characters and you've only got about 50 minutes to tell your story. I certainly sympathize with any of them who wanted more to do. They would legitimately fight me, and I would do my best to do what I had to do to give them something more meaningful than, 'Ahead, warp three,' and the rest of the usual material."

Episode #63
"The Tholian Web"
Original Airdate: 11/15/68
Written by Judy Burns and Chet Richards
Directed by Ralph Senensky
Guest Starring: No one.

While exploring the remnants of the USS Defiant, Kirk is accidentally trapped in another dimension. Most of the crew believe him to be dead, though they continue to see his apparition. Meanwhile, Spock works on trying to retrieve him when the Defiant enters our dimension again for a brief period of time. Add the Tholians, who don't want the Enterprise in their territory, to the mix and you've got

some genuine suspense in terms of whether or not Spock will succeed.

••••

"I met a student who was a physicst and told him that I wanted to write a *Star Trek* script which would be a ghost story based on fact," says writer Judy Burns. "He said, 'Why don't you use the theory of infinite dimensions?' What came out was 'In Essence Nothing,' which became 'The Tholian Web.' At the time, if I remember correctly, the very first draft of the story had Spock as the one who disappeared.

"Eventually I received a classic memo from Bob Justman, who summed up by saying, 'I think we can use it, but it should be Kirk out there. He would be schmuckishly heroic to stay behind on this other ship.' Besides that, there was another episode called 'Spock's Brain' in which Spock was out of it for a period of time and they didn't want to have him incapacitated for two scripts. So, I got a phone call that said, 'We have some interest in the piece, could you come up and talk about it?' They provided a lot of commentary and suggestions and said, 'Go off and do this.' I think it turned out very nicely, and Fred and Bob had much to do with it. Many of the suggestions Bob made in his memo caused it to become what it became.

"Some of the things I was a little disappointed in were caused by technical problems. Originally there were no space suits when Kirk and the others beamed over to the other ship. There were force field belts which kept them encapsulated in a kind of mini-force field, which included an oxygen bank. It kept them secure as long as the batteries held, but if the batteries ran out—which was the greatest threat to Kirk—then they die. They didn't have an infinite amount of time within the force field. Therefore, Kirk would have wandered around the ship looking like he looks, except for a little force field belt. I think it would have made a better ghost story. He looks silly constantly appearing in that space suit. I really had a lot of qualms about that. Not from poor designing or anything, but from a story point-of-view, it would have been better. They felt strongly that if they started something like a force field belt, it might have ramifications down the line

on other stories. I was a novice in those days, but today I probably would have countered that it was a prototype model that had been given to us this one time. In 25 years, we would get it back again."

Episode #64
"Plato's Stepchildren"
Original Airdate: 11/22/68
Written by Meyer Dolinsky
Directed by David Alexander
Guest Starring: Michael Dunn (Alexander), Liam Sullivan (Parmen), Barbara Babcock (Philana), Ted Scott (Eraclitus), Derek Partridge (Donyd)

The Enterprise proceeds to Platonius in response to a distress signal, and what they find are a race of people who have based their society somewhat on ancient Rome. The difference is that they have developed extraordinary telekinetic abilities which they use to control their jester, a dwarf named Alexander.

What the Platonians eventually detail is that they want Dr. McCoy to remain behind to tend to them should they get ill. When Kirk refuses to allow this, these self-acclaimed gods start trying to control them, forcing Kirk, Spock, Uhura and Nurse Chapel into somewhat humiliating positions. Additionally, they were basically the catalyst behind television's first interracial kiss.

••••

"The big thing," says Fred

Michael Dunn, Alexander of "Plato's Stepchildren," is perhaps more recognized for his role as Dr. Lovelace in The Wild Wild West.

••••

Freiberger, "was who was going to kiss Uhura, a black girl. We had quite a few conversations on that one, because someone said, 'Let's have Spock do it,' and I said, 'No, if we have Spock do it, we're going to have all these people screaming that we didn't have the guts to have a white man kiss her. We went through a whole thing, but it all worked out and Shatner said to her, 'It's not that I don't want to, but I don't want to humiliate you.' That's a show I'm very proud of."

In his autobiography *Shatner: Where No Man*, the actor remarked, "I remember now that they had mentioned [that this was the first interracial kiss] earlier and said, 'Would you mind?' and I said, 'Mind? No, I don't mind.' And then they kind of backed off on it, in that I was being forced to do it. It wasn't Kirk actually kissing Uhura. It was Kirk being forced by some power beyond there—to kiss her. So the edge was taken off the first interracial kiss on television by the fact that this guy was going, '...uh, argh, not me—no—kiss.

"I'm well aware that there could have been different ways to write the scene or play it," Shatner continued. "We did try some variations. There could have been a whole different story, if anybody had wanted to emphasize an interracial love story. But in fact, that wouldn't have made the point as effectively. Kirk and Uhura wouldn't even think of a kiss or a love story as interracial. That would be the *last* thing they would think about. If we did any good with that kiss or anything we did on *Star Trek*, it was to push in the direction of not having to think about that."

Episode #65
"Wink of An Eye"
Original Airdate: 11/29/68
Written by Arthur Heinemann
Story by Lee Cronin
Directed by Jud Taylor
Guest Starring: Kathie Browne (Deela), Jason Evers (Rael), Eric Holland (Ekor), Geoffrey Binney (Compton)

After drinking Scalosian water, Kirk's metabolism accelerates to a different plane of existence on a par with the Scalosians themselves. Their race is nearly dead, and they want to use the crew of the Enterprise to repopulate their species.

While Kirk does what he can to foil these plans, Spock, on the slower level, works with McCoy on a cure for the effects of the water.

••••

"'Wink of an Eye' was my favorite of the three episodes I did," explained the late Arthur Heinemann a week before his death. "Director Jud Taylor asked a lot of questions about the people in the script. What they felt, what they thought, what they were like. He and I had a thorough discussion about the people and he got his actors to project exactly what I had in mind."

The story credited to Lee Cronin, actually Gene L. Coon, was perceived as being somewhat disappointing from the man who gave audiences "Devil in the Dark" and the Klingons. Dorothy Fontana believes that the seeming drop in writing quality was due to the fact that Coon was under enormous time pressure and forced to write scripts between his other assignments. "It wasn't like being on a series where you could devote all your time to that series," she suggests. "I think the writing suffers because of that."

"If you're not producing," Glen Larson says, "somebody else takes it and does the rewriting. Knowing his attention to detail and his work ethic, I would imagine that somebody rewrote him. It would be interesting to be able to see his first draft scripts."

Episode #66
"The Empath"
Original Airdate: 12/6/68
Written by Joyce Muskat
Directed by John Erman
Guest Starring: Kathryn Hays (Gem), Alan Berman (Lal), Willard Sage (Thann), Jason Wingreen (Dr. Linke), Davis Roberts (Dr. Ozaba)

A pair of aliens named Lal and Thann (who look like they're related to the Talosians of "The Cage") capture Kirk, Spock and McCoy, and involve them in a series of experiments that include a mute woman named Gem, who has empathic abilities which allow her to absorb the pain and suffering of others. The aliens are doing so in order to determine whether or not Gem's race is worthy of being saved from a forthcoming super nova, or if a neighboring planet is worthier to survive.

Episode #67
"Elaan of Troyius"
Original Airdate: 12/20/68
Written and Directed by John Meredyth Lucas
Guest Starring: France Nuyen (Elaan), Jay Robinson (Petri), Tony Young (Kryton), Lee Duncan (Evans), Victor Brandt (Watson), K.L. Smith (Klingon)

The Enterprise is told to transport Elaan of Elas to her marriage ceremony at the planet Troyius, which will result in an alliance between the two hostile worlds. It sounds like a simple enough assignment, until one takes into account the fact that the woman has no interest in the marriage, the Klingons want to see the alliance fall apart and are doing what they can to make this happen, the Troyius ambassador is murdered and Kirk falls madly in love with Elaan due to the chemical reaction of her tears on his skin.

••••

"That was an original premise of Gene Roddenberry's," says writer/director John Meredyth Lucas. "I enjoyed the love story aspect of the show and thought it was an interesting change of pace. You didn't get to do too many of those. Basically we were doing *Taming of the Shrew*."

Recalls Fred Freiberger, "Part of the reason we did that one was because the network had told us they had done a survey in which they discovered that women, generally, were terrified of space. They needed stability, they needed surroundings. They'd rather be in valleys than on top of mountains. So we tried to get the women, which is why we did a romantic story. We tried to reach a segment of the audience we couldn't otherwise reach, and didn't succeed."

Probably the most enduring aspect of this episode is Scotty's brief mention of the Elaan during his 24th century visit to *The Next Generation* in sixth season's "Relics."

Episode #68
"Whom Gods Destroy"
Original Airdate: 1/3/69
Written by Lee Erwin
Directed by Herb Wallerstein
Guest Starring: Yvonne Craig (Marta), Steve Ihnat (Garth), Key Luke (Cory)

The inmates have taken over the Elba II asylum, and it is in that situa-

••••

Yvonne Craig, Batgirl of the Batman *television series, was a resident of the Elba II asylum in "Whom Gods Destroy."*

tion which Kirk and Spock are captured by former Starfleet captain Garth, who has acquired the power to change his shape at will. Our heroes do what they must to turn the tables. Basically, that's it.

Episode #69
"Let That Be Your Last Battlefield"
Original Airdate: 1/10/69
Written by Oliver Crawford
Story by Lee Cronin
Directed by Jud Taylor
Guest Starring: Frank Gorshin (Bele), Lou Antonio (Lokai)

The Enterprise finds itself in the midst of a chase between an alien law enforcement officer named Bele and his prey, Lokai. Half the face of each man is white while the other half is black. The only difference is the side on which the particular color is. Bele reveals that, on their world, Lokai is a criminal and lower life form because his colors are on the wrong side. Ultimately Kirk makes the discovery that the aliens are sole survivors of their homeworld, the population having killed itself.

••••

"That was originally a Gene Coon story that was brought to me," relates writer Oliver Crawford. "It dealt with racial intolerance, and I thought it was a marvelous visual and cinematic effect. The whole point of the story was that color is only skin deep. How could

any writer not respond to that? That fit right into today's scene, and I was very pleased with the episode."

Recalls Fred Freiberger, "Gene originally had a devil with a tail chasing an angel. We used actor Frank Gorshin and thought, 'What an idea it would be to do black on one side and white on the other, and the other guy has it the opposite way.' *That's* the stupidity of prejudice. There's a wonderful moment when Kirk says, 'What's different about him?' And he says, 'He's white on the other side.' That was a big morality show and I liked the idea of it. As a side note, we ran a little short on that show which is why it ended with a chase that went on forever. I thought it was a hell of a creative situation."

It also marked Gene Coon's final effort for *Star Trek*, though Freiberger was grateful for the contributions made to the series.

"Gene Coon was a lovely, talented guy," says Freiberger, "who came up with certain stories and said do what you want with them. He worked as much as he could with us and he was a complete gentleman and completely professional about the whole thing."

Episode #70
"The Mark of Gideon"
Original Airdate: 1/17/69
Written by George F. Slavin and Stanley Adams
Directed by Jud Taylor
Guest Starring: Sharon Acker (Odona), David Hurst (Hodin), Gene Kynarski (Krodack), Richard Derr (Admiral Fitzgerald)

Kirk attempts to beam himself down to the planet Gideon, but is shocked to find himself back on the Enterprise, with the difference being that he is the only person on board. This turns out to be the work of the inhabitants, who have created an exact duplicate of the starship (how they pulled this off is anyone's guess) to trick Kirk. It seems that the planet is suffering from overpopulation because the citizens are disease-free. Kirk, though, carries the remnants of a disease that nearly killed him. They want the captain to infect one of their people so that disease, and then death, will spread across the planet.

••••

The plot of this episode could very well have inspired the feature film *Zardoz*, whose story is quite similar.

"One of my pet themes is over population," relates Fred Freiberger, "and I thought this was a good idea. We were taking a shot at something fresh and gutsy, and it worked out pretty well. That one was also shot entirely on the Enterprise. I felt that if we had to do the show under those restrictions, we had to come up with good stories and that one worked."

Actress Sharon Acker, as related in the *Official Star Trek Fan Club Magazine*, enjoyed playing Princess Odona. "I thought she was fun," said Acker. "I was really looking forward to playing her. Odona was a little out of my field. I mean, I never thought of myself as a princess, I never thought of myself as particularly exotic, so to play the role of somebody who was both of those things and who also came from another planet was a real exciting challenge for me. But I didn't necessarily see her as different from me emotionally, except, I guess, from the point of view of her commitment to be willing to give her life for the people of her planet. She was willing to die to bring death and dignity back to the people of her planet. From that point of view I don't know if Sharon Acker could ever take such a step. So I think she was heroic and grand and very special and rather beautiful and quite a bit beyond the Sharon Acker that was playing the part."

Episode #71
"That Which Survives"
Original Airdate: 1/24/69
Written by John Meredyth Lucas
Story by D.C. Fontana
Directed by Herb Wallerstein
Guest Starring: Lee Meriwether (Losira), Arthur Batanides (D'Amato), Naomi Pollack (Lt. Rahada)

While exploring unique geological conditions on an unnamed planet, Kirk, Spock and McCoy confront the holographic image of a woman named Losira. She is actually a warning device left behind by an ancient civilization to repel their enemies, the Kalandans. Her "touch" is death, and it is up to the crew of the Enterprise to shut down the com-

Lee Meriwether, decked out here in Catwoman's traditional leather outfit, was the lethal Losira in "That Which Survives."

puters that continue to generate her lethal image.

Episode #72
"The Lights of Zetar"
Original Airdate: 1/31/69
Written by Jeremy Tarcher and
Shari Lewis
Directed by Herb Kenwith
Guest Starring: Jan Shutan (Lt. Mira Romaine), John Winston (Lt. Kyle),
Libby Erwin (Rindonian)

Lieutenant Mira Romaine, who Scotty has fallen in love with, is possessed by the lights of Zetar, a cloud-like being that is actually the collective existence of a now-dead race. Enjoying physical existence again, they decide to keep their human host at the expense of her own life.

• • • •

"I haven't seen [the episode] since the first time it aired," said director Herb Kenwith in *Starlog* #179. "I remember going to the first cut, and at the time, directors didn't have that much say about it, and I was disappointed. It wasn't telling the story the way I had hoped it would be told. You get 10 people in a room who read a script, and you get 10 versions. It's like *Hamlet*. There are so many ways to play it. Since *I* was directing it, I wanted *my* version told. I felt there was a lot of distortion to it upon seeing the first cut.....I was so dismayed and hurt by it. I

didn't have the kind of shell you need to observe your work when it's done for the efforts of someone else.

"I liked the script," Kenwith added. "I though it was interesting and so far removed from anything I had done, because I had done theater and plays. While doing *Star Trek* we all laughed at a lot of it. We throught, 'Oh, this is silly, but let's do it.' Of course, it turns out to be a classic. It wasn't so silly after all."

Episode #73
"Requiem for Methuslah"
Original Airdate: 2/14/69
Written by Jerome Bixby
Directed by Murray Golden
Guest Starring: James Daly (Flint),
Louise Sorel (Reena)

While searching for a cure to a rare disease, Kirk, Spock and McCoy beam down to the surface of Holberg 917-G. There they are surprised to find a man named Flint, who turns out to be an immortal. Kirk falls in love with Flint's daughter, Rayna, and is horrified to learn that she is actually an android, as are all the "people" living there.

• • • •

"I always wanted to do a story about a Neanderthal who found himself gifted with immortality," reflects Jerome Bixby, "who lived up to the present day. Learning, learning, learning throughout this enormous lifetime, mastering the arts

and sciences through philosophy. I wanted him to have been Beethoven, because Beethoven has kind of a Neanderthal cast to his face. And so I had that story kicking around that I had never done. Why not do a story about a virtually immortal man for *Star Trek*? So I came up with Mr. Flint, which by the way was the name of my Neanderthal. It pleased me very much when I wrote it, [and] there is a story behind that. I have a habit, and I can make this work very well in prose, and that is alliteration. I can make prose jump through hoops, and when you start uttering these things aloud, they often sound somewhat contrived and sometimes ludicrous unless you are deliberately writing poetry.

"Some of my dialogue near the end between Spock and McCoy where McCoy is really coming down on Spock and saying, 'You poor schmuck. You have no emotions. You can't live. You'll never know what love is like. That hope doesn't exist for you,' etc. I pulled out all the stops and wrote about 15 pages of dialogue that De Kelley absolutely refused to utter. He said, 'This sounds like poetry!' 'We are the hollow men, we are the stunted men,' like T.S. Eliot. So whoever was directing that—Murray Golden—wanted to do the tag. He wanted to do that ending. But he said, 'We can't do that without dialogue. It just won't play.' So I said, 'Give me three minutes,' and I went over and sat down in Captain Kirk's chair on the Enterprise set and rewrote the speech right there, because I didn't want to lose that ending either. Five minutes later they had a draft."

"Some good emotion there," says Fred Freiberger, "and the reveal of her being an android was well handled. I liked the idea of walking into a factory and seeing the woman you love being replicated."

Episode #74
"The Way to Eden"
Original Airdate: 2/21/69
Written by Arthur Heinemann
Story by Michael Richards and Arthur Heinemann
Directed by David Alexander
Guest Starring: Skip Homeier (Dr. Severin), Charles Napier (Adam), Mary Linda Rapelye (Irina, Victor Brandt (Tongo Rad), Deborah Downey and

• • • •

Phyllis Douglas (Hippies)

A group of space-hippies attempt to take over the Enterprise so that they can be transported to the mythical world of Eden, a realm supposedly of paradise. You haven't lived until you've seen Mr. Spock in a jam session.

••••

As originally conceived, "The Way to Eden" was entitled "Joanna" and dealt with Dr. McCoy's daughter, who was among the "space hippies."

"The producers didn't care for that idea," says Dorothy Fontana, who removed her name from the story, "so they made it Chekov's Russian girlfriend. And then they shifted the focus of the story. I've never seen the episode."

Fred Freiberger sheepishly admits, "I didn't like it at all and I don't blame Dorothy's original story. We probably did it all wrong. I'm unhappy to take the blame for that one, but there's no one else to blame."

Arthur Heinemann, who wrote the teleplay based on Fontana's story, added, "It was my idea to inject the element of deadliness in Eden. The original story did not have any deadly aspects. It just dealt with space-age hippies who wanted to find a romantic place to live. I wanted to make a comment that underneath all that beauty was a deadliness. I enjoyed that too, because I wrote some lyrics for some songs that the hippies sang. As a matter of fact, I get a royalty from EMI for it. About once a year a check comes for $3.47.

"I wasn't particularly pleased with the episode itself, though. It was directed in kind of a one, two, three manner. Over simplistic, if I remember."

Episode #75
"The Cloud Minders"
Original Airdate: 2/28/69
Written by Margaret Armen
Story by David Gerrold and
Oliver Crawford
Directed by Jud Taylor

The Enterprise arrives at Ardana to obtain zienite, cure for a plague on Merak II. What they find is a divided race, with the elite living in a city in the clouds while the "have-nots" mine the zienite mineral, and they seem quite insane. Kirk realizes that the gas of the mines is causing this madness and he sets about getting both sides to talk out their differences.

••••

Writer David Gerrold recalls,"I submit a story later on called 'Castles in the Sky,' and the point of the story is that there are people living in the sky cities and it's like Beverly Hills. Then there are people working in the cotton fields down below and it's Watts. They're working the mines for the dilithium crystals. The point of the story is that McCoy in the shuttlecraft crashes on the surface of the planet and he ends up helping the children of the people on the surface who are suffering from high pressure disease. When the rebels come to kill McCoy [because] they represent the sky people, the parents of the children stand in front of him, like the scene in *The Ugly American*. Meanwhile, in the sky city, there's Kirk and Spock, and the official representative arguing about the shape of the table, just like the Paris Peace Talks. Finally we run the action in the story appropriately, and it's a lot of moving around and finally a confrontation.

"It wasn't a bad story. It really was a story that addressed the issue of 'haves' and 'have nots.' The problem was that at the end we get into the starship and we head away. Kirk says, 'Well, another good job. We didn't solve the problem totally, but we got them talking to each other and that's a lasting solution, because they will solve their problems.' And McCoy says, 'Right. But how many children are going to die in the meantime?' And nobody has an answer. In other words, you're expecting a happy ending, and McCoy gives you a little nudge. I felt that *Trek* had established that it was capable of doing that kind of story.

"What happens is Freddy Freiberger saw this as a polemic, and it annoyed the hell out of him. He wanted to do a nice, safe story where everything was wrapped up in the end. I said, 'It doesn't quite work that way in real life. Let's do a story with a little grit to it,' and he said, 'Alright, you've had your one shot on the outline. I want you to take on a co-writer.' I talked to my agent and he said, 'Take the co-writer, otherwise he'll cut you off.' So suddenly I'm working with

Ollie Crawford on the next draft of the outline. He forced him on me. I thought that since Ollie was the story editor on the last show he produced, maybe he'll know what Freddy will buy. 'Ollie will keep me from making mistakes. I'll learn from him and we'll definitely go the distance on this one.' Ollie's a good guy."

Oliver Crawford adds, "I recall Freddy calling me up and saying, 'I want to put an old pro together with a young writer.' Writers are constantly wounded, but television is very much a collaborative medium. To get the happy circumstance where everything gels and everybody's talent enhances everybody else's is tough to achieve, but worth it when you do. When people go off on tangents, you find that you don't have much of anything. I know very few writers who are happy with all of their work as produced, unless they're in a position of power and not too many of us are. I thought 'The Cloud Minders' was right in line with the good work and thrust of the series. It was almost like a *Brave New World*. The key thing there was exploitation, and that's something we must deal with all the time."

Margaret Armen explains, "The reason that I ultimately did the teleplay is that Freddy Freiberger called me in and said that he had two writers, he didn't tell me who, that he had gotten this story from. He said, 'I don't want you to look at the teleplay, Margaret, because it doesn't work. It's all philosophizing and talk. We need something with action. It's a good basic theme and a good basic story, and we're going to tell you the basic story. From that we want you to start from scratch and do a scene breakdown and, hopefully, a teleplay.' All they told me was that part of the society was living on the surface of the planet in great luxury, and the larger part of the society was down in the caves working like slaves and kept that way. As I say, I never saw David Gerrold's screenplay nor did I see Oliver Crawford's rewrite, so I don't know that it was static and didn't work. So I wondered how in the world I could build action into this philosophical notion, and that's why I added the gas in the caves which numbed the minds of the people so that they appear to be stupid. I

••••

told the story against the background of rebellion, in which Kirk and Spock become involved and it worked that way. For all I know, the first draft of the story and teleplay may have been even more acceptable than mine, but mine happened to be what the producer wanted."

Says Gerrold, "I hinted in one of those meetings with Fred Freiberger that I didn't want to sell out to television, and he said, 'I've been in television for 20 years and I've never sold out.' In television it's not whether or not you sell out, but how badly you sell out. The giveaway is when they say they've never sold out. Obviously you've never challenged anyone. You've sold out before you got there. You look at 'The Cloud Minders' now and it's kind of harmless, but at the time it was suddenly a story that said 'We're right to be in Vietnam, we're right to send the troops into the ghettos, and we're right to do whatever we want. Yes, they have some valid concerns, but if we give them gas masks, they'll stay in the ghettos.' That pissed me off, because it ignored the fundamental issue that these are human beings and there is an unfairness in who is living in the sky cities and who is living down below. And the issue was never resolved in the story. I was very upset about the way that turned out. I didn't like the episode. So it was an unhappy experience, particularly for a new writer, who needs reassurance that he can succeed in the industry."

Today, Fred Freiberger keeps his thoughts on the whole situation rather succinct. "I liked the story when David came in with it, but nobody was thrilled with the script," he says. "We fought to save Gerrold's credit on that to which, I'm sure, we got no gratitude. There was no appreciation on his part in that we told every writer that came in that we wanted to save his credit."

Episode #76
"The Savage Curtain"
Original Airdate: 3/7/69
Written by Arthur Heinemann and Gene Roddenberry
Story by Gene Roddenberry
Directed by Herschel Daugherty
Guest Starring: Lee Bergere (Abraham Lincoln), Barry Atwater (Surak), Phillip Pine (Colonel Green), Nathan Jung

(Genghis Kahn), Carol Daniels Dement (Zora), Robert Herron (Kahless)

The ultimate battle between good and evil as Kirk, Spock, President Lincoln and Vulcan pioneer Surak go up against mad scientist Zora, Genghis Khan, murderer Colonel Green and the Klingon that inspired the Empire, Kahless. The mediator is a rock creature named Yarnek, who is curious as to which side will prove victorious.

••••

"Gene Roddenberry wrote half a script," explained Arthur Heinemann, "and I don't know if he couldn't figure out how to end it or got tired and had other things to do. He was in and out of the show at the time. His script was handed to me and I wrote the last two acts, and rewrote some of the first two acts. I guess I must have liked it, otherwise I wouldn't have taken it. Although at that time I found myself capable of making myself like anything that they gave me. It wasn't hard to sell. If somebody says, 'I love you,' you just have to believe them.

"The story was interesting because the four greatest heroes in the history of man, or the universe, were pit against the four worst. How could you end that thing except by having them fight? I tried to inject some sort of moral underpinnings to it by saying that the good guys were fighting for the safety of other people, whereas the bad guys were just fighting for the sake of fighting; for the game. But I wasn't happy with the final execution of that episode. It was written toward the end of the season. The final fight scene was supposed to take place in a huge canyon, but they figured the daylight hours at the time weren't long enough to shoot on location, so they had to build rocks out of canvas and paint, and nobody could climb on them because you'd fall through. Maybe it was the only way. Who knows?"

Episode #77
"All Our Yesterdays"
Original Airdate: 3/14/69
Written by Jean Lisette Aroeste
Directed by Marvin Chomsky
Guest Starring: Mariette Hartley (Zarabeth), Ian Wolfe (Atoz), Kermit Murdock (Prosecutor), Johnny Haymer

Mariette Hartley was Mr. Spock's third love interest in the annals of StarTrek. The actress is seen here in Gene Roddenberry's Genesis II.

(Constable), Stan Barrett (Jailor), Ed Bakey and Al Cavens (Fops), Anna Karen (Woman)

A landing party beams down to Sarpeidon to remove the inhabitants from a forthcoming explosion of their sun. What they find is a massive library, and a librarian named Mr. Atoz (A to Z). Quite by accident, Kirk, Spock and McCoy step through a portal and are transported back in time. Kirk appears at the time of witch-hunts in a Salem-like setting, while Spock and Bones go back much farther to a more savage time where Spock actually falls in love with a woman trapped there, Zarabeth. The trio must make it back to their own time before the sun explodes and they are trapped forever.

••••

"I love that episode," smiles Fred Freiberger. "The woman who wrote it was a librarian at UCLA. I remember that when Leonard Nimoy read that script he came to me and said, 'I'm a Vulcan, how can I be passionately in love with a woman with emotion involved?' So I said, 'This is way back in time, before the Vulcans had evolved into a nonemotional society.' He accepted that, for which I was very grateful. One of my favorites.

Episode #78
"Turnabout Intruder"
Original Airdate: 6/3/69
Written by Arthur Singer
Story by Gene Roddenberry
Directed by Herb Wallerstein

••••

Guest Starring: Sandra Smith (Dr. Janice Lester), Harry Landers (Dr. Coleman)

Kirk finds himself the victim of Dr. Janice Lester's hatred. She was once romantically involved with the captain, and has been unable to assume a command of her own. Now she wants revenge and has found it in an alien device which is able to transfer her mind to Kirk's body and vice-versa.

• • • •

"I have to tell you, Shatner is a very creative guy," enthuses Fred Freiberger. "When I say creative, I mean he's willing to try *anything.* He loved 'Turnabout Intruder.' I was, frankly, a little concerned when Gene Roddenberry came up with a story where Kirk changes places with a woman. When I originally read it, I had said to Gene, 'I wonder what Shatner is going to say about this,' and Gene said he wouldn't have any problem with it. He was right. When I mentioned it to Shatner, he just loved the idea."

William Shatner (Captain James T. Kirk) and Leonard Nimoy (Mr. Spock) together at the Academy Awards.

• • • •

••••

CHAPTER SEVEN
The Remaking of Star Trek 1970-1978

Network cancellation was the best thing that could have ever happened to *Star Trek*. Had NBC renewed the show for a fourth or even a fifth year, the series would have undoubtedly continued to chug along. But, with considerable budget cuts each season, there would have a diminishing quality about the whole project and it would have undoubtedly faded into the annals of television history.

Star Trek had been such a ratings disappointment for NBC, that the final episode, "Turnabout Intruder," was not aired until summer reruns of 1970. In the fall of that year, Paramount began offering the show to independents, hoping that they would be able to recoup a few lost dollars on this "dog." Despite a slow beginning, the number of stations interested in carrying the series gradually increased, with the audience, in turn, growing as well.

Shortly thereafter, it had become obvious that there was something brewing. With Neil Armstrong's boot gracing the lunar surface the previous July, outer space suddenly became vogue. Space was the place, and *Star Trek* was the ticket to get there.

"*Star Trek* probably came along too early," explained Gene Roddenberry in *The Making of Star Trek: The Motion Picture* [1980, Wallaby Books]. "Had man landed on the moon during our first or second year, the idea of space flight wouldn't have seemed so ludicrous to the mass audience. *Star Trek* probably would have stayed on the air. The eye of the world did not turn to space seriously as a future possibility until we were in our third year, and by then it was too late.

With the continually mounting interest in *Star Trek* came the idea of a convention dedicated to the show, which would be held in New York during January of 1972. Episodes would be shown, merchandise pertaining to the series sold, and fans given the opportunity to meet and listen to the creative talents behind the series. The promoters of

Reunited on stage for an early Star Trek *convention: Walter Koenig, George Takei, William Shatner, DeForest Kelley, Nichelle Nichols, Leonard Nimoy and Arlene Martel.*

the con were expecting, with a little luck, maybe two or three hundred people. They were not prepared for the two thousand that actually showed up.

A year later, a second convention was held, with guests including James Doohan, George Takei, and *Star Trek* and science fiction writer David Gerrold. Again, the promoters took what they thought would be adequate precautions, and again they were wrong. This time between six and seven thousand fans showed up. The same thing happened in 1974 when what is estimated to be between ten and fourteen thousand people attended. A firmer grip was placed on crowd control for the 1975 convention when registration was closed at approximately eight thousand, and those people lucky enough to get in experienced William Shatner's first (and now all too rare) con appearance. The next year's convention was limited to six thousand people, and guests included DeForest Kelley, Gene Roddenberry, Majel Barrett, James Doohan, Nichelle Nichols and George Takei.

Throughout the "convention years," the syndicated episodes were breaking all kinds of records, easily equating itself with the most popular

shows in reruns. Paramount noted this with interest, and was somewhat more than intrigued when the public began to demand a revival of the show. Rumors abounded, with the general feeling being that *Star Trek* would either come back as a new television series or perhaps even a feature film.

Still, Paramount made no official move. It's likely that they viewed the phenomenon as little more than a fad; that any such revival would, in effect, "miss the boat," and they would stand to lose even more money. They were wrong. *Star Trek* was no fad.

While fandom flourished, as did the merchandising of the show, animation production companies began to approach Gene Roddenberry and Paramount Pictures with the idea of doing an animated version. Many of these suggestions were turned down, but Filmation came to them with a package that they liked. Most important to Roddenberry was that he would have complete creative control, thus being able to insure that the series did not resemble any other kid vid on the air at the time.

"That was one of the reasons I wanted creative control," said Roddenberry

••••

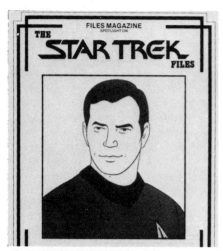

FILES MAGAZINE
SPOTLIGHT ON
THE
STAR TREK
FILES

The animated William Shatner/Captain James T. Kirk as seen in this publication that covered Star Trek-Animated.

at the time. "There are enough limitations just being on Saturday mornings. We have to eliminate some of the violence we might have had on in the evening shows. There will probably be no sex element to talk of either, but it will be *Star Trek* and not a stereotype kids cartoon show."

The idea was to do a series that would air on Saturday mornings, but would also feature the basic ideals of the original show. Both Roddenberry and Paramount agreed that this would be a good idea, and to that end the original cast was signed to provide the vocals to their animated counter-parts. Additionally, many of the writers involved with the live-action series were hired to pen scripts. Former *Star Trek* story editor Dorothy Fontana was signed to repeat her duties here, and take on the new ones of associate producer.

"When Gene approached me to do the show," she explains, "he asked me if I would like to come on as story editor and producer. Since I wasn't a part of another regular staff at the time, I decided to do it. I had not worked in animation, which I do enjoy, so I had a good time on the show. I left after the first season, because I wanted to move on to something else and not get stuck in animation. The business is funny. If you stay too long in one thing, people start to buttonhole you there and say, 'You can't do anything else,' regardless of all your other credits."

Roddenberry believed that the animated series would be the first step in getting a *Star Trek* feature film made, but DeForest Kelley wasn't so sure. "I questioned it at the time," he explained back in the '70s, "and he said he was going to do it. I thought it was the death blow. Gene said, 'No, I don't feel that way at all. I think it's important to keep some form of *Star Trek* alive and in the minds of people.' It's not the network, it's Paramount. The network wants the show again, and would love to have it back. But Paramount, the studio that owns *Star Trek*, doesn't want to make *Star Trek* prime time because they're making so much money in syndication with it. They feel they would be competing with themselves."

Opines James Doohan, "[The animated series] is forgotten. I think it was ordinary. It was ordinarily drawn. It was fun doing it because I did three characters and in ten of the episodes I did four. I pushed for that, because once you did more than three they had to double your pay. Strangely enough, I didn't use any accents. I just changed the tone of my voice. It's kind of like being back in radio again. Also the very fact we did it and made a little money. We certainly hadn't made any on the series because the residuals ran out in April 1971. The unions remedied that situation because of *Star Trek*, absolutely. They never thought any show would run like *Star Trek* has run."

One person not included in the animated series was Walter Koenig. "I was upset about the way I found out about the series," admits the actor. "It was at a convention. Everybody thought someone else had told me apparently. Dorothy thought Gene had, Gene thought Dorothy had. Apparently to save money, Filmation wanted to have Majel do Uhura's voice and Jimmy do Sulu's voice—this because in cartoons at the time you got paid one check to do two character voices. To Leonard's credit, he said he would not do the series unless they hired George and Nichelle since they had been there from the beginning. I wrote a script for it and in fact they asked me to write another one, but I wasn't interested since I was still upset over not being part of the series."

Twenty two episodes were produced in all, and, for the most part, Fontana's efforts in securing the finest possible talent paid off. Those scripts, penned by Fontana herself as well as veterans from the old show and the genre, proved themselves to be quite literate, and certainly a bright spot on the Saturday morning schedule. Unfortunately, like its predecessor, *Star Trek: Animated* was cancelled prematurely, with Roddenberry and the original cast once again going their separate ways, apparently forever.

The Cast

Prior to *Star Trek*, William Shatner had carved an impressive niche for himself as an actor, having scored quite successfully on stage, screen and television. Incredibly, his most difficult time came immediately after his three year-stint on *Star Trek*, following a divorce which left him in a precarious financial position.

"There was a time, before *Star Trek*, when I wouldn't accept a role that I didn't think worthwhile enough to play. Then, because things are so cyclical in show business, I needed to take those roles," Shatner explained in his autobiography, *Where No Man*. "There even came a point when I thought—I don't know whether I'm ever going to break through—

William Shatner in one of his early post-Star Trek films, The Devil's Rain.

• • • •

Leonard Nimoy co-starred with Donald Sutherland and Brooke Adams in the remake of Invasion of the Body Snatchers

to get those roles that I think I should be playing. That was just before *Star Trek*. *Star Trek* hit. And after *Star Trek* I've had the opportunity to play a few of those things that I thought should be coming my way. But, I was in a financial bind and had to accept a lot of things that I wouldn't have done in an earlier day."

Following the release of *Star Trek: The Motion Picture*, Shatner's fortune would take a definite upswing, leaving the tumultuous '70s behind him.

Leonard Nimoy, who would have seemingly been the most typecast from *Star Trek*, had actually gone on to the most successful career of all the cast members during the ten year period between cancellation and revival. He immediately shifted from *Star Trek* to a co-starring role in the hit series *Mission: Impossible,* on which he played make-up genius Paris. "I thought it was an opportunity to do a wide variety of characters so that I would, perhaps, become better known as a character actor rather than a Spock actor," he said in *The Star Trek Interview Book.* "It didn't really work out that way, in fact, but that was one of the reasons for doing that show."

Nimoy quit the series after three seasons to pursue other roles. "Quitting the show was kind of a dangerous thing to do, but I felt confident," he admitted. "But '71 was the first year out of six years of TV series and it

turned out to be a perfect year with a mix of all the things I wanted to do." Among them was the film *Catlow* and the lead in the national touring company of *Fiddler on the Roof.* Eventually his career led him to tackle another "logical" character, that of Sherlock Holmes on stage.

In addition, he began directing episodic television, narrated the syndicated series *In Search of....* and received acclaim for his one-man-show *Vincent,* based on the life of Vincent van Gogh, as well as for the books of poetry he wrote (including one called *I Am Not Spock*) and his Broadway role in *Equus.* Prior to the filming of *Star Trek: The Motion Picture,* he starred in Phil Kaufman's remake of *Invasion of the Body Snatchers,* which he described as "a frightening aspect of image-making modeled on preferred roles that people play as dictated by the media." Naturally it would be his return as Spock that would garner the most attention, and ultimately lead to a fruitful directing career.

DeForest Kelley has the most easy to summarize post-*Star Trek* career of anyone: he did a feature film entitled *Night of the Lepus,* about giant killer bunnies, and retired, with the exception of the animated *Trek* spinoff and feature films.

James Doohan made a comfortable living for himself throughout the '70s via the *Star Trek* convention circuit, as well as roles in such films as *Pretty Maids All in a Row* (produced by Roddenberry) and as a regular on the CBS Saturday morning series *Jason of Star Command`,* which he left after one season. "They really didn't give me anything to do so I said, 'Goodbye.'"

George Takei certainly diversified following *Star Trek.* Not only did he make appearances on a variety of television series, but he wrote a pair of science-fiction/swashbuckler novels and threw his hat into the Los Angeles political arena.

Nichelle Nichols parlayed her *Star Trek* success as Lieutenant Uhura into a singing career, and a position with NASA and its astronaut recruitment drive. "When I began," she pointed out, "NASA had 1,500 applications. Six months later, they had 8,000. I like to think some of

those were encouraged by me. I did do a lot of traveling, speaking to universities, to professional and minority and women's groups, sometimes just to one person I found to be a particularly good prospect. The aim was to find qualified people among women and minorities, then to convince them that the opportunity was real and that it also was a duty, because this was historic. I really had this sense of purpose about it myself."

Walter Koenig, like his costars, did his fair share of episodic television work following his two seasons as Chekov, and even co-starred in the Gene Roddenberry television pilot, *The Questor Tapes.* Additionally, he served as an acting teacher, directed plays, wrote novels and penned the scripts for such primetime television fare as *Family* and *The Class of '65.*

It's unlikely that the ensemble could have known in 1969 that their lives would continue to be drawn together over the next two and a half decades, fueling a 30-year phenomenon.

Gene Roddenberry

For the fans of the little science fiction show that refused to die, it probably seemed as though Gene Roddenberry came out of nowhere when *Star Trek* premiered, and had done nothing from the show's cancellation in 1969 until the release of *Star Trek: The Motion Picture* a decade later. Nobody can say the guy didn't try.

Roddenberry, who prior to *Star Trek* had worked on westerns, police

James Doohan spent one season co-starring in the Saturday morning series, Jason of Star Command

shows and even produced a show about the Marines called *The Lieutenant,* did his best to equal the ultimate success of *Trek.* His feature film *Pretty Maids All in a Row* was a disappointment, and his efforts to create a realistic version of *Tarzan* never got beyond the scripting stages. His supernatural television pilot *Spectre* went nowhere, and a proposed film project with Paul McCartney fell to the wayside when the revival of *Star Trek* seemed to be becoming a reality. He did, however, manage to create a pair of television pilots that came *this* close to becoming weekly series: *Genesis II* and *The Questor Tapes.*

Shortly after these tentative series were cancelled, the word from Paramount was that there might indeed be some kind of revival of *Star Trek.*

The Trek Begins Anew

Roddenberry was given his old office at the studio and told to write a movie script for a low-budget feature film.

"They turned me down a couple of times," Roddenberry said, "then finally they said, 'Write a script and we'll give you an office on the lot and think about it.' They were not that serious about [it] when we first started. I think they had in mind a $2-$3 million picture. We debated a long time whether it would be a two-hour TV film or a movie for theatrical release. I didn't want to do it for television. When the original *Star Trek* ended, Paramount thought it had a real loser on its hands, a stinker. Oh, they'd make a couple of bucks on reruns but they *knew* the show would never amount to much. They destroyed all the sets. Everything. Even Spock's ears. I felt that for TV, the limited budget allowed just would not suffice for the rebuilding of the sets and of the Enterprise. It would be the same quality as on the old show and, after all these years, I felt that they wouldn't be good enough. They said, 'Okay, we'll do a theatrical release. Go write a script.'"

Although little is known about the resulting script, entitled *The God Thing,* reports have stated that the premise questioned the very nature of God and the universe around us.

Paramount was apparently not interested in a script which, essentially, pit Captain Kirk against God.

Director Richard Colla, who had helmed *The Questor Tapes* TV movie pilot, was very familiar with that particular screenplay, and recalls it fondly.

"That script was much more daring," he says. "They went off in search of that thing from outer space that was affecting everything. By the time they got on to the spaceship and got into its [the alien's] presence, it manifested itself and said, 'Do you know me?' Kirk said, 'No, I don't know who you are.' It said, 'Strange, how could you not know who I am?' So it shift-changed and became another image and said, 'Do you know me?' Kirk said, 'No, who are you?' It replied, 'The time has passed, and you should know me by now.' It shifts shapes again, and comes up in the form of Christ the Carpenter, and says, 'Do you know me?' And Kirk said, 'Oh, now I know who you are.' And he says, 'How strange you didn't know these other forms of me.' Really, what Gene had written was that this 'thing' was sent forth to lay down the law; to communicate the law of the universe, and that as time goes on the law needs to be reinterpreted. And at that time 2,000 years ago, the law was interpreted by this Carpenter image. As time went on, the law was meant to be reinterpreted, and the Christ figure was meant to reappear in different forms. But this machine malfunctioned, and it was like a phonograph record that got caught in a groove, and kept grooving back, grooving back, grooving back. It's important to understand the essence of all this and reinterpret it as time goes on. That was a little heavy for Paramount. It was meant to be strong and moving, and I'm sorry it never got made."

"I handed them a script and they turned it down," Roddenberry stated matter of factly in 1980. "It was too controversial. It talked about concepts like, 'Who is God?' [In it] the Enterprise meets God in space; God is a life form, and I wanted to suggest that there may have been, at one time in the human beginning, an alien entity that early man believed was God, and kept those legends. But I also wanted to suggest that that might have been as much the Devil

as it was God. After all, what kind of god would throw humans out of Paradise for eating the fruit of the Tree of Knowledge? One of the Vulcans on board, in a very logical way, says, 'If this is your God, he's not very impressive. He's got so many psychological problems, he's so insecure. He demands worship every seven days. He goes out and creates faulty humans and then blames them for his own mistakes. He's a pretty poor excuse for a Supreme Being.' Not surprisingly, that didn't send the Paramount executives off crying with glee. But I think good science fiction, historically, has been used that way—to question *everything.*

"[Anyway,] the movie then sagged for quite some time," he continued. "It really got bogged down. I didn't hear anything for over three months. Meanwhile, unknown to me, the executives then in charge were interviewing writers, accepting outlines. I found out about all this quite by accident. None of the outlines were accepted. I think the main reason for all the problems with those scripts rested in the fact that most of the people making decisions concerning the film knew little or nothing about *Star Trek.* As it turned out later on, several of the principals had never even seen the show."

Despite this statement to the contrary, according to *The Making of Star Trek: The Motion Picture,* some script activity took place between Paramount's rejection of *The God Thing* and their soliciting story ideas from other writers.

Jon Povill, who would eventually go on to be story editor of the proposed *Star Trek II* television series and associate producer of the first film, had worked with Gene Roddenberry as a researcher for what was then planned to be a novelization of *The God Thing.*

"Gene went to work on that script in May of 1975," details Povill, "and it was his first attempt at a *Star Trek* feature. By August it was shitcanned by [Paramount President] Barry Diller. Gene, who had gotten to know me pretty well by then, suggested that I take a crack at writing a treatment, which I did."

The resulting treatment dealt with the people of planet Vulcan going mad, and the Enterprise's mad-dash through time to set things right by combatting a psychic-cloud that is affecting the population. It, too, was rejected.

The studio's search for the proper vehicle to launch the first *Star Trek* film began around this time, with those writers approached including John D.F. Black, who has served as story editor of the original show's first season and penned "The Naked Time," and then wrote the story for the "Justice" episode of *The Next Generation*; famed author Harlan Ellison, whose sole contribution to the show had been its most popular episode, "City on the Edge of Forever;" and science fiction veteran Robert Silverberg.

John D.F. Black describes the storyline he pitched with a good-natured shrug. Something in his voice conveys the feeling that he still can't believe the way the studio handled the proposed film.

"I came up with a story concept involving a black hole," recounts Black, "and this was *before* Disney's film. The black hole had been used by several planets in a given constellation as a garbage dump. But with a black hole there's a point of equality. In other words, when enough positive matter comes into contact with an equal amount of negative matter, the damn thing blows up. Well, if that ever occurs with a black hole, it's the end of the universe—it'll swallow everything. The Enterprise discovered what's happened with this particular black hole and they try to stop these planets from unloading into it. The planets won't do it. It comes to war in some areas and, as a result, the black hole comes to balance and blows up. At that point, it would continue to chew up matter. In one hundred and six years Earth would be swallowed by this black hole, and the Enterprise is trying to beat the end of the world. There were at least twenty sequels in that story because the jeopardy keeps growing more intense."

Paramount rejected the idea. "They said it wasn't big enough," Black notes wryly.

In his excellent nonfiction assessment of horror and science fiction, *Danse Macabre*, Stephen King reported the rumor that Harlan Ellison went to Paramount with the idea of the Enterprise breaking through the end of the universe and confronting God himself. And that wasn't big enough either.

Ellison gave Stephen King a little more information on his story meeting with Paramount.

"It involved going to the end of the known universe to slip back through time to the Pleistocene period when man first emerged," he said. "I postulated an alien intelligence from a far galaxy where the snakes had become the dominant life form, and a snake-creature who had come to Earth in the *Star Trek* future, had seen its ancestors wiped out, and who had gone back into the far past of Earth to set up distortions in the time-flow so the reptiles could beat the humans. The Enterprise goes back to set time right, finds the snake-alien, and the human crew is confronted with the moral dilemma of whether it had the right to wipe out an entire life form just to insure its own territorial imperative in our present and future. The story, in short, spanned all of time and all of space, with a moral and ethical problem."

Paramount executive Barry Trabulus "listened to all this and sat silently for a few minutes," Ellison elaborated. "Then he said, 'You know, I was reading this book by a guy named Von Daniken and he proved that the Mayan calendar was exactly like ours, so it must have come from aliens. Could you put in some Mayans?'"

The writer pointed out that there were no Mayans at the dawn of time, but the executive brushed this off, pointing out that no one would know the difference.

"'I'm to know the difference,'" he exploded. "'It's a dumb suggestion.' So Trabulus got very uptight and said he liked Mayans a lot and why didn't I do it if I wanted to write this picture. So I said, 'I'm a writer. I don't know what the fuck you are!' And I got up and walked out. And that was the end of my association with the *Star Trek* movie."

The Robert Silverberg story, entitled *The Billion Year Voyage*, was more of an intellectual foray as the Enterprise crew discovered the ruins of an ancient, but far more advanced, civilization, and must battle other aliens in order to take possession of the wondrous gifts left behind; gifts which would surely benefit mankind some day in the future when he is ready to

accept that responsibility.

This trio of stories were fascinating attempts at reviving the show, and it seems unimaginable that all of them were turned down. The revival game was destined to continue for some time to come.

Ten Years And Counting

By 1976, *Star Trek* was celebrating its ten year anniversary, and the show's fan following was continuously growing larger, with the demand for a new film or television series growing more vehement. It had been seven years since the last new episode, and the only difference was that the idea of reviving the show, in one format or another, was actually being considered by Paramount.

If any attempt to do so seemed likely to happen, it would probably be the one initiated in July of 1976. Jerry Eisenberg was hired as producer, with Phil (*Invasion of the Body Snatchers, The Right Stuff*) Kaufman directing. Scripting were a pair of English writers named Allan Scott and Chris Bryant, whose credits included *Don't Look Now* and *Joseph Andrews*. Their experience in science fiction was non-existent, but what they lacked in knowledge, they made up for in enthusiasm, and a willingness to learn.

Kaufman, in particular, was thrilled with the prospect of being involved. "George Lucas is a good friend of mine," he had told one reporter. "He told me before he made *Star Wars* he'd made inquiries as to whether *Star Trek* was available to be bought. I thought George had a great thing going. When I was asked if I would be interested in doing *Star Trek*, well...I felt I could go through the roof."

In addition to all of this, the original cast had essentially been signed to reprise their original roles, with the exception of Leonard Nimoy, who, at the time, had refused all interviews pertaining to *Star Trek*. William Shatner, however, had no problem in discussing the situation.

"Leonard Nimoy has a beef, and it's a legitimate one," Shatner said in 1976. "It's about the merchandising and it's something that irks me as well. Our faces appear on products all over the country, all over the world, and we've not really been compensated fairly for it. Leonard was walking in London, England. He stopped to look at a billboard. The billboard's divided into three sections. The first section is Leonard's face with the ears—Spock—the ears are drooping. The second section of the billboard has Leonard, with the drooping ears, holding a tankard of ale. The third section has an empty tankard of ale, and Leonard's face, with pointed ears straight up in the air. So Leonard and I have had this battle, with whoever licenses *Star Trek*, for a long time. I mean, kids are walking around with my face on their shirts. Occasionally I see a postcard with my face on it. People are exploiting us. So anyway, Leonard goes back to the studio and says, 'There's a demeaning billboard of me out there. Did you guys okay it?' So he goes to his lawyer and tries to sue. Right now Paramount wants Leonard, and Leonard wants fair recompense. It's only reasonable that Paramount meet his demands. Something has happened here. Someone has made a lot of money from the show, and the people who were the show have seen very little of it. I think Leonard is totally in the right."

While Nimoy would eventually agree to do this attempt to resurrect *Star Trek*, the format would again be changed and he would, again, drop out.

The Scott/Bryant screenplay opens with the Enterprise investigating a distress signal sent from the USS DaVinci. By the time they arrive in that quadrant of space, the other starship is gone. Suddenly, Kirk's brain is struck by electromagnetic waves, which results in erratic behavior and his commandeering a shuttlecraft. He pilots it towards an invisible planet and disappears. Three years later, Spock leads an expedition back to that area of space, and they discover what they believe to be the planet of the Titans, an ancient, but highly advanced race which had been thought extinct. Problem is that the planet is being drawn towards a black hole, and it becomes a race against time between the Federation and the Klingons, who are both interested in that particular world. The one who saves the planet will receive the fruits of their knowledge.

On the planet's surface, Spock discovers Kirk, who has been living there as a wild man. However, the captain is

This advertisement raised the ire of Leonard Nimoy, who launched a lawsuit against Paramount Pictures for using his likeness without paying a royalty.

restored to normal in short order, and together they discover that the planet is actually populated by the evil Cygnans, a race which had destroyed the Titans. The story concluded with Kirk, in an effort to destroy the hostile Cygnans, ordering the Enterprise *into* the black hole. As Susan Sackett noted in *The Making of Star Trek: The Motion Picture*, "During the trip through the black hole, the Cygnans are destroyed and the Enterprise emerges in orbit around Earth. But it is Earth at the time of the Cro-Magnan man, the dawn of humanity. The ancient Titans, it would seem, were the men of the Enterprise."

Jon Povill, a writer as well as Gene Roddenberry's assistant, noted the project with interest, though he wasn't convinced it was right for *Star Trek*'s debut on the movie screen.

"It was an interesting script in a certain sort of way," Povill explains. "It was not *Star Trek*. People would have gone to see it, and it would have done as well as we did with *Star Trek: The Motion Picture*, but it's just as well that it didn't get made. Chris and Allan even felt that it was something that wasn't quite successful. They didn't feel they had brought off a script that was just right. They didn't feel confident about it. Then Phil Kaufman decided that he wanted to take a run at the script. His treatment was, I think, worse than the script. Then the whole thing kind of fell apart."

Reflects Allan Scott, "The difficulty for us was trying to make, as it

were, an exploded episode of *Star Trek* that had its own justifications in terms of the new scale that was available to it, because much of the show's charm was the fact that it dealt with big and bold ideas on a small budget, and of course the first thing that a movie would do, potentially, was match the budget and scale of the production to the boldness and vigor of the ideas. Of course we spent weeks looking at every episode of *Star Trek*, and I would guess that more or less every member of the cast came by and met us.

"We were surprised that it didn't go, because it seemed that it would. It was absolutely a 'go' picture. But it was a very exciting project to be involved with. I'm sorry it didn't work, because we would have enjoyed it even more if it had. We had a lot of fun and it was really an enjoyable time. I don't feel unhappy about it at all. It was just one of those deals that happens at studios from time to time that fell down the middle."

Phil Kaufman's reaction to the cancellation of the film was not quite so idealistic. "We were dealing with important things," he said. "Things that George [Lucas] has a smattering of in *Star Wars*. We were dealing a lot with Olaf Stapledon. There were chapters in *Last and First Men* that I was basing *Star Trek* on. That was my key thing. Gene and I disagreed on what the nature of a feature film really is. He was still bound by the

••••

things that he had been forced into by lack of money and by the fact that those times were not into science fiction the way they are now. Gene has a very set way of looking at things. My feeling always was that he was anchored in a 10-year-old TV show which would not translate for a feature audience ten years later with all that had been done and could potentially be done in a feature scope. For years I had walked around San Francisco with George Lucas talking about what *he* was doing. I knew what the potential of this kind of stuff was."

Perhaps most shocking to him was the feeling that Paramount canceled the film because of the success of *Star Wars*, which was released in May of 1977, and the belief that they had blown their opportunity at the box office. "They didn't even wait to see what STAR WARS would do," Kaufman said incredulously. "I don't think they tried to understand what the phenomenon of *Star Trek* was."

"We considered the project for years," summed up then Paramount president Barry Diller. "We've done a number of treatments, scripts, and everytime we'd say, 'This isn't good enough.' If we had just gone forward and *done* it, we might have done it quite well. In this case [the Scott/Bryant/Kaufman version], it was the script. We felt, frankly, that it was a little pretentious. We went to Gene Roddenberry and said: 'Look, you're the person who really understands *Star Trek*. We don't. But what we should probably do is return to the original context, a television series.' If you force it as a big 75 millimeter widescreen movie, you go directly against the concept. If you rip *Star Trek* off, you'll fail, because the people who like *Star Trek* don't just like it. They love it."

So, once again, the Enterprise's destiny was being charted towards the television screen, although no one had any idea—though they should have suspected—that she would never complete the voyage.

TV Trek-Take 2

And the Earth shook. If it didn't, then it must have been a movement of damn near equal proportion to the fans of a little television series they had refused to let die. They had taken "control" of the show's destiny by generating an unprecedented amount of enthusiasm, resulting in a phenomenon whose closest relative was probably Beatlemania circa 1964. They gathered together at conventions, met their idols, penned original fiction dedicated to the characters and ideals of the show and never stopped hoping for the day when it would be resurrected on either television or the movie screen. In the middle of 1977, it seemed as though their efforts had finally borne fruit: *Star Trek* was returning to television.

After numerous attempts to bring the show back as either a feature film, television movie or weekly series, it finally seemed that a revival would come to pass. The original cast, with the exception of Leonard Nimoy, who for career and litigation reasons did not wish to play the role of Spock on a weekly basis, had actually been signed to reprise their most famous roles, scripts were being developed and sets constructed for the brand new starship Enterprise. Everything was coming together, allowing *Star Trek* to touch a new generation in the same way as it had the previous one.

For some time, Paramount Pictures had dreamed of starting a fourth network to compete with the three majors, much as the Dumont Network did during television's Golden Age. To this end, they contacted independent stations all over the United States and began offering product to fill one night a week with new programming, cornerstoned by the series entitled *Star Trek II*.

Robert Goodwin had been with Paramount Pictures for two years. Originally he was assistant to Arthur Fellows, who, in turn, was the Senior Vice President in charge of television production and had taken over Playboy Enterprises, whose name had been changed to Playboy-Paramount. Goodwin spent approximately one year as the Director of Development.

"Then a guy named Gary Nardino came in and took over as President of Paramount Television, and made the decision to start a fourth network," Goodwin details. "The plan was that every Saturday night they were going to do one hour of *Star Trek* and then a two hour movie. My interest had always been more in the long form rather than the series side of television. Nardino decided that he was going to put me in charge of all these two hour movies, which was great for me."

At that point, forces were at work which would pull Goodwin away from this choice assignment and bring him over to Roddenberry's team. Meanwhile, Roddenberry himself grew more vibrant with each passing day, as a seven year battle to bring *StarTrek* back seemed at an end, and he was essentially being given the opportunity to top himself, although he never really looked at it that way.

"Those [original] episodes will always be there for what people want to make out of them," he told *Starlog* at the time. "We're making a new set of them ten years later under very different circumstances. I think neither takes away from the other. The worst that can happen is someone would say that Roddenberry couldn't do it a second time. That doesn't bother me, as long as I did my damndest to do it a second time."

What was truly exciting to him was the opportunity to deal with different social issues in a new and fresh style, as television had been altered considerably by such series as *M*A*S*H* and *All in the Family*. Gone were the days when you *had* to hide your ideas within entertainment, for fear that network censors would not allow the show on the air. Things had changed to such a degree, that television was actually *challenged* to express itself in new and different ways.

"Dialogue is more naturalistic on television today," Roddenberry explained. "Direction is more sophisticated. There are better methods of optical effects. There are better methods for special effects. The audience is certainly more sophisticated and able to reach their minds out further. The audience is ready for statements on sex, religion, politics and so on, which we never would have dared to make before."

Star Trek II was envisioned as a dream come true, and efforts were made to secure the proper creative team. First choice was the aforementioned Robert Goodwin as producer.

"They were looking for someone to come on as producer," says

Goodwin, "and Gene Roddenberry had heard about me. To be perfectly honest, I wasn't anxious to do it. My real interest, as I said, was the long form, and I was supposed to supervise all those two hour movies. I was pretty much strong-armed to do it, and not given too much of a choice. Paramount said, 'Forget the two hour movies, you're doing Star Trek.' So I went over to see Gene and initially I got kicked out of his office. His assistant, Susan Sackett, thought I was an agent or something, and she didn't know that I had an appointment to see him. She wouldn't let me in, and I said, 'Fine,' and walked out. I was about a half a mile away at the other side of the studio, when Gene Roddenberry came running after me. To make a long story short, he wanted me to go in as one of the two producers. They were going to hire a writing producer and a production producer. It was kind of a strange situation."

Roddenberry found his "writing producer" in Harold Livingston, novelist and television writer.

"I had never met Roddenberry," admits Livingston, "but I think I was working at Paramount at the time. Bob Goodwin and I were both going to work under Gene. If I remember correctly, there were a lot of interviews and bullshit that went on, but Gene and I kind of hit it off. We had similar backgrounds. We had both been in the Air Force during the war and we both worked for civilian airlines after the war, so I think that's one of the reasons that Gene, in the beginning, liked me.

"I had never paid much attention to Star Trek," he smiles sheepishly. "I'd always considered it something of a media event. I was totally unwashed. Anyway, the object of the new series was very vague. All they knew was that the studio had some kind of arrangement with what was then going to be a fourth network. I suppose it would take the form of some kind of syndicated program. So thirteen episodes plus a pilot were ordered, and it was then my job to develop these stories, which I set upon doing."

To this end, he began to utilize Jon Povill, Gene Roddenberry's assistant.

"I wanted Jon Povill to be my story editor," Livingston explains, "and Gene wanted him to continue cleaning his

garage or something, so we had a big thing about that. I eventually got my way."

"Harold was primarily responsible for getting me the story editor job," concurs Povill. "Gene was reluctant to move me 'that far, that fast,' to use his words. Harold was adamant that I was doing the job of a story editor and, by God, I should be getting paid as one.

"Harold had not been very familiar with the old series at all," he continues, "and kind of relied on me to be the monitor of whether something fit with Star Trek or not. Once everything got rolling, and we were in a lot of writer's meetings, I sort of took over as the person who pointed out where there were holes in the stories, and where they did not conform to what Star Trek was supposed to be."

Rounding out the early cast of behind the scenes characters, was Jim Rugg, a veteran from the original series who was to handle the special effects, and production designer Joe Jennings. Matt Jeffries, who had designed the original Enterprise, but was, at the moment, tied up on Little House on the Prairie, would serve as technical consultant.

On July 15, 1977, Gene Roddenberry issued a memo telling the production crew that they needed to come up with a new bible for potential writers. Bob Goodwin, Harold Livingston, Jon Povill and several others began making contributions to this item, which had proved a successful tool during the course of the original series. The "bible" which eventually evolved, stated that the series would chronicle the second five year mission of the Enterprise. While in drydock following its initial mission, the vessel had been completely refurbished.

James T. Kirk, we learn, has refused a promotion to admiral so that he can command the starship on its newest voyage. All of his original crew have been reassigned to him, with the exception of Mr. Spock, who has "returned in high honor to Vulcan to head the Science Academy there." In updating the series and attempting to fill the void created by Spock's absence, three new characters were added and hopes were high that actor Leonard Nimoy would frequently reprise his role of Spock for guest appearances.

The guide detailed the intricacies

of the Enterprise's weapon and defense abilities, followed by a character breakdown, focusing on the new additions.

Lt. Xon, a full Vulcan, has taken the place of Mr. Spock as ship science officer. This twenty year old, who is "a genius even by Vulcan standards," was destined to prove himself as capable as his predecessor. The primary difference between the two is that Xon has virtually no knowledge of the human equation, and realizes that the only way he will be able to equal Spock is by making an effort to touch his repressed emotions, thus allowing him to more fully relate to the crew. Roddenberry wrote that "we'll get some humor out of Xon trying to simulate laughter, anger, fear and other human feelings." Interesting to note is that the Spock-McCoy feud would have carried over to Xon and the doctor, with the difference being that McCoy believes their "feud is a very private affair...and McCoy has been known to severely chastise (in private) those crewmen who have been unfair to the Vulcan in comparing his efforts to Spock's."

The second new character mentioned is Commander Will Decker, Enterprise first officer who is something of a young Captain Kirk. The son of Commodore Matt Decker, who met his demise tackling "The Doomsday Machine," he comes quite close to worshipping the captain, and would "literally rather die than fail him." This is in direct contrast to the somewhat antagonistic Kirk-Decker relationship demonstrated in Star Trek: The Motion Picture. Essentially Decker is a captain in training, and the idea was that the audience would watch his gradual growth during the five year mission. In many instances, he would lead landing parties, thus alleviating the perpetual logistical flaw of the initial Star Trek TV series: a ship's captain would never beam into potential danger as often as Kirk did, and it's a format change which would eventually be incorporated into The Next Generation.

The final new addition to the crew would have been Lieutenant Ilia, the bald Deltan, whose race is marked by a heightened sexuality that pervades every aspect of their society. Additionally, Ilia, as is common among her people, is abnormally intelligent, second, perhaps, only to Xon, and gifted with some rather unique esper abilities. As noted, "unlike the mind-meld of Vulcans, it simply is the ability to sense images in other minds. Never words or emotions, only images, shapes, sizes, textures. On her planet, sexual foreplay consists largely of lovers placing images in each other's minds." Like Decker, Ilia made it into the first feature film, and remained, essentially, as the guide depicted her.

These character profiles were followed by a breakdown of the original crew, an explanation of the standing sets, description of equipment and an explanation of terminology.

With the guide having been written, Harold Livingston began contacting writers and agents in an effort to get the first thirteen scripts in motion.

"I wanted to make *Star Trek* more universal," explains Livingston matter of factly. "I felt that success not withstanding, the show had a restrictive audience. There was a greater audience for this. I felt that almost all of the stories seemed to be allegorical, and I wanted to make them a little harder and a little more realistic. My broad intention was to create a series that would attract a larger audience by offering more. We would still offer the same elements that *Star Trek* did, i.e. science fiction and hope for the future, and do realistic stories.

"I just thought they had reached a certain barrier with it," he continues. "How much could you do before it becomes totally redundant, and then where do you go? I wanted to bring it down to Earth...figuratively. They had so many stories which, to manipulate or move the plot, this goofy thing appeared out of nowhere. I'm thinking specifically of some Greek with an echoing voice that came on and saved them. That was done too often. And I simply also wanted scripts that were interesting and made sense and moved from a literary standpoint. I felt that too much of that was neglected or overlooked, because they had their science fiction themes. I wanted to do both, although I don't know if it would have worked. I have a great fear of these cultist series-films, because they're really self defeating in the end. You're going to have a limited audience. That

was my feeling, right or wrong."

Famed science fiction author Norman Spinrad wrote to Harold Livingston regarding a story the two men had discussed, that essentially dealt with the search for ultimate knowledge as well as personality changes in some of our crewmembers, some of which pick up traits of the others

On August 4, Gene Roddenberry referred to the story by saying, "We could use any ideas [which] might make this story work. Spinrad is brilliant and he is onto the right thing." Negatively speaking, he noted that the production probably couldn't afford the maze as described in the story. "Also," he explained, "it is largely a two-man story with them interacting with a 'hidden power.' It is hardly action adventure. The jeopardy is mostly intellectual."

The entire *Star Trek II* company was very excited by Spinrad's full treatment which came later on. Roddenberry in particular was extremely positive, suggesting that perhaps the alien power could sway the Enterprise crew over by offering to give the individual whatever it was they desired most. This, he pointed out, was similar, but different to the premise of the original show's first season episode, "The Naked Now." Interestingly enough, the idea of trying to sway the crew by offering them whatever they desire, was picked up in the "Hide and Q" episode of the *Next Generation*.

"I don't remember where the idea came from," Spinrad admits, "except that I've always been fascinated with the high-mind concept, which I have dealt with in books. It would have made a great TV piece, because it's all in the acting. They all take on each other's characteristics, which .is something really weird and strange, that wouldn't be as interesting in a novel, but would as a film or play. Something oral. Something with acting."

Several sub-standard script ideas caused Roddenberry to note, "Apparently the past has a way of repeating itself. During our first three years, a principal problem in most story ideas received was that they usually presented our captain and crew with no particular *jeopardy* or *need*. In other words, it is not sufficient for a story idea merely to have

our people in starship running into something interesting while out in space. In fact, it is not even sufficient to have them run into merely something fascinating!

"The above is why the typical story of 'two interesting civilizations' rarely works out," added Roddenberry. "Too often a writer thinks he has brought in enough if there are needs created for other characters in the story. This simply doesn't work. Yes, we want our *Star Trek* story to involve fascinating things we meet out there, but those fascinating things *must* create an important need for one or more of our characters. That need can be for something to happen—or something *not* to happen. That need should grow steadily more and more important so story moves toward climax. Also, the resolution of that need must grow more and more impossible. Admittedly, all this is fairly elemental and stuff every writer knows. But I think that *all* of us (including yours truly) often tend to forget it when doing science fiction."

One of the writers contacted was Alan Dean Foster, author of numerous genre novels, including the *Star Trek Log* series for Ballantine Books.

Foster adapted a Roddenberry *Genesis II* story idea to the *Star Trek* format. "Robot's Return" dealt with a space probe returning to Earth after hundreds of years, and in search of its creator NASA. "In Thy Image" took this basic premise and placed it in the *Star Trek* universe, enlarging the overall threat along the way as Kirk and company must save the entire planet from this deadly machine.

"At that point," interjects Bob Goodwin, "they had spent about four years trying to get a script for a feature, but they couldn't come up with anything that Michael Eisner liked. We had various options on the two hour premiere [which would be released theatrically in Europe], and I suggested to Gene that since it had never been done in the series before, we should come up with a story in which Earth was threatened. In all the *Star Trek* episodes before, they never came close to Earth. 'In Thy Image' fit that criteria perfectly. I remember that one day we went into the administration building. In there was Michael Eisner, Jeff Katzenberg, Gary Nardino, me, Gene and a bunch of other people. In the course of that meeting, I got up and pitched this two-hour story. Michael Eisner slammed his hands on the table and said, 'We've spent four years looking for a feature script. This is it. Now let's make the movie.'"

The plan still called for a two hour television film, but no one in that room realized that the groundwork had just been laid down for *Star Trek: The Motion Picture.*

The Meeting

The atmosphere of that meeting, held on August 3, 1977, was a combination of joy and sobriety. On the one hand it was proof that *Star Trek* was very much alive in Paramount's eyes, and on the other it revealed how problematic resurrecting the show actually was.

Meeting with Michael Eisner, Jeff Katzenberg and other key executives, Gene Roddenberry stated at the outset that he expected to have up to ten scripts in development within a two week time period. Michael Eisner felt that their primary concern must be the two hour opening episode for the simple reason that it would kick off the new series and tap into the "enormous amount of worldwide potential in the first return of *Star Trek.* A February 1st answer print is vital, and the film must be superb."

While Roddenberry agreed with this, his general feeling was that the more stories they get into development, the wider their choice of an opening story. "The intention," he said, "is to give the best material to top established writers."

Michael Eisner, without hesitation, pointed out that he had no problems with paying whatever writing cost was necessary to insure the best possible script. He even went so far as to state a willingness to pay up to two hundred thousand dollars. Another concern was the lack of director, although Gary [*The Black Hole*] Nelson was being talked to, with Bob Collins as a backup.

Eisner continued to emphasize how important it was for them to meet the February 1st date, and for the story to be finalized so preproduction could begin.

"We'd be kidding you if I didn't say we have some problems on the February 1st date, but we're hoping to overcome them," Roddenberry explained.

"Look," Eisner responded, "I'm willing to go with a three million dollar budget, if the script is good enough. I'm not encouraging extravagance, but I am concerned that we meet the target date and the film be visually fabulous. We need a writer who can make the characters come alive, with a terrific director and a terrific story."

Changing the subject for a moment, Gene Roddenberry admitted that he was bothered by the idea of tailoring the opening script to both William Shatner and Leonard Nimoy, as the latter would not be a part of the regular series. "I'd prefer to eliminate Nimoy completely," he said.

Eisner disagreed, stating that it was absolutely necessary for them to have both actors reprising their original roles, and that they must be signed even at unreasonable figures.

"I don't agree," countered Roddenberry. "I can almost promise us that the excitement generated by the return of *Star Trek* with most of the original crew, aided by a publicity campaign to hype excitement over the new, different type of Vulcan, would cancel out any disappointment over Nimoy's absence."

The Paramount chieftain would not accept this. The actor, he insisted again, must appear in the film, even if only briefly during the opening scenes. Both Roddenberry and Goodwin agreed, feeling that it would be a preferable way of handling the situation, because it would satisfy audience demand while at the same time allowing them the freedom to work with the new story and characters.

As stated earlier, one of the reasons that Nimoy did not wish to appear on the series stemmed back to a lawsuit launched because the actor felt he should be compensated for the money Paramount was making from his likeness on *Star Trek* merchandise. Gary Nardino explained that a deal had been offered to the actor which would include the opening film, select episodes and a settlement of his lawsuit against them. In response, Eisner said that he would be willing to pay the actor up to $100,000 for three days work, but the deal with Shatner should be closed first so as to keep his cost down.

"It's understood," he added, "that there's no interest in him for the series, although we may have to make a pay-or-play PTS [Paramount Television Service] commitment as incentive for the two hour film."

Roddenberry again stated that he was concerned about making the February 1st date, and Eisner explained that he was attempting to generate money abroad on the property before it went to television. Approval was given to put thirteen scripts into work for series delivery in March 1978, but no series problems/deadlines should affect the two hour film.

"There is only one priority at Paramount," Eisner stated emphatically. "*Star Trek.*"

Bringing New Life To An Old Show

In attempting to bring *Star Trek* back to audiences of the 1970s, the show found itself saddled with one particular problem that had to be overcome in order for the series to work effectively.

"The original series had seventy nine episodes," points out Jon Povill, "and therefore a lot of things had already been done. I think the biggest challenge was coming up with things that weren't repeats of ideas which had already been explored. What we were definitely striving for on the show was doing things that were different, and I think by and large we were successful. That was the biggest challenge, coming up with things that were fresh, and were *Star Trek* as well.

"I think we were helped out tremendously by the new characters. It's something that the features really need at this point. Someone has to start taking over. I think it's absolutely essential. They're all good people and they're just right for their parts, but if you don't start setting something up here, they're going to start...no offense to anybody...dying off. The characters of Xon, Decker and Ilia would have helped in this area. We wanted characters that could go in new directions, as well as the old crew.

"I particularly liked Xon," says Povill. "I thought there was something very fresh in having a nice young Vulcan to deal with; somebody who was trying to live up to a previous image. That, to me, was a very nice gimmick for a TV show that was missing Spock. But we *never* wanted Xon to be a Spock retread. We wanted him to be somebody who definitely had his own direction to go in, and he had different failings than Spock. Also, he didn't have Spock's neurosis regarding his human half. As far as Xon was concerned, Spock had a distinct *advantage* in being half-Vulcan and half-human in the context of where he was, what he was doing and where he was working. If he was on Vulcan, it wouldn't have been an advantage, but to be living with humans, it really helped. Xon's youth was also very important and he would have brought a freshness that people would have appreciated.

"Ilia was sort of an embodiment of warmth, sensuality, sensitivity and a nice Yin to Xon's Yang. Decker, of course, was a young Kirk. I think he would have been the least distinct. He would have had to grow, and the performance probably would have done that, bringing something to Decker that the writers would have ultimately latched on to for material. He's the one who would have had to develop more through the acting and performance than the other two. Xon and Ilia were concept characters. They would have developed too, I'm sure, because characters grow when they're performed much more than they do from just the writing. In the early writing, you don't realize the full potential. You don't know who's going to play the character, how they're going to play it and what the characteristics of their performance are going to be. If you look at 'The Menagerie,' for example, Spock laughs."

On August 9th, Roddenberry responded to Alan Dean Foster's one hour treatment of "In Thy Image."

"The principal problem in your *Star Trek* story outline is certainly not lack of imagination," he pointed out. "Rather, I believe, most of my comments will bear upon control and selective use of that imagination. *Believability* of characters, incidents and scenes is much more critical in picture/sound science fiction than in printed. Most of our story problem seems to boil down simply to getting to know our alien machine character better. Its abilities, limitations, motivations, needs, and so on. With all that

established, it should then be much easier to build a tale which rises steadily in excitement and jeopardies (to the starship *and* to Earth) to a very exciting and satisfying climax."

Ironically, this problem would plague the script even after it had metamorphosized into *Star Trek: The Motion Picture*, and it was a thematic trap that no one could extricate themselves from.

While Alan Dean Foster took Roddenberry's comments to heart and began to expand his outline, *Star Trek II* was coming to life on the Paramount soundstages. On August 9, Bob Goodwin filed his first production report.

"Work is continuing on stage 9," he explained, "with construction of the Enterprise set. All frames and platforms have been built for the bridge...By tomorrow we will have a lay-out on the stage floor for the corridor and by the beginning of next week we will start framing and constructing the corridor walls. Joe Jennings has worked out most of the design problems of the engineering room and has started working on drawings which will be ready for you to see by the end of the week. The plan now for stage 8, which will be used as the planet set is to put in the ground row and the backing, but to leave the dirt out until we see if we need that stage space for any extra sets that might needed for our first show."

As all this was developing, production designer Joseph Jennings was in the midst of creating the interior of a starship which would be completely unlike the rather primitive looking sets of the original *Star Trek*.

"I had been working at Paramount," explains Jennings, "and the Production Manager of Television called me in and said, 'How would you like the assignment?' We started preparing and that was about it. It was as simple as that."

In attempting to upgrade the ship from the original series, he says that the idea was to make the mechanics of the starship much more sophisticated. "The bridge of the Enterprise was designed to go into series, so we were designing it to be all things to all people. As a result, all of the devices were practical and they worked off proximity switches. You didn't have to touch the

board, but simply had to reach toward it and whatever effect you were tripping would show up. This was not for one specific show. What you're being asked to do is design a set that will function for at least three years of shows, so we were being a great deal more sophisticated than perhaps we would have been were it laid out to begin with as a feature film in which there were a certain given set of actions that had to be performed on that set. Then you only build those things that operate properly.

"When you talk about series," Jennings elaborates, "you don't know down the line what you're going to need. As a result, I wrote an operations manual for the bridge, which was intended to be given to guest directors who would come in and would not be familiar with the set, but in a matter of several days would have to come up with a working knowledge of it. So all of the stations and every switch, button and light flash was all spelt out as to what it did and what it was supposed to be. It was an attempt on my part to make the operation of the ship consistent from show to show. As I say, all of that effort and energy when it became a picture was superfluous. To be specific, directors walk in on the bridge of a spaceship and want every damn light winking and blinking, and now you get your spaceship in trouble and the meteor is coming. What do you add to it that's going to look dramatic? Besides, if you look on the instrument panel of any comparable vehicle we know, all of those lights aren't blinking all the time. So I thought perhaps by being very specific in making the thing operable, we could get a little more believability into it from that point of view."

On August 16th Harold Livingston filed a "writers status report," noting that those assigned included Arthur Heinemann, Alan Dean Foster, James Menzies, Margaret Armen, John Meredyth Lucas, Worley Thorne, Shimon Wincelberg and Theodore Sturgeon. Of them, only Sturgeon would not ultimately deliver a story.

In addition, Livingston met with a total of seventeen other writers, of which only Bill Lansford had a story which fit *Star Trek* requirements. Entitled "Devil's Due," the producer noted that he and Roddenberry had met with the author "concerning a story with Faustian overtones, a Devil and Daniel Webster conflict and we expect to assign Lansford after a final meeting."

While these meetings did not bear much fruit, Livingston was still quite pleased at the way things were progressing. "We find that these initial meetings are beneficial to writers," he said, "because despite the writer's guide and the two scripts we usually give as representative *Star Trek* scripts, it is always helpful when the writers discuss face to face and we explain our problems, requirements, standards and specifications. With almost no exception, writers have recontacted us and/or have reacted enthusiastically."

He added that the search had begun for a writer to flesh "In Thy Image" out to script form. His first choice, Steven Bochco (*Hill Street Blues, L.A. Law*) was unavailable and would be for several months. Two other names being considered were British author David Ambrose (who would ultimately pen the "Deadlock" script for the proposed series) and science fiction veteran William Norton. An attempt to interest Michael Cimino was unfruitful, which is probably just as well. Imagine *Heaven's Trek.*

"The problem with many name writers," Livingston opined, "is that we do not want to involve ourselves in a situation where we will sign a writer who will be tempted to 'write down' to the story. We must have someone who is actively into science fiction, namely *Star Trek*, and will be so enthusiastic he will give us the very best he has.

"After four weeks of developing stories," he closed, "talking to writers, word has come back to us now and it is very interesting to note that *Star Trek* is considered the 'hardest sell in town.' It is also considered perhaps the most prestigious credit a writer can receive. This, needless to say, we consider very encouraging. The result has been that we are very selective in our story material, and we feel that the stories we now have in work are the best possible stories we could find. Our status now is that we have eleven hours assigned. This includes two 2-hour versions. This would leave us with two one hour openings. We have request-

ed the purchase of an additional five back-up hours, and are anxiously awaiting approval on this request."

Bob Collins, in the meantime, had been signed to direct the opening episode, and began to help in the screentest process to determine who would be most suited to portray the pair of alien characters, Xon and Ilia. He elected to begin with the Vulcan, and tested hundreds of actors in pointed ears before he spotted the one he felt most comfortable with to take over the science station from Mr. Spock.

"I found an actor named David Gautreaux to play Xon," Collins recalls. "He was a nice young man and a terrific actor, and all of that would have worked, although there was some concern over how people would react to the fact that there was no Spock."

That was a question which crossed quite a few minds.

The Man Who Would Be Xon

Although the general public may not be aware of it, actor David Gautreaux was a part of the *Star Trek II* company for over a year. In fact, plans still called for him to play the role even when the TV series metamorphosized into the first feature film. But then Leonard Nimoy was signed on as Spock, and Xon was dropped at Gautreaux's request.

"I was doing a play at the time," he reflects, "trying not to think that I was going to be playing an alien for the rest of my life. Then I spoke to Gene Roddenberry and said, 'What's the story? Did you see that Leonard Nimoy is coming back to play his character? What's going to happen to Xon?' He said, 'Oh, Xon is very much a part of the family and you're very much a part of our family.' I responded, 'Gene, don't allow a character of this magnitude to simply carry Mr. Spock's suitcases on board the ship and then say, "I'll be in my quarters if anybody needs me." Give him what I've put into him and what you've put into him. If he's not going to be more a part of it and more noble than that, let's eliminate him.' They continued with the idea of Xon for quite a while."

Gautreaux's involvement began

Actor David Gautreaux as Xon, the character designed to take over the science officer position from Spock in the Star Trek II *television series.*

when he screentested for the role with hundreds of others and was chosen for the part. This occurred several months before preproduction on *Star Trek II* had begun, thus scripts for the series had been written and preparations made for the two hour premiere movie.

Upon being announced as *Star Trek*'s newest Vulcan, he felt that there were two things that had to be done. The first was for Paramount to downplay his signing aboard, with a bare minimum of publicity. The second was that he purchase a television and learn what the phenomenon was all about. The actor explains his views on both points.

"I remember when I was first cast as Xon," Gautreaux reflects. "A fair amount of the fans reacted very strangely. Somebody recently told me that actors in soap operas place themselves in serious jeopardy if they antagonize the favorite character of the show. They, the actor on the street, can be the object of the fans' wrath. That does happen in this business. When *Star Trek II* was announced and I was essentially the replacement for Spock, I received some really strange letters from people saying, 'Don't drink the water,' or somebody was going to drop LSD in my Coca-Cola. It was like poison pen letters, because Spock was God to these people.

"I personally was never a fan," explains Gautreaux. "I never watched the show. I bought a television two weeks after I was actually signed for the role, because I was given an advance large enough to actually do something like that. I was a hard working, but not making money, kind of actor. I just thought I had better start watching the show and catching up with this incredible history. Much of the time I would watch the show and say, 'I don't get it,' not thinking of what it would have looked like if I had seen it in '67 or '68, and compared to it television of the time. It was so revolutionary, but to be looking at it in 1978 or 1979, I didn't think that much of it, although it did carry a large philosophical leap of faith that was wonderful for television."

Studying episodes very carefully, Gautreaux got a firm grasp of just what makes a proper Vulcan and began intensive preparations for the role of Xon, attempting to make him the quintessential representation of that particular race. One of his greatest motivations was the initial description of the character in the screenplay of "In Thy Image," where the Vulcan, smelling rather strongly, has just beamed aboard from a meditative monastery in the Gobi Desert.

"I actually went off on a meditative trek and fasted for ten days," Gautreaux says. "I allowed my hair to grow long, I started researching to be a Vulcan with no emotion. For an actor, that's death. I was looking at it from an actor's point of view, which is how do you appear as having no emotion without looking like a piece of wood? That was my acting objective, and I went to several acting coaches. Jeff Corey is the one who gave me the key of how I could actively play the pure pursuit of logic as being my primary action. Then I felt I needed a physical equivalent, and I followed the teachings of Bruce Lee, who taught about dealing with emotions and a freedom from emotions that allowed you to live in a non-violent world. That's really what he was all about, despite the impression his films gave. His methods, his trainings and his students existed in a nonviolent life. The way to do that was to not let anything 'stick.' If somebody hits you, it doesn't stick; it just flies through you. So with a Vulcan dealing with 'lame brain' human beings....if they said something particularly stupid, or, in the case of Doctor McCoy, something particularly

antagonistic, because of the training I had gone through, it would not have the stick effect. It would not attach itself. The idea is that a Vulcan is pursuing something much larger than what is around him at that moment.

"In all honesty, I was looking forward to playing Xon. His actions were tremendous. His strength without size, and the aspect of playing a full Vulcan. When I say that, I mean somebody who had a larger presence than, say, Spock's father, who was a full Vulcan. By presence I mean a more involved presence on the show and the running of the ship. It was a very exciting premise to be playing. To me, it was a potentially good gig that didn't work out."

Gautreaux, who, as stated earlier, requested that his character be eliminated rather than diminished, ended up playing Commander Branch of the Epsilon 9 space station in two scenes of *Star Trek: The Motion Picture*. Apart from that, he left the show behind, but has managed to retain the most positive aspects of Xon and his preparation for the role.

"I have found ways to put that training to use," he says. "I was an avid bowler at the time and a pretty consistent 160 or 170 kind of bowler. Using the principles of an actor working to become a Vulcan, increased my bowling to a consistent 220. The primary goal of a Vulcan is to always be removing his energy away from himself and onto the task, the pursuit of logic or the need of the other person who needs what you have to give them. So you're constantly removing the energy from yourself, thus freeing yourself from obstacles. This is what I learned from fasting. When we remove three meals a day plus snacking, get past the third or fourth day, which is the real hump stage, the next ten days are gravy. You can go on forever as long as you have some water and some freshly squeezed juices for necessary proteins now and again. But you are so clear. You ask for something, you know exactly what you're asking for. What you find is that human beings are not very good at dealing with straightforward requests. They always want to know about the grey area and the pink area; they don't want to just give you the black and white. That's what makes life very silly and full of jokes and

shenanigans and why things don't get done as well. Vulcans are like *Zen and the Art of Archery*. There's no such thing as a target. There's no such thing as an arrow. There's no such thing as a bow. Everything is one motion, and there's no such thing as hitting the target or not hitting the target, because the bow, the arrow and the target are all one. So in bowling, you remove at least fifty percent of the effort, which is to do things correctly, and concentrate on the game itself. That kind of concentration can be done on anything you do. I use it all the time."

David Gautreaux pauses for a moment, as though trying to make sure he's expressed the enduring influence of the Xon character throughout his professional and personal life.

"I have never personally felt badly, upset or any of those things for not playing Xon," he concludes sincerely. "I've always felt that it was too bad the public didn't get the chance to see this character, given the preparation I had given to it. But for how it enhanced my own life, they paid me a hundred fold. Xon took me from a state of physical to a state of metaphysical, which is something that I've never lost."

"In Thy Image"

On August 29, Harold Livingston presented a new writers status report, and noted that they had met some twenty odd writers.

"We have also received a large number of submissions from various writers, either in one or two page outlines, and in some cases full scripts," he said. "We have investigated most of these, none have really met *Star Trek* standards. They keep coming in and the response from writers is totally overwhelming. I have recently received a submission from Thomas Ardies, who has published a best selling novel, is a well known novelist and short story writer, and also extremely desirous of doing a *Star Trek*.

"Richard Bach," the producer continued, "the author of *Jonathan Livingston Seagull*, and the current best selling novel *Illusions*, is a *Star Trek* fan. He has submitted two stories, both of which were so eminently desirable, we purchased them. One story is a tale of a society whose people are, for the most part, repressed and annually release these emotions by viewing their star ships in combat with other star ships. It is a very entertaining and provocative story, and Bach had submitted a five page outline. Almost simultaneously, Art Lewis, a very accomplished writer, came in with a similar idea. It was decided to graft both of these stories and assign Lewis to develop the story and teleplay. At the same time, Bach's second story is, what we consider a truly representative *Star Trek* vehicle, about a kind of dream world where our crew members become actively and dangerously involved in the dreams of a lady who had been in suspended animation for 200 years, kept alive throughout that time with periodic dreams. Bach is now writing the outline and actually has requested we allow him to do the script first, and if we do not like the script we can drop the project. I encouraged him to write the traditional outline and we would proceed from that point.

"Alan Dean Foster delivered the final draft of the two-hour movie. We met with him extensively, discussed the story, made numerous revisions and I am now in the process of rewriting the first act which we all, in concert, consider too slow. We should have the story ready to show a screen-writer some time this week."

In early September, several treatments arrived at the *Star Trek II* offices, including Shimon Wincelberg's "Lord Bobby," William Lansford's "Devil's Due," the Margaret Armen/Alf Harris collaboration, "The Savage Syndrome," and John Meredyth Lucas' "Kitumba."

"Lord Bobby," which would eventually be retitled "Lord Bobby's Obsession," was a good attempt which incorporated an alien being, again something like Trelene in "Squire of Gothos," as well as the Romulans.

"Kitumba" had Enterprise travelling to the Klingon home world in an effort to avert a potential intergalactic war. This story would have made a wonderful "prequel" to the sixth *Star Trek* film, *The Undiscovered Country*.

"The Savage Syndrome" had Decker, McCoy and Ilia investigate a derelict vessel in orbit around a lifeless planet. On board, they find that the crew had been driven mad and killed each other

in particularly brutal and savage ways. In the meantime, a space mine detonates in the vicinity of the Enterprise, unleashing energy that affects the crew's neural impulses. Instantly, they, including Kirk, are transformed into savages, and it's up to the trio to set things straight again.

From a production standpoint, this episode would have been quite important for the simple reason that it was primarily a ship-board story, and therefore more cost effective than the average episode. This had been a problem that occurred during the run of the original series, and had been a constant one on *The Next Generation*.

On September 2, 1977, producer Bob Goodwin wrote, "...in order to do an effective job on our stories that take place in settings other than the Enterprise, and still remain within our financial and production limitations, it is absolutely vital that we have an equal number of ship-board stories....If we don't have some good Enterprise stories in our back pockets, we could find ourselves with very serious production problems comes December."

The memo specifically cited "The Savage Syndrome" as a perfect example. For instance, the first draft of the outline had Decker, McCoy and Ilia actually land the shuttlecraft on the surface of a planet, where they studied ancient ruins as well as "several other things they encounter." Goodwin made the suggestion that the shuttle be investigating an object in space; this way it "would confine our story, for the most part, to the Enterprise." The second draft of the outline made this adjustment.

Harold Livingston came up with the idea of using 23rd Century technology to fight back against the savages. "Wouldn't it be more exciting and interesting if either Decker or McCoy—or both—used their brains to outwit [them]?" he asked. "For example, they might use the viewing screens and other instruments to completely enthrall the savages, perhaps on a level of the old 'B' movies, where the white explorer, knowing the moon was due to eclipse, filled the natives with awe and dread when he promised to make the sky dark and (as the eclipse occurred) did!" Livingston was right, and the scene would have

played most effectively. In fact, a later draft had a scene in the rec room, where McCoy threatens to bring the wrath of the gods upon the primitives. On cue, Decker activates the proper controls and "the walls become a crashing ocean, the air filled with the thunder of the waves and wind. An instant later the ocean becomes a World War II battlefield— shells bursting, cannon fire, and the deafening shrieks of the wounded." From there, the image becomes a raging fire, earthquakes and so on.

These illusionary walls were probably inspired by Ray Bradbury's *The Illustrated Man*, and would eventually make it to *The Next Generation* in the form of the Enterprise's holodeck.

Writer Margaret Armen explains the genesis of the episode from her point of view: "Alf and I started with the *what if?* motif. There's an old saying, 'Scratch the man and the savage bleeds.' So, what if these people from this futuristic, very scientific civilization have something happen to them which strips them down to the basic emotions and drives of the cave? That was the line of thought we pursued."

"Devil's Due," which was rewritten as an episode of *The Next Generation*, essentially put Captain Kirk in the form of a defense attorney, vieing for the freedom of a planet in a struggle against what appears to be the devil. Jon Povill felt that this story worked very well and that it had "all the elements necessary for a very exciting, involving episode."

While things were shaping up nicely with the various stories coming in, the opening two hour episode was proving to be something of a problem.

"William Norton was engaged to write it," said Livingston, "but on September 5th he contacted me to say that after considerable agonizing he had reached a conclusion that he could not write a proper *Star Trek* script. Although this set us back considerably in time, I think that in the end his honesty and candor and professionalism will prove beneficial. I personally feel this supports my theory that most writers find it extremely difficult writing a *Star Trek* script unless they have been completely immersed in it for some time. *Star Trek* stories require special treatment, special handling; the writers really should be well acquainted with the nuance, characterization and various other colorations that make *Star Trek* stories the unique things that they are. This situation, needless to say, leaves us in a serious state, bordering on crisis. If we are to meet the November 1st production date it is essential we receive a script no later than October 1st. We have examined and re-examined and re-examined again the names of writers considered qualified to write this initial episode."

None seemed suited for the job, so as a solution to the problem, the plan called for Livingston to work on the script himself over the next few weeks. "It is a step not taken lightly," he added, "but as something we feel we cannot avoid and leaves us no choice other than to proceed in this manner."

As he dove into the first draft script of "In Thy Image," he managed to issue yet another writer's status report in which he explained that there were only three remaining stories to be filled, and that they were being very selective as to which ones they went with.

"All of the stories," he said, "that have come in present no great problems, but all seem to need some work to get them into second draft and subsequently into script. The 'emergency' situation we are faced with slows us up somewhat now in that I am involved writing the script and am unable to devote full time to story development. However, Jon Povill has been very helpful in this area and is keeping things balanced until I can get back to devoting my full attention to this."

Regarding the development of "In Thy Image," he felt that the script was turning out "extremely promising," and that the visuals would be spectacular and easily achieve the "big screen" effect that each of them had been looking for.

"The hour episode situation," Livingston concluded, "is, as I have stated above, somewhat uncertain because of this 'emergency.' Although we would prefer some time on the back, I think with some diligent efforts on all our parts, we'll be able to overcome the time problem and when the two hour episode is in production, we fully anticipate having enough

hour scripts to go forward immediately.

"In essence, then, everything is under control."

Not exactly.

Script Wars

By the time Harold Livingston had taken to writing "In Thy Image," the working relationship between he and Gene Roddenberry had begun to disintegrate...badly.

"I don't remember when I began to pierce the Roddenberry myth," Livingston says, "but he and I suddenly started to have creative differences. I resented his interference and he, apparently, wanted someone to carry his lunch around, and that wasn't me. We became socially friendly for a while, but in any case we started to have various difficulties. Out here they're called 'creative differences.' I just didn't think he was a good writer, and I didn't like the way he was doing some of the material. We developed these stories and somewhere along the line I began to get tired of having to go to him for approval of a story, because this wasn't my understanding of my function there. It's one of those things that no one wants to touch, because it could be a very serious problem. All you can do is ignore it and hope that the problem doesn't arise. Well, it did, and I began to commission stories without his approval."

Both creative talents weathered this rapidly intensifying storm for the next two months while plans were rapidly being laid out to bring "In Thy Image" to the television screen, with much attention going to the scripts which would fill up the rest of the first thirteen put into work.

As Livingston was wrapping up his first draft, talk began that the character of Decker would somehow be done away with in the next draft, as the general consensus was: "Who needs two Captain Kirks?" What had started out as a solid addition to the crew, was turning out to be something of a headache.

"I think it would be very beneficial for us to determine as soon as possible whether or not the character of Will Decker will continue or be eliminated," said Livingston just before handing in his script. "Every story in work and those also in script contain

Decker as a very integral character. If we're going to eliminate him, I think we had better move on it now to further save ourselves much unnecessary work re-writing, and writing around the elimination of that particular character."

Later, Arthur Fellows, head of television production, issued a memo to Gene Roddenberry in which he discussed his and Michael Eisner's feelings regarding the first draft script.

"The return of *Star Trek* is an event in itself," wrote Fellows, "and we believe that this script really incorporates the elements that will be an extraordinary send off for the next 'five' years. The action and basic story are well conceived. However, at this rough draft stage a problem exists throughout in the arena of character and relationships."

Fellows believed that through the course of the script we never really felt the enormous pressure that had been placed on Xon's shoulders, nor were we given the opportunity to see him win the respect of the crew. This situation, he felt, should be rectified in order for the public to accept this new and different Vulcan. In addition, the feud between McCoy and Xon (ergo, humanitarianism versus logic) should be dealt with more fully, filling the viewer with warm recollections of the McCoy-Spock relationship.

"In many ways we face a similar task with Decker," he wrote. "[If he's] going to be around for a long time, any intensifying of the emotions surrounding his existence and purpose on the ship will only aid in endearing him to all involved."

While feelings were strong regarding Ilia, it was generally believed that the character should not be bald. "Her baldness," pointed out the executive, "may really get in the way of the audience buying the intense relationship between Kirk and the woman. We would prefer to have Ilia with hair, keeping the bald girl but giving her some other function on the show." It seems that Gene Roddenberry had a somewhat similar struggle over twenty years ago, when network executives pleaded with him to get rid of "the guy with the ears."

"The storyline presented is quite special and extraordinary," he enthused, "but somehow the ending seems to be too 'small' when we consider what led up to it. The slow, steady build-up of excitement and tension as this story unfolds is so effective that the ending deserves to soar. Right now, it is a bit anti-climactic. The final dialogue and moment when Ilia has convinced Vejur to save the servo-units is too convenient."

"Robert Goodwin's theory about the ending," muses Livingston, "is that I just pissed it away because I was so disgusted with the situation. I think the truth is that I couldn't come up with an ending. I just couldn't do it. The problem was that we had an antagonist so omnipotent that to defeat it, or even communicate with it, or have any kind of relationship with it, made the concept of the story false. How the hell do we deal with this? On what level? Everything pretty much worked in the story until we got to the ending. We tried all kinds of approaches, including aesthetic, theological and philosophical. We didn't know what to do with the ending."

Jon Povill, on the other hand, did. "We knew we had to have a big special effects ending," he says. "The problem of what was going to happen at the end and why it was going to happen, was one that plagued the script from the very start. The original treatment had a showdown between Vejur (although it wasn't called Vejur at the time) and Captain Kirk in which he draws a droopy daisy. Vejur recognizes that there is great power and value in this droopy daisy and flies off. Real deep. Then Gene came up with the idea of the machine dumping its data into Decker, with a lightshow of all the information it had accumulated. We were going to get all this amazing, incomprehensible stuff that Vejur had accumulated in its travels across the universe, and, of course, nobody could come up with these images. So that didn't work.

"It was pretty much my contribution," Povill goes on, "to say that the reason for what was happening was that this thing needed to go on to the next plane of existence; that it was transcending this dimension and going on to the next. It then became logical that the machine would need that human element to combine with. It was the only thing that could have made sense."

As Povill notes, Gene Roddenberry's rewrite of "In Thy Image" featured

Vejur unloading its information into Decker, and then using the commander to transcend this dimension to enter another.

By the time early November 1977 came along, production of "In Thy Image" was scheduled to begin in just a matter of weeks. It seemed that nothing was going to interfere with Star Trek's return.

The Motion Picture

"Gene Roddenberry's values lay in his knowledge and experience. Now if he had imparted that and allowed the professionals to do their job, they might have had a picture. Rewriting was compulsive with him; he simply could not live with himself knowing that someone else was writing Star Trek," states Harold Livingston matter of factly. "In December of '77, Roddenberry and I were really at each other's throats. My contract was up around that time and I quit before they could fire me. I knew there were too many problems. The film was in preproduction, and they had gone back to basically what I wrote, with Collins as a writer, restoring much of what he had left out, but little of Gene's."

Interestingly, Livingston would ultimately quit the Star Trek project three times—and would eventually have to fight it out with Roddenberry concerning the screenplay credit on the film—but was always coaxed back by the Paramount brass. For the moment, however, he believed that he was leaving the realm of the 23rd Century behind him forever.

As the new year came in, so did the decision—though not an absolute one—to turn the Star Trek II television series into a feature film. Jon Povill, who had taken over the writers status reports after Livingston's departure, pointed out that "all the scripts that we have in hand are in very good shape, and should Paramount at some point decide to proceed with the series, I feel that we have here the nucleus of an excellent first season."

On January 19th, Jeff Katzenberg stated that "We are currently analyzing all of the aspects necessary to move forward with Star Trek II as a theatrical motion picture. Unfortunately, much information—premature and

potentially destructive to our long-range planning—already has leaked out to the media and the public. This has become most alarming, even though we are appreciative of such wide-spread interest in the project and aware of its future value to us [a classic case of understatement, considering that Star Trek has become a billion dollar industry for Paramount]. It therefore becomes imperative that no information regarding the film be given out at this time. I must emphasize how essential it is that information concerning this show not now be given out by those associated with it in any capacity. The project at its present stage can suffer seriously. And the success of a properly timed, well-coordinated future public relations campaign can be jeopardized."

The decision to produce Star Trek: The Motion Picture came about for a number of reasons. First of all, the three networks, fearful of any new competition, reportedly lowered their advertising rates, thus making it less viable for Paramount to begin their fourth network.

Second, not only had Star Wars been released and become an unprecedented phenomenon, which had convinced Paramount to do the new series as opposed to a film in the first place (believing that their opportunity had come and gone); but Steven Spielberg's Close Encounters of the Third Kind found box office life as well, thus proving that science fiction most definitely could appeal to movie audiences of the 1970s and '80s.

"It was a combination of things," said Gene Roddenberry in regards to the decision to make a feature film as opposed to a new series. "Five years ago, Paramount began looking at the remarkable rerun of the Star Trek series—and they began to say, 'Well, gee, maybe we do have something here.' And it resulted in, four years ago, my checking into the studio with the idea of putting together a Star Trek feature. At the time, the plan was just to do a modest-budget feature; and they were convinced they had a sufficient audience. But we couldn't come up with a script that Paramount really liked. Paramount wasn't that much into science fiction at the time. I think a lot of studios at the time had a rather simplistic view of science fiction—rocket ships and blasters and high adventure—the kinds of things that, really, you saw in *Star Wars*, though probably with a few more half-nude women. I just wasn't interested in doing a space pirate type of show—a film is just too great an exertion of time and energy. The concepts I was working in and trying to get by at the same time had some fairly complex and, I thought, daring thematic material. And that just kind of shook them up, because they weren't thinking of science fiction as being a really heavy thematic thing. We finally ended up starting to do it as a spectacular for television to open up a new series. But about that time, *Star Wars* did come along and showed that there was, indeed, not only the audience that they thought might be there, but a rather unusual-sized one at that. They have been moving toward it for a number of years. Not fast enough to suit me, nor with a large-enough budget, but they were moving."

"When 'In Thy Image' became a feature," adds director Bob Collins, "we were given a budget of about eight million dollars. Somewhere around that time we were talking about special effects. Roddenberry and I went down to the Pacific Theatre and sat down for what I think was a noon performance of *Close Encounters*. We came out and were both pretty blown away by the film. I turned to him and said, 'Well, there goes our low budget special effects.' After *Star Wars* and *Close Encounters* you couldn't do those kind of special effects anymore. That meant a whole new thinking and a whole reorganization of the production and concepts. They needed a great deal more money and time, and there were only a few people who could do it. We spoke to John Dykstra and Robert Abel, and they chose Abel. So he came on board and decided that he would make it into a Robert Abel production. His budget, which had originally been one or two million dollars, suddenly jumped to seven and ten million dollars. The budget kept rising, and Paramount was getting more and more nervous as it kept pumping more and more money into it."

As the budget on the film rose, Collins began to suspect that his time with the project was limited. What he did not know, or expect, was a political back-stabbing by some of those involved.

"We were preparing to make this picture," he says, "but the writing was on the wall. I was a television director who had not done a feature film at that time. It was kind of evident that they were going to hire somebody who was used to working with big budget special effects. Paramount wasn't brave about such things, so I called up Jeff Katzenberg and said, 'You're going to replace me, right?' He said, 'No, Bob, never. Take my word for it, Bob. Trust me.' Then my agent, who at that time handled Robert Wise, called up and said, 'Look, we've got an offer for Robert Wise to replace you on the picture.' Apparently Paramount couldn't remember that we both had the same agent, so I called up Jeff again and said, 'Look, are you going to replace me?' He said, 'Absolutely not. Never. You're absolutely staying with the project.' I pointed out that Robert Wise and I had the same agent, so he said, 'If Robert Wise doesn't do it, then you are absolutely going to do it. ' I kind of laughed about that for a while. I knew it would happen sooner or later. They wanted to get somebody in place before they fired me. So they got Wise, and the first step was to redecorate my office.

"I was more angry about the way it happened. I could understand them wanting someone else when the budget escalated to twenty million dollars, but I wish they would have been nicer about it and said, 'Look, these are the facts of the situation.' But Paramount's not the only place in town that works that way either. I was angry at Katzenberg. Anyway, and this isn't sour grapes, but I never really thought the film did all that it could do. It wasn't as good as it could have been. This is not against Robert Wise, because given the circumstances, I don't know how anybody could have done. But I didn't think the script was very good in any case."

He's quick to add that any anger he felt was not really directed at Gene Roddenberry.

"Gene would often say about the script, 'This isn't *Star Trek*,'" Collins reflects. "One could argue that it may not be *Star Trek*, but it's good. At the same time, you had to realize that on a human

level, on a personal level, that he was wrapped up in it. His whole way of defining himself was involved with the series and with this project. I don't think any of us ever felt very angry at him. We all wanted to help him realize his ambition, and we wanted to make a good picture too. Paramount was kind of holding a gun to his head, saying that they were going to do it, and then they weren't going to do it. That tension, I think, flowed through all of us. I'm not sorry about calling somebody an asshole if that's what I think they are, but I liked Roddenberry and I always felt sympathetic towards him and the project."

So Bob Collins left the film, with actor David Gautreaux (as detailed earlier) soon to follow. At that time, casting had been going on for someone to portray Decker, but this was put on hold for a time.

"They went with Robert Wise as director," offers Bob Goodwin as an explanation for why he never cast the role. "Gene and I were never really informed of what the steps of the deal were. It turns out that Robert Wise is used to getting producing and directing credit. Apparently he would not accept a producer, so Gene Roddenberry was moved to executive producer and I was asked by Gene and the studio if I would stay on as associate producer. I didn't want to spend a minute of my life doing that. I was an associate producer ten years earlier, and it was like taking a step backwards, especially facing two years of production. So I left.

"What really upset me about all this," he seems to be punctuating each word, "is that at the same time I had a pilot that had gotten a go ahead. I had developed it under the Playboy job. It was a wonderful script, but I was having severe problems with the director, who was shooting down in New Orleans. I was the executive producer and had hired a producer, but no one was watching the store down there. The dailies were coming in and they were just terrible. So I wanted to go down there and try to pull it together, because I saw the handwriting on the wall, but the guys at the feature department threatened that if I went down to New Orleans, they would take me off the picture. At the same time, they were negotiating a deal that would

• • • •
95

have me off the picture anyway. So what ended up happening was that by the time I finally got word on the Robert Wise deal, I immediately got on a plane and went to New Orleans, but by that time it was just too late. So not only did I end up not doing the *Star Trek* film, but I ended up with a terrible pilot that did not sell. So there I was, literally out on the street. I came to work one day and they had taken my name off the door. My stuff was packed in boxes in the hall and the janitor told me I had to be off the lot in twenty minutes.

"That's the way they handled it," Goodwin concludes. "That's the kind of thing that can destroy you. I began to wonder, 'What did I do wrong?' Luckily, someone I knew with money had been waiting for me to leave Paramount, because he wanted to start a company with me. Thank God for small miracles."

Leonard Nimoy and Director Robert Wise at the press conference announcing *Star Trek: The Motion Picture.*

••••

CHAPTER EIGHT
Star Trek in the 1970's
An Episode Guide

Star Trek: The Animated Series

SEASON ONE
Episode #1:
"Yesteryear"
Written by Dorothy Fontana
Original Airdate: 9/15/73

Spock must travel backwards in time through the Guardian of Forever to discover why he no longer exists in the eyes of those in the present time frame. Arriving on Vulcan, he meets himself as a child and helps the young Spock through a rite of passage. The child is saved by his pet sehlat, but the beast is wounded in the struggle and, by young Spock's decision, must be put to sleep.

••••

"'Yesteryear' resulted from my looking back at the things we had done on the series and remembering the time portal from 'City on the Edge of Forever,'" states Dorothy Fontana. "I thought we could use that for a legitimate trip, but then have something happen so that Spock has to return to Vulcan to his childhood. We could probe into these characters and see the beginning of some of the trouble with Spock and Sarek, Amanda's problems back and then and part of what made Spock Spock. I also felt strongly about dealing with the death of a pet. It was a very serious thing for kids. We were trying to put across a lesson to children, that when it comes time for an animal to die, if he must go, it should be with dignity."

Episode #2:
"One of Our Planets is Missing"
Written by Marc Daniels
Original Airdate: 9/23/73

An energy cloud that consumes planets that lie in its wake is threatening the population of Mantilles, and the Enterprise must devise a way to combat this threat before it's too late. Only after the starship is pulled within the cloud

does Spock come to the conclusion that it is actually an intelligent creature that can be reasoned with.

Episode #3:
"The Lorelei Signal"
Written by Margaret Armen
Original Airdate: 9/29/73

In this variation of "The Deadly Years," Kirk, Spock and McCoy beam down to a planet within the Taurean star system, where they are captured by a race of female aliens. These women are immortals who gain their life force from others by utilizing a special headband. The trio must find a way to counteract the effect of these headbands before they die of old age.

Episode #4:
"More Tribbles, More Troubles"
Written by David Gerrold
Original Airdate: 10/6/73

All of the elements of "The Trouble With Tribbles" are back, with Kirk and company running into and rescuing Cyrano Jones. Accompanying Jones, naturally, are tribbles, but supposedly a variation of the one that appeared in the live-action episode. These tribbles, he explains, have been genetically engineered *not* to reproduce. What the con man fails to mention is that the more quadrotriticale the tribbles eat, the *larger* they get. Added to this is Captain Koloth and his Klingon soldiers.

••••

This episode was originally to appear as a live-action *Star Trek*, but never did due to third season producer Fred Freiberger's reaction to "The Trouble With Tribbles."

"I went in there with the attitude of having to prove myself to the new producer," says David Gerrold. "I said, 'I know how well "Tribbles" turned out, I know I can do it, I've got my credential, and everyone who saw "Tribbles" loved it, the episode turned out well, I don't have anything to be embarrassed about, I don't have to prove myself.' I walk in, Freddy Freiberger is looking at me and his first words are: 'I saw "Tribbles" this morning,' because he was having episode screened for him. The polite thing to say is, 'Not bad,' or 'Well done,' or 'Good job.' His words were, 'I don't

like it. *Star Trek* is not a comedy.' From that point on, our relationship never recovered. I said, 'Well, Gene said he wanted a sequel,' and he said that he had no interest in it."

When contacted by Dorothy Fontana for the animated series, Gerrold resurrected the idea.

Episode #5:
"The Survivor"
Written by James Schmerer
Original Airdate: 10/13/73

A shape shifter dupes the Enterprise crew into believing its philanthropist Carter Winston, who has been missing for five years. Once on board, it transforms itself into Captain Kirk and takes the Enterprise into the Romulan neutral zone, where the vessel is quickly surrounded by enemy vessels. The shifter, we learn, is actually a Romulan spy.

Episode #6:
"The Infinite Vulcan"
Written by Walter Koenig
Original Airdate: 10/20/73

Arriving at the planet Phylos, the Enterprise discovers a giant being who is actually a clone of Dr. Starros Keniclius, a scientist who had existed during the earth's Eugenics Wars (discussed in the live-action episode "Space Seed"). It is Keniclius' intentions to clone Spock so that the duplicate of the Vulcan can serve as a peacemaker for different worlds. Kirk's arguments that the universe is basically at peace falls on deaf ears, and the captain must use all of his resources to convince the Spock clone that he is merely a copy, and that the original might be dying.

Episode #7:
"The Magicks of Megas-Tu"
Written by Larry Brody
Original Airdate: 10/27/73

When the Enterprise is brought into another dimension, the ship and her crew is rescued by a pan-like being named Lucien who, like all his people, is in possession of a variety of extraordinary, even magical, abilities. To use these powers is forbidden, and the people of Lucien's realm, the Megans, detect what he is doing, they put him on trial. As Captain Kirk defends Lucien during a

••••

trial, it becomes apparent that Lucien had once visited earth long ago in the past and may have been the inspiration for the legend of Satan.

Episode #8:
"Once Upon a Planet"
Written by Len Jenson and Chuck Menville
Original Airdate: 11/3/73

This sequel, in many ways a retread, of live action's "Shore Leave," has the Enterprise crew return to the planet where any wish can come true. Once again things go terribly wrong as the Keeper has died and no one is left in charge of the equipment.

Episode #9:
"Mudd's Passion"
Written by Stephen Kandel
Original Airdate: 11/10/93

Kirk, despite his better judgement, rescues Harry Mudd from a group of miners that he has attempted to con. No sooner has Harry beamed on board the Enterprise than all hell breaks loose when he lets Nurse Christine Chapel know about a love potion he has in his possession, which she proceeds to use on Spock. At first her attempt fails, but following a delayed reaction Spock falls madly in love with her and the potion's influence is felt all over the ship.

••••

Stephen Kandel, who had the distinction of writing the two Harry Mudd live action adventures, penned this animated spin-off as well. "Dorothy Fontana just called me for a script. It was as simple as that," he says. "Animation is great because you direct as well as write. You could go anywhere and do anything."

Episode #10:
"The Terratin Incident"
Written by Paul Schneider
Original Airdate: 11/17/73

When the Enterprise investigates a mysterious distress signal, the starship is struck by a lightning bolt. As a result, all organic matter on the vessel begins to shrink in size. Needing to do *something* before it's too late, Kirk and a landing party beam down to the source of the distress signal and discover a miniature city which is threatened with destruction when their planet explodes. The only way they could elicit help was to infect the crew of the Enterprise with the same "disease" that affected them. The true hero of the day turns out to be the Enterprise transporters, which are able to restore everyone to their natural size.

••••

"The 'Terratin Incident' was based on a one-paragraph story idea that Gene Roddenberry had," explains writer Paul Schneider. "I took it from there with Dorothy Fontana, the show's associate producer. I just loved the concept of doing something related to *Gulliver's Travels*. I enjoyed that, as well as watching the process of the animation develop. Overall, I thought the episode turned out rather well."

Episode #11:
"Time Trap"
Written by Joyce Perry
Original Airdate: 11/24/73

The Enterprise gets trapped in the Delta Triangle, an intergalactic version of the Bermuda Triangle, which has become something of a graveyard for vessels which have disappeared, representing such diverse races as the Klingons, Gorns, Romulans, Kzin and Vulcans. What Kirk and the crew are shocked to discover is that the descendants of the crews of these various vessels are still alive, and have formed something of a government under the umbrella title "The Elysian Council." Escape from the triangle is deemed impossible until Kirk and Klingon captain Kor (who went up against Kirk in the live-action "Errand of Mercy") realize that they have to work together to discover the key to this elusive puzzle.

Episode #12:
"The Ambergris Element":
Written by Margaret Armen
Original Airdate: 12/1/73

While underwater exploring the world of Argo, Kirk and Spock are rendered unconscious. When they come to they discover that they are now water-breathers, as they've been surgically altered by the race that exists here, the Aquans. These beings believe that Kirk and Spock have come in peace, which is why they have bestowed this "gift" upon them. But when Scotty leads a rescue team, the Aquans suddenly believe they're under attack and their benevolence takes a dark turn.

••••

Admits writer Margaret Armen, "I didn't really see how an animated series could work, but they have marvelous artists at Filmation. Dorothy Fontana was the story editor and she approached me. I thought it would be fun. She said the main difference is that for the artists' sake, you must describe every scene and every action in great detail so that the artists will know what to draw. Both of my episodes were fun to write, and I enjoyed doing them."

Episode #13:
"Slaver Weapon"
Written by Larry Niven
Original Airdate: 1215/73

While transporting a Slaver stasis box (created by a race that once ruled the galaxy), Spock, Sulu and Uhura are attacked by the cat-like Kzin race who wish to possess the device. Intrigue piles upon intrigue as the box passes from hand to hand, until the Kzin results in the destruction of their own people.

Episode #14:
"Beyond the Farthest Star"
Written by Samuel A. Peeples
Original Airdate: 12/22/73

Enterprise is captured by the gravity of a black hole known as Questar M-17. There they discover a starship whose sole occupant is a evil, and formless, creature that had been stranded there by those who had built the ship. It manages to take control of the Enterprise and only after Kirk and Spock convince it that they intend to destroy the vessel and everyone on board does it release its grip.

••••

Samuel A. Peeples, who also wrote the second live-action *Star Trek* pilot, "Where No Man Has Gone Before," notes, "Dorothy Fontana used to be my secretary when I was at Universal. She was nineteen or twenty years old. I think I bought her her first legal drink on her twenty first birthday. She was hired as the Associate Producer. She called and said, 'Gene suggested that since you had done the pilot for the original *Star Trek*, maybe you'd like to do the pilot for the

••••

animated *Star Trek*.' And that's what I did. I did the pilot and it was aired later on. The *Variety* review was absolutely incredible. As far as the inspiration for the story, I don't have the vaguest idea. It seems to me that I was trying to say that it would be interesting if there was a space ship which was actually a living creature. It's alive, but it is used to going from one planet to another. They did great animated stories, and they didn't write down to children, by and large. There were a couple that were, obviously, designed for the younger market, but most of them were quite mature."

Episode #15:
"The Eye of the Beholder"
Written by David Harmon
Original Airdate: 1/5/74

While searching for the survivors of a missing starship, Kirk, Spock, McCoy and Scotty are captured by the slug-like race of Lactra VII and put into cages as exhibits in a zoo. It is only after Spock mind melds with a child Lactran that the race realizes they have captured an intelligent species.

Episode #16:
"Jihad"
Written by Stephen Kandel
Original Airdate: 1/13/74

Kirk and Spock are among the beings contacted by the Vendala, supposedly the first race ever to venture into outer space, to take part in a mission to recover the stolen brainwave pattern of Alar. This being (Alar) is the one who transformed the Skorr from a war-like race to one of peaceful benevolence. If the brainwave pattern is not restored, then a holy war (jihad) will take place throughout the galaxy.

••••

"'Jihad' was an idea I'd had for a long time," explains Stephen Kandel. "It was a message story and difficult to sell on network television. Network executives would have said, 'My God, what are you doing? That's a message story!' I jumped at the opportunity to drop it into a *Star Trek* format, which we did, and it worked very well. In fact, I won a humanitarian award for it."

Episode #17:
"The Pirates of Orion"
Written by Howard Weinstein
Original Airdate: 9/7/74

When Spock contracts a strain of choriocytosis, Kirk has three days to rendezvous with the S.S. Huron, a vessel equipped with the antidote for this disease. Enroute, however, the Huron is boarded by an Orion pirate ship which steals its cargo. Kirk must recover the cure before time runs out.

Episode #18:
"Bem"
Written by David Gerrold
Original Airdate: 9/14/74

Bem, an observer from the planet Pandros, is on board the Enterprise. Unbeknownst to Kirk, Bem is trying to determine whether or not the Federation is an alliance worthwhile for his world to be a part of. To learn the truth, he manipulates a series of circumstances which leads a landing party down to Delta Theta III, where a female voice—claiming to be a god—warns Kirk and company away. When Bem disappears, Kirk must live up to his responsibility to find the being despite the risk to himself and his ship.

Episode #19:
"Practical Joker"
Written by Chuck Menville
Original Airdate: 9/21/74

When the Enterprise inadvertently enters Romulan territory, Kirk tries to elude Romulan warships by entering an energy field. This field turns out to be alive as it proves by taking over the ship's computer and begins launching one practical joke after another.

Episode #20:
"Albatross"
Written by Dario Finelli
Original Airdate: 9/28/74

When the Enterprise delivers medical supplies to Dramia II, Dr. McCoy is arrested and charged with the murders of millions of inhabitants. It seems that nearly twenty years earlier the doctor had been part of a medical team chosen to vaccinate the populace against a Saurian virus. Shortly after that team left a plague broke out that wiped out most of the population. Now McCoy will stand trial for the crime he is accused of. Complicating Kirk's attempts to free him from prison is the spread of the virus onboard the Enterprise.

Episode #21:
"How Sharper Than a Serpent's Tooth"
Written by Russell Bates and David Wise
Original Airdate: 10/5/74

In this storyline, which is extremely similar to the live-action "Who Mourns for Adonais?", the Indian god Kulkukan captures members of the Enterprise as it has done other species from around the galaxy with the intent that they worship him as a god just as the people of earth did thousands of years earlier. He has about as much success as Apollo did in the earlier version.

Episode #22:
"The Counter-Clock Incident"
Written by John Culver
Original Airdate: 10/12/74

Enterprise first captain, Robert April, is being transported by the starship to his retirement ceremony. The ship is accidentally plunged into a nova where everything works in a counter-clockwise way, resulting in the people aboard the Enterprise growing younger to the point where they are children. April, now a 30 year old man, takes command and must get the starship out of this dimension before it's too late.

STAR TREK II
(The Television Series)

Episode #1:
"In Thy Image"
Written by Harold Livingston

In many ways, this is *Star Trek: The Motion Picture* sans Spock. The newly refitted starship Enterprise sets out to combat the mysterious energy cloud that has been destroying vessels and is on a direct heading for earth. Captain James T. Kirk, Dr. McCoy, Scotty, Sulu, Uhura and Chekov are joined by first officer Commander Decker, science officer Lieutenant Xon and navigator Lieutenant

••••
99

Ilia as the discover the truth behind this enemy: it is actually an ancient earth space probe enroute to its home world in search of its creator.

Episode #2:
"The Child"
Written by Jon Povill
and Jaron Summers

The Enterprise passes through a mysterious cloud. As it does so, an energy form penetrates the starship's hull and proceeds to Lieutenant Ilia's quarters. A glow envelops her entire body and she begins to moan with pleasure. When she awakens the next morning, she informs Dr. McCoy that she's pregnant.

Within three days Ilia gives birth to a beautiful girl, who begins to age rapidly. In a matter of hours she is ten years old and growing older. While McCoy tries to discover what's happening, the Enterprise is afflicted with one near-disaster after another, every one of which is averted at the last possible moment by the child (named Irska, which, in Deltan, means "bright light"). Kirk learns that the molecular structure of the Enterprise's hull is breaking down and will turn to dust in a matter of hours.

Xon performs a Vulcan mind-meld on Irska and learns that she must be transported directly into a bright light which has been following the ship. This is done and the hull's breakdown is instantly reversed.

Kirk and company conclude that in some strange way Ilia served as Irska's first womb, while the Enterprise served as the second. The aliens had arranged it so that the child would learn all about human emotions, wants, needs and the ability to make sacrifices for loved ones, before it metamorphosized into a higher life form.

••••

This script, which was eventually rewritten as an episode of Star Trek: The Next Generation, holds a special place in writer Jon Povill's heart.

"One of the keys to me becoming story editor on Star Trek II was that 'The Child' had to be written in a week," Povill recalls with a laugh. "I had Jaron Summers do a first draft and then I had to do a pretty complete rewrite. It had to get into shape for shooting, and the way that

script came out would determine whether or not I could be the story editor."

He got the job.

Episode #3:
"The Savage Syndrome"
Written by Margaret Armen
and Alf Harris

Decker, McCoy and Ilia investigate a derelict vessel in orbit around a lifeless planet. On board, they find that the crew had killed each other in brutal and savage ways. But why?

Meanwhile, a space mine detonates near the Enterprise, unleashing an energy which attacks the neural impulses of the crew and transforms them into savages. Primitive forces drive their every move. Decker, McCoy and Ilia return to the Enterprise to try and reverse the mine's effects before the starship and her crew are destroyed.

••••

Notes writer Margaret Armen, "Gene Roddenberry was very close to the show. Alf and I went in with three stories, and in the end it was 'The Savage Syndrome' that he liked, because he was looking for Star Trek stories that were really different."

Episode #4:
"Practice in Waking"
Written by Richard Bach

The Enterprise comes upon a sleeper ship with only a single passenger. Scotty, Decker and Sulu beam over to investigate and discover a woman in suspended animation. Scotty accidentally touches a control panel and the three collapse to the deck, only to reawaken in ancient Scotland without memory of their lives aboard the starship. In the past, they meet with the same woman and protect her from the mobs who claim that she is a witch.

On the Enterprise, McCoy discovers that Scotty, Sulu and Decker's life signs are growing progressively weaker. His prognosis is that the longer they remain in this dreaming-state, the closer they come to actually dying. Kirk and crew must somehow awaken them before they drift off into final sleep.

••••

Producer Harold Livingston noted at the time, "Getting Richard Bach

to work on Star Trek is a real score for the show. His story should make one hell of an episode."

Livingston's assessment was common among the staff. Despite never making it to script form, "Practice in Waking" was one of the most popular story ideas among the Star Trek II crew. They felt that Richard Bach would add a certain amount of class to the series and pave the way for new directions.

Episode #5:
"To Attain the All"
Written by Norman Spinrad

While trapped in another dimension, the Enterprise is boarded by a blue-skinned alien who refers to himself as The Prince. He tells Kirk and the others that if they prove worthy, mankind will be the recipient of the ultimate gift: the attaining of the "All."

Kirk reluctantly accepts the demand that Decker and Xon, representative of their respective species, be the ones who'll attempt to unlock the Prince's secret. If Kirk refused, the starship would never be allowed to return home. The duo appear in a maze-like structure within a planetoid and are told that their goal awaits them at the other end. They proceed, and at mid-journey take note of a bizarre switch in personality traits: Xon utilizes human intuition while Decker applies Vulcan-like logic to problems.

They ultimately reach the other end of the maze and the glowing spheres that await them. Xon reaches out to touch it and his mind is assaulted by an energy unlike any encountered before. Then, with the Vulcan serving as a conduit, the alien intelligence within the sphere begins spreading its influence through the Enterprise. It rapidly possesses the majority of the ship's crew and engineers a permanent switch of personality traits. It's soon obvious that they're all becoming part of a single mind.

The intelligence inside the sphere plans to force the humans to merge with the All. The All, after acquiring physical bodies, could go deep into space and merge with all intelligent beings in the galaxy. The Prince believes this is fair, for even though humanity will lose its individuality, it will gain immor-

••••

tality. The price, naturally, is too high and it's up to Kirk (and eventually Decker) to save them.

Episode #6:
"The Prisoner"
Written by James Menzies

The bridge crew is understandably shocked when the image of Albert Einstein appears on the main viewscreen, requesting that the starship help him. Einstein explains that he and many other earth scientists were kidnapped and kept alive by a "storage battery" on an alien planet. While Kirk doesn't believe that he is truly speaking to Einstein, the captain's curiosity is aroused. He orders the ship to that world.

While the Enterprise is in orbit, six scientists from earth's past (circa the early 20th century) appear in the transporter room. Xon is quick to discern that they aren't living beings, but rather highly realistic illusions. Now aware of the trap they've been caught in, Kirk orders the Enterprise to break orbit. The ship cannot. Beaming down to the planet, the captain comes face-to-face with Logos, the alien behind the charade. His goal is to assume the identity of all human life, beginning with Kirk and his crew. This, Logos feels, is only fair considering that humanity is such a savage race, constantly living under the threat of nuclear annihilation. Kirk counters that the earth Logos speaks of is ancient history. The alien refuses to believe this, insisting that man will never change.

A battle of wills between the Enterprise crew and Logos follows, with the destiny of humanity hanging in the balance.

Episode #7:
"Tomorrow and the Stars"
Written by Larry Alexander

Due to a transporter malfunction, Kirk is sent back in time to Pearl Harbor in 1941—mere days before the Japanese attack. At first he materializes in a ghost-like state, unable to touch or be touched by anything.

Kirk meets Elsa Kelley, a woman unhappy with her marriage to career-Army husband Richard. Initially frightened by Kirk's appearance, she ultimately tries to accept his story.

Meanwhile, Xon and Scotty attempt to "yank" Kirk back to the Enterprise. That fails but does have the effect of making him solid again. This in turn leads to Kirk and Elsa falling deeply in love. The dilemma arises of whether or not Kirk should alter history by warning her of the imminent Pearl Harbor attack, or merely depart with Decker and Xon when they locate him.

••••

An interesting moment in "Tomorrow and the Stars" occurs shortly after the transporter malfunction, when the ghost-like Kirk screams out, "Xon, what have you done to me?" This line seems to indicate Kirk's bitterness that Xon isn't Spock.

"Oh yeah," laughs writer Larry Alexander, "but that's only because I was able to take it one step further. In other words, Xon is not Spock even though I considered him Spock from a character point-of-view. So there is a little resentment there. It seemed the 'logical' thing to do."

This script began when Gene Roddenberry gave Alexander "The Apartment," a story he had written for the aborted Genesis II series. Alexander came up with "Ghost Story," in which Kirk and the landing team arrive on a planet that lies in ruin. There they discover highly advanced technology but no sign of a living civilization. Kirk enters a science lab and is projected backwards in time. He encounters a pair of scientists who have developed a device to scan the mind. On a human, however, it operates quite differently.

Hooked up to Kirk's brain, the machine causes him great agony. The demons from within his mind, the Id, materializes and destroys all life on the planet (resulting in the destruction the crew finds in the beginning).

Alexander freely acknowledges the debt that "Ghost Story" owes to Forbidden Planet, but points out that it goes beyond that film.

"I thought it was a wonderful story idea to have Captain Kirk responsible for the death of a planet," he enthuses, "and it's the one step beyond Forbidden Planet that had never been dealt with. It makes it much more human

and, to me, much more of an interesting irony. That's the kind of material I think is interesting and I was shocked when Gene Roddenberry said he didn't want to go with it."

It's suggested that saddling Kirk with a planet's death wasn't the right thing to do to such a heroic series character.

"In effect it wasn't his doing," Alexander differs. "He asked them not to do it. I was very strict about that. He didn't volunteer to do this, and when he realized what was going on, he did everything possible to stop it. All of that, I think, holds up on that basis. I was thinking very strictly about what happened to Kirk in many episodes where things didn't turn out the way he hoped. That's what makes Star Trek so wonderful. As heroic as Kirk was, through no fault of his own, hard choices had to be made. In Harlan Ellison's story ['City on the Edge of Forever'], Kirk has to allow Edith Keeper to die. It's a gulp at the end of the show, and it's like that when the people of this planet find that it's his demons which have destroyed their world, not theirs. It makes it that much more ironic."

Roddenberry preferred instead that Kirk go back to earth's past and chose Pearl Harbor as the time and place.

"It seemed a very obvious choice," muses Alexander. "Pearl Harbor is good, though, because you can use footage from various war films, which would work. But I didn't want to have the responsibility, because the story works as a story. It's like sending somebody back in time to kill Hitler in the crib, and he does it. The only irony you can have is his coming back and them saying, 'Why didn't you kill Kowalski like we asked you to?' History would be the same, but somebody else would do the job."

Episode #8:
"Devil's Due"
Written by William Lansford

Responding to a distress signal from a solar system "that shouldn't exist," the Enterprise arrives at Neuterra. Kirk, Xon, McCoy, Sulu, Ilia and Chekov beam down to the surface. They find a paradise, and a profound sadness amongst its people.

Meeting with the world's most blessed member, Zxoler, Kirk comments on the planet's beauty. The elderly man announces that all life on Neuterra will be destroyed in 20 days, which is the reason for the distress signal. One thousand years earlier (when Zxoler was a young man), the people had reached a point where their science outreached their wisdom to control it. As a result, the planet was ecologically raped and their civilization on the verge of extinction. Then, a being identifying itself as Komether appeared in answer to their prayers. It promised them 10 centuries of prosperity in exchange for their planet at the end of that time.

Unfortunately the prosperity of the planet extinguished the civilization's desire to develop. They never came up with a way to leave their world, choosing instead to enjoy paradise. Now their time is almost up.

While Kirk feels sympathy for their plight, he points out that the Enterprise is not equipped to transport more than a handful of extra passengers; any additional aid would arrive too late. Kirk then finds himself, as a representative of the Federation, defending the planet in a trial against Komether, who just might be the Devil himself. The captain suspects this demon may have been created from the Neuterrans' mind.

••••

In Jon Povill's opinion, "Devil's Due" could "work very well. It had all the elements necessary for a very exciting, involving episode."

"This was essentially 'The Devil and Daniel Webster'," said Harold Livingston. "The story has been developed to a point where we all feel it will be a most exciting *Star Trek*."

"Devil's Due" was later rewritten as an episode of *Star Trek: The Next Generation*.

Episode #9:
"Deadlock"
Written by David Ambrose

Commodore Hunter informs Kirk that the Enterprise will partake in war game activities. The captain is to take orders from Starfleet Science Advisor Lang Caradon. Knowing the man's reputation, McCoy points out that the tests will likely be an experiment in behavior control. This does not please Kirk.

Continuing games of manipulation ensue, culminating in a very real near battle-to-the-death between the starship and Starbase 7. Kirk, Decker, McCoy and Xon beam over to the base to see what they can do to prevent the imminent destruction. They ultimately discover that key Starfleet personnel, including Hunter and Caradon, have been replaced by alien beings. They reveal that the Federation is approaching their territory, which concerns them deeply. It's their intention to create hostilities among humans so that they'll eventually destroy themselves and never infect the aliens' part of the galaxy. Kirk must defeat this scheme while convincing the aliens that the Federation poses no threat.

••••

"David Ambrose is a British writer whom we had at one time considered for the two-hour premiere," explained Harold Livingston "His story, 'Deadlock,' concerns the Enterprise and a starbase involved in war games which turn out to be much more serious and which truly test the mettle of all our characters, our procedures and the bravery of our Enterprise crew. This should also be an extremely exciting story."

The concept of "gods" striking against man—an old standby used by Gene Roddenberry—may have been added to the story at the request of others. Ambrose's earlier treatment, "All Done With Mirrors," offered the same story with a different resolution. In this scenario, Caradon belongs to an underground organization which plans to overthrow the Federation. The struggle between a flagship and a starbase was just one of many accidents triggered by "dedicated fanatics" in key Starfleet positions, all pledged to sacrifice their lives for the cause.

Episode #10:
"Lord Bobby's Obsession"
Written by Shimon Wincelberg

Starfleet sensors detect a possible penetration of the Neutral Zone by a Romulan vessel. The Enterprise is ordered to investigate. At the Zone, they encounter a smaller ship and a humanoid who identifies himself as Lord Bobby, actually Lord Robert Standish, the Earl of

Lancashire, kidnapped from earth by aliens at the beginning of the 20th century. Somehow, these vanished aliens made him immortal. Bobby is thrilled to be among humans again.

As soon as the visitor boards the starship, five Romulan vessels surround and fire upon the Enterprise. They disable the warp drive. Kirk must convince the Romulans that the Enterprise isn't on a hostile mission, while at the same time dealing with the potential threat of Lord Bobby. An examination by Dr. McCoy reveals Bobby as an alien whose real purpose is unknown.

Episode #11:
"Are Unheard Melodies Sweet"
Written by Worley Thorne

A landing party arrives on the surface of a planet within the Haydes star cluster. It searches for the remains of the USS St. Louis, which reportedly crashed there. Xon locates the ship's log and, via tricorder, learns that the crew had been afflicted by a strange delirium from the planet and had piloted the ship into the atmosphere.

Decker mysteriously disappears while the Enterprise crew contracts the disease. Kirk must return to the ship while still attempting to locate Decker. The commander is held prisoner by an alien race with illusionary abilities, who force him to live out one sexual fantasy after another. Their lives exist only within illusions, which has resulted in their world falling into ruin. They face extinction and that's where the Enterprise personnel come in. The aliens plan to "manufacture" hormones to enhance their dream worlds and prolong their race. The earthlings serve as suppliers.

Kirk and his crew eventually learn that this race had once been extremely savage, but by focusing on the unreal they suppressed their true nature. Fantasy sex fills a void in their lives, but they no longer produce the necessary hormones. As a result, their old aggressions are returning.

Kirk must resist temptation and rescue Decker while McCoy (again) searches for a cure to the rapidly spreading disease.

••••

"Working on *Star Trek* was

something I very much wanted to do," says writer Worley Thorne, who would ultimately pen the "Justice" episode of *The Next Generation*. "I began my career the year that the original show started and I felt as though I missed out because I wasn't established enough to write for it. This was an opportunity to do something I had always wanted to do."

Episode #12:
"Kitumba"
Written by John Meredyth Lucas

The Enterprise embarks on a potential suicide mission to the Klingon homeworld to prevent an intergalactic war. Aided by a warrior named Ksia, who doesn't believe either side could survive such a conflict, they pass safely to the planet's surface. There they encounter the leader of the Klingon people, the Kitumba, a child destined for greatness.

Kirk does his best to convince the Kitumba that an invasion of Federation space would be disastrous for both sides. The captain seems to be winning the youth's confidence, but realize that there's no clear-cut way to end the potential war. The Enterprise crew falls into the midst of a power struggle between the ruler and his most trusted aides. That struggle will determine whether the ultimate war begins.

••••

"Kitumba" could easily served as a prequel to the feature film *Star Trek VI: The Undiscovered Country* in which the Federation and Klingon Empire begin the peace-making process.

Producer Harold Livingston had said at the time, "I think 'Kitumba' is very exciting, visually interesting and dramatic. It should be one hell of a show. [My notes] on it are really very minor, which illustrates the excellent flow of the story."

John Meredyth Lucas is justifiably proud of this particular effort. "I wanted something that we had never seen before on the series, and that's a penetration deep into enemy space. I then started to think of how the Klingons lived. Obviously for the Romulans we had Romans, and we've had different cultures modeled on those of ancient earth, but I tried to think of what the Klingon society would be like. The Japanese came to mind, so basically that what it was, with the Sacred Emperor, the Warlord and so on."

••••

CHAPTER NINE
Star Trek: The Movies

Paramount had never ceased to vacillate about the future of *Star Trek*, always fearful the phenomenon would abruptly end and leave them to foot the bill for an ill-advised "reunion" film or series. It wasn't until the back-to-back sucess of *Star Wars* and *Close Encounters of the Third Kind* that the studio realized there was an insatiable appetite for genre fare, thus the scuttling of the *Star Trek II* series one week before production was to commence.

When *Star Trek: The Motion Picture* was announced, Paramount Pictures envisioned it as a modestly-budgeted $15 million film. At a cost of about $5 million more than George Lucas had spent on *Star Wars*, it was imagined that the film could compete with that special effects extravaganza and win the battle hands down. Wrong! Conflicting visions, a special effects debacle that had the production begin with one F/X house then changing to others in mid-stream, and a scripting nightmare that resulted in much of the movie being shot without a completed third act, all combined to bloat the budget to $44 million, a budget only surpassed (at that time) by Twentieth Century Fox's *Cleopatra* and a Soviet screen version of *War and Peace.* Ironically, *Star Trek: The Motion Picture* reached theatres screens on December 7, 1979—Pear Harbor day. Based on the universal criticism it received, it appeared the film's release date was prophetic.

Star Trek: The Motion Picture was savaged by just about everyone, from reviewers to moviegoers drawn in by ten years worth of hype. The fans themselves were disappointed, though they were so desperate for *any Star Trek* that they turned the movie into a $175 million success and labored to have over an hour of truncated footage restored to a re-release in the hopes it would buoy the film. Although Paramount rejected the notion of a re-release in 70mm (the original hadn't been released in 70mm since

the final answer print had only been completed several days before the release date), they did include some deleted footage in the film's video release—another unprecedented sucess which helped launch the fledgling home video market.

David Gerrold, an integral part of the creation of the *Star Trek* spin-off *The Next Generation*, notes, "The fans had come off this two year high with *Star Wars* and the audience wanted more *Star Wars*, but there wasn't any more. So they went to see *Star Trek* and they were hungering for more, so *Star Trek* benefitted from the *Star Wars* phenomenon. They went and they saw it over and over again, but it was embarrassing to watch the fans because they were all apologists for this picture: 'Well, it's not that bad. It's a different kind of *Star Trek.*' Instead of really just acknowledging that it was a bad movie, they tried to explain that it was wonderful and you were an idiot for not understanding it. It was wonderful to watch them fuck their minds over to explain away a bad movie. The truth was that there was this movie that they wanted to love and they were so disappointed, but they wouldn't dare say that they were disappointed."

In fact, even *Star Trek*'s creator Gene Roddenberry, who had shepherded the film through production and been responsible for the endless rewrites that typified the shoot, couldn't defend the film from its detractors. Sitting next to Roddenberry on a plane heading towards the film's glamorous premiere in Washington D.C., Walter Koenig, who hadn't seen the movie, recalls querying the producer about the final product.

"Gene had just seen the cut and it was literally still wet," says Koenig. "I said 'What do you think of the picture?' He answered, 'It's a good picture.' It was a death knell, as soon as he said that I knew it wasn't going to work. He didn't put it down. He didn't denigrate it, but I heard it in his voice. I absolutely knew. Then you hope against hope that it's going to be good and you see the limousines and the red carpets and the spotlights. Then you see those first five minutes of the film with the music and you see V'ger and the destruction it causes. I got very excited but shortly thereafter I

began to become aware of time; that time was passing. That I wasn't involved in the picture. I was sitting in the audience and my heart sank and sank and sank, and I knew, ultimately, it was not a good film. I had no way of knowing what the critics would do. It was devastating, particularly *The Washington Post*, the first one that we saw the next day. It was the only time in my life that I thanked God for the relative anonymity that I had on *Star Trek*, because I was not mentioned in any way, shape or form."

The auteur theory notwithstanding, the individual who was saddled with the blame for *Star Trek: The Motion Picture*'s critical savaging was not its director, but producer/writer Gene Roddenberry who, although allowed to keep an office on the Paramount lot following the film's release, was considered a pariah and the prime reason that the film had spiralled overbudget and resulted in an aesthetically abysmal enterprise.

Yet when the film was originally announced, there was a great deal of enthusiasm and belief that the filmmakers would be creating a modern *2001*.

The Press Conference

"The fans have supported us and consistently written us to pull our act together," announced former Paramount President Michael Eisner to the press on March 28, 1978.

Apparently the studio had, for on that day Eisner made the announcement that production would soon begin on the long-awaited *Star Trek: The Motion Picture*, featuring the entire original cast, with series creator Gene Roddenberry serving as executive producer and Robert Wise handling the directorial chores. After 10 long years, the dream was about to become reality.

Highlights of the press conference, reportedly the largest since Cecil B. DeMille announced production of *The Ten Commandments*, included:

William Shatner on returning to the role of Captain James T. Kirk: "I somehow always felt that we would be back together. Regardless of what I was doing, or where my career was taking me at the moment, I knew Captain Kirk was *not* behind me. He still would be very

••••

Leonard Nimoy, DeForest Kelley, Stephen Collins, Persis Khambatta and William Shatner co-starred in the $44 million "epic", Star Trek: The Motion Picture. (copyright © Globe Photos)

• • • •

important in my future life—and work....I think Spencer Tracy said it best—'You take a deep breath and say the words.' Of course you have to have some years of experience to know how to say the words and suck in your breath. An actor brings to a role not only the concept of the character but his own basic personality, things that he is, and both Leonard and myself have changed over the years, to a degree at any rate, and we will bring that degree of change inadvertently to the role we recreate."

One question on the mind of the press was why Leonard Nimoy had seemed so reluctant to return to the fold.

"We've had a long and complicated relationship, Paramount and myself, for the last couple of years," Nimoy explained, "and probably the thing that took the most time was the fact that the mail service between here and Vulcan is still pretty slow. It's not really a matter of reluctance. We had a lot of details to work out. There have been periods of time when the *Star Trek* project was moving forward and I was not available. For example, last summer we had come to what I felt was an understanding about doing the movie. I went off to do *Equus* on Broadway. During that period of time, the concept changed to a TV series. It was difficult then to get together because there was a question of availability. When the project turned around and I was available again, we started talking immediately. It has been complicated; it has been time consuming. But there was never a question of reluctance to be involved in *Star Trek* on my part. I've always felt totally comfortable about being identified with *Star Trek*, and being identified with the Spock character. It has exploded my life in a very positive way. The Spock character has always been part of my life. I have never tried in any way to reject that. I'm very proud of the fact that I'm associated with the character. And I look forward to playing the character because I certainly wouldn't want either one of two things—anybody else playing it, or *Star Trek* happening without it."

One thing that Gene Roddenberry emphasized at the time was that the storyline of the film, like so many of the episodes, would bring with it a powerful message.

"It definitely will," he emphasized, "and this is one reason I was so pleased that Bob Wise joined us in the production, because he feels the same way about this motion picture. I think all good stories have something to say, and without anyone getting on a soapbox at any time in this film, we will be talking about something that we think is very important."

A Wise Move

"I thought it was time," explains Robert Wise in terms of his reason for accepting the directorial reins of *Star Trek: The Motion Picture*. "I have always been intrigued by science fiction, even though I have only done two other films in the genre, and I thought it was time that I did a science fiction picture that took place in space. Both my my other ones were earth-bound. In *The Day the Earth Stood Still* we had a visitor from outer space, coming in a spaceship....that really intrigued me more than anything else. So I was glad to have a chance to explore this further. I liked the idea of doing *Star Trek* from the beginning, the quality of it....It was really the fascination and the desire to do a film which dealt with the experience of being in space."

Wise admits that he was not familiar with the *Star Trek* universe before he accepted the picture. "Of course I knew of it," he clarifies, "but I had not become a Trekkie when the TV series had first come out and I had only seen one or two segments, which I thought were alright—but I didn't get hooked on it. After the President of Paramount asked me if I would be interested in considering directing the movie, I said, 'Well, I just don't know. I'll have to read the script, of course, and I would have to see several more of the TV segments.' I had to get familiar with what it was and what had caused it to become so immensely popular. So that's what happened: I read the script and I saw about a dozen episodes of the series so I could become familiar with it, and make my own judgement."

Given his track record, it's not surprising that Robert Wise is used to autonomy on his films, yet in the case of

Star Trek he was in the position of working closely with the concept's creator, Gene Roddenberry, which, he notes, "was comparatively easy. Of course, as much as producers and directors are separate entities, you always have little conflicts at times but, by and large, it was fine. When I came on after being asked to do the film, I said, 'What about Mr. Roddenberry? Because it's his baby,' and they said, 'Well, you'll have to work it up.' So Gene and I talked at some length about how we could work together, how he and I saw the whole thing. We came to reach a working agreement about halfway in our positions and I think we functioned pretty well on that level."

For his part, Roddenberry told journalist Tom Rogers that in terms of having control, he had "as much as I have the personality to take over. But more is not always more in making a movie. Making movies is quite different than making a television show. In television, I had directors that came and went, different directors every week. Naturally I had to assume a lot of control over the initial show because it was my idea, and I wanted all of the directors to be directing the same Mr. Spock next week as they directed last week. In a movie, however, which is a director's medium, I can hardly get a director of the quality and ability of a Robert Wise and then walk in and say, 'Listen, I want you to do everything exactly as I tell you.' When you bring in Robert Wise, you're bringing in his talent, his ability of wide-screen movies. There's a wonderful partnership between he and I, rather than one or the other trying to seize more control.

"There are a lot of places we disagree," he continued, "but in a friendly, professional way. My taste for costumes was a little different than his, but in the end I went with his taste because he was the man responsible for creating the whole visual image. If it had been more than just a question of taste, if I had thought the costumes violated *Star Trek* format, then we would have probably had a very serious fight. But we didn't, because it was just a question of taste. There are some places where he wanted to do some things, I can't remember an example right now, and I would say, 'Bob, the *Star Trek* format has always been this. I don't want to lock you into format, but let's not change unless we have some value that makes the change worthwhile.'"

In this respect, Robert Wise was in the unusual position of not only working in a format familiar to the audience but with a cast that had better knowledge of the characters and film than even he had.

"I should tell you a story first," laughs Wise. "After Paramount finally signed everybody, they had a big publicity party for the press and they set up a large table with Roddenberry, all the cast, etc. When my turn came to speak, I said, 'You know, I'm the alien here,' because I was the only one who hardly knew anything of *Star Trek*. They all knew more than I did. But it worked out very well. They're all very good actors, very professional. There were some very pleasant moments with all the actors on the set because I found that they really loved their characters and always looked for ways of improving their roles, like 'So and so wouldn't say it like that.' At the same time, they were never pushy or overly tempted to be demanding—to take the whole thing. I found all of them, and particularly Bill and Leonard, to be professional and very good actors."

Unlike his other genre efforts, *The Day the Earth Stood Still* and *The Andromeda Strain*, *Star Trek: The Motion Picture* represented an extremely complex shoot due to the elaborate special effects.

"Control was much simpler [back] then," sighs Wise. "In *Star Trek* all of this was very elaborate; very, very difficult because I had so much to deal with which was not even done yet. Scenes in which my actor had to play and react to that screen and I had nothing to show them on the screen. All that came in months later. The best I ever had for them to react to was a projection of a sketch or a picture of what the effects men were planning to achieve. That's all I had for them. I had to remind them of what was going on in terms of the action, to describe the best I could from the script and from my own ideas of the sketch and what they were supposed to be looking at. It takes some very professional actors to respond to something like that, and that made it very difficult—in fact, it was perhaps the most difficult part

of the film. And then we had, of course, the big problem of having to change the special effects people after a year."

One of the strongest criticisms levelled against the film was the fact that the interpersonal relationships—which were so integral to the success of the original *Star Trek*—were given a back seat to the F/X.

"It [wasn't as] if somebody sat down at the beginning and said, 'Listen, we want to get a lot more special effects.' It was not a deliberate move to shift the emphasis from one area to another," Wise emphasises. "That was really because of the story. That was the script, or the story we had to tell, and we didn't try to put more special effects in it. I didn't try. None of us tried. We had people reacting to things that were happening on the screen, so we had to show these things. If there is a valid criticism coming from those Trekkies who really love these characters with all their heart, there still wasn't anything we could do about it. We would have had to have a totally different story."

One would imagine that Wise wishes that they had.

The Script's The Thing

Star Trek creator Gene Roddenberry often attributed the success of the series to the fact that it showed man transcending his intolerance for his fellow man; that we as a species had moved beyond our petty differences which have, for so long, separated us, and achieved a peace amongst ourselves and the stars.

Unfortunately, what was true for a network television series and the motion picture it inspired, was not true for the real-life behind the scenes relationships which brought the magic to life. This has never been more true than in the writing of *Star Trek: The Motion Picture*.

As detailed earlier in this volume, the film began as a two-hour episode of the abandoned *Star Trek II* television series. The plot of "In Thy Image" had been derived from a Roddenberry-written premise for *Genesis II* entitled "Robot's Return," in which a NASA space probe returns to Earth seekings its creator.

Famed science fiction writer

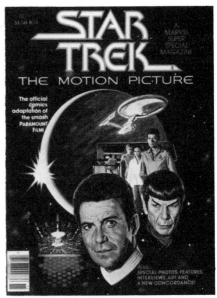

The cover of the Marvel Comics adaptation of Star Trek: The Motion Picture.

Alan Dean Foster explains, "When they were thinking of the *Star Trek II* TV series, a number of writers were called in to submit treatments for hour-long episodes. Roddenberry got in touch with me based on the *Star Trek Log* series I had done for Ballantine Books, and he said that he felt I was comfortable with the *Star Trek* universe and comfortable and familiar with the characters. So I submitted three story ideas. One of them was based on a page and a half of his notes on something called 'Robot's Return.' He thought that could be developed and wanted to see what I could do with it.

"After my treatment based on Roddenberry's page was handed in," he continues, "it was decided to open the new series with a two-hour movie for TV, which is fairly standard procedure when they can manage it for dramatic series, and it was decided that my treatment of the ones they had at hand would be the best suited to carry two hours. At least that's what I heard. I went home and developed a 32-page outline."

That outline, like "Robot's Return," dealt with an old space probe that had achieved consciousness and was now returning to Earth to join with its creator. While the story worked quite well as far as the show's production team was concerned, there was no intention of having Foster write the actual teleplay.

Harold Livingston, co-producer of the series, says, "Alan Dean Foster was a protege of Gene's and he was brought in to me to write something. So I wanted to see something he had written, and he brought me two screenplays which I thought were terrible, and I didn't want him to write. I just didn't think he was right for the job. This was obviously a very subjective judgement, but that's what they're paying me for. They either rely on my judgement or they get someone else.

"I made a deal with Alan's agent that he would write a story and agree *not* to do the script. So he wrote a story which was this business of the old machine coming back to Earth and assuming a kind of life form. I didn't know that this had also been an episode of the original *Star Trek* ['The Changeling']. By the way, at this point we're starting to come to a production date as well. I then began to look for writers to turn the story into a script. I went through two or three weeks of talking to people and I couldn't find anybody that I liked. With five weeks to go, I decided I'd write it myself.

"So I sat down and for five weeks I wrote this script of 'In Thy Image.' I finished the first draft, delivered it to Gene and Gene said, 'God, it's good. You've done your job. Now just relax and I'll write the second draft.' He writes it in a week. Then he brought it in, gave it to us proudly in a bright orange cover, and there it is, 'In Thy Image,' by Gene Roddenberry and Harold Livingston. He took first position. We all read it and I was appalled, and so was everyone else. There was [story editor] Jon Povill, [producer] Bob Goodwin, myself and Bob Collins, who was the director."

Adds Collins, "Harold and I sat there and we asked each other which one of us was going to tell him that it wasn't quite right. Finally, I said 'Hell, I'm the director,' and walked out of the room."

Harold Livingston continues the scenario, "I said, 'I'll tell him.' I went in and I said, 'Gene, this doesn't work.' Well, his face dropped to his ankles. Then I got myself wound up and I told him why it didn't work, and I said, 'Why'd you do it? When something

works, you don't piss in it to make it better!' In any case, he was pretty stubborn about this. He thought it was good and said, 'We'll give it to the front office.' Well, about three days later, we have a meeting in Michael Eisner's gigantic white office. We sat around this huge table. There was Roddenberry, myself, Eisner, Jeffrey Katzenberg, the head of television, Arthur Fellows; and a couple of other guys. Michael had the two scripts. 'In Thy Image' by me was in a brown cover, and Gene's version was in an orange cover. Michael had one script in one hand and one in the other, balancing them in his palms. And he said, 'Listen, this is the problem. This,' Gene's orange script, 'is television. This,' the brown script, 'is a movie. Frankly, it's a lot better.' Well, holy shit! Everybody was clearing their throats. The great man had had his feathers ruffled. Anyway, after some heated discussion, it was decided to let Collins write a third version using the best elements of both. So Collins did this after two or three weeks, and his was a total disaster.

"Along that time, Roddenberry and I really began to get at each other's throats. December came along and my contract was coming up. Before they could fire me, I quit. We had too many problems there. I just didn't think that Gene was a good writer. He, for his part I'm sure, considered me a total interloper. Who the hell am I to come in? I understand that, in fact I understood it, but I wanted to instill some literary value into these science fiction myths. He had his own formula which worked. He was obviously saturated with science fiction. I think he knew a lot about a lot of things, generally, and he had a great following. Here I was getting on his nerves."

One undeniable contribution to the script that came from the rewrite, however, was Roddenberry's idea of having the probe, eventually called V'Ger (short for Voyager 6) release all its data into Will Decker. Livingston's conclusion, on the other hand, merely had the probe recognizing the positive qualities of man as a species and departing the galaxy.

"Robert Goodwin theorized that I just pissed away the ending because I was so disgusted with the situation," muses Livingston. "I think the truth is that I

couldn't come up with an ending. I just couldn't do it. The problem was that we had an antagonist so omnipotent that to defeat it, or even communicate with it, or have any kind of relationship with it, made the concept of the story false. How the hell do we deal with this? On what level? Everything pretty much worked in the story until we got to the ending. We tried all kinds of approaches, including aesthetic, theological and philosophical. We didn't know what to do with the ending."

Jon Povill, on the other hand, did. "We knew we had to have a big special effects ending," he says. "The problem of what was going to happen at the end and why it was going to happen, was one that plagued the script from the very start. Then Gene came up with the idea of the machine dumping its data into Decker, with a light show of all the information it had accumulated. We were going to get all this amazing, incomprehensible stuff that V'Ger had accumulated in its travels across the universe, and, of course, nobody could come up with these images, so that didn't work. It was pretty much my contribution to say that the reason for what was happening was that this thing needed to go on to the next plane of existence; that it was transcending this dimension and going on to the next. It then became logical that the machine would need that human element to combine with. It was the only thing that could have made sense."

Upon quitting *Star Trek*, Livingston went to work at Aaron Spelling Productions, believing he was leaving the 23rd Century behind him. Under the guise of wanting to infuse the production with "fresh writer blood," Dennis Clark was hired just as the TV-movie became a theatrical film. From the writer's point of view, it was *not* a happy experience.

Clark explains, "I try never to bum-rap people. The problem with Gene is that his heart was never in the right place at the right time. It's a good heart, but he puts it aside at the wrong times. I was the subject of a practical joke from him. An awful one, and it was right at the beginning of the relationship and it set things off badly. Gene's a nice man, unless you give him some power. That practical joke was the beginning of the end. I got pissed off, Gene got pissed off and the only mediator was Bob Wise who looked at me and said, 'I'm going to have to fire you, aren't I?' And I said, 'Yes.'"

Clark's involvement with the film lasted approximately three months, two of which "I spent hiding from Nimoy and Shatner because they didn't want me to talk to them. I'd have to leave my office when they were on the lot, because actors want to tell you, 'This is how I perceive the character,' and Gene didn't want their input. He didn't want me to have their input. He didn't even like Bob Wise's input....I wish I could tell you more, but my point of view is very biased and it's a part of my life I don't even like to think about."

Paramount's Jeffrey Katzenberg, Robert Wise and Gene Roddenberry all asked that Livingston return to the film. Reluctantly, he did so.

"I had an understanding with young Mr. Katzenberg and Mr. Wise and Gene that I would do it as long as Gene didn't write," explains Livingston. "'I don't want Gene to put pen to paper. You want me to write it, I will write it. I'll do all the rewriting you want, but *I* will do it.' I had a certain style I wanted to do the script in and I had directions I wanted the characters to explore. The first thing that happened is that I rewrote 'x' number of pages and they were to be pouched to Eisner and Katzenberg in Paris. Somehow, Roddenberry got a hold of it, rewrote it and sent that to Paris. Eisner called up from Paris and said, 'What kind of shit is this?' Then Wise and I had to explain what happened. This kind of thing continued and Gene would be very remorseful and contrite, 'I was just trying to help.' I said, 'Listen, Gene, I'm not going to do this if you're going to keep this up.' Well, I quit three times. I resigned. I'm talking about $10,000 a week."

Each time he quit, Livingston was cajoled to come back to work by either Robert Wise or Jeffrey Katzenberg. Needless to say, the same problems would begin anew.

"As we began shooting," recalls Livingston, "we would get to a point where I would send in pages and then Gene would send in different pages and Wise would get two different versions. Sometimes I would write it and put my initials on them, and Gene would put 'G.R., 4PM' under mine, as though that's what should count and my pages should be ignored. This was the way the picture was made. For the third time I quit, I said, 'Screw it, nothing is worth this.' Now we weren't talking to each other. Gene has a brilliant story mind for this kind of thing, but he's a bad writer. He's clumsy. Anyway, the third time they really went behind Gene's back. I said I wouldn't have anything to do with it, and Eisner called me himself from New York and said I had to fix the script. I said I would do it if Gene promised he wouldn't do anymore writing, which of course was broken immediately. Finally, the picture was somehow filmed."

Which is not to say that the problems were over. The writing credits proposed to the Writer's Guild by Paramount was screenplay by Harold Livingston and story by Alan Dean Foster.

"They left Roddenberry out," Livingston says, "so he protested. He's the one who launched the protest. I knew he couldn't win an arbitration, because it wasn't his script. Anything he'd done was tossed out, or most of it. In any case, I blackjacked Foster into splitting the story credit with Gene. He agreed to do it and Gene wouldn't accept it. On that basis, I said, 'Okay, Gene, screw you. We'll go to arbitration.' When I said that, he withdrew, and he withdrew in a funk; he was mad. I said to him, 'If you felt you deserved credit, then you have a system for determining this. Why didn't you use it?' He said, 'I don't want to lower myself to that.' At that point, I guess, he decided to withdraw and assume this injured pose. But he would have lost this arbitration because he didn't write any script. All he did was rewrite, patch up, fool around and screw up everything."

At the time, Roddenberry explained, "It [the script] started off a bit simpler because it had been written as a two-hour television program. It got more and more complex as it got to be a bigger and bigger movie, and we started adding things on to make use of the wide-screen, big-vision, like the wing-walk, where they go out on top of the Enterprise saucer section. I put that in. I put the climax of the show inside V'ger, where the original script did not. I'm not taking

screen credit because we had a writer who worked very hard on it. He felt he deserved the credit and my policy is to never get into a credit dispute. That was my policy all through *Star Trek*. If a writer felt he wanted it and wanted it badly enough to have a Guild action on it, I'd withdraw."

Of the situation, Alan Dean Foster recalls, "The first thing they did was try to deny me screen credit. When the credits came out to be filed with the Guild, the credits read, 'Screenplay by Gene Roddenberry and Harold Livingston, Story by Gene Roddenberry.' I'm a very low-key guy. I'm an old handshake-is-my-bond kind of guy. Once it became a big budget movie, I became the non-existent man as soon as the budget increased, because it became serious money. Trying to keep my blood pressure down I called my agent and said, 'What's going on?' And she said, 'Oh, that's nothing.' 'What do you mean that's nothing?' 'Nobody's mad at you or anything, that's just the business.' I said, 'Well, it's not my business and we picked up and moved to Arizona.

"My agent suggested I file for solo credit. I said, 'Sure,' because I did 98% of the writing on the treatment. Then Harold Livingston called me and said, 'Just because Roddenberry is being a son of a bitch, doesn't mean that you have to be one too.' I thought about it and I said, 'You're right.' So I called and said, 'Look, all I'm interested in here is having it read the way that it read on the script, which is 'Story by Alan Dean Foster and Gene Roddenberry,' because it was, as I freely admit, based on his one page idea. I then get this very strange letter back saying that Gene Roddenberry is off in La Costa someplace recuperating, he's very tired, very busy and he really doesn't have time for this. I just laughed. Is this real life or kindergarten? I just threw up my hands and said, 'Fine, whatever,' and that's why I have sole story credit on the movie.

"I had only worked with people like George Lucas, who is one of the nicest people in the movie business, and Ronald Shusett, who produced *Alien*. But *Star Trek* was my worst experience. Nobody had ever tried to do that to me before. That's just the way it is, apparent-

American Cinematographer's February 1980 issue examined the making of Star Trek: The Motion Picture.

ly. They put you in the shark cage, you learn how to fight with the other sharks or you go back in the goldfish bowl. I belonged in the goldfish bowl."

Although not bitter, Foster does recall Roddenberry hugging his shoulder and saying, "You remind me of me when I was getting started. I'm going to teach you everything I know about the business."

"He *did* teach me quite a lot about the business," Foster laughs with-

out humor, "although I don't think that's what he originally had in mind."

Considering the critical scorning that *Star Trek: The Motion Picture* received, it hardly seems to have been worth all the battles, though Harold Livingston remains philosophical.

"I was upset with the film," he states. "It just wasn't what I wanted. I can't honestly say this wasn't my fault, because in the end I took the rap for it anyway. But if I do a poor job, I'll tell you it's bad. I know it's bad and I'll welcome help. I'm certainly not infallible. Gene would never admit that he wrote a bad line or couldn't write. He made an industry of *Star Trek* and he's really done nothing else. Gene's values lay in his knowledge, his experience. If he had imparted that and let the professionals do their job, you'd have had a picture."

••••

CHAPTER TEN

Star Trek II: The Wrath of Khan

Star Trek: The Motion Picture was nothing like *Star Trek*: The TV series. It was as if the powers that be decided to remake *Star Trek* by violating every principal the series' popularity was based on. Couched-in subdued, generally unpleasant hints of their former personalities, the characters wandered through an aimless and irritating plot which seemed primarily an excuse for a self-conscious special effects extravaganza. The plot was unabashedly drawn from several episodes of the series, most notably "The Changeling," and the climactic "revelation" was expounded with such numbing heavy-handedness that even the most dedicated Trekkie must have suppressed a shudder before jumping up to praise the Emperor's new clothes.

"We had no idea that the first film would be a disaster," actor William Shatner admitted in 1982. "We never knew it was falling apart while we were shooting. We didn't have an ending to the script when we started, but we had months to play around with solving it. With all the high-priced talent around, we were sure that someone would come up with a corker of a finale. Somebody would certainly create something which made *sense*. [But] we never got it together. Nobody connected with the film ever sat in a theatre and saw the movie with an audience *before* it opened. After you've spent nearly two years on a project, that's essential. By that point, you're just too close to a movie to judge it objectively. The finished *Star Trek: The Motion Picture* was really two movies: one about *Star Trek*, one about special effects. Had 15 minutes been trimmed out of the released version, I think it would have been a different, stronger film. I also felt that the characters weren't as fully realized as they could have been. We certainly were dwarfed by the special effects. It was a very confusing time for me. One felt helpless. I remember having lunch with the studio head who asked me, 'What made *Star Trek* so successful?'

I couldn't tell him anything. What was I going to say? 'Character development and story?' If I had told him that, he would have said, 'Yeah, but we need big effects to compete with *Star Wars*.' As a result, you wound up with a weak movie."

That "weak" movie cost $45 million "that Paramount will admit to," according to one film industry figure. But like the TV show, extensive merchandising saved the first movie. The myriad products created in conjunction with the movie sold very well. And when the movie finally earned back its nut—a film must gross about three times its production costs to start showing a profit—it was plain that even severe maltreatment had not killed the golden goose.

Word of a Gene Roddenberry-produced sequel began making the rounds shortly after the premiere of *Star Trek: The Motion Picture*. One proposed plotline, according to *Starlog* magazine, had the Enterprise travel backwards in time to save the life of President Kennedy. As a result, all history would have been changed. Reportedly, this tired retread of "City on the Edge of Forever" would have concluded with Spock firing a deadly phaser blast at the president to set things straight. Nothing more was heard of this premise.

"We know a little bit more about how to use *Trek* in motion pictures," Roddenberry said in 1980. "The second run in anything is easier. If you've ever played golf, the second try you can always sink the putt. It's that first shot at the hole...The sequel story is much more intra-crew, intra-character. It has many more of the difficult decisions that Kirk always had in the TV episodes; decisions about morality and ideals—but I'm not going to say anything more. It's good *Star Trek*. It would have made a good three-parter on the TV show—if I'd had the money to do it."

Many of Roddenberry's views of the *Star Trek II* script would ultimately prove themselves correct, but, ironically, he would have nothing to do with the final film.

Project Genesis

Paramount began to think once more about bringing out the sets it had

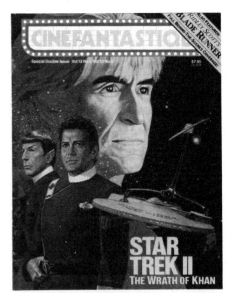

Star Trek II: The Wrath of Khan *as covered in the pages Cinefantastique's July-August 1982 edition.*

carefully stored away after the first film wrapped. This time, things would be done differently, they decided sensibly enough. This time the television arm of the studio would produce the motion picture. This time its budget would be strictly controlled and kept to about a quarter of the final cost of the first film. This time it would be *Star Trek* as it had been in the much-loved TV series: a story about people, not technology or special effects.

Gene Roddenberry, creator and executive producer of the series and producer of the first movie, became "executive consultant."

"My contract gives me the total right to produce and write all motion pictures," Roddenberry told *The Official Star Trek Fan Club Magazine*. "But I did *Star Trek* 79 times. I just can't be a creature of *Star Trek* all my life. I wanted to see bright, new people come in and put a good stamp on it and add certain differences. As the consultant, they send me everything from the first story idea to the final draft of the motion picture. I also see the dailies and rough-cuts and all of that. I make my comments to them. I have told them the only time I would say, 'no, stop, I refuse to put my name on it,' is if they should break any of the very basic things about *Star Trek*. If you're going to have good people, you've got to give good people some latitude to do it their way."

••••

Harve Bennett was chosen to serve as executive producer. Bennett has been respected for his intelligence, his articulateness and his fund of general knowledge since the days when, as Harvey Fischman, he was one of the original radio show "Quiz Kids" in the '40s. Since then, he has worked for the Sun Times in Chicago, CBS-TV, ABC-TV (where he was executive producer for *The Six Million Dollar Man*) and as an executive producer/writer for Universal. Bennett was executive producer of the *Rich Man, Poor Man* and *From Here to Eternity* mini-series.

"I came to Paramount with no anticipation of doing feature pictures at all," Bennett has told journalists. "I was here to do television. But the second week I was here I got a call from [studio president] Barry Diller. Now you have to remember that running the studio at the time was Barry Diller, who used to be my assistant at ABC, Michael Eisner, who used to be a counterpart of mine at ABC New York, and running the entire operation was the great immigrant, the last of the moguls, Charlie Bludhorn, who built Gulf and Western, and bought Paramount. Barry calls me in and says, 'Will you come to a meeting in my office?'"

At that meeting were the aforementioned executives, including Charles Bludhorn, who asked Bennett what he thought of *Star Trek: The Motion Picture*. "I....decided that the truth was the only thing I could say. So I said, 'I thought it was boring.' He suddenly turned on Michael Eisner and said, 'See, by you, bald is sexy.'"

With the script for *Star Trek II* still to be settled upon, Bennett began gathering his production staff. He selected Robert Sallin, a director and producer of television commercials and an old college chum, to produce the movie. Bennett and Sallin both attended UCLA's Film School "in the early fifties," jokes Sallin, "before it was fashionable." Sallin has made over 1600 commercials and won virtually every top national and international award, including the 1978 Clio for Most Humorous Commercial of the Year and the 1970 Grand Prix of the Venice Film Festival for outstanding commercial worldwide. It fell upon Sallin, who joined the production in February

1981, to bring in *Star Trek II* quickly and cheaply. The film's budget is officially $12 million.

Sallin says, "Before I joined Harve on the project, I sent him a lengthy memo. I had studied *Star Trek I* and I pinpointed a lot of the fundamental weaknesses of the first film. First and foremost, I felt it was too much a special effects picture and that the humanity of *Star Trek* just wasn't there. I felt that the focus of our picture should be humanity. Let the special effects support it as any effect should support basic storytelling, not be driven by the effects which so many science fiction films are. I felt that the look of the picture from a design point of view had been all wrong, the lighting was too flat and uninteresting. I made a very strong point about one thing. I said, 'Let's not attack this as though it's another film project or another television project. I want to interview every member of the crew. I want to make sure that these guys are not only mentally competent, but I want an attitude here. I want an attitude that we're all in this together. As corny as it sounds, I wanted to make sure we had a great time making this film."

Bennett also hired Michael Minor as art director and it was Minor who suggested the direction the script would eventually take. At that time the story was called *The Omega Project* and it revolved around a destructive weapon.

"Harve wanted something uplifting, something that would be as fundamental in the 23rd Century as the discovery of recombinant DNA is in our time," said the late Minor, who suggested an idea to Bennett during a casual phone call. "Then something just came to me and I said, 'Terraforming.' Harve asked, 'What's that?' and I told him it was the altering of existing planets to conditions which are compatible to human life.

"I suggested a plot, just making it up in my head while talking on the phone," he continued. "The Federation had developed a way of engineering the planetary evolution of a body in space on such a rapid scale that instead of eons you have events taking place in months or years. You pick a dead world or an inhospitable gas planet, and you change its genetic matrix or code, thereby speed-

ing up time. This, of course, is also a terrible weapon. Suppose you trained it on a planet filled with people and speeded up its evolution. You could destroy the planet and every lifeform on it. The Federation is involved with playing God, but at the same time, trying to take barren dead planets and convert them into lovely worlds. Harve liked the idea a lot. At the story conference the next day, he came over, hugged me and said, 'You saved *Star Trek!*'"

In other ways than the reencounter with his old nemesis, Khan, the past is catching up with Kirk. The script realizes that these people are no longer the same people we met 15 years ago. They've grown older. They're surrounded by a bevy of cadets who make them feel their age. Kirk, in particular, is feeling the cold breath of mortality on the back of his neck. He has just turned another year older as the story begins, and is starting to realize that he has not been exactly building an emotional nest.

"Throughout the story," explains Sallin, "Kirk goes through a great deal of introspection and reflection on his life. In a sense, he's having a midlife crisis. Throughout the film we exposed and plumbed the interpersonal relationships, which were established back on the series, to a level I don't think you've seen before."

In the script, Kirk meets his son, someone he was never particularly interested in becoming involved with, and he doesn't even recognize him. David Kirk (actually David Marcus, having taken his mother's name) is not a little boy, not a teenager, but a grown man, a scientist on an advanced project, indicating years of education and experience behind him. "I stayed away because you asked me to," Kirk tells his son's mother, but staying away and staying totally out of touch are two different things, and they both know it. Kirk has always worked hard at being emotionally superficial, and it has come home to haunt him in many ways.

Stated Harve Bennett to journalist Marc Shapiro, "The main thing that rang false about the first film was that the characters had gone 20 years and hadn't aged which, to my way of thinking, was totally unbelievable. I felt a major element in future films would be to have the characters age and to focus on what they were going through as people as they did so. At one point, I even sat down with Shatner and told him point blank that there was a real danger in having a middle-aged Kirk running around like a 30-year-old."

As the script developed, Sallin began preproduction and was determined not to let the film's special effects get out of hand, a factor which drove up the budget on the first film.

"I just applied some old commercial production techniques," he details. "I storyboarded everything. I had a chart made which listed, by scene, every special effect and optical effect, and I timed each one. I designed and supervised all the special effects. Mike Minor, our art director, sat up here in my office and did the storyboards. Then I held meetings with four or five optical effects companies, and some of those meetings ran over three hours.

"I gave them thorough information, so that when the movie was finished, the amount of deviation from the plan was very slight. As you recall, in the first movie there were quite a few problems with special effects. Because I knew how to handle and manage production, I was left very much alone by the studio. I think they were all a little intimidated by what had gone on previously, and the idea of of special effects escalating the way they did on *Star Trek I* was a major fear and concern. This time we came in so close to budget that you couldn't go out for a decent lunch on the difference."

The storyboarding process began in June, before the script had been finalized. As different scripts came in, art director Mike Minor redrew the boards. "I laid out four different features in storyboard," said Minor. "Literally different. Different plots, different characters, different events, different effects. I put in maybe 400 man-hours before we settled on what we used to get bids for the effects."

The Search For Nimoy

Harve Bennett began the process of selecting the storyline for the film by screening numerous episodes of the original television series. While quite a few of them appealed to him, the one that absolutely captured his imagination was "Space Seed," which introduced Khan Noonian Singh.

At the time, Bennett had asked himself, "Who is the heavy? Who is the black hat? We won't make this picture unless there *is* a black-hat heavy.' You know the solution the writers and producers came with with for [*Star Trek*] II: Khan. I had been watching the *Star Trek* episodes, and I said, 'Okay, where's my heavy?' Montalban, especially now that he's become 'Mr. White Suit,' is the best heavy there ever was. It's great! Great reverse casting, and it works."

Initially, Bennett wrote a one-page outline entitled *Star Trek: The War of the Generations*, in which a new generation is planning on overthrowing the United Federation of Planets. Their leader, it turns out, is Khan, who sees this as a chance for revenge against Kirk and all that the Federation stands for.

Next, Bennett had to find someone to collaborate with to expand the premise into a screenplay. "After considering other writers," said Bennett, "I found out that Jack Sowards, a great 'movie of the week' writer, was a great *Star Trek* fan. We talked and he clearly knew more about *Star Trek* than I did, so I hired him. Jack and I went to work, and I say *we* went to work because the process is like this: you talk, and you rap and the responsibility is that the writer records, in whatever fashion he chooses the fruits of the give and take of this process. His task is then to go and make it become a script. Jack made an enormous contribution to this picture."

Most notable among them was the idea of killing the Spock character as a means of enticing Leonard Nimoy to star in the film, after the star had stated he had no interest in *Star Trek II*.

"There have been times when I've been concerned about the future of my career, because of the identification with the character," explained Leonard Nimoy. "But I never had a confrontation with the studio in which I've said I would never play the part again. My only concern with *Star Trek* has been that if we're going to do it, we do it well. I don't want to just do a rip-off *Star Trek* title just because people will pay to see it. If it's going to be good, I wanted to be there. I'd hate like hell to see a great *Star Trek* movie hit the screen and not be in it. I'd feel very jealous. [At the time] I really was adamant that I would not work on *Star Trek II* because I had been so frustrated with the other and I was feeling very negative about the whole thing."

Jack Sowards continues the scenario: "When Harve and I had our first meeting, Harve said, 'Look, Nimoy has refused to do it.' I said, 'You want Nimoy to do it?' He said, 'Yeah,' and I told him to dial Nimoy's number. He picked up the phone, dialed the number and said, 'What do I say?' I said, 'You say, 'Leonard, how would you like to play your death scene?' Leonard came on the phone, Harve said, 'Leonard, how would you like to play your death scene?' And Leonard's comeback was, 'Where does it come in the picture?' Harve looked at me and said, 'Where does it come in the picture?' And I said, 'Right up front. Right in the very beginning.' Harve said, 'Right in the very beginning.' A minute or two later Harve hung up and said, 'Leonard will do it.' Of course when we wrote it, it came in the very beginning. But everytime we wrote a little bit more, we moved it back and we moved it back and we moved it back, until it came at the end."

"[Harve] caught me completely by surprise with that one," Nimoy related. "The more I thought about it, the more I thought, 'Well, maybe that's the honest thing to do. Finish it properly rather than turn your back on it.' So, eventually, we agreed that Spock would die. There was a lot of controversy over whose idea it was and why. It was even said that it was the only way I would do it and that it was in my contract that Spock would die! It got to be a messy situation.

"The only thing I can tell you is that when Harve and I started to explore the idea, I thought back to the first season of *Star Trek*, when the Spock character had taken root and been widely accepted. The whole concept of his lack of emotionality, his control of emotions, was a very interesting and important part of the character. Dorothy Fontana, who was a writer on the series, came to me on the set one day and said, 'I'm going to write a love story for Spock.' I told her she couldn't do it because it would destroy the character, destroy the whole mystique about whether or not he's emotional. The whole story we'd been telling was that he was completely in control of his emotions. She said, 'I have an idea that might work, and I'm going to try it.' She did, and wrote 'This Side of Paradise,' a beautiful episode in which Spock fell in love. At the end of it, there was a bittersweet parting and it was all over. And he had gone through this fantastic experience! "

The Scripts Of Wrath

With the Nimoy matter settled, Jack Sowards and Harve Bennett got down to business in their approach to the screenplay for *Star Trek II.*

Relates Soward, "We sat down and watched 'Space Seed' and the original motion picture. Actually, we sat through the original picture and talked. It was beautifully done, but the effects overwhelmed it. You can't have five minutes of dialogue and 15 minutes of effects, but that's what they did. We looked at it from the point of view that we wanted to take bits and snatches of those effects—the ships, spacedock, etc.—and use them in the picture. Of course we thought that nobody has really seen this. When you've got a character scene going and you cut outside, cut somewhere else, you don't linger on it for five minutes, it works. That's one of the reasons we watched the original picture, to see how many of the effects we could use without making it look like we were just cannibalizing an old picture. We both knew that it had to be told in a totally different way, and that was in terms of the characters. Fortunately, the big upside is that we eventually got Nicholas Meyer to direct, who has a talent for bringing a scene to life. With him, the characters are living their lives. That's what a director is supposed to do. A director is supposed to make these scenes a part of a person's life. Some directors point the camera a certain way and shoot the scene. They don't realize that that person has to be living a life, and the scene happens within that life. If the life doesn't exist, the scenes loses its meaning."

While watching "Space Seed,"

Sowards found himself delighting in Ricardo Montalban's performance as Khan and knew that Bennett's instincts regarding the use of the character were correct.

"I thought 'Space Seed' was wonderful," he enthuses. "Ricardo Montalban is a classically trained actor. Anybody who can deliver those lines has got to be. Most actors in town would mumble them, but the man knows just how far to go. If you've watched *Fantasy Island* or his movies, there's a smoothness. In this, he was something totally different and he knew just where to go with it without going over the edge. He *is* Khan. He brings that sort of macho arrogance to it and you believe this is a genetically engineered man who is stronger, smarter and brighter. A hero is nothing without a villain. If you overcome a slug and a snail, you haven't done anything. If you overcome something like Khan, a hero is defined."

Sowards explains that he didn't feel there was any problem in adapting the characters to changing times. "I think they're timeless," he says. "The only thing we had to do with the characters was let them age. I think they're a good set of characters you can move anywhere, and these actors are so good. They're so used to working with each other and they have such a rapport. It's almost as if they can read each other's mind. They know when the cue's coming and how to play it, and it's a pleasure to work with people like that."

The first result from the Bennett/Sowards collaboration was the December 1980 "*Star Trek* Outline," which expanded upon the elements of Bennett's one-page story idea. Added was a romantic relationship between Kirk and a bridge personnel member named O'Rourke, the death of Spock early on and a face-to-face confrontation with Khan, in which the Eugenic survivor used acquired mind control powers to try and defeat his opponent. Many of these elements, including the last one, made it to the screenplay entitled *Star Trek: The Omega Syndrome.* By the time the script was written, Khan's goals had grown considerably. He now planned on using the technology of "the Omega system" to set himself up as ultimate ruler, with the Romulans, Klingons and Federation all

under his control. In between, he wanted revenge against Kirk.

Next was a screenplay called *Star Trek: The Genesis Project*, which introduced the concept of Genesis and moved the story closer to that of the finished film. Again, Khan and Kirk had a hands on confrontation.

"Kirk and Khan may not have met in the film, but they did in my script. You bet your ass," Sowards laughs. "In my script, Khan was more of a mystic than Attila the Hun. I invested Khan with certain powers. He could make you see things which didn't actually exist. It was a battle of wills, which Kirk ultimately wins when Khan realizes he cannot control his mind. Nobody wins the fight and it ends up as a fight in space with the ships. But they do have this confrontation. It was a 12-page fight that they simply took out and threw away. The fight *would* have required a lot of special effects, because it was really a mind attack by Khan on Kirk and Kirk's being able to resist it. He would take it to different places. They would be on a shore somewhere, fighting with whips. They would be in a stone room of a castle. When you got into the whole thing, it was a very expensive process, so I can understand their dropping it. But not the face to face confrontation. I could never understand that."

Shortly after this script was handed in, Harve Bennett decided to go with another writer to develop it further. Although David Gerrold and Theodore Sturgeon were in the running, he ultimately chose Samuel Peeples, who wrote, among other things, the second *Star Trek* pilot (and the one which sold the series), "Where No Man Has Gone Before."

"Sam Peeples had done outstanding work in other areas when I was at ABC," related Bennett. "He had done two pilots that I had been involved with, and I thought he could write robustly. So I brought him in, he read the script and I said, 'Sam, you know more about *Star Trek* than I do. I want you to fix this.' He said, 'I know just what to do.' The result was his script."

Interestingly, the Samuel Peeples draft of *Star Trek II* incorporated many of the elements of Jack Sowards' version, with the *exception* of Khan.

Added were a pair of aliens named Sojin and Moray, beings from another dimension who want to use their powers to take command of ours.

Notes Robert Sallin, "Neither the Jack Sowards or Samuel Peeples script worked. It felt like television. It felt like a long television episode, and I didn't believe that the underlying humanity and the relationships between the people were very strong. There was a lot of intergalactic weirdness in the scripts which I felt were defeating."

Bennett "went right back to Jack's script and did a quick rewrite of my own, just to get everything together," he said in *The Star Trek Interview Book*. "Enter Nick Meyer. When I saw *The Seven Percent Solution*, I was so impressed with the screenplay that I went out and read the book, and I was even more impressed with the book....Nick read my rewrite of Sowards and Peeples and said, 'This has promise. What if...' He signed on and said, 'You write it, and I'll rewrite you.'..."

Robert Sallin remembers things a bit differently. "I was preparing a list of all the directors I thought might be acceptable for this film," he says. "I must have had somewhere in the area of 30 or 40 names, but I kept striking out because either they didn't want to do *Star Trek*, they didn't want to do a sequel to *Star Trek*, they didn't want to do science fiction, they didn't want to do any kind of special effects material or they weren't available. A lot of people simply didn't want to do it after what happened with the first one. Because the film was being done under the aegis of the television division, I wanted to find a director who was on his way; who hadn't hit it yet but whose heart and soul was in to it, and who would bring a certain passion to the project.

"Then," he continues, "Nick Meyer's name came up. I saw *Time After Time* and I thought it was inventive, and I very much liked the writing of the *Seven Percent Solution*. I thought that was a very fine and inventive piece of work. He seemed to come up with things with a fresh point of view. So I suggested it to Harve. We sent the script over to Nick and had a meeting with him. I remember standing in the alley, saying to Harve, 'I think the guy's dynamite. I think he has a

great vision of what can be done here.' Time moved on, the studio seemed to respond to Nick and so we went with him. It is, in all candor, Nick's uncredited rewrite that is on the screen. Contrary to what the critics may say, Harve made contributions, Sowards made contributions, I made contributions, but I think it was Nick's final version that we used. Nick never took credit for it and he told me his agent said he was crazy. But he said it was just something he wanted to do."

The Meyer Connection

Not only had Nicholas Meyer written the book and screenplay of *The Seven Percent Solution*, but he was the director behind the sensational *Time After Time*, which transported Jack the Ripper and H.G. Wells from Victorian England to the modern world. His talents were highly respected, and the attachment of his name to *Star Trek* was a major coup.

Said Meyer, "They sent me the script, which I loved. I met Harve and Bob [Sallin] and I thought they were wonderful, and I haven't changed my views since. As far as the film was concerned, I could not have been better partnered to not look like a fool because of the expertise and support I was given. The miracle of it was that we were all making the same movie. Everything really could have come unstuck if we had started going off in different directions. But there was never a substantive disagreement about the tone or the action. Details, yes."

Meyer admitted to not have ever seen an episode of the original series, noting that he didn't particularly like the science fiction genre.

"I'm interested in good stories first," he stated. "I loved *Star Wars* and *The Empire Strikes Back*, which I thought were very exciting and a lot of fun. I saw some *Star Trek* stuff after the film was offered to me, and they also ran the first movie for me. I didn't like that very much. I thought that it was spectacular in some ways, but I didn't like the way the people looked or what I considered the lamentable absence of story and human interaction. There are really two reasons to do remakes and sequels, aside from

financial considerations. One is because, for whatever reason, it's been so long and people really didn't see the original, except on late-night television. The other reason is that there was something wrong with the original. It didn't fulfill what it was supposed to, or could be improved upon. I looked at the first film and thought that there was no way that we were going to make a movie as filled with ennui as that one. I also knew we could do it for a quarter of the cost, so we would probably look like heroes!

"[Adding dimension to the characters] was definitely the aim. I have always thought, to the extent that I've had any clear thoughts about *Star Trek*, that it was something that for one reason or another never quite fulfilled its promise. Either because in terms of a TV show, they couldn't afford the sets or the effects, or because in the first movie they dropped the ball somewhere. This was an opportunity to make something right that had never quite been on the nose before. The more specific you get, the better. It was not necessary for me to see Admiral Kirk go to the bathroom, but I said why couldn't he read a book? At which point, I grabbed the first book off my shelf, which was *A Tale of Two Cities*, and for some reason or another, I just stuck with that, which was interesting because it's the one book that everybody knows the first line and the last line to. That became the bracket of the movie and it also somehow became the theme of the movie. Leonard and Shatner got excited because they always felt in some way that they had the Sidney Carlton-Charles Darnay relationship going on between them. That's very specific, and from the book we got the glasses, which was specific too, and real! From all of that came age! Interestingly enough, *Star Trek II* is not very much about science fiction, the Genesis Planet aside. Its themes are entirely earthbound—death, aging, friendship."

One of the issues Meyer was pressed with was deciding what elements of the *Star Trek* formula he should keep in the film and what should be discarded.

"Very simple," he mused. "I kept what was good and changed what was bad! I decided that I owed allegiance to what was good in either the first movie or, more importantly, the television series and that I owed no allegiance and no respect to things that were bad. What that really boiled down to was the characters. I had to keep the characters as they were but at the same time I had to redesign everything that I could—the uniforms, the sets, etc. Again, it was in the context of what they were, the overall shapes, I couldn't do anything about. But I could add twinkling lights whenever possible, I tried to get away from that grey look. Philosophically, I said that I was simply going to take these characters more seriously and more literally than anyone has ever taken them before."

Meyer was faced with his own share of problems regarding the cast itself. Nimoy had been convinced to come back, but there were near defections by George Takei and DeForest Kelley, who were not satisfied with the script.

Noted George Takei, "When I first got the script and saw the kind of participation Sulu had, I saw that he wasn't much more than a talking prop. There was no character there, and I decided that I just couldn't go back under those conditions. My heart just wouldn't be in it. I told this to Harve Bennett and Nick Meyer, and they understood, but the script was already written and there wasn't much that they could do with it at that point....Harve understood the problems and had a few scenes added that bolstered my part a little, but I was still unhappy. Filming was due to begin soon and a decision had to be made. So they made me certain promises and I was on the set the first day of filming without even a contract. The first shots included me on the simulation bridge, so I was locked in. Unfortunately, when the film came out, some of the little scenes which would have added to my character ended up on the cutting room floor."

Explained DeForest Kelley, "At first I turned it down. I strongly disliked the first script handed to me. I felt it was a busy story and didn't work, so I had a big conversation with Harve Bennett. He was upset. I said I would rather *not* be in it, because the role was not meaningful, and the script just was *not* a good *Star Trek* script. He said, 'Well, what do you think we should do?' 'I think you should hire a writer who has written for *Star Trek*

and rewrite it!' He looked at me funny and said, 'Well, who would you hire?' I said, 'Gee, Harve, I don't know, I'm not in that line of work." Meyer, as stated above, was brought in and did a rewrite. "I feel that Meyer brought it to life and really made it a kind of *Star Trek* script. When he sent me that draft, I said, 'That's more like it,' and I went with it."

Sharing Kelley's view of working with Meyer was William Shatner. "Nick Meyer had written a script and we were in love with the script and impressed by his creative ability," he enthused. "So even though it was only the second picture he had directed, we felt that his imagination should be given full flower. And so here he was. He had written the script but he hadn't directed very much. Whatever help we could give him was offered and he would accept it or not accept it, depending on whether he thought we were correct. But he had written the script and had therefore brought to it another unquestionable aspect."

He's Dead, Jim

Principal photography with the main actors began on November 9, 1981 at the Paramount Studios in Hollywood. Production ended January 29, 1982, a few days over schedule and slightly over budget, a rather remarkable feat for a production of *Star Trek II*'s scope.

From the beginning, the film was marked by keen interest from fans, seemingly fed by rumors that Spock had been killed off in a script. There was considerable speculation that publicity "leaks" about Spock's death were deliberately planted to stir up Trekkies and media attention for the film. Such suspicions were exacerbated when the TV news magazine *Entertainment Tonight* (also produced by Paramount) ran a call-in viewer poll on the subject of whether Spock should perish or be spared, and then it conducted three-days worth of interviews on the bridge set of the Enterprise.

"The studio did not generate any of the rumors about Spock's death," says producer Robert Sallin. "People have assumed that when this movie was conceived the first thing the studio did was to run out and create the rumors that

Spock was going to die, to get the Trekkies excited and generate publicity. That is contrary to my knowledge. I know that the position of the studio brass is that they would just as soon nobody said anything. Early drafts of the script were stolen and made their way into the hands of fans, and that fueled the furor."

However the rumors were promulgated, in the final analysis Spock *did* die, so at least the concern on the part of the fans was not completely wasted on cynical manipulation. What constitutes Death is a matter of semantics and debate even now, let alone in the 23rd Century. "In science fiction there are many kinds of life, and many kinds of death," Sallin points out.

Ironically, this was one death that Leonard Nimoy himself had tried to avoid as filming of that scene grew closer. "I found myself being moved by the scene early, very early, at about the point where Kirk says to Scott something about you have to get us out of here in three minutes or we're all dead," related Nimoy to *Starlog* magazine. "You see Spock hear that and react. I'm already feeling emotional about what's coming. [I] really came within a hair's breath of walking off the lot rather than playing the scene. The day we were going to shoot it, I was very edgy about it and scared of it—scared of playing it, almost looking for an excuse not to, finding something to pick an argument about. It was a very tense time. And I *still* feel that way seeing it. It's a moving scene and I'm pleased with it in the context of the film. I'm glad we did it. I think we did it well. I think we did it honestly and sincerely."

According to Nicholas Meyer, it was the filming of that scene finally made him comprehend the true power of *Star Trek*.

"The scenes which were the most difficult, or at least the most wrenching to do, were the death of Spock [sequences]," he said. "Everybody stood around on the stage in tears, which was very surprising to me because I'm not that experienced as a movie director and I was amazed at how moved they were. The next day at the dailies, same thing. Everybody cried. I come from the 'less is more' school of thinking. You can have somebody point to something and say, 'Look at that' and you don't have to cut to what he is pointing to. In fact, you can raise considerable tension by not showing the audience what the character sees. For example, once Spock enters the reactor room I deliberately didn't cut back to him for a long time. After hearing, 'You can't go in there, you can't go...', you gotta be wondering, 'What's happening to him?' You want to see what's going on there. It's a matter of choice, of taste. I would rather underplay and let the audience imagination rise to meet something halfway. From what I've seen of the series, I tend to think they overacted or showed too much.

"My attitude has changed perceptively. I don't know whether it was the actors themselves or the characters, but I finally thought, when I was watching the death scene and I realized that *I* was choked up, I thought, well, we have now transcended the subject matter. This is no longer simply about a man with pointy ears, which is how I felt because I didn't know it that well."

While George Lucas' Industrial Light and Magic (ILM) finished the special effects work on *The Wrath of Khan*, Paramount began to lift the film's veil of secrecy in an effort to publicize the forthcoming release. Public statements by director Nicholas Meyer led to some friction on the production, however. Robert Sallin took exception to off-hand remarks made by Meyer which characterized the ongoing effects work as being disorganized.

"I don't believe in taking credit for other people's work and I don't believe in making myself seem more important at other people's expense," says Sallin. "Nick did not supervise the creation of the effects storyboards, and Nick did not supervise the execution of the shots. He attended one meeting with me at ILM, at which time I ran through every frame of every shot, and that was it. He was overwhelmed with the special effects and just backed away from them."

Director Nicholas Meyer was pleased with his cut of *Star Trek II*. Traditionally, the first editing of a film is done at the director's order, but may be amended or recut later, at the discretion of producers or studio. Meyer's cut was tightened somewhat, according to Robert Sallin. "We had too much plot, essential-

ly," he explains. "Nick's background is that of a writer, and in his version there was an extraordinary amount of exposition that we didn't feel was totally necessary; so Harve Bennett and I made some changes, in response to notes from the studio. It had to do with the tempo of the film. What we have is essentially the same picture as the director's cut."

Meyer has disputed the idea that fans had any influence on the ultimate ending of the film. After a screening at a science fiction convention in Kansas on May 8, a high-placed Paramount official indicated that other endings had been considered, perhaps filmed, and that the one used would depend on fan reaction. Meyer has firmly denied this.

"The question in my mind was not whether he died, but whether he died well. His death needed some organic relationship to the rest of the movie, and a plausible connection to whatever else was going on. If we did that, I don't think anyone would question it. On the other hand, if the movie suddenly turned around a corner on two wheels and we 'fulfill Leonard Nimoy's contract by bumping off his character which he has grown tired of playing,' if indeed that was the scenario, which I have never heard, that wouldn't be so good. That stuff that we were going to have more than one ending, that we were going to let the audience decide...that was all bullshit. Art is not made by committee and it's not made by voting."

As far as can be determined, Spock always died, in every version of the script and every cut of the film. Additional scenes involving Spock's death were shot by an ILM crew, with Robert Sallin, at San Francisco's Golden Gate Park in late April, more than two months after principal photography wrapped, when the movie was, for all intents and purposes, complete. The scenes show Spock's casket, a photon torpedo casing, drifting after his burial in space, finally coming to rest on the planet created by the explosion of the Genesis device aboard Khan's ship. Originally, Spock's casket was simply set adrift in space. These extra scenes were filmed after the results of opinion screenings before carefully-selected, demographically-balanced audiences.

"One of the major conflicts Nick and I had in the making of the picture was the whole idea of reminding people, of planting the seed that Spock might come back," explains Robert Sallin. "It was not in the original script, that idea of going back to the planet. Nick hated the idea, but I think the studio wanted it because they were getting so much flack about killing Spock."

Commenting On Khan

Star Trek II: The Wrath of Khan was a critical success, with the majority of reviewers noting that this is the way the first film should have been done.

The cast, as related to various journalists, had nothing but unanimous praise regarding the film, believing it to be far superior to *Star Trek: The Motion Picture* and a much more satisfying experience.

William Shatner: "I was nervous about it. Especially after the first film. The success of your performance, essentially, rests in the words. Everything rises and falls on the script. When a script is good, it takes a heroic effort to ruin it. As this script developed, I swung wildly from awful lows to exalted highs. I began to realize that the movie might be good. By the time we were ready to shoot, I knew *Wrath of Khan* would be great. I knew we had ILM for the effects, so the movie couldn't *look* bad. We also had a very human, *Star Trek*ian script. It was a wonderful working experience. It was as if the years between this film and the old show never existed."

Leonard Nimoy: "In doing [*Star Trek: The Motion Picture*], somebody, somewhere, decided that if we're going to do a motion picture, it must be different than what we did on TV, so we must now start to work out the differences. We'll change the color of the bridge, the wardrobe, the attitudes of the characters. It seemed to me that somebody was watching *2001* a lot, and getting into a cerebral, futuristic trip rather than an adventure romp, which is what *Star Trek* is built on. Maybe it's because they felt that people would not pay to see in the theatre what they had seen on TV, that they would want something different. My opinion is that if we can do the best *Star*

Trek episode ever done, well-produced and well-acted, and put it on the big screen, it will work. I think that's what we've got this time. It's great! There's nothing wrong with success. It's terrific and I'm relieved because Bill, Dee, myself and other people who have talked about this picture before its release, felt strongly that it would be successful and that we were on the right track. What has happened here is that our perspective of what *Star Trek* is really supposed to be has been verified. The audience has said, 'Yes, that's right.'"

DeForest Kelley: "In my mind, there's no comparison [between the first two films]. This is the kind of film that in fact we had all hoped for the first time. It's not easy to convince the studio that, as successful as *Star Trek* was, the fans nevertheless have a deep feeling about the characters, and that you can't ignore it. In my opinion, that was the mistake that was made with the first film, ignoring the relationships that were so popular in the TV series."

James Doohan: "To me, this movie is *Star Trek* the way it should be. The first one was just some grandiose idea that somebody had. There is gorgeous action going on at all times. The characters all have some great things to say. It's just a beautiful blend of all of the good things that were in all of the good shows that we had in the series."

George Takei: "I think in *The Wrath of Khan* we have genuine drama because of the confrontation of two strong, cunning, inventive adversaries that are driven to an inevitable collision. You know that they are not going to avoid each other, that there is going to be some dramatic confrontation. Ricardo Montalban is an awesomely well-suited adversary for Kirk."

Nichelle Nichols: "I was both pleased and surprised [with *Star Trek II*]. I felt that, this time, they did it right. I think this is the definitive *Star Trek*. They've captured the essence of what made the show wonderful."

Walter Koenig: "I think that if you can point to one single element that makes this film successful, it is the presence of a formidable, worthy antagonist. You can't have conflict unless you have something to butt up against. V'ger was more like something you were in awe of. I think Ricardo Montalban, on the other hand, has done a wonderful job with the character of Khan. Not only is he a presence in terms of villainy, but he's also a character of depth. Even when you hate him, you feel a certain sympathy toward him. That, to me, is extraordinary. Nick Meyer was quoted as saying that he would like to direct Montalban in *King Lear*, and I can believe it. I think that is what makes this story work——the fact that he's not only against Kirk but against the whole crew. We're all heroes to varying degrees, and our opponent has to not only be the equal of Kirk but also, in effect, the equal of all of us. I think Montalban embodies that very well."

One person not overly impressed with the film was *Star Trek* creator Gene Roddenberry. "I think it was an exciting picture," he explained. "I had many problems with it, though. I thought they were very lucky they had the actor they did in Ricardo Montalban to play Khan, since it was not a well-written part. 'I will chase you through the moons of Jupiter' and so on, in the hands of almost any other actor would have gotten snickers from the audience. Montalban saved their ass. Khan was not written as that exciting a character, he was rather flimsy. The Khan in the TV episode was a much deeper and better character than the movie Khan, except that Montalban pulled it off.

"I also objected to other little things. Remember when the eel came out of Chekov's ear? What did Kirk do? He had a look of disgust on his face and grabbed his phaser and went 'zap.' Now, how dare he destroy a life form that had never been seen before! It needs studying. They had him act like an old woman trampling on a tarantula. Now that's not the Kirk we built up for three years. So many of those fine little things in the episodes, hundreds of them, are what gave *Star Trek* its quality. Unfortunately, they began doing those things incorrectly in that movie. There was also a great deal of violence. But yet, it was exciting—exciting photographically. I'm grateful that it did what it did."

At this juncture in time, the results of "what it did" are obvious. *Star Trek II: The Wrath of Khan* was quite successful, grossing a little more than half of *Star Trek: The Motion Picture*'s take, but proving itself to be considerably more profitable due to its much lower budget. Additionally, the hoopla surrounding Spock's death ultimately became little more than a moot point, as evidenced by the next film in the series, *Star Trek III: The Search for Spock.*.

The saga of *Star Trek* would most definitely continue.

••••

CHAPTER ELEVEN

Star Trek III: The Search for Spock

Beginning The Search

Leonard Nimoy's desire to involve himself with aspects of filmmaking other than acting seems to be one of the major forces which have ultimately propelled the direction of the *Star Trek* films, particularly concerning the death and resurrection of Spock.

What he never expected, and what made his career move to temporarily get away from Spock all the more successful, was that he would end up being the director of *Star Trek III: The Search for Spock*.

Getting the job was, to some degree, an accident. Prior to *Trek III*, Nimoy still wanted his contract with Paramount to include projects other than *Star Trek*, but they did not have anything specific for him to do in the future. "For many years," Nimoy explained, "my concern has been to try to build a career outside of *Star Trek* so that it wasn't that single straight line of only *Trek*-oriented work. So there was nothing for us to discuss. I said to Gary Nardino—I was being arrogant—with all due respect to Bob Wise, who directed the first picture, a top notch filmmaker; and all due respect to Nick Meyer, an extremely talented writer/director who directed *Trek II*; I know more about *Star Trek* than either of them and I said I could direct *Star Trek III* successfully. When I first presented the idea of my directing to Paramount, the response was very good—but there were certain trepidations. We had to talk them through. My position during those discussions was 'I don't want you to perceive me as a problem. I don't want you to think I'm an actor trying to build a directing career on the strength of my leverage. I want you to see me as the *solution* to your problem. You need a director, and I know this material. I will bring you a movie that will satisfy the *Star Trek* audience.' I didn't want to take the posture with the studio of, 'You want me to act in

Star Trek III? Then *I'm* the director, period.' Instead, we worked out what I felt was a constructive approach. Basically, I told them, 'Promote from within.'

"Michael Eisner [then Paramount president] got very excited about it and said, 'Great idea! Leonard Nimoy directs *The Search for Spock*!' It went downhill from there. At one point they said, 'No, we're not going to do it.' Harve [Bennett] and I kept operating on the assumption that it was going to work out and kept talking story ideas. In April of '83, I started my prep on the picture, reported on the lot and immediately went to work with Harve."

It may be hard to believe, coming from someone who has been a part of the industry since the 1950's, but Leonard Nimoy insists he honestly felt that moving out of the cast and taking over the film would not be a major concern to his fellow cast members. It was only a matter of time before he discovered that he was wrong.

Said Nimoy, "I must be really naive about this. I really must. I was surprised that there was so much interest and so much concern about that. The interests and concerns are valid. I just didn't perceive the potential problems or friction that other people perceive. My fellow actors were concerned about it before we started doing the picture. I simply took it as fact that I had their best interests at heart. That I would know their characters well, and I certainly knew their potential well and would try to explore it. That was one of the things I argued in that period of time when I was asking for the job."

One interesting thing that happened, possibly as a test to Nimoy's intentions and loyalty, was when he and producer Harve Bennett first discussed the script with friend and co-worker William Shatner. Naturally, since Nimoy was now in the position of authority, Shatner might feel a bit threatened, if not downright insecure about the situation. Before, he and Nimoy were a team. What if that changed?

"Leonard and I are the dearest of old friends," Shatner told writer James Van Hise. "We had shared a mutual struggle with the management in various stages, whether it was a script, a thought, a con-

The cover of Starlog Press' official Star Trek III: The Search for Spock *movie tie-in.*

cept or a dressing room and ask each other what we thought. We'd have a plan! Whenever we were to deal with management, we'd plan it out together. Now, suddenly, my 'brother' was saying, 'Well, you should do this and I think you should do that.' There was an awkward period of time for me, although I don't think for Leonard, where I felt alone in anything I might have objected to. From my point of view, it was more awkward in the beginning than with either of the other two directors [Robert Wise and Nicholas Meyer]. But that slowly erased itself."

In writing the script, Bennett did 12 outlines in all. It took six months. He says the last scene in the movie is the first one he wrote. "Somewhere along the line I read a fan poem in one of the hundreds of fan magazines about *Star Trek*. It was first person Kirk. It said, 'I left you there. Why did I do that? I must come back to you, my friend.' I thought, 'That's it!' I suddenly had a thrust. It got a lot easier from that point. A great motion picture has a very similar last scene. It was almost, beat for beat, the last scene in *The Miracle Worker* by William Gibson. It is the moment in which, after the entire play, little Helen Keller is at the well with her teacher and she begins to get some understanding, and finally with her hand on his face she says, 'Water.' And the teacher says, 'Yes!'

••••

"On *Star Trek III*, I said, 'Look, it's got to be faster and more efficient [than the writing of *The Wrath of Khan*]. So I was the sole writer on *Star Trek III*, [which] was the easiest writing job I ever had. The reason for that it, since it was so direct a continuation of *Star Trek II*, the outline was already in place. I knew exactly what I had to do and I did it in six weeks.

"I had to make a story out of the following 'givens': One, there is a casket on a planet that has been created by the reformation of life forces and life has been created from death. Two, 'There are always possibilities.' Three, before he died, Spock said, 'Remember.' Remember what? The puzzle was solved so easily that I think 17 other people could have written the script to *Star Trek III*. If you end a film with a Genesis device that can, in one 'poof,' create life where there was lifelessness, you have created an enormous story device that can not be ignored. Now the fans would be justified in saying, 'Well, why not just create a planet as a plot solution?' Or, 'What would happen if the Klingons got hold of this? They wouldn't use it to make a planet, they would destroy a planet.' Therefore, the final puzzle solving was the denial of the validity of the Genesis device. That was—as 'The Lord giveth, the Lord taketh away'—necessary, or we would have expanded the borders of *Star Trek*, even subliminally, that it would have had the same impact the A-bomb had on the 20th Century, so as to make conventional things no longer viable. That's fine, but who needs to restructure *Star Trek* on that basis?"

Writing the script, Bennett ran into other problems that were set up in *The Wrath of Khan*. First, there was Saavik. The original character, played by Kirstie Alley, did not want to come back to do the movie. "We didn't want to cut [her] scenes," Bennett said, "so we decided to recast the character and keep the part. How did we fare putting Robin Curtis in where Kirstie Alley had gone before? About even."

Kirstie Alley, who has achieved incredible fame since *Star Trek II* thanks to her varied movie roles as well as her continuing stint on *Cheers*, told *Starlog* magazine, "They offered me less money than they did for *Star Trek II*, so I figured they weren't very interested in me for Saavik. I thought [Robin Curtis] was at a real disadvantage playing a role someone else established, especially with *Star Trek*, which has an enormous following. I think she did a fine job. I have no problem with what she was doing except that, when I saw the film, I said, 'She isn't Saavik, *I* am.'"

Said Robin Curtis, "I did want to keep things fairly separate between myself and Kirstie Alley and as it turned out, each and every one of the people involved in *Star Trek III* were wonderful. I think Leonard set an example that everyone followed and that is to say I was never made to feel like I had to fill someone else's shoes. Never for a moment was I made to feel like that and I think that was really Leonard's kind of healthy approach to the whole thing."

Two other major script decisions, killing David and destroying the Enterprise, were rather easy for Bennett. He believes in a balance. If you get something, you have to pay for it. Kirk gets Spock back, but at what cost? He loses two very major things along the way. Is it worth it? That makes for a good script, and lots of emotion and tension.

"I confess to being old fashioned," Bennett continued. "There is in my vision such a thing as ultimate retribution. The reason David dies, structurally, is because he's messed with mother nature. He allowed himself to bend the rules at the wrong time, in the wrong place. He's there on that planet for only that reason. The whole story dates back to David putting protomatter in the matrix. The death of Spock, everything rests on his shoulders if you want to blame him for it."

One of the secondary themes of *Trek III* is don't mess with mother nature. The concept fo the Genesis device was too massive to deal with in the *Trek* universe for future stories. It had to be destroyed. "Gene Roddenberry said, 'Let's try protomatter.' It became a tool for me to solve the problem,' " Bennett explained, "which is the interjection of a human value system in an otherwise antiseptic, impossible box—the perfect scientist. The value system is ambition. That interested me. It all snapped together. Kirk changed the computer on the Kobayashi Maru scenario before *Star Trek II*. His son says to him, 'You've cheated.' His father says, 'I changed the rules.' Well, it turns out that the kettle was calling the pot black. David says it at a time when he knows he's changed the rules."

The loss of the Enterprise was the big risk in the script, the big surprise, though word of it leaked to the fans and campaigns, not unlike the ones to save Spock, were begun to save the Enterprise from its demise.

Bennett admitted, "The death of the Enterprise caused serious ripples. The death of David did not. That's....backwards for me. How could you destroy the Enterprise is a burden I take full responsibility for. I will justify it to the end and once again I think I have been playing fair. My choice was a humanistic choice. It began as a writer's problem. Usually it happens when you reach a sticky point. I had a whole justification for it. Oliver Hazard Perry of the U.S. Navy scuttled the Niagara at the battle of Lake Erie and won the battle as a result. He was rowed on a rowboat to another ship and took command. Perry happens to be one of James T. Kirk's great heroes. Actually, there is a model of the Niagara in Kirk's quarters for those who love *Star Trek* trivia. So, the scuttling of the ship to achieve the greater good is a tactic. Also, with the death of his son and the hopelessness of the situation, it seemed like the right solution, and also because in the series there had been one notable, false countdown."

Star Trek creator Gene Roddenberry made no secret of the fact that he disliked the idea of the Enterprise being destroyed.

"I'm upset about it," he said at the time. "I felt it wasn't really that necessary. I would rather have seen the saucer blow up. As all the old-time fans will know, our ship is supposed to come apart. The star-drive part is the nacelles and the underneath, and the saucer is not star-driven. If the saucer had been blown up, at the end of the picture we could have had a new saucer come down and reunite the two. Symbolic of the end of the story. They preferred to do it the other way."

Actor William Shatner saw the death of both David Marcus and the

Enterprise in a different light. "I thought the loss of the Enterprise and David's death were very clever devices used to create drama in a situation. The problem is that, in a continuing series of movies where the characters appear through all the films, we have to raise some jeopardy. But everybody knows the characters are not going to die. So, two elements that were expendable, David and the Enterprise, were killed off because nothing else could be killed off. In fact, the real problem is, what else can we kill? We're looking around for people to die! It's like the court-martials where you come into the room and if the knife is pointing towards you, you're dead."

Joked DeForest Kelley, "When I read that in the script, I couldn't believe it! You know, I thought, 'My God, the Enterprise is a bigger star than any of us! If they're shooting this guy out of the script, they can shoot anybody out!'"

"There are two elements in the making of a story whether it's on film or not," Bennett stated. "Suspense and surprise. You're either hoping a character will do something or he does something that you didn't expect. The sure knowledge of the audience saying, 'Oh, no, they're not going to do that,' and the sheer surprise of saying, 'Oh, yes we are.' There are many other moments in the film which were intended to be one or the other. The death of David is one clear example of surprise, because you're playing off the cliches of the expected. One of the joys of motion picture writing as opposed to television is that you have full use of those two ranges. In television the surprise is limited, and suspense is limited to the fact that the episode must end with the hero surviving."

One obvious aspect of the film was that Kirk and company would ultimately locate Spock, alive and, relatively speaking, well. The return of Spock at the climax, which is something Leonard Nimoy was not at all nervous about.

"I had confidence in the way the story was structured that it would work," he told *The Official Star Trek Fan Club Magazine*. "I certainly didn't want to do a ghostly Spock like Alec Guiness in *Star Wars*. I felt there was obviously a tremendous amount of interest from the fans as to whether or not he was coming

back. By the time the picture opened, I think the feeling really was, 'OK, he's probably coming back, but let's find out how.' And if it's done interestingly, then it works."

Since Leonard Nimoy's directorial credits were limited to such episodic television fare as *The Powers of Matthew Star, Night Gallery* and *T.J. Hooker*, the challenge of getting Bennett's script on film was a difficult yet exhilarating experience, from the filming of scenes to the actual editing of the movie. His love for *Star Trek* and his obsession for perfection is what made the movie work. However, that kind of dedication has a price.

"The shooting began on August 15, 1983," Nimoy stated, revealing what his workload as director was like. "It was 49 days of shooting during which the biggest problem I had was lack of sleep. I went to bed at 9:00 or 9:30, set the alarm for 5:00 or 5:30 and would be up at 3:00, the head going with ideas. I was just so super-charged and wired. It was a constant tiredness of the best kind."

There were many things he learned, too, on this project, such as how frustrating it can be to direct oneself.

"There is no question in directing yourself that you need help," Nimoy explained. He relied quite heavily on Harve Bennett, William Shatner, director of photography Charles Correll and others for that help. They are "People off-camera I've come to trust. I cannot emphasize enough that you don't make these pictures alone. You sure need an awful lot of talented support. In some cases, there is simply the fact that there are things going on behind you that you cannot see as an actor. The biggest problem I had, and this is really silly, but it happens that it was the scene in the sick bay of the Bird of Prey. Spock is unconscious and McCoy is talking to him. Now, not only am I in the scene, but I have to play the scene with my eyes closed. So I can't even look to see if the actor I am playing the scene with is looking anything like I think he should look. It drove De Kelley crazy. He swears that I was trying to direct him with the movement and flutter of my eyelids. It was very difficult. In a sense, I was very pleased and relieved that the design of the story allowed me to do a minimal

amount of performing."

Said Bennett about one moment of Nimoy's directing, "I'll tell you what was a great directorial achievement by Leonard was getting emotion over David's death out of Shatner because he wanted to play it more stylistically. It's the only scene I remember where Leonard said, 'Clear the bridge.' Literally, he said, 'Will everyone please leave. I want to talk to Bill.' I never asked him what he said to Bill. It was very personal. It was director talk to actors."

That scene was a very crucial part of the script. It was the moment where Kirk realizes he has lost a good portion of the fight with the Klingons because they have in their hands everything he loves or cares about. It called for a riveting, emotional and yet not overdone performance. Nimoy explained:

"On the day of the shooting of that scene, he and I got ourselves off into a corner and discussed it slowly in a relaxed atmosphere, and privately. What I said to him was this: 'You have to decide how far you want to go with this. How far you want to take this reaction. My opinion is that you can go pretty far and get away with it, maybe strip off some of the veneer of the admiral, the hero, always in charge, always on top of the situation, and show us a vulnerable person.' He took it further, frankly than I expected him to. And it was scary. I mean, how many space epics do you see where your hero, on receiving personal news, stumbles back and falls on the person's own ship? You don't see that a lot. It was a scary thing for all of us hoping that it would be perceived as a very touching moment. Some little kid breaks in laughter in the audience and you're dead. We did several takes and used the one where we really thought Bill lost control and stumbled and fell. It looked accidental, not a performance. I'm very moved by it. In my opinion, it is some of the best work he has ever done. It looked as though he had received a physical jolt, as if somebody had hit him with the information. He looks deeply hurt. Some of the most personal and vulnerable work I've ever seen done in the role of Kirk."

An intriguing part of the directing for Nimoy involved editing. "In the editing process, specifically, the most

• • • •

interesting challenge was how to tell the story and in what sequence. Having seen it on the screen in its rough cut form, we all came to the conclusion that there was something about the juxtaposition, scene to scene, idea to idea, character to character; it wasn't quite in its proper order. The jigsaw puzzle hadn't quite fallen into place. Gradually we worked our way towards it and discovered what the picture turned out to be.

"The flow just didn't want to come to life until we repositioned certain of the opening scenes. For example, what we came to call the caper, which was the gathering of the Samurai to steal the Enterprise. In its original form, it was scattered in pieces throughout the first third of the film and they were all wonderful, fun pieces. But somehow, when you cut away from each of the happenings, it was always as though the fun was being interrupted. When you came back to it, you had to get geared up to have fun again. And suddenly that little piece would be over and you were being interrupted and taken away from the story again.

"The one major reconstruction that took place in editing was to put much, if not all, that caper together as a piece so that once we start with the idea of Bill Shatner walking up and saying, 'The answer is no, I am therefore going anyway,' it starts. So that piece became a trump within itself whereas it had been originally constructed as several pieces. I think 14 minutes from the time we first started looking at cuts of the film were cut down to its present condition. Perhaps two or three minutes were cut after the picture went to preview audiences. So we were pretty close to what we had planned to put on the screen. I think that's due in great part to very successful writing and producing for the film."

Star Trek III: The Search for Spock completed production on schedule and under budget. For both Nimoy and Bennett, it was a job well done.

"For me," Bennett said, "this movie is about honor and friendship and decency and values higher than the complex value system we have inherited since the atomic age. It's a return to innocence."

Noted Nimoy, "I wasn't making a personal statement. The major theme in this film is about friendship. What should

a person do to help a friend? How deeply should a friendship commitment go? What price should people be willing to pay? And what sacrifices, what obstacles, will these people endure? That's the emotion line of the film. For me, that's its reason for existence."

A Fruitful Search

The "texture" of *Star Trek III: The Search for Spock* came together beautifully as far as fans were concerned. The film was released in June 1984 to generally positive reviews, though the critics weren't quite as enthusiastic as they had been about *The Wrath of Khan*. As *The New York Daily News* noted, "Installment three falls somewhere ahead of the first feature and way behind the highwater mark of [*Star Trek*] *II*. Enough exciting sparks are struck—rest assured—and now that the gang's all here, 'the adventure continues.'"

Despite the fact that the climax of the film was a foregone conclusion (there was simply no way that they weren't going to find Spock), *Star Trek III* does make a terrific episode, giving each of the characters a moment to shine and examines the depth of the Kirk-Spock-McCoy triangle.

Additionally, Nimoy's co-stars had nothing but raves for him as well.

William Shatner: "Leonard had a point of view and knew what he was doing. [He's] very organized and methodical. He's very creative. I'm looking forward to working with him on *Star Trek IV*. I thought *Star Trek III* was very good. I think it could have been a little more complicated in storyline, but very good."

DeForest Kelley: "I enjoyed watching *Star Trek III* more than I did *Star Trek II*. This one comes closer to the TV series than the others. I, for years, have

had full confidence that Leonard could direct *Star Trek*, or for that matter, anything he wanted to had he been given the opportunity. Leonard is the kind of director who will accept input from you because he knows that we know and feel certain things about our characters."

George Takei: "Leonard brings with him an intrinsic understanding of the show, the characters and the relationships. That was a great advantage. He also is a guy that is very intelligent and a fine artist, so he brought those qualities."

Walter Koenig: "*Star Trek III* is obviously a very successful film. I think it, perhaps more than either of the first two features, promotes a sense of family and congeniality and warmth. I think there's a feeling of affection generated by the members of the Enterprise crew, much more a sense of simpatico."

On his feature directorial debut, Leonard Nimoy hit the proverbial home run both critically and financially, as *Star Trek III* matched the gross of its predecessor. Things were, however, amiss in the *Star Trek* universe itself, given the death of David Marcus, the destruction of the Enterprise and the fact that her former crew were now renegades who had disobeyed Federation orders to go after Spock.

The groundwork had been laid for a fourth film, which would ultimately prove to be the most popular of all.

• • • •

CHAPTER TWELVE

Star Trek IV: The Voyage Home

The Voyage Begins

Considering the resounding success of *The Search for Spock*, it came as no surprise to anyone that Paramount Pictures was interested in dipping back into the well at least one more time with a fourth film. The trek got off to a less than smooth start when William Shatner made it plainly clear to the studio that he would not return as James T. Kirk unless the good admiral was given a considerable pay increase.

Six months passed while returning director Leonard Nimoy and executive producer Harve Bennett awaited word. As negotiations continued, a variation of the *Star Trek* formula was developed.

"A proposal was made by me that we didn't have to have Bill," said Bennett, "that we could do *Star Trek* in the beginning, which was Ralph Winter's idea. Let's do them at the academy. That picture seems to have worked in a variety of incarnations including *Top Gun*. It's a very workable picture. But the franchise wasn't the same without the stars and there is merit in that argument."

Interestingly, the story, entitled *Starfleet Academy*, would come up again shortly after the production of *Star Trek V*, a fact which will be discussed in depth further on in this volume.

Finally, after a total of eight months had passed (and this delay would ultimately have repercussions on Shatner himself when he took the helm of the fifth film adventure), Shatner signed on the dotted line for $2 million and *Star Trek IV* was back on track. By this time, however, quite a bit had happened behind the scenes, the least of which was the development of the film's tone and storyline, as well as the idea that this would be the concluding chapter of a trilogy; a trilogy which had not been intended when Bennett took over the series' production reigns.

"In moving through the trilogy,"

Bennett has stated, "I confess that every one of the major tricks I learned in television, I used. I'm out of tricks now....I've gotta find another one because we have now completed a trilogy and we have to go where no man has gone before. When you go where no man has gone before, you have to build things and then it starts getting expensive. Here are the three tricks of the trilogy: *Star Trek II*, in television we call that the 'bottle show.' The 'bottle show' in television takes place in an elevator that's hopefully trapped between two floors. Or it takes place in a mine shaft where people are desperately coming to try to save you and you have to stay down there and talk a lot. Sixty-five percent of the film was on the Enterprise bridge in one incarnation or another. It was also the Reliant bridge. And it was also part of the science station. We used that set for 65 percent of the movie and that is an incomparable savings in terms of time, dollars and moves. We'd shoot a scene, move the people out, repaint it and it would now be the Reliant.

"*Star Trek III*," he continued, "was the classic television 'the leading actor loses his memory' show. I did that on *Mod Squad, Six Million Dollar Man, Bionic Woman*, and you usually do it when your leading actor is exhausted or needs a rest. He's in a coma-like state. In *Star Trek III*, we had a man who was directing the movie, and who had never directed a feature before, and we felt that to act and so forth would kill him. We had our choice of how to utilize that asset, and what we did was we spent most of our money building one great set, the Genesis planet, and the story became let's find him while he directs. [For *Star Trek IV* we decided to use] local location. We've gotta add some size to this picture, so what do we do? We go out. How do you go out in the 23rd Century? You come to the *20th Century*."

Said Leonard Nimoy, "We decided early on that we wanted to do a time travel story. When I say we, I'm talking about Harve Bennett and I. We were asked by the studio to come up with a story, and our very first conversation was about doing time travel, which we both agreed was a good idea. We also felt that we should lighten up. The

To tie-in to the show's 20th anniversary and the release of The Voyage Home, Newsweek devoted its December 22, 1986 issue to the show.

picture should be fun in comparison to the previous three. The first movie had no comedy at all. That was intentional. It was intended to be a serious study of a problem. The second film had a little. The third film had a little. But there we were dealing with a lot of serious drama. There was a lot of life and death going on. In [*Star Trek*] II Spock died. In [*Star Trek*] III Kirk's son died, the Enterprise was blown up and people were being killed and planets were disintegrating. I just felt it was time to lighten up and have some fun. That meant that if we were going to do time travel, the best thing we could do was come back to contemporary Earth, where we could have some fun with our people. They would more or less be a fish out of water on the streets."

Shortly thereafter, Nimoy had numerous conversations with members of M.I.T. regarding communication with other species.

"We were talking about the idea that if alien intelligence was trying to contact us, it would probably take quite a long time for us to know what it is saying, and for us to communicate with it," Nimoy stated. "I became intrigued with the idea that there was some lack of communication that was causing the problem. [I was] aware that humpback

• • • •

whales sing this unusual kind of song, which we don't understand but which obviously means something to them. They communicate it to each other, they pass it on one to the other, they repeat it. It has a form, lasting anywhere from six to 30 minutes in cycles, and they sing it again and again. Then they cease periodically, and they change the song. It's quite a complex structure, and that's very interesting. We don't know, and we may never know, what the communication is all about, so supposing that something in the 23rd Century is trying to communicate with them and they're gone. That's how it all happened, and it's a hell of a lot more interesting and challenging, cinematically, to come back to the 20th Century to pick up a pair of whales than it is to pick up a plant or insect."

The search for a writer began, while the film was struck with an interesting....dilemma. Eddie Murphy, a golden boy at Paramount at the time, had been pretty vocal in the fact that he loved *Star Trek* and would be very interested in co-starring in the new film.

"Now the meeting with Eddie Murphy was a little bizarre," said Bennett. "He had a separate meeting with Leonard. Leonard said, 'He's a little strange in a room.' So he came in with two thugs, good looking thugs, and they were all in black leather. [We] told Eddie this story and the thought about it for awhile and he said, 'It's good. Let me see a script,' and he walked out. We sat there and thought, 'Wouldn't it be terrific to have Eddie in this movie?' Later, the studio started getting very anxious for a very good reason. Here you have a franchise called *Star Trek* and it performs in a certain wonderful way. Here you have a franchise called Eddie Murphy and it performs in an even bigger way. Why not take them together and form one franchise? Bad economics because you are probably diminishing by compositing. So the studio was resistant to it, but Eddie has a certain amount of clout and he said that he hadn't decided whether he wanted to do it or not and so much of the development of the story was with the very distinct possibility that Eddie Murphy was in it."

As is the norm for *Star Trek* films, word of this little news item

reached fandom, and memories of Richard Pryor's guest starring in *Superman III* sent a shudder through them. Naturally, a letter writing campaign was quickly initiated.

Said Harve Bennett, "The *Star Trek* fans who are our greatest asset, are also gigantic pains-in-the-ass. They know I love them and they know I can say that. They do have a propriety interest and to some extent they do pay for it. The fans found out about this and they got the word out."

"*Star Trek* is a lot of different things to a lot of different people," related Leonard Nimoy. "Some people watch it because they love the Enterprise, some people because they love the space battles, others because of the characters or the aliens. There are a lot of different reasons that you enjoy *Star Trek*. There have been people who have said to me, 'How could you destroy the Enterprise? What's *Star Trek* without the Enterprise?' We're doing drama. We're doing entertainment. We're doing fiction. If there's an individual who can't handle that and who steps over into a personal fantasy, that's his personal problem. I think the handling of the death and resurrection of Spock was tastefully done, dramatically done and was good science fiction. We're doing an entertainment piece. It shouldn't be taken too seriously."

Penning The Voyage Home

Based on their screenplay *The Long Way Home*, a black comedy about the plight of the Indian in America today, Steve Meerson and Peter Krikes were chosen to write the screenplay for *Star Trek IV*.

Said Meerson, "We sat in a room with Leonard and Harve, and Leonard told us that he wanted to do a departure, although they weren't sure what they wanted to do."

Added Krikes, "They wanted to do a film sort of based on 'The City on the Edge of Forever'...."

"Leonard started talking about plankton, cells, that cells become plankton, that things eat plankton and then whales entered the conversation."

"And we said, 'Why not make it

as simple as the whale and the whale song?' That was our idea, though that's not to say that Leonard hadn't done research on whales, because he had."

"Leonard has mountains of information on various things," pointed out Meerson. "I guess we were hired in February of 1985 and between that time and May or June, Peter and I did several outlines of what eventually became the story. Before we could start writing the script, we had to get the studio to approve the outline. We registered all the outlines with the Writer's Guild, and after we came up with the story for the movie, Harve and Leonard took our outline and went through it step by step with the studio executives, and we got the go-ahead to start writing."

The duo were given two instructions: keep Eddie Murphy in mind for the guest star, and make sure that the character of Admiral Kirk is the driving force behind every aspect of the story.

"The approach we were told to take is that Kirk really had to be the one to lead everyone," explained Meerson. "Not necessarily that he had to actually have the idea to do something, but it had to appear as if he has the idea. I think the perfect example in the movie is when Spock goes into the belly of the Bird of Prey to use the computers and learns that the sound is whale songs. It's Kirk who has the idea to go back through time, although Spock is the one who plants the suggestion in Kirk's mind. Kirk verbalizes it, and that's the way it had to be played. We were told Bill had to be the leader at all times. In that scene, if you're reading it, you say, 'It's Spock's idea,' but on film Spock's discovery that it's humpback whales is not as important as Kirk's idea of going to get them."

"Visually," added Krikes, "the scene between Spock and his father at the end is another example. You kind of ask, 'Why is Captain Kirk standing there listening to this?' He has to be a part of *everything*."

Naturally word reached them of the controversy surrounding Murphy's possible appearance, and the fact that the cast was not happy about the idea.

"I think all of those guys became terrified that Eddie would blow them off the screen," mused Meerson.

"They also got a lot of negative mail from the fans."

All of the "noise" ultimately came to nothing, as Murphy decided to bow out.

"I'm a Trekkie," claimed Murphy. "I've always loved *Star Trek* and *have* wanted to do one of the films. I wanted to be in *Star Trek* and that's where they got the idea of coming back in time to Earth in 1987. The script was developed, but we eventually dropped the idea. *Golden Child* came along and I decided to do that film instead, because I thought it would be better for my career. In retrospect, I might have been better off doing *Star Trek IV*."

Explained Harve Bennett, "We went through every writer we could think of. We finally found Steve Meerson and Peter Krikes, whose work was highly regarded. Nothing came of it. Some of that, in fairness to them, was because we had saddled them with what appeared to be a male character that we thought was going to be Eddie Murphy at one time. Then when Eddie Murphy fell out, we had to readjust the script. But, by then, it had turned to paste, it just didn't work. Frankly, there are two scenes in the picture that they wrote that stayed pretty much the same. One of them is outstanding, which is the hospital scene that had minor modifications by Nick Meyer and me. They had also laid down the outline for the plexiglass factory scene. But, essentially, we didn't have a script we felt good about or even submittable to the studio."

As one would suspect, Meerson and Krikes *did not* take kindly to such comments.

"Actually," stated Meerson, "every beat of the film's first, second and third acts is *exactly the same* as our script. The *only* thing that changed slightly was that our Eddie Murphy character and the marine biologist were combined. Eddie Murphy was going to play a college professor who taught English, but a professor who we probably all had in the '60s or '70s, who's a little bit wacky and believes in extraterrestrials. Every Wednesday, he would open up his class to a discussion and the room would light up with conversation."

Krikes said, "He would play whale songs, and it was the whale songs he played in the classroom that the ship locked on to."

"That was in the first draft we wrote, but the second draft was different. After you write a first draft of anything, once the director, the cast and the producers come aboard, *everything* changes, and not necessarily for the better. But the tone was pretty much a reflection of what was in the movie. For example, there was a scene where the Eddie Murphy character was trying to convince the Catherine Hicks character that aliens do exist on Earth. In the first draft, Hicks was a newswoman and there was a marine biologist as well. Gillian Taylor was ultimately a marriage of about three characters."

"Murphy believed in aliens and saw them beam into the classroom."

"It was the boy who cried wolf," Meerson noted. "No one would ever believe him, so he took it upon himself to follow the crew, and in one scene, he lifted a phaser from Kirk, took it back to the newswoman and said, 'See, they really *do* exist.' And she says, 'What's this?' and casts the gun aside, accidentally activating it. The phaser lands on the floor and her cat jumps off the couch. We follow her to her bedroom and she goes to sleep. The cat keeps phasing things out of the apartment by hitting the phaser, and when she wakes up, she sees that all the furniture is gone."

"That's just the side stuff," Krikes remarked. "If you look at our script and the movie you saw, basically everything is still there, like Eddie Murphy going to meet the aliens in the park to bring them gifts, and he runs into the invisible ship...."

"....Which is what Catherine Hicks did when she ran into the park to find Kirk. The structure really is exactly the same. Also, she grabbed Kirk's waist, Eddie Murphy grabbed his ankles. Murphy says goodbye to Kirk who starts to beam out, then he grabs him by the ankles and is transported aboard. He goes back to the 23rd Century, and he salutes Kirk when they get the Enterprise II. You know when Spock nerve pinches the guy on the bus? In our draft that took place in an underground subway system....You can't imagine the frustration of watching them take all the credit for something that was completely blocked out for them."

"Plus they removed a lot of the emotional qualities that we thought it would have," Krikes mused. "It's interesting how they downplayed certain things. We spent months trying to figure out how you could get dilithium on Earth, sincere there was none. We had put in a sequence with a linear accelerator, where they break into the linear accelerator at Stamford University and have to take whatever element we have and charge it. And Spock had to work on rearranging the elements."

"They simplified the sequence, essentially, and said, 'Let's just stick this little machine on top and it'll change it into something.' I think it was actually a good idea, because it wouldn't have fit into the movie."

That's not to say that there weren't some significant differences as well, including the idea that Lieutenant Saavik was pregnant due to her *pon farr* sequence with young Spock in *Star Trek III*.

"There was a scene with Kirk on the Bridge of the Bird of Prey," recalled Krikes. "They cut out five lines where Kirk says to Saavik, 'Have you told him yet?' And she says, 'No. I'm taking a maternity leave.'"

"That's why she's standing with Amanda when the Bird of Prey leaves," Meerson revealed. "Because Amanda *knows* Saavik is carrying Spock's kid."

"All they did was cut out five lines of dialogue, and you lost that whole thing, which, I believe, will turn up in a Harve Bennett script in a couple of years."

Stated Meerson, "You'll have a story meeting with Harve Bennett for about eight hours and you'll say something in the first hour, and in the eighth hour he'll say, 'What does everybody think of this?' And it's exactly what you said eight hours ago. But that's really what Saavik's involvement was."

Krikes recalled another change. "One of the things we had in our earlier drafts that they took out was what happened when they first went through time. Instead of that horrible time sequence that looks like Russian science fiction, we had them using the sling-shot effect around Jupiter and Mars. Also, when they first appeared in the 20th Century, they were in a fog, and as they lowered, the monitors picked up all of this cheering and applause. As they come out of the fog, they find themselves over a Super Bowl game and everyone thinks it's a halftime show. Then, they cloak and disappear."

Meerson explained, "That's how we introduced the Eddie Murphy character, because he's at the Super Bowl and he's the only one who believes he just saw what he saw. I thought that would have been a wonderful moment. Also, I love our ending better. Our sequence of events were similar. After the shuttle has picked them up and Earth is saved, we cut to this little chamber where they're waiting to stand trial."

"They discuss whether or not they would do everything the same if they could...."

"....And they say they would. We cut away to Spock and Sarek, who have that same chat that they had in the movie. It was originally much more bonding, but they removed about half-a-page of dialogue, which changed things quite a bit."

Commented Krikes, "Basically, Sarek was saying, 'You're half-human and I'll never understand that, but I accept you.'"

"So we cut from that to someone knocking on the door and saying, 'It's time to go on trial,' and they put them in a pool. They go through this endless black tunnel and come out into the docking area for the trial...."

"....And everyone is gathered by the windows of the dock, cheering them on."

Meerson smiled at the memory. "Everyone is confused, saying to the pilot, 'Where are you taking us?' That's when the pod rises and you see the new Enterprise II. It would have been much more emotional, instead of saying, 'You've been exonerated for this, this and this,' you could have done it in three sentences, and with everyone cheering, screaming and yelling, it would have been an emotional high. Harve likes bookends, which is why the film begins with a trial and ends with a trial. That was always a point of contention between the three of us, that you didn't need to do that sequence again because it would be understood why. You could

just take them to the ship so that everyone would be on a high, rather than waiting for it to happen. Structurally, I think they made a mistake."

Meerson and Krikes emphasize that they were excited when they were contacted about the film, but found that the road to the screen wasn't exactly easy. Part of it was the difficulty in giving *all* of the characters something to do, as well as what happened to their script after they handed it in.

"We were told to *only* worry about Kirk, Spock and Bones," said Meerson. "In their minds, those are the only people that matter."

Added Krikes, "They also took out a scene we wrote which dealt with the people's mortality and age."

"My favorite scene we wrote was between Bones and Scotty, where they talk about the fact that they're getting too old to be doing this. I personally think they [DeForest Kelley and James Doohan] would have loved to play it. It was two guys sitting on a park bench in Union Square, completely out of time and space, saying, 'We're really getting too old. If we ever do make it back, maybe we ought to give it all up and retire.' Then, they both decided that they'll *never* retire, because there's more to life than sitting on your duff."

As stated earlier, once Eddie Murphy left the project, Bennett turned his attention to other writers. One of his first creative decisions was to alter the Murphy character into a female marine biologist, who would also serve as Kirk's love interest.

Recalled Bennett, "I remember saying, 'Well, I know it's corny, but it would be better if it was a woman. Kirk hasn't had a woman to play to, which he does so wonderfully. The whole series is the woman of the week. Remember that whale special we saw where the girl was bidding adieu to the whales who had to leave Marineland because the female was pregnant and they could not keep them and they had to send them back to the sea and she was bereft? Remember that character? That's the lady,' and Leonard thought that was great.

"So, now we're getting down to where we've got a movie to make and a whole new script to write. That's when

we were fortunate enough to find that Nicholas Meyer was available."

In the pages of *Cinefantastique*, Meyer told journalist Dennis Fischer, "I got involved in number IV because they had another script they were not happy with. Dawn Steele, who [was] the head of Paramount and has been a friend of mine for many years, called me and said, 'Would you do us an enormous favor?' And I said, 'For Harve and Leonard? Yeah, absolutely.' They had a script written. The script, I guess, was for Eddie Murphy as a guest star. I never read it, so I don't know. But they weren't happy with it. They wanted to go back to their original story and write another script. Harve said, 'This is what I want to do. I write the first 20-25% of it, and when they get to Earth or when they're about to get to Earth, then you take it, finish the Earth stuff, and I'll do the ending.' We went over each other's stuff. My contribution begins with Spock's crack about 'Judging by the pollution content of the atmosphere, I believe we have arrived at the late 20th Century,' and goes from there to someplace after they get the whales and leave. I didn't read the other script because I just thought it would confuse me and since they didn't like it, why bother?"

Reflected Bennett, "Nick and I had written the final script of *Star Trek II* in 10 days. This one we wrote in about 20, and it was very simple to do it that way because I took act one and act three and Nick took act two. Now if you think about that in structural terms, I got us into the dilemma and into time travel, he carried us through San Francisco, and I got us back. That was like breathing for me because it's pure *Star Trek* and it was like breathing for him because his irreverence is what really makes the fun. Then we swapped pages and I rewrote him a little bit and he rewrote me a little bit and we put it all together and had a script. Nick always said, 'You know the problem with this script is you've got five endings.' And he was right, we did have five endings. He said, 'Why don't you have the whales save the Earth? That's the end of the picture!' No, I said, that's the end of the picture for the hoped for extended audience who's never seen *Star Trek* before. But for people who have seen *Star Trek* before, we have a trilogy to complete. So we've gotta get them back, get them off the hook and give them the Enterprise back. We've got to do that, so that when we finish this picture, we have brought the franchise back to square one and it can go anywhere it wants to go. That's only fair. Besides, that's what the fans want. So that's what we did. We kept every ending."

As finally rewritten, *Star Trek IV: The Voyage Home* opens with an alien probe that is threatening to destroy planet Earth. Kirk, Spock, McCoy and the rest, on board the Bird of Prey and heading home to turn themselves over to the proper authorities, discover that the alien signal is actually being transmitted in the language of humpback whales, a species extinct in the 23rd Century. They take the Klingon vessel back to Earth circa 1987, get involved with marine biologist Gillian Taylor, who plays an integral role in their obtaining the necessary whales and then joins them on the return to the future. There, and once Earth has been saved by the whales singing to the probe, she joins the crew of a science vessel, and our people have the charges against them dismissed, with their being sent aboard a brand new starship Enterprise.

As vehemently as Meyer opposed the suggestion at the close of *Star Trek II* that Spock would come back, he was against Gillian's sojourn through time.

"In my version of the script," he said, "originally, when they all leave to go back, she didn't leave. She said if anyone's going to make sure this kind of disaster doesn't happen, somebody's going to have to stay behind, which I still think is the 'righter' ending. The end in the movie detracts from the importance of people in the present taking responsibility for the ecology and preventing problems of the future by doing something about them today, rather than catering to the fantasy desires of being able to be transported ahead in time to the near-utopian future society of the *Star Trek* era."

While it's common knowledge that rewrites are a part of every produced screenplay, writers Steve Meerson and Peter Krikes were nevertheless shocked to discover that Harve Bennett and Nicholas Meyer had been nominated for lead writing credits on *Trek IV*. This led

to Writer's Guild arbitration.

Steve Meerson said, "Harve wanted to sort of roll up his sleeves and, as he called it, *Trek* it up, claiming that we weren't that familiar with *Star Trek*, which was a lie. Unbeknownst to us, he was telling the studio things like, 'They're going to deliver the first act today,' which he never told us and of course the studio got upset with us and said, 'Where's the first act?' and then Harve would say, 'I didn't say that.' Basically, you're talking to two people who did not leave this office for seven months. I'm talking we were working seven days a week, with food being slipped under the door. Our arbitration statement on the movie said, 'If a story had previously existed, what were we doing between February and May and June coming up with like seven outlines to write the script from?'"

Noted Krikes, "I don't know if you're aware how arbitration works, but within three days from the end of filming, the producer entities must turn in all the written materials to the Writer's Guild. In this case, it took two months to turn them in. They were trying to get our names off the script."

"There's actually a rule you can go by," stated Meerson. "When a script goes to arbitration at the Guild, the people that get first position—it goes to follow—did the lion's share of the work. We got first position on the script. I don't really want to get into the arbitration, *per se*, only to say that it was very political. Peter and I were lucky that we ended up with any credit at all. They have a very high-powered machine which is not very kind to outsiders, and we aren't the first people to experience that. It was a difficult pill to swallow. The reason it hasn't affected us that much is that everyone in town *knows* we did the story. They know our work, and it's such a departure from the other movies. *Star Trek IV* was so different, and we were the only new element."

Both men found their experience to be enlightening and—despite everything—something to be proud of.

"We can sum it up by saying we learned to sit with our backs to the wall, and to make sure what's on the other side of the wall first," said Peter Krikes. "It was a real roller coaster experience and, so far, it's the most successful

in the series. *That's* a wonderful feeling."

Noted Steve Meerson, "When you go into story meetings with people who are constantly claiming that your ideas are theirs, what you need to do is take notes, write memos, confirm memos about what transpired, make sure all materials are registered and make sure you're aware of the arbitration process, which is supposed to function on your behalf, but doesn't. It's very political. You learn the avenues that are open to you, and basically you grow up. You learn that you can't trust anyone.

"By the same token, I think we were both delighted that we were a part of something that will go on forever, and I also think it said some things that needed to be said. There are some important messages there, and being allowed to have that forum was very exciting. It's hard for me to say this, but it was worth all the aggravation."

Bringing The Voyage Home

Although the set of *Star Trek IV* was generally very upbeat, there was a severe falling out between Leonard Nimoy and Harve Bennett, reportedly resulting in Bennett's actually being thrown off the set.

In the pages of *Captain's Log*, Bennett explained, "I had been emotionally beat up by Leonard Nimoy. I respect him for what he has done, but in the transition between *III* and *IV*, Leonard had come to regard me as in his way, with regards to the auteurship of the film. I was not only the man who said 'No,' but the man who was conspiring to....you know. So that on one occasion, it got really mean on the stage—mean from him to me. I was smarting—'Who needs this shit?'—was foremost on my mind."

A production source wishing to remain anonymous added, "Harve, actually, was barred from the set. He and Leonard weren't speaking on literally half of the filming. They had a major argument on the set and Harve was thrown off."

While Nimoy did not discuss this issue with the press, he did detail the challenge of not only directing the film, but co-starring in it as well.

"It was hard physically," he

said. "But I had a good time doing it because I really enjoyed playing the Spock character in this picture. He's a very different Spock. A Spock who's evolving, who's confused. He's trying to figure out who he's supposed to be and how he's supposed to function. It was great fun to play, but, physically, very tough because it's a long day. If you just direct the picture, it's a tough job. If you act in it as well, it's tougher. Then you have to add on a two hour make-up job every day, which means that you have to be in at 5:00 every morning. [But] this is a funny Spock. He's also very touching. I think it's a very touching moment when Spock discovers his identity. It happens at the moment when Kirk and McCoy are talking about what to do about Chekov in the hospital, and Spock says, 'We must help Chekov.' Kirk says, 'Is that the logical thing to do, Spock?' Spock replies, 'No, but it is the human thing to do.' I hope audiences [were] touched by that. It's the kind of moment when you say, 'Ah, Spock is there. He found his way.'"

As a director, Nimoy felt that *Star Trek IV* was much more ambitious and exciting than the previous films.

"We were off the soundstages for the first time," he enthused. "The first three pictures were almost exclusively on the soundstages. In *Star Trek I*, we were off the soundstage for a couple of days; on *Star Trek III* we were off for a couple of nights for the Vulcan exterior scenes. To get off the soundstages on this one was very invigorating. It gave a lot more energy to me and the cast of the picture, and I had a little bit more time. I shot *Star Trek III* in 49 days and on this one I had 53. Actually, I had 57, and I came in four days early."

To put it mildly, *Star Trek IV: The Voyage Home* was a great success, pulling in some $126 million and quickly establishing itself as the favorite of the series among many people, including the vast majority of film critics and some of the cast members.

William Shatner: "We discovered something in *Star Trek IV* that we hadn't pinpointed in any of the other movies—and it just shows how the obvious can escape you—that there is a texture to the best *Star Trek* hours that verges on tongue-in-cheek but isn't.

There's a line that we all have to walk that is reality. It's as though the characters within the play have a great deal of joy about themselves, a joy of living. That energy, that 'joie de vivre' about the characters seems to be tongue-in-cheek but isn't, because you play it with the reality [that] you would in a kitchen-sink drama written for today's life."

DeForest Kelley: "I have always felt from the very beginning that the core of *Star Trek* was the family. It was always this group of people that were working in this bizarre-type world together. That's what made the show successful. One of the greatest mistakes in the first motion picture was that they neglected the people and went around us. It's taken some time but now it's back to normal thaniks to Leonard Nimoy."

James Doohan: "*Star Trek IV* was absolutely delightful. It was a delight to do, and a delight to watch. Our best, dramatically speaking, mostly on account of Ricardo Montalban, was *Star Trek II: The Wrath of Khan*. But *Star Trek IV* was cute and funny, and everybody loved it just for that. Also, there was the great comraderie between the characters. The fans just absolutely love the banter that goes back and forth."

George Takei: "I thought *Star Trek IV* was perhaps the most successful *Star Trek* movie we've done. It brought together the various elements that made *Star Trek* as a television series so sucessful. It certainly had the interrelationships of all the characters that the series such an accessible show....In terms of commentary on a pertinent contemporary issue, we explored the fact that there is a price to be paid when we play with our ecology."

Nichelle Nichols: "The first film was good science fiction if you don't think of it as being *Star Trek*. Unfortunately, that's what everybody thought they were getting which is why it seems to be people's least favorite film. The second film was centered around Spock dying and the third, around bringing Spock back to life so there wasn't enough time to introduce the things that made *Star Trek* on TV so great. Those elements finally came together with *Star Trek IV*. The humor and action were there. The idea of the

whales was wonderful. It was definitely a step in the direction of what the old series was all about."

Walter Koenig: "I thought *Star Trek IV* was a delightful picture. The biggest surprise was seeing Leonard's performance, because I'd never seen him work in the picture, except for the scenes in which he was behind us on the bridge, but those individual scenes....those scenes with Bill, I'd never actually seen. That was the most effective performance he'd given as Spock because he maintained the sense of emotional distance and at the same time there was a wonderful underpinning of compassion to the character. I'm pleased for him, for his success, for the picture's success, and I'm very pleased to have been part of that."

Leonard Nimoy summarized his own feelings regarding the film, by noting, "[The feeling on the first film] was that we had to do a 'motion picture.' Nick Meyer brought a jauntiness back to it. I tried in *Star Trek III* to do a dignified job of resurrection, and do it with a sense of mysticism, a sense of wonder and, above all, to really capture the loyalty of these people for each other; their willingness to sacrifice themselves and their careers for the purpose of helping Spock. Having done that, I really wanted to have a good time on this one. Somebody had been constantly dying in the films, and this time I said, 'Nobody's going to die. I don't want anybody hitting anybody, I don't want anybody shooting anybody,' or any of that stuff. If anybody was going to be injured, it was going to be accidental.

"I insisted that there be no bad guy," Nimoy closed. "We had done two pictures in a row with black-hat heavies, and I didn't want a bad guy anywhere. Circumstances would be the problem. Lack of awareness, lack of concern. Ignorance would be the problem. Not a person. I hope with this one we've really gone full circle and come home, which is why, in a sense, we're calling it *The Voyage Home*. We're saying, 'Enjoy yourself, have a good time, and don't mind us as we drop off a few ideas along the way.'"

• • • •

••••

CHAPTER THIRTEEN

Star Trek V: The Final Frontier

Captain's Log

Star Trek IV: The Voyage Home was both a critical and commercial success that achieved its goal of being the much sought after "crossover film;" a *Trek* film that appealed to the mainstream audience. As such, it was a hard act to follow, a fact that no one could deny, let alone William Shatner. The actor had, as stated previously, made a point in his contract for the fourth film in the series of being given the opportunity to direct number five. After all, Leonard Nimoy had twice been given that chance and Shatner knew that he was contractually entitled to the same thing.

In the pages of *Captain's Log*, Shatner stated, "Somewhere along the line, Leonard's lawyers and my lawyers had gotten together and drawn up a favored nations clause, which meant everything he got, I got and vice versa. Well, in the beginning, I was commanding more money, so that any raises I was getting, Leonard would get also. So I made Leonard a great deal of money on my lawyers by bringing him up to the salary I was getting. We used to joke about that, how that clause had benefitted him so much. But in the end, the fact that Leonard directed a picture, which meant that I would get to direct one, was by far the most important consequence of that clause."

"Directing has been a lifelong dream," Shatner enthused elsewhere. "My business is to entertain people, and to communicate my feelings to them, so I find the best way is to direct. Directing is the pinnacle of our business. A really good director has a point of view on his film and all his other skills emanate from that spine. I've always wanted to entertain, and I think I can do that with my point of view, so I'm under the impression that I can gather all my skills

around me to make people laugh and cry. I wanted to do more. I haven't done it to the extent that I wanted to. I think the movies have matured beyond the series and we have to give our audience that maturity. I'd like to think that's what I've done."

No sooner had production been completed on *Star Trek IV*, then Shatner began thinking of the next chapter in the ongoing saga. He definitely had his storyline in mind, beginning with the fascination he had always held for television evangelists who claim that God is speaking through them, rather than someone else. "I took the TV evangelist persona and created a holy man who thought God had spoken to him," said Shatner. "He believed God had told him, 'I need many followers, and I need a vehicle to spread my word throughout the universe.' That vehicle he needed became a starship [the Enterprise] which the holy man would capture when it came to rescuing some hostages he had taken....Finally the Enterprise arrives at the planet where God supposedly resides, in the center of the universe....Kirk, Spock, McCoy and the holy man are beamed down to the planet. It's like the drawings of Dante's *Inferno*, like a flaming hell. When God appears, he seems like God....but gradually, in a conversation between God and the holy man, Kirk perceives that something is wrong and begins to challenge God. God gets angrier and angrier, and begins to show his true colors, which are those of the devil....So essentially that was my story: that man conceives of God in his own image, but those images change from generation to generation, therefore he appears in all these different guises as man-made Gods. But in essence, if the devil exists, God exists by inference. This is the lesson that the *Star Trek* group learns. The lesson being that God is within our hearts, not something we conjure up, invent and then worship."

"The real problem with *V*," returning producer Harve Bennett told *Cinefantastique*, "was that the premise was faulty. You pick up a *TV Guide* and you read the log line which says, 'Tonight on *Trek*, the crew goes to find God.' Automatically, and unconsciously, you know we're not going to find God because no one has and no one will, and

The making of Star Trek V *as seen through the eyes of Starlog Press' official publication.*

no one would be so arrogant to say what they're depicting on screen is actually God, because others will say, 'No it's not.' So we know we're going to face an anticlimax, a trick. The nature of the trick is the only suspense in the story. But you'd say this to Bill and he's say, 'No, no, it's the greatest adventure of all time,' and I'd say, 'No, it's not an adventure because everyone is ahead of you. So what we have to do is make getting there as interesting as possible."

The Final Screenplay...?

"I would say that the trilogy probably stands because of its centering on the life, death, resurrection of Spock and his refulfillment," stated Harve Bennett to *The Official Star Trek Fan Club Magazine* (#64). "This film is continuous only in the sense of time. What we are trying to do in each picture is explore other angles and other undiscovered depths of these very legendary and familiar characters. And that's not too easy because you reach a point where you say, 'How much more can we explore these people?' But remember, these people are also aging, which they did not do in the series. So as they age, they are revealing more and more of their back and foreground stories. That's where the challenge is for me: to try to keep mining these relationships. [*Star*

••••

Trek V also] has with it an imperative of going back to deep space. *Star Trek II, III* and *IV* were all, to some extent, manageable in terms of budget, shooting time and scope. With *Star Trek V*, we have now come to the space imperative and we have some very, very difficult appetites: planetary and construction appetites—things you have to show and places you have to go, and an alien here and there. All these things make the cost and complexity of the film more difficult."

To make things a bit easier, both Bennett and Shatner began an intensive search for the proper screenwriter to bring this vision to the screen. Who they found was David Loughery, the writer behind *Dreamscape*.

"I sold an original screenplay to Paramount called *Flashback*," says Loughery. "Based on the merits of that script, Paramount offered me an overall deal, which I accepted, and one of the executives at that time asked me if I had any interest in working on *Star Trek V*. I said, 'Sure,' thinking that would be the last I ever heard of it. A couple of weeks later, they put me together with Harve Bennett. We talked and got along real well, and then we met Bill Shatner, who had already written an outline which he had turned into Paramount."

That outline, subtitled "An Act of Love," dealt with the Enterprise being commandeered by a rogue Vulcan named Sybok (as is the case in the final film), and being led to a world beyond the Great Barrier where they encounter God, who turns out to be the Devil.

"Paramount liked Bill's outline," says Loughery, "but they thought that it was a little too dark. After the success of *Star Trek IV*, they wanted to make sure that we retained as much humor and fun as possible, because they felt that was one of the reasons for the big success of that film. They wanted us to inject a spirit of fun and adventure into the story. I think they just wanted a balance between the darker elements and some of the lighter stuff. One particular change was in the character of Sybok. Originally, he was a very messianic, possessed kind of figure who was willing to trample anyone who got in his way, but he began to remind us too much of Khan and we had to take him in a different direction. It

would have been easy to write Sybok as a black-hat or a crazed Mohammed, but that was too much Khan.

"The idea of God and the Devil was reflected in the script's earlier drafts. Those drafts were much cleaner and more comprehensible in terms of the idea that you think you're going to Heaven, but you turn out to have found Hell. We weren't literally saying Heaven and Hell, but we were suggesting the idea that it was like, 'Wait a minute, is this God or the Devil?', without saying specifically that it's either, but instead is an alien entity that has tapped into our perceptions about where they're going. We did, however, run into some problems, one with Gene Roddenberry."

Roddenberry rejected the notion of the Enterprise encountering God, believing that *Star Trek* should avoid such specific religious themes.

"I didn't object to it being an alien claiming to be God," Roddenberry said in *Captain's Log*, "but there was too much in it that an audience could have thought was really God or really the devil, and I very strongly resist believing in either. I do not perceive this as a universe that's divided between good and evil. I see it as a universe that is divided between many ideas of what is."

Admits Shatner, "[Gene] did come down strongly against the story and set up circumstances that were negative and unfortunate. There's nothing wrong with a good story about the search for the meaning of life. That's basic to any great storytelling, no matter what form it takes whether it's *The Bible* or a myth or a fairy tale. I was hoping to be able to accomplish that with *Star Trek V*."

Loughery quickly adds that as fascinating as the theme of "meeting God" may be, it was the exploration of the relationship between Kirk, Spock and McCoy that appealed to him the most.

"To me, God was never the most important part of the script," he explains. "Yes, it was part of the story, but my focus and concentration was on the relationships. The whole God idea was almost a subplot. We had to tread a fine line, because we could really become very pretentious and pretend that we're saying something infinitely important. What I think we're really say-

ing is something that's very simple, which is that if there is a God, he's not a place you go to in terms of outer space. He's a place you go to inside yourself. We also wanted to challenge the audience's imagination and expectations when they realized that this is what Sybok's divine mission was. We really wanted the audience to stir around, look at each other and say, 'Are they serious? Can they possibly mean that we're going to see God?' Because, for me, *Star Trek* is probably the only arena in which you might actually try to do that. *Star Trek* has always been big enough to encompass almost any kind of concept, so we thought when we dropped the bomb and said, 'Oh, by the way, we're going to see God,' it would be something the audience would be excited about and say, 'Gee, maybe they will....who knows?'

"In terms of the Kirk, Spock and McCoy relationship, one of the things that occurred to me," he states, "is that if you look at *Star Trek*, you see these three men who are in middle age, and their lives have been spent in space. They're not married, they don't have families, so their relationship is with each other. They represent a family to each other, maybe without always acknowledging it. That, to me, was the most attractive thing, saying, 'What is family?' If it's not three people who care about each other, I don't know what it is."

Nobody Said It Was Gonna Be Easy

There was a point in the development of *Star Trek V* in which William Shatner had to go off to act in Ted Turner's *Voice of the Planet*, while David Loughery and Harve Bennett wrote yet another draft of the screenplay. This version was *so* different from the original concept, that Shatner felt betrayed upon his return.

"In truth," explains David Loughery, "we had gone too far, but sometimes you need to go too far in order to really see where you need to be. We found a median that was satisfying to all of us. We had some interesting ups and downs. I did lots of drafts over two years, and each one was a little different from the one before. What Harve and I had written—where we had really gone off from the original concept—was where we began to deal more with the idea of this legendary planet, this mythic place called Sha Ka Ree, being Sybok's goal and thinking of it more in terms of Shangri-La. It's a kind of Eden that existed, and a place one could reach by passing through this ordeal called the Barrier. We were leaning in the direction of it being more a mythic and heaven-like place, and dealing less with the idea that a physical God existed there. We were shying away from the idea of going to see God, and thinking more in terms of achieving Heaven. What we ended up with, as you can see in the film, is a balance between those two things."

The resulting screenplay chronicled Sybok's abduction of representatives from the Federation, Klingon and Romulan Empires, and using them as bait to lure a starship in. Naturally that starship is the Enterprise, which Sybok (who improbably turns out to be Spock's half-brother), utilizing great prowess in Vulcan mind control, gains command of. By freeing crewmembers from their greatest personal pain, he is able to enlarge his army of God-seeking followers. Even Spock and McCoy are swayed to his side, leaving Kirk to take on Sybok alone.

Both Leonard Nimoy and DeForest Kelley were unhappy with the way their characters were portrayed. In Kelley's case, it was a flashback sequence where Dr. McCoy performs euthanasia on his father. For Nimoy, Spock had been written in such a way that Sybok revealed to him his greatest pain, which was coming to grips with his human half, resulting in his betraying Kirk and the Enterprise to partake in Sybok's divine mission.

William Shatner explained, "After De read the script, he didn't want to do the scene. So I took him to lunch and tried to convince him it would work. I said, 'De, this is the best scene you've had to play in a long time.' He's such a wonderful actor, and I really felt he hadn't had a chance recently to show what he was capable of doing. Finally, after much talking, I convinced him to do it. His one stipulation was that we add an explanation of why McCoy committed the euthanasia. We added a short bit of

dialogue where Sybok asks, 'Why did you do it?' and McCoy answers, 'To preserve his dignity.' With these new lines, De felt that McCoy's motivations were clearer and more understandable. Once we solved De's objections, we were then closer to getting the scene I had envisioned."

In #71 of The Official Star Trek Fan Club Magazine, Kelley explained, "When the scene was first presented to me, it was a little harsher. Once we smoothed it out, I still knew it was going to be a difficult scene to do and I felt if that scene didn't come off absolutely right, we would be in trouble....I don't know whether the public realizes it or not, but a character that people have watched for over 20 years was being stripped in front of them of a very private and secretive situation that took place in his life....That moment of McCoy's privacy in Star Trek V would have been divulged to Kirk before anyone. His opening line in the scene was, 'Oh my God, don't do this to me!' And that meant many things: he knew that it was happening to him there, in front of these people, plus the fact he had to relive it again was tough.....The more I looked at it and studied the scene, the more important it became to me because it's a topic that goes on today. I thought it would be interesting to lay it out in the presence of a motion picture audience and let them decide within themselves what is right or wrong."

Leonard Nimoy wasn't at all happy with the flashback Sybok takes Spock on, nor his betrayal of Kirk.

Explains David Loughery, "Leonard had some problems with the earlier drafts, feeling that there were things that Spock would not do. His suggestions were very helpful, and along those lines we made the change that Spock had previously come to understand his human self, and does not betray Kirk. The way it turned out, I think is interesting because it really shows that the bond between these guys is strong and can't be broken. Rather than have Sybok walk off in a snit, he kind of admires this. His reaction is not really one of disappointment when it turns out that Spock won't go with him. He really kind of understands that Spock couldn't go with him. I think he sort of admires

that in a way. I was surprised, actually, when I eventually watched it with an audience. When Spock told Sybok he couldn't go with him, the audience let out a cheer. I wasn't anticipating that. And when McCoy sheepishly says, 'I guess you better count me out too,' they went for that. Then you go to Bill, who has this look on his face that says, 'Eat it, Sybok!' And they loved that too.

"One of the smart things we did early on was bring Leonard and De in to go over the script, because we wanted their input. These guys have lived with these characters for more than 20 years, and have very strong opinions on what their characters would and wouldn't do. There were problems with this too, however. As originally conceived, only Kirk held out against Sybok, which gives you more of a one man stands alone kind of thing, betrayed by his best friends. Leonard and De objected and it was changed. Suddenly there were three guys against Sybok. When you start doing that kind of stuff, bit by bit you remove and dilute the real strength of the original vision and finally you end up with a bit of a mish-mash. It would have been great for Kirk to have squared off against Spock in some way. But you find the script beginning to accommodate the needs of the actors who know their characters and say, 'Spock wouldn't do that.' It's kind of indefensible. You don't really have an argument that can turn them around on something like that."

The script—which had been finished shortly before the 1988 Writer's Guild strike that lasted some six months—was only part of William Shatner's problems. During its long development, Leonard Nimoy accepted the assignment of helming The Good Mother, thus delaying production by several months. Rumor had it that Shatner threatened to shoot the film without Nimoy, but everyone knew that this was a threat without meaning. One can't help but wonder if, in some way, Shatner was being paid back for prolonging negotiations on Star Trek IV, thus delaying production on that film.

To make matters worse, Paramount announced that Star Trek V was overbudget and that cuts would have to be made. The natural place to cut was special effects, the majority of which occurred toward the end of the film. A frustrated Shatner related, "My original concept for the movie had the characters descending into the equivalent of hell. The angels surrounding 'God' turned into horrible gargoyle-type figures and chase Kirk, Spock and McCoy into a burning chasm. I was quickly told that my idea was much too expensive. So we changed the gargoyles into Rockmen. That is, as Kirk, Spock and McCoy are running away, these huge, twisted shapes break free from the rocks surrounding them and pursue the characters. I had in mind six Rockmen, six hulking, strange creatures—terrifying! But each of those Rockmen were incredibly expensive....so the first thing I was told was that I could only have one Rockman. So here I had gone from this fantastic image of floating cherubim turned into flying gargoyles, then to six hulking Rockmen, now down to one Rockman. It was one of the first lessons I had in the realization that the movie in my head was going to be different from the one in reality."

Ultimately production snafus would cost the actor-director even his one Rockman, and much of his original vision. There were times when the production was in chaos, and it was all that everyone could do to stay as close to schedule and budget as possible.

Noticing what was happening, Leonard Nimoy on *The Tonight Show* said, "I gave him one piece of advice the first couple of days of shooting. I said stop talking so fast. It's the sign of a first-time director. You come on a stage the first day on the set and you're excited and you've got the adrenaline going and you're nervous and if you want to spot a first-time director, you look for the guy with the sweaty palms and he's hyperventilating and he's talking too fast. He thought that by talking fast it would speed up the schedule but you couldn't understand a word he was saying."

Assessing The Final Frontier

Kirk stands alone. As he races back towards the shuttlecraft, a horde of unspeakably evil gargoyles are unleashed by the malevolent god-creature intent on

devouring him. They pursue Kirk relentlessly while Scotty desperately tries to repair the damaged transporter—disabled by a phaser blast when the chief engineer accidentally beamed a gargoyle on board the ship and vaporized it.

For Shatner, the loss of his grand vision for *The Final Frontier*'s ending was a major disappointment. His substitute idea also went unrealized in which a Rockman, the god-thing's creature formed out of solid rock, attacks the Shuttlecraft Copernicus. The footage, first shot on location in the desert and later on a soundstage at Paramount, was deemed unsuitable and considered a major disappointment to both the crew and its director.

"I was required to reduce the budget and I kept slicing away at the ending," says Shatner. "I didn't realize until we got there how much of the ending I had lost and what a disservice I had done to the film. That was lesson number one."

Explained screenwriter David Loughery, "When the torpedo came down and explodes the hole, it's like the bottle is uncapped and all the imps spill out, free, and chase our characters back to the shuttle. That was our original concept. A movie, especially a movie like this one, goes through so many transformations from original story to final film. Because of all the hands involved in the making of these movies, it sometimes starts to take on a committee atomosphere to moviemaking. Things don't turn out exactly the way you originally wanted them to, but there are reasons for that. We certainly wish we could have hung on to some of that concept. The area of the movie that has always been in flux is *how* we represent the god-being. That sequence got lost when it became financially impossible for us to create the gargoyle creatures. You're always sorry to see those things go, because your imagination is one thing and the budget is something else. In various places, we had to make certain cuts and rearrangements based on how much we could afford."

"What the final result was, was the final result," says Shatner. "I have certain regrets but I feel in total that a lot of the vision was there. I made one major compromise at the beginning which was mitigating the original idea of the

Enterprise searching for God and instead finding an alien pretending to be God. The enormous thrust of the idea was eviscerated and that was my first compromise. It seemed that was a necessary one due to the fact that everybody was very apprehensive about the obvious problem. I thought [the film] was flawed. I didn't manage my resources as well as I could have, and I didn't get the help in managing my resources I could have. I thought it was a meaningful *attempt* at a story and I thought it was a meaningful play. It carried a sense of importance about it. Technically it went well, I thought. We hired a lot of different people. We went to New York and got other special effects people. So we experimented and I had to learn a great deal, not only about film but the politics of film. I don't think I'll make those same errors again. The experience has made me froth with ambition."

"In retrospect," offers David Loughery, "you always look back from the distance of a couple of years and I've always felt—it was always in the back of my head—that one of the problems is that it's a reactive story rather than an active one. What I mean by that is that our guys are kind of required to stand by and be dragged along on somebody else's quest. In this case, Sybok's. It's sort of *his* quest and *his* passion, and Kirk, Spock, McCoy and the rest of the crew are dragged along almost as though they were a supporting cast to this guy. If it had been Kirk who suddenly had this vision of God and hijacked his own ship and turned against the Federation, *then* you've got this much more active, passionate kind of story."

Co-star Leonard Nimoy diplomatically offers, "Bill worked very, very hard and he directed it as well and as capably as any of our other films. He was not riding on a good script. If you're not riding on a good script, you're the person people point fingers at. And he was responsible, it was his story. I've had that experience. I did a movie for Paramount [*Funny About Love*] that didn't work at all. I wasn't successful with the script."

Of the screenplay for *Star Trek V*, Nimoy points out, "I complained. I said, 'I think you've got some problems here,' and the message I got back is, 'We know what we've got and we know what we want to do.' Having sent in my notes, once they got them it's not my place to say, 'You must do the following.' Once the tank starts rolling, it's tough to stop it. It's very interesting. You cannot draw a rule and say, 'It must be done this way.' Sometimes things bubble together and sometimes they don't, even though you've got very well paid and professional people doing the job. Sometimes it works and sometimes it doesn't, and that's why some pictures succeed and some pictures fail."

To criticisms levelled against Shatner's sometimes unorthodox approach to direction, he has an immediate response.

"It's like youth," defends Shatner. "I wish I were able to say it was because of my youth. A first time director knows no boundaries and it's not knowing them that you shatter them. Rather than accepting the status quo, I tried to break the boundaries and make the camera do things that it wasn't supposed to, not because I didn't know how, but I thought that by standing firm and being as adamant as possible it would happen. But there came a point where I had to compromise. I was rushing around trying to save what I thought was my movie, but I had spent days and weeks with Harve telling him the story and him telling me his version of the story and going over and over and over as we built the story and the script and we worked in a very close and intimate way. It got to the point where we were talking about the death and birth of people close to us and there were times where tears passed between us in the intimacy of his office. These moments are part of the making of Star Trek V for me. If anybody else is doing another trip, that's their problem."

Another problem that helped torpedo the acceptance of Shatner's installment in the Star Trek mythos were the widely criticized special effects of Bran Ferren and Associates, which was hired to replace the more expensive Trek veteran effects teams of Industrial Light & Magic.

"I took a lot of personal hits about that and I feel a tremendous sense of responsibility and it hurts," says Star Trek V Executive Producer Ralph Winter. "At the time I made the decision on what

I felt would be best for the picture. It was not a capricious decision. It was based on testing we all did. There were a number of people involved in that decision, but I was leading the process. I felt like we were going to get something better and, in the beginning, we did...but it didn't work out that way."

Shatner shared Winter's regrets about the film's visual effects. "We had problems that we might not have had if we had different personnel," he admits. "I followed other people's leads because I did not have first-hand knowledge of these things, but I was in on the decision so I make no excuse for that, but it is an instance where my lack of experience showed."

Trek V Producer Harve Bennett disagrees that choosing Ferren to provide the film's visual effects was a mistake. "I think that's peripheral," says Bennett. "You should have seen ILM's test for God, they were silly. We went with the creative judgement that Bran had a more vigorous attack to help us sell the illusions and it was a picture that needed fancy footwork. In addition, it's important to note that when were ready to start ILM was overcrowded, we would have been the fourth or fifth major picture at ILM and we would have received their D team instead of their A team, which was a very important consideration. All the people we had worked with in the past were booked."

Bennett holds the success of Star Trek: The Next Generation partially accountable for the failure of Star Trek V to meet financial expectations. "In my opinion, and marketing never agreed with me, there are only so many hours in a Star Trek fan's life," says Bennett. "You've given the cult, where they were used to having turkey dinner every two years and old turkey sandwiches in between, a fresh turkey sandwich every Saturday and Sunday, big moviegoing nights. I know from a lot of mail I've received that people felt about Star Trek V that maybe they'd see it next week because they didn't want to miss The Next Generation. After all, turkey is turkey. I think the appetite for Star Trek movies was seriously impacted by the success of the series, not destroyed, just kind of subdivided and the feeding frenzy

we experienced on Star Trek II, III and IV did not exist on V, even if it had been a better movie."

In addition, Bennett feels that the growing popularity of The Next Generation ultimately hurt the success of Star Trek VI as well. "There has been an erosion and a conversion in the Star Trek cult," he says. "At first they tended to be resistive of The Next Generation and then, as the show improved and the habit accrued [and] they were getting fresh material as opposed to reruns and the inevitable wait for movies, I think they became very interested. You can see in all the publications where the letter ratio is shifting where the minority opinion is that the original characters were more interesting and the majority opinion is, 'Hey, let's get on with it.' Sitting in a theatre and watching the trailer for Star Trek VI you didn't get the electric shock that you did watching the promos for the other movies, that we've got to be there. On the contrary, you got some titters, talk back to the screen and I was startled to find the audience restless. That may mean nothing, but it may mean I don't want to go see a funeral."

David Loughery has his own theories as to why the film warped out of theatres almost as quickly as it warped in.

"That was the summer of Batman," he reflects. "I don't know how many movie-spending bucks there are out there, but I think that everybody had a weekend that summer. We had an opening weekend where we made $17 million, and everybody thought we were all right, but it just didn't continue that way. Frankly, it was the kind of summer where the money was divided among a handful of films, and Star Trek V didn't turn out to be one of them. We were all taken by surprise.

Regardless of the film's reception, for Shatner exploring The Final Frontier was one of the most rewarding experiences of his career.

"Directing film is a wild adventure for anyone equipped to do it," says Shatner. "I made compromises on Star Trek V thinking I had to do that, that's the nature of the business and it is the nature of the business to compromise. But the line where you do not compromise I couldn't tread because of a number of

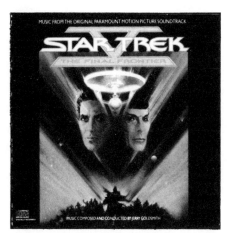

The jacket adorning the Star Trek V: The Final Frontier *CD, music composed by Jerry Goldsmith.*

factors, not the least of which is my own nature. I got to learn when it's time to stand and when it's time to turn and that, really, for a knowledgeable person in the business is a more important lesson than where the camera is and how to play a scene and what your establishing shot is. Those mechanics of making a film no longer become a point of discussion, it's automatic, it's there creatively. The political point of a director is a constant learning process because of the interpersonal relationships between the director and the rest of the people; the cast, the crew, the management and that is constantly changing from day to day and moment to moment, depending on how confident you feel and how confidently you express that feeling. It changes from job to job. I had the most joyful time of my life directing *Star Trek V.*"

Favored nations clause not withstanding, the subject of Shatner's possibly directing STAR TREK VI never came up.

CHAPTER FOURTEEN
Star Trek VI: The Academy Years

After the chilly box-office reception of *Star Trek V* and the continuing chorus of naysayers criticizing the cast as being too old to continue, many suspected the silver screen voyages of the starship Enterprise had truly passed into the final frontier. But Producer Harve Bennett, in conjunction with *Star Trek V* screenwriter David Loughery, was hard at work creating a new vehicle to continue the *Star Trek* movie missions.

"Every time they go to make one of these *Star Trek* movies," notes Loughery, "the producers and the studio always run into the same problem in getting the original cast together. The reasons for that are money, power, creative differences, ego, health, unavailability....all of those things. Harve always had this ace up his sleeve, which was if we can't get everybody together for one of these *Star Trek* movies, we should do a prequel."

Called *Starfleet Academy*, the proposed film would have chronicled a young Kirk, Spock and McCoy's days at the Academy, as part of *Trek*'s 25th anniversary celebration. Instead, a sixth and final film featuring the original "classic" cast was put into production by Paramount, resulting in Harve Bennett's departure from the series.

"We had a better movie and we had a film that would have allowed them to make the same *Star Trek VI* eighteen months later," says Bennett of *Starfleet Academy*, which was aborted after objections from fans made the project untenable.

"I think there was a fat chance of that happening," comments Walter Koenig. "I can't read Harve's mind, but if *Starfleet Academy* had done well, they would have gone on with that group. If it hadn't, they probably would have abandoned the whole project."

"Because of the way *Star Trek VI* is being sold, don't miss your chance to say good-bye, it's unlikely that *Starfleet Academy*, which asks 'Would you like to know how it all happened?' will be made," continues Bennett, whose previous producing chores included work on *The Mod Squad*, *The Six Million Dollar Man*, the Emmy Award winning miniseries *A Woman Called Golda* and *The Jesse Owens Story*.

Starfleet Academy chronicled the story of a young James T. Kirk, a Spock who is estranged from his parents and becomes the first Vulcan to attend Starfleet Academy, and Leonard McCoy, a 30 year old doctor who attends the Academy after having pulled the plug on his terminally ill father and is searching for meaning in his life. Michael Curtiz's 1940 film, *The Santa Fe Trail*, served as an inspiration for what Bennett envisioned as the classic triumvirate's first trek. The film which could have been made, according to Bennett, for $27 million would also have avoided the hefty multi-million dollar salaries of its leads—Shatner and Nimoy—as well as Kelley's take-home of nearly a half a million dollars and the $125,000 paychecks the supporting players pocketed.

"I pitched the idea to Harve at his daughter's Bat Mitzvah," recalls *Trek VI* producer Ralph Winter. "We had already locked in the *Star Trek IV* storyline with the whales and I said, 'You know, I have a great idea, let's do a prequel' in the middle of this reception for his daughter. I suggested we develop a series of films to be another franchise, another tent pole that we could open. We could do a prequel and find out how Kirk and Spock met at the Starfleet Academy. When we were doing *Star Trek V*, we got the studio to approve work on the script. It is an excellent story, but it has been misperceived. It's a great story finding out about this young cocky character on a farm who goes to flight school and meets up with the first alien that comes from Vulcan and how they meet the other characters. It would have been a gift for the fans on the 25th anniversary."

David Loughery notes, "When I heard about the idea, I thought it was terrific. Not from the point of view of recasting, but from the point of view of storytelling, because I worked so closely with these characters on *Star Trek V*, that the idea of doing an origin story—where you show

them as young cadets and kids—was tremendously exciting. What it was, was a real coming of age story. In outline form, it was the story of Kirk and Spock meeting for the first time as cadets here on Earth. We've got a young Jim Kirk, who's kind of cocky and wild. He's not exactly what you might think starship captain material might be. He's like one of these kids who would rather fly hot planes and chase girls. Spock is this brilliant, arrogant, aloof to the point of obnoxiousness, genius. It's this mask he's hiding behind to cover his own conflicting human emotions. He's an outcast, he left Vulcan in shame against his father's wishes and, like all adolescents, he's trying to find a place to fit in, but he keeps screwing it up.

"Over the course of this story," he continues, "which is one year at Starfleet Academy, Kirk and Spock are sort of put to the test and they begin as rivals and end up as friends and comrades who learn that they have to combine their talents for the first time to defeat a deadly enemy. In the final scene, where they say goodbye at graduation and go their separate ways, we're able to see the legends that these two boys are going to grow up to become."

But for Bennett, who had spent a decade living with *Star Trek*, *Starfleet Academy* was not to be. The rejection of the project was a big disappointment for the veteran producer who planned the film as his freshman directorial effort.

"It meant a lot to me because I came out of UCLA film school wanting to be a director and other winds blew me to to other ports," says Bennett. "It was a desire of mine to direct and it was accepted by the studio and, the fact is, part of the deal was for us to do a *Star Trek VI*, with the original cast after *Starfleet Academy*."

But once word leaked out about the project, support was marshalled against the film and vociferously denounced on the convention circuit by members of the supporting cast, as well as *Star Trek* creator Gene Roddenberry.

Said Roddenberry in the pages of *Cinefantastique*, "I didn't like it. Who was going to cast the new Kirk and Spock? No one has ever cast a *Trek* character besides me that's worked. Braggadocio or whatever, that is the history of *Trek*. It wasn't good. Some of it was like *Police*

Academy. You could hardly do this without the magic of a group of characters tailored for *Star Trek*, which this was not."

Letters began to pour into Paramount decrying the planned feature as heresy.

"We were really caught off guard and surprised by the fans who reacted so negatively to the idea of this movie," admits David Loughery. "Somehow they conceived it as sort of a spoof or a takeoff. That's where we got off on the wrong foot. The fans had misinformation, which may have been put out there by people for their own reasons. Certainly if we were going to make a movie like that, it meant that Walter and whoever wouldn't get that job a year or two down the line that they had come to expect. I don't know if that's the case, but I do know that the misinformation released had people convinced that we were going to do a cross between *Police Academy* and *The Jetsons.* It was never that kind of story. I think it's traditional that the fans have objected to different things. Harve's always been smart enough to double-cross them; give them what they've objected to, but surprise them with something that makes it good and worthwhile. We felt that there was a powerful story there, one that the audience would be interested in. We're always interested in young Indiana Jones and young Sherlock Holmes, and how they started and came to be who they are. This was sort of the way to explain Kirk and Spock and where they came from."

"There *was* pressure from a lot of people not to do this," Bennett emphasizes. "I don't think there was any question that the self-interest of the supporting cast was not served by it and if I was George Takei, I would do exactly what he did and if I were Jimmy Doohan, I would be a really unhappy man. The only one I'm really furious at though is Jimmy Doohan. He said I was fired and I can't abide lies. My term was up and I was offered $1.5 million to do *Star Trek VI* and I said, 'Thanks, I don't wish to do that. I want to do the Academy.'"

Responds Doohan, "I was impressed with Harve when he first came in and did *Star Trek II* and *III,* but I think he got a little greedy. He wanted things his own way. He wanted to take over *Star Trek* for himself. What the heck, you don't do that sort of thing, trying to destroy instead of building. He obviously did not realize the strength of the old cast. The whole thing would have been starting out as if from scratch. I think it was [Frank] Mancuso who didn't realize we were not going to be in it. When he found out, [he] said good-bye Harve."

"My last words to Mancuso before he was asked to leave [by the then recently installed head of Paramount, Stanley Jaffe] was if it was a question of anyone's concerns about my directing, I'd back off on that," says Bennett. "They then offered me *Star Trek VI* and gave me a pay or play commitment to direct and produce *Starfleet Academy* afterwards. My position was, and I think it was correct, that they would pay me to do *VI* and make the movie which would have been a real big, fat check for me and never made *Starfleet Academy.* To be paid off because the movie I might have done, which is being done by others, would close the franchise was not my intention. I had a life, it's not like I hadn't done anything else before *Star Trek.* The *Star Trek* curse is something that the poor supporting cast has to live with, but I don't."

Opines William Shatner, "Harve was striving to find an answer for the studio's question 'Are these guys too old to continue?' So he tried to find a solution as a storywriter and he must of said here's a way of going. Apparently everybody agreed, but at some point they shut him down after preparing this production for a year and he got very upset about it and left. I wasn't too clued in on the politics of what was happening. I had heard about the prequel and was considering my options, but it was never approved and we didn't know whether or not there would be another *Star Trek* until the last second."

For Ralph Winter, *Starfleet Academy* would have ushered in a new approach to the *Star Trek* franchise for the studio in which a coherent plan would be created for producing the *Trek* films on a semi-regular basis as opposed to the sporadic, fitful stop and go start-up on a new film every three years with the arduous contract negotiations that initiating each new chapter entailed.

"*Starfleet Academy* may have looked like a mistake," says Winter, "but look at the franchise as a whole. We have a successful series of feature films, then a new television series and with the film series ending it made sense to start a new series of films. You could have opened a whole new frontier. When *Star Trek: The Next Generation* came out, the people said this will never work, how can we have a new Captain? It will never equal Kirk and Spock. But they've achieved their own success. It could have been the same with a prequel cast, now you would have three different fronts. Make the successful features with the original cast, features with a prequel cast and the television series with the new cast. That's what could have happened. You look at the long term and you develop two or three scripts at a time and you maximize production. The unfortunate part about today's economy and the thinking of these big companies is let's see how this one does and then we'll decide on the next one. There was never a plan after any of these films to do another one. *Star Trek II* was the last picture, Spock was dead. That was it. It's just getting too expensive to drag out all the wardrobe, sets, models. With a long term plan you could milk this forever and the fans would be thrilled, but if you go one step at a time and don't know where you're going, then the films are expensive and maybe it does make sense to the do the sixth film with the original cast."

As for the *Star Trek VI* that did materialize on the screen, Bennett has mixed feelings, having hoped that Nimoy and his confederates would meet with success, but is dubious. "I'm sure glad that it's not my movie," mused Bennett. "I was presented with the choice of doing *Star Trek VI* in 11 months and I didn't want to do a conventional film and I didn't believe I could do it in that time. The fact that they have done it is a tribute to all my buddies, and they are good buddies. Nicholas Meyer is the fastest writer in the world, Ralph Winter is the most ethical and perfect producer of special effects movies anywhere and one of the nicest men I've ever know. It wasn't easy to walk away from that, but if your heart is not in something and you've earned the right not to have do things that cause you pain, then you don't do them."

In terms of the future of *Starfleet Academy,* as the saying goes in the *Star Trek* universe: "There are always possibilities."

• • • •

••••

CHAPTER FIFTEEN

Star Trek VI: The Undiscovered Country

"On the Beach"

During the Christmas 1991 movie season, while Oliver Stone was pinning the murder of President John F. Kennedy on the CIA and the military-industrial complex, simultaneously grabbing the covers of every major magazine from *Esquire* to *Life* to *GQ* to *Newsweek*, *Star Trek* was not only attributing the assassination of its architect of the new frontier to these familiar and conveniently nebulous 20th century arms merchants, but perhaps the very fabric of galactic peace to their nefarious machinations.

But, of course, no cover stories here. It's only sci-fi, right?

The genesis of *Star Trek VI* began when Leonard Nimoy, at the behest of then Paramount studio chief Frank Mancuso, set about to revive the floundering film series for its 25th anniversary. In essence, he became the newest in a long line of perennial great birds of the *Star Trek* galaxy.

"Frank Mancuso had called Leonard into his office and said, 'Leonard, help me make this film,'" recalls *Trek VI* co-writer and novelist Dennis Martin Flinn, author of a number of well regarded detective novels including *San Francisco Kills, Killer Finish* and *Lady Killer.* "At that point, Leonard was the producer, writer, the director, the star and it was up to him to discharge those duties or pass them onto other people. Mancuso apparently knew he could trust him to get the whole thing going and to get it going quickly, and I think that had something to do with *Star Trek V.* Let's face it, nobody wanted to have anything to do with anybody who had anything to do with *V,* except as necessary. I don't think *Star Trek V* was entirely Shatner's fault by any means. Moviemaking is a very collaborative business, but no one was happy with it."

In total agreement with Flinn is screenwriter Mark Rosenthal, who, along with partner Lawrence Konner, are the unsung heroes of *Star Trek VI.* It was this team that came up with the original storyline for the film, a fact that did not become apparent to the public until about a week prior to the film's opening when newspapers heralded, "Story by Leonard Nimoy, Lawrence Konner and Mark Rosenthal." Even the paperback adaptation does not feature their names amongst the credits.

"We were under contract at Paramount and the feeling was that they were not going to do another *Star Trek* movie," reflects Rosenthal, whose credits include *Jewel of the Nile* and *Superman IV.* "The guys were getting old and *Star Trek V* was a disappointment. Everybody was disenchanted with Shatner's direction. There was a bad taste in everyone's mouth and no one wanted to go out like that. They knew the 25th anniversary was coming up, and we were approached by the vice president of production, Teddy Zee, who's now at Columbia. Teddy called us up and said, 'Frank Mancuso has spoken to Leonard, Leonard was still upset because of the last one and he was floating out the idea of one last adventure.' He asked us what we thought about it. The reality was that I am a Trekkie and my partner is incredibly non-science fiction oriented. We were kind of a Yin-Yang but we liked that idea, because Larry would provide a good balance.

States actor-writer-executive producer Leonard Nimoy,"The Berlin Wall had come down. The Russian government was in severe distress. Communism was falling apart. These changes were creating a new order in our world. I thought there would be a new kind of dialogue, a new thinking of these relationships. And a whole new military vision and a whole new vision of hardware. Realizing that over the 25 year history of *Star Trek*, the Klingons have been the constant foe of the Federation, much like the Russians and Communists were to democracy, I wondered how we could translate these contemporary world affairs into an adventure with the Klingons. I thought it was an ideal way for us to have our closure too, because the Klingons for us have always been the

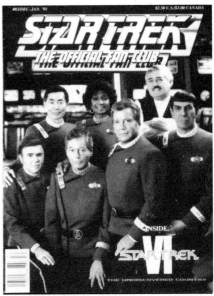

The official **Star Trek** *fan club provided indepth coverage on the making of* **Star Trek VI: The Undiscovered Country.**

Communist Block, the Evil Empire. It just made sense to do that story."

"The main thing we were concerned with," Rosenthal says, "was that we had never really gotten details about the Klingon Empire. There was a whole question of whether we should go to the actual home planet. What happened was that they felt in terms of budget, recreating the entire planet would be impossible, so it became this prison concept. The original idea was to go to the actual capital city. I still think it was a better idea, but you can see how this process happens. The first *Star Trek* had a horrendous budget and it was a bad movie. Paramount began to realize that the Europeans did not grow up with *Star Trek*, so there's a very small market for it. The studio always feels that they have to make their money in a domestic situation, which for a big-budget special effects movie is tough. When you write, you try to come up with stories that take place in one ship, because that's pretty cheap to do. When you start talking about sets and locations, the budget gets very high.

"At one point we had a discussion about using Chernobyl, and that really opened the floodgates," he enthuses. "Then we began to look at specific events and, of course, recent Soviet histo-

••••

ry serves as some kind of basis for the movie. Once you get on that track of thinking, we said, 'What's really going on?' Everyone is paranoid that someone is going to try and sabotage peace between the Soviet Union and the United States. Why not have the same thing occur between the Klingons and the Federation? It all kind of led to the idea of assassination. What if Gorbachev was assassinated and the blame fell on Kirk? That was really the key. We were also trying to see what else had happened in *Star Trek IV*, what kind of threads could be picked up. Everybody remembered that a Bird of Prey had crashed into San Francisco Bay at the end of the movie, and the Bird of Prey was equipped with a cloaking device. That led us to thinking. One of the rules about the Bird of Prey was that they had to decloak when they fired. What if, given the Stealth Bomber, they could fire while cloaked? That became an important element."

Nimoy returned to the studio and pitched the idea: a peace overture between the Federation and the Klingon Empire triggers a hostile reaction from those on both sides who had invested the most in the existing state of belligerence. The studio was hooked. This time there was no hokey science-fiction concept, no search for God, just Klingon battle cruisers and starships slugging it out in the stars...for peace.

The man who had once declared "I Am Not Spock," and whose character had been killed off in hopes of luring him back into the fold for one final film in *The Wrath of Khan*, had now assumed a paternal, nurturing role over the series. Nimoy had shepherded *Trek* for half a decade and now recruited *Star Trek II* savior Nicholas Meyer to co-write and direct the film. Hiring Meyer was an inspired choice. Not only did the veteran *Trek* helmer work and write fast, but bringing him onboard would help avoid any problems with Nimoy's co-star and fellow director, William Shatner, who was itching to get behind the camera again and whose ire would surely been raised had Nimoy attempted to direct his third *Trek* film.

Shatner admits to a degree of disappointment over not captaining from the director's chair of what could

be the Enterprise's final voyage. "I felt a sense of loss that I couldn't be the problem solver," he says. "I would have loved to have been immersed in those very same problems and bring to bear what I had learned on the previous film. But on the other hand there was a sense of tremendous relief, as I was only too aware of the pressures on Nick Meyer both from a production point of view and a political view from the studio and, as time would get short, the anxiety that was involved in trying to get it done on time. I was very sensitized to the things he needed to accomplish."

Shatner is quick to point out that he was very pleased with the film's storyline. "It's a really good idea," he says. "It's a classic *Star Trek* idea in that the important issue of the day is incorporated into the story of *Star Trek*, and by doing so—and because we put it into the future—we're able to comment on it as though it has nothing to do with today, yet it makes a commentary."

Going to the beach in Cape Cod, Leonard Nimoy shared the premise credited to him, Rosenthal and Konner. with the vacationing Meyer, who co-written *Star Trek IV*, but rejected overtures to helm *Star Trek III* and *V* in years past. This time Meyer was hooked, partially because the film he was in post-production on, MGM's *Company Business*, shared a similar glasnot-inspired theme, but had been "butchered" by the studio, according to Meyer.

"Leonard said to me, 'Let's make a movie about the wall coming down in outer space.' His statement just spoke to me," Meyer admits. "What I wanted to do with it, was to widen the world of *Star Trek* before closing out the series, if that's indeed what's happening. The thing I've learned from these movies is that your only chance of succeeding is not to repeat yourself, not to try the same exact thing. I didn't want to go mano-a-mano because I had done that with *II*; I didn't want to make a comedy because I felt *IV* was the most broadly comedic of any of them. So I thought, 'I want to make an ensemble piece and I want it to be a political thriller.' Like everybody else, I was fascinated by the events of the last few years from 1989 on. I had been

in Berlin working on another film and I had seen the wall coming down. God, what are the possibilities? What are the potentials for greatness or disaster? Who would have thought it? It's a bright spot, but it's filled with the potential for real disaster, and this is the theme of the movie, because change is *real* scary. In this film, the intention is certainly to deal with what people do when they are confronted with the prospect of radical change. There are some people who are capable of embracing it, and some who have a lot of trouble with it."

It was in May of 1990 that Mancuso had first called Nimoy to his office to recruit him to have a new *Star Trek* film featuring the "classic" cast ready for the show's 25th anniversary. By October of that year, Flinn and Meyer were completing their first draft script based on the Konner and Rosenthal story.

"Nick was involved with *Company Business* in London and wasn't going to be able to write the screenplay in time to get the film into production for the release date that would coincide with the 25th anniversary," recalls Flinn. "So he told Paramount that the only way he could do it is if he could co-write the script with me, and that's how it came about. He was kind enough to trust me, and while he was in London we communicated via computer. When we turned in our first draft in December of last year, the studio greenlighted it."

The screenplay evolved constantly, not least of all to reflect the myriad of comments from Nimoy, Shatner and Gene Roddenberry who, according to Nimoy, was very much involved in a creative consultant capacity.

"I'm a Roddenberry disciple," says Nimoy, who was reportedly one of the stumbling blocks in the release of Roddenberry's book celebrating 25 years of *Star Trek*. "He was very much involved. I went to him for regular meetings on this script. Everytime we had a draft, I met with him and we discussed it. He was very intrigued with the idea that we would be exploring the relationship with the Klingons. He was concerned in this particular story about the prejudice question, because it's an interesting issue. Sometimes when you show people showing a prejudice, even though your intention is to show that they're wrong, there are going to be people who identify with them. Here you've got a couple of guys saying, 'What do you think of the smell? Only the top of the line models can talk.' Gene was concerned about that stuff. He said, 'I don't feel good about Enterprise crew talking that way.' We pointed out, 'These are bad people who are racists and who turn out to be assassins.' 'I'm just uncomfortable with a couple of guys walking around in Federation uniforms talking that way about another race.' And I understood it. It's a danger. By and large, he was quite taken with the idea of a Klingon detente. It was his idea to put a Klingon in the Federation on *The Next Generation*, and this was the beginning of that link."

Co-writer Dennis Martin Flinn notes, "When *Star Trek* relies on science-fiction, it's a big failure. Maybe that's part of why nobody likes *Star Trek I* and *V* very much. Gene Roddenberry originally called *Star Trek* "*Wagon Train* to the stars" because westerns served the purpose in our society of being morality tales about good guys versus bad guys and, in many cases, in those thousands of westerns it was irrelevant that the setting was the Old West. What was important and great in a movie like *Shane*, for instance, was the story of the individual in society, and *Star Trek* is best when it's a morality play. That's what Gene called the original episodes, so when Leonard came up with the idea that the Klingons could stand in for the Russians and we could deal with the end of the Cold War, we were home free in terms of fundamentals that we knew worked."

Distilling the action/adventure plot was even more attractive to Flinn, who relied on familiar cinematic conventions to drive his metaphoric storyline.

"The idea sprung up from what would happen if someone attempted to assassinate Gorbachev," says Flinn. "In our story, Kirk might be blamed for that. Then comes something that I grew up on in movies, which is 'I've got to get out of here so I can clear my name.' I thought that's a good way to go and it worked for forty years in westerns and detective stories."

Flinn offers that had *Star Trek VI*'s story been pitched as a contemporary allegory, the studio would never have greenlighted the production. "Science-fiction allows you to do that," he says. "You can hide it from the executives; they don't get it. Nobody would touch it. The studios would say the military industrial complex goes to see movies and they would come up with a reason not to make a movie that exposes this. That's the kind of advantage science-fiction offers. Issues have gone to television, but they're the exception and not the rule. Our advertisers don't want you to insult anyone, they don't want you to insult serial killers. They may be watching."

Both Meyer and Flinn were not afraid to wield their pen to take the 25 year old characters in new directions. In addition to Spock's attachment to his Vulcan counterpart, Valeris, Kirk, who had always represented the best qualities of 1960's America in the finest Kennedy-esque tradition, was set-up as a bigoted right wing zealot, prejudiced against a very evil empire for having slain his son in *Star Trek III*.

"In the script there's a wonderful line," says William Shatner. "'In space, all warriors are cold warriors.' Both sides have come to define themselves by their antagonism. 'What will I be without my enemy?' The best *Star Trek* stories have their genesis in real life. For this story, you just have to pick up the daily newspaper."

"There are three kinds of people in the universe of *Star Trek VI*," Flinn points out. "The people who wanted peace, the people who did not want peace for their own self interest, and then there were the people, like Kirk, who had lived a certain way for 25 years vis a vis with the Klingons, but were intelligent enough to say what does the future have to offer? Maybe this isn't wrong. I think we were lucky to be able to see Kirk as a man who, if he was rigid at all, at least recognized his own rigidity. That in itself was flexible and not rigid. And of course it allowed us to create a character that, in essence, was a spokesman for the uncertainties and the whole idea of the undiscovered country. The future, being scary, got nailed down because we had a character that could say that."

Nicholas Meyer opines, "I think the heroic thing about Kirk and the rest of the crew is their effort to acknowledge, to confront and ultimately try to overcome their prejudice. If a man leaps into a raging torrent to save a drowning child, he performs a heroic act. If the same man leaps into the same pond to save the same child, and does so with a ball and chain attached to his leg, he must be accounted not less heroic, but more heroic still because he overcomes a handicap. And that's what heroism and drama is about. I think Kirk is more of a hero for being a human being and not less because he's super human, which I never believed."

"The portrayal of Kirk," adds William Shatner, "attempts to show a man who has spent a lifetime imbued with the idea that his mission in life is to subdue, subvert and make the enemy submit to his nation's or his Federation's view. That's his whole training and that is the military training. He learns differently and that is the classic dilemma that *Star Trek* has sought to present in its most successful shows."

It was the central dichotomy in Kirk's character, and in the film, that Cliff Eidelman attempted to capture in his score for the movie. "It gave me a theme for the opening," says Eidelman. "It's Kirk taking control one last time and as he looks out into the stars, he has that spark again one last time. It's his one last spark into space, but there's an unresolved note, because it's very important that he doesn't trust the Klingons and he doesn't want to go on this trip even though the spark is there that overtook him."

Nimoy, too, felt that the script's underlying theme was effective. "Spock experienced prejudice growing up half-Vulcan and half-human," states Nimoy. "In *Star Trek VI*, Spock becomes an emissary against prejudice and discovers, during the course of the story, his own prejudices."

Despite the strength of its script, *Trek VI* was far from a sure thing. Once the word got out that *Star Trek VI* was indeed underway, while the fans rejoiced the cast became the butt of a many jokes. "The talk shows were making fun of us for weeks," remembers Flinn. "David Letterman was doing the search for geritol—so it was risky already. Two of the actors are 71 years old, but, hell, they're healthy."

With the realization that the previous film had been a commercial and critical disappointment, the producers of *Star Trek VI* sought to make the new film as different from its predecessor as possible.

Ralph Winter elaborates, "*Star Trek IV* reached out to an audience that had never seen a *Star Trek* picture before. We increased our audience 30-40% and *Star Trek V* didn't do that. Everybody started out to make a good movie, a lot of people read that script and thought it was going to be great, but we stumbled. Has that affected our thinking about this picture? Yes, it has. We have a different composer, a different look. We're doing everything we can to give this film a fresh look."

According to a member of the new film's production team, "They got ILM on the project very fast because they didn't want the problem that they had the last time and Lucas can deliver fast."

"We went away from the visual effects on *Star Trek V* because we thought we were going to get something new and different from another guy, which didn't happen," Winter says. "We went back to what we know is proven and the stuff that ILM did is spectacular. We were the benefactors of technology from *T2*. The look of the picture, the cameraman, the set dresser, the designer, everything about this film is trying to stretch and be something the other films haven't. I was a key member of *Star Trek V*, and when someone talks about it, it hurts. You didn't like it? Fine. We're trying to fix it. We wanted to make a film that the fans are going to like for the 25th anniversary. We looked at the areas of the picture where we could make it distinctive and different and not just the fifth sequel to a motion picture. Where we could do it and not spend a tremendous amount of money, we did."

Adds director Nicholas Meyer, "A lot of people said *Star Trek II* was such a terrific movie and had a lot of unkind things to say about *Star Trek I*, but I don't think they realize that *Star Trek II* wouldn't have been so good if someone hadn't gone boldly where no one had gone before and showed us, in effect, what not to do when it was really impor-

tant. It's damn hard work to make those movies and I'm not going to look down my nose at any of them."

However, even with a suitable script, having a major feature film ready in less than a year was a difficult challenge. With the studio vacillating for months over the future of *Star Trek*, now it was up to the assembled team of director Meyer, executive producer Nimoy, and producers Winter and Steven Charles Jaffe to have a film ready by the end of 1991.

"We got a go on February 13th and we had to have it in theatres by December 13th," says Winter. "That's really a short amount of time and money for the expectation level. The fans don't think about how much the budget was, they just want to know why the picture wasn't good, if it wasn't good."

Problems resulting from the tight shooting schedule typified the production from its inception. Recalls Nicholas Meyer, "I told them it would take 55 days. They said you have 51 and I yelled and screamed and they finally gave me 53...and I came in at 55."

But the tight production schedule was not the only daunting obstacle. With the recession cutting into box-office receipts and the failure of a crop of big-budget action movies in the summer of 1990, all the major film studios were preaching fiscal prudence when it came to their pictures. *Star Trek* was no exception. With box-office for most of the films in the series averaging in the $70-80 million range, Paramount balked when they were handed the budget for the latest Enterprise mission. The studio halted pre-production in order to cut its inflated budget, threatening to discontinue work on the film unless extensive production costs could be severely curtailed.

"This picture almost didn't get made," Winter explains. "It almost died a number of times. It's being made for less money than the last one and it's quite a feat. The above the line [cast and other non-technical related expenses] is substantial with the number of stars we have, so the money I have available to make this picture is a lot less than you have to make *Alien 3* or *Terminator 2*."

Rejecting the nearly $40 million price-tag for the film, Paramount had put *Star Trek VI* into turnaround in early

1991, hitting the brakes on a project which was screeching toward production at warp speed. "Bill and Leonard made concessions to get this picture made because they wanted to make it, we all did," Winter details. "Everyone made concessions and, frankly, Nick and Steven and I deferred a significant portion of our salaries to get this picture made, because we believed the story was worthwhile."

Says co-producer Steven Jaffe, "One of the ways that Nick and I have worked together as producer and director in the past is that I have directed second unit on every movie we've done together from *Time After Time* to *The Day After*, where I was hired exclusively as a second unit director. On *Star Trek* the pressures we were under to do this project were greater and for less money than the others. It's a sensitive subject to me because it's something that comes up every single movie, and we've prided ourselves in the past on bringing in all of our movies on budget and on schedule or under, beginning with *Time After Time*. It's kind of disturbing when you have an enormous amount of pressure put on you as though you weren't going to try and do it that way."

Scrambling to reduce the film's inflated budget, set-pieces were cut from the film and instead of building all-new Enterprise interiors, it was decided that redressed sets from *Star Trek: The Next Generation* would stand-in for the Enterprise 1701-A. "Those sets were built for *Star Trek: The Motion Picture* in 1978 and I've used them on every one of these pictures," says Winter. "We were fortunate to schedule the sets as soon as they wrapped for the season and we were in there ripping out walls and changing lights. As soon as we were done, we had to repaint, slap it back together and recarpet them. They were used for hallways, transporter rooms and stuff like that."

With the budget trimmed to a manageable $26 million, Paramount greenlit the picture on February 13th, 1991 with a mandate that the film be ready for release by the end of the year. The cameras starting rolling on April 16, 1991 but before then, the production team had to round out the supporting cast.

• • • •

"Wanted: Master Thespians"

Once Flinn and Meyer fulfilled their first qualification for good *Star Trek*, creating a solid action/adventure story with a message, the second hurdle awaited and that was finding a strong guest cast. With the assist of casting director Mary Jo Slater, they loaded the last *Trek* with a cast of all the Hollywood heavyweights they could afford.

"Nick wanted an all-star ensemble cast and in addition to the seven stars that have been in *Star Trek,* he wanted to populate it with stars on every player that wasn't a regular, even if you couldn't recognize them," says producer Steven Jaffe. "What's important to Nick, especially with the aliens, is that he wanted them to be very articulate and great actors that could project through the make-up. I think that's a very smart way of making it not just a really good *Star Trek* movie, but a good movie in general. It's very hard for an actor with a couple of pounds of make-up on his face to project through there. A great actor like Chris Plummer has the range and power to blast through it. You feel a personality and not just like you're looking at a guy with a mask on. To that degree, we achieved our goals. There were some people that we wanted that we couldn't afford. In the long run it may have worked out for the best, because I think David Warner is extraordinary in the movie, which would have been totally different from Jack Palance. I was also happy to work with him again, [as] the last time we worked together was on *Time After Time.* Kim Cattrall is extraordinary. We were very happy she wanted to be in the movie."

On being able to achieve the casting for the film he did, Meyer says, "I hunted them down and twisted arms and I said, 'Read the script.' When people read the script, then they wanted to do it. That was a good sign. Christopher Plummer's last day of the movie I felt myself going into a deep depression, and going over to have a cry in the corner of the soundstage. I was so upset when he left. First of all, he's great. Secondly, he's a really terrific guy. We were having fun and it was such a thrill to work with him.

David Warner's an old friend of mine. I'd use him everytime I make a movie if I had my way. I think Kim Cattrall is the most underrated actress of her generation. I'm always surprised to find out that she was in this movie or that movie, and then I realize she's so good that she sort of disappears into the role. I loved working with her. I think she's a great actress and a real beauty too."

For Cattrall, who was initially wary of taking the role of Valeris, *Star Trek VI* was an exciting experience made even more intriguing by the constantly evolving script. Time pressures forced the film into production before Meyer could finish his revisions.

"Things changed dramatically," says the actress. "The final scene Leonard and I had together on the page was written as one thing, but [in] he and I doing it, it took on a life of it's own. It's an exciting scene to experience because not until the last moment did either of us know what was going to happen. You've never really seen Vulcans mind meld. The only other instance that Leonard could recall was when he was brought back to life and there was a mind meld. There is such an infusion of two people's chemistry and energy caught between incredible pain and pleasure. It's the closest thing to a sexually heightened experienced that you would get in a *Star Trek* movie."

Says Flinn, "*Star Trek* is known for great guest stars. I think [having] a regular cast helps enormously, because what people want more than anything in movies, and maybe in all art, is something old and something new. When the audience is comfortable they're happy, but at the same time that doesn't allow for any originality. So in *Star Trek II* you have Ricardo Montalban. Here we have Christopher Plummer, and you have the best of both worlds. Even in the episodes, whether it was Joan Collins or Teri Garr, they would always meet some alien out there who, on a pure entertainment level, would provide something new so that you could tune in not just for your favorite characters, but the weekly surprise as well. We definitely have that with Christopher Plummer, who is such a marvelous actor."

"The thing that I can say *Star Trek VI* has going for it that none of the other films had, is the preponderance of quality guest performers," admits Walter Koenig. "We have some really strong people. Kim was wonderful. There's a mind meld scene that the first time a mind meld is really sexy. It's very sensual. Rosanna DeSoto, Chris Plummer, Brock Peters, David Warner are all great."

"I've worked with Christopher Plummer and he's just a fabulous actor," adds Jimmy Doohan. "I saw him at Stratford doing Cyrano in Canada, and he just wiped the floor with every other Cyrano in the business. He's just sensational. Thank God, we had a great supporting cast because that's what this movie called for."

Decades before, Shatner had understudied for Plummer in *Henry V* in Canada, and now the two were squaring off among the stars in *Star Trek VI.* Unlike *Star Trek II* where Khan and Kirk never met, Kirk got to spar Shakespeare with General Chang face to face. "Mary, Queen of Scotts and Elizabeth the First never met and playwrights have been putting them together ever since," reflects Meyer. "Did they [Kirk and Khan] really never meet? They should have met."

Flinn was at first worried that Meyer's propensity for injecting classical quotations may have been overdone until he saw what Plummer was able to do with the polished prose. "Once we got this guy, Nick said, 'This guy can really do this stuff,' and kept adding more and more," says Flinn. "Whether it's pretentious or not, I think it depends on how it's used. It's a case of writing for the actor or getting the right actor for the role, which is a very grey line sometimes. Nick did polishes and rewrites right up until the night the scenes were shot. I don't quite agree with using too much of that sort of thing, but once you get Chris Plummer, suddenly it's working. In *Star Trek II,* he put the book in Shatner's hands and the bifocals and he made a marvelous statement that, no matter how information is delivered to us in the 23rd century, great literature will still exist and I thought that was a marvelous statement. In terms of literary allusions, I can only say to you that Nick is very, very well read with an education that is certainly classically oriented. I happen to have appreciated that for some time, and kind of went with the flow when I began working on the script myself."

One of the surprises that the film's casting offered was Christian Slater as a member of the Excelsior crew, serving under Captain Sulu. Notes George Takei, "I have a new puppy and it's the cutest thing. Its tail wags, it just bounces up and down. Well, that was Christian Slater. He was so happy. He lobbied to get on the set because he was a *Trek* fan from a child. My childhood dream was to swashbuckle in Sherwood Forest. He did that, but his dream was to wear a Starfleet uniform. He was like my puppy, bouncing up and down, dashing down the corridor, climbing up a ladder and saying, 'This is where Scotty did so and so.' He was literally a 21-year-old kid in his fantasy land."

Offers producer Ralph Winter about the film's casting, "Nick wanted to go for a classy approach. He wanted to go with actors who were going to make a contribution and really wanted to work with us. Despite not having the budget of some of the enormous pictures, we didn't want to be deterred by that. We wanted to find people who liked the material and would treat it as if it was the biggest picture ever made. We went for the best actors in each role. We were not looking for someone to say, 'Okay, I'll do it,' but people who got excited about the material, who were *Star Trek* fans and would love to be in the picture. That's what attracted us to Kim Cattrall, Christopher Plummer, Rosanna DeSoto and Kurtwood Smith. In other places, we went for a specific look, and also a good actor—Iman."

As for the comely chameloid, writer Flinn envisioned a somewhat different approach to the last woman to stir Kirk's loins. "The person I had in mind was as different as night and day from Iman," says Flinn. "I had Sigourney Weaver in mind, but I'm not sure we didn't come up with a better choice. I didn't imagine that we could ever afford her, but I just saw the character as a big, ballsy space pirate; a female version of the dark side of Han Solo. She turns out to be rather villainous, but a kind of swashbuckling female space pirate, and I thought of Sigourney."

Equally taxing was finding a place for each of the supporting players who demanded their share of screen time. Not surprisingly, in a cast that has been lauded and extolled for nearly 25 years with a nearly religious fervor, tempers and egos have periodically flared and often festered. One of the unique challenges of crafting a *Star Trek* film is providing the ensemble with their share of the action to appease both the actors and their respective cheering sections.

"You've got a picture with seven stars and you want to give everybody a meaningful role," notes Ralph Winter. "That is the challenge of doing something like this as opposed to doing James Bond or Indiana Jones, where it's clear there's only one hero with a lot of supporting characters. You've got a team of seven people that have to be given something meaningful to do. Nick [Meyer] has done a great job of weaving that together. We know who the core audience is and we've got to satisfy them, but beyond that it's got to be fun, it's got to be entertaining and capture your imagination."

One could hardly imagine Bernard Lee clamoring for a larger role as M in the James Bond film series, just as one would have found it equally outrageous if Denholm Elliot had held out for expanding the role of Marcus Brody in the Indiana Jones trilogy. But when George Takei expresses dissatisfaction with his navigating chores as Sulu, people take notice.

"Accommodating them is part of the assignment," Dennis Martin Flinn states. "If you hate it, don't take the assignment. We had to make sure both Leonard and Shatner were satisfied and they both had notes from the first draft. In this one circumstance, the actors probably have a leg to stand on. In any original film or work of art, the play's the thing and if somebody says my part isn't big enough, that's just ego talking. What a writer or a director tries to do is tell the story as effectively as possible, but maybe in *Star Trek* part of it is the story and you're adding to the 25 years of lore of these people. The audience wants to know what happened to Uhura and Sulu and we made a conscious effort to promote Sulu, maybe partially because he's

been complaining about being a navigator all his life and certain things fell into place and maybe others didn't."

"It's a terrific picture for everybody," Jimmy Doohan remarks. "George finally got to be somebody on his own ship and Leonard had a lot to do with that."

In *Star Trek II*, Chekov was given a larger role as a member of Captain Terrell's crew. In *Star Trek V* it was Uhura whose nude dance captured the attention of a desert scouting party. Spoiled by *Star Trek IV*, the entire cast got into the action as the reconnaissance parties looked for whales in '80s America. For Koenig, these opportunities to work away from his William Shatner were a godsend.

"*Star Trek II* was a delight from start to finish and one of the greatest delights was working with Ricardo Montalban and Paul Winfield, and not being on the Enterprise having to be judged by our leading man," says Koenig. "It was great not having scenes reblocked by our leading man, which I found very oppressive. I was working with actors who give as well as take. Totally professional. There's no question Ricardo has a strong ego and that's great. He's very colorful. He's really very flamboyant. Working with him was a pure delight. He was always there for your close-up and always very giving. I remember Nick [Meyer] saying something to him about his performance needing fine tuning, and I thought, 'Oh shit, here it comes,' and he said, 'Ah, you're right.' It was beautiful. That's the way every theatrical experience should be. With us, unfortunately it wasn't. The two weeks I worked with Bill as the leading actor wasn't as much fun."

Shatner, who along with co-star Nimoy, has been the principal beneficiary of *Trek*'s success, having segued into other roles successfully as well as that of a popular science fiction writer, is not surprised to be the butt of criticism and is diplomatic in responding to the criticism. "If the original concept of the show was still in effect and the series was still going today, the situation would be exactly the same," he says. "There are people whose names and parts are above the title and people who aren't. That's the nature of the business and that's the way these stories are told."

As for the criticism he has received on the convention circuit and in the press from not only Doohan and Koenig but other members of the ensemble, Shatner is puzzled. "It's coming from a couple of people," he says. "I don't understand that. I'm not even aware of it, quite frankly. Occasionally I'll hear something from an ardent fan of mine who'll say so and so said this about you, and it bewilders me because I have had no trouble with them. Nothing certainly bad, nothing particularly good either. We have done our job and gone on and I have never had bad words with anyone. I don't know what vitriol is spilling out. The people who I see a lot of—Leonard, DeForest and the people in management and the directors—I've heard nothing bad from."

Ralph Winter, who had initially expressed trepidation over working with Shatner on *Star Trek V*, has nothing but praise for the actor turned director. "It went a lot smoother than I thought. I had a great time with Bill. He was terrific and he was a lot of fun."

Kim Cattrall also was positive about her dealings with Shatner. "He's sort of a technical shark," she says. "He can technically do almost anything as an actor. He was a gentleman with me and it doesn't matter how I feel about him personally. We're both Canadians and I had a professional relationship. I never told him that when I was first starting out as an actress I was a day-player in a series of commercials he was doing. I don't think anybody does better what he does. He *is* Captain Kirk and he's amazing in what he does. I can't say I'm the same kind of actor he is. His technical expertise is like somebody doing a skill extremely well and you know that's what he's going to do. I never had any problems with him or his outcrys. I found him respectful, he runs his lines a lot, over and over and over again, which is kind of annoying, but everybody has their own way of working."

"Bridging the Generations"

When *Star Trek V* went into production, it was easy to ignore the upstart interloper, *Star Trek: The Next Generation*, but with *Star Trek VI*, it was executive producer Leonard Nimoy who gave impetus to bridging the generations and establishing continuity between the series.

According to *Next Generation* producer Rick Berman, "They're interested in getting right what we have defined so there are no contradictions. We have a wonderful relationship with Nicholas Meyer and Leonard Nimoy, and they have been terrific in coming to talk to us. There's much more of a family-like atmosphere than there was with *Star Trek V*. They want the movie and our show to have a symbiotic relationship."

Perhaps realizing the surging popularity of *The Next Generation*, Nimoy agreed to guest star in an episode ("I thought it was time," he said), giving his tacit approval to the venture by acknowledging its success and possibly hoping to bolster interest in the flagging feature film series by starring in a story linked to the events of *Star Trek VI*.

"I had a number of conversations with Gene Roddenberry over the years about appearing in a *Next Generation* story," he relates. "We both had agreed that it was a good idea and that all we needed was to come up with the right idea. The idea of doing it never really went away. Frank Mancuso brought the subject up when we sat down to discuss *Star Trek VI*, I went to *Next Generation* executive producers Rick Berman and Michael Piller. I said, 'This is Frank Mancuso's idea. Do you have any thoughts?' Their response was whether I would do the show. I told them that if they got the right story, I would do it. They came up with this terrific story and I said, 'Let's do it.'"

Star Trek VI is peppered with references to its syndicated offspring. Not only in its storyline, which paves the way for eventual peace between the Klingon Empire and the Federation, but references to the Khitomer Outpost and, of course, Michael Dorn playing his great, great grandfather, a Klingon defense counselor named—what else?—Worf.

For Dorn, who downplays his affinity for the old show, appearing in the film was a treat. "It was a lot of fun," he says. "It was an honor. I liked the show when I was growing up and I like doing our show very much, but you don't think about it till it happens and then you realize how important it is. The best thing about being in this business is working with really good actors. It gets the old creative juices going."

Says Denny Martin Flinn, who co-wrote the script and had even considered having the classic crew turning over the Enterprise at the end of *The Undiscovered Country* to Picard and company until he realized the difference in timelines, "The genesis was really Nick saying 'How about if we get Michael Dorn to play the part of Worf?' and everybody said 'Nick, *The Next Generation* is 75 years later!' and Nick said, 'Okay, we'll make it his great, grandfather' and that was it. Nick had not created the part of Worf for a particular actor, but we got Michael Dorn and they explained to him he couldn't play himself."

For Dorn, playing one of his ancestors meant subtly altering his performance in the role. "I felt Worf was more at peace with himself in *Star Trek VI* than Worf on the television show, because he's a Klingon, all Klingon," the actor explains. "He is a Klingon and he's from Klingon, he's never been taken away from his family. He's spent all his time with Klingons and was more in touch with himself. He was more even-keeled and not quite as racked with inner turmoil."

For special effects make-up artist Richard Snell, approaching the challenge of creating Worf's great grandfather required some thought. "Originally they thought they were going to possibly use his old prosthetics from the series. It was decided not to because it was too much of a tie-in," says Snell. "My Klingons are different than the series TV Klingons, and I have a different idea about it. Like all art, it's subjective and so it was decided there should be some tie-in in design, but for the subtlety of motion we were going to sculpt it very thin over the eyebrows so you could get in very close with a camera. We definitely felt there should be some tie-in, a genealogy and blood line involved. We refined it for film work, but I'm not the type of person who would throw out someone else's designs and say this is going to be mine."

Originally it had been intended

that *Star Trek VI* and *The Next Generation* would be even more closely linked with *The Undiscovered Country* being the Enterprise's "classic" cast's final mission. In the last Captain's Log as originally scripted, Kirk stated, "...This ship and her history will shortly became the care of a new generation. To them and their posterity will we commit our future. They will continue the voyages we have begun and journey to *all* the undiscovered countries, boldly going where no man...where no *one* has gone before."

However, reportedly after Michael Dorn gave an interview stating that *Star Trek VII* would definitely feature the *Next Generation* cast, Leonard Nimoy, irked over Dorn's comments, had the ending changed. Instead, when the Enterprise is called back to spacedock, Spock joins Kirk in disobeying orders and continuing on their mission. The final log now is changed to simply refer to *The Next Generation* as "another crew."

Ironically, despite *Trek VI*'s myriad references to *Next Generation*, no one involved with the production claims to follow the show except for Nicholas Meyer, who labels himself a fan. Even he insists that he was not concerned with developing a continuity. Members of the "classic" cast are still less than effusive in their praise for their 24th century counterpart.

"I originally thought it would be detrimental to the feature films," says Walter Koenig, who plays Chekov. "I had this propriety feeling based on my own insecurities and neuroses. I looked askance at the show, hoped it would fail and was comforted by the fact that a couple of the episodes first season were trading on stories we had done, which reassured me that they weren't as good. I am aware that my reactions weren't objective and perhaps to this day they are not. I still like the best of our show better than theirs, but their show has definitely shown enormous progress and has considerably more merit than I ever attributed to them, and the actors are all very strong performers. I would love to have the resume of Patrick Stewart. These are very talented people. What I sense is missing, and maybe it's because of my territorial feelings, is the dimensionality of characters and the sense of fun that

Kirk, Spock and McCoy had. Their interchanges, their human weaknesses, the way they reacted, the fears exposed by Bill Shatner in his character. I don't see those things in *The Next Generation*. They seem more straightforward, more in control and in command. Kirk, for all his heroics, what made him appealing to me were his anxieties, his concerns, his fears, his amorous interludes. All of that made him very human to me."

In a *TV Guide* poll celebrating the original *Star Trek*'s 25th anniversary, the magazine asked readers to vote on who they would feel more comfortable captaining the Enterprise if earth was in peril. Readers came down firmly on the side of James Tiberius Kirk. Responding to the poll, William Shatner says, "It's unfortunate that they perceive it as a competition, which it isn't because it's two different shows and two different characters. But, on the other hand, wouldn't it have been awful if I had lost?"

And for Shatner, who professes not to have had the opportunity to watch *The Next Generation* at any great length, he finds "classic" *Trek* far more appealing. "My perception is that it's more interesting storytelling to have passion and have one person in a dilemma. It's a more personally effective way of telling a story to my way of thinking. A story told by committee is not as exciting. There's more distance between you and the audience."

Koenig would be hard-pressed to disagree with Shatner. "I do recognize that my initial feelings about *The Next Generation* were fairly mean spirited," he acknowledges. "I had propriety feelings and didn't like the idea of somebody else taking over. I still feel a twinge when I realize that future films will be with the *Next Generation* and even though I'm not anxious to do anymore *Star Trek*, I still have those vestigial feelings about not giving it up."

"I think they're doing a darn good job," says Jimmy Doohan, *Trek*'s Chief Engineer Montgomery Scott who reprised the character in the sixth season *Next Generation* episode "Relics". "They're good stories, but there's no messages. I think maybe the messages are what make the older ones so great. When I talk to people about *The Next Generation*, they tell me they always wonder what the

message is. The original always had a message and there's no message. To me, this movie has one of the greatest messages that we can possibly imagine, particularly in light of our present day situation and this brilliant story talks about where we are going today."

Doohan's optimistic appraisal of *Trek VI*'s message and *TNG*'s moralistic failings is a philosophy that is not shared by Michael Dorn. "I have a tendency to talk about reality and there are a lot of things going on in the real world that are compelling and inspirational," says Dorn. "There's also a lot of things that *Star Trek* is trying to say which is the same thing. If you want to get a message out of *Star Trek*, then I think that's good. But the whole purpose of the thing is good, exciting entertainment. I think the more that Gene was involved with it, the more we were trying to exploit things and bring across messages and show there's something out there. The same with Nick and the movies. Our show has that message, but it's more like good television. No matter what I think, it's highly rated and doing very well. I would say it's basically good television, we don't show anything that isn't known. Maybe it brings to light some things, but we're just a mirror of society."

Dorn rejects the notion that the original series could be more progressive in addressing social issues because of the preponderance of socio-political concerns which America grappled with in the '60s, and that the '80s offer less of an opportunity for *Star Trek* to deal with topical issues as has been suggested by many involved with the series. "That's wrong," says Dorn. "*Star Trek* is the perfect forum for those types of things to deal with new, fresh, untried ideas. How can you say everything has been done? The fall of Eastern Europe, famine, these are contemporary issues. What about a society that is the richest in the world where people are starving and dying on the streets with nothing, or a society that puts so much emphasis on arms and protecting our country that our schools are going bankrupt? I think our show is the perfect forum for entertainment and to deal with social issues. We've just scratched the surface and it's good televi-

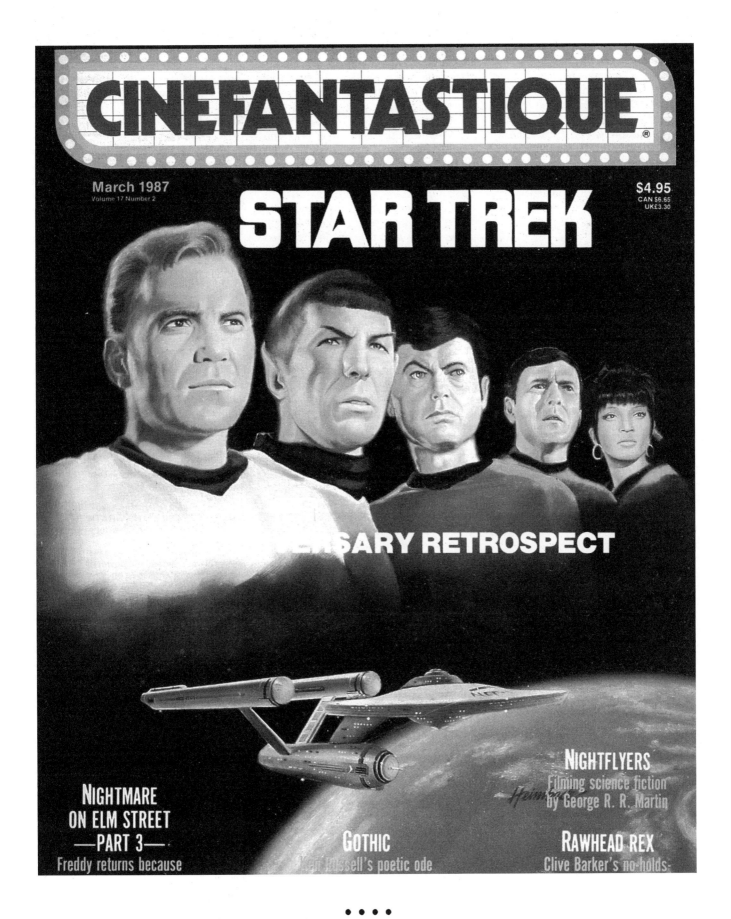

CINEFANTASTIQUE

March 1987
Volume 17 Number 2

$4.95
CAN $6.65
UK £3.30

STAR TREK

...SARY RETROSPECT

NIGHTMARE
ON ELM STREET
—PART 3—
Freddy returns because

GOTHIC
Ken Russell's poetic ode

NIGHTFLYERS
Filming science fiction
by George R. R. Martin

RAWHEAD REX
Clive Barker's no-holds-

sion, but we're not really trying to break any ground."

For Dorn, *The Next Generation* and his two week stint on *Star Trek VI* have afforded him some of his most cherished acting experiences. "*Star Trek* really is wonderful," he says. "It's a dream come true, but it's still acting. How do you act in front of a blue screen? How do you act as a doctor if you've never been a doctor before? It's [pure] acting."

"This is the End.... Or Is It?"

With the idea in mind that *Star Trek VI* would be the classic cast's swan song, co-writer Dennis Martin Flinn devised an ending for the film in which the characters would sign their names to their final log aboard the starship Enterprise, which not only ended the series with an emotional flourish but passed the baton to the next generation, both literally and figuratively. And although the signatures remain in the final cut, several changes were made.

"They reversed the order of the names so Shatner's is last, like an opera," says composer Cliff Eidelman. "It's a minute of signing off, which is real emotional music."

However, the only emotion writer Flinn experiences when he sees the signatures is anger. "They are different than how I conceived them originally," says Flinn. "My original script read the signatures were James T. Kirk, Mr. Spock, etc. What we were doing is offering them a chance to sign the final log. I thought that would be rather touching, especially since it's the last film and all, but it got changed to the actors instead of the characters and I personally dislike it very, very much. One of the actors who's executive producer, who shall go unnamed, likes it since I suppose he'd rather see his own name than his character's name up on the screen. A lot of people have argued both sides and I guess we lost. Frankly, I think no one gives a fuck about Leonard Nimoy and William Shatner and those people in any substantive *Star Trek* sense. Those people are Mr. Spock and Kirk and Dr. McCoy, and I don't see any point of the actors signing their name to the log of the U.S.S. Enterprise. I'm

upset that other people on the production haven't spoken up more who carry more weight than I do, like the producers who I know damn well agree with me but just did not fight it strongly enough. We're certainly in the majority, but the situation was not easy because I think the director and Leonard are the only two people who wanted that, but nobody wanted to argue except me."

And with the final flourish of Cliff Eidelman's score as the house lights came on in theatres, *Trek* fans were left to wonder if what they had just watched was truly the final mission of the original crew of the starship Enterprise. That question had become an equally hot topic among the members of the *Trek VI* production team prior to the film's release, with rumors running rampant that the ending was changed to be left more open-ended.

"I heard the same thing with *Star Trek II*," says director Nicholas Meyer. "I had nothing to do with bringing Spock back to life and if it had been up to me, my picture would not have ended ambiguously. This movie has only had one ending from the very beginning and that ending has never changed. I remember all the rumors that we filmed multiple endings for *II*. We never did that either. This film was written from the first draft the way it ended. There has never been any studio pressure or suggestion to change that, and I suppose that's because the ending doesn't preclude anything."

Flinn recalls a somewhat different coda for *Trek VI*'s climactic moments. "In rewrites and polishes Nick did the night before shooting, the final, final scene was rewritten. I honestly don't believe this came out of any desire on Nick's part to leave the door open, but out of the story and the metaphorical way that he writes. The nice thing that he wanted to do was a Peter Pan line—I guess he was in an optimistic mood that night—and the way the scene is structured there's no door being slammed, but, of course, you could always finesse that. It's up to the studio—and probably Leonard and Shatner as well."

Like most people both on and off the crew, Flinn, had been under the impression that Paramount had officially

sanctioned *Star Trek VI* as the final chapter of the "classic" cast's voyages, so he was surprised to find then recently installed studio head Brandon Tartikoff mulling *Trek*'s future after an early screening of the film for executives.

"I had always heard that this was the last film," recalls Flinn. "We had a very early screening for the executives [and] they liked it very much. They were all just standing around afterwards and Brandon Tartikoff, who had just literally taken over the studio, and who had virtually nothing to do with the film until that day, said 'Why is this the last film?' Everybody looked at each other saying 'Gee, didn't you tell me this was it?' and then everybody looked at Leonard, who really is the key, and he did not say 'No more from me.' I sort of thought he was saying, 'Well, it's your studio. Make me an offer.'"

"Brandon was very happy with the picture. He said 'You guys have given me an unexpected Christmas present'," agrees Ralph Winter, who adds, "I had watched *Star Trek* as a kid and thought it was fun. It was a thrill to be involved with the picture. If you had asked me ten years ago that I would be producing the sixth *Star Trek* film, I'd think you were crazy. It's fun to think that this is really a part of American culture and to become a part of that and to make a contribution to that is fun and rewarding. But the biggest reward is to go to opening night at 8 o'clock and to sit down with an audience that has waited for months, avoided reading the script, wears a costume, brings a phaser and sits there and laughs, cries and has a good time. We do it for ourselves as much as everyone else and if we're entertained, we think everyone else will be. That's the reward."

Cinefantastique's December 1991 issue celebrating Star Trek's 25th anniversary, highlighted one of Gene Roddenberry's last interviews.

Cinefantastique magazine begins their yearly visits to the set of Star Trek: The Next Generation

••••

CHAPTER SIXTEEN

These Are
the New Voyages....

"While the original *Star Trek* looks primitive now, it still has a lot of content. The idea for *The Next Generation* was to provide the same content in a 1987 capsule; with 1987 parameters. The difficulty has been that the public is extremely sophisticated, and the ideas that seemed new and revolutionary in the early show are no longer revolutionary...The whole experience has been very stimulating, because we're trying to cover new ground"
—Bob Lewin, former producer of
Star Trek: The Next Generation

In 1988, the *Trek* flame was once again rekindled with the return of *Star Trek* to the small screen. The year was 1986 and Paramount Pictures feared there would indeed be a final frontier in their future. The franchise which they had at first ignored, then exploited and finally cultivated into a monetary bonanza seemed to be heading toward permanent space drydock.

Despite the fact that it was the 20th anniversary of *Star Trek* and the studio was anxiously awaiting the word on their forthcoming *Star Trek IV: The Voyage Home* feature film, which would eventually become the most successful of the movies, there was deep concern over the fact that *Star Trek* was losing ground in syndication as well as beginning to look extremely dated as television had became bigger and more sophisticated. The future was starting to look old. After all, regardless of the fans' devotion, how many times could they watch the same 79 episodes before their fervor began to dissipate?

In fact, the television series that had put the phrase "off network syndication" in the dictionary, was getting tired. Independent stations were running it less, and the studio's prize goose of the past decade and a half looked as though it was nearly deplete of golden eggs. Some of the blame can be shifted to the December 1979 release of *Star Trek: The Motion Picture*. Although a financial

success, the film was a milestone in an important respect. It was the last time fans would lop up whatever they were force-fed by the Paramount machine. If *Trek* was new but not improved, the windfall might turn to a trickle.

The thinking in 1986 was that even if *Star Trek IV* went on to great success (which it did), a hit every two years was not the same as cash pouring into the coffers on a weekly basis from the syndication of a series. It was clear that a new *Trek* was necessary, and with a near-geriatric and exorbitantly priced ensemble of talent in the form of the original cast out of Paramount's reach on a weekly basis, it was decided that it was time to build a better starship.

During the hoopla of the shows' 20th anniversary, Paramount Pictures announced the anticipated means of pumping artificial life into the waning phenomenon.

"The speculation is over," said Mel Harris, then President of Paramount Television. "The answer is yes. *Star Trek* lives. Starting next fall, beginning with a two hour telefilm followed by 24 one-hour episodes, *Star Trek* will return to television in the form of a new series, *Star Trek: The Next Generation*. Although this is a new starship Enterprise, a new cast and new stories, the man at the helm is still the same: the creator of *Star Trek*, Gene Roddenberry. And we're proud to have him once again supervising all aspects of production."

What Harris had failed to mention was that Roddenberry was third on their A-list of producing choices for the series. First they had gone to father and son team of Sam and Greg Strangis (who went on to produce Paramount's syndicated *War of the Worlds*), whose take on the show—which dealt with Starfleet Academy and space cadets—was not what the studio was looking for. Leonard Nimoy, whose evolution from *Star Trek* actor to director and fiscal frugality had earned him critical kudos and respect among the Paramount hierarchy, was approached next. He rejected the offer because he did not want to get tied down to the rigors of producing a weekly series when his directorial career was first taking off. With nowhere else to go, Paramount reluctantly turned to

The late Gene Roddenberry at one of his generally infrequent convention appearances. (photo copyright © Karen Witkowski)

Roddenberry. Their reluctance was quite understandable, considering the image that Gene had painted of the studio's executives throughout the 70's, blaming them for the aborted attempts at reviving the show.

David Gerrold points out, "Roddenberry would go out to various speaking engagements and would say 'It's difficult. How do you convince the studio executives that what you're talking about is changing the world?' And he'd do it very sly. Studio executives are maligned by everyone who works for them. If a studio makes fifteen hit pictures a year, who gets the credit? The directors, the actors, the executive producers of the picture, but the studio executive who said, 'I'll buy this picture, I'll finance it', he's just lucky enough to be sitting there when they brought the project into him. They can tell the difference between a good story and a bad story. They get excited when they work with exciting people. You don't get to be the head of a studio by accident. Admittedly there have been stupid men as studio executives who do make mistakes, but twenty years at Paramount? Paramount is the most successful studio in the industry. Down the line they're doing all these great pictures like *The Godfathers, Saturday Night Fever*...and

••••

Patrick Stewart in the persona of a knight in shining armor in John Boorman's Excalibur.

they can't get *Star Trek* on the boards? Give me a break. Finally, they get *Star Trek* going and what does Gene do? He spends their money like there's no tomorrow. He makes a $40 million epic. An awful movie."

Paramount hoped that Roddenberry could be contained this time out, despite the fact that they had been forced to cede full creative control to obtain his cooperation. Eventually the studio's saving grace would be a young producer named Rick Berman who would ultimately become the real winner in the power struggle that was to ensue involving the studio, Roddenberry and a cadre of writers. Berman would be the one responsible for shaping the series and turning it into a bonafide sensation in its own right. Ironically, Berman who has become the prime force behind the success of Next Generation hadn't sought to run the series and was only handed the producing reigns when the division of Paramount he presided over, longform and miniseries production, was phased out by the studio, leaving the executive nowhere to go. When he was offered the chance to steer the new *Star Trek*, he took it despite being advised against it by his peers.

"I had a lot of people who told me I was nuts," recalls Berman. "But I had a feeling it was going to work and I

decided it was worth the risk of leaving a well paying job at a movie studio to work on a science-fiction sequel syndicated television series."

Berman's most recognizable production credit prior to *Star Trek* was his years spent on PBS' children's educational show *Big Blue Marble*, which hardly prepared him for the rigors of riding herd over a technologically complex and expensive one hour dramatic series pioneering the first-run syndicated television market.

But by the time the first script for the pilot episode was finished, the conceptual template for the new show had been firmly embedded. Whether this template could make for riveting drama was beside the point. The show's two-hour pilot, for instance, was widely considered a disappointment and derivative of episodes of the old series and the first motion picture, even though writer D.C. Fontana's original drafts were far more original and compelling until Roddenberry began rewriting it, but the viewers continued to watch.

There were a number of obvious difficulties in bringing *Star Trek* back to the small screen. First and foremost was the tremendous affinity and loyalty that fans had for the original cast. The new series intended to completely eschew Kirk & Company for an all-new crew of Starfleet officers, set nearly a century after the voyages of the first starship Enterprise.

Numerous ideas had been bandied back and forth during the early discussions between Roddenberry and the team he had brought together, largely veterans of the first series, including writers David Gerrold and D.C. Fontana, producer Robert Justman and Eddie Milkis and newcomers Herb Wright and Rick Berman. It was finally decided that the setting would be a new incarnation of the Enterprise with a cast which wouldn't include any vestiges of the original. Rather than attempt a retread of the first series, Roddenberry was intent on presenting all-new Starfleet officers.

"Gene had to create a new television show from 25 years of mythology that had grown up over an old one and he had to do it all out of whole cloth," says Berman of the creation of *Next*

Generation. "You have to understand what it's like to write a stylized 24th century script and know what words can be spoken and what words can't and how to go about all of the things we do to create this television show as opposed to if you were creating *MacGyver*. He also had a lot of people who felt they knew more about *Star Trek* than he did and he had to get pretty tough about it. We had a group of writers that came in and didn't have the benefit of someone as strong as Mike Piller. People had no idea what *Star Trek: The Next Generation* was going to be about. Gene felt the obsessive necessity to put his own print on everything to get the show going and I applaud him for that. By the time I was sort of in control of the series, in the second year, Gene had pretty much cemented his idea of what the show was going to be about and it was my job to continue, to keep it going and not to formulate it because he had done that."

After moving into spacious offices in the Hart Building on the Paramount lot [now occupied by Michael Piller and his baseball card collection], Roddenberry used his newfound stature to arrange for a non-stop unspooling of classic science-fiction movies to set the stage for what would be the fruitful discussions from which the new ensemble of *Trek* characters would spring. The producers decided early on that there would be no Vulcans onboard the new ship and late in the production Rick Berman and Herb Wright championed the addition of a Klingon officer. Roddenberry hated the idea. He wanted to stay clear of any characters from the first series, but was eventually swayed to include the character in a supporting role although the officer, Worf, as he was named, would grow in importance over the years to become a major part of the show.

Roddenberry directed his efforts towards refining the stories and the scripts for the series, leaving the massive logistics of keeping the show on schedule and on budget in the hands of producers Robert Justman and Rick Berman, who oversaw the day to day operations ranging from scheduling to color correction. Justman who shared Roddenberry's emotional reasons for returning to the show nearly twenty years after its cancellation, says, "When I left *Star Trek* in 1968, it was a disaster. It was a failure as far as the network was concerned and the industry. The only thing that saved *Star Trek* two years in a row were the people who cared about it. By the time the third season rolled around, the handwriting was on the wall and Gene and I both know that it was so. I had a need to return to prove that the show did have value and was successful and could be successful again, and that you can go home again and prove to the people who doubted you that there was value there all along; that this was a worthwhile, if you'll pardon the expression, enterprise."

Working with veteran casting director Junie Lowry, the producers embarked on a massive search to personify the characters created by the new *Trek* production team. A massive talent search led to the casting of English Shakespearean actor Patrick Stewart as the new Captain, Jean-Luc Picard, a Frenchman. The casting of Stewart was an audacious choice since the actor was not only an Englishman playing a French captain, but in his fifties and distinctly bald. Discovered by producer Robert Justman while performing at UCLA, casting Stewart was one of the series first coups.

Rounding out the ensemble were veteran actor LeVar Burton as the blind navigator, Geordi LaForge; acting coach and choreographer Gates McFadden as the new doctor, Beverly Crusher; second-in-command Riker was to be played by Jonathan Frakes, security chief Tasha Yar was portrayed by Denise Crosby, who left the show at the end of the first year; Michael Dorn could be found under heavy prosthetics as the Klingon officer, Worf; and Wil Wheaton, who had made a strong impression on movie audience's in *Stand By Me*, played precocious acting ensign Wesley Crusher, the doctor's young son. Another triumph in casting for the show was the hiring of Broadway actor Brent Spiner to personify the show's resident Spock-substitute, android Data, who, like Pinnochio, sought to become human.

Production Designer Herman Zimmerman suggests that the new ensemble is more faithful to Roddenberry's original hopes for *Star Trek* before the casting of William Shatner and Leonard Nimoy turned the show into a star vehicle. "If you want to go back to Mr. Roddenberry's original ideas, he wanted to create an ensemble cast and he did, but because of the really strong ability of Bill Shatner and Leonard Nimoy and the romance of those characters and the relationships between each other and Dr. McCoy, it became more of a star cast than an ensemble cast. In *Next Generation*, Gene achieved what he was really striving for in the first place. He has the strength of Picard in Patrick Stewart, but he has a very level competent cast all the way through. I think he was more pleased than he was the first time around with the casting of *Next Generation*."

"I was very involved with the original casting on *Star Trek* and if I could pride myself on any casting coup it had to do with Patrick Stewart," adds Berman. "Bob [Justman] discovered Patrick Stewart and brought him to the attention of Gene Roddenberry and Roddenberry said no. I met Patrick Stewart and said to Bob Justman, 'We have to convince Gene to use this guy,' and Bob said to me, 'We can't, it's a waste of time. When Gene makes up his mind it's a waste of time to try and change his mind'. But in my case, ignorance was bliss. I didn't believe that and I was the guy who basically bugged Gene into realizing that Patrick was the best Picard."

Roddenberry's first choice for the role of the Enterprise captain in *The Next Generation* was *Cagney & Lacey*'s Stephen Macht. "As far as the other characters, they were far more the selection of Bob Justman and mine than they were of anybody else," says Berman. "Gene basically approved, like the studio did, the people that Bob and I chose, and he was not all that involved in it. He was very stubborn about who he wanted to be Picard and, in the case of Marina Sirtis and Denise Crosby we selected them for the opposite roles, and he said I want Crosby to play Tasha and I want Marina to play Troi and that was his idea. Frakes was my choice. He liked Frakes, but his first choice was Bill Campbell [*Rocketeer, Crime Story*]. Gene liked him and we brought him into see Paramount executive John Pike and he said no. The next person we chose was Frakes. He felt very strongly about what he wanted Frakes to be but he was never very stubborn about the casting."

Unlike the original show where friction and tension between the ensemble typified its three years of production and only elevated during the making of the feature film's involving well-documented early feuds between Shatner and co-star Leonard Nimoy, the cast of *The Next Generation* was quite enamored with each other.

"One of the reasons this show didn't take the dive we all feared it would in the back of our minds in comparison to the old show," Jonathan Frakes points out, "is because the characters were so well thought out ahead of time. I don't know how they cast this so well. We go out to dinner after 14 hour days. They hired actors who like to act instead of hiring movie stars or models. For virtually all of us, this was the biggest job of our career and we're so happy about that. It was an ensemble and I think it was a good ensemble."

"We're landlocked on this planet Earth," says Herman Zimmerman, *Next Generation*'s original production designer who was charged with remaining faithful to the original production design of the sixties show while updating the technology and aesthetics for a saavier television audience. "Whether we put them in costumes of the future and generate imaginative settings, we are still dealing with good and evil, love and hate relationships and all of the basic emotions and problems that human beings are running into daily. That's one of the things that makes Roddenberry's view of the future so believable. It's a republican view of the future, where life can be easy. You don't have to work at something you don't like. You can find the thing that allows you to contribute and that is what you can do for a living."

Star Trek's standing sets which spanned two huge soundstages on the Paramount lot are astounding in their level of detail and one could actually believe they're aboard a spaceship when they become lost in the maze of corridors

• • • •

This mock-up of the new Enterprise bridge featured toy figures in the place of the ship's crew.

that connect the various sets on Stage 9. Nearby was Stage 16 which serves as the locale for various swing sets, planetary exteriors and locales. The level of craftsmanship which was involved in bringing a *Next Generation* episode to life is gargantuan and with a budget of nearly $1.5 million an episode, the show strove to achieve a feature film quality look while stretching the boundaries of a television budget.

"The new bridge design evolved, as did the exterior of the ship, from two basic concepts," says Herman Zimmerman. "One is it is unnecessary to have aerodynamics because space is a vacuum. It is, by the 24th century, in Mr. Roddenberry's mind, entirely possible that technology has reached such a state of proficiency that it has become an art form. Point two is that instead of a five year mission we have a 30 year mission with women, children and families aboard. We wanted to make the whole environment of the starship more comfortable. It never was a battleship. It's a far cry from an all gray militaristic starship. It's indeed a state of the art, comfortable machine that we're proud to call home."

Ultimately, the old adage that the more things change, the more they stay the same is borne out. *Star Trek* for all its newfound glitz and modern maturity, still harkens back to the essential elements which encompassed it in the '60s,

and it continued to wrestle with the same issues that have intrigued audiences for the last twenty years.

"I think the content is much the same as it ever was," says former producer Robert Justman. "While our techniques may be a little slicker [and] the shows may have a better look, I think the show's content is much the same. Just because centuries have passed, we haven't dispensed of the Ten Commandments. They still work. I can't say I was ever satisfied. I'm pleased. I'm never satisfied. You can't turn out a Picasso every week. Supposedly we're dealing with some kind of art. It's not possible in a collaborative effort to turn out a work of genius once a week.

"Some people were afraid of the new *Star Trek* because the old people wouldn't be in it," recalls Justman. "It was a threat to them. But I don't think that lasted very long. You form new relationships all through life. Sometimes the old relationships are the best, sometimes they're not. But there's room in this world for diversity. People resist change for various reasons. It's just a natural reaction to put a show or an enterprise down out of hand, but it's not very science fiction. The great thing about people interested in science fiction is that they have open minds. They're eager for new ideas. Otherwise, why do anything different? Let's do *Space Patrol*. It was on

and people liked it."

The first 13 episodes were considered a disappointment. Indeed, the new Enterprise probably would have been mothballed by any of the trigger-happy networks, which favor terminating any expensive drama whose numbers don't justify their exorbitant license fees if they don't muster up to Nielsen standards early on. But Paramount, having anticipated a difficult start-up, side-stepped such dire and inevitable consequences by bartering the show into first run syndication, guaranteeing some well-needed breathing space to steer its wayward little starship that apparently couldn't back on course.

This proved no mean feat. Despite protestations that the new *Trek* would not replicate its progenitor, several of TNG's early episodes bore distinct similarities to those of the classic series, or dealt with Roddenberry's by-now familiar pet issues. including his perpetual God-fetish addressing judgmental alien beings, while at other times indulging his lust for exploring sexual issues in the basest of terms.

"First year of a series is a very exciting time to be aboard," says Herb Wright. "Its the riskiest, but also the most exciting. That's when you're making the rules. There's no one saying 'I've got the secret', because you're all trying to figure it out together. There's a sense of it becoming. On *Star Trek* you really had excitement, a new ship, a new cast and an opportunity to do shows that you couldn't have done 20 years ago with a much healthier effects budget and no more rubber monsters and cardboard walls. You walk on those sets and you think you can fly, but there was so much strife and turmoil the first year I couldn't deal with it anymore. First season, no one got protected. Everyone had a target drawn on their chest when they came in."

Recalls Wright of the infamous revolving door policy which typified the series in its first two years and saw myriad writers join the show only to be fired or leave several weeks—sometimes days— later . "It was like Vietnam, you didn't want to get close to them because you knew they wouldn't be there very long; Johnny Dawkins, Sandy Fries. They'd be given a script to write and direction and before they could learn what the show was about they'd be torn apart by the staff and thrown to the wolves or Gene would just say I hate them and they'd be out the door. It was very strange. I remember Sandy Fries thought he was king of the mountain for five minutes. He went home and had champagne and a big party and Monday morning he walked in and he was fired."

In fact, it is because of *Star Trek*'s idealistic and utopian view of the future that Berman suggests *Trek* has had such extraordinary turnover on its writing staff throughout the years. "We had to manufacture our conflict from other than interpersonal conflict among our characters and that does make it very difficult to write. The language had to be stylized, we don't know how people are going to speak in the 24th century and so we have them speak in a sort of stylized generic fashion. It's not 24th century, it's not contemporary and on the other hand its not medieval either. We have to deal with science fiction and a lot of people don't understand what SF is and a lot of people are interested in dealing with fantasy and the writers have to deal with a lot of technical elements. Any dramatic television show has a set of rules that you've got to follow. If you're writing *St. Elsewhere*, you've got to know about medicine. If you're writing for *L.A. Law*, you've got to know about juris prudence in the state of California. On the other hand, with *Star Trek* you've got two sets of rules. A set of rules dealing with physics and astrophysics and astronomy that we follow or try to follow as accurately as we can and then you've got a set of rules that have to do with *Star Trek*

Next Generation's *former co-executive producer Robert Justman walking past the model of the starship Enterprise.*

which are made up rules, they're not real. There's no such thing as a dilithium crystal or people transporting. There's no such thing as warp drive and Romulans and Ferengi and Klingons. These things don't exist and as a result it's fantasy but it's 25 years worth of established rules and they have to be followed. So you've got the rules of science and the rules of *Star Trek*. Writers have to be willing to follow both sets of rule and its difficult."

However, Berman is the first to admit that while he may be at the forefront of staying true to Roddenberry's vision of the future, it is not one he personally shares. "I believe that for the pur-

poses of our show Gene's vision of the 24th century is dramatically correct and it works for us. I probably have less. I don't think we're going to be living in a *Blade Runner* society but I think we'll be living in a future which will be very similar to the world we're living in now. Then again, this show has nothing to do with my vision of the future, I have become an expert in Gene Roddenberry's future, it's like learning a language and I'm fluent in it now and I can protect it and police it and nurture it in the same way that Gene did."

• • • •

CHAPTER SEVENTEEN
Season 1 Episode Guide

"Encounter at Farpoint"

"The Naked Now"

"Code of Honor"

"The Last Outpost"

"Where No One Has Gone Before"

"Lonely Among Us"

"Justice"

"The Battle"

"Hide & Q"

"Haven"

"The Big Goodbye"

"Datalore"

"Angel One"

"11001001"

"Too Short a Season"

"When the Bough Breaks"

"Home Soil"

"Coming of Age"

"Heart of Glory"

"The Arsenal of Freedom"

"Symbiosis"

"Skin of Evil"

"We'll Always Have Paris"

"Conspiracy"

"The Neutral Zone"

Episodes #1& 2:
"Encounter at Farpoint"
Original Airdate: 9/26/87
Written by D.C. Fontana &
Gene Roddenberry
Directed by Corey Allen
Guest Starring: John de Lancie (Q), Michael Bell (Groppler Zorn), Colm Meaney (Battle Bridge Conn), Cary Hiroyuki (Mandarin Bailiff), Timothy Dang (Main Bridge Security), David Erskine (Bandi Shopkeeper), Evelyn Guerrero (Young Female Ensign), Chuck Hicks (Military Officer), Jimmy Ortega (Torres), DeForest Kelley (Leonard McCoy, "The Admiral")

The maiden voyage of starship Enterprise NCC-1701-D, introduces us to the new crew that will begin the next "ongoing" mission. First out, Captain Jean Luc Picard is to investigate the mysterious and somewhat miraculous Farpoint Station, a staging planet deemed vital to the interests of the Federation.

Enroute, they are boarded by the all-powerful Q, who feels that mankind has ventured far enough into space and will not allow further contamination. To this end, he places Picard and his crew on trial for crimes against humanity. It is the captain's suggestion that Q allow them to prove the worthiness of their species by completing their mission at Farpoint Station. Intrigued, Q agrees and is shown just how far man has come as the truth behind Farpoint is revealed.

••••

"Encounter at Farpoint" writer Dorothy Fontana contributed some of the original STAR TREK's most popular episodes, including "This Side of Paradise," "Journey to Babel" and "Charlie X." Additionally, she was the associate producer of the 1973 animated spin-off, and penned one of that show's most enduring episodes, "Yesteryear." Bearing this in mind, it's not surprising that she was chosen to script "Encounter at Farpoint."

"Roddenberry wanted to do a story that took place on a staging planet at the edge of space with a new station," she explains. "We were working on the characters at that point. The preliminary outline really broke out the possibilities. It was not what you now see. The crea-

ture that first appears is a spaceship, but it is a space-going gun platform. That is the threat. Then we find out that it is a creature. It shows up as a gun platform, and it's being used because it was weakened and nearly dead from starvation, which is a characterization I carried on. Of course we do manage to break the creature out of its enslavement. That was the very beginning idea, and then Roddenberry wanted one with the creature down on the planet, because he liked the idea of a mate.

"When we originally discussed it, I thought it could be its child, or an old creature that is dying and is captured, and the creature that comes to rescue it does so out of respect for its elders," she adds. "You could go many ways. I didn't think the only way you could go was a mate."

"The first episode really felt like two stories forced together," says Jonathan Frakes (First Officer Riker). "I feel that the later episodes were better, if for no other reason than that the company was better and knew their characters better and were less worried finding out if the show would succeed. I think the look of the pilot had the quality of the original."

Offers Marina Sirtis (Counselor Deanna Troi), "I watched the pilot with my hands over my eyes. I didn't feel it was working. I got some really good feedback from people, but personally, knowing what I can do as an actress and what was up there, I wasn't really happy. I was really pleased to make changes. I personally thought that if I continued to play Troi that way, it would get really boring because if you're telepathic, a psychologist, who is hugely super intelligent and has that kind of background, she would be so understanding, so nice, so forgiving, so laid back and perfect that I'd be the Linda Evans of *Star Trek*. What I wanted more of was Alexis."

Director Corey Allen, who received an Emmy Award for an episode of *Hill Street Blues,* was highly enthusiastic about helming the show, particularly the "Q" plotline.

"The script turned me on immediately," he enthuses. "'Q' is what you're doing right now. You're 'Q' and I'm 'A.' Every one of us has a constant Q pounding on the back of our head, saying,

John de Lancie, the man who would be Q at one of his frequent Star Trek convention appearances. (Photo copyright © Karen Witkowski)

'What about that? How do you feel? Are you really worthy?' It's the question we pose ourselves; it's a constant looking at ourselves, a questioning of ourselves and a probing. Many times we'll manifest that probe by getting involved in outside circumstances, saying, 'I'm tired of asking myself all these questions in my head. I think I'll go to the theatre and let the actors on stage do it. Or go to the boxing match and let two gladiators do it. I'm tired. I need their help. I think what Gene Roddenberry did was put two adversaries on the screen so they could effectively deal with those questions.

"The 'Q' is in all of us. It's a question of worth. For many people the attitude is, 'If I'm worth something, it's because of my purpose, because of my birth or my humanity, or because I'm alive.' People meet that question in different ways, but it's usually, 'What is my question of myself, however I couch it? What is the question I constantly pose myself?' Most of us probably ask, 'Should I be here?' That *should* is the human part of it. *Why* am I here? is a little more clinical. Do I have the right to be here, probing space, captaining a ship, leading people, taking responsibility, living? I really

••••

believe that my understanding of that human questioning is what I brought to the episode. It's something that I do understand very well, and I feel good about my compassion about that question and my universalization of it. Essentially I was sharing myself.

"[The Farpoint scenario] wasn't as important to me as the concepts we've been talking about. There had to be an issue for the Enterprise to face, and it was okay with me that that was the issue, but the best part for me was that at first we *failed* to see that there was sentience; that there are passionate beings other than those that resemble ourselves. I thought that was a very nice issue to raise. We don't always recognize other sentient beings, and it's analogous of the way we treat each other. No one feels as deeply as I do, I keep thinking, and naturally that's bullshit. So I like the point it made, although it could have been any issue there."

Opines former executive producer Maurice Hurley, "I thought the execution was herky-jerky, because it was the first show. Having, basically, God tell man you've come far enough; that everywhere you've come, everything you've touched, you've sullied. I love that. I thought that was just awesome. There were also a lot of little things in it that I loved. Beyond that, it has the problems of the first episode of any show."

Episode #3:
"The Naked Now"
Original Airdate: 10/3/87
Written by Michael Bingham
Story by John D.F. Black
Directed by Paul Lynch
Guest Starring: Brooke Bundy (Sarah MacDougal), Benjamin W.S. Lum (Jim Shimoda), Michael Rider (Transporter Chief), David Renan (Conn), Skip Stellrecht (Engineering Crewman), Kenny Koch (Kissing Crewman)

The Enterprise is sent to investigate the status of the S.S. Tsilkovsky, which was investigating a collapsing star when all communication was lost. Upon arrival in that sector of space, an Away Team investigation learns that the entire crew is dead and that they had been gripped by madness.

Unbeknownst to anyone,

Geordi LaForge is infected with the disease and brings it aboard the Enterprise. The virus spreads rapidly through the crew, having the effect of alcohol and freeing them of their inhibitions. It is Commander Riker's vague (and highly improbable) memory of a similar occurrence on Captain Kirk's Enterprise that leads them down the road to a cure before the starship is caught in the wake of the collapsing star.

Naturally things work out in the end, though not before practically everyone has gotten laid.

••••

Star Trek fans are well aware of the fact that "The Naked Now" was a remake of the original series' first season episode, "The Naked Time."

The science fiction genre is not an unfamiliar one to director Paul Lynch, whose credits include episodes of *Werewolf, Beauty and the Beast, War of the Worlds, The New Twilight Zone* and, of course, *The Next Generation* and *Deep Space Nine.*

While outsiders may see his being saddled with "The Naked Now" as an unfortunate roll of the dice, Lynch himself doesn't agree.

"The same basic story [of 'The Naked Time'] holds true," he explains, "in that the Enterprise contracts something from another ship and the crew begins to change. Because it's a new cast, they change accordingly. Everybody drops the way they are and lets their inhibitions come out. I'd say that 'The Naked Now' is slightly more adult and a lot more comic than the original. In that show, one of the guys [Sulu] picked up a sword and started running around with it. In this it's much more of a character change in the way of romance and strangeness leading towards humor. Everybody in the show is affected by it in different ways, but not that dissimilar. For instance, while one person might be affected by becoming amorous in a serious way, someone else becomes amorous in a lighter sense. It's all quite subtle compared to the original, because the original episode was quite heavy-handed, like most of the original episodes were.

"The main difference," he continues, "is that the production has

changed over the years. The production design of the ship and the costumes and all of that are so much more futuristic 'modern' than the old series. The original show always looked like it cost $1.98, with four walls painted blue. The engine room in the old ship was a painting. The new engine room looks like it belongs in a spaceship in reality. It's wonderful and quite stunning."

A moment of controversy in the episode was the liaison between a "fully functional" Data and a scantily clad Tasha Yar. "That was the one moment I remember the most," says the director. "It was risqué and it was something *Star Trek* never did. Everyone had a great deal of fun doing it and ever since I've gotten the feeling they would like to do something like that again."

Notes Maurice Hurley with a groan, "That, to me, represented, 'Don't we have a new idea?' I didn't like that show at all. It just wasn't very good. What it did show, though, was that the new ensemble could interact, and that there were relationships between them that worked. But doing it was terrible. It was a warmed over premise. Why do it?"

Episode #4:
"Code of Honor"
Original Airdate: 10/19/87
Written by Katharyn Powers and Michael Baron
Directed by Russ Mayberry
Guest Starring: Jessie Lawrence Ferguson (Lutan), Karole Selmon (Yarenna), James Louis Watkins (Hagon), Michael Rider (Transporter Chief)

The Enterprise is in the midst of negotiating an invaluable medical vaccine from the people of Ligon II, when that world's leader, Lutan, kidnaps Tasha Yar and decides that he wishes to keep her, as she has smitten him.

What eventually unfolds is a classic game of political manipulation, as Lutan sets events into motion in such a way that his wife, Yareena, challenges Tasha to a death battle. Picard is in the difficult position of having to protect one of his own while preserving the peace and obtaining the vaccine.

••••

"I bought my first television specifically so I could watch *Star Trek*,"

Denise Crosby, first Tasha Yar and then the Romulan Sela on Next Generation, seen here in The Eliminators.

reflects writer Katharyn Powers. "I was a starving actress in New York at the time—so that was like putting out blood—but I had to watch the show. I've been a *Star Trek* fan for years. When I finally became a professional writer, there was no *Star Trek* to write for. So, for me, doing this script was like an 'If only....' that came true....The inspiration for 'Code of Honor' was to combine interesting characters with interesting problems, juxtaposed with this wonderful new cast. And even though it's a new cast, they still wanted to have the same kinds of *Star Trek* stories, the same feeling of camaraderie and family. To prepare for the script, we watched many of the old episodes and the movies to immerse ourselves in 'space.'"

Adds co-writer Michael Baron, "'Code of Honor' underwent many changes, but the idea was to create an alien civilization with an interesting look and a central theme to it. We based them somewhat on the Samurai culture in Japan and made parallels, which was fun to do. I've always been fascinated by Japanese culture and history."

"An execution problem," states Maurice Hurley matter of factly. "A good idea, but the execution, to me, just fell apart. Again, if you take that script and if the actors had been told to give it a different twist, that show would have been different. But it became too baroque and fell apart. But the concept

of having a guy saying, 'I have to have somebody kill my wife and this is the person,' is a good idea."

Former creative consultant Tracy Torme notes, "I felt like it was a '40s tribal African view of blacks. I think it was kind of embarrassing. Not only was the ending like [original series episode] 'Amok Time,' but it came dangerously close to *Amos & Andy*."

Episode #5:
"The Last Outpost"
Original Airdate: 10/17/87
Written by Herbert Wright
Story by Richard Krzemien
Directed by Richard Colla
Guest Starring: Armin Shimerman (Lebek), Jake Dengel (Mordoc), Tracey Walker (Kayron), Darryl Henriques (The Portal), Mike Gomez (Daimon Taar)

The Enterprise is in pursuit of a Ferengi vessel which has stolen a T-9 energy converter from a Federation outpost. The chase leads to the orbit of a planet in the T'Kon Empire, where both vessels suddenly find themselves held in stasis, all power rapidly draining. Each blames the other, but evidence soon points to the planet below as the source of the power drain.

After a beam down, humans come upon Ferengi for the first time. Together, they encounter the Portal, guardian of the Empire who puts them to

a test. The species which passes this test will survive, while the other will be disposed of.

••••

"In the script they're confronting the Portal, who is something of a cloaked creature," says Richard Krzemien, the writer who supplied this episode's original story. "He represents the entrance to the T'Kon Empire. Originally, that Portal was a small guy named Dilo, who was the caretaker of this planet, and he was meant to be a light, upbeat kind of character who got caught in the fact that he was asleep when his entire group of planets died. This is where the interesting thing about successive drafts comes in. The concept of that still exists, but it's how Dilo is embodied that's changed."

Maurice Hurley recalls when he was working on a film location once when the crew had to pass through an orchard. In the garden was a watchdog who would wag his tail and jump around while the crew was walking through. When they left, the dog would start barking ferociously. "The owner would look and see the dog barking and people leaving and make the assumption the dog was doing a helluva job. Really, the dog was just as lonesome and friendly and sweet a dog as you'd ever meet and that was the kind of image we wanted to put on 'Last Outpost.' I thought it would be

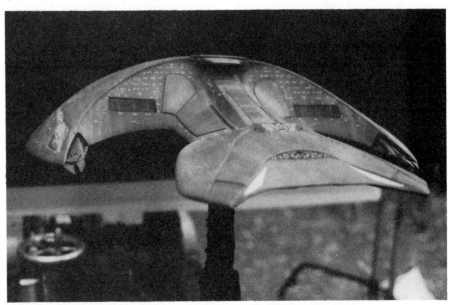

A model of the Ferengi ship, which would first be used in "The Last Outpost."

••••

great, but it turned into this silliness with the Ferengi."

Director Richard Colla admits to having a difficult time evaluating the episode.

"My experience and relationship to a picture is that I start with a piece of material," Colla explains, "I read it and I am struck one way or the other on the positive side, and those are the highlights of the piece for me. Those areas that might have lapses in logical continuity are places that I need to fix, hopefully, in the story, because once we start to put it on the stage and start to make it, you're always compromising. You know you're going to compromise, but the struggle is to simply make a creative compromise so that you don't destroy the emotional essence of that moment of the story. In episodic television especially, the struggle is to try to maintain a level of quality of excellence at least to the point where you don't fall below an unacceptable level. You don't want to be in that terrible situation where you've just got to get it done. Given all of that, when you put it together, there are still going to be moments that don't work. Moments where you say, 'Gee, I really wish I had time to shoot a close-up over there,' and so on. When you're finally through the final phase, you're always fixing the mistakes. So the experience always is from the initial reading to the final, delivered product. It becomes a series of trying to solve problems, and the only thing that you really see are the problems. When you finally run the picture as an answer print, there's joy that it's done, but, boy, the real emotional experience for me is that I'm pissed I didn't fix the things that needed to be fixed. So I have no objectivity in the final analysis. I just have to do the best work that I can, finish it, put it behind me and let other people say whether or not they liked it."

Armin Shimerman, who portrays a Ferengi, has also portrayed a Newcomer in *Alien Nation*, and underground denizen Pascal in *Beauty and the Beast*. He is seen weekly as the Ferengi Quark in *Star Trek: Deep Space Nine*.

Episode #6:
"Where No One Has Gone Before"
Original Airdate: 10/24/87
Written by Diane Duane and
Michael Reaves
Directed by Rob Bowman
Guest Starring: Eric Menyuk (the Traveler), Stanley Kamel (Kosinski), Herta Ware (Mother Picard), Biff Yeager (Argyle), Charles Dayton (Crewmember), Victoria Dillard (Ballerina)

A Federation propulsion expert named Kosinski and his alien assistant, the Traveler, come aboard the Enterprise to enhance the warp capabilities of the starship. Something goes horribly wrong, and after two warp accelerations, the Enterprise finds itself over 350 million light years from home. Returning to their own galaxy would take over three centuries!

Things go from bad to worse when, in this sector of space, reality breaks down, and the crew begins to hallucinate. The only way back is through the unexplained powers of the Traveler, who was actually the one responsible for this journey in the first place. The problem is that he is dying.

• • • •

The script for "Where No One Has Gone Before" read that the Enterprise has reached the end of the universe, "a concept that can't be described because it can't be understood," then Visual Effects Supervisor Rob Legato. "You sit there and scream that it can't be understood, but I've got to shoot it in three weeks. To them it's an eighth of a page and that's nothing. The trouble is that you come up with an idea and it's all in pieces until the final composite. You don't have any time to say, 'Okay, this is a good story point, let's add this or that.' It better be acceptable right off the bat. Then you have hours, not days, to embellish it."

"I did a page one rewrite of 'Where No One Has Gone Before,' and they absolutely hated it," smiles Maurice Hurley. "I think they wanted to fire me, and they would have if I didn't have a guaranteed contract. I said, 'Wait a minute, I'm used to writing from this point of view of vulnerability. I just write the most outrageous shit in the world and then we sit down and work it out. But don't attack it and don't attack me.' And

that's what happened, so I took it and started rewriting it some more, and it eventually turned out to be what you saw on the screen, and a show that I liked a lot. Everything about that episode worked. That's when everybody started to hit their stride a little bit. The casting was good, the Traveler was wonderful, the optical effects were excellently outstanding. You could feel things starting to come together."

"[Diane Duane and I] really lucked out," admits writer Michael Reaves. "It was our concept and everything, but we were massively rewritten. I will agree that it was the best episode [at that time]. Yes, they had an all-powerful alien, but at least he was not a cranky child. One of the things we liked about the show as aired is that there was some honest emotion involved, although not nearly as much as we had. I've only seen a few episodes of the show, but it was very one-note to me. At least this alien had some problems; some things he wanted to accomplish that were viable within the *Star Trek* universe. Also, one thing they did keep from our story is that this was a problem that was not solved by slowing something up, which I kind of liked. Production-wise it was wonderful, and the acting was all very good. It came together much better on the screen than we thought it would when we read the script. We were lucky, because it was out of our hands."

Director Rob Bowman recalls, "It was the fourth episode and the writers were really fresh, It was a very enlightening script, the likes of which you don't very often see on television. I felt very fortunate that it was such a great script but, personally, I was terrified because it was my first episode and I wanted to make a good impression. I worked on that show every day I had the script, which, including the shooting, was like 20 days for me. I used lots of storyboards, blocked the sets, walked around them for several weekends to get used to them, and thought out every possible angle. But for the first couple of days of shooting, it was pretty terrifying, mostly because of my being so new to the show, and also being so young I had to prove....it was a very good Hollywood crew, but there's always a couple of days of testing that

• • • •

you go through, especially when you're young. So there were the first two days where I was proving I had an idea of what I wanted to do. Once I felt the connection was made on the second day, we took off and I started to get lots of good input from the crew as well. Bob Justman and Rick Berman were very creative and very helpful. It was one of the tightest ships I've ever seen, and that was a real change."

Episode #7:
"Lonely Among Us"
Original Airdate: 10/31/87
Written by D.C. Fontana
Story by Michael Halperin
Directed by Cliff Bole
Guest Starring: John Durbin (Badar), Kavi Raz (Singh), Colm Meaney (Security)

In a plotline extremely similar to the original series' "Journey to Babel," the Enterprise is transporting Selay and Andican delegates to a peace conference on the planet Parliament. It's everything that Riker, Tasha and ship security staff can do to stop them from killing each other.

At the same time, the starship passes through a cloud which, unknown to anyone at first, consists of living entities. One of them is accidentally caught in the ship's computer and it moves from Worf, to Crusher and, finally, to Captain Picard, who, while under the alien influence, decides to have himself beamed into open space to rejoin the other cloud creatures.

••••

"In 'Lonely Among Us' I pulled from myself," says Dorothy Fontana, "some elements from 'Journey to Babel' in that the mission was to transport these diplomats from here to there. The flow was entirely different. They were a subplot to be, in point, a fun kind of thing as opposed to serious 'drama,' like in 'Babel.' So what I did was pull from myself and switch it around. I felt that was acceptable. A lot of people said, 'That's "Journey to Babel",' but, no, it's not. I wrote 'Journey to Babel' and I wrote this, too, and I feel there is a difference. There's a definite delineation and separation here, both in intent and content."

Offers director Cliff Bole, "I don't recall that being one of my better shows, but I worked as hard on that as I

worked on anything else. The subject matter affects the end product. There's some better written shows, obviously."

Episode #8:
"Justice"
Original Airdate: 11/7/87
Written by Worley Thorne
Story by Ralph Willis (John Black) & Thorne
Directed by James L. Conway
Guest Starring: Brenda Bakke (Rivan), Jay Louden (Liator), Josh Clark (Conn), David Q. Combs and Richard Lavin (Mediators), Judith Jones (Edo Girl), Eric Matthews and David Michael Graves (Edo Boys), Brad Zerbst (Medical Officers)

The Enterprise deposits a colony on a planet in the Strnad system and then proceeds to Rubicum III for possible shore leave. The people there, the Edo, are extremely loving and sensual, and they make the crew welcome.

What the Away Team finds is that this is an idyllic world of paradise where everyone seems to have exactly what they need, and there is no crime whatsoever. Unfortunately what they learn as well is the reason for the lack of crime: all illegal actions, from the most minor to the most severe, are punishable in one way: death. This point is driven home when Wesley accidentally crushes some plants and is sentenced to die.

Picard must allow justice on this world to be carried out or ignore the Prime Directive and rescue Wesley. Complicating matters is a vessel in orbit around the planet claiming to be the god of Edo and demanding that the Enterprise leave this sector of space, and retrieve the colony it had so recently deposited on a nearby world.

••••

Although John D.F. Black, who wrote the original story for this episode, finds little redeeming about the final product, he does recall his initial thoughts on the idea's genesis.

"'Justice' is about the human answer to what you do when violence in the streets becomes rampant," he explains. "What do you do if you're a colony? What do you do, and how would it look to somebody else when you have responded in the only way you can?

"The story has to do with justice

Wil Wheaton (Wesley Crusher) parties down at a Star Trek convention appearance. (Photo copyright © Karen Witkowski)

for everybody, and how you deal with terrorism and anarchy. How do you stop it? And once you've stopped it, what happens next? Let's say that what we do is kill everybody who is a terrorist or suspected of being a terrorist. Now the people who have killed everybody, what do they do? We're talking about a society dealing with some aspect of itself. And this society [as originally conceived] is made up of Earth people who went out there to set up their own democratic society. It's what corrupted the Greek democracy."

"A great idea, though it got a little fanciful for me," says Maurice Hurley. "It was a part of the contemporary culture we're talking about here. If you want to start controlling crime, maybe the answer is, 'Listen, if you commit a crime at a certain level, it's the death penalty.' And where does that level start? Where does it stop? Why not any crime? Get rid of all the criminals, get rid of the criminal genes, let's whack them down and let's go. You can make that argument, and if a culture like our culture keeps going the way it's going, it's an argument that people may start pushing forward. There's a resurgence of people saying, 'We're not using the death penalty as much as we should be.' You hear that every day, and when you hear the arguments, it's hard at some level not to buy them. You say, 'Wait a minute, maybe there are some machines that are flawed at the factory and should be recalled.' Then you take it to its logical absurdity, and you can have a society like the one in 'Justice.' I thought the *idea* of that show was wonderful. It got too fanciful, sexual and there was an innocence that was missing. It got looney tunes for me. And I didn't like the machine-god idea at all."

Episode #9:
"The Battle"
Original Airdate: 11/14/87
Written by Herbert Wright
Story by Larry Forrester
Directed by Rob Bowman
Guest Starring: Frank Corsentino (DaiMon Bok), Doug Warhit (First Officer Kazago), Robert Towers (Second Officer Rata)

Ferengi Daimon Bok offers a gift to Picard: the somewhat battered Stargazer, which Picard had commanded years earlier. The ship's final mission had been the battle of Maxia, where, after being severely damaged but still managing to destroy its Ferengi opponent, it was set adrift. Unknown to Picard, Daimon Bok's son died at Maxia, and the Ferengi has held the captain accountable ever since.

To this end, he utilizes an alien mind-control device to get Picard back on board the Stargazer to relive the battle, only this time the Ferengi vessel has been replaced by the Enterprise.

••••

"'The Battle' was pretty good," comments Maurice Hurley, "because Patrick Stewart did such a good job. I thought he made that work. Originally I wasn't too hot about the episode, as I've seen it since. I think it's better than I originally thought. I still think the Ferengi were a waste of time. Goofy. No bushido involved; it was a joke. We had these arguments from the beginning. I was the lone voice screaming in the wilderness. If somebody's interested in gold, they're not much of an adversary. If we can make gold in our replicator—and we can—then it's like sand at the beach in Santa Monica. Who cares? Give 'em all the sand that they want. Get them out of here. They want gold? Here, take a truck

load and get out."

Rob Bowman smiles, "I love 'The Battle,' because there's so much to it. That was my second show and it was kind of a broad episode. The story seemed to have a lot of scope to it. I'm not sure why I felt that way, but it was a little bit intimidating when I first got the script. I was going to be dealing with Patrick Stewart, whose knowledge is unending, and I really wanted to tap that; I really wanted to get in there and make that man work. At the same time, I was concerned that I didn't have enough notches on my belt to bring the best out of him. I think what I ended up doing was making my own little version of that movie, while not letting Patrick do his version of it. The only thing I could be comfortable with was my version, so I'd say, 'This is what I want in this scene,' and Patrick just gave it to you. I think at that time, no other show had that look. We went dark in a lot of scenes and we did different angles and things the show hadn't done yet. For me, it was a real creative stretch and it felt great for the show. They loved how dark it went in some spots. Also, nobody ever used Steadicam on that show, and we used it on the Stargazer, which was actually a redress of the films' Bird of Prey bridge."

Episode #10:
"Hide & Q"
Original Airdate: 11/21/87
Written by C.J. Holland and Gene Roddenberry
Story by Holland
Directed by Cliff Bole
Guest Starring: John de Lancie (Q), Elaine Nalee (Survivor), William A. Wallace (Adult Wesley)

Intrigued by the Enterprise crew from the events of "Encounter at Farpoint," Q and those of his continuum want to study the species more closely. To this end, he decides to bestow a gift and chooses Riker as the recipient. As a result, the commander is given the same powers as Q, and must learn how to cope with them.

••••

"That was a turning point script, and now I'm talking about personalities," says Maurice Hurley, who used the pen name C.J. Holland. "I wrote that script

Jonathan Frakes (Commander William Riker) takes to the stage at a Star Trek convention. (Photo copyright © Karen Witkowski)

and Gene rewrote it, so I took my name off of it. That's where Gene and I had our little talk about the future. Mine was more action-oriented and less philosophical, if I can say that. It was more direct, a little more playful. I didn't think it was necessarily a better version, because that's a subjective choice. It was a matter of procedure of how the show was being done. It had nothing to do with who's right and who's wrong, because that's a subjective call. When you have people on a show who are your staff writers, you don't take work away from them. You get them to modify it to closer to what you want, rather than just do a rewrite."

"Nobody knew what these demons Q conjured up were going to look like until I walked onto the set with them because there was no time to show anyone the concept beforehand," says make-up supervisor Michael Westmore. "I didn't even know myself until I got it done."

Looking back, one can't help but note that the set construction looks extremely archaic compared to what they're doing on the show today.

"That was part of the shakedown," says director Cliff Bole. "We used a set that was similar to the look of the old show, and of course we didn't want to do it. One of the mistakes is that maybe we should have shot that at night, and not had it in day and showed the dimension of the set. But all that's changed. I think it had to do with the producers that were there. The more guys you have, the more stuff you have to spin off of them and things tumble when you do that."

Episode #11:
"Haven"
Original Airdate: 11/28/87
Written by Tracy Torme
Story by Lan O'Kun
Directed by Richard Compton
Guest Starring: Majel Barrett (Lwaxana Troi), Rob Knepper (Wyatt Miller), Nan Martin (Victoria Miller), Robert Ellenstein (Mr. Miller), Danitza Kingsley (Ariana), Anna Katarina (Valeda Innis), Raye Birk (Wrenn), Michael Rider (Transporter Chief), Carel Struycken (Mr. Homn)

The Riker/Troi relationship is thrown into disarray when Troi's mother, Lwaxana, beams aboard to put into motion her daughter's pre-arranged wedding. This is as surprising to Deanna as it is to everyone else.

Shortly thereafter, her soon to be husband, Dr. Wyatt Miller, beams aboard and the two of them try to establish some kind of relationship before they take the plunge. Wyatt seems distant, however, due to the fact that for years he had a mental impression of a woman in his mind, and Deanna is *not* who he envisioned.

All things become clear when a Tarellian plague ship attempts to enter orbit around the planet Haven, despite the protests of the people on its surface, and one of the crew people is the woman of Wyatt's dreams.

••••

"'Haven' was originally called 'Love Beyond Time and Space,' and was written by a writer who I really don't think understood science fiction," says Tracy Torme, the son of crooner Mel Torme. "When they offered it to me, there was good and bad. The bad was that I couldn't even get through the outline he had written, and the good was that I thought it was so unusable, that anything I did would be an improvement. It was kind of like a no-lose situation for me in a way, so I basical-

ly told them that I thought the story would only work as a comedy. I think it was originally serious, and I wanted to do sort of a broad comedy about these two families who couldn't really stand each other, but wanted to go through with this wedding. My version was more caustic; the comedy had a sharper edge to it. 'Haven' was rewritten maybe 20 or 30 percent, and a lot of the comedy was softened and taken out of the original piece, so the net result was that I didn't particularly like the episode when it first aired. It's still one of my least favorite shows that I've been involved with. But for some reason, it's been pretty popular amongst fans. I'm grateful for that. When I see it again in repeats down the road, maybe I'll feel better about it than I do right now."

Episode #12:
"The Big Goodbye"
Original Airdate: 1/9/88
Written by Tracy Torme
Directed by Joseph Scanlan
Guest Starring: Lawrence Tierney (Cyrus Redblock), Harvey Jason (Felix Leach), William Boyett (Whelan), David Selburg (Lt. McNary), Gary Armagnal (Dan Hill), Mike Genovese (Desk Sergeant), Dick Miller (Vender), Carolyn Allport (Jessica Bradley), Rhonda Aldrich (Secretary), Eric Cord (Thug)

Captain Picard, driving himself to distraction in preparation for the Federation's first contact with the Jarada in 20 years, goes to the holodeck to relax. What he recreates is the fictional world of '40s detective Dixon Hill, but relaxation is out of the question as a malfunction alters this supposedly safe "game" of role-playing. Imagery and reality become one. Bullets are suddenly real...and so is death.

••••

"When I wrote the original treatment and draft of 'Haven,' the staff was really nice about it in their feedback," reflects Tracy Torme, who penned the Peabody Award-winning episode. "I think they were very pleased, and very quickly I knew they were going to offer me another one, which they did, and that became 'The Big Goodbye.'

"Gene wanted to utilize the holodeck and had thought of the idea of doing a detective story there," he

adds. "I have always been a big Raymond Chandler fan, and even more of a *film noir* fan. So I thought it would really be fun to do something like that. I'll just say that 'The Big Goodbye,' more than on any other script I've ever worked on for feature or TV, just fell into place almost magically for me. When I turned the first draft in, it's the closest I've ever been to being satisfied with a draft that I can remember. I just felt very relaxed about it, and felt that it was really going to work. Some scripts are a struggle and some scripts aren't. This one very definitely was not much of a struggle compared to some of the others, and so I have quite an affection for that show. I think everyone had fun making it. The actors, I believe, had a great time getting out of their uniforms. I was really very pleased with the way the technical people handled the show and a lot of the little touches they put in, and how they left the script alone. My only real complaint was about the Jarada aliens. They were much more interesting in the script, and because of budgetary reasons they ended up being sort of a plot point in the story as it is."

Smiles Maurice Hurley, "I thought it was just great. It was a use of the holodeck, it was a use of the cast, a use of the ensemble. I thought the acting in it was exceptional, the direction was wonderful and so was the lighting. It was like a breath of fresh air. It may not have been a breath of air for the audience, but it was for us. It was just fun to do. It's got humor and life to it. The thing is that *Star Trek* can't brood. If it broods, it gets self important and self-indulgent and preachy, like it has a tendency to do if it's not careful. But if it has some life to it, some humor, then it just jumps up and flies. It's different, but absolutely locked in the *Star Trek* format. Everything in there worked."

Director Joseph Scanlan found a variety of appealing aspects of "The Big Goodbye," thus making his entrance to the *Star Trek* realm an extremely satisfying one.

"The '40s setting was appealing, number one," he says. "It was a parody of *The Maltese Falcon*. We had a Sidney Greenstreet-type character, a Peter Lorre-type...they were all there. We had an office that was identical to the office that Bogie sat in in the 1940's. There was the same window, the same venetian blinds...just a great deal of fun."

One would nonetheless think it was difficult to combine the future with the past while maintaining the show's reality for the audience.

"Had you asked the question the other way...in other words, combining the past with the future world, I would say that it's a little difficult, and that is indeed what we had to do," Scanlan explains. "My problem, as I said to Gene, Rick and Bob, was that I'm not a fan of the show, so I'm bringing a different perspective. The holodeck was never, in my opinion, totally clear as to its function to the audience, and it's the first time that people, in effect, got trapped in it because of a malfunction of the equipment. They're trapped in the past, and yet it's not a time warp. It's very tough, I think (and, again, I'm a neophyte at this) to tell the audience that this is not a time warp when we are deeply involved with a subplot which really became the main plot in a holodeck image of San Francisco, where bullets start flying and somebody gets hit and starts to bleed. That's pretty tough not to consider a time warp, even though it was not. It was just an emotional and visual experience in the holodeck as equipment screwed up. I guess I'm answering the question, not directly, because I treated the two pieces as entirely different pieces. I, in actual fact, did all of the 1941 stuff as if Picard is indeed playing Philip Marlowe, or rather the name they gave him, Dixon Hill, and play that for all it was worth as a genuine thing. The only key, the only balance to keep the audience's memory of being on the ship is the dialogue that Tracy put in. There's a point when Captain Picard says to the doctor, 'We should be getting back to the Enterprise,' and she says, 'We're on the Enterprise.' He replies, 'Of course, it's becoming so real that I forgot.' That kind of thing."

Episode #13:
"Datalore"
Original Airdate: 1/16/88
Written by Robert Lewin & Gene
Roddenberry
Story by Bob Lewin and Maurice Hurley
Directed by Rob Bowman
Guest Starring: Biff Yeager (Argyle)

The Enterprise heads back to Data's home world to discover what happened to the colonists that had disappeared. There they find the remnants of what appears to be another version of Data, which they retrieve. Back on board, the science officer reactivates his "brother," Lore.

Apparently Lore is an exact duplicate of Data, with one notable exception: he is equipped with emotion.....as well as a twisted psyche, which threatens the entire crew of the Enterprise as he leads them to a trap involving a tremendous crystalline entity in space; the same entity responsible for the death of the colonists two decades earlier.

••••

"The sets, the design of it and the look of that show was brilliant," notes Maurice Hurley. "I thought that might have been the best looking show of the first season. There were some things back and forth in there that I didn't like in terms of the characterizations, but basically it was alright."

Recalls Rob Bowman, "The whole story behind 'Datalore' was that after 'Too Short a Season' [which would air later] I had no other *Star Treks* lined up. Bob Justman called me into his office at the end of that and said, 'We've got a script that you should really do,' and it was 'The Big Goodbye.' I read it and said, 'Hey, I'd like to stay and do this.' So we worked it out that I could. In the meantime, the next show that was going to start shooting after 'Too Short a Season' was going to be directed by Joe Scanlan, but the script they had was not in good shape. This was 'Datalore.' They got to a point in preproduction where they said they couldn't have the script ready in time and that we would have to switch scripts. So they switched 'Big Goodbye' with that, and I got 'Datalore.' Boy, was I ready to do 'The Big Goodbye.' It was going to have a different look and different texture, and was going to be a real different episode. But it was very well done by Joe, so the show didn't suffer.

"I took on 'Datalore' and said,

'Here's a show they don't think will work, and I'm going to make it work,'" he adds with a smile. "'I'm going to prove to these fuckers that they made a mistake with this show.' It got rewritten and there were some problems with the script, but it was a difficult one to write. Brent [Spiner] and I had a lot of discussions on it, because neither one of us was that thrilled about it. He was not very pleased, only because it has his character doing things that he didn't feel he would do or things he had developed in other ways. He didn't think it was completely in sync with his interpretation of what the character was. It was a learning experience, and we had lots of discussions with Rick Berman and Bob Justman. In a sense of working technique, there's lots of visual effects and split screens. It was a technically difficult show to do, and we had an extra day to shoot it because of that. I thought it was excellent. For me to tell somebody the plot, there's nothing unusual about it. It's the way that Brent played the character that made it unique. He did the one scene in his own office with Brent sitting down and Lore discussing what it's like to be human. He did one side, we shot through a double, then turned around, read it the other way and shot the other half of it. Those two characters in those scenes are different people, and that's three and a half pages. This is what I mean about these guys being open to new stuff. He really painted those characters differently. Lots of good communication with Brent on that show."

Episode #14:
"Angel One"
Original Airdate: 1/23/88
Written by Patrick Barry
Directed by Michael Rhodes
Guest Starring: Karen Montgomery (Beate), Sam Hennings (Ramsey), Patricia McPherson (Ariel), Leonard John Crofoot (Trent)

Searching for survivors of a freighter ship named the Odein, the Enterprise arrives at Angel One, a matriarchal society in which men are deemed a lower form of life. Riker leads an Away Team to the planet's surface, and finds that he must sleep his way to the top, so to speak, in order to discover the whereabouts of those he seeks.

••••

Meanwhile, the holodeck suffers yet another malfunction as Wesley Crusher catches an alien flu and spreads it swiftly throughout the Enterprise, leaving his mother, Beverly, the task of finding a cure before everyone on board dies.

••••

Comments from the crew regarding "Angel One" are rather succinct.

Says story editor Melinda Snodgrass, who wasn't aboard first season, "If the holodeck was really this untested, they would have shut down every one in the fleet!"

Notes Maurice Hurley, "Terrible. Just terrible. One of the ones you'd just as soon erase."

"'Angel One' was about a reverse role society," explains producer Herb Wright, "in which women ruled and men are subservient. It's been done a thousand times already, including Gene Roddenberry's *Planet Earth*. So the major issue that we wanted to make sure was straightened out was that I didn't want to do Amazon Women that are six feet tall with steel 'D' cups. My feeling was that the hit taken on this should be apartheid, so that the men are treated as though they are the blacks of South Africa. Make it political. Sexual overtones, yes, but political. Well, that didn't last very long. The sexual places it was dragged to were absurd."

Episode #15:
"11001001"
Original Airdate: 1/30/88
Written by Maurice Hurley and Robert Lewin
Directed by Paul Lynch
Guest Starring: Carolyn McCormick (Minuet), Gene Dynarski (Orvil Quinteros), Katy Boyer (One Zero), Alexandra Johnson (Zero One), Iva Lane (Zero Zero), Kelly Ann McNally (One One), Jack Sheldon (Piano Player), Abdul Alaam El Razzao (Bass Player), Ron Brown (Drummer)

The Enterprise stops off at a starbase for repairs, which are to be initiated by members of the computer-interdependent Binars, a race that functions as one. While these repairs are being implemented, much of the crew is granted shore leave. Picard and Riker head to the holodeck for some recreation, where Riker falls head over heels for a "woman"

named Minuet. Simultaneously, and unbeknownst to the captain or his first officer, the Binars have faked a containment shield breakdown, which results in the ship being evacuated. Once empty of all personnel (except our two heroes), the Enterprise is stolen out of spacedock and sent to the Binars' home planet, where it is hoped that the memory of the starship's computer will reactivate the main computer of that world, which has been damaged by sunspot activity.

••••

Says director Paul Lynch, "The Binars were great. Nobody seemed to know they were four very small girls we found. It was also interesting that they all talked in that kind of connective fashion. Carolyn, who played Minuet, was terrific, and she's in *Law & Order* now. A wonderful guy we dug up that they let me hire was a jazz pianist who was the leader of the group. He used to be the other guy on *The Merv Griffin Show* and he had this dry wit. We had him as the leader of the musicians and he was wonderful. It seemed to me at the time a very nice easy episode."

"Loved it," enthuses Maurice Hurley. "There were some things in there that came off so well. When they were sitting in the bar and talking about love, and how you fall in love with the image and the illusion....It just worked on that level, and then the Binars were just wonderful science fiction creations; that they dealt in this binary language and had their little buffers. [Make-up supervisor Michael] Westmore did some wonderful work on that. Jonathan was just great. He really did a terrific job and it may have been the first time he had been given a chance in the series to do something; to show who he is a little bit as a person and an actor. The holodeck worked great in that episode, and the episode was about when you realize your mate bears no resemblance to the illusion you fell in love with."

Smiles Jonathan Frakes, "A fabulous show. Those were the kind of chances we took first season that when they worked, they worked great. It was a very chancy show and I loved it. Those characters, the Binars, why haven't they returned? That was a very well conceived idea. They should have them as a regular

on the ship to fix the engines or whatever the hell they do."

Episode #16:
"Too Short a Season"
Original Airdate: 2/8/88
Written by Michael Michaelian and D.C. Fontana
Story by Michael Michaelian
Directed by Rob Bowman
Guest Starring: Clayton Rohner (Admiral Mark Jameson), Marsha Hunt (Anne Jameson), Michael Pataki (Karnas)

The Enterprise responds to a hostage situation on Mordan IV, where the lead terrorist, Karnas, demands that negotiations be handled by the 70-year-old Admiral Jameson. The admiral, it's revealed, had been on that world four decades earlier and negotiated another hostage situation, which ultimately resulted in decades of civil war on the planet.

Now, Karnas wants to extract revenge against Jameson, but fate may have beaten him to the punch. Jameson has taken a youth elixir which is rapidly de-aging him, though the side effects could be fatal. Now, the admiral has to face Karnas as well as his own wife, who feels betrayed in that by getting younger, he is stealing himself away from her.

••••

Explains Dorothy Fontana, "The high concept Michael Michaelian came in with was male menopause, which is a subject not often touched in television. Michael said, 'Well, I've been going through it lately, and I can really sympathize with the whole idea of wanting to go back to the man that he was and coming to grips with the man that he is and will be.' It was interesting, but he wanted to do it with reverse aging; someone seeking out that youth for a purpose. Of course using a science fiction gimmick, you can do it in a matter of days. Michael did a treatment and a first draft script, but the key element that always went a little wrong with it was the terrorist angle; why were we going to that planet? The Macguffin. A lot of what I put in at the end was also in Michael's story and drafts, but approached with a different emphasis. Also, instead of it truly being terrorists, it's all a trap, pulling Jameson to the planet. Those were pretty much the changes."

••••

163

"That was a show with a lot of dialogue," Rob Bowman recalls. "I considered it sit and tell, rather than show and tell, and I prefer to show the audience. I believe in the word, but one of your tools in making movies is visual aspects, and just as there is verbal dialogue there is visual dialogue. One without the other can get very monotonous. But the real treat for me was working with Clayton Rohner. He and I got together on weekends, and I think that's the most I ever spent with an actor off the clock, developing a character. We just decided to do it, and it was pretty much his episode, with all of them reacting to him. He was the saving grace of that episode, although he didn't really interact as well with the other characters as I would have liked. He really took it as his own episode. I remember all the other actors saying, 'This is not our show, it's Clayton's,' and I said, 'I know, but we can't change that now.' I think it was a solid episode, with lots of make-up challenges, special effects and a wheelchair that never worked. That thing became a joke. It is still a joke. People say, 'I hope this isn't going to be another wheelchair.' I think people may have lost their jobs over that thing. The prop people built it up and it was nothing. I had to shoot around it and couldn't move that guy anywhere, so it really was kind of a bummer."

Episode #17:
"When the Bough Breaks"
Original Airdate: 2/13/88
Written by Hannah Louise Shearer
Directed by Kim Manners
Guest Starring: Jerry Hardin (Radue), Brenda Strong (Rachella), Jandi Swanson (Duana), Paul Lambert (Lettian), Ivy Bethune (Katie), Derek Torsek (Dr. Bernard), Michele Marsh (Leda), Dan Mason (Accolan), Phillip N. Waller (Harry), Connie Danose (Toya), Jessica and Vanessa Bova (Alexandra)

As an act of desperation to continue their species, the people of Aldea (who are sterile) kidnap a variety of the Enterprise's most promising children, including Wesley Crusher. At first, they honestly believe that the starship will be willing to let them have the children for a price, but when Picard is unbending, they use their massive computer to hurl

the vessel three day's distance away. While Picard continues to try negotiations, Beverly does her best to discern the reason for the world's sterility, hoping that there will be a way to reverse the situation and get back the children.

••••

"I wasn't on staff yet when I pitched it, but I love writing about children," recalls writer Hannah Louise Shearer. "I thought it would be fascinating to deal with an aspect of the show that hadn't been dealt with which was all these families in space. It evolved in that way. Of course, it's my favorite episode. Gene [Roddenberry] and I talked about doing something contemporary [and] I think we managed to deal with a society that had lost its humanity in favor of technology. Wil Wheaton was just wonderful in that show. Alas, poor Wesley got the brunt of a lot of criticism, but he was really extraordinary with those kids and turned them into a little family on the set, and I think it really translated. He was a character growing up, and in any century that's a very difficult time, so why not use it?"

Maurice Hurley states, "That had a nice quality to it, sad and poignant at the same time. Again, it was done in seven days and you always say, 'God, we could have done this better, we could have done that better.' You've got to remember that these shows...this is a point that has to be made over and over and over again. You start thinking about the differences in these shows. It isn't another dope bust, another murder mystery, another lost kid. Each one of these shows is so completely different, one from the other, and yet they were executed in seven days on the stages. In the first year, for reasons I don't want to get in to, the show shut down for two days, but that had nothing to do with the show or anything else, but for two years the show virtually never had a shut down. In all of those shows that were turned out, they are so different one from the other, and it's astounding to me."

Episode #18:
"Home Soil"
Original Airdate: 2/20/88
Written by Robert Sabaroff
Story by Karl Guers, Ralph Sanchez &

Robert Sabaroff
Directed by Corey Allen
Guest Starring: Walter Gotell (Director Kurt Mandi), Elizabeth Lindsay (Luisa Kim), Gerard Prendergast (Bjorn Benson), Mario Roccuzzo (Arthur Malencon), Carolyne Barry (Female Engineer)

The Enterprise arrives to give medical exams to the terraforming scientists of Velara III, just as one of them is killed by an errant laser weapon, which almost dispatches Data as well. It turns out that the terraformers have disturbed a previously undiscovered life form which quickly takes control of the Enterprise, dismissing the humans as "ugly sacks of mostly water."

••••

"They just called me to do another, and I was happy to do so," says Corey Allen. "I think we struggled with that script for a very long time. The 'Q' in that one was, 'Do I recognize that there could be other life forms than the kind of life I'm used to?' To ask that question was okay, but I don't feel it was asked as strongly as it had been in 'Encounter at Farpoint.'"

Maurice Hurley adds, "An interesting idea, but the execution fell apart. I thought it was a wonderful idea. If you could think of all the problems you could possibly put together in one episode, we had it in that one. Casting, sets, location, time, the fact that the director was getting pages the day before we had to shoot....that was a real tough show to do."

Casting note: Water Gotell, who portrays the head terraformer, is perhaps best known as General Gogol in the James Bond films.

Episode #19:
"Coming of Age"
Original Airdate: 3/12/88
Written by Sandy Fries
Directed by Michael Vejar
Guest Starring: Ward Costello (Gregory Quinn), Robert Schenkkan (Dexter Remmick), John Putch (Mordok), Robert Ito (Tech Officer Chang), Stephen Gregory (Jake Curland), Tasia Valenza (T'Shalik), Estee Chandler (Ohana Mirren), Brendan McKane and Wyatt Knight (Technicians), Damel Riordan (Rondon)

Wesley Crusher attempts entrance into Starfleet Academy by undergoing a series of written, psychological and behavioral examinations. Meanwhile, Picard is offered a position as the head of the Academy. Simultaneously, Admiral Quinn and his assistant, Lieutenant Commander Remmick, begin interrogating various crewmembers in their hopes of determining whether or not the good captain is a part of a conspiracy that Quinn feels is building within the Federation.

••••

"We left the ending open deliberately as to whether it was an external or internal Starfleet plot," says former story editor Hannah Louise Shearer, who did an uncredited script rewrite. "They already had an invasion story in mind."

"There were three stories in there that all came together in a wonderful way," opines Maurice Hurley. "I like that one a lot. It worked very well. Wesley was good, the kid who stole the spaceship was good, the whole testing program, how it worked, why he failed, why he didn't get into Starfleet Academy—that's the lesson. That's the kind of lesson you want to do when you're making a show like that. Not every show has a lesson, but there was some nice ones in that show about how to win and how to lose. What is winning? What is losing? What's important? What isn't?"

Episode #20:
"Heart of Glory"
Original Airdate: 3/19/88
Written by Maurice Hurley
Story by Michael Michaelian
Directed by Rob Bowman
Guest Starring: Vaughn Armstrong (Koras), Charles J. Hyman (Konmil), David Froman (Captain K'Nera), Robert Bauer (Kunivas), Brad Zerbst (Nurse), Dennis Madalone (Ramos)

A trio of Klingons are rescued from a damaged freighter within the Romulan Neutral Zone. One of them dies as a result of his injuries, but the other two, it turns out, are fugitives from the Klingon Empire. They try to convince Worf to abandon the humans around him, and help them capture the Enterprise. Admittedly, there are a few

brief moments of doubt as to what Worf will do.

••••

"I consider 'Heart of Glory' to be an information episode," explains actor Michael Dorn, who plays Worf, "because it gave you everything you wanted to know about what happened with the Klingons. Why did they become allies? Why is Worf there? How did he get there? That type of thing. It was very good, although I felt it could have been taken a little further. What I wanted was an epic battle in the end, but it was a good show for me, because it showed them that people are as interested in Worf as they are in the other characters."

Maurice Hurley, credited with writing the episode, states, "That's where I came as close to putting me on *Star Trek* as I possibly could in philosophy, point of view, position. I put my philosophies on paper, and it all worked together perfectly. That's where Rick Berman and I were hitting our stride; that's where we were locked at the hip in putting these shows together. When I had a problem, I could go in and we could sit there, close the door, yell and scream. I'd pace, he'd make suggestions. The two of us made stories work in that room that had to be shot within a couple of days. We were under enormous time pressure, and we were working hand in glove. We had a wonderful time, on that show especially."

Sighs Rob Bowman, "That was near the end of my season, and I was very, very tired. I was looking forward to time off. I was at a state of mental fatigue that I had never been in before. It was a very late script, Maurice wrote it in two days. I read it and said, 'Holy shit, this can be very good if you let me do this and let me do that.' That show was, I think, one of the easiest of my shows, because everything worked so well. Once I got the script, ideas on how things should look came very quickly. The final battle in engineering was supposed to be played on the first deck. Worf shoots [the Klingon] and he falls down. But nobody had shot in that chamber vertically, so we did some things in the end with the camera that hadn't been done before. Some ideas we tried worked very well. It was just a show where every hand we had was a 21. It just worked."

Michael Dorn (Worf) looking very un-Klingon like in this publicity shot.

Episode #21:
"The Arsenal of Freedom"
Original Airdate: 4/9/88
Written by Richard Manning and Hans Beimler
Story by Maurice Hurley and Robert Lewin
Directed by Les Landau
Guest Starring: Vincent Schiavelli (Salesman), Marco Rodriguez (Paul Rice), Vyto Ruginis (Logan), Julia Nickson (Lee Ann Su), Georges de la Pena (Solis), Marco Rodriguez, Vyto Ruginis, Julia Nickson

When the U.S.S. Drake disappears in orbit around the planet Minos, the Enterprise is sent to investigate. An Away Team reminiscent of the original *Star Trek* (Picard, Riker, Data and Dr. Crusher all take part) beam down and are immediately in trouble. They are attacked by various defensive weapons which view them as intruders, and in the midst of fleeing, Picard and Crusher fall in a pit, where Crusher is severely injured. Meanwhile, Geordi is in command of the Enterprise, which is coming up against orbital defensive weapons. A solution must be discovered before the Enterprise and her crew are destroyed.

••••

"In the original version, Picard fell and hurt himself," recalls director Les Landau. "In reading it, I suggested maybe

Gates McFadden (Dr. Beverly Crusher) administers some behind-the-scenes gossip at a Star Trek *convention. (Photo copyright © Karen Witkowski)*

the doctor should be the one who gets hurt and Picard, being out of his element, should have the wherewithal to help her. That was a suggestion they took."

"It started out as a vastly different show," says writer and former *Next Generation* producer Robert Lewin. "It was originally going to be a love story in which Picard was dying and Beverly [Crusher] was going to reveal how she really felt about him. I tried to deal with that in a very sensitive and moving way, but it gradually changed because of Gene. He did not want to do a love story."

Maurice Hurley notes, "You look at that show and see that it's done in seven days, and it's unbelievable. If we'd had another couple of days, we could have made it even better. It was an attempt to look at a contemporary problem with a future perspective. We're kind of arm dealers to the world now. We make our F-14s and then we go over to the Persian Gulf and have to track the F-14s on radar because they're going to attack our own ships with our own missiles. There's some insanity going on here, and if you keep taking it to its ultimate conclusion.... We've got it boys; we've got the ultimate weapon here. It only kills people, leaves all the buildings.

It's better than a cobalt bomb. 'How do you know it works?' 'Well, come on, we'll give you a little demo.' Good night. Turn off the light. It's over."

Casting note: Julia Nickson, who plays one of the bridge personnel under Geordi's command, portrayed Sylvester Stallone's girlfriend in *Rambo: First Blood Part II* and appeared in the first season of *Babylon 5*.

Episode #22:
"Symbiosis"
Original Airdate: 4/16/88
Written by Robert Lewin, Richard Manning and Hans Beimler
Story by Bob Lewin
Directed by Win Phelps
Guest Starring: Judson Scott (Sobi), Merritt Butrick (Captain Tejon), Richard Lineback (Romas), Kimberly Farr (Langor)

The Enterprise comes across a disabled Omaran ship and decides to provide aid, until they discover that a supposed plague cure being carried in canisters is actually a highly addictive drug that the Omarans have been supplying to neighboring Bracca for over two centuries. Picard abruptly finds himself embroiled in a battle between the drug suppliers and their clients, and he is torn between cutting off the supply and obeying the Prime Directive of non-interference. Ideally, he develops a unique approach that combines the two: by not providing the necessary repair equipment to the Omaran ship, the drug will not be delivered to Bracca and in a matter of time the people of that world will realize that their dependency is something that can be overcome.

••••

"It came about, coming off *Miami Vice*, as an interrupted drug bust," says Maurice Hurley, also a veteran of the once-popular cop show. "We came across a drug deal in progress and how does that play out? There were some nice *Star Trek*ian kind of problems that needed to be solved."

One problem that the vast majority of people felt could have been solved was not having Tasha Yar deliver a "just say no" speech to Wesley Crusher.

"That was Hurley who forced that one in there," the writer admits. "I take the blame for that. I jammed that in over everybody's objections. They were

screaming on the set, the actors were screaming, they were puking, they were yelling, 'We can't do this.' I said, 'No, there are kids out there. If we're going to make the message, let's make the message.' If it offends the adults or bothers some adults but it hits home with a couple of the kids, then, by God, we're going to do it. I'll take the heat on that one, but I'd probably do it again the same way for the same reasons."

Episode #23:
"Skin of Evil"
Written by Joseph Stefano and Hannah Louise Shearer
Story by Joseph Stefano
Directed by Joseph Scanlon
Guest Starring: Mart McChesney (Armus), Ron Gans (Voice of Armus), Walker Boone (Leland T. Lynch), Brad Zerbst (Nurse), Raymond Forchion (Ben Prieto)

A shuttlecraft containing Deanna Troi crashlands on a previously unexplored planet. An Away Team beams down to learn her fate, when they are confronted by what can only be described as an oil-slick, which is also a sentient being. This creature, which can rise from an oil puddle to a figure some six feet tall, is the personification of evil stripped off of the race that had once populated this world. Left behind, the creature has spent an eternity alone and now takes great pleasure in torturing anyone it comes into contact with. To this end, it kills Tasha Yar simply because it wants to. Now the crew has to figure out how it will rescue Troi while avoiding the creature's deadly touch.

••••

Writer Joseph Stefano, veteran of *The Outer Limits* and *Psycho*, says of "Skin of Evil": "I don't think I've ever said this before in response to a journalist. No comment."

"Infinite problems," groans Maurice Hurley. "Some of it worked, some of it didn't. I thought the funeral scene did. We just didn't have the opportunity to do that show correctly to make it what it could have been. I think the biggest problem was the slime creature. If he had been better, if we had been able to really do that, it would have taken three or six weeks. It just looked like what it was. It was too ambitious. When we try to do

••••

creatures, horror show stuff, it falls apart; just falls on its ass. You just can't make that stuff work in the time available. You can't do *Aliens* on *Star Trek*."

"I liked the idea," says Robert Lewin of Tasha's early and undramatic demise. "It was not my idea, it was actually an idea that came from the outside. It was from a person who was not on the staff and he suggested treating it that way and not having any real martyrdom. The attitude was that it's dangerous in space, that's what happens. Let's not get sentimental about it, we have a lot to do even though there was a slightly sentimental ending to it. I personally would not have done it that way. But when it was suggested, I saw it was a very good and clean way to do it."

Hannah Louise Shearer, who rewrote Joseph Stefano's original draft, explains, "Gene wanted an episode that dealt with sudden death. The other aspect was dealing with the character Stefano had created of pure evil. I have to admit I got sick when I rewrote the script, because it was very difficult to deal with a creature of pure evil. Gene and I had agreed that the crew of the Enterprise has no right to make judgments about other creatures out there and kill indiscriminately because of what they do. The job was to make the character of Armus believably evil and give it a basis for its horribleness that was understandable in a way. Not to destroy it, because we have no right to destroy life simply because we don't understand it, but to sentence it to a kind of karma that it deserves. I use the word karma, Gene didn't. I don't remember who came up with the idea of the hologram at the end of the show, but I ended up writing it. The act of writing it was a great catharsis and I felt also a wonderful opportunity to identify who these characters were. The most important thing was to get the emotions out of it. An opportunity to kill a main character in a series doesn't come along very often, and it was something I relished. What I wanted to deal with is how that affects those around her."

Jonathan Frakes cites "Skin of Evil" as one of his favorite episodes. "I think we took greater chances then than we did later. The shows may be better, the level of it, but 'Skin of Evil' was

absurd. We had Patrick sitting and talking into a black oil slick—but what was wrong with that? I suffered physically like a fool with Mikey, sure I'll get in that black fucking metamucil shit. That was absurd. That was a time first season when they took chances, some of them missed, but some were great. Like 'Naked Now,' the episode which we've never done anything quite like where everyone got drunk and horny. That was risky. All the early stuff with Brent as Sherlock Holmes. Bowman's work, that first Klingon show, those were all great."

Offers director Joseph Scanlan, "When you read the script, it has a wonderful intellectual quality to it, forgetting the complications of creating the creature. This entity had such an ironic quality. I thought his dialogue was extremely interesting and found his one on one with Picard to be the ultimate face off. I was very enthusiastic about doing it.

"When I was talking to the producers," he elaborates, "I said, 'If we don't make this monster believable, we are in deep water, because this could be a most wonderful concept, but he's a very sympathetic character.' It was important that we not have the audience feel sorry for him when it's over, but I would guess that if you and I took a poll, half the audience would feel great empathy for him. The poor guy is there in this little puddle and that's that. I think the producers really wanted him to be so evil that you'd say, 'Leave him there. Fuck him,' but of course it never happened that way. There was no way to avoid empathy for him, which led to the irony of the situation. He killed Tasha, he damn near killed Riker, and I still wasn't mad at him. Look at what his people had done. How could you not feel sorry for him?"

While this element plagued the director's mind throughout most of the episode's shooting, more problematic was the actual design of the creature.

"What the special effects department was going to do," he says, "was create an eight or ten inch scale model of the figure. They'd put him on a hot plate, shoot it and melt it, and then reverse print that so that when he stood up, he absorbed all of the blackness and there was nothing left on the ground. The downside is that any time you wanted to

Marina Sirtis (Counselor Deanna Troi) entertains the gathered audience of fans. (Photo copyright © Karen Witkowski)

shoot the figure, we would have to shoot this ten inch thing in whatever artificial set we could create. Very difficult to do, and tie in with the actors. I'm capsulizing here a bit, because I never had so many special effects meetings in my life. Does he have a head? Is there a clearly defined neck and shoulders, or does it all slope off? Is he drippy and gooey, as if the oil never ceases to run? There are a million possibilities.

"Anyway, we finally settled on building a ten foot pit in the studio floor. Ten feet deep by about six feet in length...about the size of a grave. One side of it went all the way down, and the other side had a hydraulic platform that went down about halfway so that the stunt guy could stand on it, full figure, on the surface of the planet, be reduced to about waist high and then, through his own ingenuity, submerge himself even further, either by crouching down or stepping off the platform and further into the abyss."

Despite all the preparation, he doesn't believe that the effect was pulled off successfully.

"If we had a four million dollar budget and were doing *Alien*, we had the potential for a very intelligent piece of work. But to do it in seven days is very tough. My first cut was just barely ade-

Former "Mama" Michelle Phillips portrayed Captain Picard's first Next Generation *love interest in "We'll Always Have Paris."*

quate and it took input from the producers to make it better. I had always wanted a Roddy McDowall-type of venomous evil coming out of the mouth of this guy, but the producers leaned more toward what you got, which was the throaty presence, but always somewhat ominous. The bottom line is that it became a caricature, I think, and as a result, as close as it came to being a good show, it was not a good show."

Episode #24:
"We'll Always Have Paris"
Original Airdate: 4/30/88
Written by Deborah Dean Davis and Hannah Louis Shearer
Directed by Robert Becker
Guest Starring: Michelle Phillips (Jenice Manheim), Rod Loomis (Dr. Paul Manheim), Isabel Lorca (Gabrielle), Dan Kern (Lt. Dean), Jean-Paul Vignon (Edourd), Kelly Ashmore (Francine), Lance Spellerberg (Transporter Chief)

Captain Picard is reunited with a former love (Michelle Phillips) when the Enterprise investigates the research outpost of Dr. Paul Manheim, whose experiments have resulted in a series of time distortions. If not corrected, the very fabric of time will be torn apart, destroying all reality.

• • • •

"A very good friend of mine suggested it and we needed a script in five days," explains Hannah Louise Shearer. "It was an interesting experience based on that. We wanted something that was utterly romantic [and] that explored the character of Picard, [giving] some insight into why he was who he was. To me, unless you find out over the years who these people are, they're cardboard characters. I'm going to say something that's probably heresy: as much as we identify with the archetypes of the original *Star Trek* characters, I don't think we know very much about them. You know who the archetypes of Kirk and certainly Mr. Spock were, and when I was a kid I had a mad crush on him—all women did—but I didn't know who he was. I think the characters this time evolved much more quickly.

"Deborah [Dean Davis] and I had a great time writing this show, because we were probably writing the most romantic episode in the world," she adds. "It was toned down 75% and it's very interesting, because women say it was their favorite episode, but men find it very uncomfortable. I think that was true on staff as well. The women in the office loved it, they loved the idea of Picard being in love and wanted him to make love to this woman, which was in our original draft. The men backed off from it very powerfully. So I think it was definitely a compromise episode which was successful in its own way. That romantic perception was mine and Debra's, not shared by Patrick, who had to play the role and who has a very clear vision of what his captain should be, so our perception in the original draft probably went too far and it was toned down to fit what his needs were and what his beliefs of the character were. I still think that men are more uncomfortable with it, but men are generally more uncomfortable in romantic situations than women. I think there is such an underlying sexism in everyone's viewpoint, it's very pervasive in our society. Debra and I had wanted to do something about a professor whose work wasn't appreciated and had to go off on his own. Maury wanted to do something about a time anomaly and dimensional changes, and we married the two elements which worked very well. It was not an easy show to write."

Casting note: Michelle Phillips, of course, is late of the 1960's-70's band, The Mamas and the Papas.

Episode #25:
"Conspiracy"
Original Airdate: 5/7/88
Written by Tracy Torme
Story by Robert Sabaroff
Directed by Cliff Bole
Guest Starring: Henry Darrow (Admiral Savar), Ward Costello (Gregory Quinn), Robert Schenkkan (Dexter Remmick), Ray Reinhardt (Admiral Aaron), Jonathan Farwell (Walker Keel), Michael Berryman (Rixx), Ursaline Bryant (Tryla Scott)

The conspiracy hinted at in "Coming of Age" becomes reality when Picard is mysteriously summoned by several other starship captains, and informed of a plot to infiltrate and subvert Starfleet. The Enterprise proceeds to Earth to get some answers, where Picard and Riker and reunited with Admiral Quinn and Lieutenant Commander Remmick. In the tradition of *Invasion of the Body Snatchers*, they learn that key members of Starfleet have been taken over by members of an alien race hell-bent on ruling the galaxy.

• • • •

"It was alright, but I hated that horror show crap at the ending," says Maurice Hurley. "The thing is, and I've got to take the blame for this as much as anybody, I said, 'Let's do it, let's do it to a bust.' The problem is that *Star Trek* has to have, at the end, elevation. You have to feel an uplift at the end, somehow. And that show didn't even come close to giving you any feeling like that. There was no sense of feeling better about yourself. That's not a show that you would want to sit down and watch with your six year old kid. It was a mean show to me; just a mean little show."

Explains writer Tracy Torme, "The situation was similar to the one involving 'Haven' in that they had a show called 'The Assassins,' which had gone through a few drafts and was really not close to anything they wanted to do. It was sort of just sitting there. Again, I agreed to take it over, with the condition that I could really turn it upside down and basically create a new story. Originally it was a *Seven Days in May* kind of story about a coup inside of Starfleet, and various officers felt the Prime Directive was too restrictive and that the Federation was getting soft; that the peace with the Klingons had sort of made us complacent and somewhere down the line there would be a threat and we had better be prepared for it. The leaders of it were all friends of Picard. I really liked that story. It had nothing alien in it at all, and was really a paranoia story. Gene rejected it. Although he liked it, he didn't want to open that can of worms with the Federation. I was thinking 20th Century as opposed to 24th Century.

"I instantly knew that the story just had to change. Then what dawned on me was that this was the next to last show of the season and I really felt that although the show had improved a great deal, that we were still too comfortable and weren't pushing the limits of what we could do. I wrote 'Conspiracy' with the idea of doing something different; something with an unhappy ending, a harder edge, horror elements....I thought that if people hated it, it was only one *Star Trek* and we could always go back to what we always do next week. I wrote it intentionally to be different. I figured it would cause controversy, but I wanted it to be a different type of show. Thanks to Bob Justman and Rick Berman, especially, who really got behind it, it managed to keep 95% of the original hard edge. Because of that, it's a special show for me. I'm proud of *Star Trek* for being willing to take a chance. Die hard fans who want a nice, neat, comfortable universe at all times might be a little upset about it, but that's okay."

Executive Producer Bob Justman offers, "When I read the first version of 'Conspiracy,' I thought it was wonderful and it did things one would not have assumed that we would have done. It took some chances and I was just thrilled with what I read, and I was very happy that we were able to accomplish what we did. It was a grisly show, very chilling and very effective. It leaves you hanging. You know there's more to come. Those kind of things can work very, very well and in this case it did. It was strong and we couldn't have done what we did on network television."

"Maybe they were experimenting with a lot of stuff on the screen in motion pictures at the time," reflects director Cliff Bole. "I certainly felt the difference shooting it, but the way I looked at it was just another little test to see if the public would buy it."

Tracy Torme named the character of Ryan Sipe, one of those mentioned by Commander Tryla Scott (Ursaline Bryant) involved in the conspiracy, after his favorite football quarterback, Cleveland Browns Brian Sipe.

Episode #26:
"The Neutral Zone"
Original Airdate: 5/14/88
Written by Maurice Hurley
Story by Deborah McIntyre and
Mona Glee
Directed by James L. Conway
Guest Starring: Marc Alaimo (Commander T'Bok), Anthony James (Subcommander Thei), Leon Rippy (I.Q. Sonny Clemons), Gracie Harrison (Clare Raymond), Peter Mark Richman (Ralph Offenhouse)

The Enterprise comes across a vessel containing a group of people in suspended animation, much as was the case with the original show's "Space Seed." Instead of finding genetically engineered supermen, the Enterprise awakens a yuppie stockbroker, a housewife and a country singer from the 20th Century who cause almost as much havoc as Ricardo Montalban's Khan did. This story serves as the backdrop for the first confrontation with the Romulans in over half a century, in which outposts are being destroyed along the Neutral Zone. As the Romulans make clear in the episode's final moments, "We're back."

••••

"A slambanger," laughs Maurice Hurley. "That was written in about a day and a half. That was the last show of the season and the strike deadline was on us. I think that script was written literally in a day and a half. The characterizations were good. I think there were some nice things in the casting and it was interesting, but it was pretty much a slapped together show. It was set up to be a three-pronged episode. The first prong was setting up this situation with the Romulans [and] these destroyed outposts, and this would lead to a little kind of alliance with the Romulans which ended up with us confronting the Borg. But we never had a chance to play that out. We set it up and it could have been fun. The Borg were a good concept. You've got to have the planning time to lay the foundation, but we didn't have the time second season [because of the Writer's Strike]. That was disappointing since some of the stories we thought were going to work out and develop, we didn't and that was unfortunate. We couldn't do it because of the strike. An alright episode, but nothing great."

The Romulan, T'Bok, was played by Marc Alaimo, who subsequently returned twice on *TNG*, making a lasting impression and leading to his being cast as Gul Dukat on *Deep Space Nine*.

• • • •

••••

CHAPTER EIGHTEEN
SEASON TWO

An Introduction

It's ironic that *Star Trek's* Writer's Guide is referred to as "The Bible" since Roddenberry's "thou shalt nots" abounded and those who violated his commandments were either struck down or left the show of their own volition.

"I think those people who have survived on the show are the people who are comfortable with the concept of what it's all about," says Rick Berman. "First season there were a group of writers who had friction with Gene, but it was not personal. It was over how people wrote the show. There were some personality conflicts, but no more than there are on most television series. It was all blown a little more out of proportion than I thought it deserved to be."

With Roddenberry's control of the show severely diminished after a variety of Writer's Guild problems during the first season and the departure of Robert Justman as Supervising Producer, due to health reasons late first year, Rick Berman took over as the "great bird" of the new galaxy class starship. Filling the void on the story side was Maurice Hurley, a veteran of *Miami Vice* and *The Equalizer*, who Roddenberry had brought aboard early first season. Despite botching a rewrite of "Where No One Has Gone Before", Hurley was allowed to stay aboard and quickly rose up the ladder to fill the power vacuum in Roddenberry's absence.

"Cop shows, lawyer shows and hard drama are my homefield," Hurley says. "I took *Star Trek* because of the challenge. It was something I had never done before."

By second season, Hurley was the head writer, having furiously completed rewrites first season to keep the teleplays coming in as filming on stage caught up with the material that was written. Complicating matters had been the impending Writer's Strike forcing Hurley to dash off a script for "Neutral Zone", the first season capper, in a matter of days. By the time second season was ready to go before the cameras it was already late into the season due to the prolonged Writer's Strike forcing the staff to dust off an old script intended for *Trek's* 70's revival, "The Child". Substituting Troi for Ilia, they fine tuned the premise for *The Next Generation* and launched into the first couple of episodes.

"You don't look at the ensemble as characters on the show," says Hurley. "The ship is a character, the ensemble is a character. It's a strange way to look at it when you write the show. You don't, for instance, find one of the characters in violent verbal opposition to another character on what they're seeing or what they're doing. And you have to write it that way because that maintains the unity and integrity of the crew, which is critical. The show's been criticized by writers because there are no internal conflicts. Riker does not want Picard's seat, Geordi does not dislike Data because he has this advanced intellect, etc. Those conflicts and pettiness is not there, so you can't do *thirtysomething* in space. If you were to say, 'I think I can do better,' you probably can, but it's not *Star Trek*. If you're going to do *Star Trek* these are the rules you have to go by."

First year, lines were often being rewritten on stage and sometimes overdubbed in post-production to try and make sense of confusing storylines. Although second season was not as troubled, Hurley feels that the end of the first year was his best time on the show and that the Writer's Strike ruined the show's second season for him.

"The second half of the first season was great," says Hurley. "If we could have kept on that roll I might still be there. It was just rocking, too much fun to believe. There were problems, people yelling and screaming, but it didn't matter. We were all pulling on the oars and driving for the same goal. Everybody was busting their butt and it was great fun. If we had been able to kick in and keep going second season there would have been no telling.

"We had a lot of things we

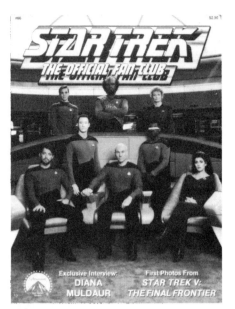

This cover of the official Star Trek *fan club magazine highlighted the show's second season, including Diana Muldaur as Dr. Pulaski.*

wanted to do," he says of the second season. "I like to move a character from one point at the beginning of the season to another at the end of the season, and one of the problems with *Star Trek* is the characters never change. If you look at the old series, they go through all these incredible adventures and they are still the same characters at the beginning that they are at the end. That's not the way life is. I wanted to arc the characters through the second season, but we didn't have the time to build the foundation. That was disappointing."

Hurley's strong arm tactics, however, were alienating a number of writers onboard, including Hannah Louise Shearer who ankled at the end of first season and Tracy Torme, the young writer who had earned critical kudos with his scripts for "Haven", "The Big Goodbye" and "Conspiracy". It was only with the help of Berman, Justman and Roddenberry himself that Torme was able to have his script 'Conspiracy' produced over the vocal objections of Hurley, who was opposed to the graphic violence and decidedly downbeat tone of the episode in which parasites invade the bodies of the leaders of the Federation on Earth, resulting in the Enterprise being brought home to combat the menace. Another producer who left the show

••••

claimed of Hurley, "He didn't want a fresh outlook and we carried out meaningless assignments dutifully."

Hurley also had many proponents, including Story Editor Melinda Snodgrass. "I learned a lot from him," says Snodgrass. "He was great because he always let me make my own changes. If he didn't like a scene he would tell me why and talk it over. But he always let me go away and fight with it. It was painful, but I really learned a lot about screenwriting in the crucible of a fast, hard apprenticeship."

Whoopi Goldberg was added to the cast as a recurring regular who would be the bartender at *Trek*'s new interstellar bar & grill, the Ten Forward, built only a few soundstages away from Paramount's *Cheers* set. At the same time, Gates McFadden was unceremoniously fired and replaced by Diana Muldaur as Dr. Katherine Pulaski.

Despite the announcement that *Trek* would be honored with a Peabody Award for Excellence in Television for its episode "The Big Goodbye", a first season film noir set in the holodeck written by Torme, the second season was rife with turmoil. Shortly after the airing of "Elementary Dear Data", another holodeck adventure in which Data takes on the role of fictional detective Sherlock Holmes, the estate of Arthur Conan Doyle warned that they would sue the show if they used the Sherlock Holmes character again. The initial episodes were received poorly and the stunt casting of comedian Joe Piscopo as a stand-up comedian was eviscerated by fans. Gone were the Ferengi, who had been replaced at the end of the first season with the familiar *Trek* villains the Romulans. Disturbingly, whenever the new show faltered, it resorted to the original as a crutch. Unable to successfully create new villains, the Romulans began to serve as a primary source of conflict for the Federation despite Roddenberry's early vows that these alien antagonists would not be a part of his next generation. Likewise, the highly touted ensemble was reduced second season to a triumvirate clearly reminiscent of the first show. Picard, Riker and Data shared the spotlight as the gang of three that would dominate the stories throughout year two, while characters such as Worf, La Forge, Troi, Wesley and the newly added Muldaur were relegated to supporting status.

Muldaur was earning her share of disdain from fans who rejected the acerbic doctor who would continually admonish and torture the innocent android Data in much the way McCoy belittled Spock in the old show, but while Spock could easily defend himself and often got the last word with as little as a raised eyebrow concealing a sinister devilish Vulcan smirk, Data was like a child being abused by his foster parents.

Under Hurley's reign the show took on a darker tone, and although adhering to the strictures of Roddenberry's universe governing the interpersonal relationships of the characters, he was quick to point out that space was not always a happy and cheerful place to be. In the second episode of the season, "Where Silence Has Lease", the Enterprise is turned into a floating dissection laboratory by a curious alien creature who brutally kills the first red-shirted security guard of the new series on the bridge. If Roddenberry's stock and trade had been judgmental God-like beings, Hurley's take was slightly more malevolent. In "Loud As A Whisper" three ambassadors are killed, in "Matter of Honor" Riker finds himself unwelcome aboard a Klingon ship as part of a Federation exchange program, "Contagion" highlighted the dangers of technology when a computer virus results in the destruction of an entire starship, in "Time Squared" the Enterprise is faced with destruction when a Picard from the future warns of the ships impending destruction and, most importantly, Hurley devised the Borg, a race of omnipotent, cybernetic super foes who appeared invincible in the dark and threatening "Q Who."

Joining the show was Melinda Snodgrass, a popular fan writer whose *Tears of the Singer* had been a bestselling *Trek* novel for Pocket Books. Snodgrass' "The Measure of the Man", sold on spec to Hurley, was one of the standout episodes of the season. Opting out however was popular fan writer Tracy Torme, whose second season scripts "The Royale" and "Manhunt" had—according to the writer—been so mutilated by Hurley that he had to use a pseudonym on both works. Torme, who had served as a Creative Consultant in year two and had once been groomed to take over the reigns of the show, was not prepared to carry on the meaningless

assignments and suffer through the endless divisive rewrites that had characterized Hurley's tenure on the show, which had led such Producers as John Mason, Mike Grey, Burton Armus, Leonard Mlodinow and Scott Rubenstein to flee after as little as one episode's work.

"We didn't have the time we needed," Rick Berman says of the truncated season brought on by the Writer's Strike. "The quality of the first several episodes suffered in that we did not have the time that we would have liked to develop and polish the early scripts."

"I thought that the second year of the series, in general, was a year in which they had some real writing problems," offers third season writer Dennis Russell Bailey. "I think there were some really good episodes like Melinda Snodgrass who wrote what is probably the best episode of the series', "Measure of the Man," but in general I thought they had a real writing problem and they were going around forever blaming it on the Writer's Strike, which was nonsense. Every show on television had to deal with the writer's strike that year and it wasn't easy for anybody but they recovered."

But by mid-season, *The Next Generation* finally seemed to hit its stride. "We seemed to find a direction second season," says Melinda Snodgrass. "Once I came on board there suddenly seemed to be this climate of discussion among the writers about what we wanted to do with the show. My impression was that this was a new phenomenon. We were a little bit more on the same wavelength."

The season ended with a cost-cutting collection of clips episode, "Shades Of Grey" which did not bode well for the oncoming season. Hurley, who had grown tired of the infighting at the show, gave notice that he too would be leaving through the same revolving door he and Roddenberry purportedly had put in place. At the end of the second season, *TNG* was without a helmsman yet again.

"Two years was enough time in space for me," says Hurley who returned to Universal to develop shows and eventually landed at Warner Bros. producing the new *Kung Fu* for first run syndication. "I did some good, some bad, some mediocre, but it's not a show that I could continue to do. It's not where I come from."

• • • •

••••

CHAPTER NINETEEN
SEASON TWO

Episode Guide

"The Child"

"Where Silence Has Lease"

"Elementary, Dear Data"

"The Outrageous Okona"

"Loud as a Whisper"

"Unnatural Selection"

"A Matter of Honor"

"The Measure of a Man"

"The Schizoid Man"

"The Dauphin"

"Contagion"

"The Royale"

"Time Squared"

"The Icarus Factor"

"Pen Pals"

"Q Who?"

"Samaritan Snare"

"Up the Long Ladder"

"Manhunt"

"The Emissary"

"Peak Performance"

"Shades of Grey"

Episode #27:
"The Child"
Original Airdate: 11/19/88
Written by Jaron Summers, Jon Povill and Maurice Hurley
Directed by Rob Bowman
Guest Starring: Seymour Cassel (Lt. Commander Hester Dealt), R.J. William (Ian), Colm Meaney (Transporter Chief), Dawn Armenian (Miss Gladstone), Zachary Benjamin (Young Ian), Dore Keller (Crewman)

Deanna Troi is impregnated by an alien presence, and comes to term with the child in a matter of days. She gives birth to what appears to be a normal child, but he ages rapidly from an infant, to a toddler and then a ten year old. The boy takes in everything around him for analysis, and inadvertently affects the growth of a deadly organism within holding canisters, which threatens to engulf the ship. Rather than put anyone in danger, the child decides that it's better he join his own kind, and dies.

• • • •

With a writer's strike delaying production on a second season, Paramount dusted off this script which Jon Povill and Jaron Summers had written the series' aborted '70s revival with the classic cast that led to *Star Trek: The Motion Picture.* During a hurried rewrite, Ilia became Troi. Additionally, Gates McFadden was let go as Dr. Crusher, with Diana Muldaur joining the cast as Dr. Katherine Pulaski.

"'The Child' suffered from being the first episode of the second season more than anything else," says Maurice Hurley. "I never even looked at the first script. It was a premise that had been written up for a series that was never done, and I never even looked at it."

States Rob Bowman, "I know that the idea of carrying the bug on board in the containment grid came from the movie *Sorcerer,* which came from a French movie in which wet dynamite had to be taken across the jungle. That was our thread of jeopardy. As far as my involvement, I think that being the first episode of the second season, my thrust was to make sure we gave the audience something that would justify their wait over the summer for the first episode. Simply put, it was just that. Here's our

audience of loyal Trekkies who watch our first season, and then have to sit through summer reruns waiting for what we are going to give them next season. I said, 'We must give them a great first episode to welcome them back, instead of kind of resting on our laurels.' That was the agreement between Rick Berman and I, and we went a little bit extra on quite a bit."

Episode #28:
"Where Silence Has Lease"
Original Airdate: 11/26/88
Written by Jack Sowards
Directed by Winrich Kolbe
Guest Starring: Earl Boen (Nagillum), Charles Douglas (Haskell), Colm Meaney (Transporter Chief)

The Enterprise is trapped in a void that serves as a laboratory experiment for a super-powerful alien being. Nagillum (Earl Boem) is intent on experimenting on the Enterprise and experiencing the crew's emotions. When Picard realizes that the creature will need to destroy at least half of the crew's complement before attaining its desired results, he threatens to self-destruct the ship. A thinly veiled attack on animal research.

• • • •

"I love that show," says Maurice Hurley. "You know where Nagillum's name came from? We wanted to get Richard Mulligan for the role, and if you spell his name backwards, you've got Nagillum. It looked terrible, just didn't work at all, but the first two or three acts of that show are just a humper. Unfortunately, the ending didn't work at all. But that's the whose sense of scientists out in the unknown, doing what they really relish, what they want to do more than anything else. What that show was to me was our guys at three in the morning, they hear a noise in the attic. I put a pillow over my head and go back to sleep and hope it's nothing. They got up to find out, 'Oh boy, what is it?' That's what the show was. And then, again, I hate to keep saying it, monsters and creatures just didn't work. One of things that sometimes has to be remembered, and I forgot it as much as anybody, was that you forget these are scientists out there, not soldiers. They're out there to learn, so that sense of learning and investigation is

really important, more important than all of the running and jumping, more important than the Ferengi, more important than the Borg, more important than any of that stuff is to deal with an idea or something new."

Explains director Winrich Kolbe, "I kind of like this one, but don't ask me why. To me that episode was kind of a baptism by fire, because I'd never done any science fiction before. Suddenly I come on to this script where I go from the same bridge to the same bridge to the same bridge to the same bridge. We spent five days on the bridge. One of the unique challenges of doing *Star Trek* is that you're basically shooting the same sets over and over again. It's not like a cop show where there's a day or a day and a half in the squad room and the rest is out on location. So for me 'Where Silence Has Lease' was five days on the bridge.

"The bridge is intriguing when you step on it for the first time and you look at it for about ten minutes," he continues. "Then it becomes an utter crashing bore, because it's nothing but tan walls and a few twinkling lights. I did a lot of choreography on that show. It's probably the script that has the most notes on where actors move—every step, which I very rarely do. I usually like the actors to drive themselves where they have to go. On something like 'Where Silence Has Lease' you have to keep the camera constantly moving, and that was a hell of a challenge. I spent a lot of time on that bridge on my belly, hanging down from the rafters and in any other position to try and figure out what I would do with the camera.

"As far as the idea of the alien studying them, I kind of like it. It's a different perspective and basically every story that we're telling, it doesn't matter if it's book form or movies or TV, it's just a matter of perspective. The problem with this kind of story that I have is that I want to make it a two-hour episode and really push it. The different perspective is so intriguing to me. We look at things in our little universe and interpret people in a certain way and they make sense of us or they don't make sense of us. A foreigner, for instance. The way he or she thinks or sees things. You put that in outer space and have a totally different organization looking at us, now it seems to me that you want to push it further. You want that experiment to go further and us become almost like whatever they want us to be. Unfortunately it didn't go that far. That is probably my major beef. The problem is you only have 44 minutes and in those 44 minutes, unless you do story arcs, if you have to go out there and come back in 44 minutes you're kind of handicapped. You don't want to go out too far so you lose your audience and never catch them as you come back."

Episode #29:
"Elementary, Dear Data"
Original Airdate: 12/3/88
Written by Brian Alan Lane
Directed by Rob Bowman
Guest Starring: Daniel Davis (Professor James Moriarty), Alan Shearman (Inspector Lestrade), Biff Manard (Ruffian), Diz White (Prostitute), Anne Elizabeth Ramsey (Assistant Engineer Clancy), Richard Merson (Pie Man)

Realizing Data's familiarity with the canon of Arthur Conan Doyle hardly challenges Data's deductive capacities, Geordi attempts to create a worthwhile opponent in a Sherlock Holmes recreation within the holodeck. As a result, LaForge inadvertently gives life to a powerful, sentient Dr. Moriarty (Daniel Davis), who takes control of the Enterprise and kidnaps Dr. Pulaski.

••••

Reflects Maurice Hurley, "Wonderful episode. It was triggered off for Data by the experience of 'The Big Goodbye,' which was organic to the show. It wasn't a writer saying, 'Let's do this.' It was one of the people living on the Enterprise. And we did that show in seven days. We had carriages, old London, and I thought the guy who played Moriarty was just wonderful. I've never seen anybody play Moriarty better than that.

"By the way, there was an ending cut off of that show by Gene. We had a large fight about it. In that ending, Picard knew how to defeat Moriarty. He tricked him. He knew all along that Moriarty could leave the holodeck whenever he wanted to, and he knew because when Data came out and showed him a

drawing of the Enterprise, if that piece of paper could leave the holodeck, that means that the fail-safe had broken down. In turn, this means that the matter-energy converter which creates the holodeck, now allowed the matter to leave the holodeck, which was, up to that point, impossible. When he knew that paper had left the holodeck, he knew that Moriarty could as well, so he lied to him. The doctor says, 'How could you lie to Moriarty?' Picard basically says, 'Well, after all, dear doctor, it is Moriarty, and until we know whether he is saying what he's saying because that's how he really feels or if it's more of his guile and deceit, it's best to be very safe with this.' It was better than I'm saying, but that whole rationale was missing. Gene basically thought it made Picard look deceitful, dishonest and it hurt the character. I thought it made him look clever, and since you are dealing with maybe the most profound criminal mind in literature, you've got to be careful."

Director Rob Bowman remembers the episode extremely well. "That came about pre-season with Rick Berman," he details. "We got together and he told me some of the shows they would be doing, and if something sounded good I should stop him. He said they were doing a Sherlock Holmes episode, and before he could say Holmes I told him it was mine. I said, 'That will be my payback for 'The Big Goodbye.' So I kind of went with that with the vengeance that I would make it something great. It was a *huge* production. They built that whole street from the ground up on stage. Indoors. It's an awesome episode.

"The thing that became absolutely ludicrous about it as far as I'm concerned, was a poor decision on the part of those who made it. They went from an eight day schedule down to a seven day schedule for an enormous show. They made the shooting process one of the most unpleasant I've ever been through. I thought it almost killed the episode. The speed we had to shoot....it's like the script was an eight or nine day shoot. I don't mind doing a nine day shoot in eight days, as long as it's not a ludicrous schedule. But seven days is the least amount of time you can probably do an episode anyway that still looks

good. Of course you could do bottle shows, like I did on the season's last episode ['Shades of Gray'], where you just scramble for three days and shoot everything as fast as possible.

"Here was a show where we had all this great production value. Brent Spiner was about to do the best work I've ever seen him do. We had all these sets and they said seven days. I think that show is when I started to pull away from *Star Trek*, because I felt that it was a great opportunity to make a wonderful episode, and there was an arbitrary decision because the sets cost so much—I think $200,000—where they said, 'We'll save money by taking a day off the schedule.' It's like, 'Wait a minute, guys, first you have to take a day out of the script. You don't just take a day off the schedule to save $60,000.' As you can tell, I was pretty angry about it, and still have a little hostility towards what I went through on that show to make it happen.

Certainly Brent Spiner came through with flying colors and everybody did. The original draft of that script was so eloquently written; absolutely beautiful, but it was probably a two hour episode at least and was written way, way down, but that was a wonderful script. We pulled the episode off."

Episode #30:
"The Outrageous Okona"
Original Airdate: 12/10/88
Written by Burton Armus
Story by Les Menchen, Lance Dickson and David Landsburg
Directed by Robert Becker
Guest Starring: William O. Campbell (Captain Okona), Douglas Rowe (Debin), Albert Stratton (Kushell), Rosalind Ingledew (Yanar), Kieran Mulroney (Benzan), Whoopi Goldberg (Guinan), Joe Piscopo (the Comic)

A space rogue named Okona (William O. Campbell) hitches a ride aboard the Enterprise, striking up a relationship with Wesley and a number of eligible female ensigns. Concurrently, two feuding races seek him for his crimes, accusing him of having impregnated the daughter of one, and having stolen a valuable national treasure from the other. Meanwhile, holodeck comedian Joe Piscopo and barmaid Guinan

Joe Piscopo attempted to teach Data a thing or two about humor in "The Outrageous Okona".

(Whoopi Goldberg) give Data a lesson in humor, as the android continues on his quest towards humanity.

Episode #31:
"Loud As a Whisper"
Original Airdate: 1/7/89
Written by Jacqueline Zambrano
Directed by Larry Shaw
Guest Starring: Howie Seago (Riva), Marnie Mosiman (Woman), Thomas Oglesby (Scholar), Leo Damian (Warrior/Adonis), Colm Meaney (Transporter Chief), Richard Lavin and Chip Heller (Warriors), John Garrett (Lieutenant)

A deaf mute negotiator, Riva (Howie Seago), who telepathically shares his thoughts through a chorus of interpreters, is sent to negotiate a peace on a feuding planet. When his chorus is killed during an ambush, he is forced to learn to communicate by using sign language. He is counseled by Troi, who helps him overcome his handicap and negotiate a successful peace.

● ● ● ●

"Troi got to show her claws and she gives this guy a boost," says former story Melinda Snodgrass.

"An okay episode," muses Maurice Hurley. "I had higher expectations than the way it turned out. It should have been more effective."

Episode #32:
"The Schizoid Man"
Original Airdate: 1/21/89
Written by Tracy Torme
Story by Hans Beimler and Richard Manning
Directed by Les Landau
Guest Starring: W. Morgan Sheppard (Dr. Ira Graves), Barbara Alyn Woods (Kareen Brianon), Suzie Plakson (Lieutenant Selar)

Dr. Ira Graves (W. Morgan Sheppard), a dying, egomaniacal scientist, places his consciousness in Data's body to preserve his life. When the android begins acting strangely, the crew suspects that something is amiss. Joining the Away Team is Vulcan doctor Selar, the first appearance by Suzi Plakson on the show.

● ● ● ●

"I had wanted to do a story about Data having hidden memories of the dead colonists from the planet he came from," reveals Tracy Torme. "A woman comes aboard who once had a triangular love affair with these two men from the colony. Their memories instantly come alive in Data whenever he sees her, and their personalities basically take him over. One was an Italian Don Juan-type, and the other was sort of an overzealous and very jealous kind of nerd, so Data would suddenly break into these personalities and become very jealous, possessive, amorous, or whatever, around this woman. I couldn't do it because Richard Manning and Hans Biemler already had a story they had sold, about genius Ira Graves and how he ends up transmitting his intellect into Data. So what we ended up doing, when Richard and Hans were not going to work on the show for whatever reason, was I combined the two stories. I used Ira Graves as a character and the setting on his planet, and put a lot of elements from my story into it. In their story, the scientist puts his intellect into Data and everyone knows about it ahead of time, so when he comes on board, it's not a secret that there's somebody else inside Data. That made the whole story play differently, so that was one of the major changes. A lot of the specifics from the show were taken from my original idea. It was a story I wanted to do, and I wanted to do it for Brent, who I admire a great deal. This was really the only way I could do it."

Dismisses Maurice Hurley, "That was science fiction bullshit that didn't work for me, basically for one reason. We talk about Gene saying he didn't want Picard to be deceitful with Moriarty. My problem with 'Schizoid Man' is that once you take Data out of character and allow him to be somebody else, we really hurt the character. He was injured in that episode. To see him playing somebody else really damaged the character, for me. You can do that with a lot of characters, but Data is ingenuous, and this took some of that shine off of it. It's the little 14 year old girl and all of a sudden she's giving some guy a French kiss. Something's just a little bit off. There's that incredible innocence of Data that gets damaged."

Casting note: Suzie Plakson would reappear as Worf's love interest in "The Emissary" later in the season and has subsequently become a co-star of *Love & War*.

Episode #33 :
"Unnatural Selection"
Original Airdate: 1/28/89
Written by John Mason and Michael Gray
Directed by Paul Lynch
Guest Starring: Patricia Smith (Dr. Sara Kingsley), Colm Meaney (Chief O'Brien), Patrick McNamara (Captain Taggart), Scott Trost (Transporter Ensign)

A genetic mutation on an experimental colony begins to rapidly age the colonists, and holding the clues to a cure is a genetically created being. Pulaski beams aboard a shuttlecraft to find an antidote, when she discovers that she too has been affected with the malady and is rapidly growing older.

● ● ● ●

"I liked the episode a lot," says Colm Meaney, who plays Transporter Chief Miles O'Brien. "I thought it was really good. It held your interest, it was a marvelous sort of detective story in a way, while at the same time it was making a statement about the dangers of these wonderful scientific developments that can be used for great benefit. It also said something deeper about the dangers of them, and in a sense it begged

● ● ● ●

Diana Muldaur (Dr. Katharine Pulaski) seen here with Richard Daysart on the set of L.A. Law.

the question should we really be trying to do this?"

Of working with Diana Maldaur in her short-lived stint as Doctor Katherine Pulaski, director Paul Lynch notes, "She was a lovely lady. She did have trouble remembering her lines, though. We solved it by putting them on cue cards for her."

Episode #34:
"A Matter of Honor"
Original Airdate: 2/4/89
Written by Burton Armus
Story by Wanda M. Haight, Gregory Amos and Burton Armus
Directed by Rob Bowman
Guest Starring: John Putch (Ensign Mendon), Christopher Collins (Captain Kargan), Brian Thompson (Lieutenant Klag), Colm Meaney (Chief O'Brien), Peter Parros (Tactics Officer), Laura Drake (Vekma)

As a part of a Federation exchange program, Riker transfers aboard a Klingon warship where he is challenged by the unaccepting warriors. Striking up a friendship with Lieutenant Klag (Brian Thompson), Riker slowly begins acclimating to their alien ways. But then the Klingons discover a structural breach they believe has been caused by the Enterprise. The captain, Kargan (Christopher Collins), attacks the starship

and demands Riker's allegiance to him, while the commander must attempt to save his former ship without betraying the oath he had taken upon joining the Klingon crew.

••••

"'A Matter of Honor' was just a good idea," Maurice Hurley smiles. "It dealt with a social problem. One of the things that the old *Star Trek* did that the new *Star Trek* can't do as well, was make comments on issues. Back then, opinions were changing, things were changing, times were changing and it was very volatile and dynamic. Now we're into a period where it's stagnant; there's no dynamic change happening. People have settled in to opinions on problems that have no clear cut solution. What's the solution to AIDS? How do you capsulate, in a word, the solution? There isn't any.

"Now you take a show like 'A Matter of Honor' and say, 'We're going to do a little culture swapping,' so we explore what it must be like to be the only black face in a room of 40 white people," he adds. "That must be kind of tough. That's what Worf, in a sense, is doing. He's the only Klingon on a basically human ship. So we said, 'Let's spin it. Let's put somebody on an all Klingon vessel and see how that works.' What's it like to be a fish out of water? What is it like to be the only white face in a meeting in Harlem? That's got to be a little funny, a little different, a little tense. That's how that show started, it was a way to look at a contemporary social problem and give it a spin. At the same time, when you watch that show, there are wonderful things in it. When Riker is sitting with the Klingons, the Klingon says he's surprised at Riker because he has a sense of humor. Riker looks at him and says, 'Son of a gun, I was thinking the same thing.' If Riker had said, 'I'm surprised you guys have a sense of humor,' it wouldn't have meant anything. But spin it, and all of a sudden it became the point of the whole show."

Recalls Rob Bowman with a smile, "Jonathan Frakes and I really got into that episode. That was a fun one to do. I think Jonathan was waiting to do something that was rough and had action, and it also had the bonding between he and Klaag. Every day was

Jonathan and I doing high-fives and trying to put forth on film all the energy and spirit and adventure that was in that script. It was great to do. I guess there's a spirit inherent in the Klingons that seems to push it forth in a certain direction with the characters and with the camera

"I was going through my divorce at that time, and was escaping into the world of space for some happiness. Probably helped me to concentrate a little better. I know I was very aggressive at that point, so we put that on screen. When we did the fight on the bridge, I wanted to be as rough as I could possible make it. We even had to pare it down a little bit, because what we had in mind was too much."

Episode #35:
"The Measure of a Man"
Original Airdate: 2/11/88
Written by Melinda Snodgrass
Directed by Robert Scheerer
Guest Starring: Amanda McBroom (Captain Philipa Louvois), Brian Brophy (Commander Bruce Maddox), Clyde Kusatsu (Admiral Nakamura), Colm Meaney (Chief O'Brien), Whoopi Goldberg (Guinan)

Commander Bruce Maddox (Brian Brophy), a gung-ho cybernetics expert, wants to disassemble Data in order to learn more about his inner-workings. Picard defends the android in court to establish his sentience, coming up against court appointed litigator Riker.

••••

"It's interesting about 'Measure of the Man,'" observes Melinda Snodgrass. "Everyone seems to view it as a Data script, but it's really a Picard script. Data is the catalyst, but the stress is all on Picard."

"Stunning," Maurice Hurley exclaims. "That's the kind of show you want to do. You get one of those shows done and you say, 'Okay, good, we got that one done.' You don't need too many of those to feel real good about a season. It just worked great, everything about it. And it dealt with an issue in a very interesting way. I thought Whoopi's place was good in that. She's a wonderful actress."

Enthuses director Robert Scheerer, "'Measure of a Man' is one of the greatest episodes we've done and it

••••

has nothing to do with me. It has to do with the content, what it had to say, how it deals with it, the depth that it goes and the way it's resolved. I love that show. It is indeed my favorite show. I guess you would have to say that what I enjoyed is the dilemma that they're put in to, especially Jonathan and Patrick having to deal with Brent not as a dear friend but as someone whose worth has to be resolved. And Jonathan had to take the other side. It was all just beautifully crafted. It was not typical episodic television and had a great deal to say about man, humanity, what our problems in the world are today and hopefully what we can do about it in the future."

Episode #36:
"The Dauphin"
Original Airdate: 2/18/89
Written by Scott Rubenstein and Leonard Mlodinow
Directed by Rob Bowman
Guest Starring: Paddi Edwards (Anya), Jamie Hubbard (Salia), Colm Meaney (Chief O'Brien), Peter Neptune (Aron), Madchen Amick (Teenage Girl), Cindy Sorenson (Furry Animal), Jennifer Barlow (Ensign Gibson), Whoopi Goldberg (Guinan)

Salia (Jamie Hubbard), an alien princess who beams aboard the Enterprise, must learn how to accept her responsibility as a mediator in a planetary dispute, and sacrifice a chance to live her own life. She is accompanied by her protector, Anya (Paddi Edwards), a shape-changing alien woman, who warns an infatuated Wesley to stay away from the girl, fearing she will be encouraged to stay aboard the Enterprise and relinquish her regal duties.

••••

Opines Rob Bowman, "Decent show about Wesley Crusher falling in love for the first time. In the first reading of the script, I felt that we had no show. I thought, 'Oh, shit, here's the one. This is where we all fall on our faces.' I just felt that there was no real conflict and the dialogue was more people talking *at* each other instead of *to* each other, just making statements back and forth. There really was no character evolve. It was basically you do that, I'll do that, you do that...and I just don't find that good char-

acter writing. I loved that girl. I was in love with her by the end of the episode. I enjoyed that shoot very much. The only thing I was embarrassed to shoot was the scene where the two monsters come together. I closed my eyes and photographed them, and when I saw it all with music, I thought it came out really nicely. And the end with Whoopi and Wil was a gem. But those costumes....When they showed me those costumes, I said 'You're going to save money, but you're going to make me photograph these?' I said, 'When the audience sees these, they're going to change the channel.' We cut them down so they were just seen on screen for blips—but geez!

"We did some neat effects, we were fortunate in the casting of the nanny. She came off great and Wil Wheaton, I thought, did a real fine job. I think it was just one of those episodes they wanted to make inexpensively, so it was just trying to make the best that we could out of a simple story."

Maurice Hurley is not a fan of the show either. "Again, we're dealing with a monster show, and we don't do well with monsters. The idea was good, but the execution didn't work. If we had more time, I think that show would have been better."

Freelance writer Marc Scott Zicree (season four's "First Contact") feels, "They really missed the boat with Wesley. In those early shows when Wesley was fifteen and going out and playing ball with the blonde aliens and falling in the bushes, they were writing him like he was five years old. He should be looking to get laid instead of playing ball. Then he falls in love with that girl and they share chocolate mousse—give me a break."

Episode #37:
"Contagion"
Original Airdate: 3/18/89
Written by Steve Gerber and Beth Woods
Directed by Joseph Scanlan
Guest Starring: Thalmus Rasulala (Captain Varley), Carolyn Seymour (Subcommander Toras), Dana Sparks (Weapons Officer), Colm Meaney (Chief O'Brien), Folkert Schmidt (Doctor)

A Federation starship, the

Yamato, is destroyed by a deadly computer virus which soon infects the Enterprise, while also threatening a Romulan warship. The clue to saving the ship lies on the legendary planet, Iconia, where Picard and Data beam down in hopes of unraveling the superior technology of a long dormant computer network of an ancient civilization.

••••

"One cannot escape the impact that this series and the whole *Star Trek* mythology continues to have," says Patrick Stewart. "I have been overwhelmed and made extraordinarily proud to continue to be associated with a program like this, because I have been reminded everyday of the continuing impact in all possible areas of what this show does."

Episode #38:
"The Royale"
Original Airdate: 3/25/89
Written by Keith Mills (Tracy Torme)
Directed by Cliff Bole
Guest Starring: Sam Anderson, Jill Jacobson, Leo Garcia, Noble Willingham

An Away Team beams down to a mysterious planet where a Las Vegas casino is vividly duplicated. Losing communication with the ship after passing through an antique revolving door, they explore the bizarre gambling establishment and discover the body of a long-dead American astronaut. What they also discern is that they are trapped in the plot of a pulp gangster novel called *The Hotel Royale*, created to entertain the lone survivor of the ancient Earth space expedition. Only by taking on the roles of the novel's characters—a group of foreign investors who purchase the hotel—and assuming their personas through the end of the book, can the Away Team escape being trapped in the alien simulation.

••••

There was quite a bit of behind-the-scenes dissent over this episode, particularly between Maurice Hurley and Tracy Torme, who was so disappointed with the former's rewrite that he used a pen name.

"I thought the script was weak in terms of the story premise," says Hurley. "I found out after we were in the middle of it that it was a take-off from the old series, about a society based on a book. 'A Piece of the Action.' There were gangsters in this one, gangsters in that one, and both based on a book. It seemed derivative to me, but I didn't know it was derivative until we were in the middle of it."

States Torme, "When I came in to pitch to Bob Lewin, he really liked that story which was at the time called 'The Blue Moon Hotel.' It was a story that I had always liked. There had been a lot of talk about doing it in the first year, but finally [second] year they gave me the green light and told me to go ahead and do it. It became 'The Royale,' and I wrote a draft which was, again, a bit of a departure for *Star Trek*. It was kind of a surrealistic piece, with a lot of comedy and a lot of sort of subtle satire in it.

"One of the executive producers and I had a severe disagreement about how the show should be done, and for reasons which I believe are personal rather than professional, I was informed that I was being removed from the script. At that point I immediately told them that I wanted my name off the script, because I knew the direction they were going to go in, and I just knew with all my heart that it was a bad choice. I've completely disowned the piece. I suppose skeletally it's my story, but when I started to reread the rewrite, I got ten pages through it and I got sort of a cold chill and had to put it down. An interesting thing is that the cast, the crew and even secretaries went out of their way to tell me how much they liked my draft, and they asked me in a totally puzzled manner, what on Earth had happened and why we had changed it. All I could do was shrug. Of course this is all my opinion, and you'd probably hear something different from the other side. Basically there's one person who had this disagreement with me and removed me. I felt like a lot of the comedy was taken out. A lot of the surrealism was taken out. I feel that it's very heavy-handed now, and it's gone from being a strange episode to being a stupid episode."

Admits director Cliff Bole, "I thought Tracy's original story was much better. Different strokes for different folks. Sometimes you get a story and there's no backup to go to. If you have two on hand, you might make the move to do another

one while you repair the first to make it better. Other times, time just crawls up your back and you have to shoot these every goddamned day. Once you start shooting, it goes straight through until you finish 26 of them. It's like a factory. Hollywood is a factory town, and every episodic show is like that. You can't shut down. 'The Royale' was one of those things that happen in television, where you have an idea and you have to get out there and shoot it because time is coming on you. It was a quickly put together show, but received well."

Episode #39:
"Time Squared"
Original Airdate: 4/1/89
Written by Maurice Hurley
Story by Burt Michael Bensmiller
Directed by Joseph Scanlan
Guest Starring: Colm Meaney (Chief O'Brien)

The Enterprise rescues a disabled shuttlecraft and finds an incoherent Captain Picard aboard. Reviewing the ship's logs, they discover the vessel was sent back in time to warn the crew of the Enterprise's impending demise in a deadly space anomaly. As the time of the ship's destruction nears, the Picard from the future begins to revive, while the Jean Luc of the present grows more and more uncertain for fear of endangering the vessel and repeating the steps his future self made, thus resulting in the ship's end.

••••

"Somebody else's idea," says Maurice Hurley, who wrote the script for the episode. "We've seen a lot of people do time backs and forths and jumps around. They're always coming back 500 years or 1,000 years. Nobody's ever really come back six hours. Six hours is what fascinated me. Also the idea that it was originally a prelude to the episode 'Q-Who?', but Gene didn't like it.

"Originally," he elaborates, "the events of the episode was put together by Q. He had manipulated all of them as a way to introduce himself. The way it was originally designed, is that three episodes later they're going through space and all of a sudden Picard finds himself stuck in a shuttlecraft in a flash, and he sees the ship falling into the top of the vortex and exploding. He thinks he's lost his mind;

he doesn't know what's going on. Q appears and says, 'Hey, how ya doing?' Picard says, 'You caused that and all these other things?' Q says, 'Ah, well, surprised you didn't put it together earlier. Oh well, you *are* slow. Just a kind of calling card, something to do. Interesting, wasn't it?' And now he's into it. 'What do you want?' 'I want to join you.'

"So it was like the first one ended as a total, 'What the hell was that? It doesn't make any sense. I can't figure it out. Why would that happen? It would just be illogical as hell to have it happen.' But you go through an hour of being driven by this plot, and then you solve it, but you don't really solve it because you don't know what happened. Why would going forward be any different than going backward? Why would going into the center of it save you? It did, but why? It doesn't make any sense. But it does if Q is pulling the strings. Then the whole thing works. Those two were supposed to be tied together. It was a nothing ending, but if you realize at the ending that something happens where Picard says, 'This is a bullshit ending, everyone, it shouldn't have happened. What does it mean?' It means that there's something else here.

"The thing that I liked about it is that from the audience's point of view, since people follow the show so closely, the next time they see the vortex they say, 'Here we go again,' and they would connect those two shows instantly. And then to have Q jump in and have Picard make the conclusion at the same time the audience is making the conclusion, I thought was a way to involve them at a level they hadn't been involved with the show before, where they're in a decision making process with Picard. It's a goofy way to do it, but it's different. Admittedly the ending of 'Time Squared' was confusing. The rationale behind it was gone."

Episode #40:
"The Icarus Factor"
Original Airdate: 4/22/89
Written by David Assael and Robert L. McCullough
Directed by Robert Iscove
Guest Starring: Mitchell Ryan (Kyle Riker), Colm Meaney (Chief O'Brien), Lance Spellerberg (Ensign Herbert)

Riker is offered his own command, and the news is delivered by his estranged father, Kyle, a legend in the annals of Starfleet. Meanwhile, Worf begins acting strangely and must undergo the Klingon Age of Ascension. Both Riker and Worf achieve a personal catharsis with the first officer battling his father in a match of ambu-jetsu in the ship's gym, and the Klingon, accompanied by his human friends, in a recreation of the ritual aboard the ship's holodeck.

••••

"It was an emotional piece, a character piece between two people," points out director Robert Iscove. "The father has deserted Riker for 25 years, then he comes back and they have this confrontation. Well, according to Roddenberry, by the 24th Century we've all kind of resolved those feelings of anger. So it's very hard to play. If you're not going to serve the resentment and the anger, what happens once the two of them get together, you can't get into any real human drama. I did it because I'm a Trekkie and wanted to be involved. The original series was much more humanistic in its approach.

"The future *isn't* perfect," he adds. "But every time you push against it, the immediate people—Berman and all of them—agree with you, but then it goes to Roddenberry, the ultimate voice, who says you can't do that. I was supposed to do some more of them, but I said, 'Thank you very much, but I can't.' There's just no place to go with it. If you can't deal with the emotion, what's the point?"

Casting note: Action fans will recognize guest star Mitchell Ryan as the villain in Richard Donner's *Lethal Weapon*.

Episode #41:
"Pen Pals"
Original Airdate: 4/29/89
Written by Melinda Snodgrass
Story by Hannah Louise Shearer
Directed by Winrich Kolbe
Guest Starring: Nicholas Cascone (Davies), Nikki Cox (Sarjenka), Ann H. Gillespie (Hildebrant), Colm Meaney (Chief O'Brien), Whitney Rydbeck (Alans)
Data receives a distress call from an alien girl on a planet in the throes of geographic turmoil, and

responds to her communique, thus violating the Prime Directive. Wesley, given his first command, in this case of a geographic survey team devoted to study the phenomena, must face the dilemma of whether to save the planet and restore its tectonic balance, or allow it to be destroyed.

••••

"In 'Pen Pals,'" says Melinda Snodgrass, "you can picture Data becoming entranced in answering [the] question, 'Is there anyone out there?' First, he's an android and if you ask him a question, you're going to get an answer. Secondly, the whole thing would be so charmingly intriguing to him, that he would do it. We kicked around who else to put in the role of the person communicating with the child and, finally, I said Data was the only one and everyone agreed with me. You never could picture any of the other characters doing that, but Data can make the mistake, and I don't mean that in a pejorative sense, and step out of his careful Starfleet training because he's really just growing up. He's more of a child than Wesley."

According to producer David Livingston, "Pen Pals" represented one of the first times that the series utilized a second unit to shoot ancillary footage for an episode. "We got to the point where we were going to do the walls disappearing," he recalls. "The midnight hour was rapidly approaching and I went up to Rob Legato and said, 'This is crazy, we can't do this.' He said, 'Right, let's do it second unit,' and I went up to [director Winrich] Kolbe and said, 'We're going to do this second unit,' and he said, 'Great.' That all became second unit, otherwise we'd still be shooting that episode."

Notes Maurice Hurley, "My second favorite premise, the first being 'The Last Outpost.' Somebody's out there, some little kid on some little planet sending out a CQ. Just like I did in my bedroom when I was ten years old with my little crystal sets, sending out CQs and never getting it back. But here somebody says, 'Anybody out there?' and a voice replies, 'Yes.' Wait a minute! Then the rest of it kind of got muddled around, mucked up and lost its purity, although it worked okay."

"An intriguing episode, though I'm not quite sure I did it justice," con-

cedes director Winrich Kolbe. "Something goes through my mind when I look at 'Pen Pals.' It seems to me that there was another script floating around then it got changed during the production, and I don't think it got changed for the better. It was one of those situations where I said, 'Come on, guys, let's push the damn thing. The relationship between this little girl and Data is something you want to explore. Data is a machine, how far can he go before he becomes a threat either to himself or the little girl or somebody else?' I don't think it ever came through and I don't consider it one of my better shows. I think we all did a damn good job, but it could have been better."

Episode #42:
"Q Who?"
Original Airdate: 5/6/89
Written by Maurice Hurley
Directed by Rob Bowman
Guest Starring: John de Lancie (Q), Lycia Naff (Ensign Sonya Gomez), Colm Meaney (Chief O'Brien), Whoopi Goldberg (Guinan)
Q returns, commandeering Picard in a shuttlecraft. Warning the captain of human complacency, the omnipotent superbeing transports the ship to the deepest recesses of the galaxy. There they encounter the unstoppable, cybernetic super race known as the Borg, who slowly begin to disassemble the vessel with their superior technology. Unable to defeat the collective race of hive creatures, Picard reluctantly tells Q that he's learned his lesson and asks him to transport the ship back home before it's obliterated.

••••

"It was thought we needed some kind of new threat, with the Klingons uncomfortable allies, that we could take seriously," says Melinda Snodgrass. "The Borg are in many ways Maurice Hurley's. It was his script and he was coping with creating this new villain. We kicked around a lot of different ideas and I realized that what we were really kind of describing was cyberpunk, so I talked a bit about that movement in science fiction, the idea of augmenting humanity. We felt we wanted to come up with a villain you just couldn't reason with."

••••

Maurice Hurley offers, "A good one. It was an attempt to create some new jeopardy, a new villain. You have to have an adversary that's worthy, so you made it impossible to defeat them. What we really wanted to do, but couldn't because of money, was insects. Insect mentality is great, because it is relentless. The Borg are a variation of an insect mentality. They don't care. They have no mercy, no feelings towards you. They have their own agenda and that's it. If all of them die getting   there, they don't care. If you want some bad assess, there you go!"

Offers Rob Bowman, "The avant garde tone I think we understood very well. We communicated a great deal. I think Maury knew better than anybody what we should do. The working relationships were essential. It was a very unusual show. We didn't know day to day if we were making a stinker or a winner. It was just too weird. When I saw the final answer print with the effects and the music, I thought, 'Wow, Maurice was right. It really is disturbing.' I don't know how he got it past Roddenberry. Maury was adamant about this. He championed this thing through with a fervor which couldn't be stopped and he was, basically, like a bull in a ring. Everybody got out of his way and a lot of people thought he was dead wrong. There were some angry arguments about this show. It was an incredibly difficult episode. Patrick even got a little bit hostile that the rest of us were not taking it seriously enough, we were a little bit too jokester and he was right.

"We wanted to make a great episode. The script was very unusual and the Borg were, we thought, really quite threatening and we wanted to get that across; the production value that was in the script. But time is always something you don't have enough of in television. The post production on that show is really what saves it. The matte shots, the stuff in engineering....we were able to do a pan with the phaser where Worf hits the guy and knocks it back. What we did in that shot, which has never been done before, is that we actually panned with the shot. They pulled it off and it looked great. I think that was a very abstract, almost avant garde episode with Q and

whatever the hell he was trying to prove with the Enterprise, telling Picard to be aware because there are some bad asses out there that you're not prepared for no matter what you think. This is just a lesson to you to keep your eyes and ears open, because there are things out there that you don't understand, and here's an example. For television, it's big stuff. But in order to make it big stuff, it's a lot of investment by everybody."

Episode #43:
"Samaritan Snare"
Original Airdate: 5/13/89
Written by Robert McCullough
Directed by Les Landau
Guest Starring: Christopher Collins (Grebnedlog), Leslie Morris (Reginod), Daniel Benzali (Surgeon), Lycia Naff (Sonya Gomez), Tzi Ma (Biomolecular Specialist)

The Pakleds, an apparently dim-witted race of beings, recruit Geordi's help to fix their malfunctioning drive unit and threaten him with violence unless he stays aboard to assist them with their technological incompetence. At the same time, Picard is escorted by Wesley via shuttle for a life-saving heart transplant. Enroute, he recounts his formative years, much to Mr. Crusher's great joy.

• • • •

"Very strange but nice," Maurice Hurley muses. "That was very different. It gave Geordi a nice turn, and the more you use LeVar, the happier the show will be, because LeVar is wonderful to work with."

Says Les Landau, "I dealt with a race of what appeared to be ugly and slow people. They have a need for things, which can be a reflection of our society. That's what *Star Trek* tries to do, take an almost unbelievable situation in an unbelievable time and somehow make all of us realize that's what's happening today, and what we can do to make the planet and the universe a better place. I think that is the essence of *Star Trek* and the tradition Roddenberry is trying to carry on."

Ironically, "Samaritan Snare" served as the impetus for writers Dennis Putnam Bailey, Lisa Wilke and David Bischoff to write third season's "Tin Man."

"The point at which we became

serious about trying to write a script for the show was about five minutes after watching 'Samaritan Snare,' which in my personal opinion was the most abysmal piece of *Star Trek* ever filmed," says Bailey. "My objections to it were that it always resorted to idiot plotting to make the story work, and that offended me a great deal worse than some of the awful shows which were done on the original series. I thought the way in which it was plotted and the way it was dealt with was an insult to the intelligence of the people who watched the show and the actors and characters in the show. None of the plot could have happened if all of the characters hadn't suddenly become morons that week.

"Someone must have been aware of how hokey it was, because they wrote obvious questions into the script which they chose not to answer," Bailey continues. "For instance, before Geordi beams over, Worf says explicitly to Riker, 'Do we have to send them our chief engineer because they have a little problem?' and it's never answered. If you don't want to answer it, don't bring it up. Another thing that is stupid is Deanna Troi comes on the bridge and says to Riker, 'I don't sense fear or confusion. Geordi is in danger. Bring him back,' and no one even responds to that. They simply act as if it wasn't said. On the trip over to the starbase, where Picard and Wesley have this long heart to heart talk, Wesley says why would anyone use a defective heart transplant. That's a minor point. A major piece of stupidity is they send him to a medical facility where it turned out that no one was qualified to handle the operation if it went at all wrong. I can't believe they expect viewers to be so stupid as to not ask about that. The fact that the routine was repeatedly said, throughout the show, to be an absolutely routine procedure and when it went wrong, it went wrong for no reason that was mentioned, except that it had to go wrong to have the climax. Then it turns out they have to call the Enterprise to bring Pulaski over to do the operation because she's more qualified and the people there weren't."

Casting note: Lycia Naff (the three-breasted mutant woman from *Total Recall*), returns as the bumbling ensign Sonya Gomez she first portrayed in "Q Who?"

• • • •

Episode #44:
"Up the Long Ladder"
Original Airdate: 5/20/89
Written by Melinda Snodgrass
Directed by Winrich Kolbe
Guest Starring: Barrie Ingham (Danilo O'Dell), Jon de Vries (Granger), Rasalyn Landor (Brenna O'Dell), Colm Meaney (Chief O'Brien)

Originally entitled "Send in the Clones" ("They didn't have the guts to stick with that title," says actor Jonathan Frakes), "Up the Long Ladder" has the Enterprise serve as a rescue ship transporting a primitive rural farming community away from their doomed planet, along with an advanced race of clones. The clones, realizing they are nearing their extinction due to the lack of sufficient genetically replicable material, plan to copy the DNA of Pulaski and Riker in hopes of restoring the race, this in spite of the duo's objections.

••••

"It was intended to be a commentary about immigration, because I hate the current American policy," says Melinda Snodgrass. "I wanted it to be something that says sometimes those outsiders you think are so smelly and wrong-colored, can bring enormous benefits to your society because they bring life and energy. That's what I was going for. Now my boss, at the time, was Maury Hurley, who is a major Irishman and leads the Saint Patrick Day's parade. When I was describing to him what I wanted to do, I was trying to come up with an analogy, and I said it was like a little village of Irish tinkerers, and he loved it so much he made me make them Irish tinkerers. I said okay, and that's how it came about.

"It is ironic, because I got enormous flack from the right to life coalition because they destroyed the clones," elaborates Snodgrass. "They thought I was condoning abortion. In fact, I did put a line in Riker's mouth that was very pro-choice and the right to life coalition went crazy. He says I told you that you can't clone me and you did it against my will, and I have the right to have control over my own body. That's my feeling and it was my soapbox, and it was one I got to get on. I was supported by Maurice all the way."

Episode #45:
"Manhunt"
Original Airdate: 6/17/89
Written by Terry Devereaux (Tracy Torme)
Directed by Rob Bowman
Guest Starring: Majel Barrett (Lwaxana Troi), Robert Costanzo (Slade Bender), Mick Fleetwood (Antedian Dignitary), Carel Struycken (Mr. Homn), Rod Arrants (Rox), Colm Meaney (Chief O'Brien), Rhonda Aldrich (Madeline), Robert O'Reilly (Thug), Wren T. Brown (Transport Pilot)

A sequel to "Haven" and "The Big Goodbye," in which a horny Ms. Troi (Majel Barrett) is on the prowl for a mate. She attempts to seduce Picard, who takes haven (no pun intended) in the holodeck as Dixon Hill to hide   from her amorous advances. Also aboard are a band of alien delegates bent on sabotaging an upcoming diplomatic conference.

••••

As was the case with "The Royale," Tracy Torme was so disenchanted with the rewrite to "Manhunt" that he took his name off the script.

"The original concept was that it was a sequel to two of my shows from the first season. Two sequels in one," he smiles. "They had been talking to me for a long time about bringing Mrs. Troi back. Since 'Haven' wasn't one of my favorite episodes, I thought maybe somebody else could do a better job with the character, even though I had basically created it. Then I started thinking about it and realized that there was another element from another one of my shows that would fit in nicely, and it would be kind of fun to do two sequels in the one show. That really appealed to me, and Gene was very supportive.

"The problem is that some of the best writing I did on that show was for 'Manhunt' in the Dixon Hill segment," Torme continues. "I was determined to make different than 'The Big Goodbye' and to have part of the show on the holodeck where nothing goes wrong, nothing malfunctions. I love Raymond Chandler and I love *film noir*, so I wrote all of these very cynical, typical Chandleresque voiceovers for Picard to use and I had him program a specific Dixon Hill book, *The Long Dark Tunnel*.

Majel Barrett, perhaps best know as Lwaxana Troi, the Auntie Mame of the Galaxy, often entertains fans at conventions. (Photo copyright © Karen Witkowski)

The first one was based on *The Maltese Falcon*, this was *Farewell My Lovely* and a little bit of *Little Sister*. The Dixon Hill rewrite was as bad as 'The Royale.' I turned green when I saw it. They got on this kick where Picard kept saying it was based on this book he just read. He kept saying, 'That didn't happen in the book I read.' Not only was it like *Battlestar: Galactica*, but it was like 'The Royale,' where they had [said] everything was from a book. I was desperate, I went to Gene. It really got to me. 'The Royale' I just shrugged off, but they were just mutilating 'Manhunt' and, once again, I thought maybe with Gene stepping in he could save it. But he was out of the picture and everything would have to go through Maury [Hurley] and he didn't want to hear it. The Dixon Hill stuff was a complete turkey. The Troi stuff worked okay. I took my name off because I didn't want people thinking I wrote that."

"Ah, yes, the return of Dixon Hill," remembers Rob Bowman. "This one was to be Majel's episode, and she's a fascinating woman. I was asked to make sure that she does her best, so everyday that's what we worked on. There's really no story tie between her want, which is a mate, and Picard going to Dixon Hill. It was just a way for us to get to the old stuff. There's no

••••

reason for him to particularly go there. We had a great time doing the '40s stuff. I'd looked forward to that since 'The Big Goodbye.' It was a little disconnected, there was no reason for the *film noir*, but it was entertaining. I think I didn't have enough pace in the show, it was a little boring for me, but that may have just been the tone of the show. Torme had warned me ahead of time and said this is what's going to happen and it did. They changed it a great deal to accommodate Majel and sacrificed what Tracy and I thought were some of the *noir* nuances to the show. The emphasis was shifted from the *noir* to Majel. This is the boss' wife and she only does it once a year, so it should be accommodating for her and that's what you did. "

Episode #46:
"The Emissary"
Original Airdate: 6/24/89
Written by Richard Manning and Hans Beimler
Based on Unpublished Story by Thomas H. Calder
Directed by Cliff Bole
Guest Starring: Suzie Plakson (K'Ehleyr), Lance LeGault (K'Temoc), Georgann Johnson (Admiral Gromek), Colm Meaney (Chief O'Brien), Anne Elizabeth Ramsey (Ensign Clancy), Dietrich Bader (Tactical Crewman)

A ship full of Klingons is being released from cryogenic freeze, believing that the Empire is still at war with the Federation. Only the Enterprise is within interception range of the ship, which will be in position to attack a system of Federation colonies if it is not stopped. A Klingon ambassador, K'Ehleyr (Suzi Plakson), the half-human/half-Klingon former lover of Worf, is shuttled aboard the ship to assist in a peaceful awakening of the Klingons in hopes of persuading the ship to return home without incident.

••••

Of "The Emissary," Maurice Hurley says, "Great idea and one that worked. Hard for that one not to work, but it worked well all the way through. With the Klingons you're dealing with emotion and passion. You've got somebody who can say something. You need that balance in the show sometimes. The show gets so intellectually smug and self-serving, and you need something like that to break it off; someone

willing to storm the barricades. The idea of the half-Klingon was fun."

Notes director Cliff Bole, "I liked the show and thought Michael Dorn did a real good job in it. I think I let [Suzi Plakson] get overboard a little bit. She was a little too broad, but she's a talented lady. I think the Klingon shows are fun to do, because you can go a little broad with them. Who the hell knows what a Klingon is anyway? Who knows how Klingons make love? In 'The Emissary' I came up with that thing where she digs into his hand and there's all that blood. I did that on the set. I was wondering what these people do, and I had the image of bones breaking and felt that's what they do when they get it on."

K'Ehleyr was played by Suzi Plakson, who had made an impression as the Vulcan Dr. Selar in Tracy Torme's "The Schizoid Man." Torme had wanted to develop a romance between Selar and Worf, an idea that was nixed by the producers because "The Emissary" was being planned. But Torme decried the show's premise as "obvious. Had it been a Vulcan, it would have been a lot more interesting."

Episode #47:
"Peak Performance"
Original Airdate: 7/8/89
Written by David Kemper
Directed by Robert Scheerer
Guest Starring: Roy Brocksmith (Sirna Kolrami), Armin Shimerman (Bractor), David L. Landers (Tactician), Leslie Neale (Ensign Nagel), Glenn Morshower (Ensign Burke)

As a result of his confrontation with the Borg, Picard consents to a war games drill in which Riker takes command of a Starfleet frigate. Riker makes use of a team of ancillary officers, including Worf and Wesley, to fend off the Enterprise in mock combat. During the engagement—which is being overseen by a master tactics strategist—the ship, with its weapon systems deactivated for the drill, is attacked by the Ferengi.

••••

"I loved that script," says Melinda Snodgrass. "When I came in, I thought it was a wonderful vehicle for Jonathan [Frakes] and I had a lot of fun doing the rewrite. I really enjoyed writing action, but we had a hard time selling it, because it costs a lot of money to have spaceships fight."

Notes Maurice Hurley, "A good idea that worked. The war games were fun, and the characters were good."

"A fun episode," says director Robert Scheerer. "And I love [guest star Roy] Brocksmith. He is just a wonderful comedic actor. I've used him two or three times on other shows."

Episode #48:
"Shades of Gray"
Original Airdate: 7/15/89
Written by Maurice Hurley, Hans Beimler & Richard Manning
Directed by Rob Bowman
Guest Starring: Colm Meaney (Chief O'Brien)

On an Away Team mission, Riker is disabled by a deadly virus and is put into stasis while Pulaski attempts to combat the disease before it kills him. In order to fight its spread, Riker must relive memories of previous missions, which segues into a series of clips from the first two seasons.

••••

"Piece of shit," states Maurice Hurley, who co-wrote the episode. "It was supposed to be a bottle show. Terrible, just terrible, and a way to save some money. I was on the way out the door. I wrote it, and Beimler and Manning did the rewrite."

Director Rob Bowman shares the consensus. "All we shot was three days of framework and they just stuck in flashback, and the only reason they do it is to save money. That's what it was about and all we did. I never saw a final cut. All I can say about the show is I shot it in three days...and it was a nice set. I told them it was going to take five days of shooting, not three, so they tried to pare it down. When they asked, 'How can you do it in three?', I said, 'We can't change sets. If you want to get a maximum amount of filming done in three days, you can't move me all over the ship. Let's just stay in sickbay. I remember spending at least two full days in sickbay. I tried to be as interesting as I possibly could be with the camera, so it didn't seem like we just stold their money. It was Paramount saying, 'We gave you more money for 'Elementary, Dear Data' and for the Borg show. Now do us a favor and give us a three-day show.' So that's what you do. It's an accepted part of the medium."

••••

CHAPTER TWENTY
SEASON THREE

An Introduction

Third season is widely considered the best season of *Star Trek: The Next Generation* ever produced, and signaled a dramatic change from the policies and dramatic tone of the first two seasons.

When Hurley announced he was leaving the show, Rick Berman brought aboard a science-fiction veteran, Michael Wagner, who had headed the writing staff on the short lived ABC series *Probe*. Wagner came aboard in hopes of charting a new, smoother course. But soon after joining the staff as an executive producer, he was off the show.

"I just don't think it was his [Wagner's] cup of tea as far as the way the show worked," opines director Cliff Bole, "and the way Rick and everybody knows the show so well that they all rely on each other. Input even comes in from the technical guys, who seem to have almost been in space. I just don't think it was the way he'd been operating in other places."

Wagner, who had toiled on the final frontier for only three weeks before departing, was replaced by Michael Piller, a former journalist, TV executive and censor who had worked briefly with Wagner on *Probe*, and who had also contributed to *Miami Vice*. Fresh from a four-year-stint on *Simon & Simon*, Piller arrived already a fan of *TNG*, and embraced the idea of reinvigorating the sputtering starship. It was Piller's conviction, in fact, that *TNG* already ranked as one of the best shows on television, comparing favorably with such critical darlings as *thirtysomething*, *Wiseguy* and even *L.A. Law*.

The classic *Star Trek* had not survived its third season. And Piller understood that its successor would have to last at least four for it to be profitably stripped in syndication. The writer/producer was therefore anxious to put his own imprimatur on the show.

Helped by old *Trek* hands Hans Beimler and Richard Manning, who had worked on the show first season but had left over creative altercations with Hurley; and by Melinda Snodgrass, who had been honored with a Writer's Guild nomination for her "Measure of the Man" script, Piller began to craft some of the series' finest episodes.

With Hurley's exit, Berman also involved himself more with the writing, bringing Piller under his administrative and creative aegis. Unlike his predecessors, however, *Trek*'s new Caesar asserted his authority subtly, at first ordering costume changes and replacing several production crew-members. Berman was seeking a new and more distinct look. Piller, meanwhile, complemented Berman with his keen eye for strong spec material and although the two didn't always agree, they worked synergistically and continued to boldly take *Star Trek* where it had never been before.

The two producers inevitably directed their attentions to casting. Berman lured Gates McFadden back to reprise her role as Dr. Beverly Crusher, citing Muldaur's "lack of chemistry" with the rest of the cast. The fifty-something actress Muldaur soon found a role more suited for her personality on NBC's *L.A. Law*, where she was cast as the scheming and acerbic Rosalind Shayes.

Although under Piller and Berman *Trek*'s ratings improved, harmony did not always prevail behind the scenes, as the revolving door continued to swing. Story editor Richard Danus barely lasted a month and Trekkies Beimler, Manning and Snodgrass, responsible for some of third seasons' most distinguished episodes, quickly found themselves at odds with Piller, who had his own ideas about running a starship. By the end of the season, all were gone.

The performers, too, began to entertain notions about how to conduct business. Patrick Stewart, for instance, was unhappy with his role. On the original series, William Shatner had asserted the predominance of his character, excluding his supporting cast from most seminal dramatic scenes and episodes, but Stewart simply wanted a "piece of the action", pointing out that Riker and Data seemed to be receiving the most

Mark Lenard's portrayal of Sarek has spanned Star Trek's original series, animated spin-offs, film sequels and The Next Generation. (Photo copyright © Karen Witkowski)

attention. Distressed, Stewart felt Picard talked too much, he complained, but when anything happened, he was invariably left on the bridge while his subordinates got the call to action. "Watching Picard is like "visiting a social worker," concurred right-wing science fiction writer Ben Bova.

By mid-season, the new show was sufficiently secure with its place in the *Star Trek* pantheon to reintroduce Sarek (Mark Leonard), Spock's father from the original show and feature films. However, scandal erupted when guest star Michael Rappaport attempted suicide on the third day of shooting an episode, "The Most Toys" (He would successfully kill himself in a second suicide attempt several weeks later) which was hastily recast, forcing actor Saul Rubinek to step in to replace the actor.

The mood on the set had turned dour, and would infect the tired and weary cast for the rest of the season. Cast and crew were burned out by the prolonged shooting schedule necessitated by the Writers Guild Strike and anxious for summer hiatus.

"I've done television for 11 years and there is no show more difficult that I've ever been involved with than *Star Trek* on a number of levels," says third season writer/producer Ira Steven

••••

Behr, now co-executive producer of *Deep Space Nine*. "It's just difficult because you're not just trying to tell a story that could work or not work, you're trying to tell a story that works within very special, limited parameters. The only thing I can compare an episode of *Star Trek* to is another episode of *Star Trek*," says Behr. "The rules are so clear and it's such a unique kind of thing that in the third season of *The Next Generation* I would come up with ideas that I would think would be really good and work that other people would say you can't do. Every writer whose ever had an ax to grind, and there are definitely axes to grind, has complained about that, but having been through that fire, that ordeal, I'm not quite at that same place."

Behr had first been approached by Maurice Hurley second season when he was working at Paramount on the NBC series *The Bronx Zoo*, but rebuffed his overtures to join the series when he went out to lunch with the former *Trek* producer. "He told me what it would entail to work on the show and I said 'goodbye, thank you'," notes Behr. "It was just very different than I was used to doing on series television."

Behr was eventually persuaded by Michael Piller to join the writing staff during the series' third season and left at the end of his first year after penning "Captain's Holiday" and "The Vengeance Factor" and contributing to numerous other rewrites.

"When I left *Next Generation* they had offered me a two year deal for the fourth and fifth season which, after going back and forth on, I decided not to take," recalls Behr. "The third season was such a demented time. It was so difficult for everyone involved, including Michael, to get it all together. The show had fallen way behind because of the things that happened in the beginning of the season and it was a long and unpleasant season. It was a time that the pressures of doing television were getting to everyone and they aren't a lot of fun to begin with. On the third season on this show it got ugly. I'm just talking about the pressures and I think we all reacted in ways that did not show anyone at their best. That's totally understandable and if it happened all over again, I'm sure no one would act any better. It was just a very difficult situation."

Tempers were not improved when in a lackluster third season episode co-written by Roddenberry's long-time secretary, Susan Sackett, the press latched onto a scene in which an ostensibly naked Troi and her mother are stripped naked by the Ferengi according to their custom. In fact, actresses Sirtis and Roddenberry's wife, Majel Barrett, donned body stockings throughout.

By season's end, Piller, too, contemplated departing. Berman and Roddenberry persuaded him to stay on. The reinvigorated writer/producer contributed a season-ending cliffhanger, a critical and ratings smash in which he injected some of his own personal dilemmas about whether to leave the show or remain onboard. In this script, "The Best of Both Worlds," he used Riker as his fictional surrogate and shattered traditional *Trek* rules by employing extensive special effects and vicious character conflict.

By now, TNG was boldly on its way to where *Star Trek* had never gone before — a fourth season. It was already being stripped in many markets, delivering ample doses of *Trek* to *Trek*-hungry fans hitherto satiated only by reruns and infrequent feature films.

••••

CHAPTER TWENTYONE
SEASON THREE

Episode Guide

"Evolution"

"The Ensigns of Command"

"The Survivors"

"Who Watches the Watchers?"

"The Bonding"

"Booby Trap"

"The Enemy"

"The Price"

"The Vengeance Factor"

"The Defector"

"The Hunted"

"The High Ground"

"Deja Q"

"A Matter of Perspective"

"Yesterday's Enterprise"

"The Offspring"

"Sins of the Father"

"Allegiance"

"Captain's Holiday"

"Tin Man"

"Hollow Pursuits"

"The Most Toys"

"Sarek"

"Menage a Troi"

"Transfigurations"

"The Best of Both Worlds, Part I"

••••

Episode #49:
"Evolution"
Original Airdate: 9/23/89
Written by Michael Piller
Story by Michael Piller and
Michael Wagner
Directed by Winrich Kolbe
Guest Starring: Ken Jenkins (Dr. Paul Stubbs), Mary McCusker (Nurse), Randal Patrick (Crewman #1), Whoopi Goldberg (Guinan)

A science experiment of Wesley's goes awry when he accidentally releases intelligent micro-organisms, "nannites," into the ship's computer system. This accident jeopardizes the success of an important scientific mission under the auspices of Dr. Paul Stubbs (Ken Jenkins), an obsessed scientist who will stop at nothing to proceed with his career-saving experiment.

••••

Coming aboard to replace short-lived producer Michael Wagner was Michael Piller. Also beaming back aboard was Gates McFadden, who returned as Dr. Beverly Crusher after a brief hiatus. Departing was Diana Muldaur, who had not proved as appealing to fans of the show, but would soon go on to tremendous success as Rosalind Shayes in the once critically acclaimed NBC drama, *L.A. Laws.*

Of the episode, Piller explains, "I felt it was a real opportunity for some character growth for Wesley. I wasn't quite sure what that was when I started writing; I didn't know how everything quite fit together. I had this story about nannites. Once I got to know the scientist and realized who he was, I realized that the scientist is Wesley in forty years if he stays on the course of being the smart kid who is dedicated to his work and seems not to have much else going on in his life. I said, 'If I use that relationship to get it down to a more human level, I can help Wesley grow. I can help Wesley move into a relationship with a girlfriend.' There were ten minutes of romance between he and the little girl on the Enterprise that got cut out because the show was too long. But at the end, you saw him sitting down with her and the mother saying, 'That's what he ought to be doing.' That became the key ele-

ment to Beverly's re-entry into the series, which was, 'My son is not having a normal childhood.' We know a lot of kids like that. I saw that and had a sense that was needed.

"[Overall] I felt it was a B-episode. I thought it worked okay, but I didn't have an ending for it and neither did Mike [Wagner]. There are some character scenes I'm very proud of. I didn't dislike it. I was proud of the episode, but I thought it didn't quite come off."

States director Winrich Kolbe, "I didn't think that much of the show. It was basically Wesley Crusher's episode and that was intriguing in a way. But maybe I should just resign myself to the fact that in 44 minutes there are many interesting stories which cannot be told. I liked the fact that we had a scientist who tried to push an issue and then suddenly found out that there are ramifications he hadn't thought of, which is the lack of control of the nannites. So there was a certain amount of immaturity, cockiness or whatever. I liked that, but maybe due to the fact that it was Wesley and everyone considered it a child's show, even the writers, the issue wasn't dealt with properly. It's a very serious issue.

"Recently I was in Georgia," he continues, "and you can't avoid seeing the kudzu, a vine which was brought in from Japan for a variety of reasons. It's a very fast growing vine and it was supposed to be great for holding down enbankments. The only thing they didn't consider was that that vine in the more humid, warm climate of Georgia is taking off and devouring tracks of woodland. You can actually see it grow. We put a mark down where I wanted to put the camera and a day later we came in there and the mark was gone. Now that is something where somebody said, 'This would be very good.' The DNA cloning going on right now. Those are things that are the responsibility of the scientists that are very important. I think by making it a mother/son show and putting that element in there, that particular element of scientific responsibility got lost."

Episode #50:
"Ensigns of Command"
Original Airdate: 9/30/89
Written by Melinda Snodgrass

Directed by Cliff Bole
Guest Starring: Eileen Seeley (Ard'rian Mackenzie), Mark L. Taylor (Haritath), Richard Allen (Noe), Colm Meaney (Chief O'Brien), Mart McChesney (Sheliak)

Data is given his first command responsibility on a planet whose human colonists are in danger. The Sheliak, a violent alien race which stringently adheres to legal precedent, plans to colonize the world, which legally belongs to them. When the population refuses to evacuate, Data must improvise in order to persuade the populace to leave before the Sheliak reach the planet and destroy the colony. Aboard the Enterprise, Picard attempts to find a loophole in the Federation's treaty with the Sheliak to stall the attack.

••••

"I wish you could have seen my version," says Melinda Snodgrass. "I wanted to take Data one step further in his development as a human being. I wanted to stress him and have him face a situation where logic isn't enough, to show that in order to command you have to have charisma. You have to learn how to wave your dick and hope your dick is bigger than the other guy's."

Notes Cliff Bole, "That was one of those shows where we started off with these illusions of grandeur, and at the last minute we had to cut $200,000 out of it. It's the budget crunch."

Episode #51:
"The Survivors"
Original Airdate: 10/7/89
Written by Michael Wagner
Directed by Les Landau
Guest Starring: John Anderson (Kevin Uxbridge), Anne Haney (Rishan Uxbridge)

When the Enterprise finds only two survivors of an alien attack which destroyed the entire population of Rana 4, they are suspicious of the story told by Devin Uxbridge (John Anderson). Uxbridge maintains that he and his wife were the only ones to survive the raid, and that they are safe and should be left alone. Ultimately, Picard discovers that this seeming pacifist is actually a powerful shape-changing alien entity who assumed human guise to marry an earthling, and when she was killed by the invaders, he destroyed their attackers' entire species across the universe.

••••

"We were on location for a day," recalls Les Landau. "It made not only the audience but the crew happy. When you're tied to shooting indoors every day, it gets monotonous. We were lucky enough to go out to Malibu and we had a beautiful summer day. I think it was a unique story for *Star Trek* and one of my best works to date."

The episode was written by Michael Wagner, who warped out of the *Star Trek* offices as quickly as he warped in as executive producer, only to be replaced by Michael Piller.

Director Cliff Bole, who has helmed numerous *Next Generation* episodes, opines, "I just don't think it was his [Wagner's] cup of tea as far as the way the show worked, and the way Rick and everybody knows the show so well that they all rely on each other. Input even comes in from the technical guys, who have almost been in space. I just don't think it was the way he'd been operating in other places."

Episode #52:
"Who Watches the Watchers?"
Original Airdate: 10/14/89
Written by Richard Manning and Hans Beimler
Directed by Robert Wiemer
Guest Starring: Kathryn Leigh Scott (Nuria), Ray Wise (Liko), James Greene (Dr. Barron), John McLiam (Fento), Pamela Seagall (Oji), James McIntyre (Hali), Lois Hall (Dr. Warren)

When the Enterprise leads a rescue team to a Starfleet outpost that is studying a primitive culture, they inadvertently allow the atheist race a glimpse of their futuristic technology and are mistaken for gods. Wary of violating the Prime Directive, but needing to rescue a wounded Federation officer, Troi and Riker beam down in native garb. Although Riker escapes with the lost member of the science team, Troi is captured by the Nantokans, who have adapted Picard as their god.

••••

"We did *Henry VIII* in New York," says Jonathan Frakes of co-star Ray Wise (Liko), who is probably best known as psycho-daddy Leland Palmer

on *Twin Peaks*. "We went out to Vasquez Rocks where they used to shoot some of the old shows. Everybody feels better when we go out on location, even if it's only a day."

Casting note: Kathryn Leigh Scott portrayed Maggie Evans, the love of vampire Barnabas Collins in the horror soap opera, *Dark Shadows*.

Episode #53:
"The Bonding"
Original Airdate: 10/21/89
Written by Ronald D. Moore
Directed by Winrich Kolbe
Guest Starring: Susan Powell (Lieutenant Marla Aster), Gabriel Damon (Jeremy Aster), Colm Meaney (Chief O'Brien)

A shipboard story of a boy, Jeremy Aster (*Robocop II*'s Gabriel Damon), who must cope with the death of his mother, Marla (Susan Powell), who died while on an Away Team mission. Worf feels compelled to play surrogate father, since he led that mission, but everyone is shocked to find Marla alive and well aboard the ship. The crew learns that she is a re-creation, transported there by the guilt-ridden alien race which was responsible for the officer's death.

••••

Recalls Michael Piller, "I came in without any shows to shoot. There were no stories and no scripts in the works, which is the greatest nightmare you can imagine. There's nothing to fall back on and the appetite of any weekly show is voracious, because as soon as you've got a script done you have to have another one right behind it and it continues that way. I went through every scrap of paper to see what was here from past administrations that I could develop. The first thing that came to my attention, the first thing I saw that had any value, was a speculative script that had been sitting around called 'The Bonding.' It appealed to me enormously. It needed a little work and hadn't tied the alien story into the other story quite right. But I like that show a lot and am very proud of it. I think it struck the heart of *Star Trek*, exploring the human condition. This was a marvelous example of that."

Writer Ron Moore notes that the biggest change in his script was that when the boy first learns his mother had

Kathryn Leigh Scott, seen here as Maggie Evans on Dark Shadows, believed Picard to be a god in "Who Watches The Watchers?"

been killed, he recreates her on the holodeck. "The thing I was playing with is what are the dangers of the holodeck," says Moore. "A kid goes in and recreates his dead mother. What do you do in that situation? They felt that they didn't want to do another holodeck show at that point, that it moved the focus away from the aliens. What sparked the idea was that we have this shipload of a thousand people, and this time they've brought their families. It never seems the series has dealt head-on with some of the questions a family ship would inevitably bring up. I wanted to write a story about what happens when someone's mother dies, and what happens to that kid and our family on board the ship. That process naturally led to Worf, because he's an orphan as well."

"Interesting show," says Winrich Kolbe. "I'm a little bit ambiguous about the little boy who I used to call Clark Gable, Jr. because of his ears. Again, it was a cute episode and a good one for Michael, but again it's not something that intrigued me that much. It's just not as strong as some of the others."

Episode #54:
"Booby Trap"
Original Airdate: 10/28/89
Written by Ron Roman, Michael Piller

••••

and Richard Danus
Directed by Gabrielle Beaumont
Guest Starring: Susan Gibney (Dr. Leah Brahms), Colm Meaney (Chief O'Brien), Albert Hall (Galek Dar), Julie Warner (Christy), Whoopi Goldberg (Guinan)

When the Enterprise is trapped in a futuristic minefield which rapidly drains the ship's power, LaForge must devise a means to escape. He enlists the holographic aid of the ship's designer, Dr. Leah Brahms (Susan Gibney), by recreating her and the Enterprise design labs so that they can devise a means to navigate the ship to safety.

••••

"When we got the first draft of 'Booby Trap,' it was Picard talking to some woman in the back of the Enterprise, helping him to solve a problem," says Michael Piller. "It just said to me, 'Picard should be on the bridge, not chatting with some woman.' I said to myself, 'It should be Geordi, because Geordi is in love with the ship and this is a story about a guy in love with his '57 Chevy.' That played into Geordi's character, who's always been a fumbling guy around women, but if he could just marry his car, he'd live happily ever after. He gets to create the personification of the woman who created the engine he loves. It's sort of a relationship between he and his Pontiac."

"*Star Trek: The Next Generation* is what it is," says *Deep Space Nine* producer and *Next Generation* fifth season story editor Peter Alan Fields. "It's a science-fiction show. It doesn't mean illusion or fantasy. I think we need to do shows that you don't see on *thirtysomething* and I think the audience expects things with a science-fiction twist to them that doesn't make them less believable. I think the best kind of science-fiction is rooted in your own life, what can happen now and is a reasonable extension. To do a character story and blend it with science-fiction is that pinnacle we reach for and the one that comes to mind which I thought was a marvelous was 'Booby Trap.' You couldn't have seen it on *thirtysomething*. As science-fiction it worked and it was full of character, full of humanity and full of life."

Episode #55:
"The Enemy"
Original Airdate: 11/4/89
Written by David Kemper and Michael Piller
Directed by David Carson
Guest Starring: John Snyder (Centurion Bochra), Andreas Katsulas (Commander Tomalak), Colm Meaney (Chief O'Brien)

LaForge is lost on an Away Team mission to a hostile planet, where the Enterprise detected a downed Romulan shuttle. While being unable to communicate with the ship, Geordi encounters a wounded Romulan Centurion, Bochra (John Snyder), who takes him prisoner. Meanwhile, in sickbay, Crusher attempts to revive a dying Romulan and is led to Worf, who is the only person on board with the compatible blood type that can save him.

••••

Michael Piller was heavily involved in the rewriting of this episode. "I would say it ended up one of our furthest off scripts, and in a period of about seven days the staff and I turned it into what I think was one of the best shows of the season," he points out. "I would say that 'The Enemy' was about something, it helped Worf's character grow by a foot. When I originally made the suggestion that we let the Romulan die, there was a gasp in the room. Michael Dorn said to me, 'What are you doing to my character?' Of course after he realized what we were doing, and saw the reason for it, he fell in love with the idea. Rick Berman knew instantly it was the right thing to do. Once he was behind me, it was a race to the finish line. And it was absolutely the right thing to do. You knew the audience was waiting for Worf to come around, because they always do in television. But the character wouldn't do that and I think we made a really good decision. At first, though, it was quite a shock and a controversial decision. But you end up talking about survival and survival among enemies. I think it was just a natural character development. The character called for it."

Of his involvement in the episode, Michael Dorn explains, "I called the producers and said I didn't agree. I thought [giving blood] was the honorable thing to do. I thought people would look at

Andreas Katsulas, seen here in Someone to Watch Over Me, *portrayed the Romulan Commander Tomalak on several episodes.*

him [Worf] as a murderer. The producers felt that Worf was getting to be too human...just a guy with a big head. When the opportunity came for them to show that Worf was not human, that he is not bound by the same morals as we are, they felt it was a wonderful opportunity."

Now Dorn realizes they were right. "They had a great reason for doing it and that it made sense. I got into it. I think it's my favorite episode, even though I only have three scenes. It really showed three different sides of Worf. It was an exceptional show for that."

Episode #56:
"The Price"
Original Airdate: 11/11/89
Written by Hannah Louise Shearer
Directed by Robert Scheerer
Guest Starring: Matt McCoy (Devinoni Ral), Elizabeth Hoffman (Premier Bhavani), Castulo Guerra (Mendoza), Scott Thomson (DaiMon Goss), Kevin Peter Hall (Leyor), Dan Shor (Dr. Arridor), Colm Meaney (Chief O'Brien)

The Federation negotiates with the planet Crystalia for control of what is believed to be the first stable wormhole, when the Ferengi led by DaiMon Goss (Scott Thomson) intervene in the negotiations hoping to place their own bid. One of the negotiators, Deviononi Ral (Matt McCoy) becomes intimately involved with Troi, who learns he is half-Betazoid, giving him a special edge during the negotiating sessions against Riker.

••••

••••

The pre-airing hype regarding a scene in which Troi beds alien ambassador Rol caused quite a stir among fans.

"It was never meant to be outrageous television," says Michael Piller. "We got quite a few letters from outraged people before it aired, but nobody wrote after it aired. I listen very carefully to those complaints."

Of the episode Piller adds, "One of the best scripts we had. I think if you listen to that show and don't watch it, you can really have fun with it. I really thought it was a disappointing episode. It just didn't make it and was not a great show. As far as servicing the character of Troi, it was quite a wonderful vehicle and she was marvelous."

Notes director Robert Scheerer, "The thing I remember most about that episode is working so closely with Marina, because I hadn't really worked with her that extensively. There was a very human quality to her and the show. Another show I thought she was wonderful in, which I didn't see, was 'The Loss.' Damn, she was wonderful in that. I was thunderstruck by that because it's not an easy thing to play."

Episode #57:
"The Vengeance Factor"
Original Airdate: 11/18/89
Written by Sam Rolfe
Directed by Timothy Bond
Guest Starring: Lisa Wilcox (Yuta), Joey Aresco (Brull), Nancy Parsons (Sovereign Marouk), Stephen Lee (Chorgon), Marc Lawrence (Volnath), Elkanah J. Burns (Temarek)

Picard mediates a dispute between a pirate band and the Sovereign (Nancy Parsons), the leader of their homeworld, in order to allow the renegades to return under a grant of amnesty. The murder of one of the band's clansman is perpetrated by Yuta (Lisa Wilcox of *Nightmare on Elm Street 4* and *5*), Riker's latest dalliance and the Sovereign's servant, who's seeking vengeance for the destruction of her clan.

••••

Timothy Bond, a veteran *TNG* director, helmed the installment. "If we had rehearsal it would be great, but we don't," says Jonathan Frakes about acting

in the show. "Everyone has come to realize that they're only so many ways to shoot the bridge, so let's get on with it. We all know the room and where we're going to go, and if you try to get too artsy-fartsy, you get yourself into what they affectionately refer to as the toilet."

The episode had a decidedly dark tone, particularly the teaser in which Riker leads an investigating Away Team that comes across numerous corpses.

"It was fun to do," laughs Timothy Bond. "The dialogue was of little consequence, and I think some of it was even cut. There's a tendency in television to say, 'I'm opening the door now.' Well, just open the door. It's not a radio show. So we were able to make that quite visual and the art department came up with this bizarre painted backdrop. They lit it with green light and there was smoke. That show also featured the best set I've ever had. We only had it up for two days and it was such a shame to tear it down."

The conclusion of the episode was somewhat controversial for two reasons: first, that Riker is forced to kill Yuta and, second, that Captain Picard has no reaction whatsoever to this action.

"They [the producers] *were* worried about the ending and the idea of Riker doing something like that," concurs Bond. "Regarding Picard, I'm afraid there is a reason for his lack of reaction: opticals. He couldn't move for that one period where she gets vaporized. In retrospect, maybe it was kind of a mistake of mine. I just had this idea that it would be really neat that when she's vaporized, Picard was there, in the shot. That meant putting several layers of elements into the shot and in order for it to work properly, Picard had to stay still. Not a good reason. When I saw it, I actually regretted the decision, but by then the ship had sailed. Believe me, Patrick noticed too. He even asked, 'I'm just supposed to sit here and do nothing?' The other problem is what *could* he do? We knew Riker had to kill the girl and we didn't want to get Picard shot by the phaser. In retrospect, what I should have done is what you usually do—don't have him in the shot. If he's not, then the audience doesn't think, 'Why doesn't Picard react?' We had a lot of rationales at the time, but we were wrong. Overall, though, I'm real

Nancy Parsons, co-manager of Motel Hell, was Marouk in "The Vengence Factor."

proud of the episode."

Episode #58:
"The Defector"
Original Airdate: 12/30/89
Written by Ronald D. Moore
Directed by Robert Scheerer
Guest Starring: James Stoyan (Admiral Jarok/Setal), Andreas Katsulas (Commander Tomalak), John Hancock (Admiral Haden), S.A. Templeton (John Bates)

Romulan Commander Tomalok (Andreas Katsulas), returns while chasing a Romulan defector. Sub-Commander Setal (James Stoyan) warns the Federation of a Romulan incursion in the Neutral Zone which will set the stage for a massive invasion. Picard, wary of the logistics clerk's story, discovers the officer is actually the legendary Admiral Jarok. As they charge into the Neutral Zone, Picard discovers no outpost and a fleet of Romulan ships waiting to take the Enterprise back to their homeworld for study.

••••

Ron Moore's second effort for the series was one he pitched to the producers after they bought his spec script, "The Bonding." On its strength, he was offered a staff job as story editor.

"They really liked the idea of having this sort of Cuban Missile Crisis at the Neutral Zone," says Moore. "I wrote the first draft and was involved in the rewrite. About two weeks later, after the show was put to bed, they had an opening on the staff. They called me up and said, 'We would like you to come

••••

aboard.' I said, 'Well, I don't know, maybe—I'm getting my shoes polished this week.' Meanwhile, I'd have stepped over my dead grandmother."

"Not an easy script to write," opines Michael Piller, "because the middle of it was very soft. It had a good ending and a good beginning. The first several drafts of that show had a lot of talking in the middle, questioning whether or not we trusted him. It was nice to come off of 'The Enemy' with a little bit of an echo. We don't do that a lot and I like when we can. Ultimately it was a combination of circumstances where a nice thing happened. One, we punctuated it with some little techno-babble stuff, detective work, messages from Starfleet and little pacing things that really helped the middle of that show. Second, we didn't know how to open the show. We wanted to open it with another Sherlock Holmes gag which probably would have been rather irrelevant. At the last moment, we got a phone call from the studio saying that we couldn't do Sherlock Holmes anymore because there's a lawsuit from some other show or movie...some other Paramount lawsuit involving the estate of Sherlock Holmes. Paramount didn't want another one, so Sherlock Holmes was out.

"We sat down a day or two before we started shooting to figure out what we were going to do. Someone suggested Shakespeare, so we went to Patrick, who's obviously our scholar, and said, 'What would be a good Shakespearean play that would echo the script?' Actually there was a Shakespearean play called 'The Defector,' but it was too unknown for our purposes. So he came back with *Henry V*, and he picked out the scene and section and we condensed it to use it as an echo. If you watch that episode, there's a scene where Picard and Data are talking about how the crew is holding up, and then Picard says a line or two that echoes the play. Then, in the confrontation with the Romulans, there are suggestions of *Henry V* in Picard's stance, bravery and decisions, and what the argument is about. If you are a musician, as I am, it is a trick that you throw into arrangements to echo other songs and play on a melody that reminds you of something else. I was very proud of that. I also liked

the tension, the decision making, lonely at the top. It almost became Picard's show as a result of adding King Henry to the mix. I was very pleased with it."

Offers Robert Scheerer, "There were a couple of extra scenes in that episode which had to be cut for time. I was sorry about that. There was a second interrogation scene that I just loved that, unfortunately, we couldn't use because of time problems."

An audience-pleasing moment of the episode is where it's believed Picard is outnumbered, when a group of Klingon warships decloak around the Romulans.

"You know, it's very frustrating at times on this show because, obviously, directorially one is on the stages and can only lead up to and away from those effects that make the show what it is. With Rob Legato and Dan Curry you just get the most magnificent effects, but I never see them before hand. I'll offer suggestions of what I think it should look like and Rick [Berman], of course, is deeply involved in that as is Michael Piller. First of all it's wonderful knowing you're going to get something terrific and always what thrills me is that there are always surprises, things I didn't expect were there which just absolutely knock me out. But it is a strange feeling leading up to something you don't know what it's going to be."

Episode #59:
"The Hunted"
Original Airdate: 1/6/90
Written by Robin Bernheim
Directed by Cliff Bole
Guest Starring: Jeff McCarthy (Roga Danar), James Cromwell (Prime Minister Nayrok), Colm Meaney (Chief O'Brien), J. Michael Flynn (Zayner), Andrew Bickell (Wagner)

Genetically altered veterans of a war on Angosia 3 have been consigned to exile on Lunar 7, a prison colony soldier Roga Danar (Jeff McCarthy) flees from before being captured by the Enterprise. Escaping from the brig, he attempts to lead his fellow officers in a coup against the government, which is petitioning to join the Federation. Troi learns that the soldiers which had once fought for Angosia, have now been banished and are pariahs from

their homeworld.

••••

Michael Piller admits to having mixed feelings about the episode. "I thought the story was thin and we filled it out with a good cat and mouse chase," he says. "I thought it played well on screen and was very action-oriented. 'Vengeance Factor,' 'The Hunted' and 'High Ground' were all shows which I developed, and was not really happy with any of them. I felt that they did touch on themes of importance and did ultimately deal nicely with those, and there's quite a bit of controversy about the ending [of 'The Hunted.']

"At first we were going to have a huge shoot out and have everyone wiped out in the end, but that didn't really make anybody a hero. Picard goes down there and we're caught in a stalemate. We've now created the character of this planet's society in such a way that Picard can make the statement at the end, 'This is not our affair. You guys are going to have to solve it. When you're ready, come back to the Federation and we'll reconsider your application.' I thought it worked. There are people on the staff to this day who think it doesn't. I think it's an important theme that you cannot explore enough, but I don't think we really got to the heart of it because the story was one-note, and it could have used a little more texture. Again, if we had a little more time....I give that about a B-. The whole theme of the show was let's look at how society treats its returning veterans. I thought from a conceptual level we handled that well, and we came up with good science fiction to make it interesting. There's some argument that the best soldier ever created bringing the Enterprise to its knees is a little hard to believe, and that might have been the weakness of the show. I enjoyed it, and was not ashamed of the show."

Offers director Cliff Bole, "I liked the story, because the premise was dealing with an issue in space that has happened and is happening in our present time. Originally, Danar was going to come back and there was going to be a big confrontation. That was cut due to budget and time. We simply did not have the time in seven days to do that. I thought the loss of that confrontation took away a little bit, making

••••
190

"The High Ground"
Original Airdate: 1/27/90
Written by Melinda Snodgrass
Directed by Gabrielle Beaumont
Guest Starring: Kerrie Keane (Alexana Devos), Richard Cox (Kyril Finn), Marc Buckland (Waiter), Fred G. Smith (Policeman), Christopher Pettiet (Boy)

Dr. Crusher is kidnapped by a band of terrorists who are demanding independence for their territory, and believe the Federation has allied themselves with the government. They've created a method for instantaneous teleportation—which is slowly killing them—and transport aboard the Enterprise in hopes of destroying it. Meanwhile, Crusher attempts to save Kyril Finn (Richard Cox) and his fellows from the tissue degeneration which is destroying them.

••••

Says Michael Piller, "Another show that I wasn't particularly happy with. We set out to do a show about terrorists.. What was the statement we made about terrorism in this show? Was it the point where the boy puts down the gun and says, 'Maybe the end of terrorism is when the first child puts down his gun?' It was effective in the context of that show, but is certainly not a statement that provides any great revelation. You must be prepared to say something new about social issues. I would love to do a story about the environment. I would love to do a story about urban gangs, yet the dangers of starting a show with a concept that is socially motivated is that you better damn well find a personal story to tell and something new to say about that issue, otherwise you're not enlightening anybody. You're retreading old ground, and I think that's what we did in 'The High Ground.'"

Adds Melinda Snodgrass, "What I wanted to do was the American Revolution. They wouldn't let me, so we ended up doing Northern Ireland, which I felt made our people look incredibly stupid. I wanted it with Picard as Cornwallis and the Romulans would have been the French, who were in our revolution, trying to break this planet away. Suddenly Picard realized he's one of the oppressors. Instead, we do 'Breakfast in Belfast,' where our people

decide they're going to go off to Northern Ireland. That's what I was told to do."

Brannon Braga, fifth season story editor and an intern at the time of "The High Ground," relates, "Very rarely do we start thinking about an episode in terms of an issue. Let's do a show about AIDS, let's do a show about terrorism. We rarely think in those terms. We usually think in terms of neat science-fiction twists and that's what sends us in the direction of what's this story about and who's in it?"

"When we have started by saying let's do a show about terrorism, you get things like 'High Ground' which is an abomination," says Ron Moore. "It's our one terrorist show. We didn't have anything interesting to say about terrorism except that it's bad and Beverly gets kidnapped—ho hum. They take her down to the caves and we get to have nice, big preachy speeches about terrorism and freedom, fighting and security forces versus society. It's a very unsatisfying episode and the staff wasn't really happy with it. It's just an example of what happens when you start at the wrong place."

Adds Braga, "It's very on the nose, it's very obvious. It wasn't a Star Trek. The irony of the show is we can do anything. There's no reason for us to tell a mundane story. On L.A. Law you don't have a science-fiction element so you can't tell it any other way. But the frustrating thing about it was we desperately want science-fiction elements. It's hard to come up with those vital science-fiction twists."

Episode #61:
"Deja Q"
Original Airdate: 2/3/90
Written by Richard Danus
Directed by Les Landau
Guest Starring: John de Lancie (Q), Richard Cansino (Dr. Garin), Betty Muramoto (Scientist), Whoopi Goldberg (Guinan)

Q has been stripped of his powers (and his clothing) and deposited aboard the Enterprise for his indiscretions by his disenchanted peers in the Q continuum. Picard promptly places the powerless Q in the brig. Shortly thereafter, the Enterprise is pursued by a race of aliens seeking revenge against Q for his vicious practical jokes against them, and

he's saved by Data. Selflessly sacrificing himself to protect the Enterprise, Q's powers are restored by Q2 (Corbin Bernsen), and a joyous Q celebrates by materializing a Mexican mariachi band on the bridge, along with a bevy of beauties and cigars for all.

••••

"I always think of Q as Lokki," says Melinda Snodgrass. "He's chaos. [Producer] Maury Hurley always thought Q was here to teach us a lesson, to guide and instruct us. I can understand that to some extent, but I really see him as a mischief maker. He really just wants to foul Picard's head."

Director Las Landau notes, "Needless to say, John de Lancie is a delight. He took a role, which granted was an exceptional part, and made more of it than was on the page. He made himself a recurring character. He's a dynamic personality and the character of Q is an unbelievably Trekkie, attractive character. The optical effects took a lot of time and effort on everyone's part. He arrives suspended in the air, he snaps his fingers and things happen. In order to make it happen right, aesthetically and creatively, it takes time. Q was always a fascinating character and very popular with the Star Trek audience. He kind of melds with Picard in a very unusual way in a battle of wits to see who will ultimately triumph. Although I think it's a standoff in its conclusion each time, Picard seems to always have the slight edge, which is as it should be."

"Wonderful show and a very difficult one to get on its feet," Michael Piller details, "but once it got there, we were very proud of it. Our first take on it was that Q lost his powers, came on board and we developed a whole story about how we were about to come into a war with the Klingons. It turns out that Q didn't really lose his powers after all, he was just playing with us and pulling our strings just so that he could make himself a hero, become an officer and prove his value. It wasn't a bad story, but ultimately we sat down with Gene and Rick Berman, and Gene said, 'If you're going to do a story—Godlike and brought down to Earth—then do it. Do a story about what it's like to lose everything that you are and have to discover your own humanity.' He kind of threw cold water on us and suggested we do it straight forward and that's what we did. We made it a comedy, we made it fun, but I think it has some extraordinary things to say about humanity."

Episode #62:
"A Matter of Perspective"
Original Airdate: 2/10/90
Written by Ed Zuckerman
Directed by Cliff Bole
Guest Starring: Craig Richard Nelson (Investigator Krag), Gina Hecht (Manua Apgar), Mark Margolis (Dr. Nel Apgar), Juli Donald (Tanya), Colm Meaney (Chief O'Brien)

Riker is accused of murdering an alien scientist, Dr. Apgar (Mark Margolis), and destroying a scientific space station. Picard arbitrates over a holodeck recreation of the events to establish whether or not there are sufficient grounds for his first officer to receive extradition to the planet, where the penalty for his alleged crimes is death.

••••

"Probably the hardest story to break," opines Michael Piller. "It was a technical nightmare for the director. I was very, very happy with the script and I thought the show was disappointing. I guess it didn't translate properly. It was very ambitious, but it got overly convoluted. The casting was off. If you had put Lana Turner in the role of the woman in that show, you would have understood it all—but I don't think it played as it was intended.

"That's about the best murder mystery I've been involved in developing in my career," he continues, "because every detail falls into place, every line comes together to explain how, what, when and where, and it really worked from a mystery standpoint. It's so complicated a mystery. In fact, it's like *The Big Sleep* in space. It's very complicated, yet if you take that script apart, nothing falls out of it. It ought to win an Edgar Allen Poe Award for best mystery of the year. I've been involved in a lot of crime caper shows, but this was a very proud script turned out. I just didn't think it was great television. "

Cliff Bole admits that, directori-

ally, "A Matter of Perspective" was not easy. "One of the toughest shows I've ever shot from the standpoint of keeping continuity and having to shoot something three different ways."

Episode #63:
"Yesterday's Enterprise"
Original Airdate: 2/17/90
Written by Ira Stephen Behr,
Richard Manning, Hans Beimler and
Ronald Moore
Story by Trent Christopher Ganino and Eric A. Stillwell
Directed by David Carson
Guest Starring: Denise Crosby (Tasha Yar), Christopher McDonald (Lieutenant Richard Castillo), Tricia O'Neill (Captain Rachel Garrett), Whoopi Goldberg (Guinan)

During a conflict with the Romulans, the Enterprise NCC-1701-C is propelled forward in time through an anomaly and history is changed. Our crew is unknowingly thrust into an alternate universe in which the Federation is still engaged in a bloody war with the Klingon Empire. Only Guinan suspects something is wrong and urges Picard to return the Enterprise-C back in time where it will open the door for peace with the Klingons, or forever change history and thus doom the Federation against the superior forces of the triumphant Klingon Empire.

••••

Enthuses Michael Piller, "That was a classic episode. I never met Denise Crosby in person, but I am sure an admirer. She did a great job for us. That's just about as neat a show as we could do. It was as entertaining and unique a time travel show as you'll ever see. I don't know that there was a better episode third season. Hell, Picard sends 500 people back to their death on the word of the bartender. Come on, that's hard.

"I was very happy with it and, frankly, I give the credit to the director and the cast and the people who post-produced it," Piller elaborates. "The script was not one of the best scripts we wrote that season. Conceptually it was marvelous, coming out of the heads of some people here. I thought conceptually it was the most exciting show we did. Because Christmas was coming, we had

actor schedule problems, Whoopi was going off to do something after the first of the year, and so on. We had to rush that up in the schedule and gang-bang it out. There are little holes in the episode that we couldn't fix. It was such a complicated and fascinating premise, but it was ultimately the character material that really made everybody proud. It was a wonderfully produced show."

Two points posed to Piller is that the harder-edged Enterprise in the time altered future was much more reminiscent of the original series; and that as Enterprise-C went back through time, the audience should have seen the same time dissolve that took place in the episode's beginning.

"There are a lot of people who like that Enterprise a lot better," he laughs. "The 'blending' from one Enterprise to another was done as an after thought. After the show was cut and everybody looked at it....if you recall, the sequence of events, you're inside the Enterprise, you cut outside to see the ship coming through the hole, and then you see the crew blend into the time-altered Enterprise. Originally, you cut outside, and then match cut to a different Enterprise. Tasha is in place and everyone looks different. When people looked at it, they were saying, 'People are going to think we're cutting inside the other ship.' So we had to come up with an idea—which the guys in post-production did a marvelous job on—that showed the transition on camera, which was never scripted. Sometimes marvelous things happen because of emergency needs; a band-aid to cover up a mistake."

"To this day I do not understand 'Yesterday's Enterprise,'" confesses Jonathan Frakes. "I do not know what the fuck happened in that episode. I'm still trying to understand it—but I liked the look."

Co-writer Ron Moore explains, "I've heard from time to time, I wish you'd do some war stories, but this is the reality of war. It's not a pretty piece. But it was a lot of fun to watch that ship move, and see Picard biting Riker's head off. I wrote a couple of different story outlines on it. Somewhere during the course of that I came up with the idea that the alternate universe would really be nasty and awful

••••

The original generation: DeForest Kelley (Dr Leonard "Bones" McCoy), Leonard Nimoy (Mr. Spock) and William Shatner (Captain James T. Kirk) as seen on Star Trek. (Photo copyright © G. Trindl/Shooting Star)

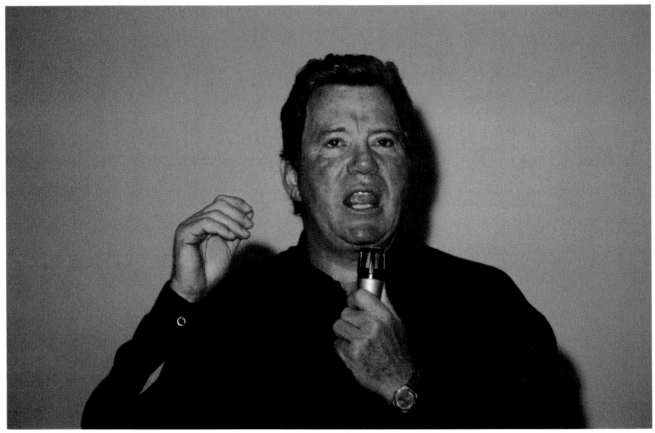

Top: Leonard Nimoy, William Shatner and assorted Vulcans in a behind-the-scenes shot from season two's "Amok Time". (Photo copyright © Trindl/Shooting Star)   Bottom: William Shatner in an all-too-rare convention appearance. (Photo copyright © Karen Witkowski)

William Shatner, DeForest Kelley and Leonard Nimoy reunited as Kirk, McCoy and Spock on the set of the first feature film, Star Trek: The Motion Picture. *(Photo copyright © Trindl/Shooting Star)*

From Top Left: Making the convention circuit are DeForest Kelley (Dr. McCoy), Majel Barrett (Nurse Christine Chapel) and Leonard Nimoy (Mr. Spock), who delivers the Vulcan salute to the gathered fans. (Photos copyright © Karen Witkowski)

From Top Left: James Doohan (Scotty), Nichelle Nichols (Uhura), Walter Koenig (Chekov) and George Takei (Sulu).
(Photos copyright © Karen Witkowski)

Captains Picard and Kirk (Patrick Stewart and William Shatner) are brought together at a New York Star Trek convention. (Photo copyright © Karen Witkowski)

Top: *The first season cast of Star Trek: The Next Generation, including Denise Crosby as Security Chief Tasha Yar and Wil Wheaton as Wesley Crusher. (Photo copyright © G Trindl/Shooting Star)* **Bottom:** *Wil Wheaton, Denise Crosby, Gene Roddenberry and Marina Sirtis answer questions from fans. (Photo copyright © Karen Witkowski)*

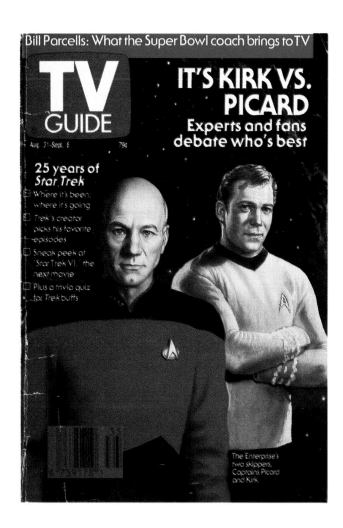

TV GUIDE

Aug. 31-Sept. 6   79¢

IT'S KIRK VS. PICARD
Experts and fans debate who's best

25 years of Star Trek
- Where it's been; where it's going
- Trek's creator picks his favorite episodes
- Sneak peek at 'Star Trek VI,' the next movie
- Plus a trivia quiz for Trek buffs

The Enterprise's two skippers, Captains Picard and Kirk.

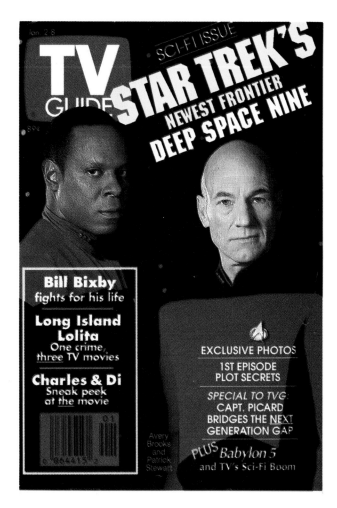

Jan. 2-8

TV GUIDE

SCI-FI ISSUE

STAR TREK'S NEWEST FRONTIER
DEEP SPACE NINE

89¢

Bill Bixby
fights for his life

Long Island Lolita
One crime, three TV movies

Charles & Di
Sneak peek at the movie

EXCLUSIVE PHOTOS
1ST EPISODE PLOT SECRETS

SPECIAL TO TVG:
CAPT. PICARD BRIDGES THE NEXT GENERATION GAP

PLUS *Babylon 5* and TV's Sci-Fi Boom

Avery Brooks and Patrick Stewart

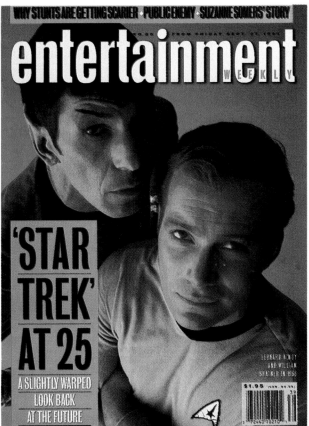

entertainment WEEKLY

ON SALE FROM FRIDAY SEPT. 27 1991

'STAR TREK' AT 25
A SLIGHTLY WARPED LOOK BACK AT THE FUTURE

LEONARD NIMOY AND WILLIAM SHATNER IN 1966

$1.95 (CAN. $2.50)

From Bottom Left: Leonard Nimoy and William Shatner grace the cover of Entertainment Weekly to celebrate Star Trek's 25th anniversary; TV Guide features Patrick Stewart and William Shatner on the cover in a battle of the captains (Kirk won the poll hands down); Avery Brooks and Patrick Stewart are pictured together in order to launch Star Trek: Deep Space Nine.

The late Gene Roddenberry, creator of both Star Trek *and* The Next Generation, *appearing at the dedication of the building named after him on the Paramount lot. (Photo copyright © Albert Ortega)*

From Top Left: Patrick Stewart (Picard), Jonathan Frakes (Riker), LeVar Burton (La Forge) and Brent Spiner (Data).
(Photos copyright © Karen Witkowski)

From Top Left: Michael Dorn (Worf), Denise Crosby (Yar), Wil Wheaton (Wesley), Gates McFadden (Dr. Crusher).
(Photos copyright © Karen Witkowski)

Top Left-Right: Marina Sirtis (Deanna Troi) and Michelle Forbes (Ensign Ro) take questions from the audience. (Photos copyright © Karen Witkowski)   Bottom: Whoopi Goldberg (Guinan) joined Patrick Stewart (Picard) on the set of Ten-Forward beginning in season two. (Photo copyright © Fred Sabine/Shooting Star)

Top: The cast of Deep Space Nine, *from L-R: Nana Visitor, Terry Farrell, Cirroc Lofton, Avery Brooks, Colm Meaney, Armin Shimerman, Rene Auberjonois and Siddig El Fadil. (Photo copyright © Celebrity Photo Agency) Bottom: Rene Auberjonois poses with Odo's bucket at a convention. (Photo copyright © Karen Witkowski)*

Actress Kate Mulgrew portrays Kathryn Janeway, captain of the starship Voyager *on Star Trek: Voyager. (Photo copyright © Albert Ortega)*

Top: Tim Russ (Tuvok), Kate Mulgrew (Janeway), Robert Duncan McNeill (Paris) and Robert Beltran (Chakotay) toast the launching of Voyager.
Bottom: Ethan Phillips (Neelix) and Roxann Biggs-Dawson (Torres), seen without their alien makeup. (Photos copyright © Albert Ortega)

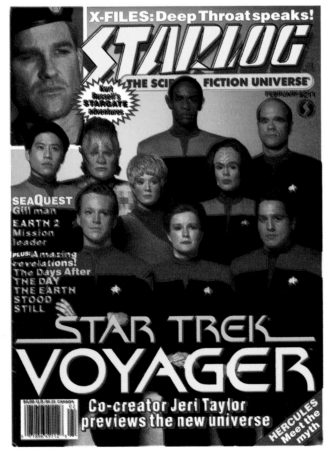

Top: Voyager navigator Harry Kim (Garrett Wang) and nurse-in-training Kes (Jennifer Lien). (Photos copyright © Albert Ortega) Bottom: Starlog magazine introduces the crew of Voyager, while Cinescape heralds the premiere of the motion picture Star Trek: Generations.

and militaristic and that we're losing the war with the Klingons."

Note: The map Picard holds which displayed the Neutral Zone between the Romulan and Federation territories is identical to the map that appeared on the Enterprise viewscreen in classic *Trek*'s "Balance of Terror." This was due to the efforts of graphics wiz and unofficial *Trek* historian Michael Okuda.

Episode #64:
"The Offspring"
Original Airdate: 3/10/90
Written by Rene Echevarria
Directed by Jonathan Frakes
Guest Starring: Hallie Todd (Lal), Nicolas Coster (Admiral Haftel), Judyann Elder (Lt. Ballard), Diane Moser, Hayne Bayle, Maria Leone and James Becker (Ten Forward Crew)

Jonathan Frakes' first directorial effort in which Data creates a daughter for himself (Lal, played by Hallie Todd). Although hoping to tutor his new and improved cyborg in humanity, Data's plans are upset when Starfleet Admiral Haftel (Nicolas Coster) announces his plans to take Lal back with him for study. Picard is swayed to defend Data, who is reluctant to give his "daughter" up to her Federation foster parents.

••••

"The perfect show to follow 'Yesterday's Enterprise,' and a totally different kind of episode," points out Michael Piller. "The script and performances were great, and it was marvelously directed by Jonathan. My taste, it was as good a show as we had all year. When you have good character stuff, you've got my support. It's a very challenging concept. It was a concept I wanted to do, so we sat down with Gene and he came up with a number of suggestions and said this is what would make it fit into the *Star Trek* bible. Rick Berman added some crucial pieces to the puzzle. We are very determined to protect the uniqueness of Data as a character, but at the same time, it seemed to make perfect sense that one of the human traits that Data would have observed and perhaps covet, is procreation and parenting. He would also know that his value to Starfleet was so great that if he were ever in an accident, he's too valuable to end

with himself."

Melinda Snodgrass differs with the assessment. "I felt it was fairly obvious and tired and stupid and I didn't want to do it. I did a page one rewrite and Michael [Piller] did another rewrite. It had a lot to do with 'The Measure of a Man,' which I don't think we needed to do again so soon. It was a good show for Jonathan to start with. It was a nice bottle show and he didn't have to cope with alien cultures."

"I went to [Rick] Berman and said I'd like to do a show," recalls actor turned director Jonathan Frakes. "He said I'd have to go to school, and so I spent about 300 hours in the editing room and on the dubbing stage learning about that side of it. Editing was the side of things I felt weakest in. I naturally looked over the shoulders of all our regular directors and took some seminars, read textbooks and finally I didn't go away. Rick was kind enough to give me 'The Offspring' and I was thrilled, because I got a Data show and those always work. It was wonderfully satisfying and I'm very happy with that episode."

Chip Chalmers, who would subsequently become a director in his own right, served as assistant director of "Offspring."

"One of the more pleasant memories for me was 'The Offspring,' which was Jonathan Frakes' first directing job," reflects Chalmers. "Working with Jonathan, who is one of the funniest and kindest people that I know, was just a pleasure. To watch his eyes light up when he realized he could make his own vision happen was a real joy. It was really magical to watch him....play.

Episode #65:
"Sins of the Father"
Original Airdate: 3/17/90
Written by Ronald D. Moore and
W. Reed Moran
Based on the Teleplay by Drew Deighan
Directed by Les Landau
Guest Starring: Tony Todd (Commander Kurn), Charles Cooper (K'mpec), Patrick Massett (Duras), Thelma Lee (Kahlest), Teddy Davis (Transporter Technician)

Worf returns to the Klingon homeworld to defend his late father against charges of treason. He is prompt-

ed to do so by his younger brother, Kurn (Tony Todd), who is still alive and has transferred aboard the Enterprise as part of the Federation exchange program. Victimized by political infighting, Worf accepts excommunication from Klingon society to protect the council, which is rife with deceit. Council member Duras (Patrick Massett), plots to keep the truth of *his* father's dishonor and Worf's father's framing, in hopes of ascending to one day head the council.

••••

Michael Piller admits, "It was complicated, because we were combining characters and scripts, trying to put together a Worf story we liked. I think we came out of it fairly well, with a good show."

"I thought Tony Todd did a wonderful job as Worf's brother," says writer Ron Moore. "I was kind of worried, because there's always that hesitation when you're bringing in other family members no one else has ever seen. Half the audience is ready to throw things at the screen, and you're thinking, 'This better work.' I was there when he stepped on the stage and made it his own. I was in love with 'Sins of the Father' and I fought for it when there was some question about which way we were going to go with it. I really like the fact Worf took it on the chin that episode. It said he was willing to stand up and do the right thing for his people, even if they weren't going to do the right thing by him. Patrick and I were at the Saturn Awards together, and he made a really good suggestion. He felt that when Worf is asking Picard to be his chadich, Picard originally says a single Klingon word, but Patrick thought it would be nice if Picard knew the whole line of ritual. At that time there wasn't a formal ritual, and there wasn't one for Kurn either, so I went back and wrote a line for him to say in Klingon and I tied it into Picard."

Explains Michael Dorn, "There was a lot more involved in it than the writers realized. Things that have to do with Klingon loyalty and honor. They didn't give it its due. You look at Worf in a different light, and I've played him in a different light since that episode. This is now something they have come up with. I'm doing this on my own. Hey, it's their fault. They wrote it. So now, I'm going to carry on with it."

Director Les Landau enthuses, "Here was an opportunity to explore the Klingon world in depth from beginning to end. Meaning that Ron Moore came up with a wonderful story which Richard James, the art director, and Jim Meese, the set decorator, had to visualize in terms of set design and set decoration. Additionally, to which Marvin Rush, the cameraman, had to conceptually find a visual representation of what the Klingon world was all about. I think all three of those gentlemen accomplished that task totally. In fact, Richard and Jim went on to win Emmy Awards for that episode, which I'm very proud of. Marvin's work speaks for itself. It was visually one of the most dynamic episodes ever done. It looks like a feature film. There were long detailed conversations about how, conceptually, we should deal with them. Ultimately, Rick Berman gave the final approval for each and every one of the ideas and details, and we showed a world that was heretofore never seen before, and which the audience craves to see more of. I was never one of the original *Star Trek* fans, however. My attitude was, is and always will be to never see what has come before, but go where none have gone before and visualize what is in my thinking and mind as to what the visuals should be, which is dictated by the storyline. We must always come back to the words and what the story is, because without it, we have nothing to tell. After all, film and episodic television is nothing if not telling a story."

Episode #66:
"Allegiance"
Original Airdate: 3/24/90
Written by Hans Beimler and
Richard Manning
Directed by Winrich Kolbe
Guest Starring: Stephen Markle (Tholl), Reiner Schone (Esoqq), Joycelyn O'Brien (Haro), Jeff and Jerry Rector (Aliens)

Picard is abducted by aliens as part of a futuristic lab experiment, and replaced by a duplicate who acts in an atypical manner: seducing Dr. Crusher and singing drinking songs with the crew in Ten Forward. Meanwhile, Picard along with three other captured aliens attempt to escape from their containment, discover-

ing that one of them is actually the lab-keeper.

••••

Michael Piller admits that the series needed a show to balance the budget of "Yesterday's Enterprise."

"'The Offspring' helped us a lot and so did 'Allegiance,'" he says. "I'm a great fan of intimate shows, and it was a simple show from a production point of view, because you needed one set. With trying to come up with good, solid stuff for Picard....we'd done a good job treating Picard as a captain, but he hadn't gotten to do the holodeck fantasies he likes to do, and he hadn't been able to have fun. We wanted to come up with some real fun for both Patrick the actor and Jean Luc the character, so we came up with this idea. It might have been two ideas put into one. One was Picard gets stuck in a no-exit situation, and a false Picard takes his place on the Enterprise. I loved the stuff on the Enterprise, wonderful character stuff and Patrick was wonderful. I thought it was a good, solid show and immediately following that was 'Captain's Holiday,' which, again, was borne out of the fact that we wanted to give the captain some characterization. Delightful episode."

"Picard does some things that had only been in the real Picard's mind," says Ron Moore. "Watching him sing in Ten Forward gave everyone a kick. And the scene with Beverly in his cabin was kind of fun. I like the fact we've taken him apart more and really are seeing what makes this guy tick."

This episode represents director Winrich Kolbe's favorite of the numerous he's directed. "I like it because we did something stylistically interesting in the lit room where the four people were incarcerated. It was Patrick's show and I always know when it's going to be Patrick's show it's going to be a good one because he's so damn good in everything that he does. If I had to choose a particular *Star Trek*, that would likely be it. I look the look of it and what Marvin Rush was able to do, and Richard James the set designer. What you have to consider in directing any kind of entertainment concept is time and money. We were so far behind after the first two days that basically the whole hierarchy of Paramount

was camping out on my set. Then we went into the new set, the octagonal chamber and suddenly we were taking off. We came in under budget and under time. It was a set that was terrific to shoot in and I could put the camera anywhere I wanted to. I think the only thing I would change right now is I would get a steadicam in there so that we could have even more mobility than we had in that show. I really liked the episode."

Episode #67:
"Captain's Holiday"
Original Airdate: 3/31/90
Written by Ira Steven Behr
Directed by Chip Chalmers
Guest Starring: Jennifer Hetrick (Vash), Max Grodenchik (Sovak), Karen Landry (Ajur), Michael Champion (Boratis), Deirdre Imershein (Joval)

Picard is conned in to taking a vacation on Rysa, the Club Med of the cosmos, where the captain becomes an unwitting pawn of the unscrupulous Vash (Jennifer Hetrick). She is seeking the legendary tax-u-tat treasure and being trailed by former ally, Ferengi Sovak (Max Grodenchik), who hopes to retrieve it as well. Also searching for the powerful treasure are two Vorgon time travelers from the 27th Century, Ajor (Karen Landry) and Boratis (Michael Champion).

••••

Given the plot of "Captain's Holiday," it would appear that the experience of "Yesterday's Enterprise" uncorked the show's seeming fear of doing time travel stories.

"Time travel must be handled with delicacy," says Michael Piller. "I think it must be handled with a great deal of understanding, because there are so many problems. Rick Berman feels very strongly about that as well. The fascinating thing about 'Captain's Holiday' is that that really was the turning point in the script development. Ron Moore made a suggestion. Originally it was a *Maltese Falcon* kind of story where an old, rare thing had been lost and a bunch of people are looking for it on this island. The first draft of that had nothing to do with it. It was originally a good script, but it could have been *Magnum*. Ron was in here with the staff and said, 'Instead of it being from the past, couldn't it be from

Corbin Bernsen (who had a bit part in "Deja Q") and Jennifer Hetrick (Vash in "Captain's Holiday") were married in L.A. Law.

the future?' And I said, 'Which also means that the guys who are chasing it are from the future,' and that started putting a whole new spin on it. We actually came up with an extra tag that we cut out of the show. We never start a show off of the Enterprise, but we broke the format here. The guy shows up from the present and says, 'Is Jean Luc Picard here yet?' And they say, 'No, but he will be...' At the end of the show, we see these guys come back from the future again to replay the whole drama. We thought it was a little confusing and we cut it. It was sort of a *Twilight Zone* ending, and it didn't quite work."

"I really don't watch much television at all," says Jennifer Hetrick, who portrayed Vash in "Captain's Holiday" and returned in fourth season's "Q-Pid". "I had watched the original *Star Trek* when I was a kid on and off. I was never a Trekkie and was not really familiar with this show, but have since taken to it. I thought it was quite funny. It seemed like a *Romancing the Stone/Raiders of the Lost Ark*-type story. I did use that as an example, but not specifically for my character. I just used my own imagination and what I know of myself and found her very adventurous and conniving to a degree, but also vulnerable and committed. I loved the Ferengi, Sovak. I

was spared the make-up fortunately. When I saw what everyone else had to go through, I was thrilled. Thank God, I was human."

"Captain's Holiday" represented Chip Chalmers directorial debut, a rare case of an assistant director taking control of an episode.

"'Captain's Holiday' is one of my favorites because it was the first," he enthuses. "This episode was also terrific because Patrick is such a wonderful actor. The other thing for me is that I got a wonderful actress, Jennifer Hetrick, and we had such a good time working on the show. What stands out for me is that I got very, very sick for a couple of days and during those two days we were shooting 'on' Rysa, actually stage 16, I was running a 102 degree temperature. These wonderful people put up a cot with lots of padding and a pillow right behind Rycea. We'd come out, rehearse, I'd muster up as much energy as I could while they were lighting, I would go lay down on my cot and pass out for 15 or 20 minutes while they set up. I'd go out, say action, shoot and we made it through those two days with everybody rallying around. I can look back at that show and smile for a lot of reasons, but certainly the happiest result is that we proved Patrick Stewart is extremely funny."

Episode #68:
"Tin Man"
Original Airdate: 4/29/90
Written by Dennis Putnam Bailey
and David Bischoff
Directed by Robert Scheerer
Guest Starring: Harry Groener (Tam Elbrun), Michael Cavanaugh (Captain DeSoto), Peter Vogt (Romulan Commander)
A telepathic Betazoid, narcissistic Tam Elbrun (Harry Groener), is assigned to the Enterprise to communicate with a new life form, a living space vessel dubbed "Tin Man." Complications arise with the intervention of two Romulan warships intent on keeping the life form from falling into Federation hands.

••••

"I was disappointed with 'Tin Man'," admits director Robert Scheerer. "It was an interesting show, but I don't think that I pulled off the sense sufficient-

ly of the living ship. God knows I tried. We struggled and struggled with it, but we ended up a little bit insufficiently fulfilled—I thought. An interesting show, but I don't think I did my best work in that show."

"I had gone to the sets a year before and Eric Stilwell told us 'Bottle shows, all they want is bottle shows,'" recalls uncredited co-writer Lisa Wilke. "'Don't go to another planet, make it as cheap as possible and maybe they'll buy it.'"

Dennis Putnam Bailey, who collaborated with his partner David Bischoff on the teleplay, says, "I wanted to demonstrate that we could turn in work they could use. The upshot of this was that they had reached a point third season where they really needed an extra show. Michael Piller and the rest of the staff were pulling stories out of nowhere and making them better than had been seen first and second year. Piller and the people he handpicked turned the show entirely around and they were up against the wall every week. They wrote 'Yesterday's Enterprise' in three days with five writers and it came out wonderfully.

"There came a point," he continues, "where we were told they wanted a script that was ready to shoot, so they could spend more time working on the scripts they thought had a lot of potential and needed rewriting. They had no expectations they could find a script out of nowhere. But Melinda Snodgrass read our script and brought it to Michael Piller and said, 'I think we can use it with very little rewriting.' Piller read it and decided they could use it. He passed it on to Rick Berman and, at this point, we were told we were on Rick Berman's desk. It took about a week and I was running into walls. All I could think about was will they buy it? We got the call on a Monday night that they had bought the show and that they were going to start shooting it a week later. When we were doing 'First Contact' we went through the more normal process of developing story in script. It's a lot more stressful way to work than sitting in Maryland and mailing exactly the story you want to see and having them send you a check and say we'll film it next week."

••••

Some have criticized the story as bearing a striking resemblance to 1979's *Star Trek: The Motion Picture*, but as Bailey points out, "Tin Man" is based on a story written by him and David Bischoff in 1975.

"In 1975 Dave and I wrote and sold to *Amazing Science Fiction Stories*," the writer says. "It was a short story called the 'Tin Woodman' and we were nominated for a Nebula. It was a short story and the thrust was a deep space, interstellar exploring ship encounters a living organism space craft orbiting a star with which they cannot communicate. One of the characters in this story is an empathic woman who is a part of the bridge crew of this spacecraft and her job is to monitor the emotional states of the other crew members. They consider her useless for first contact because her abilities are so limited. They fall back to earth have this teenage telepath who can't shut off listening to other people's minds pulled out of a psycho-ward basically and put in a missile and sent out to them. He joins with the creature and goes off. We wrote this in '75 and when we wee developing stories for *The Next Generation*, I said to Dave we have a story that would fit into the series really well. We wrote it 20 years before with no intention of ever doing anything else with it."

Episode #69:
"Hollow Pursuits"
Original Airdate: 5/5/90
Written by Sally Caves
Directed by Cliff Bole
Guest Starring: Dwight Schultz (Lt. Barclay), Whoopi Goldberg (Guinan), Charley Lang (Duffy)

Barclay (Dwight Schultz), an introverted crewmember—introspective, shy and incompetent—retreats to the holodeck to spend his life in a fantasy world he creates for himself. This despite LaForge's persistent attempts to shape him into a superior officer. When Barclay misses an important staff meeting, Geordi invades his holodeck environs and discovers a recreation of *The Three Musketeers*, in which the characters are based on the command crew, including Troi as the goddess of empathy and Riker as a fearful knave.

••••

Laughs Jonathan Frakes, "That was a riot, and the goddess of empathy...."

Michael Piller agrees although he discounts the widely perceived view that the show was a jab at self-absorbed *Trek* fans who are so obsessed with the show that they are oblivious to reality.

"It was a wonderful hour of television," he says. "Splendid, original, fresh ideas. You can't get better than that. It really was not intended directly at *Star Trek* fans. It was certainly about fantasy life versus reality. More than any other character in the three years I have been at *Star Trek*, that character of Barclay was more like me than anybody else. My wife watched that show and saw what was going on, and said that's [me] because I'm constantly in my fantasy world. Fortunately, I make a living at it. I have an extraordinary fantasy life and use my imagination all the time. It's real life that I have the problems with. I was delightfully happy with the episode. That's the one I would like to have in my biography when they write it.

"Dwight Schultz had been a *Star Trek* fan for a long time," continues Piller. "He told Rick Berman, 'If you ever get something for me, I'd love to do the show.' Dwight had just done a feature with Paul Newman and was very hot, and we didn't think we'd get him. It was a marvelous character piece. It's a Geordi show, but Dwight is at the center of it. This was a script submitted by a speculative writer."

Director Cliff Bole also differs with the purported fan-inspired storyline "I didn't feel that, and I would have heard if it was intended. I certainly didn't approach it that way. Dwight Schultz was excellent. He really comes to work prepared and has a direction. He did a great job. The fantasy part of it was fun too. Technically, I had fun on that show. I also enjoyed the illusion within an illusion, like the Three Musketeers. I think the *Star Trek* fans respond to that more than they do to anything else. They like those little period fantasies."

Episode #70:
"The Most Toys"
Original Airdate: 5/12/90
Written by Shari Goodhartz

The A-Team's *Dwight Schultz and Mr. T prior to Schultz's occasional appearance on* Next Generation *as Barclay.*

Directed by Timothy Bond
Guest Starring: Saul Rubinek (Kivas Fajo), Jane Daly (Varria), Nehemiah Persoff (Toff)

Data is abducted by alien Saul Rubinek, who collects rare and valuable items and intends to turn Data into a museum piece, while the Enterprise crew is deceived into believing he has perished in a shuttlecraft explosion. Attempting to escape and warn the Enterprise, Data commandeers a shuttlecraft and, brandishing a phaser, realizes that sometimes it is indeed necessary to kill.

••••

Among the many mementos of Rubinek's collection were a Mickey Mantle baseball card and an otherworldly critter.

"The creature was a hand puppet that Michael Westmore created," reveals producer David Livingston. "It was this little creature that Saul Rubinek went up to and said 'bidi-bidi-bidi.' That was his call to the creature and that became a running gag. People on the set still say, 'bidi-bidi-bidi.'"

"[The late] David Rappaport was supposed to play a very key role," reflects Michael Piller, "and he attempted suicide during production. We had to recast and reshoot, and were lucky to get a good actor. I'm very pleased with the way the script came out. It was a rather sick character he's playing, but fascinating."

Reflects director Timothy Bond, "When I arrived, David [Rappaport] and I started talking about putting the show together and he seemed in good spirits. We did a couple of days shooting that went quite well and then, over the weekend, he tried to kill himself. Nobody quite knows why. He had been doing a wonderful job. Then on Sunday night at midnight I got a call from my assistant director who said, 'Our guest star is in intensive care and we don't know why. So we have to shoot around him tomorrow.' By the time I went in the next morning, there was a story going around that they had found him in his car with a tube running in from the exhaust. Obviously I had to replace him. The guy who ultimately played the part, Saul Rubinek, is somebody I went to school with. It just happened that he was passing through town as was just about to start Bonfires of the Vanities, the ill-fated film, and he's a Trekkie. He called me and asked if I could get him in to see the sets. I said I would try and would call him on Monday. So I called him and said, 'How much do you want to see these sets?' He never goes guest shots on television, but I persuaded him to do it.

"Recasting changed the character," he adds, "because David Rappaport was quite small. The requirement, dramatically, is that people had to be afraid of him. That was very trick for someone of David's size to pull off, and we had to do it through a different approach in the photography and the sense that he could always get a weapon and blow people away. David underplayed it, but I always had guys in the background who were pretty beefy. As a matter of fact, when I first started working on the episode, I had this idea—which I still think is brilliant, but they wouldn't let me do it—to build his spaceship to his scale, so the ceiling would be about four feet from the floor. When anybody got in, they would have to bend over. It would have made it a nightmare shoot, but I thought it would have been a powerful visual. When we lost David, thank God we didn't have the small sets.

"What I loved about the show was the hung jury at the end. Would Data have killed him? Did Data try to kill

him? And the final push in on Data when he gets to tell the guy that they've confiscated all his belongings. The guy says, 'You're enjoying this,' and Data says, 'No.' It was fun with Brent Spiner because he's such a good actor. He knows to show just enough for the audience to ask, 'Is he enjoying this?' It was fun to get that sort of feeling."

Episode #71:
"Sarek"
Original Airdate: 5/19/90
Written by Peter Beagle
Story by Marc Cushman and Jake Jacobs
Directed by Les Landau
Guest Starring: Mark Lenard (Sarek), Joanna Miles (Perrin), William Denis (Ki Mendrossen), Rocco Sisto (Sakkath)

An aged Sarek (Mark Lenard) is escorted aboard the Enterprise to a diplomatic conference, where it is discovered that his mind is gradually deteriorating with lapses into senility and illogic. Only his assistant, played by Rocco Sisto, can keep his emotions in check. When the tirade of emotions proves too much, Picard volunteers to mind-meld with Sarek to give him the time to successfully complete negotiations.

• • • •

"I think in some ways, it's even better than 'Journey to Babel,'" says writer Ron Moore. "Mark Lenard has a chance to do some solid acting. It's a character-driven show and that's different for us."

Opines Michael Piller, "The key to the whole season is in personal stakes and personal drama. The Sarek story touches a lot of people. The generation of this episode came from an idea that had been submitted to this show from outside. It was not an idea about Sarek, however. It was an idea about an ambassador who begins to have mental problems as he is being taken up on some mission. As we started talking about it in house on staff, we said what would really be interesting is if you took a very powerful member of either Starfleet Command or the Federation, and have them going through a time of their lives, like so many of our parents, where they're beginning to have problems with aging. From that point, it was two or three steps of somebody saying, 'How can we turn it into a

science fiction show?' Somebody said, 'If it were a Vulcan, you could have some real telepathic impact from some kind of disease,' and from that point it was really short-stepped to, 'What about Sarek?' Sarek is an extraordinarily honorable character who we felt obliged to protect and deal with in a very respectful manner. At the same time, this becomes an extraordinarily personal story. A real stunning show."

Notes director Les Landau, "There are some great moments in that show. When we first see Sarek listening to the concert and reacting to Data's beautiful playing of the violin and we, finally, see the tear fall from his eye....it reaches such a point within him that he can no longer take it and must leave the environs of the Enterprise theatre, which surprises the captain and Troi especially. There was just something about the way Mark Lenard played this moment and reacted that just made [it] extra special. The other moments that particularly come to mind in that episode is the mind meld between Picard and Sarek. Trying to come up with a way to conceptualize and shoot that became a frustrating point. I think, ultimately, when the two actors got to the set and showed me what they wanted to do, it just melded together and became a wonderful moment within the show. You always come to the set with a prepared framework for a particular scene, but you use that only as a schematic. When actors get to a set, all your planning can go out the window, and such was the case when Sarek finally says to Picard, 'Illogical, illogical,' to shed some kind of emotion. The dynamics between Picard and Sarek reach a level that I think is classic in Star Trek history. I think the most outstanding moment is when we finally see Picard sitting with Beverly, where he is the mind of Sarek thinking about his life that has come before, his former wife and the one and only reference to his son, Spock. If you watch what Patrick did in that scene, it is truly spectacular. I have had many great experiences on the show, but certainly that was one of the best. Patrick is so capable on so many different levels that one just let's him go. There is some discussion prior and after, but his ability is so right on, that one is reluctant to make any adjustment."

Episode #72:
"Menage A Trois"
Original Airdate: 5/19/90
Written by
Fred Bronson and Susan Sackett
Directed by Robert Legato
Guest Starring: Majel Barrett (Lwaxana Troi), Frank Corsentino (DaiMon Tog), Rudolph Willrich (Reittan Grax), Ethan Phillips (Dr. Farek), Peter Slutsker (Nibor), Carel Struycken (Mr. Homn)

Riker, Troi and her mother, Lwaxana, are kidnapped by a lovestruck Ferengi who not only wants the elder Troi for her body, but her brain—for its unique telepathic powers. Pursued by the Enterprise, the Ferengi captain is willing to release Troi and Riker in return for the hand of Misses Troi. Picard woos Lwaxana in an attempt to convince DaiMon Tog (Frank Corsentino), that he is truly in love with her. Meanwhile, Wesley makes a second attempt to gain entry to Starfleet Academy.

• • • •

"It's a comedy," says co-writer Susan Sackett. "It's not Shakespeare. We pitched a lot of stories and the last one was Mrs. Troi. At first, we were going to do O'Henry's "The Ransom of Red Chief' and it kind of evolved. We developed the story and the premise with Gene, and we would run things past him. His criticism helped make the characters believable. When we came up with something he thought would run, he said, 'Now take it to Michael Piller."

"I did a polish and the boys and I did another," adds Melinda Snodgrass of her re-write with former story editors Richard Manning and Hans Beimler. "I had asked to be let out four weeks after, because I had worked straight through a year and a half without a break and I wanted to come home to New Mexico."

Before the episode aired, a moment which aroused the ire of *Star Trek* fans was the alleged nude scene in which Troi and her mother are disrobed, according to Ferengi custom, while Riker looks on helplessly.

"We weren't nude, of course, at all!" Marina Sirtis, who along with Majel Barrett was garbed in a full body stocking, exclaims. "The Paramount publicity machine goes into action and they try and find something different to draw the

public's attention to that particular episode. It was the same thing with 'The Price.' There was this big ho-ha about Troi being in bed with somebody. For the first time ever in *Star Trek* you see two people in bed together—but when you actually saw it, it was pretty tame. But that's their job, publicity, and that's what they do."

For the record, those who want to see the busty Betazoid in the buff are advised to check out Michael Winner's dreadful version of *The Wicked Lady*, starring Faye Dunnaway, the same director's *Death Wish III* or the equally inane *Blind Date*, starring Kirstie Alley. No body stockings included.

Episode #73:
"Transfigurations"
Original Airdate: 6/19/90
Written by Rene Echevarria
Directed by Tom Benko
Guest Starring: Mark La Mura (John Doe), Charles Dennis (Sunad), Julie Warner (Christy)

An amnesiac alien being, dubbed John Doe (Mark Lamura), is saved from certain death by the Enterprise and Dr. Crusher discovers he is undergoing an evolutionary process. The doctor gains an affectionate attachment for the ailing alien, who helps Geordi find self-confidence with women after a talk about the book of love with Worf proves unsuccessful.

• • • •

"We wanted to do a show where we get to see 24th Century medicine up close and personal," offers Michael Piller. "Beverly Crusher uses all her skills to save an alien, reconstructing him and putting him back together and sort of falling in love with him. It's a very spiritual kind of show."

Explains episode writer Rene Echevarria, "After selling 'The Offspring' to the show, I went back to New York and Michael [Piller] called me a couple of weeks later and said he had a story that was dead in the water. It was a premise they had bought involving us finding some crashed ship on a little moon and there's a man who's basically dead and we use miraculous 24th century medicine and bring him back to life. We practically grow him back, but who

is he and what's the story? I thought about it for awhile and came up with the basic idea of 'Transfigurations,' that someone was evolving out of their human form into an energy being. We've seen both of those stories before, but we've never seen the intermediate step. So Michael went for it and commissioned a story and then I came out and did a break and wrote the first draft. That script also was the second to last episode of the season, so there was a huge time constraint. After the first draft, I went back to New York and he called me and said come back and help do the polish and rewrite, and it was broken up by acts. Every one on staff at the time wrote an act, and then it was all put together and Michael did a polish on it.

"Next," he continues the scenario, "Michael said he wanted to do an environmental story and I came up with something for which I wrote many, many drafts, but it never got off the ground. Towards the end of that process, he said he had a script that he wanted me to write. It involved every environmental story that people had done and seemed fairly obvious. They in fact commissioned a teleplay that was literally smokestacks, and it would have been very obvious to the audience that it was the cause of the blindness and mutations in a tribe that was kept on a little island called the Island of Tears. They were kept there, hidden from view, in order for the rest of the society to be able to maintain its mode of production, which was highly exploitive and environmentally unsound. The audience would have guessed at the end of the first act what was going on. What I came up with was a Federation colony that mined dilithium and they're natives to that planet. The twist was that what was causing the problems were these organisms that had evolved in the presence of electromagnetic fields of dilithium. Its removal was creating mutations."

Episode #74:
"The Best of Both Worlds, Part I"
Original Airdate: 3/18/89
Written by Michael Piller
Directed by Cliff Bole
Guest Starring: Elizabeth Dennehy (Shelby), George Murdock (Admiral Hanson), Whoopi Goldberg (Guinan)

• • • •

Ambitious Borg expert Shelby (Elizabeth Dennehy) hopes to become first officer of the Enterprise, assuming the seat she believes Riker is vacating to take over the captaincy of his own ship. Then they discover the return of the Borg, which have destroyed Federation colony Jure 4. Confronting the Enterprise, the race of cybernetic beings kidnap Picard, and transform him into a spokesman by which they can announce their intentions to conquer the Earth. Leading a daring rescue attempt, Shelby, Data and Worf find that Picard has been turned into Locutus, the king of the Borg. Upon the Away Team's returning to the Enterprise, Riker prepares to unleash the force of the ship's main deflector dish in hopes of destroying the Borg vessel....and Captain Picard.

••••

"The conversations we had during the year about the Borg always seemed to come back to what ultimately did not come to pass," says Michael Piller. "We felt there had not been a worthy successor to the Klingons as adversaries in the new generation, and that was a very serious problem that a show like this has to wrestle with. Third season we spent a great deal of time developing the Romulans, and to a lesser degree the Ferengi, to be a continuing threat and a worthy adversary. But we also had always known that the Borg were there and that there had been a good response from the audience about them. But when the Borg came up, most of the people here felt they were boring because there was no personality you could put your teeth in to. The fact is because they were all one and there was no spokesman or star role, every time we talked about doing a Borg show, we said, 'Why don't we create a 'queen bee' that can be the spokesman for this group, and make her a character instead of just cold steel?'"

That idea did not sit well with Piller, who appreciated the unique quality of the Borg as villains and he was reluctant to conventionalize the alien menace.

"I really liked 'Q Who?', and so I resisted those suggestions," he says. "I never really came around to trying to do it, because to me there was something special and frightening about the Borg

that their lack of character brought. For a show that dwells and specializes in character to be challenged and possibly destroyed by a characterless villain seemed, to me, to be a special kind of threat. But when we started talking about the cliffhanger and the Borg, we really did talk about who was going to be the queen bee."

And it was Piller who came up with the notion of a king bee: namely Jean Luc Picard—or Locutus, as he came to be known for a while.

"It all just fell into place," relates Piller. "I said, 'I've got it. Picard will be the queen bee.' There was actually an early draft of the story in which both Data and Picard were taken and combined as a Borg. Someone said why should they do this, and we didn't have a good answer so we dropped that idea."

But the challenge was what would happen on the Enterprise once Picard was abducted. Even with the extra money for space battles and sets, Piller was determined not to have "Best" turn into *Battlestar: Galactica*, but rather maintain the human drama which would serve as a backdrop to the epic drama he was weaving.

"We had no idea it was really a Riker story when we started out," Piller emphasizes. "I came up with the idea of having the Shelby character come onboard to challenge Riker. That seemed to play into the Riker emotions and the conflict over whether to take the other job or not, and that builds into the issue of whether or not he was big enough to fill the center chair. [This] led to the second part, which is the master versus pupil dynamic we set up, some of which was cut out of Part II for length, including a scene between Riker and Troi where Riker expresses is concerns and doubts about Picard. We lost a little character to justify all the action that had to go in there."

Admittedly, Piller has always found it easier to write character than *Trek-Speak*, that mystical science fiction language that *Next Generation* perfected. Writing about Riker's dilemma over whether to accept the captaincy of the USS Melbourne or remain with the Enterprise came easily, particularly in light of his own personal decision that he was wrestling with as to whether to

remain on the show or move on himself.

Notes Piller, "Good writing usually draws upon something that means something to the writer. At the end the third season, I had decided not to return to *Star Trek*. Rick and Gene asked me to come back because things were going very well, but I had so many other things I wanted to do. I wanted to write features and create my own shows. I had always told myself that I couldn't commit long term to anything, but as I was writing this script, I found myself in the position of Riker, who was trying to decide whether he was going to leave the ship or not. Much of what happened in Part One was about what was going on in my head."

In one scene taking place in Ten Forward, Riker confides to Troi that he might be afraid of "the big chair."

"Riker is talking to Troi about why he hasn't left," says Piller. "'What am I missing that I used to have? I don't seem to have that drive that I used to have,' and ultimately he comes to the realization that ambition isn't everything. If you're happy and comfortable and find the rewards of the people you work with, then it's something that counts for a great deal. We push ourselves and push ourselves, and sometimes it is good to do that—it has certainly been healthy for me and my career—but there are also times when you sit back and enjoy your successes, and being with the people you love. That was really me speaking through Riker."

Making production of the episode easier was the lesson taught by second season's "Q Who?"

"The set had been a problem," says David Livingston, "because we didn't have the money to build a complete one, and the Borgs had taken a long time. We made a lot of changes on them after they were first put together. The technical part of figuring out how to stick on all this tubing to these guys was a big deal. The R&D, so to speak, was really done on 'Q Who?' in the look of the Borg. When we got to 'Best of Both Worlds,' we knew what the problems were. We knew we had to build a different kind of set and it worked out really well."

After production wrapped, the Borg set lay idle on stage 16, collecting dust while cast and crew enjoyed their

••••

199

summer hiatus and fans pondered the second part of the saga, wondering what would happen after Riker ordered the Enterprise to fire on the Borg ship.

"When we finished the first half, we had no idea what the second half would be," admits Rick Berman. "Michael Piller, with a little help from me, resolved it. It was a lot of fun to be able to stretch the format and do something that was two hours as opposed to one."

Unlike fans who had spent the entire summer wondering how the Enterprise would defeat the Borg and rescue Picard, Michael Piller had waited considerably longer to start thinking about how he was going to write himself out of a seemingly impossible-to-solve cliffhanger.

"After my contract was signed," he laughs. "I never try to think of these things until I have to. I'm a very instinctive writer and the people I don't work with are the people who need all the answers laid out before they start writing. I find the discovery process is what the life of scripts is about. Yes, you need to have the broadstrokes and have a direction so you know where you're going, because television is too expensive and goes too quickly to run all the way down the road only to realize you don't have anything when you get to the end. But I do honestly believe that you let the characters take you and just listen to what the voices are saying when you write a script. Ultimately you'll find wonderful things. The danger, of course, is when you get a block, you can't figure out what the hell they're trying to say."

Guest star Elizabeth Dennehy recalls her experience on "Best of Both Worlds" quite well.

"The first part was the hardest," Elizabeth Dennehy, who portrayed Shelby, explains. "I didn't know anything about the show and I had to look like I knew, because I was in charge. I was a commander and the hardest thing in the world to do was making that dialogue

sound like I spoke that way all the time. It was impossible. It's so easy to remember and memorize lines when they make logical sense or when you get blocked and you say when I move over here, I say this. But this was just memorizing timetables. It was just 2x2 is 4. I didn't know what a manipulation effect in the Borg ship's subspace meant. That's not English! It was like learning a foreign language by phonetics. It was just grueling and my first day was the hardest day of all. It was a scene in a big conference room where I'm talking to them about what the Borg do, and they're like tongue twisters. LeVar and Brent have the hardest stuff to learn. I don't know how they do it. You have to sit down and drill yourself, and that was the hardest thing. By the second show, I knew how to do it. On top of all the other things, you need to think about the person you're working with and the character and hitting your mark and don't block him there, and all those kind of things. But, geez, those lines. I yelled at Michael Piller when I first met him. The day he visited the set I had to say, 'Separate the saucer section, assign a skeleton crew,' and I asked him, 'Can you lay off on the alliteration a little, Michael....please.' He laughed. It was hard.

Remembers then assistant director Chip Chalmers, "'Best of Both Worlds' was definitely a get down and dirty show. I also remember the moment when Patrick, dressed in a Borg outfit, first walks up to the viewscreen and says, 'I am Locutus of Borg.' He came on to the set—everybody was wowed with what they had done to Patrick—and we got everyone settled down and did one rehearsal. All he had to do was walk up to the camera. He did so and towered over everyone. It was just so creepy and so spooky, and he said, 'I am Locutus of Borg. Have you considered buying a Pontiac?' And everyone was on the floor. That's the kind of thing that makes it wonderful to work on the show; those people have a wonderful sense of humor."

••••
CHAPTER TWENTY TWO
SEASON FOUR

An Introduction

In *Star Trek*'s fourth season, *Next Generation* faithfully continued to fulfill the mission of the starship Enterprise in boldly going where no man, woman or Andorian has gone before, while improving on the quality of its impressive third season voyages.

"Fourth season was the best season so far," said director Les Landau at the time. "The quality of the writing and the storylines have improved so much over the last four seasons, climaxing in what was delivered to the audience this year."

Michael Piller says, "I don't think there was one clinker in the whole group. Certainly third season we had some. Arguably you could say there were better shows third season, but week after week we maintained a much higher consistency of quality than we had or most shows ever achieve."

"The show has gotten better and better each year," agrees Rick Berman. "We all take it extremely seriously and that's the only way you can do it because its such hard work and the second you start getting sloppy the audience sees it instantly. The fact that we have kept up the quality and integrity of the show and simultaneously the audience has gotten bigger is a wonderful achievement. It's wonderfully good luck as well."

Surprisingly, third season—despite being widely regarded as a success for *Trek*—was also riddled with its share of problems which included an unhappy captain named Jean Luc-Picard.

"Patrick came to me in the middle of the season and said 'I'm bored, you haven't given me anything interesting to do' and he was very unhappy about it," reveals Piller. "He was upset with the way Picard was being treated and he had every right to be, but third season we basically were just trying to

keep our head above water because we didn't have anything in development. If you look back at [the fourth] season I don't think Patrick's had one complaint. He's got to die, been Borgified, all kinds of things."

Ron Moore, who returned to the show for a second year as the show's Executive Script Consultant, agrees that the shows improving quality was a result of more time spent refining the scripts. "We were able to get ahead on scripts fourth season," says Moore. "Last year time was short and we were off and just ahead of the gun. We had a better handle on it going into the fourth season so we never really got to that scary point where you're writing madly on the stage."

Upon reflection, fourth season was at times overthought, Piller offers. "One of the things that I would say about the first half of the season is that we had a few gimmick shows," he says. "They were really good adventures and had good hooks — things that are easily described in *TV Guide*. I think every series needs those and I look at the series as a whole and I would say the entertainment value of the first half of the season was very high, but I don't think there was much substance to it. The second half of the season I think was sterling television and we really reached the best television has to offer."

In prepping the fourth season in the summer of 1990, Berman, who had championed the series through stormy seas during its early shakedown period, did not have a detailed personal agenda for the show's new season.

"We did not really set a fourth season goal," says Berman. "We knew which characters we wanted to focus on and what kind of stories we wanted to do in very broad strokes. We knew Wesley was going to be leaving and, of course, we knew we had to start off with a show that finished up the Borg experience. Our ultimate goal was to do good episodes as opposed to working on a seasonal arc of some sort."

"There was no formal sit down," adds Ron Moore. "We had a lot of discussion with Michael and Rick about different stories. Right off the bat we were talking about the idea that we wanted to followup on 'Sins of the Father', the Borg shows

Cinefantastique covers the fourth season of Star Trek: The Next Generation.

and, at some point, do a 'Day In the Life' show. We also talked about doing something more with O'Brien and getting somebody married."

Jeri Taylor, who joined the show as a Supervising Producer after Producer Lee Sheldon left the show over the familiar "creative differences" which had sidelined so many of his predecessors, also had her own ideas regarding what she wanted to see happen on the Enterprise's latest treks.

"I didn't feel I needed to come in and fill any sort of vacuum," says Taylor. "My tastes are very much in synch with Michael Piller's and we really perceive the stories in very much the same way. If there's anything I wanted to do more of, it was developing the characters of Crusher and Troi because I thought they were underused and would like to flesh them out and make them more rounded and interesting people. There is a very small way in which I sometimes remind people about the role of women and sometimes they remind me. I'm not saying that this was a staff of men and I had to come in and show them the way, but maybe it was something a little more in the foreground with me than some of the others."

Taylor's perceptions of the role of females on *Star Trek* are shared by its main female protagonist, Marina Sirtis, who plays Counselor Deanna Troi.

"I don't think we've addressed feminism," says Sirtis. "The women on the show were very non-threatening and I don't think it's realistic, I don't think it's realistic in the 20th century so it's definitely not realistic in the 24th century. Ever since Denise left the show the two woman that are left are both doctors in the caring professions so we don't see women in power positions. We do see female admirals but I have to say the fans don't really care about our guest stars, they care about the regulars and what they want to see are the regular women having more power."

Sirtis felt that despite the continuing attention her character had received from the show's writers, Troi was still underutilized and underdeveloped. She refers to an original draft of the third season episode 'The Enemy' in which Geordi is stranded on a planet with a hostile Romulan soldier as an example.

"In the original draft which I happened to read which we're not allowed to see so we don't make conversations like this," Sirtis says, "it was Troi and Geordi stranded on the planet and because Geordi was blinded by the electromagnetics preventing his visor from working when we came across the Romulan it was actually Troi who incapacitated him. I felt very excited about this. I finally got to do something interesting and different and, of course, when the final script came not only was I not on the planet, but I had one line at the end of the show — and that was actually cut. That's the kind of thing that happens and I wish it wouldn't."

Michael Piller acknowledges that servicing the lesser-used members of the *Trek* ensemble was a consideration going into the fourth season.

"One of our goals from the beginning of fourth season was to find stories for each character, Troi among them," says Piller. "I think the last two years have seen her develop a great deal and that does not mean it's sufficient or there shouldn't be more done, but I believe that she used to be a character who looked at the screen and said 'I sense anger out there' and we've given her a chance to actually do therapy, to do some very serious stories and make

some critical contributions to the solutions or problems and really become a counselor in the best sense of the word. I don't really think that she's an underdeveloped character anymore. I feel very good about Troi. She's a really sexy lady who provides an enormous amount of emotional support to our other continuing characters."

Ironically, one of the main objectives fourth season was not only delving into *Trek*'s future, but its past and the 1991-92 season boasted the return of a number of characters from *Next Generation*'s first several years on the air. "We informally decided to go back into our own universe and bring back some of the more interesting characters that were created over the first three years," says Piller. "We created a whole universe here and we have a tendency to go onto the next new discovery, which is great. At the same time I think we have created some very interesting problems and characters which should be revisited. We're not serialized by any means, but we like the idea of doing revisits and that's why you saw so many of the characters from prior seasons make a comeback this year."

Not only were there the persistent references to the Daystrom Institute, the Tholian Wars and the like, but even to such obscurities as the nannites Piller introduced in his script to "Evolution" the previous year, and the ability of the main deflector dish to channel energy as established in "Best Of Both Worlds".

"I like continuity and those references," says Ron Moore. "The danger is you don't want to serialize the show. This isn't *LA Law* or something where you can carry stories over week to week. A first time viewer who sits down and watches 'Reunion' [Moore's sequel to 'Sins of the Father' in which Duras returns to assume the mantle of leadership of the Klingon Empire] will have to work and follow it pretty closely, but he can do it. I think you can watch that show and not have known what happened in 'Sins' because I don't think it's as important, it's just knowing that Worf has this problem. Of course, it's nice to know the backstory just as it's nice to know about his relationship with K'ehleyr, but all you need to know is *something* happened."

One of the most talked-about returns of the season was K'ehleyr, played by Suzi Plakson (who also starred as Dr. Solar in second season's "The Schizoid Man"). In "Reunion", Worf finds out he is a father and is reunited with his former love, K'ehyler introduced in second season's "The Emissary".

"All the comments were I loved the show, but why did you have to kill off K'ehlyr?" says Ron Moore, who co-wrote the episode. "That's usually the only comment I get. I loved it and I think it works just fine and if that wasn't there you'd be missing a big part of the story where Worf has to embrace his son in the end and finally getting to go after Duras."

Killing K'ehylr however was not the biggest risk the producers took fourth season, although few incidents on the show have engendered more outraged mail than her slaying. In fact, probably one of the points of contention which the creative team wrestled with early on in the season was the follow-up to Michael Piller's two part Borg epic, "Best Of Booth". Upon the second part's conclusion, a clearly shaken Picard trembles upon reflection on his seizure by the Borg.

"It was my intention to wrap up the two parter with the feeling that although everything is solved," Piller says, "life isn't so smooth and a man does not walk away from something like that and go back to work without having a little extra flashback nightmare. It's just that little uncertainty, the moment of discomfort that I wanted to leave the audience with."

Some of the staff were equally uncomfortable with the notion of Piller wanting to continue the story of Picard's abduction by the Borg into an unplanned third part. "The biggest decision of the hiatus was to extend the storyline of Picard's kidnapping into the third episode," says Piller. "That was very controversial and there were a lot of people who were very hesitant about doing a threesome and going down to earth. People felt it was not *Star Trek* and I have friends who are fans of the show who called and said I hope you never do that again. But I've got to tell you, for my money, 'Family' was one of the best pieces of film we did fourth season and it was also consistently the lowest rated in both the original and reruns. Maybe my friend was right — if you're not out in space, you're not hitting the audience where they want to be hit."

Director Winrich Kolbe who has been with the show since second season and contributed a number of episodes, weighs the challenges of helming a *Star Trek* adventure.

"There are certain advantages and pitfalls to doing this show," Kolbe says. "One thing I like about *Star Trek* is when I'm prepping an episode I go in at nine in the morning and I leave whenever I'm finished, but I stay basically in the studio and read the script. If I want to take a break I walk over to the stage and lay out my shots and take a walk back and read the script."

This is very different than most one hour dramatic series where Kolbe would spend a large amount of his time in the back of a van scouting locations for a show such as *Hunter*, for which he frequently directed. In the world of *Star Trek* where nearly everything is created within the confines of three soundstages on the lot, the need to drive around looking for locations to shoot is virtually eliminated."

"Television has grown up a lot," says Berman. "The cynical element of television. I think our show is a lot more believable than the old show and that's due in large part to the creator of the old show too because it was Roddenberry who was very vehement when we created *Star Trek: The Next Generation* that it had to be believable. That it would not deal with swords and sorcerers or be melodramatic. The old *Star Trek* had people who wore togas standing under arches and our *Star Trek* is much more contemporary and believable."

"They're still cardboard rocks," laughs producer David Livingston. "The creative people on this show are so talented that they're able to make cardboard rocks that are still all fake into a reality which I'm sometimes just blown away by. After all, as one of our coordinator's says, the Enterprise is just plastic on a stick. The only time you are ever disappointed is when you know that you've had to cut the money and, in our minds, we know that it could have been substantially better."

The budget for the year is deter-

Left-Right: NextGeneraton *writers Brannon Braga, Lolita Fatjo and Ron Moore.*

mined by the cost of the previous year's expenses. Livingston who is involved with the planning of the show's annual pattern budget elaborates.

"We do a cost analysis at the end of each season and find out what we spent and if we spent that amount of money last year then we budget the same amount for the next year," he says. "If Peter only spends $10,000 for opticals on a very simple show the money he saves I get to put into construction and vice versa. We have maintained the amount of money in all of our departments and increased them accordingly due to cost of living. It's not like there's any kind of contest going on about who gets the most money. We have tried to maintain— and have been successful in keeping— the money level at a sufficient level for our departments."

Larry Carroll, Co-Story Editor fourth season, was not too put off by the budget constraints, having had a history working in low-budget features which included the notoriously cheap Charles Band's Empire Pictures, the successor to the Roger Corman legacy of shooting on a shoestring.

"The average episode of *Star Trek* probably costs more than most of Charlie's pictures combined," jokes Carroll. "Michael Piller and Rick Berman really know what they can do and what they

can't do and they're masters at keeping the show within totally practical limits and then maximizing what they can do and squeezing every bit of production value out of it. It's really amazing."

"It's amazing because our budgets are still so tight," adds David Carren. "Whatever they do they really do it with such top quality that we're always struggling to keep it under budget anyway."

"We have what David and I have come to call the 'M' effect named after the Fritz Lang film, *M*, where he did everything off camera with Peter Lorre," says Carroll. "People come in here and pitch these stories with these fantastic things we could never begin to produce, and its simply because this show is so well produced and so well thought out that they don't miss those things and believe they're all part of *Star Trek*. They don't realize how incredibly sophisticated, lean and spare the storytelling is."

And even if the writers have visions of extraordinary space battles and vast planetscapes, those are ideas which are soon dismissed by Livingston upon his initial review of the first draft teleplay. "Scripts can always be cut," says Livingston. "Obviously Michael does not want to prevent the writers from having their imaginations flourish and if they think that they need 1000 people for something, they should write that, but it's going to come down to 10 people pretty quickly.

Generally, the writers have been very responsible in knowing how big the show is and what they can write to."

The bottom line demands of the show's budget often force the show to remain shipbound where standing sets already exist and do not require additional construction, thus resulting in an unofficial ratio of ship to planet shows even higher than the original series.

"We have to do ship shows for cost," Livingston says. "We try and balance that off and save enough money to do the big shows like our season finale, 'Redemption', in which we built the Great Hall again and had a couple of ships and a Klingon home. We try and keep the construction budget on par with the optical budget. They're not the same money but in terms of each year we try and allocate as much money to construction as we possibly can. To me the two most important parts of spending the money on the show are the opticals and construction. It does cost an awful lot of money to build those sets, but the goal is not to have the show take place on the ship all the time."

Often sets will be redressed and used in other episodes to help cut costs. "We use sets over and over again," says Livingston. "We can build a huge set and keep using it. We use sets over and over again and nobody in the audience has a clue, I hope. We are attempting not to have that quality of being a ship show. You would be surprised what we turn around and make happen. There was one set this year that we used three times in a row and I defy anyone to tell me that they were the same set because Richard James did such an amazing turnaround. It shows how well we're able to do it, Marvin Rush lights them differently and they're dressed differently by Jim Meese and they're shot differently. The money we get from Paramount is all up there on the screen."

The desire among the directors to continue to advance their craft and utilize the newest in advanced film technology often taxes the budget as well as the varied resources of *Trek*'s production team often bringing them into conflict with Livingston.

"The directors know coming in that we have a pretty good budget on this show," says Livingston. "They know that they are going to get a lot of goodies and if they're willing to fight for it, great. Let them come in and scream and pound on my desk, I want this set. When I shot my episode, I did. Sometimes though you just have to say no. Richard James will have designed something like the Taj Mahal and I use my red pencil, which is a cliché and a joke, and I start scratching it all up and saying we can't have this and this and out of that Richard sometimes comes up with something that's even more inspired. Budget limitations and schedule force everyone's creativity to go up one notch and they have to really figure out how to make this better. It's easy to spend tens of millions of dollars and, I think, we've seen enough feature films which have been horrible where they've just thrown caution to the wind and not really thought about what they're doing and spent a lot of money. We don't do that. Working on episodic television forces you to be more creative."

"They want a movie and they want it for $1.2 million," says director Kolbe. "Nothing ever goes smooth. They're very few shows where everything seems to come together. 'Identity Crisis' was going fine until we hit Stage 16 and then it was 17 hour days. I know that they were quite worried about us going over and it ended up going over by a half a day."

"He drives you a little crazy because his shots take a long time but he pushes it to the max and takes every second that we'll allow him to get and then probably more," Livingston says of Kolbe. "He's excellent with a camera and has a wonderful eye. He was a pointman in Vietnam and that's good training for a director. God bless him, he's technically a master and does his homework. He knows how to pull off that technical stuff."

Despite the turmoil which has shaken the writing staff over the years, the technical team has remained consistent except for some changes in crew made by Rick Berman at the beginning of third season. It is their devotion to bringing *Next Generation* to life that has been a truly unheralded triumph in reviving *Star Trek* for the small screen. "What we do is fake, it's not real," says Livingston. "Even though we work on a show that presents a positive image for the future and says there's hope for all of us, when you read the headlines that's reality. Gene's the idealist and I guess we'd all aspire to be that way, but unfortunately we're not. That's why a lot of people are on this show and stay here. It's uplifting and we have a good group of people. If this show was *Blade Runner* I don't think the people would last, they'd all be so depressed."

The fourth season in which the new characters have become firmly established in the minds of its viewers have provided a chance to break some of the rules which bound both the makers of the original series and the new. This new series equivalent of *Trek Classic*'s dreadful fare like "Turnabout Intruder" seems to be a thing of the past.

"I think it was a natural process of evolution," says fourth season Story Editor Larry Carroll. "Obviously, you say you're going to make a sequel to *Star Trek* and that's a pretty gutsy thing. You have a tremendous weight and there were a lot of brilliant decisions that were made in terms of the casting, the structure, the definition of the 24th century that when you look at them are amazing. They were not decisions people would normally go for. It was really gutsy getting a bald English actor to play the French captain of the Enterprise. It took a while for the show to come together and for it to really get up and get rolling but it's been a gradual process of evolution to find the stories that work right."

Carroll's writing partner, David Carren agrees. "There's one basic thing that never really changed and part of that evolution was the new *Star Trek* finding its way to being a family," he says. "The old show worked because it basically was a family. It was more like Kirk was a big brother than a father figure and everyone else was kind of his siblings and Spock was the wise Uncle. There were all kinds of interesting dynamics to their relationships. The family didn't really jell per se on this show until deep into the second season or even third where it really came together. I think Ten Forward was an important part of that, it was like that family milieu and all those elements fell into place and you saw there's Picard and he's the father and here's the rest of the members of his family."

"On the original series Roddenberry had that basic kernel of an idea which is that the Enterprise is one big happy family," says Marc Scott Zicree. "Harlan Ellison and he had all those enormous arguments because when Harlan wrote 'City on the Edge of Forever' he had drug dealers and all that on the Enterprise. Roddenberry took it all out and said 'No, these are the cream of the crop' and, in retrospect, you see Roddenberry was right and that's why you've got all these Trekkies dressing up in their uniforms and dreaming of being on the Enterprise. At least, he had the wisdom to realize there should be family spats because that's realistic, but by the time he got to the new show and he was pushing 70 I guess he wanted lukewarm farina and wanted there to be no conflict ever.

The *Star Trek* audience however is unique in the annals of television history and was more tolerant of the early flaws in the series' first two years and has endured through the early disasters and has been richly rewarded for their patience in the show's third and fourth season.

"I think is some respects the show has gotten better," says Marina Sirtis. "In other respects it's stayed the same. I'm going by what the fans say, because it's very hard to be objective when you're in the show. The fans tend to say that the writing and the storylines have gotten much better over the last four years, but I think that's possibly to do with the fact that now we have more or less a fixed writing staff. In the first couple of seasons the turnover was so immense that I don't think they could ever get a hook, they were here for ten minutes and then they were gone which wasn't really long enough to establish any kind of continuity or character development in their scripts. The writing has improved because we have a stable of writers that we've had for a while."

"When it clicks it's one of the best shows on television," says Zicree. "It's one of the few shows I watch and one of the few I want to write for. The episodes that really work are the ones that shake up the structure like Yesterday's Enterprise', which did this wonderful What If scenario. I like those kind of stories, but still the show has improved each year and the ratio of good episodes to bad has gotten better each year. In the first few years it was one good episode in every blue moon and if I saw another episode where superior aliens put them on trial..."

"I think we have to go back to the original idea and concept," says director Les Landau. "Gene created the model for what *Star Trek* is and will continue to be, and he has proven that it will exist on its own forever. I would hate to see the Enterprise lose Captain Picard, Number One, Data, Beverly, Troi or Geordi, but the idea, the universal concept of what *Star Trek* is about will endure because its a timeless story. What Gene created, Rick has followed up on and Michael puts down in words, will endure forever because we're dealing with universal themes about the human condition."

• • • •

CHAPTER TWENTY THREE
SEASON FOUR

Episode Guide

"The Best of Both Worlds, Part II"

"Family"

"Brothers"

"Suddenly Human"

"Remember Me"

"Legacy"

"The Reunion"

"Future Imperfect"

"Final Mission"

"The Loss"

"Data's Day"

"The Wounded"

"Devil's Due"

"Clues"

"First Contact"

"Galaxy's Child"

"Night Terrors"

"Identity Crisis"

"The Nth Degree"

"Q-Pid"

"The Drumhead"

"Half a Life"

"The Host"

"The Mind's Eye"

"In Theory"

"Redemption, Part I"

Elizabeth Dennehy, who portrayed Commander Shelby in both parts of "The Best of Both Worlds."

Episode #75:
"The Best of Both Worlds, Part II"
Original Airdate: 9/24/90
Written by Michael Piller
Directed by Cliff Bole
Guest Starring: Elizabeth Dennehy (Shelby), George Murdock (Admiral Hanson), Whoopi Goldberg (Guinan)

In the season premiere and conclusion of "The Best of Both Worlds," Riker's plan to use the Enterprise's deflector dish to disable the Borg ship fails. The alien vessel continues on its direct heading towards Earth, destroying a fleet of 48 starships. The Enterprise once again engages the Borg and rescue Picard/Locutus. Once aboard the Enterprise, Data accesses Picard's mind and plants a suggestion in the Borg collective consciousness that it is time for them to regenerate, resulting in the ship being put to sleep and the Borg self-destructing. Dr. Crusher successfully removes Picard's cybernetic implants, although memories of the abduction still haunt him.

••••

"I thought Part One was much better than Part Two," says writer and executive producer Michael Piller. "The reason was that Part Two had to deliver the goods promised by Part One, but they were not as interesting. If you look at it as a two hour movie, it's really quite effective. As an episode by itself, I don't think Part Two really has a lot of character stuff. It has to have the battles and all the stuff I don't like writing. The one thing I will say about Part II, about which I was extremely pleased, was how I figured out to defeat the Borg, because, frankly, when I was writing it I had no idea. I basically discovered the solution at the same time the characters did. It just occurred to me that their strength was their interdependency, [so] why not make their weakness that same interdependency?"

"I actually had much less to do in the second one than the first," recalls actress Elizabeth Dennehy, who returned to the Paramount soundstages after a three month hiatus to pick up seconds after the first show ended. "I had the show on tape so I watched it quite a few times before we went back. The hard thing was remaining the same weight, because my weight goes up and down and those spacesuits are merciless. I'm sure I put on some weight between the first and the second one. The costumes are so awful, it's very hot on the Paramount lot. It's like you're on a frying pan and you walk around in this one piece outfit. They're dark and everyone walks around with them unzipped between takes. They have stirrups on the feet and big shoulder pads, so it's like you're being compressed and pulled by a rubber band together, and you just want to be put on a rack afterwards. It was so awful, I hated them. It's a rite of initiation that the whole cast will say, 'Elizabeth, say I hate my space suit,' and I said, 'I hate my spacesuit,' and they said, 'Okay, welcome.' It's a rite of passage there. And the fact you can't live like a human being, you can't eat and drink is probably good because it keeps you in shape, but it's a form of slavery which I'm not sure I could deal with knowing I could never go on a binge. I don't know how the girls do it all the time. And the wigs...I looked like Jane from *F-Troop* with that hairdo...and poor Michael Dorn and Brent. I don't know how they do it. I'd go insane. I was so lucky I played a human."

Notes director Cliff Bole, "I enjoyed doing those two shows more than anything I've ever done. They turned out really well. The Borg is like a Klingon. You can do anything you want with them. They're fun and *real* expensive to play with. The two episodes do go together, and I wouldn't put it past Paramount to do that in the foreign markets. Part II's ending was a little bit of a cop out. We ran out of time. We only shoot 42 minutes. God, the old hours we used to deliver were like 51 or 52 minutes. There's just not a lot of time. You'd like to do a bigger ending. I don't have an answer for it, but it was just a real quick ending for such a big show. Paramount, at the beginning of the year, had pulled back a little bit budget-wise. It was also an attempt to do big and fast. They let us go a little bit on the first one because it was the first time we'd done a cliffhanger."

Episode #76:
"Family"
Original Airdate: 10/1/90
Written by Ronald Moore
Premise by Susanne Lambdin and Bryan Stewart
Directed by Les Landau
Guest Starring: Jeremy Kemp (Robert Picard), Samantha Eggar (Marie Picard), Theodore Bikel (Sergei Rozhenko), Georgia Brown (Helena Rozhenko), Whoopi Goldberg (Guinan), Dennis Creaghan (Louis), David Tristan Birken (Rene Picard), Doug Wert (Jack Crusher)

While the Enterprise is refurbished in spacedock, Worf's adopted human parents, Sergey and Helena (Theodore Bikel and Georgia Brown), visit the ship; Wesley is given a recording made for him by his late father, Jack (Doug Wert), and the captain returns to Earth to visit his jealous brother, Robert (Jeremy Kemp), in France. There, Picard undergoes a painful catharsis to purge the bitter memories of his Borg experience.

••••

"'Family' was really different for the series," agrees Ron Moore. "It was a very atypical show for the *Next Generation* and the original series too. I don't think they could have gotten away with a show like that either. Aside from the location work, conceptually it was very different for us. I think it's the only episode of *Star Trek*—old, new or movies—that never went to the bridge of the Enterprise once in the entire show.

••••
207

["Family"] began with Michael Piller when he was doing 'Best.' He surfaced the idea early that it would not be quite fair to wrap everything up neat and tidy at the end of Part II—that we had made such a point of saying this is such a really horrendous thing that had happened to Captain Picard, that it was psychologically and physically raping the man and it wasn't fair to go on like nothing had happened. He thought here was an opportunity to do something we've never done before: we'll be at Earth, we can go home and do a story about the captain sort of finding himself again."

Offers Piller, "The normal objections were that we were not serialized. We try to tell stories that can be told in one hour and that's what we do very well. When I got to the end of Part II, we made the decision not to extend it and I called up Rick and said, 'Hey, listen. Next week Picard can be fine, but for a show that prides itself on its realistic approach to storytelling, how can you have a guy who's basically been raped be fine next week? There's a story in a man like Picard who's lost control. Delving into the psychological crisis that a man like that has to face, and what does he have to do?' Finally, I was persuasive enough to talk Gene and Rick into taking the chance, and I think everybody is glad we did."

Piller was able to champion "Family" without making some concessions to Rick Berman that would force it to conform to traditional *Star Trek* formula.

"When Rick said 'I'll let you take Picard to Earth,'" Piller reflects, "he told me 'I want a science fiction story going on aboard the ship at the same time.' So we struggled for weeks and weeks trying to come up with an interesting science fiction story that we could match with Picard going down to Earth. One version of it had a child stowaway that causes problems [but] we didn't like that, and then we came up with this idea that we went to Rick with. We said that while Picard's on Earth, up on the ship people are disappearing for no apparent reason and, ultimately, it's because of this wormhole, and he liked it, but said he didn't feel there was room for both stories. He said he thought we should do them as separate shows and come up

with something else. He decided we're not going to ruin the episode with Picard by trying to put some ridiculous scientific thing in, and we decided to do it the way it was originally conceived, and do it as a whole show about family."

Ron Moore recalls, "We decided as long as we were there at Earth, let's make it a show about people's families and do some other character's on the ship and explore their backgrounds. It became a very off-concept show, [looking] at the characters and how they got to be who and what they are."

One character, oft talked about but never personified, made his first appearance on *Trek*: Wesley's father, Jack Crusher (Doug Wert).

"Every fan and their cousin has written letters about Jack Crusher and wanting to see him," remarks Piller, who had suffered through reams of story proposals from prospective *Trek* writers "pitching" scripts about Beverly Crusher's late husband. "We had gotten a spec script about Jack Crusher in the holodeck, and Ron Moore came down and said maybe we should use it so we bought the premise from the people who wrote the script. We felt if we were going to do a story about family and really make that the theme of an episode, it was an element we really should explore and use as part of a script to sort of speak to the theme of family and how the reach and embrace of family can extend across even death. What Jack said in the scene about looking down at the newborn child Wesley, and seeing in his face all the people he had ever loved, was something I was feeling and going through at that time having just had a baby daughter. I think this particular season and, in general, my career and my work has always tried to reinforce family values, because to me as the world gets more technologically smart, we find more and more ways to separate us as family. It's a terribly important part of my life and my work."

Says director Les Landau "I think it was certainly one of my best episodes and one of the best episodes of *Star Trek* ever. 'Family' was the perfect follow-up to the Borg shows and the conclusion of that storyline. Picard was in a dilemma, what to do and what better place to do it than in the environs of

one's 'home.' After all, his home is the universe, but his specific home is La Barre, France. This was a story that was opened up. It was about Earth and a place that we could identify with human beings and no aliens. That opening moment where Picard walks into the vineyard and see his brother on his hands and knees picking grapes [and] his brother doesn't even acknowledge him, gives me chills just thinking about it.

"It was my first episode of the season, but it was the fourth episode to be filmed," recalls Landau. "Patrick ended the third season with the Borg show and then started the fourth season with a Borg show, and went on to two other shows that had relatively little to do with the result of the culmination of what had happened during the Borg incident, which was unbelievable. Patrick Steward had to adjust and say it's four months later, I have to go back to what did I feel, what was I going through, and relive all the events and make it believable that he had just come back from this incident and was going home. I think it was certainly one of my best episodes of *Star Trek* and one of the best *Next Generation* episodes ever. I'm not talking about my work, but the story, the acting, the production values. Everything about that show worked."

Episode #77:
"Brothers"
Original Airdate: 10/8/90
Written by Rick Berman
Directed by Rob Bowman
Guest Starring: Cory Danziger (Jake Potts), Brent Spiner (Lore & Dr. Noonian Soong), Adam Ryen (Willie)

Data commandeers the Enterprise and beams down to a mysterious planet where we find he has been summoned by his creator, Dr. Soong (Brent Spiner), who intends to plant a chip in his electronic circuitry which will give him humanity. Then Lore (Spiner, again), Data's evil twin brother from season one's "Datalore," arrives.

Lore, pretending to be Data, deceives Soong into planting the chip in him, depriving Data of his chance to be human. When the Away Team beams down they find Lore gone and Soong dying.

•••

"In fact, at one point it looked very hairy that we weren't going to be able to pull it off with Brent playing all three roles and we began a casting process of Chinese, elderly male actors," says Rick Berman, *Next Generation*'s guiding force, Executive producer and author of "Brothers," his first script for the show. "Keye Luke was one of the people we were thinking about, but we ended up finding a way production-wise we could do it. It would have been a lot less expensive to have done it with another actor, but we ended up doing it with Brent and that made it a little more fun. As for Lore, I would love to bring him back. We left him with a new chip in his head that was wrongly placed there, and so he is even more demented than before and he's off doing God knows what. I think we may hear from him again."

Adds Michael Piller, " Rick said, 'I'm writing this episode so Data can play every character,' and he stuck by his guns and we pulled it off. That's the only show where we had rehearsal. I said to Rob Bowman and Legato, 'You've got to rehearse this,' and they rehearsed for two or three days with Brent, figuring [it] out both for Brent as an actor and in terms of staging. They worked out some of the motion control shots and did a lot of preparation in terms of figuring out what to do, because that kind of preparatory time on the stage when everybody is standing around is not a good idea. What we did was we tape out the floor like in a stageplay, or a videotaped multi-camera show. We actually taped the floor and brought in steps and had props and pieces of furniture and they actually blocked it out and staged it. I'm glad we did, although we've never done that on this show before because it saved us a lot of time, if we hadn't it would have been really dicey.

"The story that Rick wrote did not have Lore in it," points out Piller. "We have a process that we call breaking a story where we put all the writing staff in a room and we look around and whatever the writer came in with serves as only a starting point. Everybody sits down and we go to a board and break it down into acts and scenes and we try and see how the show is going to lay out. I tell everyone that in this room it is a

safe environment and that they are to speak out with whatever ideas they have, even if it's stupid or wrong, because it may spark an idea in someone else that leads us to the solution of a particular problem in a script."

In the case of "Brothers," it was decided that the script needed an additional element of jeopardy. Enter: Lore, Data's twisted android brother introduced first season in "Datalore."

"Lore demanded to come back into that show," says Piller. "I'm very much into Zen writing and I believe these things. It was something that had to happen to make that show work and it was the right thing to do. And, of course, it made it a must-watch episode. We were standing around going through Rick's story and my feeling was that after reading his first draft that the idea of Data going back to see Dr. Sung and the story of the child who was hurt in the practical joke were not enough elements to hold up the episode. Once Data goes back to see Dr. Sung, it's basically a chat and without some jeopardy or another event to go on I was afraid it was going to be flat. We talked about what we could do and, ultimately, the obvious thing was that we bring Lore back. It wasn't said let's ring Lore back and do an episode with him, it was let's go see Sung and Lore. I knew from the moment we came up with it that Brent Spiner in three roles was going to make for an unforgettable episode and I think it was."

"Brothers" was so complex that director Rob Bowman and visual effects supervisor Rob Legato extensively rehearsed actor Brent Spiner prior to shooting the episode, thus requiring multiple exposure shots with motion control camera in which Spiner plays three different characters.

"That's the only show where we ever had rehearsal," says producer David Livingston. "I said to Rob Bowman and Legato you've got to rehearse this first. They rehearsed for two or three days with Brent figuring out both for Brent as an actor and in terms of staging how they would shoot the motion control shots. What we did was we taped out the floor like in a play or a multicamera show, and then actually blocked it out. I'm glad we did because it saved us a lot of time. If we hadn't, it would have been really dicey."

ALL-NEW STAR TREK ADVENTURES *Published by STARLOG Magazine* VOLUME 19

STAR TREK
THE NEXT GENERATION
THE OFFICIAL MAGAZINE SERIES

SPECIAL ISSUE!

Journeys past & present: How they made the series' most acclaimed episodes

Episode #78:
"Suddenly Human"
Original Airdate: 10/15/90
Written by John Whelpley and Jeri Taylor
Story by Ralph Phillips
Directed by Gabrielle Beaumont
Guest Starring:
Sherman Howard (Endar), Chad Allen (Jono/Jeremiah Rossa), Barbara Townsend (Admiral Rossa)

A human teenager, Jono (Chad Allen) is found aboard a damaged Tellerian ship and brought back to the Enterprise along with his comrades. Jono is responsive only to Picard's command authority. The captain tries to reacclamate him to human culture when his adopted father and commander of the Tellerian fleet, Endar (Sherman Howard), demands his return. If not, war will be declared against the Federation.

Jono, despite the desire of his grandmother—a Starfleet admiral—for him to return to Earth, rejects his heritage and rejoins Endar.

••••

A subplot involving Jono's injuries and the ambiguous manner in which they were attained, stirred some controversy on the show and generated some heated comments from viewers who perceived the episode as condoning child abuse.

"We got some pretty angry letters on that show," says Michael Piller.

••••

"They said, 'How can you let an abused child go back to the people who are abusing him?' We really brought the child abuse issue up because it was the right and natural thing to bring up in the context of the story. There are real parallels to stories that go on in today's world about parents who fight over custody and one says there's been abuse. Who do you believe? But, mostly, it was a cultural clash story. It was a story of someone who was human who had been raised in a totally alien environment. Is he human any longer? That's really what that story was about."

Adds Rick Berman, "We wanted to make the point that the interpretation of broken bones was nothing more than normal childhood broken bones, and that these people were sort of prejudiced in this direction. It was in no way intended to be an episode that had anything to do with child abuse. It was the Wild Child. It had to do with a boy being brought from one culture to another and not fitting in with either, and the inevitable need for him to return back to the world in which he grew up."

"I thought we made it clear that he had a loving and protecting father in the alien," Michael Piller interjects. "We did have Picard make his own concerned confusion evident to the audience and I am a very great believer in grays and that there are not always answers to the tough and difficult questions. It was part of their culture and a normal loving thing that wasn't meant to imply child abuse. If we didn't say that, it's too bad. I think that episode was marvelously written by Jeri Taylor and it was strong enough to hire her on staff. I was disappointed by the show primarily because the aliens weren't alien enough. I felt there was some miscommunication on some level. The whole idea of that show was missed because these savage, different alien type creatures turned out to be very human."

Episode #79:
"Remember Me"
Original Airdate: 10/22/90
Written by Lee Sheldon
Directed by Cliff Bole
Guest Starring: Eric Menyuk (The Traveler), Bill Erwin (Dr. Dalen Quaice)
Dr. Crusher becomes trapped in

a parallel universe in which the crew of the Enterprise is seemingly disappearing off the ship, while the real crew desperately tries to rescue her. The fear is that one of Wesley's warp bubble experiment might turn deadly, trapping Crusher in the alternate universe.

Once the entire crew has disappeared, the doctor races against time to escape from inside the warp bubble. Only with the help of the Traveler does she succeed.

••••

"That was a very interesting high concept episode," says Rick Berman. "I thought it was possibly a little bit overly confusing. You're fooling the audience a little and I don't like to do that. They were looking at one world when, in fact, we were dealing with parallel universes and that was potentially confusing."

Making a return visit to The Next Generation to serve as a deus ex machina to get Beverly back for next week's episode, was "Where No One Has Gone Before" fan fave, the Traveler (Eric Menyuk). "I think that was an afterthought," admits Berman. "That was a question of finding a way to resolve the story."

Interjects Cliff Bole, "They added the character of the Traveler at the last minute. They added him because he's big at the conventions. He was just a walk-on. They were searching for some way to patch up the ending, so the Traveler came in."

"The first two drafts did not have the Traveler in it," explains Michael Piller. "The first draft ended with the realization of what had happened turning out to be a dream episode. We didn't find that satisfying, so we decided at the end of act three to pull everything from the first 60 pages into the first three acts and tell the audience what's going on on the other side of the warp bubble and how they're trying to get Beverly back. We spend the next two acts deciding how to get her back. At the beginning of the year we said that we wanted to bring the Traveler back for something, so why not use him in this episode to help Beverly back."

Episode #80:
"Legacy"
Original Airdate: 10/29/90
Written by Joe Menosky
Directed by Robert Scheerer
Guest Starring: Beth Toussaint (Ishara Yar), Don Mirrault (Hayne)
The legacy of Tasha Yar continues to haunt the Enterprise crew when they come upon her sister, Ishara (Beth Toussaint) on the late Tasha's warring homeworld, where a Federation ship's emergency shuttle has crashed.

Offering to assist the Away Team in rescuing their stranded comrades, Ishara hides a secret agenda which will allow her to disable the defenses of her clan's enemies and lead an offensive strike against them. As she prepares to disable the generator during the rescue mission, Riker stuns her with a phaser before she can betray them all.

••••

"It was a good episode because of the performance of the girl and the relationship between her and Data," says Michael Piller. "There's nothing as poignant as seeing the betrayal of an innocent, as Data is. I was very happy with this show, but it doesn't stay with me. It's a show that has great entertainment value, but it doesn't stick as one that I'll always remember."

"'Legacy' was fun to do," says director Robert Scheerer. "First of all, I had Beth Toussaint, who prior to that episode I had used on an episode of Matlock. She was quite wonderful, very attractive, sexy and a good actress. We were having trouble finding someone for the role and I mentioned Beth and showed the tape. Everyone said she was wonderful and she came in and did it. A great pleasure to have her be accepted and the fact that she was good.

"Obviously," he continues, "I had to go back and watch those first season episodes featuring the Tasha Yar character because I didn't know anything about her. That kind of research was interesting."

Episode #81:
"Reunion"
Original Airdate: 11/5/90
Written by Thomas Perry, Jo Perry, Ronald D. Moore and Brannon Braga

Story by Drew Deighan, Thomas Perry and Jo Perry
Directed by Jonathan Frakes
Guest Starring: Suzie Plakson (K'Ehleyr), Charles Cooper (K'Mpec), Patrick Massett (Duras), Robert O'Reilly (Gowron), Jon Steuer (Alexander)

K'Ehleyr (Suzie Plakson from second season's "The Emissary") returns to the Enterprise, surprising Worf by bringing his illegitimate son (first Kirk, now Worf—didn't they ever hear of condoms in the 24th Century?) aboard. At the same time, K'Mpec (*Star Trek V*'s Charles Cooper), the head of the Klingon High Council, confides in Picard that he has been poisoned and that the fate of the Klingon/Federation alliance rests with Picard, who must decide whether the treacherous Duras (Patrick Massett) or Gowron (Robert O'Reilly) will rule the Klingon Empire.

Jockeying for power, Duras discovers K'Ehyler's attempts to investigate events which imply that his father betrayed the Klingons to the Romulans (not Worf's as the character stated in "Sins of the Father") and murders her. Seeking vengeance, Worf slays Duras aboard his ship and Gowron prepares to ascend to rule the High Council.

••••

"Rick's been throwing me nice episodes," says director/actor Jonathan Frakes. "Three people got killed, there was murder and revenge. I've been lucky. Suzi [Plakson] was great. A lot of people are sorry she's dead. It's a character that people really loved or hated because she was so big and shameless in her performance. I loved it."

"We love Suzie and that character, but it worked because you cared about her and we made an effort not to do it capriciously and for no reason, just to get her off the show so Worf wouldn't have to deal with her," says Ron Moore. "I have pals that like the show and they were upset. It took Worf's character in a different direction, which is sort of what we did with 'Sins.' Anybody who watches that episode is moved and outraged by the killing of K'Ehleyr. You're mad and you have that same need for vengeance that Worf does. If we've tapped into those feelings so when Worf goes back to his quarters and grabs that sword and the

audience is screaming for Duras' head, then you've done it. You really had to do that scene in the Captain's Ready Room where Picard calls Worf onto the carpet for what he did and puts it to him."

"I killed K'Ehleyr," says Michael Piller proudly. "The original idea was about Worf's kid and bringing K'Ehleyr back, who was having a relationship with Duras. But when we started talking about how to make the story work, I'm the one who said she should die. Finally it was clearly what seemed to want to happen in the story, that she should be trying to find out what Duras was up to and he kills her. Worf, enraged, kills Duras. You wanted to get to a place where Worf was going to take Duras apart, and there's no real good reason for him to do it unless she dies....he had it coming."

Episode #82:
"Future Imperfect"
Original Airdate: 11/12/90
Written by J. Larry Carroll and David Bennett Carren
Directed by Les Landau
Guest Starring: Andreas Katsulas (Tomalak), Chris Demetral (Jean-Luc/Ethan/Barash)

After beaming down to a mysterious planet, Riker awakens in sickbay and finds that 16 years have apparently passed. He has a son, and peace negotiations are continuing in earnest with the Romulans. Riker's fears that this could be a Romulan plot to discover the secret location of Outpost 23 actually turns out to be the fantasy of a lonely little boy.

••••

"It was an opportunity for Jonathan to take charge of an episode and it just shows the dynamic quality of Riker to have to deal with not only having aged fifteen years, but to discover that you have a son and have been married and [are] captain of the Enterprise," says director Les Landau. "Can you imagine waking up one day and finding out that you've skipped fifteen years on your CD? There were lots of tricks and false leads, and yet there was something universal about the theme of this alien at the end which was the embodiment of this little boy. The final moment where Riker sees this alien being in the caverns of this other world and says I will take you with

me and you will always be a part of me, goes back to the basics of what *Star Trek* is all about. It's that caring for the human condition, love for the universal being. It sounds very esoteric and snobbish to talk this way, but that's when *Star Trek* is at its best."

"We've had some amazing pitches, but the most notable we ever heard was in 'Future Imperfect,' where the team came in and said we have a story where Riker wakes up from an accident 15 years in the future," recalls Brannon Braga. "It's 15 years in the future, Riker has a son, is the captain of the Enterprise and has no idea what happened. Mike Piller said, 'Stop, we'll buy it.'"

Adds Michael Piller, "We got for months without hearing good ideas. Larry and David came in on one hot week and brought a couple of ideas. The first thing out of their mouth was Riker wakes up and it's 15 years in the future and he has a son. I said sold and they did it and did a real good job on it. The Romulan gag of it being a double switch was added by accident. The first draft was a little flat after we got into the story, just like 'Remember Me.' You had a situation where you are into it and something strange is happening and yet it can't just turn out to be a dream at the end of the show because it's not satisfying. What you do is you get to the third act and you need to do something that moves the action forward. This is one of the best examples of the notion that you shouldn't censor yourself. I just talked and David Carren said, 'You mean that he thinks it's a real Romulan plot for an act?' and I said, 'That's not what I mean at all'—then I said, 'Stop, wait a minute, what if that's exactly what we do and play it out as a Romulan gag for an act.' That's what I think made that show work."

"We pitched the major story elements," says David Carren. "The only major element that came up was that it was a Romulan plot and you find out it's a fantasy within a fantasy. Originally it basically went through five acts and then you found out that it was the little boy's fantasy."

Notes Piller, "Ideas just come in waves. For some reason, everyone seemed to be coming in with an amnesia story and you saw three of them on the air this year on our show and one of them we saved for next year. 'Future Imperfect' was one of our better amnesia stories. For a while everyone seemed to be coming in with stories about children and we had more children in the first 12 episodes than ever before. The only thing they didn't come in with was amnesiac children stories. It became a great gag around here."

Guest star Andreas Katsulas, playing Romulan Centurion Tamalok for the last time, says, "I felt much more comfortable when he was an incredible giant on the screen, just a face. Suddenly when I had to account for everything else, I didn't feel support and nothing was supporting what I was doing. I was happy not to recur unless it would have gone back to a screen character."

Episode #83:
"Final Mission"
Original Airdate: 11/19/90
Written by Kasey Arnold-Ince
and Jeri Taylor
Story by Kasey Arnold-Ince
Directed by Corey Allen
Guest Starring: Nick Tate (Dirgo),
Kim Hamilton (Sonji)

Wil Wheaton's swan song to *Star Trek*, in which a shuttlecraft carrying Picard and Wesley to a negotiating conference crashes on a desert planet. When they attempt to gather water from a shielded fountain, Picard is critically wounded and Wesley must take charge.

The shuttle captain, Dirgo, persists in his attempts to raid the water spring and is killed by the system's defensive mechanism. Wesley must rely on his wits to figure out a way to obtain some water before Picard dies.

• • • •

"The idea had originally been to have Wesley and Picard crash together on a planet and do a role reversal, but it had been an ice planet," reveals writer Jeri Taylor. "The nature of the planet changed because we felt we could make it a much more realistic dry planet than ice planet. It would look hokey and fake and we don't like to do that. That's the episode I probably put more work on than any all year long, because it was a combination of a very delicate kind of interpersonal story, and the dreaded technical story which is the garbage

scow in space. So I had this supertechnical thing going on at the same time as this delicate kind of interpersonal story."

Michael Piller relates, "There had been a lot of very bad feeling around here about the way Tasha Yar was sent off. So we were determined to give Wesley a send-off that had real value and something that stayed with us. We finally decided that he would go to the Academy, which I think was Gene's idea [and] the most reasonable and easiest idea, which also keeps him alive for future episodes. I think Jeri did a wonderful job on the script and Corey Allen, who is one of my favorite directors, gave you the best pieces of film you can get. If it gets an A- instead of an A, it's only because the story itself, of two guys trapped on a planet and how do we get off, in general is not very original, and the story of the garbage scow was no great shakes either. But I think we handled it pretty well."

"The only thing I said they couldn't do was they waned to go back outside again, and I said we had to do it inside," explains David Livingston. "They wanted to do the fountain outside, but we ended up doing the rest on Stage 16. It was Rick's idea to change it from ice and that was a great, great idea, [and] very critical to the episode's success. The crane shot in the beginning is great. I could hear Maurice Jarre's score in the background."

Says Rick Berman, "It was a little more expensive because we went on location and the opticals. We had huge optical problems with the fountain. It was a nightmare. It was something we built and it didn't work. Then we were going to do it optically and that didn't work. So we had a lot of technical problems. That's one of my favorite episodes. I think it was very poignant and the acting on the part of our guest cast, Nick Tate, Patrick's work and Wil's, was just excellent. I thought it was just a terrific piece of drama."

Episode #84:
"The Loss"
Original Airdate: 12/21/90
Written by Hilary J. Bader, Alan J. Adler
and Vanessa Greene
Story by Hilary J. Bader

Directed by Chip Chalmers
Guest Starring: Kim Braden (Janet Brooks), Whoopi Goldberg (Guinan)

Troi loses her empathic powers due to a cloud consisting of two-dimensional creatures which are leading the Enterprise into a deadly cosmic string fragment.

Faced with being human, Troi announces her desire to resign as ship's counselor and, despite the sympathy of the crew, turns curt and hostile as she drowns in her own self-pity. It is only when the creatures are freed from the ship's perimeter that Troi regains her powers and asks to resume her regular duties.

• • • •

"I pushed for this episode a lot," says Rick Berman. "It was fascinating to me that someone would lose one of their senses and be unable to explain it to others because they didn't have it in the first place. If you were the only sighted person in a colony of blind people and suddenly you lost your vision and they all said 'So what?'...that's what this was. I think Marina did a really good job. We create conflict by infecting people with weird space anomalies and alien microbes and making people act differently, so when people are off character, they can have a little bit more conflict. In this case, it came out of her losing one of her senses."

States Michael Piller, "It was a very difficult story to get right. I felt the script was adequate, it's not one of my favorites. The problem in conception was that you have a phenomenon that nobody can identify with. We said this is our blind show, but we can't do a blind show like other shows. This basic idea has been pitched to us every season, with Troi losing her sense of empathy. Finally, because we needed a Troi show, we said let's do it here."

A B-story, which is a term used to describe an additional story paralleling the main plotline, involves two-dimensional creatures which have caught the Enterprise in its field. This was incorporated into the Troi story.

"We had gotten the 'B' story from our intern, Hilary Bader," Piller says. "I said let's match this to the Troi story, and it was difficult to satisfy all of us, because everybody said she's going to get her sight back, or rather her insight back, by the end of the episode. We toyed briefly about not giving it back to her, but the bottom line for me was that these shows work because the journey is interesting and that what she learns and what she goes through has to be interesting and involving and, ultimately, educational in that we are showing off the stages of someone who has a serious disability, and what they go through when they are suffering this."

"The handicapped people came up and thanked me," Sirtis smiles. "That's exactly the way they feel, it's the way I expressed their emotions. 'The Loss' was very, very popular."

Chip Chalmers enthuses, "An episode with some character conflict. There was that scene where Deanna went storming into sickbay and really got it on with Beverly, 'If I were you, I wouldn't have sat on my butt and would have been trying to do something about this,' and she goes storming out. People who saw that scene loved it. Whoopi Goldberg was also in that episode and, of course, she's a gem. She came after the show and said she wanted to do it. Obviously they immediately said, 'You've got it.' She *makes* the time. Whoopi's got a feature film opening every three months it seems, and she makes the time to do *Star Trek*. When she was a little girl, she saw the original show and a world where different races got along. A black woman could be sitting at the communication controls of a spaceship. That's not only okay, it's great. I think that was impressed on her at kind of an early age and she's always had a tremendous amount of admiration for the concept."

Episode #85:
"Data's Day"
Original Airdate: 1/7/91
Written by Harold Apter and
Ronald D. Moore
Directed by Robert Wiemer
Guest Starring: Rosalind Chao (Keiko),
Sierra Pecheur (T'Pel), Alan Scarfe
(Mendak)

A day-in-the-life episode which follows Data around the ship as he prepares for Chief O'Brien's (Colm Meaney) upcoming wedding nuptials, that prepa-

ration beginning with Dr. Crusher teaching him to tap (the scene was choreographed by Gates McFadden herself, who, among other accomplishments, choreographed *Dreamchild* and *Labyrinth* for the late, great Jim Henson).

Meanwhile, a Vulcan ambassador beams aboard to lead secret negotiations with the Romulans. When it appears that she has been killed in a transporter accident, Picard discovers that she is actually a Romulan spy coming out from the cold.

••••

"'Data's Day' was a show I had supported us doing for quite a long time," says Executive Script Consultant Ron Moore. "The idea of doing a day in the life is a fairly common television convention that you kind of get around to doing. To do it on this show was very challenging and we've never done a show even remotely like it. Harold Apter pitched that in the third season and we've been trying to get it off the ground ever since. At one point, it was going to be a Picard day-in-the-life, then a day-in-the-life of the ship and it went through a lot of changes until we came to the decision that Data was the perfect vehicle to do that with, because he's the only one who's up 24 hours a day."

"We've had more people come in with the average day-in-the-life of the Enterprise story," notes Rick Berman. "It's a story that never works. Then we decided to do it all from the point of view of Data with logs and I was skeptical about it, but the writers were interested and pursued it. I ended up being pleasantly surprised, but it was an off-episode."

One of the early considerations had been to replace Wesley after "Final Mission" with a female conn officer who would get romantically entangled with Transporter Chief Miles O'Brien, an idea which was ultimately rejected.

"I was against that because I felt that O'Brien was too good a character and potential benefit to the show to make him another star's supporting character," says Piller. "I felt he would always sort of be a sounding board for someone else to talk to and I didn't want to waste him on that. So we never did get around to replacing Wesley and O'Brien emerged on his own."

Surprisingly, rather than create a new female conn officer who would marry O'Brien, the chief was married off to a new supporting player, Keiko, ship's botanist who was played by Rosalind Chao.

"It all grew out of doing a day in the life story," says Ron Moore. "When you're talking about doing that, you sort of say what are the things that happen behind the scenes? What happens during a day on the Enterprise? Some of the things that come up are a baby gets born, maybe somebody dies—maybe not. Then somebody said what if someone gets married and that sparked. We obviously didn't want any of the regulars getting married, because that's a big thing and we didn't want it to be a faceless nobody. Everybody was delighted with the work Colm Meaney had been doing for us and we did want to do more with him as the series was going on. So we said this is a neat idea—we'll marry O'Brien."

The marriage to O'Brien was not the only problem in the story for "A Day in the Life of the Enterprise," which would ultimately become "Data's Day." In addition, there was the question of what else would happen to keep audiences glued to their television screens.

"We thought we needed to provide a frame," says Ron Moore, who rewrote Harold Apter's original script. "Otherwise you'd be left with a lot of little vignettes and there's no common threads to take you through the day. We needed an over-arcing story going on that we could refer to every once in a while, and also that gave us the opportunity to show that although the viewer at home gets to watch the entire episode, how it would be different from just Data's point of view where they would get just a little bit of information here and another briefing here. Obviously Picard knows everything and suddenly there's all this jeopardy happening, but Data hasn't been in on the whole thing all the time."

"Rick believed that you cannot have a show that has no jeopardy or drama on *Star Trek*," Michael Piller says. "I agreed with him, otherwise all you're doing is a scrapbook. It was a story that we kept over from last year and nobody could really figure out what to do. The story went through the various permutations a day in the life story always goes through. Are we going to do everybody? Are we going to do Picard? Ultimately we decided that Data would give us the most unique perspective of life on the Enterprise and it also gave us insight into Data. My feeling was if you take a show like 'The Defector' from last season and instead of showing the audience everything that everybody sees, you only take it from Data's point of view and he only gets to see the tail end of scenes and certain things that he's exposed to....What if there is actually a major story playing out and Data's only on the fringe of it? To me, that's a fascinating concept."

Episode #86:
"The Wounded"
Original Airdate: 1/28/91
Written by Jeri Taylor
Story by Stuart Charno, Sara Charno and Cy Chermak
Directed by Chip Chalmers
Guest Starring: Bob Gunton (Captain Ben Maxwell), Rosalind Chao (Keiko), Marc Alaimo (Gul Macet), Tim Winters (Glen Daro), John Hancock (Admiral Haden), Marco Rodriguez (Glen Telle)

A dark, fatalistic episode for Trek. A rogue starship captain launches a one-man war against an alien race with which the Federation has recently negotiated a peace treaty.

Attacking the alien Cardassians, the captain (Bob Gunton), whose wife had been brutally killed, is talked out of his path of vengeance by a former member of his crew, Chief O'Brien. Picard warns the Cardassian leader that he realizes they have been rearming and that Captain Maxwell was right. He intones ominously that the Federation "will be watching."

••••

"It was sort of Heart of Darkness with the rogue captain out of control," says producer/writer Jeri Taylor. "It started with the idea that if you had been at war with a country and now you are not at war with them anymore, you can't just immediately become friends. If you're trained to look at people as the enemy, it's hard to now be their friends. While in the 24th century people have a much more expansive view of the galaxy and are able to do

it a little better, we planted the idea that some people had just a little more residual problem with that sort of thing, and harbored some resentment. [It's] a very provocative kind of area to get into. The material was somewhat epic in nature, which is always fun to do, and yet at its core was this very personal story between him and Picard, where two strong and able people tee off against each other. And there is the wonderful device of the song at the end of the episode, in which Colm Meaney really came into his own and did a wonderful job. When he and Maxwell sing that song at the end, I really just loved that moment."

"That was a wonderful English hymn that was used in The Man Who Would Be King," says Rick Berman. "I always loved it and we worked it in where O'Brien and Gunton's character sing it together. It's another episode that's constantly pitched to every television show where you've got to bring back the guy who's lost it, but we dealt with prejudice in that episode. Some people felt Gunton [as Captain Maxwell] played it very soft, but I thought he did a great job."

David Livingston comments, "I thought that was the best makeup for an alien race that Michael had done. They looked so realistic and unique and powerful. He astounds me, he does all of his own sculpting. He's a real sculptor and he designs all these things and gets a piece of clay and sits there with his little knife. Two hours later, he's up in the office showing us his head. He makes a mold and they pour the mold right from his sculpting to the pieces. The best contribution I made to this show was hiring Michael Westmore. That's my one coup. My best coup. He's hung in here because he gets to do so many different things—it's not like Rocky, where he kept making noses for Sylvester Stallone. After a while, how many noses can you make? Michael is a true artist and he loves his work and just blows me away."

Points out director Chip Chalmers, "This episode aired during the Gulf War and was about Picard doing everything he could to prevent a war, happening during a time when the United States of America was doing everything it could to start a war. I thought it was a real interesting

dichotomy of ideas. That was one of the best written shows that I've seen in a while. We also had to deal with the Cardassians, which meant new ships, new aliens and we introduced a new enemy that's finally able to speak on the level of Picard. They're not grunting, they're not giggling, they're not mutes or all-knowing entities. Here are the Cardassians who also graduated first in their class and they're able to carry on highly intelligent conversations with Picard, but they're sinister as hell. It was fun to introduce a whole new alien race."

Episode #87:
"Devil's Due"
Original Airdate: 2/4/91
Written by Philip Lazebnik
Story by Philip Lazebnik and William Douglas Lansford
Directed by Tom Benko
Guest Starring: Marta DuBois (Ardra), Marcelo Tubert (Acost Jared), Paul Lambert (Dr. Howard Clarke)

Reworked from an original premise for the aborted Trek '70s TV revival, "Devil's Due" plays like a 1966 Enterprise voyage in which Kirk, er, Picard, must argue in court that a woman, Arda (Marta Dubois), claiming to be the devil, is really a charlatan. His goal is to prove this in order to nullify a contract she has on that world and the Enterprise.

Picard challenges the validity of her claim. Data serves as arbitrator in a contest of wills which could cost Picard his soul...or something equally valuable, his self-esteem.

••••

Ironically, this traditional Trek was, at the time, the highest rated show of the series since "Encounter at Farpoint," and whether that's due to the show's special effects-laden trailer, a sultry female protagonist (in early drafts, a male) or, as David Livingston speculates, "the fact there was no basketball game on that night," we can only guess. Even more than the usual litany of writers had a hand in crafting a rewrite of this decade old teleplay: Philip Labebnik (Wings), William Douglas Lansford, Lee Sheldon, Melinda Snodgrass, Larry Carroll, Dave Carren and Michael Piller.

••••

"It was a very difficult story because it's such an atypical story," explains Larry Carroll, "and it was a very hard story to get a handle on, but Michael really believed in it. It seems like every other writer in the Writer's Guild worked on this episode."

"It was like an old *Star Trek*," says Jonathan Frakes. "It's ironic that it was an old *Star Trek* story, because it's really a Kirk story. It was so 60's."

Says Michael Piller, "'Devil's Due' was a story that had been put into development third season when we had no stories and no scripts in development. We owned a script from the failed attempt to bring *Star Trek* back. Basically, because I had no product, I told Melinda Snodgrass to go out and get that script, which I had been told was a decent script, and rewrite it, [sticking] our characters' names in. That didn't work at all, and we started talking about how we could change it to better suit our show. We never succeeded in breaking it last season and, during the hiatus, I gave it to Philip Laezbnik, who is a writer for Paramount on *Wings* and a real *Trek* fan. He turned it inside out and made it a delightful show. It was too funny, though, and the people felt it was playing it all for laughs. I loved that draft of the script, but not everybody did. It was put into rewrite by approximately 15 people between Phil's script and the final draft, which I took, changing the male devil into a female devil for fun. [I] put back as much of Phil's original script as I could, and the bottom line was I felt the script was very funny and satisfying. It was very off for our show, and I thought it's origins showed, but ultimately it was a funny little show and a nice part of our mix."

David Livingston states, "That went through a lot of revisions and they changed it to a woman, which was a great fix. We brought her in for a lot of sessions and never found the right part for her. She came in and just blew us all away. Like, how do you do better? Let's just start shooting. Where's her wardrobe? We want more of that. I'm always pushing for more humor on this show. I think we get a little too serious sometimes. It's nice to be a little lighter. We talk about it and get a lot of sour looks. Certainly Brent offers a lot of

comic possibilities and we're exploring them more and more."

Episode #88:
"Clues"
Original Airdate: 11/11/91
Written by Bruce D. Arthurs and Joe Menosky
Story by Bruce D. Arthurs
Directed by Les Landau

The crew of the Enterprise gradually discovers that they have "lost" 24 hours since encountering a mysterious wormhole in space. Data begins to exhibit suspicious signs pointing to a cover-up.

Following the clues, Picard learns that the Enterprise crew's memories were erased by a xenophobic race intent on preserving their solitude. The ship returns, and the aliens threaten to destroy the Enterprise unless they can assure them of success in erasing all knowledge of their existence.

••••

"It was a very difficult episode to do," says director Les Landau. "It's a story that repeats itself three or four times. How do we make it interesting and still tell the story? As it unfolds, we find that we are repeating ourselves in time, and, again, it's for the benefit of another species. Directorially, it was the most difficult assignment I've had on *Star Trek* and probably one of the most rewarding. In order to show different points in time and flashbacks within flashbacks was very difficult. I tried to create a style that was very fluid and singular in its point of view, until the very end when we came back to normal time [and] the camera work and editing became very cutty.

"There was a fluidity to all of the earlier sequences and a rhythm that, as the show developed before our eyes, became more tempoed to show that we were getting closer and closer to real time. There are long takes early on and longer camera moves in the first flashback. In the second one they're less fluid and long. Finally, when we come back to real time in act five, there are static shots where there's hardly any movement and a great deal of editorial cutting to show that we are back in real time.

"You try and fine a thread in every episode that you can use to tell the

story. It was shot in such a way that it demonstrates what the story's all about, but there are always a shot or two or three that I fall in love with that I put in my cut, that don't make it to the screen. It's like playing golf. When you play golf, you remember every shot you hit. Filming an episode is exactly the same thing. You remember every shot you hit, and when it's missing from your scorecard at the very end, you know you've either bogeyed, parred or birdied your round. It's a perfect analogy."

Michael Piller enthuses, "I really loved that show. It's one of my favorites of the year. It was a perfectly realized classic mystery put together into a *Star Trek* format, which came together into a very satisfying episode. It was written by a writer we hired off a spec script, who is a mailman in the Phoenix area. He gave us a very good story, [but] the script needed some work. Mostly restructuring caused by the departure of Wil Wheaton and a major dialogue polish. Joe Menosky came in during the hiatus and did the polish. [He] did such a good job, that I thought he deserved to be on staff.

Episode #89:
"First Contact"
Original Airdate: 2/18/91
Written by David Russell Bailey, David Bischoff, Joe Menosky, Ronald D. Moore and Michael Piller
Story by Marc Scott Zicree
Directed by Cliff Bole
Guest Starring: George Coe (Chancellor Durkin), Carolyn Seymour (Mirasta Yale), Michael Ensign (Krola), George Hearn (Berel), Steven Anderson (Nilrem), Sachi Parker (Tava), Bebe Neuwirth (Lanel)

The Enterprise must make "first contact" with an alien world on the verge of attaining warp technology. When Riker is injured on the planet, Picard must accelerate his plans to retrieve his wounded first officer or risk violating the Prime Directive.

Ultimately, the minister of the planet rejects the Federation's overture, realizing that by embracing other cultures in the galaxy, he will jeopardize his homeworld where the citizenry is not ready to accept that they are not the center of the universe.

••••

"That had a different bent because it was a story about the guest and the point of view is from another culture," muses Jonathan Frakes. "I'm not sure that the writing in that episode was as good as it could have been. I really liked the story idea, [but] it had loopholes. It was loaded with great actors; George Coe and George Herr and Bebe, who was a delight. What a funny woman. I loved that scene. Cliff Bole directed that one, and he had me do it a lot of ways, some of which were really not good. I was thankful that they chose the takes that worked."

Reflects Cliff Bole, "Originally, when I read it, my challenge was how to handle all the talking, because it was a very talky show. Real talky, and sometimes between only two people. I think we came out alright with it. I'd like to do one that gets into a nice big conflict. I think that's a story idea that can deal with an issue. They make contact and really step into it. Picard actually made reference to that in the dialogue [of 'First Contact']. He said something about that happening with the Klingons, that the first contact with them resulted in a hundred year war."

"First Contact" began with writer Marc Scott Zicree, who was one of the first freelancers to propose story ideas to the fledgling *Next Generation* in 1986.

"It's very hard to sell to *Star Trek*," explains Zicree. "They've gone months without buying any stories. I had done up something like 50 or 60 stories in pitching to the show. Usually I sell on the first or second story. I must have run fifteen stories by them before we hit 'First Contact.' Piller liked the stuff so he kept saying keep going. At one point Ira Behr was joking and said this guy is an idea machine, we should just lock him in a room and have him slip paper out from under the door. It was the day before Thanksgiving in 1989, and the meeting was at 5:00 in the morning. Everyone was sick of being there and wanted to go home, and it was a hard pitch for a while."

And with Zicree's pitch for "First Contact," Piller was hooked. It was an irresistible concept that had never been done in the *Star Trek* mythos and seemed so obvious—the Enterprise makes first contact with a planet to arrange its entry into the Federation.

"It may be the most important episode of the season," enthuses Piller. "I can't tell you if it's the best or not. It was pitched by a very good writer, but he just couldn't find the right tone of the show. We gave it to the writers who did 'Tin Man' for us, and the way they wrote the show it didn't work either. The story was something we had around from last year, which nobody could quite solve. Eventually I said I have the vision of this show in my mind. I sat down and, ultimately, it was my version that made it to the air."

Michael Piller concedes that the difficulty of the episode was not the idea itself, but rather the rules of writing *Star Trek*.

"Our rules told us we never have open shows, and we wrote the first two drafts from our point of view and I realized it wasn't working," says Piller. "The thing that was holding us back was a rule, and I'm very much a supporter of the rules of Gene's universe, but I also love to break them if they're in the interest of the show. I went to Rick [Berman] and said that even though I know he doesn't like to break format, this could be a special show if he would let me write it from the alien point of view. He did, as long as I let everyone know that we weren't going to ever break this rule again. No other show in the history of *Star Trek* has taken the alien perspective of our characters, and I think that makes it very special and very unique. I was very pleased with the way it turned out, and I think it's thought provoking and a fresh and original idea."

Adds Marina Sirtis, "I thought it was one of the most interesting episodes of the season. It was something so obvious that we hadn't addressed, and an issue that hadn't been brought up in 150 episodes of *Star Trek*. Of course there are going to be people who are going to get warp power and are going out into space. How do we deal with this? I thought it was a really good episode and Patrick agreed that we were exactly the right two people to go down to the planet and say hi."

Most people involved concur with the notion that "First Contact" is lit- tle more than *The Day the Earth Stood Still* transplanted to the 24th century with the Enterprise crew as the aliens landing in Washington.

"That was really the concept that I always saw," says Piller. "I said it was a '50s space movie except we're the aliens and that's really the way I tried to write it."

David Livingston, the show's producer responsible for bringing the alien world to the screen, agrees that "First Contact" is indeed a 24th century take on the aliens landing, with better special effects than any 1950's movie ever had.

"It's the first episode where we really broke the mold," he opines. "From a visual standpoint, we tried to create sets, wardrobe and medical instruments that looked evocative of our culture today, but were different, and add enough that they didn't say we just rented a gurney from Central Props. We took a lot of pains in terms of talking about the props and the set dressing, so that it looked a little bit odd. I think we were pretty successful. It was very hard, but I think the audience identified with these people. It was how I would feel at first contact."

Episode #90:
"Galaxy's Child"
Original Airdate: 3/11/91
Written by Maurice Hurley
Story by Thomas Kartozian
Directed by Winrich Kolbe
Guest Starring: Susan Gibney (Dr. Leah Brahms), Whoopi Goldberg (Guinan)

Maurice Hurley, former *Next Generation* executive producer, returned to contribute a teleplay in which the Enterprise accidentally kills a pregnant space creature, whose offspring attaches itself to the Enterprise hull. Also returning is Leah Brahms (Susan Gibney), first introduced in season three's "Booby Trap" as a hologram who helps Geordi navigate the ship from a minefield. Now the real McCoy (pun definitely intended) beams aboard the Enterprise in the flesh. Geordi courts her, only to discover that the fetching scientist is married. Together they nonetheless save the space baby.

••••

"They're two great stories," says Rick Berman. "First, that of the fantasy woman Geordi thinks he's met, but didn't, and now he actually has to meet her; and the simultaneous story of the space baby latching onto the ship. They were two very nice stories that worked well together. A lot of the baby effects, especially once it latched on to the ship and went swimming out with its friends at the end, was all computer animation, which is something we rarely use because it's not usually all that believable, but it's wonderful in this show."

"I always felt that the idea of having reality versus fantasy was an interesting theme to explore and the Leah Brahms character allowed us to do that in this episode," details Michael Piller. "This to me was one of the best concepts we had all year. *Star Trek* is a show of ideas and although we've had good shows the first half of the season, the second half had some really great ideas and this was one of them. The writer who brought it in and pitched it, couldn't really make the story work, so we needed somebody else to go to work on it. Maury [Hurley] had expressed an interest in writing a script or two for us this year, and we were delighted to have the opportunity to work together again. I sent it over to him and said, 'Can you make this work?', and he did. I just thought the idea of an alien creature adopting the Enterprise as its mother is something you can't do on any other show."

A scene that consistently elicits guffaws among the cast is the inevitable shaking of the ship caused by phaser fire and other space hazards. "I've got that down now," laughs Marina Sirtis. "It was kind of embarrassing in the beginning, but maybe I've become more Americanized. Americans are much looser than English people and you have to just relax and let go, which is actually easier said than done for an English person because we're so reserved."

For director Winrich Kolbe, the production problems created by shaking are far more significant than the embarrassment felt by the actors.

"In 'Galaxy's Child' Marvin Rush designed a special head which had a strong set of springs and you really could rattle the head out of the camera. The only problem was that in the style we have in dramatic television, which is

single camera, you shoot a master or a master that movies and various close-ups, and you've got to make sure all those moves synchronize at the same strength or you're going to end up with Picard shaking like crazy and Worf right above him barely moving."

Episode #91:
"Night Terrors"
Original Airdate: 3/18/91
Written by Pamela Douglas and
Jeri Taylor
Story by Shari Goodhartz
Directed by Les Landau
Guest Starring: Rosalind Chao (Keiko),
John Vickery (Hagan), Duke Moosekian
(Gillespie)

The Enterprise crew, trapped in Tykin's Rift, is affected by sleep deprivation and starts imagining their worst nightmares. Through a series of eerie dreams and communications with a comatose Betazoid survivor of a ship whose crew went insane from the same malady, Troi discovers and contacts an alien ship also trapped in the rift. Together, they work to escape before it's too late.

••••

"That was a yawner, wasn't it?" muses Jonathan Frakes rhetorically. "That was a shitty piece of special effects work when Troi was flying with those cloud around her. That was below our standard."

"A great deal of all that work was done second unit in post production in that Rob Legato had a great deal to add to those sequences," explains Les Landau. "We designed all these wonderful flying sequences where Troi would come in and out of the clouds, and see something off in the distance. It was Rob's ability and artistic wherewithal to lay in the various layers of what she was going through and what she was seeing and, yes, it was time consuming. Fortunately, the production decided that this was something we should do second unit without the main crew since there was very little sound work to be done and it was one of the rare instances where we had a full blown second unit. The cameraman who shot that was Tom De Nivi. It was like doing another day's work on *Star Trek* with a totally different crew. 'Night Terrors' was a seven day

shoot with one day of second unit.

"You want to create an illusion, and the scene that comes to mind is the scene where Beverly is examining all the bodies in the morgue, and suddenly is it real or is it fantasy? What has her lack of dreams and sleep done to her mind? Again, I think that sequence is very effective in what happens to an individual under such circumstances. I think that sequence really worked and made the point. There were other little moments that each character tried to find in order to show that dilemma."

Muses write Jeri Taylor, "This was a real tough episode. It was convoluted, it was a little mysterious, technical, quasi-supernatural. It was all over the map and there were a lot of different episodes to try and make cohesive. I rewrote and rewrote it, and I never thought that we were ever going to put that one to bed. It was strange. Troi's dream sequences are not something you get to see every week."

"Sleep disorder stories are the most commonly pitched stories we have here," says Rick Berman. "The sleep disorder was that our people were not getting enough REM sleep [and] they were all going mad which, in fact, is what would happen. It was all medically accurate, but it was kind of hard to follow and got convoluted. I don't think there was anything very terrifying in it."

Michael Piller states, "It deals with dream deprivation, which I think is an interesting phenomena to explore, but it was the first show right after Christmas hiatus and I don't think everybody was quite back on their feet yet. As a result, the energy level was way down and the timing was off and the nature of the problem made everybody start reading slowly. When the film was finished, it was nine minutes too long [*Trek* episodes must clock in at 43 minutes] and we had to cut huge pieces out of it in order to make it fit into an hour. The bottom line was that it was no longer a script because they were dream deprived. They were all talking slowly and after a while that gets pretty boring, and the middle of that show sagged and was slow, boring and disappointing."

••••

Episode #92:
"Identity Crisis"
Original Airdate: 3/25/91
Written by Brannon Braga
Story by Timothy De Haaf
Directed by Winrich Kolbe
Guest Starring: Maryann Plunkett (Commander Susanna Leitjen)

The crew of an Away Team mission Geordi was on five years earlier while serving on the USS Victory, are all disappearing. He finds out his friend and colleague, Susanna Leitjen (Maryann Plunkett) is metamorphosizing into an alien creature, and that he's next.

As Geordi begins to unravel the mystery via a holodeck recreation of the mission, he begins his startling transformation. It's only with the help of Leitjen that the Away Team is able to return him to the ship before his transformation is complete.

••••

"It was a very tough script to solve," admits Michael Piller. "The script was originally bought as a spec script submitted by a fan. It was very heavy on point of view and [contained] stylistic devices we didn't want to do. The original script had two non-*Star Trek* characters going through what Geordi and this woman eventually went through. It was a very complicated, complex production that the director did a terrific job on. It had scenes within scenes and I was very happy with the show. It may not have been one of the best scripts we wrote, but it's a great example of how those guys in production can really turn out a helluva product."

Utilized in the filming of the episode was a state-of-the-art ultra-violet lighting system.

"We were talking about how we're going to make these guys glow and Peter Lauritson said to me, 'Why don't we try ultra violet?'" recalls David Livingston. "I said because we had done a test the year before. I almost dismissed it, but then pulled out the tape and looked at it and said this stuff is great. [I] went to Michael Westmore and Bob Blackman and said we want to do this, and they designed these suits and we painted them with u/v and put these contact lenses in to this woman's eyes that glowed. It was fabulous and we got Mark

and Brian [the LA radio deejays who were given their own short-lived series on NBC] to walk around in these suits. LeVar looked fabulous.'

"We used heavy blue light for the set lighting, and it's different lighting than you see elsewhere, because all the source coming from behind the camera is blue light. That's a decision we made and it should look harsh, and unrealistic and not well lit because it's not lit from one single blue source. It's basically a beacon shining out. It looked different than anything else and that was intentional. What I was surprised at was how powerful the u/v reflected back, and MTV is using it a lot now. I liked our use because it was integrated into the story. We used it to make it work dramatically rather than doing it as an effect. To me, that was a major accomplishment. We didn't do it to just be glitzy, we did it because it tied in dramatically with the story."

States director Winrich Kolbe, "That was an interesting show and a lot of. First of all, LeVar Burton is a hell of an actor and it's a lot of fun working with him, even though I'm sure there was a lot of pain and agony on his part going into that suit. Technically speaking we didn't make things any easier for him because we had to light everything with black light. So we're kind of restricted camera-wise to do what we wanted to do because of all of those tremendous black light units. It was a hell of a set, but a technical nightmare. But everybody seems to be happy about it."

Episode #93:
"The Nth Degree"
Original Airdate: 4/1/91
Written by Joe Menosky
Directed by Robert Legato
Guest Starring: Dwight Schultz (Barclay), Saxon Trainor (Larson), Jim Norton (Einstein)

Barclay from "Hollow Pursuits" returns and has his intellect enhanced by beings attempting to bring the Enterprise to the center of the universe to say hi.

Engaging in discussions with a holodeck recreation of Albert Einstein and hooking himself in to the ship's computers, Barclay propels the ship into the center of the galaxy.

••••

"We had sort of put in our laundry list of things we wanted to bring back fourth season," says Michael Piller. "'Hollow Pursuits' was a wonderful episode last year, and [Barclay] is a very interesting character and a great actor. We were having trouble finding something that would make it worthwhile to bring him back. Joe had this concept of somebody who became super intelligent and said, 'Maybe this could be our Barclay show,' and we weren't sure what we were going to do with our premise at first, but we finally got a story together and I was really pleased with the way it turned out. Joe Menosky has said he was really proud to have his name on that show, more so than any other show. That's Rob Legato's second episode and Rob did a masterful job in terms of interpreting the story. I think Rick came up with the idea of doing Cyrano. It was kind of a con on the audience. I think the most interesting thing in that was the room where he attached himself to the computer. We've used laser beams in post production for firing things and lighting effects, and we've had several meetings where we've wanted to use them in production but have never done it. Rob suggested it on this episode and it was a wonderful idea—all those beams coming down and hitting his head are all laser beams and mirrors. It's all live, it's another effect we want to use more of. It's the first time on stage that we've done it. It's really weird and it allows you to move the camera. If it was laid in in post, you wouldn't be able to. It has a real immediacy and in terms of technical stuff that was a real advancement in terms of using lasers on stage.

"Rob came up with that thing too. Part of it was shot at eight frames per second, and part at six frames. Then we harmonized the voice down to that speed so that the voices work within that eight frames. It was a wild effect. It was a great episode for him to do so he could draw on all of his tricks."

Says Brannon Braga, "We struggled for a year with how to have Barclay come back. We didn't want him to play the nervous chap in the holodeck again and Joe Menosky came up with the science-fiction notion of a probe which is essentially a ship in a bottle. It was a good twist on that particular character which you could only get to with a science-fiction gag."

Rob Legato utilized live laser effects on the stage in "The Nth Degree."

"We've used laser beams in post production for firing things and lighting effects," says David Livingston. "We've had several meetings where we've wanted to use them in production but have never done it. Rob suggested it on this episode and it was a wonderful idea. All those beams coming down and hitting his head are all laser beams and mirrors. It's all live and done on the stage. It's really weird and allows you to move the camera. If it were laid down in post-production, you wouldn't be able to. It has a real immediacy and in terms of technical stuff was a real advancement for us in the use of lasers on stage."

Episode #94:
"Q-Pid"
Original Airdate: 4/22/91
Written by Ira Steven Behr
Story by Randee Russell and Ira Steven Behr
Directed by Cliff Bole
Guest Starring: John de Lancie (Q), Jennifer Hetrick (Vash), Clive Revill (Sir Guy)

Vash (Jennifer Hetrick from "Captain's Holiday") joins an archaeological conference aboard the Enterprise and is reunited with Picard. Meanwhile, Q returns as a matchmaker who puts the two lovebirds and the crew of the Enterprise in a recreation of Robin Hood to teach Picard a lesson about love.

Picard storms Sir Guy's castle, where he and the Away Team rescue Vash's Maid Marian from Guy's evil clutches. Q essays the role of the Sheriff of Nottingham.

••••

"It had everything that I liked as a director," says Cliff Bole. "It had Q, who's a very entertaining guy and character. What more would I love to do than *Robin Hood: The Movie?* Here I was able to do that. I stepped back in time, there was sword fighting, some boisterous 12th century characters and also the spaceship. What more can you get? That's the ultimate as a director. Some guys like to do the man in the gray flannel suit, and I

like to do fantasy.

"It was a show where Picard falls out of character a little bit," he emphasizes. "He's not as stoic as he usually is and falls for a beautiful woman, who was raised to do that. I got a few letters about 'Q-Pid' that the women who wrote asked why weren't the ladies involved in a more modern way with the fighting. It was my feeling that we went back to the 12th century and we wee doing the 12th century, and I can't change history."

"Marina and I have always laughed about the fact that both of us can do fencing and that sort of thing," says Gates McFadden. "We're the ones who bash pots over warriors' heads, instead of doing karate or whatever. I personally love going on the Away Team missions and would love to do more of them."

"Everytime it's in *TV Guide* this episode gets a Close-Up," laughs Michael Piller. "I'm not sure why. I just think we came up with the idea of a love triangle between Q, Picard and Vash, and to bring her and Q together, which I thought was a great premise, but we couldn't lick it. It came together in a meeting with Ira Behr, who had created Vash, and we said why doesn't he do it. While we were trying to break it, someone said if we want to do a love triangle, let's throw these characters into one of the classic love stories. King Arthur was discussed with Guenivere, and then Robin Hood. Brannon [Braga] said something about wanting to do Robin Hood and Robin Hood was about to be released by about 15 motion picture companies. We said why don't we steal all their thunder? It just seemed to be that Ron Hood and his band of merry men was a very nice group to put our guys into, and then we just played it for fun. That was what was so great about the fourth season and wasn't so great about the fifth season. Each week you were never quite sure what was going to come on."

Episode #95:
"The Drumhead"
Original Airdate: 4/29/91
Written by Jeri Taylor
Directed Jonathan Frakes
Guest Starring: Jean Simmons (Admiral Satie), Bruce French (Sabin), Spencer Garrett (Simon Tarses), Earl Billings

Jean Simmons, seen here as Elizabeth Collins-Stoddard on the revival of Dark Shadows, played a futuristic Joe McCarthy in "The Drumhead."

(Admiral Henry), Henry Woronicz (J'Ddan), Ann Shea (Nellen)

A Klingon is caught on board the Enterprise spying for the Romulans, resulting in Admiral Satie coming on board to get to the heart of a suspected espionage ring. What develops is a witch hunt for his collaborator; a witch hunt that eventually leads all the way to Picard.

••••

Ironically, "The Drumhead," one of *Next Generation's* most provocative episodes, originated as a money-saving installment. The same monetary considerations that gave us the dismal "Shades of Grey" resulted in this timely and passionate (and inexpensive) story.

"We saved $250,000 on this episode," smiles actor/director Jonathan Frakes. "It was the lowest budget of the season, but the risk is that shows like this are too chatty and people like a little action. But if you like dialogue and acting, this is certainly the episode. It's the McCarthy trials, a real guilty until proven innocent approach that Satie takes and she [Jean Simmons] was brilliant. She's an enormous Trekkie and watches the show every week, and then gets on the phone with her friends and they talk about the episode. The people who are fans of this show never cease to amaze me."

Writer Jeri Taylor, who essentially started from scratch on an episode

David Ogden Stiers, with M*A*S*H co-stars Alan Alda and Mike Farrell, portrayed Dr. Timicin in "Half a Life."

Ron Moore had proposed called "It Can't Happen Here," notes, "It's basically a witch-hunt with the idea it's taking the McCarthy era and the Salem witch hunts that can happen even in our enlightened 24th Century, and how these individual personal liberties can be stepped on. If you do that ever so lightly, even in the name of freedom, liberty and the preservation of the Federation, that becomes disastrous. It's a very provocative story and one which is a little darker than some of the others. It's nothing but talk and it was a real challenge as a writer to make that work."

"That should have been a 'Shades of Grey,'" Michael Piller adds pointedly. "The studio asked us for one. They wanted a clip show to help them out with financial problems and to make sure we balanced our budget, since we spent a lot of money on some of our shows. Rick [Berman] and I discussed it and we both hate, *hate,* clip shows. We think they're insulting to the audience. They tune in and then you create this false jeopardy and then flashback as their memory goes to the wonderful time they had before they got trapped in the elevator, and that bullshit. We just absolutely said if there's anyway to avoid this, can we come up with an episode that will cost the same but at least will be a story with integrity because clip shows don't have any integrity. The studio finally

agreed to let us try, and we came up with 'The Drumhead,' which is obviously a very inexpensive episode without any special effects. But it gave us a chance to tell a very important story."

Episode #96:
"Half a Life"
Original Airdate: 5/6/91
Written by Peter Allan Fields
Directed by Les Landau
Guest Starring: Majel Barrett (Lwaxana Troi), David Ogden Stiers (Dr. Timicin), Michelle Forbes (Dara), Terence McNally (B'Tardat), Carel Struycken (Mr. Homn)

Mrs. Troi falls in love with an alien scientist, Timicin (David Ogden Stiers), who is supposed to kill himself on his 60th birthday in accordance with the rules and rituals of his planet's culture.

••••

"It's a much different type of Mrs. Troi episode," says actress Marina Sirtis. "It's not quite as flippant or light as they tend to be. It starts off quite light, but then it has a real message with a little morality play, which is something I like to do. I didn't have much to do, which is good since I don't want it to be a given that every time mom comes aboard, I have to deal with her. I think it's more interesting that when she does come back, other characters have to deal with her."

Offers director Les Landau, "It showed a whole new side to Majel Barrett as an actress and the character of Mrs. Troi. She's usually this flimsy, whimsical Auntie Mame of the universe, but in this episode she's a very sensitive, warm and caring individual. It deals with the whole issue of growing old and how society deals with the elderly and, in my mind, it was one of the most pertinent storylines I have done. The opportunity to work with Majel and David Ogden Stiers was great. He was totally supported in casting by Rick and Michael, and this episode probably has less to do with our regular characters than any other episode in the history of the show. It goes back to the 'Family' situation, which is the beauty of dealing with people like Michael Piller and Rick Berman in that they are open to exploring, not only the universe, but new ideas within the confines of that universe. That is the beauty of what *Star*

Trek is and what Gene Roddenberry created, which is a commentary on the current issues of our time. I think it has become Rick Berman's mandate to continue that theory and put forward the best possible entertainment with a subtext of something that is relevant to today's society. Again, I'll refer to 'Half a Life,' which brings back to us the character of Mrs. Troi and the fact that she—for the first time—falls for another being from another planet, who at the age of 60 is destined by his society to be put away because when one reaches the age of 60, one is put to sleep. That's an issue which is very current in how do we deal with, and what do we do with, our elders. They may have reached an age where by numbers they are old, but mentally, physically, emotionally, sexually, professionally, they are, if not at their peak, certainly have a lot to contribute. That was a very poignant episode, which goes back to dealing with issues at hand, like 'Sarek,' which deals with senility and diseases of the mind."

Writer Peter Allan Fields, later promoted to co-producer of *Deep Space Nine*, did a crash course in Lwaxana lore to prepare himself for writing "Half a Life."

"I saw both 'Haven' and 'Menage a Troi' quite a while before I even began writing and I didn't refer to them at all when I was writing my first Lwaxana Troi story except to find out her title was 'holder of the chalice...', and all of that sort of thing," says Fields. "I went through the script for 'Haven' to find out who the hell I was writing about and that wasn't difficult to accomplish. I couldn't figure out at first how much rank and privilege she had and then I realized you give her as much as they'll let her have. She takes it."

Episode #97:
"The Host"
Original Airdate: 5/13/91
Written by Michael Horvath
Directed by Marvin V. Rush
Guest Starring: Franc Luz (Odan), Barbara Tarbuck (Leka), William Newman (Kalin Trose), Nicole Orth-Pallavicini (Kareel)

Dr. Crusher falls in love with a Federation ambassador, Odan (Franc Luz), who is being ferried aboard the

Enterprise to negotiate a planetary dispute. When Odan is injured, the crew discovers a parasitic creature inside his body which is the real ambassador.

••••

"The Host" was directed by series Director of Photography Marvin Rush, who negotiated his camera around the ever expanding stomach of the pregnant Gates McFadden.

"The episode had to be shot in such a way that we couldn't see her stomach," says Jonathan Frakes. "They would not address the fact that the actress was pregnant. It was an interesting problem. You really found yourself more concerned with hiding her with furniture or with your body, or shooting from her boobs up. That was very restrictive."

"It's one of the most outstanding stories we've ever done," says story editor Brannon Braga. "Being in love with someone is not very fresh. Having the parasite as the real intelligence and the body as the host is. It was not originally pitched as a love story, it was pitched as a squirmy worm who's really the intelligence. What's ironic is that the most repulsive story ever pitched to us ended up being the most touching love story and that's why this show is so unique."

Elaborates Ron Moore, "The addition of Beverly to that story is the vital component. A lot of freelancers would take that premise and say this is a show about the ambassador and the struggles of the parasitic creature and the war negotiations. No one really cares about that. But when it becomes a Beverly problem, who's in the position with the problem, and to some extent Riker, that's how it became a *Star Trek* story."

Ultimately 'The Host' has become one of the most popular *Trek* episodes in light of its non-polemic, but effective, advocacy of tolerance and acceptance.

"I had no advance knowledge of the story I was going to direct and I don't believe the company does a great deal of that," says Marvin Rush. "I'm sure they have in mind who might be good for a particular episode, but sometimes directors who have planned for an episode don't get the episode they wee going to be given because they're not ready and there are rewrites and revi-

sions. There are things that affect those choices. I believed, in my case, I was given a ship show that involved something that was a challenge that the cameraman would be good at. That one thing was that Gates, who played the romantic lead opposite Odan, was seven months pregnant and the one trick you need is someone who can figure out how to photograph that and not give away the fact the leading lady is in fact pregnant. That may or may not have been a factor to them. I suspect that it was a consideration. I think it was ready, the script was ready to go."

Although many questioned Dr. Crusher's rejection of Odan, once transplanted into a female body, as homophobic, Rush disagrees vehemently.

"Most of the people that I have talked to thought the show worked pretty well and were entertained. Some comment was that they were unhappy with the ending because it was left a question. There was, or could have been, a sort of homosexual aspect to is and we chose not to go that route with it. I felt that it was more about the nature of love, why we love and what prevents us from loving. To me the best analogy is if your beloved turned into a cockroach, could you love a cockroach? It's the same person, if the person is the personality and core within, but can you get past the outside? We as humans are affected by the whole package, including the outside shell, and Gates in her last scene talks about maybe someday our ability to love won't be so limited. She says mankind may one day be able to deal with this, but I can't. To me that is about the nature of love and I think it's an interesting, worthy discussion. Rather than deal with the fact it was because of any homosexual bent per se, it's just that in our culture and our society people who are heterosexual who want the companionship of a male because they are a female, wouldn't be able to deal with that opposite situation."

Episode #98:
"The Mind's Eye"
Original Airdate: 5/27/91
Written by Rene Echevarria
Story by Ken Schafer and
Rene Echevarria

Directed by David Livingston
Guest Starring: Larry Dobkin (Ambassador Kell), Edward Wiley (Governor Vagh), John Fleck (Commander Taibak)

In this 24th Century retelling of *The Manchurian Candidate*, Geordi is cast in the role of Laurence Harvey and—who would have thought?—Data is Frank Sinatra in a story that has LaForge brainwashed by the Romulans to assassinate a Klingon governor. The objective is to undermine the alliance between the Federation and the Empire.

••••

"The Mind's Eye" is notable for introducing Tasha Yar's daughter as the silhouetted sub-commander quietly observing Geordi's torture, played by an uncredited Denise Crosby.

Enthuses David Livingston, "I couldn't ask for a better episode to do as my first directorial assignment, since it didn't have scenes with eleven people in the observation lounge talking for ten pages. Every scene had something going on, some action. They were all short scenes and I could do some weird stuff and was thrilled. I'm kind of hyper and nervous and uptight, and I had always been afraid of directing, but I finally said, 'David, if you're going to have the opportunity, it's on this show, so go for it.' I had the best professional time of my life on that episode. I got to make all the decisions and you get to do what you want within the constraints of the budget."

Keeping an eye on the bottom line, and filling in as producer while Livingston played with his new toy, was Merri Howard. "She acted as line producer and ran a tight ship," Livingston says. "She challenged me at all the right places and we had our battles, just like I have with the directors, but we worked everything out amicably. But you sure get a different perspective on the production people. I used to say that directors have the conscience of rattlesnakes, but I've now added to that—at least they have [a] conscience, unlike production people...and I'm one of those people."

Donning his director's hat, Livingston is quick to point out that there's little graphic violence, only psychological violence as opposed to such episodes as "Yesterday's Enterprise" and "Conspiracy."

••••

"In Theory" had Ensign D'Sora (Michelle Scarabelli, seen here as Susan Francisco in Alien Nation) fall in love with Data.

"I saw the gashes on the set of 'Yesterday's Enterprise,' and I said I don't know if I should let Westmore do it," Livingston recalls. "I knew I was going to hear from Rick in dailies, but he loved it. I was afraid it was a little too grotesque. In 'Conspiracy,' Dan [Curry] really pushed it there when he blew the head up. We have to be a little prudent about violence, and I don't think we would do something that strong again. The violence in 'Mind's Eye' is all psychological. It's like *Manchurian Candidate* in that respect. I rented the movie before I shot this episode. I love it. I screened the film on two successive weekends, and took notes and studied it. [*Candidate* director Frankenheimer] shot everything in oners on that movie. He has some others that go on for four or five minutes. I think it's John Frankenheimer's best movie, Frank Sinatra's best movie, Laurence Harvey's best movie and Angela Lansbury's best movie. But, of course, it's not Janet Leigh's best film...she did something in a shower once."

Episode #99:
"In Theory"
Original Airdate: 5/27/91
Written by Joe Menosky and Ronald D. Moore
Directed by Patrick Stewart

Guest Starring: Michele Scarabelli (Jenna), Rosalind Chao (Keiko), Whoopi Goldberg (Guinan)

The long-anticipated Data love story is finally consummated by the show's two executive story editors (writers Ron Moore and Joe Menosky), in which an Enterprise cadet, Jenna (Michele Scarabelli of *Alien Nation*), on the rebound from a bad relationship, falls for the didactic Data, the stoic android devoid of emotion.

• • • •

Ironically, it was the captain who turned to his first officer for advice when he took the helm of an episode for the first time.

"We had a couple of conversations," admits then three-time director Jonathan Frakes of Stewart's directorial debut. "He was fabulous and took to it beautifully. He's a very sensitive man and he did a great job. He was also lucky that he got a Data show as his first. Brent really is an incredible actor with unbelievable range and technique, and certainly the most popular character, so it's a real plus to get that combination."

"I was a virgin then," laughs Patrick Stewart of directing his first episode of *The Next Generation*. "Those seven days that I worked on 'In Theory' were seven of the most exciting days of my career. They were so intense. I was very fortunate that I got that episode. The way the series works is that the directors and the episodes are not carefully assigned, with the exception of the pilot and the final two-hour show where Corey Allen and Rick Kolbe were carefully chosen. It's all a lottery as to who gets to direct an episode, and I was very lucky to get a simple little love story to direct. I was lucky to have Brent Spiner as my leading man and indeed Brent was to be my leading man in the first three of the five episodes I directed. I had a fabulous guest star performance by Michelle Scarabelli. I had no big sets or Klingon Great Halls or shoot 'em ups; there were no epic scenes. I had to simply concentrate on the basics of camera movement and structure and, more than anything else, work with the actors on the scenes. Each time, before I'm about to go in to direct a new episode, I rerun each one of the previous episodes I directed, particu-

larly to look at all the things I thought I got wrong and wanted to improve. 'In Theory,' I think, still has a great deal of charm about it."

Episode #100:
"Redemption, Part I"
Original Airdate: 6/17/91
Written by Ron Moore
Directed by Cliff Bole
Guest Starring: Robert O'Reilly (Gowron), Tony Todd (Kurn), Whoopi Goldberg (Guinan), Barbara March (Lursa), Gwynth Walsh (B'Etor), Ben Slack (K'Tal), Nicholas Kepros (Movar), J.D. Cullum (Toral), Denise Crosby (Romulan Commander)

The conclusion to the triumvirate arc dealing with Worf's Klingon dishonor, which began with "Sins of the Father" and continued with "Reunion." The Enterprise returns to the Klingon homeworld so that Picard can fulfill his role as arbiter of the Rite of Succession and allow Gowron (Robert O'Reilly) to accede to the role of ruler of the High Council. Meanwhile, Worf attempts to clear his family name.

• • • •

Returning for an encore performance was the new Klingon super-starship first designed for "Reunion." Since 1979, *Trek* has been recycling stock footage of the battle cruisers that got KO'ed by V'ger in *Star Trek: The Motion Picture*, and the Bird of Prey cruiser from *Star Trek III*. During fourth season, money was finally budgeted to give the Klingons a new ship.

"It's a great model," says David Livingston. "We've used a lot of stock footage from the features, but at some point it just gets old. Peter came in and said we have to do something, and we finally did. Discussions had been going on for a while and we decided we just needed something larger and more menacing. In 'Redemption,' it looms very large in the legend. The problem is it's not just building the model, it's also having to shoot all the new motion control shots with them, so it's a big deal. But we put money into each season to do refurbishing and do the new ship shots. Peter uses the money to develop those things, and what we got out of fourth season was the new cruiser."

• • • •

•••••

CHAPTER TWENTYFOUR
SEASON FIVE

An Introduction

Ironically, what was perceived by many as one of *Next Generation*'s finest seasons did not materialize easily. Starting in 1991, after part one of the season finale's cliffhanger "Redemption" aired, the writing staff was already scrambling for new ideas after having exhausted their supply of teleplays at the end of fourth season.

"We all just looked at this empty script status reports and said how the hell are we going to come up with 26 stories?" says staff writer Brannon Braga, who was promoted to Story Editor for the show's sixth season. "We had some real gems come from freelancers and a lot of gems came from the staff. They didn't come easy, but they did come."

"There are some series where it's easier to develop ideas like a contemporary show," says then Supervising Producer Jeri Taylor. "*Simon & Simon* or *Murder She Wrote* where you can just devise a location and say I think we'll have it take place at the ballet and you set a murder mystery there. We don't have that option, we don't have a ballet or a rodeo. Every story needs to be unique with a science-fiction phenomenon and have an emotional base and all those kinds of things. When you've done as many as we have, they get harder and harder to scratch for. It's true of any series, you can never stay ahead of it because production is like this giant maw that just eats scripts. We fantasize that during the summer hiatus we'll get ten scripts done but they're treated with tender loving care that you can't just churn them out. Each one is molded carefully and scrutinized line by line and it's just such a careful effort that the time it takes doesn't allow you to accumulate a trunkload of scripts ready to go."

Facing the task of completing work on another season's worth of

Treks, considering the paucity of good material, is a daunting prospect for the Supervising Producer who was promoted to Co-Executive Producer for the show's sixth season.

"It is the single most difficult challenge that we face," explains Taylor. "I would wake up at three in the morning saying 'Twenty six stories! Twenty six stories? Where are they going to come from?' We take pitches constantly, we have a completely open script submission policy, the staff brainstorms and we ask for help from the outside. We knock ourselves out. We do whatever we can to scratch around and somehow there have always been 26 stories, most of which are quite wonderful, some of which are extremely special and some of which are not quite as terrific as they might have been. Looking at the mix the fifth year, it's a very solid and respectable effort, but it's real, real tough."

A number of scripts and stories had been purchased by the staff as a result of their open script submission policy, which required a signed Paramount release form with any submissions and did not require teleplays to be submitted by an agent. This resulted in Script Coordinator Eric Stillwell being deluged with over 3,000 spec scripts a year from fans, the large majority from starstruck Trekkies who have little idea of how to craft a legitimate screenplay.

Jeri Taylor confesses to being extremely happy with the quality of the show in its fifth season. "I was very pleased," she says. "None of them is ever easy to mount and complete and there have been any number of points along the way where all of us say 'Gulp, are we going to have any ideas?'. Ideas are the hardest thing to come by for this series. We started fifth season with only a few things in the works and never had a big, comfortable kind of reservoir of scripts and stories. We always felt like we were scrambling during the season but that's kind of par for the course. There were anxieties along the way, but I look back at the season now and think 'We really did some good stuff' and I'm very proud of it and would hold it up against any of the other years. I think the last four or five shows of the season are some of our strongest efforts and they may even become classics,

Season five as covered in the pages of Cinefantastique magazine.

although the fans will determine that."

Through the years, the difficult challenge in adhering to the strict *Star Trek* formula has seen many writers arrive and depart quickly on the show. Few have been able to adhere to the stringent parameters set by Producers Rick Berman and Michael Piller based on the guidelines drafted during the show's genesis by Gene Roddenberry.

"It's so easy for these scripts not to be believable and to make them contrived and make them fantasy like, to make these scripts hokey and illogical and muddled," states Executive Producer Rick Berman, who completely oversaw the production of the show since its second season. "The writing of the show at every level; the story level, the structural level, the dialogue and the polishing, is so tricky. It's so difficult for writers to write dialogue that's not contemporary and also not sword and sorcery. Gene in the first year was incredibly particular to the point where the writers hated it. Today, I am as particular as is Michael. We have to be, we've learned."

"There was a lot of turmoil in the first year as all television shows have and a lot of turmoil came out of the writing staff," recalls Berman. "Gene's [Roddenberry] perfectionist attitude towards first season scripts was such that it was very difficult for the writers and a lot of them left either willingly or not. I now, all these years later, totally understand and so does Mike Piller what Gene was after. This is a very difficult show to write and we had to work so carefully with new writers and we had to work very hard in making these scripts work unlike many other shows and it was very difficult."

Ironically, it was a first season writer, Herb Wright, who had segued from *Trek* to Paramount's *War of the Worlds*, who Berman recruited back to the show fifth season to juice up the science-fiction content of *Next Generation*. Wright departed several months later over creative differences in the show's direction with Executive Producer Michael Piller.

When Wright returned to the show in 1991, he found things had changed dramatically, both on-screen and off. "Fifth season was no comparison," he states. "People were so much happier and calmer and quieter and really helping each other. It was a kinder, gentler place to be. The first year I was the kinder, gentler guy and the fifth year I came back and I was suddenly the hawk. In story meetings people would say 'In this scene let's kiss the baby and I'd say, 'Bullshit, let's kill the baby' and everybody would look at me and say what's wrong with him?"

Wright recalls meetings during the first season in which Roddenberry's attorney would be involved in story conferences. "It was so bizarre," Wright says. "Gene was bringing his attorney to staff meetings and he was giving us notes on scripts and secretly rewriting them at night and taking people's names off and putting other people's names on. He would call up writers at home, free-lancers, ask them what was going on, how they were doing. It was horrible, one of the principle reasons I left. And [first/second season Producer Maurice] Hurley was the last straw for me. He was basically playing drinking buddies with Gene. Meanwhile, Robert Lewin had fallen all the way upstairs to the small office Brannon is now in.

"I was the kid on staff then," he adds. "I came back and all of a sudden I was the old man. It's radically

different, not only in content, but in the make-up of the staff and the way it's put together. They're such pros, I can't tell you how difficult it is to turn out a *Star Trek* each week and keep it the kind of quality they get."

"The first year was very chaotic," agrees Berman. "But the second year Gene stepped away and Maurice Hurley and I took the reigns and there was additional shakedown but things smoothed out a little bit and in the third year Piller came and it was shaky at first and then started to stabilize and it was very stable ever since. It was stable on all fronts. The post production people, the editors, the visual effects specialist who do such wonderful things for the show. It was a well oiled machine and it got better and more consistent and the key is that everybody continues to be as demanding upon themselves and take it as seriously as they have taken it.

"To produce a show that is this complex you have to be an incredible stickler for detail and you have to be very hard on yourself to continue to take it that frighteningly seriously and everybody did and that is true from the top right down to the production assistants," elaborates Rick Berman. "We've got some writers in Jeri Taylor, Ron Moore, Joe Menosky, Brannon Braga and now Peter Fields who are really starting to get a feel for the show. They've gone through a very long process in learning, but they are all learning it now and we're all pretty much in agreement about what the show is and what makes it work and what doesn't work and what is contrived and what is not good science-fiction and that's a key part of the ingredient too. It's really not a question of if the show had gotten better or that it was a different show, it's just a little bit more mature. The people who were doing it had gotten a little bit better at it. The thing that I'm most proud of is the general sense of consistency. We've gone through a number of regimes and the show had not necessarily gotten any better, but been more consistently good. I think since the beginning we've turned out some wonderful episodes; there are some wonderful episodes in the first season, in the second but, on the other hand, I think we do more wonderful episodes now. That

comes out of the process of experience. I think more so than any show in this town we had had very little fall off of key personnel; we pretty much had the same people working on the show that we'd had working for two, three and sometimes five years."

"It is a different process," says Brent Spiner, who portrays the unemotional android Data, of the show's evolution from first to fifth season. "There was less experimentation. I think there was less stretching of the envelope than we did in the first few years. We were looking to find the show in the first two years and what worked and what didn't and what seemed to be appealing and what wasn't and the powers that be seemed to make their decision about the format and what worked and what didn't work and kind of went with that. I'm not sure that's as exciting to work on in a creative aspect. To me it doesn't feel like a particularly creative process as much as a recreative process. That's not to put down the efforts of our writers and producers, because I think they've done a miraculous job and it's very, very difficult to turn out 26 quality episodes every year. I do think they have managed to get a high number of quality episodes on the air in a very short amount of time, which I think is difficult. But for an actor I think the fun is exploration. Particularly for me. I've always enjoyed when I've done plays' rehearsal more than performance because I think discovery is the fun and the playing of it is the job. It's a large ensemble, but I have no real huge complaints. It's been a very rewarding piece of work and I never before have done a job for this long. When I've done Broadway I've always taken three month contracts, because the fun for me is the rehearsal and the performance becomes routine. I grow tired of the routine after a few months and I never imagined I could do a show for seven years and play the same character. The good thing is that I got to play a different show every week and that keeps it interesting. There was always the hope that the next episode was going to be a great, great episode and that kind of kept us going."

However, even among the staff there was not universal accord over the fifth season's Enterprise missions. Michael Piller has mixed feelings when assessing the success of the shows broadcast during that period, but attributes this largely to the order in which the shows were broadcast. High concept episodes like "The Game" and "Disaster" aired back to back as did the personal dramas of "New Ground" and "Hero Worship", and the politically charged "Redemption" and "Unification" were only separated by a few installments.

"It's no secret that I've had mixed feelings about fifth season," says Piller. "If you were to look at the season week by week, I think that every week we delivered an entertaining hour of television and reliable, fun viewing and I'm not sorry we did any episode. What I'm not happy about as I look back is the mix. There were too many political shows in one block, too many personal dramas in one block, we were light on science fiction in the first half of the year and then I think around the last ten shows we really hit our stride. If you were to take those last ten shows and spread them out through the season, mix up the other ones and hold two or three to next year, it would have been a delightful season. I had a real sort of melancholy in the middle of the season saying, 'Darn, I felt like a championship basketball team that couldn't get its fast break together.' We did a lot of very good shows, but I didn't feel like we were really scoring the big wins. Then I think we put together probably five at the end of the season which could almost be considered up there with our best work." Helping to energize the series was the addition of Michelle Forbes to the ensemble as Ensign Ro, a character whose backstory would pave the way for *Deep Space Nine* a year later.

• • • •

CHAPTER TWENTYFIVE
SEASON FIVE

Episode Guide

"Redemption II"

"Darmok"

"Ensign Ro"

"Silicon Avatar"

"Disaster"

"The Game"

"Unification, Part I"

"Unification, Part II"

"A Matter of Time"

"New Ground"

"Hero Worship"

"Violations"

"The Masterpiece Society"

"Conundrum"

"Power Play"

"Ethics"

"The Outcast"

"Cause and Effect"

"The First Duty"

"Cost of Living"

"The Perfect Mate"

"Imaginary Friend"

"I, Borg"

"The Next Phase"

"The Inner Light"

"Time's Arrow"

Episode #101:
"Redemption II"
Original Airdate: 9/23/91
Written by Ronald D. Moore
Directed by David Carson
Guest Starring: Denise Crosby (Sela), Tony Todd (Kurn), Barbara March (Lursa), Gwynyth Walsh (B'Etor), J.D. Cullum (Toral), Robert O'Reilly (Gowron), Michael G. Hagerty (Larg), Fran Bennett (Admiral), Nicholas Kepros (Movar), Colm Meaney (O'Brien), Timothy Carhart (Hobson), Jordan Lund (Kulge), Stephen James Carver (Helmsman), Clifton Jones (Ensign Craig)

Picard discovers the Romulans are secretly providing aid to the Duras family, which is plotting to take over the Klingon Empire. Meanwhile, Worf joins his brother, Kurn (Tony Todd) as they try to keep the empire together under the leadership of Gowron (Robert O'Reilly).

••••

For director David Carson, it was not very difficult following the first part of a story which was directed by someone else.

"I do think I did my episode quite a bit differently in style from the way Cliff Bole did it," explains Carson. "I prefer to use very long lenses on the camera and I tend to make the picture very grainy, exciting, interesting and I like to throw the background a little out of focus, just to keep an element of mystery. I like to use as much mystery as I can, given the gritty nature of the story. So I like to use images, smoke, darkness, shafts of light. I find that very dramatic and I went for that as much as I could on 'Redemption.' Maybe more so than was done on the first part. But when you're doing a part two, one has to always look at the first part to see where the story's going and how it's been approached. You can't just depart from it completely because both parts have to go together.

"I find the more gritty stories fascinating," adds the director of such episodes as "The Enemy" and "Yesterday's Enterprise." "Not only do I enjoy the stories and the suspense of storytelling, but I also like the pictures that some stories produce. I think the Enterprise represents some of the 'cleaner' aspects of *Star Trek*, given this amazing, futuristic ship. Obviously the feeling is more gritty on the Klingon ships.

"I particularly enjoyed the Klingon warrior bar in 'Redemption,' because we've never seen one before. Rick Berman encouraged me to invent new ways of behaving, which is why they banged their heads together as a game; or arm wrestling with pointed daggers attached to their wrists. It was totally Klingon and it's an interesting world to work in. When you have the good fortune to have an episode like 'Redemption,' you are able to make this wonderful contrast between the clean, optimistic world of the Enterprise, and the down and dirty world of the Klingons. That's just great for a storyteller."

"I thought it was a good opportunity for me," says actor Michael Dorn. "But they also packed a lot of things into one episode...a lot of things. It was too much. I thought the Data story should have been a whole episode; it was an interesting story in which he encounters prejudice and that's a really strong point that needed more time, but they chose not to. There was also the story of how I get back to the Enterprise and the whole thing about Denise Crosby. That's three big stories for one episode, but they're the people who write it and are in charge."

"Some fans wrote and said they thought Data was really emotional in 'Redemption'," reflects Brent Spiner. "I didn't think so at all. What I was playing was a character who was in a command situation for the first time and the only model he had was the man he served under, Captain Picard. So when he yelled 'Do it!', it wasn't because he was emotional but because he thought it would engender a response because that's what Picard would have done."

Recalls writer Ron Moore, "I had more fun writing Part II than I. We knew there were a lot of stories to tell but I didn't want to lose any of those threads, and the Data thing was the most fun of all of them. I wish there were a couple more minutes because you watch it and it blazes along, [but] it was a little constrictive. The parallels to the coup in the Soviet Union was very ironic. It was something that resonated around in my mind. Part II had a little more life than part I. The problem is explaining the Sela/Tasha backstory. It was tough to write and I knew it would be confusing and that, in essence, is the difficulty with doing continuity on the show. It's fun and gives us the sense of being a real place, but you have to explain it to people who haven't seen all those other episodes. It was not an easy explanation—that all came from Denise. She came up with the concept, which I rolled my eyes at the first time I heard. But as we started to get into story on 'Redemption Part II,' I needed some sort of Romulan thing to actually happen this time since we kept saying they're doing this stuff. It just seemed natural. It fit and we did it."

Says Co-Executive Producer Michael Piller of Denise Crosby's unorthodox encore, "Sela was not created to be a new regular character on the show. I would disagree that her return was botched. I found it quite effective, I found Sela's backstory to be quite emotionally touching. The only objection that I had to the show was that in the critical moment of the fifth act, exposure of the Romulans charge, we missed one important shot that didn't sell the remarkable nature of what Data had accomplished. Otherwise, I rather liked the opening episode of the season."

"It was a terrific episode," adds Executive Producer Rick Berman. "We've played out our Klingon political trilogy to a point where we can take a rest for a while. But I thought it was delightful and [director] David [Carson] did a marvelous job."

"I think it was the bigger of the two episodes," says Co-Producer David Livingston, responsible for the physical production of the series. "It was a more ambitious show. We didn't have the Klingon bar [in the first part] and that was a tough set to light and very cramped. It looked great, we added atmosphere on the set. The other sets were repeats. Because of money, we weren't able to build the whole Klingon Hall, which was kind of unfortunate. Richard James also wanted to make some modifications to the hall, so it was kind of tough for both Cliff on Part One and David on Part II to cover it because they literally didn't have half the set. They had to turn people around and shoot it into the other

Damnation Alley's *Paul Winfield was the alien captain Dathon in "Darmok", a highlight episode of season five.*

walls. We changed the tapestry on the back wall and things like that. We did a lot of cheats."

Episode #102:
"Darmok"
Original Airdate: 9/30/91
Written by Joe Menosky
Directed by Winrich Kolbe
Guest Starring: Paul Winfield (Tamarian Captain)

Picard is transported to an unknown world, where he encounters an alien captain played by *Star Trek II's* Paul Winfield, who communicates through metaphors. Unable to understand the captain, Picard doesn't know if his intentions are hostile or not.

••••

"I just think 'Darmok' is the prototype of what *Star Trek* should be," says Co-Executive Producer Michael Piller. "It dealt with a very challenging premise and many of our best shows are scripts that have been around a long time. 'Darmok' had been around for two years. It was a script that was curious and interesting, and one which Rick hated and wanted to abandon. I said 'No, I want to make it work' and finally I gave it to Joe [Menosky] and asked him if he had any ideas on it, because he's a very bright and intellectual kind of guy. He came back with a memo

that had a stunning piece of philosophy about language and communication. He created a whole language for that episode and it's just astonishing. The episode worked on every level; it had the philosophy dealing with language and what it does for us; two: great acting performances, it had a monster and a space battle—it had everything."

Offers Director of Photography Marvin Rush, "I thought 'Darmok' was pretty challenging, primarily because night was done on soundstage and it has a very believable, beautiful look to it from my point of view. It doesn't look it but because Paul Winfield walked all the way around the fire and appeared to be lit from within the fire, that was a real tricky shot. I had two or three of those shots in the sequence. You only see parts of them in the edit but we did them as complete circles so that any one take would stand on its own. It was a very complicated bit of floating flags and dimming lights up and others down, and when the torch was tossed we had lights that dimmed up on cues. It was a very complicated show and it was all done on really long lenses."

Admits director Winrich Kolbe, "I have mixed feelings about that episode. I like it as a story. I feel that I was hampered as a director in many areas because of the many obstacles, especially when we finally went down to the planet and went into the battle. The battle is something rather physical and you want to be there with your camera where it belongs. If you have to pan, you have to pan. The moment you go into opticals that's over. First of all, it was kind of a downer. Even somebody who knows what's supposed to happen will look at the dailies and say, 'Wait a minute, what is this thing?' I finally said, 'Guys, let me just stage the thing the way I see it, and then let me explain to you what I want to do, because you can't write out every shot and I can't shoot the shots the way you write them anyway because there's always one element missing—which is the monster.' So everything had to be shot in certain angles and you had weird set-ups in there. You had half a head looking up

and unless you knew that was a shot that goes into that particular area with the monster coming down. The editor freaked out and said, 'I don't know what to do with this stuff.' I said, 'Just relax, when I'm finished you and I will sit down and put this episode together because I know the staging.' Then, because of the expense of opticals, I had to edit in the camera with the understanding that the editors would never know what the other side of the editorial process was, the monster.

"Storywise, it was a hell of a story. It was almost flawless. It tangled a very interesting subject and a very complicated subject as well, and I think it did it well. The other difficult thing for me was....can you imagine not speaking Russian and, in your case, having to write an article in Russian? It makes it kind of difficult. Even though I had a translation of the dialogue, it wasn't quite there and for me it was like directing a Russian movie without speaking the language, but you work your way through it. So that was an additional challenge. The episode seems to have struck a chord. It's a show we can all be proud of."

Episode #103:
"Ensign Ro"
Original Airdate: 10/7/91
Written by Rick Berman and
Michael Piller
Directed by Les Landau
Guest Starring: Michelle Forbes (Ensign Ro), Ken Thorley (Barber Mot), Cliff Potts (Admiral Kennelly)

The Enterprise is sent to negotiate a peace between the Cardassians and the militant rebel leader of the Bajorans, Orta, after the rebels are suspected of having attacked a Federation colony. Meanwhile, Starfleet Admiral Kennelly secretly plots with the Cardassians to destroy the Bajoran leaders.

••••

"What was in the back of our mind was the need for a character, and we thought we needed another woman on the show," says Michael Piller about creating the enigmatic Ensign Ro. "When we talked about what kind of woman we would want, we thought it would be nice to have someone who had a little back-

••••

228

story and somebody we could use to create some conflict. So Rick and I worked on the concept of Ro and it was a show I was very satisfied with."

Introducing a new character into the *Trek* ensemble was not the easiest of tasks, particularly in light of the drubbing the introduction of Sela took from the fans.

"It's a terribly difficult thing," offers Piller. "It's one of the season's greatest accomplishments. Not just by Rick and I, but by the acting of Michelle, who is just a wonderful performer. You don't just throw in new people because this audience is really particular about who they're going to make part of the family, but I've heard almost no resistance to Ensign Ro."

Piller feels that by having Ro embraced my Guinan in her freshman outing, viewers immediately were prepared to accept the new character regardless of what the crew of the Enterprise perceived as her myriad flaws. "I think Guinan embraces Ro in a very personal way. She basically took Ro by the hand and said she deserves your attention and deserves to be embraced by you. When she took Ro to Picard for that very reason, in essence, she was doing that to our audience. It was not a very easy show to write; it was not until we found that relationship between Ro and Guinan that I was personally satisfied that we really had done something magnificent."

"Mike and I felt very seriously that we wanted a character to be introduced to our mix that had a little bit of an edge and had a backstory that wasn't Starfleet Academy sweetness and light, red, white and blue," says Rick Berman. "We wanted a character whose life had enough conflict in it that they could have a little bit of an attitude but fit within the structure of Roddenberry's dictum that these characters are developed in such a way that they don't have attitudes. So we created this character and gave her a backstory and a good introductory story in 'Ensign Ro' that I think established her rather quickly."

"I've become very attached to *Star Trek*," says the energetic and slender Forbes. "I love everyone who works on the show. The stories are very interesting. It's a wonderful place where imagination just runs wild. That's rare and a lot of fun. On all levels, in writing, acting, sets, it's a wonderful place to be and be around."

Episode #104
"Silicon Avatar"
Original Airdate: 10/14/91
Story by Lawrence V. Conley
Teleplay by Jeri Taylor
Directed by Cliff Bole
Guest Starring: Ellen Geer (Dr. Marr), Susan Diol (Carmen)

The Crystalline Entity returns from "Datalore" and destroys a fledgling Federation colony. The Enterprise pursues the entity and attempts to communicate with it, while a Federation expert on this destructive force, Dr. Marr, whose son was killed on Omicron Theta, Data's planet of origin, is intent on destroying it.

••••

Director Cliff Bole does not necessarily agree with the notion that attempting to communicate with the entity after all it had done was a ludicrous extreme of an optimistic future.

"It's not, if you can control the fact that it won't happen again, and I think Picard made it clear that he wouldn't destroy anything until it was explored. And it did finally show that it had another side, and I think that's what he was saying," Bole opines. "It can be characterized with modern society's attitude, 'Let's make sure we're not making any mistakes,' knowing full well they can handle it if they were wrong.

"I'm pretty satisfied with it," he adds. "If I could go back and shoot it again, I'd make some changes. A little bit of character change. I think I would have made Marr stronger in places and in the ending I thought we were weak. Then again, she was over the edge. You know, when you've only got 40 minutes of picture, it's tough to take a character and go all the way through the change and what happens to somebody. We're doing short stories here. Why does she do what she does? Sometimes you just don't have the film time to explore it properly. We're selling nine minutes less than the old

show. You can do a lot of character development in those nine minutes.

"But you stand on what you've done and it's like theater in the round. It's not like a feature where you look at the footage and say, 'I'm going to change this and reshoot it.' You don't have that time. It's theater in the round, it's impromptu and we do good work with the resources we have available."

"I didn't think it was a very good episode," confesses Brent Spiner. "If this was to really conclude the story of the crystalline entity, I don't think it was really the way to go. Apparently, they were having problems getting the next episode ready for production and this script was ready to go, but it wasn't very remarkable."

"It was a great premise," adds Michael Piller. "The idea of the crystalline entity as Moby Dick really appealed to me. I don't think the show was as effective as I wish it could have been."

"I enjoyed working on it a lot," says Supervising Producer Jeri Taylor, who wrote the episode's teleplay. "The crystalline entity was no one's favorite optical or bad entity, and there were doubts as to whether we should even resurrect it. Along came this story from a very young, inexperienced writer, Lawrence Conley, and he tapped into something that made us say, 'This works, this is a story that really has to be done.' I wanted to do it because I felt—being a mother and a woman—I could identify with what would have to be the worst kind of loss anyone could ever suffer, which would be the death of a child. I was really able to tap into those feelings and tell a story about a woman whose vendetta over the loss of her son ruined her."

Episode #105:
"Disaster"
Original Airdate: 10/21/91
Story by Ron Jarvis and Philip A. Scorza
Teleplay by Ronald D. Moore
Directed by Gabrielle Beaumont
Guest Starring: Erika Flores (Marissa), John Christian Graas (Jay Gordon), Max Supera (Patterson), Colm Meaney (O'Brien), Rosalind Chao (Keiko), Michelle Forbes (Ensign Ro), Cameron

••••

Arnett (Ensign Mandel), Jana Marie Hupp (Ensign Monroe)

The Enterprise is struck by a deadly natural phenomena which disables the ship, trapping members of the crew throughout the vessel while the magnetic field containing the anti-matter in the engine room faces imminent collapse.

••••

"'Disaster' was pitched by a couple of outside writers and it's something we had never done before," says Jeri Taylor. "I believe in variety. I think that it freshens a series. If you see the same story week after week it becomes deadly dull. We have things on the air which hardened fans would say is not a *Star Trek* and I say, 'Who says?' It may not fall in the mold of what people call a traditional *Star Trek* or fit some formula. I'm very much for breaking formula, changing something and doing a different kind of story. It was let's do something different—stop them dead in space and give them lots of problems. I thought some fans thumbed their nose at it, but in a mix of varied stories it was a good infusion of life."

"I thought let's just have fun with it," says episode writer Ron Moore. "We put our people in interesting and fun situations. It was nice to put Troi in the captain's chair and Picard in the elevator shaft. It was very episodic, and I remember the best moment was when we were breaking the story. Michael left the room and we were looking at different elements—Data and Riker in the powertube, in particular—and somebody said 'What if Riker takes Data's head off?' Michael came back in and we said, 'You're going to hate this, but what if we took his head off?', and he laughed and rolled his eyes and said 'Do it. No one will let us do it, but go ahead, it'll be fun'. I wrote it and Rick [Berman] never said a word. It's amazing that we got away with it."

Says Piller, "I think 'Disaster' was a fun show, it achieved everything that we set out to do. Ron wrote a nice script, I loved the stuff with Data's head disembodied. It had a real pace and rhythm. It didn't reach the upper echelon of episodes for me because it didn't really have a mystery

or science fiction base to it. I think we made a mistake in that show with Ensign Ro. We gave her the role of the disbeliever who had no where to go but lose in the end because she didn't believe Troi. I think, as I wrote in a memo, it would have been much better if she'd been around a year with some victories before we threw her right in to that situation to look rather foolish. And I didn't like the moment where she had to come back and say, which was almost the same arc as that character in the opening who apologized to Data, 'Gee, you were right, Counselor and I was wrong, and I respect you.' To me, after Troi made the right decision in a crisis, Ro's character, and I'm not sure if anybody would agree with me on this, would have said, 'You still could have killed him and I still think I was right and you're just lucky it came out this way.' That's the way I would have ended it with her. The bridge sequence was my least favorite part of the show because it seemed very predictable to me. Everything else I thought was really quite wonderful."

Episode #106:
"The Game"
Original Airdate: 10/28/91
Story by Susan Sackett and Fred Bronson and Brannon Braga
Written by Brannon Braga
Directed by Corey Allen
Guest Starring: Wil Wheaton (Wesley Crusher), Ashley Judd (Robin Lefler), Colm Meaney (O'Brien), Katherine Moffat (Etana), Diane M. Hurley (Woman)

While on shore leave, Riker is given an addictive electronic mind game that rewards the player with an orgasmic-like physical sensation. He begins to distribute the device aboard the Enterprise, making the crew pawns of the alien race who have created "the game."

••••

"'The Game' kicked around for quite a while and went through lots of permutations," recalls Ron Moore. "They turned it upside down and Brannon struggled with that for quite a while and they landed on this concept. Like 'Darmok,' it was long in development with different approaches."

"'The Game' was not one where we said let's do high concept," says Jeri Taylor. "It had been in development for two seasons and we had many, many approaches and writers taking cracks at it. It had a very long development history. Through an evolutionary process—without really intending to ape that movie [*Invasion of the Body Snatchers*]—this insidious spread of a game had its origins in kids being addicted to video games now, and what happens to them. That was the original intent and that's what drove the final story and script. That insight followed the development."

"We were going for fun and high concept," says writer Brannon Braga. "It's an atypical show in some ways and a lot of people had trouble believing Picard would become addicted and all these people would get hooked, but that's the story. Either you tell it or you don't. Not that we didn't give a lot of thought to how the characters became addicted. The characters only become addicted because they were getting the game from people they trusted, which is exemplified in the notorious chocolate scene, which had a very mixed reaction, but I had a lot of fun writing it. We were going for a fun show and thought it would be the perfect one to bring Wesley back in. It's ironic to have the adolescent come back to find all the adults are addicted to a game which is something you'd expect the other way around. And it was an opportunity to give Wesley a girlfriend. When I was writing the teleplay, I tried to relax him a little bit and took the opportunity to make him a more relaxed character with some personality and some spunk. He's more savvy because he was at the Academy and has gone through some changes and he'll pick up on Robin Leffler."

"I thought that was a great episode," says Michael Piller. "That was an episode that dealt with my fascination in watching my two sons with their obsession for video games and doing a show that dealt with a non-world shattering issue but people's obsession, almost addiction, to certain types of games. There's another show that was abandoned. It had been around for a year and we had actually had two drafts of it written and I said this cannot be fixed. The tables were reversed [when] Rick [Berman] said that I kept saying we didn't have any science-fiction premises and I was groaning and kvetching. He said what about that 'Game' story, and I said I can't make that work, we abandoned it. He said 'Why don't you give it to that kid, Brannon?' He'd been interning and staff writing. He delivered that script and did some wonderful things. He wrote scenes that didn't depend on action but went straight to character; and a two minute scene with Troi and a chocolate sundae which was wonderfully written. He has an extraordinary talent to find the moments in script where you can throw in character development and spend the time doing that for the sheer delight of getting to know that character better—and *not* interrupting the flow. He grew up this season into a full-fledged professional writer and I'm delighted that he'll be coming back next year with a credit."

"That's a fun episode," adds Jonathan Frakes. "A friend of mine asked me if I still had the game. He wanted it as a present. It was like O.D.'ing on Nintendo. They told me it was going to be this incredible graphic, and all it was a tuba on a checkerboard."

Episode #107:
"Unification, Part I"
Original Airdate: 11/4/91
Story by Rick Berman and Michael Piller
Teleplay by Jeri Taylor
Directed by Les Landau
Guest Starring: Graham Jarvis (Dokachin), Erick Avari (B'Ijik), Joanna Miles (Perrin), Mark Lenard (Sarek), Stephen D. Root (K'Vada), Malachi Throne (Pardek), Daniel Roebuck (Romulan #1), Norman Large (Neral), Mimi Cozzens (Soup Woman), Leonard Nimoy (Spock), Karen Hensel (Admiral), Majel Barrett (Computer Voice)

When the Federation suspects the legendary Ambassador Spock (Leonard Nimoy) has defected to the Romulans, Picard and Data are sent to Romulus to ascertain his true motives.

••••

"Originally it came out of Frank Mancuso, the chairman of Paramount at the time, who said to Leonard when they were planning *Star Trek VI*, why don't you figure out some way to pass the baton," says Rick Berman of Spock's visit to *The Next Generation*. "Maybe you could make some elements of *Star Trek VI* that reflect on *Next Generation*, and work with Berman to make *Next Generation* reflect *Star Trek VI* to have some backpacking. I sat down with Leonard and Nick Meyer, and we discussed elements of our show. Nick looked at at least a dozen episodes and we tried to find a way to join the two in certain respects. That was done in subtle ways in *Trek VI*. And then we sat down with Leonard and we said we'd like you to do an episode or two. We needed to do something in the 24th century that reflected something that happened in the 23rd century without giving away any elements of the movie, because our episode was going to run before the movie came out. We talked about it and went away. Mike and I spent a lot of time kicking things around and finally we came back to Leonard with an idea he didn't particularly like. We made a big change while we were talking in the room and he loved it. He was very kind to agree to do it and did it for a very reasonable sum of money, considering the kind of money he demands.

"We sat down and wrote the two episodes. I think the fix had to do with the idea that unification of Vulcan and Romulan societies was something that Spock realized was happening and had been happening for centuries, and that it had to be nurtured along. The idea of him staying behind to continue that process and that the Romulans were in fact—unbeknownst to themselves—going through the same evolutionary early metamorphosis in their culture that the Vulcans had those many centuries ago. He had to be there to help them work with it. It became more of a show that dealt with a peaceable as opposed to a warlike element, and Leonard felt very strongly about that. We futzed with it here and there based on Leonard's notes and, mostly, our own."

Adds Berman, "These were the two highest rated episodes we've ever done since the pilot and I think they were quite good. I was happy with both of them. Surprisingly, I felt Part 1 worked out a little better than Part 2. Understandably, Part 2 was pretty talky, but Leonard did a great job. It was a bitch to shoot Leonard's scenes since we had to have him do it all in 5 days—his part in two episodes. Granted he only had one scene in Part One, but it was difficult and we put in long hours. But we did it."

One pre-occupation that didn't concern Berman was how to acknowledge the show's progenitor, "*Classic Trek*", during Spock's foray into the 24th century. "I don't have any great belief in paying homage to the original show. The Spock we were dealing with in those two episodes was much more the Spock from the movies than from the original series. I certainly feel very strongly about being accurate. The fans of *Star Trek* would be let down if we were not to do our very best to be true to the nomenclature and rules of the two series. We have to treat it with respect. We were dealing with a character that was based on 25 years worth of development and, specifically, on what this character and his world was doing in *Star Trek VI*."

Opines Ron Moore, "I think the Sarek scene in Part One is great, and I was really happy that they did it and had the courage to kill the character and send him out that way."

Differs Jonathan Frakes, "I thought it was a real cheat. You expected Spock to be in the first part and he doesn't show up until the end. It was deceptive, but it was nice to see some sense of continuity between the two universes. To me, the highlight of the two episodes was the scene where Picard was trying to sleep and Data stood by watching him. That was funny. Leonard's a classy guy. I thought it was very nice of him to do our show. He didn't have to, and he exhibited great class when he was here."

"I was really gratified when Michael asked me to write one of the episodes," says "Unification Part One"

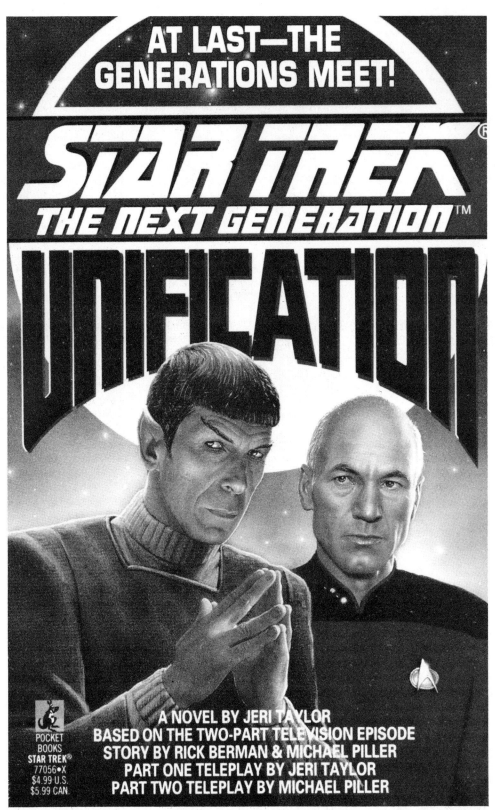

AT LAST—THE
GENERATIONS MEET!

STAR TREK ®
THE NEXT GENERATION ™
UNIFICATION

POCKET
BOOKS
STAR TREK®
77056•X
$4.99 U.S.
$5.99 CAN.

A NOVEL BY JERI TAYLOR
BASED ON THE TWO-PART TELEVISION EPISODE
STORY BY RICK BERMAN & MICHAEL PILLER
PART ONE TELEPLAY BY JERI TAYLOR
PART TWO TELEPLAY BY MICHAEL PILLER

The cover of the novelization of "Unification," the two-part episode of Next Generation that allowed Mr. Spock to meet Captain Picard.

writer Jeri Taylor. "He had set out to write them both, but they were back to back and it was overwhelming. He turned to me and I felt very complimented that that project, which was so important, was entrusted to me. He and Rick had worked out the story for both episodes and I fleshed it out in our script breaking process. He had come in with a lot of the philosophical, political discussions and what I got of course was the prolonged tease to Spock's appearance. He came on at the very end and the challenge was to tap dance well enough to sustain interest, even though this highly anticipated character was not there. I was really pleased with how the episode turned out. Once you have Spock and Picard and Spock and Data, you have gold, so the challenge was are we going to be able to keep the balls in the air enough to make that first episode work? I thought it was exciting, the mystery worked and it was a well-realized episode in its own right—almost to everyone's surprise, since it was felt this is the one we have to do to get to the good stuff. But it held its own in very equal terms with the second part."

Episode #108:
"Unification, Part II"
Original Airdate: 11/11/91
Story by Rick Berman and Michael Piller
Teleplay by Michael Piller
Directed by Cliff Bole
Guest Starring: Leonard Nimoy (Spock), Denise Crosby (Sela), Stephen D. Root (K'Vada), Malachi Throne (Pardek), William Bastiani (Omag), Daniel Roebuck (Romulan #1), Susan Falldender (Romulan #2), Vidal Peterson (D'Tan), Norman Large (Neral), Harriet Leider (Amarie)

Picard, who has found Spock on Romulus, learns that the Vulcan has come to the Romulan homeworld on a secret mission to reunite the Romulans with their progenitors on Vulcan, but quickly learns that he is a pawn in Sela's plans to invade Vulcan.

••••

"Les Landau did part one, but I did part two first," explains director Cliff Bole. "We shot out of order due to availabilities. If this is an education for the people who watch television, sometimes

you have to do crazy things. We shot two first, which was the conclusion, and then said, 'Okay, now we've got to come up with number one.' It takes a lot of talent to do that writing wise. This was only because we had a certain amount of availability with Leonard that we had to deal with.

"I admit that I have some disappointment with the story," he adds, acknowledging the fact that episode writer Michael Piller is highly critical of his own script, "but I think Michael is being a little hard on himself. We were dealt a hand and we had to deal with it. We had a certain amount of time and I think Michael did a real good job with it. Again, he's being real self-critical and we do that. We could have done better. But we had an assignment and had to do it, and I think we filled that gap real well. I'll defend that to the end.

"The strengths of the episode, are probably the things that don't show on the screen," Bole continues. "We pulled it together with the limited availability to an actor and we knew damn well that people were going to watch this show. The things that stand out in my mind are that it was a joy to work with Leonard. I don't find a lot of weaknesses with the show. I really don't. A lot of people thought it was a little slow in places, but Leonard's been playing this character for 30 years and he has a delivery. That's Spock. By the way, he was 100 years older in this episode than in anything we've seen. Negatively speaking, that show we should have opened up. We should have gone out. We should have put some air in that show. We shouldn't have been in a cave so long, we should have gone out and had a little more action."

"It's no secret I was disappointed more by my own work on it than anything else," says "Unification II" writer Michael Piller. "I thought it was a historic opportunity and I don't think we delivered what the potential of it was. I remember watching it for the first time cut together and saying, 'This is dark, it's flat, who cares, it's talky.' I'm a writer who depends a great deal on his instincts and they almost always lead me in a good direction. This time I don't think they did. If I had it to do over, I would do

a science-fiction mystery with weird stuff and get Spock involved in some form or fashion. It was unfortunate that we chose to do another political story so close to the stuff we had just done on the Klingon Empire. It was a politically heavy opening of the season. It came out of lofty goals, and goals that were very true to the nature of the show.

"It was our feeling that if you're going to bring Spock out of retirement, it should be something of cosmic significance. The unification of the Romulans and the Vulcans really struck me as the appropriate story to tell, because we're really telling the story of the unification of the original series and *Next Generation*, symbolically closing the gap that had always been in the fans' minds, if no one else's, between the two shows. I said what a great way of having this metaphor and building the series around this reunification. I thought that was marvelous, so we built the story and we had to make a decision whether we were going to do two parts or one, and we made a decision to do two parts. Right or wrong, we would have never been able to produce—for our budget—that story for an hour, though it would have made a much better hour show than two hour show. I was very pleased with Part One, oddly enough. I know a lot of people were very angry that they didn't get to see Spock until the last beat of the last scene, but I thought there were more interesting elements in Part One than there were in Part Two. I liked the stuff with Sarek, I thought it was very moving."

"We all broke the story together and we sat around and gave notes and discussed different things about Spock," says *Classic Trek* fan and *Next Generation* Producer Ron Moore. "My only real involvement was that I was a little bit more steeped in the old *Star Trek* than most people. I gave Mike [Piller] little insights, nothing really heavy, but little questions about Vulcans and I talked to Jeri about the relationship between Sarek and Spock. I was happy to see mention made of the original show. I didn't push and didn't mention anything because I wanted them to just do it. When we did work on 'Sarek' third sea-

••••

son, there were a couple of little references that I asked for to the old show which I got. Now and again I slip in something as a reference."

"I thought the mystery we set up was interesting, the character we met with Riker and the scene between Data and Picard on the Klingon ship is perhaps the single best relationship scene that this series has ever done," says Michael Piller. "I think that was classic. To me it was a good roadshow. My plan for Part Two with Rick—and I'm trying to take the blame, not the credit—was I wanted to tell a story about the maturity of one of drama's great characters. What happens to a Spock in the 85 years between then and now? How has logic and emotion played a part in his life? What is the growth of the man beyond logic? What was the conflict between he and his father and the death and passing of generations? I thought they were meaningful pieces of business to explore the man. I did not want a lot of plot to get in the way of the examination of the man and I felt that the show would be carried by the conflict between Spock and Picard, with Picard ironically representing the father through the mind meld. In fact, it was Picard who represented the original philosophy of *Star Trek* and Spock who was moving onto the future, so when the two came together it was sort of a reversal. It was all great stuff and it sounded wonderful in my mind and on paper, but the bottom line for me was that the relationship between Picard and Spock didn't have the chemistry. I don't think it was in the script and I don't think it came out on screen. There was not enough plot to pick up the slack when that didn't work. Throwing Sela into the mix didn't help. I thought it would be nice to have her as the archenemy, but it didn't really work out. It was talky without action, and it had some good scenes."

Says Brannon Braga, "I felt overall it was a little bit talky. Personally, I don't have a predilection to political stories. I find them inherently dry and the political elements of 'Unification Part One' I found somewhat dull overall. I thought it succeeded with some wonderful scenes in both episodes, mainly character scenes like between Data and Picard where he [Picard] is trying to

sleep; and there's a great scene between Spock and Data that everyone was waiting for. On the whole, I didn't care for the plot and the fan response was mixed. I know Michael was disappointed. It's hard to say any of our shows are bad, because if nothing else, they look great. I thought Part One was good. The death scene was very moving, the final scene between Spock and Picard was very moving and that arc I would have rather seen explored rather than the political stuff with Sela. I would have liked to have seen that Romulan subplot take a backseat and wish that Leonard Nimoy would have played the role less old. Mike wrote it much more lively. It should have had some of the feel of the original series where he's the guy whose onto everything and super alert. He seemed a little zoned out."

Episode #109:
"A Matter of Time"
Original Airdate: 11/18/91
Written by Rick Berman
Directed by Paul Lynch
Guest Starring: Matt Frewer (Berlingoff Rasmussen), Stefan Gierasch (Hail Moseley), Sheila Franklin (Ensign), Shay Garner (Female Scientist)

A mysterious visitor, historian Berlingoff Rasmussen, who has materialized from the future in a time pod, says he is observing the Enterprise crew on a critical mission to save an asteroid devastated planet from environmental destruction.

••••

"I am fascinated by all the episodes that have dealt with the implausibility of time travel," confesses Rick Berman. "I have always had in my head the idea of an episode that had someone who was capable of time travel and professes he is from the future, and we find out he is actually from the past. It's part of that Mark Twain feeling of what Leonardo Da Vinci could have done with a calculator or Alexander the Great with a shotgun. I developed the show with Robin Williams in mind for the role. He had said he wanted to do the show, but when it got finished his wife was 8 1/2 months pregnant and he had just finished *Hook*, and was starting something else. He couldn't do it, but I was very pleased with the direction it went in and very pleased with Paul Lynch, who

Matt Frewer, best known as Max Headroom, was Berlingoff Rasmussen in "A Matter of Time."

we hadn't used as a director since the second season."

"Nobody ever just hands in a script—not me, not even Rick," says Michael Piller. "It was a delightful change of pace and tone from the grimness and darkness of the Spock episode. It was just at the right time. Rick and I and the staff worked long and hard with him on the script and he had a lot of challenges to overcome. That fourth act where Picard and Rasmussen have a one scene act is wonderful and I enjoyed that a lot.

"In 'A Matter of Time' I was dealing with a B story that involved a world that had a series of volcanic problems, and the need for the Enterprise to come and do something that would hopefully fix it but would eventually screw it up. The solution Data comes up with will hopefully fix it, but could eventually destroy the planet," says Berman. "To sit with the scene guys and research and develop it and to try and come up with something that would work, you get lost in the technical elements of it. You need other people to come and hit you over the head and pull it back. Sometimes we succeed with that and sometimes we don't."

"It was more of a comedy than a drama," says director Paul Lynch. "Matt Frewer [who played the role originally written for Robin Williams] was wonderful as a space con man. He's an actor who left Canada to study in Britain and had been part of the theatre scene there. He got the reputation of being large for his comedy roles, but he was a consummate actor and he found the level of comedy and realism of the character which is what makes him such a good character. He was never schticky."

Episode #110:
"New Ground"
Original Airdate: 1/6/92
Story by Sarah Charno and
Stuart Charno
Teleplay by Grant Rosenberg
Directed by Robert Scheerer
Guest Starring: Brian Bonsall (Alexander),
Georgia Brown (Helena), Sheila Franklin
(Ensign), Richard McGonagle (Dr. Ja'Dar),
Jennifer Edwards (Lowry)

Worf's mother brings his son, Alexander, back to the Enterprise when she realizes that she and her husband can no longer give the youngster the attention he needs. Meanwhile, an experiment with a new warp field soloton wave goes awry, jeopardizing the ship.

••••

Enthuses director Robert Scheerer, "I love that show and I love working with Michael. Michael and I have a fun relationship. I was so proud of him in this episode and I'm very impressed with the kid, Brian Bonsall. Brian was very nervous the first day, but he loved the make-up and he's a very bright boy. The first day both of us were kind of feeling our way, seeking a common ground, and from the second day on it was just a joy. And Michael just grows by leaps and bounds on the show every year. It's a joy to watch an actor grow like that."

And what does he think of the Soliton Wave aspect of the storyline? "I've gotten to the point after doing so much episodic material that I find it hard to take one total anything and judge it. What I tend to look for more and more are moments and pieces and successes dealing with a part of an episode, or a character or character relationships. Otherwise it gets so damn depressing because you so rarely get something that comes all together. I suppose the wave

wasn't a powerhouse, but the relationship between father and son was so strong for me, that that was the joy of that show."

"I think it was something we had been thinking about since we saw him last year," Michael Piller says of the introduction of Alexander, Worf's son, as a member of the ensemble. "We thought it would be a lot of fun to have a young Klingon and to see what Worf would be like as a father, and to use Alexander to see different parts of the ship. I think Brian Bonsall did a wonderful job acting in the role. It's been an interesting addition."

"I was involved quite a bit with that script," says Ron Moore. "We had talked about leaving Alexander on the ship in 'Reunion,' but it was one more plot element we didn't want to have to deal with. The idea of bringing him back was something we kept in the back of our mind and we just decided to do it. I thought it was a good decision for the character of Worf. The idea is to keep in mind who these people are. Worf is more Klingon than the Klingons are. He doesn't seem to have a real good sense of humor, he doesn't laugh a lot. The Klingons are these boisterous Vikings in space, and his whole relationship with his son is geared towards making him the perfect little warrior. The fact that Alexander's mother didn't share any of those ideas immediately puts the two in conflict, which was good because that's the essence of drama and it's built in stories of the two of them knocking heads."

"We got a lot of negative response to the episode," recalls Brannon Braga. "Ron did as good a job as anyone could have done. I liked the relationship that was developed between father and son and I think that's an episode where you could complain it's getting to be like a soap opera on the ship. Perhaps because the B-story was just that, a B-story, with the soloton wave. There's a feeling that you need that jeopardy story and it's something Mike Piller advocates, and I think he's right. You need something to drive the story forward, but our best episodes successfully integrate the two; 'Darmok' had an A-B story, but they were vital to one another. Not only were they vital in terms of plot, but in themes as well, which is why that show worked

so well. A show where it didn't work was 'In Theory.' I just wanted to see more of the Data arc. I didn't want to see that other story at all. It was interesting with that woman through the floor, nice imagery, but that's it. You really want to go back to the other thing. Then there are shows with only one plot."

Offers Rick Berman, "I thought it was well done, but it doesn't stand out for me. Our greatest desire is to have shows where either the A-B story stands so well alone that they can be intermingled the way two plots on *LA Law* are, or the A-B story have a reason to intermingle with each other. Then there's the other event where a show is strong enough to have one story with the science fiction and character drama. The shows that I find the most disappointing are the shows where we have a wonderful character piece and a weak science fiction story. It's a wonderful character development piece of drama and some parasite, or some dripping goo or some asteroid disaster that's looming has to be forced into the story. We do our best to avoid those, but sometimes they happen."

Enthuses Michael Dorn, "I've been very lucky. Worf has been busy. He had a mate, lost her, has a son, adoptive parents and real parents that were killed, and he was paralyzed for a while. I've been very fortunate where they have touched on a lot of Worf's character."

"New Ground" was written by *Time Trax* executive producer and co-creator Grant Rosenberg.

"The good thing about *Star Trek* is I'm good friends with Rick Berman and I've known Mike Piller for years as well as Jeri Taylor," says Rosenberg. "They're so smart and so good at what they do that it was just a delight working with them. The contributions they all made were very good. But it's a lot easier being on this side of the desk. I was a writer/producer under contract at Paramount and I was writing *MacGyver* and various other shows. Rick Berman called me and said, 'We need a *Star Trek*, would you like to write one?' and I said, 'I'd love to.' They said do not come in with ideas. The chances of you coming in with a fresh idea that we haven't heard or rejected or done is slim. So they gave me an idea which had been developed by a writing team which never went from idea to script and they handed me a story and we stripped it down to its bear bones. The idea dealt with Worf's son and we built back up from there."

Episode #111:
"Hero Worship"
Original Airdate: 1/27/92
Story by Hilary J. Bader
Teleplay by Joe Menosky
Directed by Patrick Stewart
Guest Starring: Joshua Harris (Timothy), Steven Einspahr (Teacher), Sheila Franklin (Ensign), Harley Venton (Transporter Chief)

The Enterprise discovers the sole survivor of a destroyed research vessel, the Vico: a boy whose parents have been killed when the ship was exploring a Black Cluster. The youth, in attempting to cope with his pain, begins to emulate Data.

••••

"I like 'Hero Worship' the best of all the kid shows because it's the most interesting," says Brannon Braga. "Good performances and an intriguing mystery, thinking that aliens had destroyed the ship. It's an offbeat premise in which an emotion recluse tries to emulate Data's personality. It's always nice when you have a new twist, and this twist is Data confronting someone who wants to be an android as opposed to him wanting to be human. Picard's saying, 'Make him the best android he can be,' and the scene where Data confesses to wishing he knew what the taste of malted was like, is very touching."

"I thought it was a great premise," enthuses Michael Piller. "It wasn't a memorable show, but I thought it was very entertaining. What made this interesting was Data has always been emulating human behavior, and here a human is emulating android behavior. One of the goals of the script was for Data to appreciate more of what he is and who he is, and that there's something to learn from and appreciate. I think 'Hero Worship' and, as a whole, this has been a very good season for Deanna Troi. We have used her as a counselor as well as she has ever been used. She has certainly had more time on screen and what I think has come out of it is proof that she is really a wonderful actress and has levels of credibility

and truth on the screen. I'm a big fan of hers and she really rose to the challenge this year."

"On 'New Ground' we had a fire on Stage 16 and on Patrick's show we did go over to the other ship where the kid had to be rescued," says David Livingston. "Deceptively, even though the rest of the shows take place on ship, those scenes we shot on 16 take up a lot of time and add production value to the show. Very rarely do we ever just do a bottle show. There's always some kind of element that will be visually interesting. "

Episode #112:
"Violations"
Original Airdate: 2/3/92
Story by Shari Goodhartz & T. Michael and Pamela Gray
Teleplay by Pamela Gray and Jeri Taylor
Directed by Robert Weimer
Guest Starring: David Sage (Tarmin), Ben Lemon (Jev), Rosalind Chao (Keiko), Eve Brenner (Inad), Craig Benton (Crewman Davis), Rick Fitts (Dr. Martin), Doug Wert (Jack Crusher), Majel Barrett (Computer Voice)

A telepathic alien race, the Ullians, who have the unique gift of probing humans' long-forgotten memories, are being ferried aboard the Enterprise when members of the crew begin to fall into unexplained comas.

••••

"It's true that every one of these scripts goes through a very protracted and difficult development process," says Jeri Taylor. "Nothing you ever see on the air started that way. We have a very free flowing exchange of ideas in the staff, people don't agree with each other, which is extremely healthy. We hash it out, we fight, we argue, we rend our hair. It becomes very passionate and I think that's a healthy thing to happen. 'Violations' was very dear to my heart, because it was a rape story and we felt we wanted to avoid the classic rape story, which is someone gets raped and then we do the emotional aftermath. That's a story that's been told and told and told and told. We felt we had nothing fresh to offer. This was one of the first of the episodes that made us go on a course we will be going on next season in terms of the feeling and the style of the

story material. It was spooky, weird, alien, unusual. It worked so well we said maybe we need more of that and maybe the science fiction aspect of *Star Trek* is not getting all the play that it needs. Sometimes we get political, we get emotional, but are we really going with the weirdness of the Roddenberry universe? Are we seeing aliens that are truly alien? There were other writers involved, many different approaches. We ultimately came to the show that was on the air, and it was miles from where it started."

"'Violations' was a story we had in development for quite a while," says Ron Moore. "It always hinged on trying to find a way to tell what is in essence a rape story from a science-fiction standpoint. Then it became an issue of what are those little dream sequences going to be and how are we going to present the antagonist and the victims, and what are they saying about the characters and what are going to be the things that are intimate and personal to them? With Riker it was a decision to be more action-oriented, and you didn't want the guy to have such a keen insight into everybody that he'd know what the most personal moment would be. We just wanted them to all look a little different."

"We knew that about Beverly and Troi, but where did Riker rushing people out of engineering come from?" asks Jonathan Frakes. "That's a no-brainer. Riker would just say, 'That's the way it is. People die, shit happens. His worst fear is *not* rushing people out of engineering. That didn't come out of character. Bob Weimer really had a field day, though. He got to use all these science-fiction techniques, 60mm lenses and everything, and that let him give it the look that it had."

"You have to make sure you don't misinterpret what this guy was doing," says Michael Piller of the nightmare hallucinations precipitated by Ben Lemon as Jev. "He was basically going into your memories and playing in them for his own amusement, pleasure and fulfillment. He was not going in and exploring any character's greatest fear. He might go in and feel that today he wants to see Troi's sexual secrets and tomorrow he may want to see Riker's unhappiest memory and see him suffer. I don't think

••••

it's something Riker carries with him as a burden for the rest of his life. It's a memory that's part of his life, just like Tasha's first death would be for him."

Adds Brannon Braga, "I would have rather seen Geordi in the burning house memory. His flashback wasn't as powerful, but it's a great science-fiction show and I'm a big fan of surreal imagery. The show's picking up speed now and this episode is *Star Trek* at its best. It started with the premise and then the rape analogy started to come into play. This is the best kind of *Star Trek* development which is in story. We had a good story—mind rape, mental violation of memories—and it becomes an oblique science-fiction metaphor for a compelling issue of today. Beautifully directed; stylistically, the most daring show we've done."

"'Violations' was a very interesting concept," Rick Berman states. "It was one that I was a little bit critical of at first until it started to wend its way into a script. I thought it worked out quite nicely and Bob Weimer did a lovely job. It was his ability to get quite abstract in filmic techniques. I'm a great believer in *Star Trek* not using filmic techniques that call attention to themselves. *Star Trek* has enough 'gee, wow' to it just by the nature of its story elements and the nature of its visual effects. On the other hand, on an episode like this where we had to do abstract memory sequences, we let Bob go hogwild. As a result, I think we had a wonderful episode with some great acting. It was very mystical and very interesting."

Episode #113:
"The Masterpiece Society"
Original Airdate: 2/10/92
Story by James Kahn & Adam Belanoff
Teleplay by Adam Belanoff and
Michael Piller
Directed by Winrich Kolbe
Guest Starring: John Snyder (Aaron Conor), Dey Young (Hannah Bates), Ron Canada (Marcus Benbeck), Sheila Franklin (Ensign)

A genetically altered society living in a biosphere is threatened by the approach of a stellar core fragment while Troi falls for the planet's leader, Arron Connor.

••••

"This was the beginning of me feeling better about the season," confesses Michael Piller. "It was another one of these shows that had been around for a while and a lot of writers had taken a shot at. It dealt with genetic engineering and abortions and interesting things for Geordi to do, and the relationship between Troi and the leader of the society. I think it's a real classic tragedy, because everybody was trying to do the right thing in that episode and it ended up in destruction. Aside from some disappointment in casting, I was rather pleased with that. I think a lot of people were rather pleased they liked it as much as they did."

"It's a very philosophical issue that we felt seriously about, and a show that I thought was disappointing and didn't turn out as well as I had hoped," admits Rick Berman. "It was slow and talky and we had casting problems. As for the abortion issue, that's nonsense. It was totally unintended. I think that there are a very few people on our writing staff who would be involved with something that would be a non-choice outlook."

Jeri Taylor agrees. "Michael and I are at odds about it. It was an idea I didn't like from the beginning. I didn't like the concept. I wasn't wild about the script. I thought it was one of our weakest episodes of the season."

Says Ron Moore, "This is another example of a show that doesn't really work too well. We sort of show up at a genetically perfect colony—which in and of itself is starting to bore me—and when we get there, it's 'Gee, Troi falls in love with one of the people.' You can't wait to get up and get a beer."

Visualizing the biosphere was a challenging task for the production team, which utilized blue screen to create the unusual environment. "Rick wanted to make sure we could see the effects outside the window," says David Livingston. "He didn't want to do what we normally do on stage, which was something tangible and real. That presented some challenges to the director, because the blue screen was right in the middle of the set, but he shot around it a little bit and I think it worked out successfully."

Admits director Winrich Kolbe, "The people were too damn perfect, and

I don't think perfection makes for good drama. I wasn't too intrigued with the lead actor either and that turned out to be kind of a flat episode for me."

Episode #114:
"Conundrum"
Original Airdate: 2/17/92
Story by Paul Schiffer
Teleplay by Barry M. Schkolnick and
Joe Menosky
Directed by Les Landau
Guest Starring: Michelle Forbes (Ensign Ro), Liz Vassey (Kristin), Erich Anderson (MacDuff), Erick Weiss (Crewman), Majel Barrett (Computer Voice)

The crew suffers a collective cause of amnesia after they are scanned by an alien ship and are led to believe they are at war with the Lysians, a technologically inferior race who, they are told by Executive Officer Keiran MacDuff, they are supposed to destroy.

••••

"I think what made that episode worthwhile to me as a creative person was if you strip away everything that our memories give us about ourselves, then we're stripped of inhibition and parts of us that we might use to define ourselves in social interaction. How would we see ourselves?" suggests Michael Piller. "There's a psychology that says you have an outer self and an inner self, and if the outer self is stripped away and the inner self is all that's left, you're dealing in a very raw way in seeking your place in this strange and extraordinary universe. When you have Riker and Ro suddenly engage in a romantic relationship, that's sort of their raw inner selves coming out and that made it fun."

"It was fun working with Frakes," ponders Michelle Forbes. "It's an interesting problem for a character, because you have a very defined character that leans one way. When you have amnesia you wonder if that brings out a side of you that's always wanted to come out. Would you really be comfortable with that? It's an interesting thing. I had a really good time with that episode."

Opines Brannon Braga, "It was a leftover from last season, since we had already done two amnesia stories ['Future Imperfect' and 'Clues']. It was a tough show to lick and Joe Menosky finally made it work. The stuff about the character triangle is great, and it was well directed. The one problem I felt that could have kept the story moving was the mystery of the Number One who wasn't Number One. For some reason his character didn't work. I wish it would have been stronger, because this would have been a classic. We always want to explore characters in some capacity. I hope that's why people tune in. Certainly we'd like to come up with more conundrums and situations. I'd like to find more challenges which feature a science-fiction confrontation like in 'Conundrum.'"

"The most interesting thing to me was the whole Riker/Troi/Ro triangle that was going on," says Ron Moore. "It was interesting to see Ro with the tension gone and to see that she was in fact attractive to Riker and vice versa. The two of them, if they were different people, would have had a great relationship. There was a lot of fun there. I liked the last scene with Riker and Troi and Ro. That was the most interesting element of the show to me. It was a bottle show, we couldn't go very many places, but watching the actors do different takes on their characters was interesting. It's always been a question of this is our show and we want to remain true to what our vision of Star Trek was, and try and tell good drama. Sometimes we get a little too serious ourselves. There are times to tell other types of stories. I think we could loosen up a little bit. It's not a comedy, but we can have more humor."

"'Conundrum' was around for a couple of years," says Jeri Taylor. "It was a tough show to do. Everyone took a shot at writing that and what it gave us was some marvelous character development with Ro, Riker and Troi. It invigorated the relationships and showed another side of Ro in that she plays comedy very nicely."

"A high concept idea where everyone wakes up," says Rick Berman. "It's a thought provoking episode, I thought. Not one of the greats. It's based on that whole concept of what if? If you have nine people who don't know who or what they are, will they find themselves? Will they find the pecking order? Will the captain become the captain?"

Episode #115:
"Power Play"
Original Airdate: 2/24/92
Story by Paul Ruben and Maurice Hurley
Teleplay by Rene Balcer and Herbert J. Wright & Brannon Braga
Directed by David Livingston
Guest Starring: Rosalind Chao (Keiko), Colm Meaney (O'Brien), Michelle Forbes (Ensign Ro), Ryan Reid (Transporter Technician), Majel Barrett (Computer Voice)

Troi, Data and Riker investigate the disappearance of the starship Essex two centuries before via shuttlecraft, but a fierce storm forces the ship to crashland. O'Brien transports through to rescue the others but as they beam out, the spirits of the planet's exiled prisoners which inhabit the ionosphere possess Data, Troi and O'Brien.

••••

"There were two challenges in filming 'Power Play,'" says producer and episode director David Livingston. "I told other people that the best two things about it were that it was an action show, which we don't have a lot of. You just can't do 26 of those a year, they're too expensive. The other great thing was taking three of our continuing characters and having them play something entirely different. It was a chance to work with them and create totally new characters, and that was a lot of fun. We came up with names for them on the set. Marina was Slash, Data was Buzz and Colm was Slugger. It was fun working our way through that and they were all great. That script went through a lot. The writers are conscious of how difficult it is for the director once we're actually shooting, especially with an action piece, to keep changing. The two times I've directed I've done most of my prep over the weekends. I just need quiet and to sit on the stage all by myself and draw stick figures. I need to draw out each show and how it connects editorially for me to be able to have a picture of how the whole scene is going to fit together. In doing that, I will be, hopefully, open-minded enough to adjust once I see what the actors bring to it in terms of staging. But I have to have some kind of plan. And I had a lot of time to prepare—my show fell over the Thanksgiving Holiday and I

had four days there and two other weekends involved during prep. So I had a lot of time and the script was pretty well together by the time we started prep. But, boy, I think there were seven writers involved over the period of a year."

"The first time I wrote it, I thought bottle show: Ten-Forward, Picard and Troi talk," recalls Brannon Braga. "Mike Piller said don't be afraid to write seven or eight page scenes with Picard and Troi. I said, 'Okay, Mike, I won't.' Jesus! Seven or eight pages? I had a tough time writing that and when I turned it in, Piller said he felt that we'd taken it as far as it could go and we shouldn't produce it. If it had been produced as I had written it, the episode would have been a little too familiar as a hostage show. So what happened was Herb Wright had just come in and Mike said we need some new blood, and gave it to Herb. Together we came up with the twist of them claiming to be the ghosts and that's what I think brought the show level up and gave it a dimension of mystery and twists that it really needed. In the end it turned into a really great action show. To me, it was a breath of fresh air. It had no pretensions. Instead of exploring some theme or idea, it was just action and phaser blasts. What are you going to do, deny that and say it's not fun?"

For the episode's early scenes in which Troi, Riker, Data and O'Brien crash in the shuttlecraft, Livingston braved the treacherous terrain of Stage 16.

"It was tough because we had atmosphere and wind and lightning," he says. "One of those elements is hard enough. Just being on Stage 16 is hard enough. But we had all of those elements and eventually all the actors had to lie down in them. The stage floor had a sandy surface, so when you have the wind blowing, the sand starts blowing around and I was real concerned about it getting into people's eyes. In fact, Marina's make-up became so messed up that she had to have a complete redo before we could continue shooting that day. We had to go over to Stage 9 and wait for her make-up to be done. Not through any fault of hers, just the fact that she wasn't presentable on screen, because the sand had sandblasted her and she looked like a house after the guys come through with their hoses. But 16 allows you to do stuff with a camera that you can't do anyplace else. Certainly you don't get to do it on the bridge. You get to use toys, as we call them. On that show, we used the python crane arm, which allows you to reach deep into the set and then crane back and not reveal the tracks, so you can do shots that are expansive, interesting and challenging. If you're going to direct, no one just wants to show people just sitting across a desk for four pages."

Once onboard the Enterprise, the majority of the action took place in Ten-Forward. "It was real hard," says Livingston. "We had to do a lot in there and that's where everyone was held hostage. It's like shooting on an aircraft carrier, it's a big empty room. I tried to keep it active and I look at the show now and it gets pretty static at times. I wish I had figured out a way to move people around a little bit more later on in the show. Structurally, from a writing standpoint, it's really great all the way through. Act two is really good. It's all action and then after that it settles down a little bit. You kind of wish it could have been that way all the way through for a teaser and five acts, but you just can't sustain that on episodic television."

"'Power Play' had the distinction of being one of the best directed episodes of the season, but only made me angry because it was empty," says a disturbed Michael Piller. "We need to do bottle shows on this series in order to pay the piper. We need to do contained non-optical direct shows and this was always intended to be one of them. It was meant to be a show that was dark and brooding, and the shows I've always used as prototype were 'Key Largo' and 'The Petrified Forest.' Very contained situations. We had a hard time making that work and making it interesting for five acts. It's not a difficult premise, it's been done on a lot of shows, a lot of times and television has found a way to make those premises kind of work. Brannon and Herb came in with a twist that I liked about making them seem like ghosts from a past ship, which gave us a spin on it. Ultimately it became a major action show and instead of helping us get even, knocked us into the stratosphere. I wasn't very fond of that

show, but very fond of David's direction. If that show had any merit at all, it was because he directed it with an extraordinary sense of style. The three actors who were given the job of being the aliens carried it with wonderful performances. The script came together very late, and I don't think the actors got the script until the day before and they were unhappy about it. They had a right to be. Brent, Marina and Colm really put together interesting performances, but I was not happy with the script."

Points out Brent Spiner, "I always love to play another type of character. The challenge here was to make sure my character didn't sound or act like Lore, and I don't think he did. It's really fun to get those curves, because so much of Data is already defined. When you get to play someone else and let loose like Leonard Nimoy occasionally got to do in the old show, it's really rewarding."

Episode #116:
"Ethics"
Original Airdate: 3/2/92
Story by Sara Charno & Stuart Charno
Teleplay by Ronald D. Moore
Directed by Chip Chalmers
Guest Starring: Caroline Kava (Dr. Russell), Patti Yasutake (Nurse Ogawa), Brian Bonsall (Alexander)

Worf is paralyzed when a support beam breaks in the cargo bay and a container falls on him. Despite the assistance of a renowned neuro-geneticist, Dr. Russell (*Born on the Fourth of July*'s Caroline Kava), Worf insists on committing ritual suicide rather than accept living his life as a cripple.

••••

Notes director Chip Chalmers, "The interesting thing about 'Ethics' is that for the first time that I can remember, there have been some *serious* inter-personal conflicts on the ship. That's one of the rules, nobody gets in each other's face. We had some pretty serious conflicts, and I think that was of huge redeeming value to that particular episode, because for the first time people saw Riker and Worf yelling at each other. We also saw real tears and real emotions.

"As a matter of fact," he adds, "they decided at the last minute that we'd gone a little too far at one point.

Riker says, 'Do you remember all the people that died in the line of duty? At least they died trying. Here you are lying on your hospital bed,' and he circles around the bed and he's nose to nose to Worf and literally yelling, 'Why don't you just get off your ass and take the challenge!' And Worf screams, 'Enough, enough!' Then Riker backs off a little bit. The general thought was that it had just gone a little too far and it was cut."

"I wanted to show two sides of a difficult debate," explains Ron Moore. "There's been a lot of criticism of this show and I've heard feedback from people who thought we were advocating euthanasia. Other people thought we were saying bad things about the disabled and the value of people with a disability. Other people would say, of course, Dr. Russell was absolutely wrong, she was as bad as Dr. Mengele and others would say how dare Beverly get in the way of Worf's right to die. The balancing act was to make sure both sides of the argument had validity, were compelling and real positions. It was not my favorite show to work on and I found it very difficult. The medical stuff is not what I'm drawn to and it's hard to make interesting."

"I love grays," muses Michael Piller. "I don't love black and whites. I don't like answering questions so easily for the audience. That was one of the things that I liked so much about 'Masterpiece Society.' The answers were not so easy to come by, and with 'Ethics,' again, we went out of our way not to make it easy for the audience to know what the right thing to do was. I think we succeeded pretty well with that one. We wanted to explore the issue and it's only fair to explore it if you give both voices the equal fairness that they're voice and opinions deliver. Now if you're on your toes, you'll say what about the voices of prejudice in sexual orientation in 'The Outcast?' My answer is I don't think there is another side that's easily supportable. I think that bigotry is bigotry, prejudice is prejudice, and it can be said with all the fervor and belief, but it still comes out as prejudice. I don't know how to make an intolerant person attractive."

"It was basically the doctor show," says former *Trek* producer Herb

Wright. "I think Ron did a good job on it within the parameters he was given, but one of the things I thought we should do was something more grotesque. My suggestion was that instead of doing a whole new spine, they had to release little creatures into his bloodstream which would eat away what was wrong with him and see that happen. You can take a turn in the road, but they wanted to stay with something that's a more traditional doctor show than science-fiction."

Visualizing 24th century medicine at work was the daunting task faced by David Livingston. "The medical operating room was pretty elaborate. That was a pretty big set on 16, and Chip did that wonderful wide angle shot at the beginning of the operation where you really saw it. There were a lot of inserts because of doing an operation. The cargo bay scene was pretty big where we had all the bodies and patients laid out, but from a production standpoint I didn't have a lot to do with that show because I was shooting 'Power Play' while that was prepping."

Episode #117:
"The Outcast"
Original Airdate: 3/16/92
Written by Jeri Taylor
Directed by Robert Scheerer
Guest Starring: Melinda Culea (Soren), Callan White (Krite), Megan Cole (Noor)

While working with Soren, a member of an androgynous alien race known as the J'naii, Riker and Soren begin to fall in love despite a prohibition by the planet's leaders which forbids relationships with other races that have gender. Violation of this law has dire consequences for the perpetrator.

••••

"Fascinating show," comments director Robert Scheerer. "It kind of broke the mold of other *Star Treks* in that it's two people—only. Yes, other people were there momentarily, but I had never done an episode where two people were so totally in the show throughout. They were in every scene with the rarest exception. It was one moment after another with them and watching this relationship grow, and then the kicker at the end when she is 'treated.' God, that show was exciting to do. Again, treating

the whole sexuality in a wonderful almost comedic way, I thought, in many instances was delicious. I guess it was one of the most commented on shows they ever had."

"I really wanted to write this episode," says Supervising Producer Jeri Taylor. "It came out of staff discussion. We had wanted to do a gay rights story and had not been able to figure out how to do it in an interesting science-fiction, *Star Trek*-ian way. It came up with the idea of turning it on its ear and I really wanted to do it because, partly, it would be controversial and I welcome that. The idea of any drama is to touch people's feelings and engage them, whether you make them laugh, cry, angry. As long as you stir something in them, then you've been successful and I knew this would touch a lot of buttons in a lot of people. I am not a gay person, but as a woman I do consider myself in a particular minority; I know what it feels like to be disenfranchised—not in that precise way—and I felt like I had a touchstone to some of the feelings that must be involved. On a personal level I wanted to write it. It's the episode of the whole two years I'm the most proud of and the most glad that I could be associated with. We've gotten every range of response, but largely positive."

"I didn't think they were gutsy enough to take it where they should have," says Jonathan Frakes. "Soren should have been more obviously male. We've gotten a lot of mail on this episode, but I'm not sure it was as good as it could have been—*if* they were trying to do what they call a gay episode."

Counters Rick Berman, "It was very interesting figuring out what to do. We were either going to cast with non masculine men, non feminine females or females who could play an androgynous character. Obviously you wouldn't pick a 6'4" muscle-bound man nor a voluptuous woman. We knew we had to go one way or another, so we read both men and women for the roles and decided to go with women. It might have been interesting to go with men, but it was a choice that we made."

"I'm delighted to hear Jonathan say that," remarks Brannon Braga. "If it would have been a man playing the role, would he have kissed him? I think

Jonathan *would* have because he's a gutsy guy. I think they would have preferred some more androgynous looking actors—they looked like women and the actress who played it did so unemotionally. While Jeri's script was rich with humor and the character had banter and spark and wit, the actress, although she did a fine job, played it a little too unemotionally as if androgyny meant emotionless as well. Why should it?

"A very special episode. I think that there are no subjects taboo for this show and what's so risky about making the statement that intolerance is bad? What's so risky about that? Some people reacted to the show in a way that I didn't understand. They thought we were advocating a particular sexual preference. I don't think that's true at all. I think we were advocating tolerance, I think the show could have been in a completely different arena. We could have used a show that dealt with racism rather than sexual preference and it could still be an interracial relationship. But that didn't seem to have the cutting edge or the science-fiction feel of an androgynous race. The risks were what Jeri did with the gems of the episode, like talking about sexual organs on the shuttlecraft. I felt they could have gone further [and] Picard could have been less passive. Riker's a big boy and he sparks conflicts in ethics among the characters. To get someone in there whose a catalyst for conflicts among our characters is a rare thing."

"I was very happy with 'The Outcast,'" says Michael Piller. "I thought Jeri [Taylor] did a marvelous job on the script and to me this was the turning point of the season and this was where I thought we started doing excellent television again. We had been the target of a concerted organized movement by gay activists to put a gay character in the show. What it came down to was Roddenberry had been barraged by letters and had discussed with us before his death the possibility of having two men hold hands in some scene, which was totally irrelevant to the issue of homosexuality. I didn't think, nor did Rick, that was an appropriate way to do a story that addressed the issues of sexual intolerance, which I felt was really what the broader issue was about. And so that's what we decided to do, and we decided to tell a story that was about sexual intolerance. The twist, I thought, turned out very well."

Berman concurs, "We'd been spending a lot of time wrestling with all the elements of the requests of the gay community for us to involve a gay character on the show. It got a lot of publicity both good and bad. We wrestled with a lot of different stories, and came up with a very obvious metaphor for the gay community and the intolerance they receive on this planet. It's very difficult to show people being tolerant—it's much easier to show people being intolerant—and to have people relate to them. In this instance we felt it better to draw the parallel, and the story that came in was wonderful. The acting was very well done. I think we dealt with well meaning people and their intolerance and our people in the 24th century's absolute lack of acceptance of their intolerance and the frustration of fighting it. It did not satisfy certain remnants of the gay and lesbian community because it was not what they were asking for, which was to introduce a gay or lesbian character in a normal and acceptable way as one of the members of the crew. But I think it did deal with the issue of intolerance towards sexual orientation and it met that objective well."

"Mail has been very split on this episode," says Ron Moore. "We have people across the spectrum; people who salute us for doing it, then there are people that say we didn't go far enough—that it was too subtle, it was too oblique and wanted it to be more upfront, blunt and obvious. Other people were just freaked out that it was an assault on values and that they hated it and how dare we do something like this and they'll never watch the show again. It was the best of the ways we'd like to do these shows. You have an interesting issue, a good science fiction premise, conflict and its an exploration of our characters in different ways."

Episode #118:
"Cause and Effect"
Original Airdate: 3/23/92
Written by Brannon Braga

Directed by Jonathan Frakes
Guest Starring: Michelle Forbes (Ensign Ro), Patti Yautake (Nurse Ogawa), Kelsey Grammer (Captain Bateman)

The Enterprise becomes trapped in a time warp in which the crew is forced to endlessly repeat the same experience in which the ship faces inevitable destruction after a collision with another starship from the past.

••••

"I was supposed to be prepping 'Cause' at the same time I was shooting 'The Outcast'," recalls director/actor Jonathan Frakes. "But I was in every scene of it so I didn't follow an ordinary pre-production process, but I got the script, took it home and broke down how I wanted to shoot it. I had no casting to do since we offered the part to Kelsey [Grammer], who accepted. It was just a matter of deciding how I wanted to shoot it and finding a different way to shoot each scene. In a conversation with [DP] Marvin Rush, we came up with the famous Waverly Smothers bungee cord camera, bungi-flex. It was just working at home at night and finding ways to make each scene look different in spite of the fact the words were the same. The problem was, of course, that it could become monotonous showing the same thing several times."

Says writer Brannon Braga, "I love time travel stories and I don't know who doesn't. We wanted to do a time travel story that had never been done before. Being trapped in a time loop is one I've never seen before. It was a high concept show that, frankly, when I wrote it didn't have all the elements in place. I didn't know how to get out of it. I didn't have the poker scene and Joe Menosky told me half-jokingly, 'Man, you're in trouble'. I said 'You really think so?' and he answered, 'Man, you're in big trouble.' When I did a preliminary beat sheet, I came up with the idea of the poker game and a message in the poker scene. I didn't know what the message was. The break session lasted two full days, but it was fruitful and gratifying because we came out of there with a structure that was working. I came up with the poker game while I was eating pancakes and pouring syrup. I had no idea how it happened—because it was before the sugar rush. I

knew then that the poker game would somehow be utilized for once, and lay it in so the viewer thinks it's just a poker game and it turns out to be the key to saving their entire existence. Three didn't really come into play yet. I didn't want the numbers to come up later and Riker was going to win the hand with three Aces, which was going to be an additional indicator that Riker's the one.... it's his suggestion. Eventually that was dropped because Rick felt Data could program in three but not give Riker three aces, and he's right and that was dropped."

Finding the catalyst for getting the Enterprise out of the time loop was Braga's biggest problem. "I didn't know what the message was," he says. "But it was the most fun to write of all the episodes I did this season. In a way, doing the same scenes over was comforting; it was fun to come up with different takes and to think how I could get that glass to break each time. It wasn't until I got to the final draft that I thought to have the glass break over the intercom on that final loop through. So it was finding those little nuggets and pathways and weave through as we were structuring it. That was a terrific challenge. It was fun to watch."

"You will never beat that teaser," enthuses Ron Moore of the episode's opening in which the Enterprise explodes. "That's the definitive one. I like it, it's a neat episode. I was talking to Brannon when he was writing it and to see the ship blow up and then Captain's log, it's really fun. We knew the structure of the show was going to be kind of monotonous, and the challenge was always going to be for the writer to find a different way in and to make it the same but different. Also a big challenge for the director, which I think Jonathan really rose to. Each time through the loop has a different feel, a different nuance, a different look. I think he did a wonderful job on making it an interesting show. Brannon laid different clues and feelings through the episodes. The poker games for a while was the cliché padding. If the show was short, it was to time to write a poker game. Because we had written it so much, we stayed away from it and now it got used for a reason. It actually had a function."

Herb Wright agrees, " We had a lot of fun running through the room on that one. It's a helluva challenge because when the audience has seen it once and you show it to them the second time, the temptation for them is to jam the button on the remote. The challenge is how do you keep them excited, motivated and involved and wondering what the fuck is going on. And in the teaser you're starting off and you've destroyed the ship so if that isn't going to get you to tune back in, I don't know what will."

"It was dangerously repetitive by definition and I thought it could be misinterpreted like a clip show," says Rick Berman. "That's why I made it very clear to Jonathan that he couldn't use any footage again and that everything had to be photographed again and done in a slightly different way. I think it was a popular episode and worked well."

Says David Livingston of Frakes' efforts on the episode, "Jonathan had to shoot each of those repeated actions in an entirely different way. That was the challenge and what he did to that show was masterful. He was able to visually interpret each of those events each time so it didn't seem repetitive and he pulled it off. From a directing standpoint, it was a difficult show to do. Once you get past that, from a production end it wasn't that tough in terms of having to build stuff. What was tough was the post on the show and the second unit that went on to blow up the ship. Rob Legato had Stage 10 and we built large scale mock-ups of the Enterprise and of the other ship, or at least the nacelle on the other ship and we kept blowing up stuff on Stage 8. getting these tremendous explosions which we can hopefully use in the future. But Rob and Dick Brownfield were in heaven. They were like kids in a candy store. Nothing better than just being able to blow up something. Everything there was newly created just for that episode. We had a bunch of Enterprises, they didn't have all the detail but they had enough that when you cut to them you believed them."

Episode #119:
"The First Duty"
Original Airdate: 3/30/92
Written by Ronald D. Moore and
Naren Shankar

Directed by Paul Lynch
Guest Starring: Wil Wheaton (Wesley Crusher), Ray Walston (Boothby), Robert Duncan McNeill (Nicholas Locarno), Ed Lauter (Lt. Commander Albert), Jacqueline Brookes (Admiral Brand), Richard Fancy (Captain Satelk), Walker Brandt (Hajar), Shannon Fill (Sito), Richard Rothenberg (Cadet)

At the behest of his squadron leader at Starfleet Academy, Wesley agrees to cover-up the true facts behind an accident in which one of his fellow flight team members was killed when his shuttle collided while attempting to practice a prohibited maneuver for the Academy commencement activities.

••••

"It was very difficult and ultimately we knew we were taking a big risk," says Jeri Taylor of the moral quagmire Wesley wrestles with in "The First Duty". "There were arguments pro and con. We didn't start out developing the story that way. Through an evolutionary process there were many different endings and approaches which were discussed and all of them somewhat inflammatory. We knew it was a gamble, but we have to keep pushing at the edges and stretching ourselves and I felt this episode humanized Wesley in a way that he never has been and maybe now would allow fans to actually like him. He wore this awful mantle of the genius child who always saved the ship and in that sense seemed remote from a real person. He was the perfect Wesley, and that was hard for people to identify with. He made a mistake, a bad mistake; he's flawed. People are and I think in enriches him as a character, it gives him texture, maturity. It gives him something he now has to work through. That makes you a finer person in the end instead of just being a plastic perfect teenager."

"I like what we did with Wesley in 'First Duty' a lot," says Ron Moore. "I was strongly in favor of what we did with the character in that show and I was glad it was supported by Rick and Michael. We took that character in a really interesting direction and I think it helps him grow as a character a lot and makes him more accessible and human. I'm just really happy with what the episode became. It's probably my favorite

episode of the year. It had a lot of meaty stuff; the Picard/Wesley scene is powerful. When he looks up from behind the desk and gets up you think he's going to slug him. Picard just had a real heartfelt anger in his face."

"It's interesting when you don't feel you're obliged to do a show around a character and you find an idea that just seems to work for him. It seems like sometimes the most natural thing in the world," adds Michael Piller. "This is a great show and we almost didn't do it. When we pitched it to Rick, he said, it's not a *Star Trek. Star Trek* is about going off into space and exploring new planets. It's not about going back to earth. He's right, of course, and no one's going to argue that he's not, but I looked at him and said 'Look, to me we have the opportunity to do something special. We have the chance to explore an issue that is extra meaningful to a lot of young people. If you're involved in drugs or teenage misbehavior or crime, and you may know that it's the wrong thing and you have the choice of being loyal to your friends or doing what is honest—that is a great issue for us to explore. And I said to Rick it gives us a chance to go to Starfleet Academy for the first time and I, got to tell you, with a show that desperately seeks good ideas, I don't think we can afford to pass on this one. And he said 'Sold, as long as you only have three sets.'

"I remember the most interesting part of that script was when Nareen and Ron were here elaborating on what they wanted to do and Ron said Wesley can't turn in his friends. I said 'Ron, this is about truth and doing the right thing.' Ron is a very good young writer and he was right in the place that he needed to be in order to explore the other side of that issue. We had a long argument about whether it was the right thing to do and basically Ron felt that we were assassinating Wesley's character and no one would ever forgive him for turning in his friends. We went through a lot of elaboration about what was really important and what was the message we wanted to give to our audience. It was not a question of loading the dice, you want to make the other side as strong as you possibly can. Ultimately you have to make a decision to dramatically resolve the conflict with your

••••

character. Ron reluctantly agreed to go forward with this ending in mind—that the truth is the most important thing—which is what I want my kids to believe. Ron hasn't had any kids so he doesn't know that yet. What is most interesting is he got into the script and the issue of protecting the friendship was the hardest for him to get right, that for whatever he started, I'd say remember the way you argued that he shouldn't turn in his friends? I need that in the script to balance it. I need that sentiment to be in there, and strong and its got to be sold. Ultimately he got there. Great script, and very well cast and very well directed.

"It's interesting that one of the things that was late coming into that story was Picard's sin," says Piller. "We had to have scenes with Boothby and Picard and we had scenes where they talked about the case, they talked about things, but the scenes weren't clicking and they were the weakest parts of the show. We started talking about maybe he helped Picard out with a problem and maybe he got into trouble, and we tried to figure out what it was. Rick said it doesn't matter what Picard's trouble was. We keep that part of our character a mystery, which we like to do every once in a while. That was a great decision and what it did for us was put in perspective in a life cycle sort of way that if you make a mistake when you're young and its found out, you have to pay a price for it. It doesn't mean your life is ruined. It means you can still become Jean Luc Picard. It gave a much broader perspective to the story. It's interesting of course that in the very first scene Picard's being called to the principal's office and that was just a gag, a throwaway Ron had come up with. It wasn't until much later that we said, you know, it's already set up in that first scene that he was in trouble. Why don't we use it? It's very interesting the way some things just seem to fall into place. It was like it was waiting to be discovered."

"I made a real pain of an ass of myself with the writers on this one," admits Rick Berman. "If I recall, in the early stages, they wanted Wesley's crime to be a little more heinous, the cover-up more obvious and Wesley's punishment to be more severe. I found that unaccept-

able. Wesley is Wesley. He is one of our characters and heroes and he's capable of lapses in judgement, capable of making decisions on an emotional basis as opposed to thinking them out, but not capable of some of the more severe things that were suggested. And not capable of overt cover-up, lying to Starfleet Academy officials. So we basically tempered it down, still keeping it believable and the crime that was serious and would result in a punishment. But it was very difficult dealing with the relationship between Wesley and Picard. If Picard says to Wesley you're going to tell what happened, and if you don't I will. That puts Wesley in a very weak position dramatically. *If* he tells, he does because he was forced to and if he doesn't, Picard will. There was a lot of fine tuning to keep it from becoming too contrived. I think the direction by Paul Lynch was excellent and the casting was great. Getting Ray Walston to play Boothby was fortuitous and the casting of the three other Starfleet kids was successful. It was not a typical episode, it was not science fiction in nature, it was earthbound and it was a very dramatic character piece and courtroom drama. As filmmaking and one hour dramatic television, I thought it was riveting. It was a terrific episode and by dealing with some of the hi-tech abilities to detect what they were doing, we got elements of science-fiction in there as well."

"The thorny issue was does he lie or does he just admit to tell the truth," says Herb Wright. "Is it a lie of omission or is it an open running lie and the story waffles back and forth because the danger was that somehow we were going to paint this guy as a liar and never be able to redeem him again. To be able to balance the peer pressure that one would face in a situation like that, an adolescent show-off maneuver that ends up in tragedy, to say hey aren't we better than every one else and that Wesley was in on it....it was a tough show to figure out how to do that and not diminish and harm the character forever. It was a very heated discussion. He was young and he had certain frailties and he had mixed loyalties. This would be something he'll have to learn, that we're not all perfect—even in the 24th century—and we would have to go through some bumps and grinds to become the perfect people we are."

Reflects director Paul Lynch, "I thought Wil Wheaton rose to great heights in his performance. He worked great for me as did the other boy Robert McNeill, who I had worked with on *The New Twilight Zone*. He and Wesley played very well off of each other. It was a good, intriguing story, and a mystery that dealt with futuristic things. I had a great time with it, although I don't usually like doing trials just because of the amount of time you have to spend on a trial to do it well. You have to cover the audience and everybody in the audience listening as everything goes through in order to make it play. I think, although I'm not sure if it still holds true, that at the time it was the most film they'd ever used on an episode of *Star Trek*. If an average episode used 35,000 feet, I used 75,000 feet. That was mostly because of the coverage, because when I shoot a trial I shoot the people listening to everything that's said. I don't just take reactions. I used an awful lot of film, but the show turned out well. When I was doing it they were a little upset because I was using so much film.

"Mostly, though, the episode came out well because of Wil Wheaton, who really showed his stuff. It's nice to see because he was a good young kid actor when we first started *Next Generation*, and now he's matured into a good first-rate actor. It's nice to see the difference over the years."

Guest Star Robert Duncan McNeill would go on to co-star in *Voyager* as Lt. Tom Paris.

Episode #120:
"Cost of Living"
Original Airdate: 4/20/92
Written by Peter Allan Fields
Directed by Winrich Kolbe
Guest Starring: Majel Barrett (Lwaxana Troi), Brian Bonsall (Alexander), Tony Jay (Campio), Carel Struycken (Mr. Homm), David Oliver (Young Man), Albie Selznick (Juggler), Patrick Cronin (Erko), Tracey D'Arcy (Young Woman), George Edie (Poet), Christopher Halste (First Learner)

Mrs. Troi returns to the Enterprise in order to marry Campio (Tony Jay), a visiting dignitary she's never met, while a cloud of parasitic particles released from a destroyed asteroid in the Pelloris Field begins to wreak havoc aboard the starship.

••••

"I think it was something one needed to have there rather than something that was an intrinsic part of the show," says writer Peter Allan Fields of the science-fiction B-story. "I'd be lying if I said that didn't bother me somewhat. I'm sure it bothered Michael and Rick Berman as well at first, but once we got into it, the story seemed to work all right. It's true thought that the so-called dreaded B-story was, in this case, something that almost didn't belong. Because we wanted to develop the personal story as much as we could rather than flesh out a convenient jeopardy story, we felt in this particular instance even though the B story was valid and researched just as carefully as the others, the personal story should take precedence. We don't want to do them all like that. This is a science-fiction show and the science is fun, but in this case it was the personal story that was most important."

Rick Berman admits to an initial wariness over the show's atypical premise.

"I had a lot of trepidation about it," says Berman. "I was extremely pleased by the way it turned out. The first draft of the script was absolutely wonderful and Peter injected charm and heart and humor into the characters and wonderful dialogue. As we revised the script, I felt it wasn't getting any better, the revision process was hurting it in terms of some of the wonderful dialogue. But we had other problems within the story we had to deal with . I had some problems, some costuming and make-up things that troubled me, but by the time we put it together and added some wonderful visual effects to the show, I found it utterly charming. It had heart and warmth. This is a show that was premised as Auntie Mame arriving aboard and taking Worf's son under her wing to bring him out of his shell in her own flamboyant way, and its delightful, funny and wonderful.

"Dorn gives a funny, great performance," continues Berman. "There are problems that exist with Worf. We turned him into a dad and a character who has to deal with the frustration of a some-

times troublesome son which is not really *Star Trek*. It has its good points and its bad points, but the relationship between the little boy and Majel, Troi and her mother and between Worf and his son, are delightful here. Michael wasn't even guaranteed all episodes in the first season and I feel that Michael as an actor and the character of Worf have both grown more than any other one of our characters or actors. and I'm delighted with the direction Michael's acting has gone. It's a shoe-in character. What's more delightful than a Klingon onboard the Enterprise? And the writers have been taking advantage of it and Michael has been running with it."

Creating the environs of Mrs. Troi's holodeck Disneyland meant a lot of research and development for the production team to build a mudbath and visualize the menagerie of alien entertainers. "It's a kid's fantasy world and Richard [James] just kind of went for it," says David Livingston. "We went for it in terms of costume and make-up, a lot of wild hairdos and this set which included a mudbath which took a lot of R&D, but Dick Brownfield pulled it off. Majel and others were concerned that it wasn't going to be warm enough, but it was warm and toasty and everyone loved getting in to it. It was very goopy, but it wasn't real mud. It was a special solution that we're allowed to use in the movies which wouldn't be harmful to anybody and it was an approved solution they could be in. They all got kind of a kick out of it and it was fun seeing all those actors sloshing around in it."

Winrich Kolbe points out, "That was fluff, but nice fluff. It was a comedy written for Majel and I think she did a hell of a job in there. I wouldn't consider it a *Star Trek* episode *par excellance*. It fulfilled a certain function, but it was not *Star Trek* at its best.

Episode #121:
"The Perfect Mate"
Original Airdate: 4/27/92
Story by Rene Echevarria &
Reuben Leder
Teleplay by Reuben Leder &
Michael Piller
Directed by Cliff Bole
Guest Starring: Famke Janssen (Kamala),

Tim O'Connor (Briam), Max Grodenchik (Par Lenor), Mickey Cottrell (Alrik), Michael Snyder (QOL), David Paul Needles (Miner #1), Roger Rignack (Miner #2), April Grace (Transporter Officer), Charles Gunning (Miner #3)

A beautiful empathic mesomorph, Kamala, who is intended to serve as a peace offering to end a centuries-old war, is freed from stasis by a Ferengi and seduces Picard.

••••

"On a positive note, I think, like the Borg show, it showed that Picard has a flaw, you can cut into his character," offers Cliff Bole. "When I say that's positive, that means you can continue to make that character work. I think this is a real case for Picard, because he normally wouldn't have allowed himself to be so vulnerable."

"What was interesting was I was writing myself out of this funk," says Michael Piller. "I had started feeling good about stuff with 'Masterpiece Society' and I think the staff was following and feeling the same way with the material they were starting to turn out. Jeri was starting to turn out some wonderful material with 'The Outcast.' We were stuck and this ["Perfect Mate"] was a script a lot of people had put a hand to, and it wasn't working very well. The relationship between Picard and this woman wasn't working. She is an empathic metamorph and has the ability to be whatever a man wants her to be. For all those people who thought we were so sexually open-minded with the other shows, they're going to start sending in their letters and saying what's wrong with you guys on this one? This is the adolescent male fantasy of all time. But I think there's room for all kinds of shows and, essentially, if you come up with a character and throw her into a situation, you see how it works. I think the challenge of the show is if Picard is confronted with his perfect mate, could he resist her? The fun is to see him resist and he's doing all these things to try and resist and does he resist? You have to decide. The thing is complicated by the fact that he knows she just does it for him and for him the idea is, 'How do I deal with that when I find that there's something

••••

Tim O'Connor, Briam of "The Perfect Mate," seen here in the television version of **Buck Rogers.**

about her that I'm attracted to?' In a long memo to Rene Echeverria, I said this show does not work if the audience, at least the men, do not fall in love with this woman too. She must be fully rounded, bright, engaging, with a great personality and the audience should say, 'I see the problem for Picard.' If there's no magnetic electricity between the two of them and it doesn't happen for me as a man watching her, then the audience will not accept for one second that Picard would even give her a second thought."

"I'm very pleased with it," says Rick Berman. "The actress is about as beautiful as any woman any of us have ever seen and she gave a delightful performance. It's an episode which, during the final stages of writing by Michael, went through a lot of changes with a lot of heated discussions that went on, and a lot of different things that could have happened to this woman. We shot two different endings and there were two more we didn't shoot. None of us will ever know which of the four would have been best."

A disappointed Michael Piller explains, "The trick ending which no one liked but me and Patrick, may have been the product of a writer who was trying too hard, but I was overruled. I felt at the end of the show Picard has to

deliver this woman into the hands of her arranged mate. By this time in the picture he has become very close to her and I wanted to do an ending which, in fact, had three endings. I wanted to do an ending where he stopped the ceremony and said, 'No, she's staying with me.' The way that it was written was Par Lenor delivers her, Picard cringes as she kisses this man who she doesn't love. The second ending was he interrupts and says, 'I'm sorry, I can't allow this to continue,' and so while they're walking down the aisle and it seems each time it's the end of the show, we in fact cut back to them walking down the aisle so it's continuing and we understand these are things happening in Picard's mind. Finally he gets to the end, and the third ending is she interrupts and tells both of them she isn't staying for either one of them. She says through Picard's influence she's been enlightened and is going off in search of adventure, leaving both men standing there. I was overruled. I think that those who overruled me would say that her leaving was not justified by anything else in the script, but I would argue with that."

Episode #122:
"Imaginary Friend"
Original Airdate: 5/4/92
Story by Ronald Wilderson & Jean Matthias & Richard Fliegel
Teleplay by Edithe Swensen & Brannon Braga
Directed by Gabrielle Beaumont
Guest Starring: Brian Bonsall (Alexander), Noley Thornton (Clara), Shay Astar (Isabella), Jeff Allin (Daniel Sutter), Patti Yasutake (Nurse Ogawa), Sheila Franklin (Ensign)

The imaginary friend of one of the crew's young daughter, Clara Sutter, becomes a frightening reality when she threatens to destroy the ship.

••••

"I was always very turned on by the idea," says Rick Berman. "Where else but in science-fiction could you do an idea about an imaginary friend who turns out not to be imaginary? It's a story about an alien who takes the form of a little girl's imaginary friend and begins to perceive our world through the eyes of a child. I think it turned out quite nicely,

and we got two great performances. It's very difficult to work with kids because they're not as experienced and you only get them for a few hours a day, but in the case of this episode we got two very nice performances. I would not rank this as one of my favorites for the season, but it was a lot of fun."

Less generous in his praise is former producer Herb Wright. "It's not a show that dealt with our regulars and not a show that needed to be on *Star Trek,*" he asserts. "I think Michael [Piller] was trying to do *E.T.,* but what made that film work is hard to do on *Star Trek* aboard the Enterprise. E.T. was an alien in a suburban neighborhood trying to get home. It was like the lost pet that turns out to be a genius alien. But 'Invisible Friend's' problem was how do you have, in effect, an adolescent alien? I think the problem is that when you narrow your focus to what kind of show you want to do to the point where you're doing 90 percent personal stories and you're trying to do them in outer space on a 24th century starship, you're going to run into a brick wall and there's only so many times you can do that."

"I did the final rewrite on it and 'Imaginary Friend' was the most gratifying script I wrote this season," recalls Brannon Braga. "It wasn't quite working in its original guise and Jeri Taylor and Pete Fields and I broke the story and tried to make the imaginary friend more of the bad seed. Before, it was more like Puff the Magic Dragon and it was that the alien was simply curious and didn't have an evil intent. It just kind of laid there and was playful fluff. We decided to make the alien malevolent, where it's mean to the kid. I've taken to calling it Romper Room: The Next Generation. Kid stories appeal by their very nature. There's an innocence to kids and kids can have conflict. The funny thing about kid shows in the *Star Trek* universe is you can get conflict with kids because they're not developed yet like our perfect adults. In a strange kind of way, kids can have more problems and conflict than our regulars. They can still be imperfect. It is a fun episode and hopefully people won't be so sick of seeing children on the show."

••••

Episode #123:
"I, Borg"
Original Airdate: 5/18/92
Written by Rene Echevarria
Directed by Robert Lederman
Guest Starring: Jonathan Del Arco
(Hugh Borg)

A wounded young Borg is taken aboard the Enterprise and taught humanity by the ship's crew. Meanwhile, Picard and Guinan confront their own personal demons relating to the cybernetic, super race.

••••

"The minute I saw the story I fell in love with it," says Rick Berman. "The dramatic relationships are so vivid. Guinan, who comes from a people that were destroyed by the Borg, Picard who was brutalized and violated by the Borg—both are put in the position of being prejudiced. Geordi and Dr. Crusher are in the position of being open-minded and eventually sympathetic to this young man and the end result is a wonderful series of relationships and wonderful scenes between Guinan and the Borg. There's another arc that deals with Geordi and the Borg, Geordi and Picard, and Picard and the Borg, and they are all wonderfully strong, small two-character scenes. The writing was wonderful and the acting great. It was directed by Bob Lederman making his directorial debut, and I'm very pleased with it."

Uncredited co-writer Jeri Taylor agrees, "I think it will become a classic. I think it's a wonderful concept and it's just real special. It's *Edward Scissorhands* in a sense. The Borg will never be the same again."

Michael Piller, whose "Best of Both Worlds" was the Borg's first return visit and widely regarded as one of the new *Trek*'s finest hours, agrees that "I, Borg" was a satisfying follow-up. "I think it's just a great premise which forces both Guinan and Picard to confront their own prejudices," says Piller. "And you would think these are two characters who have none, but when it comes to the Borg the old issue is 'know your enemy.' It's a lot harder to hate them if you know them and it deals with the issue of what happens to these communal Borgs which cannot be treated as anything else but

parts of the whole when one is separated and becomes an individual. How do you treat him when he is an individual? I feel that if you take the unstoppable villain, the stereotype and you turn it inside out, that's great dramatic storytelling. Because you don't allow the audience to ever get comfortable with what they expect the Borg show to be. 'You think you know what the Borg are, well you've got the prejudices too, pal.' You think they're unstoppable villains and now you're going to look one in the eye and decide whether you're going to kill him or not."

"I think this is a real good way to bring the Borg back, because they're very limiting in the way they are," says Ron Moore. "They're this huge collective with no voice to communicate to and you can't relate to these guys. We keep saying they're unstoppable and if we keep stopping them it undercuts how unstoppable they truly are. They're very mindless, they don't have personality, they're hard to deal with dramatically. In 'Best of Both Worlds' you take Picard and make him Locutus and you've got something. This was a chance to take him out of that and make him a person. What are your responsibilities with that person? One of the analogies we used were the experiments where they were teaching chimps sign language and then the experiment is over and what do you have? Someone who's sort of on the cusp of intelligence or communication skills, but what do you do? You've taken this animal and broadened it to something else, but you can't just throw it back into the jungle. We tossed that around. I thought it was a real good show to do."

Episode #124:
"The Next Phase"
Original Airdate: 5/11/92
Written by Ronald D. Moore
Directed by David Carson
Guest Starring: Thomas Kopache (Mirok),
Susanna Thompson (Varel), Kenneth
Meseroll (Ensign McDowell), Michelle
Forbes (Ensign Ro), Shelby Leverington
(Brossmer), Brian Cousins (Parem)

Ro and Geordi are apparently killed in an explosion aboard a disabled Romulan warbird, but are actually "phased" into another dimension where they encounter an evil Romulan

Centurion. The duo have to convince the Enterprise crew that they're not dead before the ship is destroyed by a Romulan trap.

••••

Admits director David Carson, "This was an extremely difficult episode to do, because it dealt with special effects of a type people were familiar with from *Ghost*, which *Star Trek* had never attempted before. It was one of the most difficult technical episodes they'd ever done just by the nature of having people walk through people and an environment where people exist in different phases. I thought the story hung together quite well, and it turned out in quite a good way."

"I hate that title, but I'm very pleased with the episode," says Rick Berman. "It's a wonderful high concept story. The story really pumps along and there's great Romulan mystique and some wonderful things with people running through walls and the audience gets to see two different realities. It was very difficult to shoot in blue screen with people putting their hands through consoles and walls. It looked relatively easy on paper, but took a lot of time to make the visual effects work. It's a great piece of science fiction."

Michael Piller was also pleased with the final result, despite initial trepidation. "I get a little tired of Romulans and I was a little reluctant to make this a Romulan show," he says. "It's Ron [Moore's] script's attempt to do a bottle show, but it turned out to be a high budget special effects intensive show. It had been pitched as actually similar stories by two people. We bought the ideas and combined them into one and Ro developed the story and wrote it. I think it's terribly important to give credit to Ron Moore for the work he did this season. Last year I said Ron Moore was the best Klingon writer I had on staff, but, god forbid, he should ever work on a show that had human beings. This season Ron has put it all together. He is a complete writer now and certainly one of the strongest elements of any staff you could possibly hope for. It's been a pleasure watching him grow."

"It was fun," offers Brannon Braga about the Ensign Ro vehicle which was originally written for Geordi and Troi. "Troi's had enough running and jumping this year. We felt why not give Ro something and I'm glad she did, because she kicks a Romulan in the chest and does a kick worthy of Bruce Lee. She's some sort of acrobat. That scene in my opinion makes the whole show."

Episode #125:
"The Inner Light"
Original Airdate: 6/1/92
Story by Morgan Gendel
Teleplay by Morgan Gendel &
Peter Fields
Directed by Peter Lauritson
Guest Starring: Margot Rose (Eline), Richard Riehle (Batal), Scott Jaeck (Administrator), Jennifer Nash (Meribor), Patti Yasutake (Nurse Ogawa), Daniel Stewart (Young Batal)

A mysterious space probe disables Picard and sending his unconscious body to the deck of the bridge. When he awakens, he seems to be somebody entirely different and experiences a lifetime of memories in a matter of twenty-five minutes.

••••

"This episode allows us to bring Picard and a wonderful group of guest actors together and create a world," enthuses Rick Berman. "We see Picard at half a dozen different ages involving wonderful prosthetics and a man's lifetime in the course of an hour. It's quite dramatic and well written and [Peter] Lauritson did a lovely job directing it."

Opines Michael Piller, "It's a great premise about a man who lives 45 years of his life in 25 minutes. Patrick gives a remarkable performance. He gets to be six or seven different ages and it works. As we were breaking the story with the writers, I remember putting all the lines on the board and with each one creating the blocks to have connections and relationships grow in this other life for Picard, so that by the end of the show when they die or they are lost, there is an emotional impact that the audience should absolutely be heartbroken that he's lost these other people he loved and spent his life with. I actually had tears in my eyes when we were breaking this story and I hope we were on the money."

For Patti Yatsuke, who plays

Nurse Ogawa, assisting Dr. Crusher on the bridge was a novel experience. "My big game on this show was that all I did was work in sickbay. I had one scene where I finally got to see another part of the ship. I told them I was so excited about this one because I'm actually on the bridge now. That's been kind of my game, seeing how many rooms of the ship I can get into. I can't wait to be transported."

The big-budget "Light" came as a surprise to producer David Livingston, who was hoping to end the season with some budget-savers. "It put me into kind of shock because we had all these big shows at the end, but what happened was we didn't have other scripts that were in the pipeline. Fortunately we had the money to be able to do it. We had to make some substantial changes, especially on the last show. We made a lot of changes and adjustments to be able to pull it off in terms of the time and the money."

As "Inner Light" demonstrated, Patrick Stewart had become a much more active participant in the show's fourth and fifth seasons than he had been in the first three.

"I've been seriously hurting people for about two years now, and that's given me deep satisfaction," says Stewart. "Also, they addressed the romantic, the real romantic side of Picard. Perhaps, if there's one area which I would personally enjoy because it gives me a lot of pleasure and they haven't had much of it in the past, is the humorous, ironic, wittier side of our good captain. Two or three seasons ago I might have been complaining about being too much of a desk captain, a brief-case captain. My body count has risen dramatically in the last few episodes."

Writer Morgan Gendel is quick to point out that his initial take on the material was a "wrong-headed" thought which paved the way for the story to come. His initial concept involved the Enterprise coming across a probe in space which, when contacting a ship, would transport those with whom it came into contact into a distant realm. "It zapped this interactive thing into your mind and puts you in a different place," says Gendel. "Instead of advertising, 'Come to Maui,' you find yourself on a beach somewhere else. That was my original thought."

Like most scripts for *Star Trek*, he points out, the story went through a wide variety of permutations before shooting began. "I really liked the notion of an alternate reality, so when I went in to pitch a probe zapping their brains, I came up with an anti-war message," explains Gendel. "My thought was what if some civilization had been through some terrible war and didn't want others to repeat it. Picard and Riker are hit with the probe and find themselves on a planet with storm troopers coming. They have to finish the story and get back to the Enterprise. It seemed entirely real to them while they were there and they had to escape these marching soldiers and a war which was leading up to a nuclear holocaust. Meanwhile, aboard the ship, they're in comas. What intrigued the staff was this idea of an alternate reality, that you're lying there on the ship while experiencing something else."

As the script developed, the anti-war message was eschewed. The latest version of the story involved a community that had been wiped out in a war who wanted to pass on their story through the probe. This was the first time that "Inner Light's" overarching theme was broached. Producer Ron Moore was equally taken with the idea that Picard would experience an entire lifetime on a planet while only a few minutes had passed on the ship. By the time Gendel was ready to pitch Michael Piller the idea, he had several strong backers among the writing staff.

"Michael knew immediately it should be Picard alone," recalls Gendel, who got the go-ahead to do a story treatment from Piller. "That's where the heart of the story was, with him leading this other life."

Gendel then wrote a five-page prose outline which eventually laid the groundwork for "Inner Light," although it has major differences from the produced episode. "I still had the anti-genocide thing in my mind," he says. "I had an idea that this technologically advanced culture is about to be inducted into the Federation and everybody wonders how they became so technologically sophisticated so fast. You find out they did it on the backs of these people they wiped out, the Kataan, whose technology they stole. Meanwhile, Picard is experiencing this other life. Michael rightfully said, 'We're not going to need to cut back to the ship that much. The story is going to be with Picard.'"

Piller's next suggestion was to have Picard marry one of the Katannians and grow old and have children. "That's when everything took off," Gendel enthuses. "Even in the next pass, we had Picard meeting this woman and courting her, but it became more and more compressed."

The idea was to create connections and relationships for Picard in this other life so that by the end of the show, when they die or they are lost, there is an emotional impact that the audience should feel.

Several important decisions were made during the story break, including the fact that Picard's aging as Kamin would only take place after cutaways to the Enterprise or coming back from commercials, rather than using the hokey device of a lap dissolve to indicate the passage of time. "We knew there were certain notes we wanted to play as well," says Gendel. "We knew we wanted there to be sexual tension between him and Eline and that she'd have to die. We also wanted to show her necklace, which was in the same shape as the probe."

Gendel admits that much of "Inner Light's" premise involving the need for a culture to pass down its heritage was influenced by his Jewish upbringing as well as the subtext involving Picard carrying on the traditions and memories of Kataan, in the wake of the planet's destruction, which could be considered similar to the feelings and desires of Holocaust survivors. Indeed, even the birth of Kamin's son, Batai, playing by Patrick Stewart's son Daniel, and subsequent baby-naming was analogous to a bris in the Jewish religion by the writer.

After finishing the first draft of the script, Peter Allan Fields took over the second draft.

Executive Script Consultant Peter Allan Fields explains, "Someone named Morgan Gendel wrote the story and the first draft as well when I started to work the premise and structure from the story and made up my own sort of

relationships. It was an opportunity to give Captain Picard an entire lifetime which is the antithesis of the kind of life he had always lived aboard the Enterprise. I understand Patrick enjoyed playing it very much, and it was a delight to be able to write it. Picard doesn't change, even though he's not the captain his personality doesn't change. But now he has a life he's never had; he has love, a home, marriage, a family and things that are not burdens; things he never thought he needed before. He not only has them but he loves them and is used to them and loses them. We cover a period of 30 years all in the space of 25 minutes of time of supposed unconsciousness. I think it turned out pretty darned well."

"Peter did a great job," enthuses Gendel, who admits some disappointment over not writing the final draft, which was necessitated by the fact "Inner Light" was the penultimate episode of the fifth season, and as such faced a time crunch before the summer hiatus. "These guys from Michael on down had a take on this, that's a rare experience in television where everything comes together. We knew walking out of the story meeting that this was going to be an emotional episode."

"Inner Light" was directed by Peter Lauritson, whose most upsetting experience on the episode was being forced to cut seven minutes of footage from the final cut. "That really was a difficult thing," remembers the director. "There was definitely some blood on the floor when it was over."

Production designer Richard James, who built all the sets for the show, found the episode to be one of his most challenging. "We considered location when it was still a possibility, but we did it interior. I wondered how we were going to do the show. It was a very ambitious script and goes through a time period of 30 years, so it was a matter of showing plants that were healthy and then weren't and then started dying and then were dead. The set had to go through all these different changes and we, literally, didn't have the turnaround time. We had about fifteen minutes between set-ups, so that episode was ambitious in that regard as well as costuming and make-up."

While Gendel has gone on to write other episodes of Next Generation and Deep Space Nine, one of his most cherished ideas has gone unproduced. In the proposed storyline, a starship would encounter another probe from Kataan and summon the Enterprise when they find it holds three people in cryo-stasis. One of those aboard is the scientist who played Eline in Picard's probe fantasy. "Picard was married to this woman, made love to her and grew old with her, so it's not like a dream," says Gendel. "It's real to him and now his dead wife has come back to life, which is a really powerful thing made more so by the fact she doesn't know who the hell he is and she's married to one of the scientists also onboard the probe.

"I have a personal attachment to this episode and I thought my passion for that would get it through," he admits. "The idea is so powerful. His whole family has been destroyed in a natural holocaust, a nova explosion, and now he finds out his wife is alive. I pitched my heart out and they thought it was best not to tamper with the memory of 'Inner Light.'"

As for the mystical title "Inner Light," which seems to harken back to some Zen philosophy or spiritual guru, Gendel smiles as he reveals that the moniker is actually drawn from a George Harrison song. "It was the B-side of 'Lady Madonna,'" he laughs. "I thought it would be fun to give every Star Trek episode I wrote a title that's from a different, obscure Beatles song. I wanted to call 'Starship Mine' 'Revolution,' but they had already used 'Evolution.' It was a little joke between me and me."

Episode #126:
"Time's Arrow"
Original Airdate: 6/15/92
Story by Joe Menosky
Teleplay by Joe Menosky &
Michael Piller
Directed by Les Landau
Guest Starring: Jerry Hardin (Samuel Clemens), Michael Aron (Bellboy), Barry Kivel (Doorman), Ken Thorley (Seaman), Sheldon Peters Wolfchild (Indian), John M. Murdock (Beggar), Marc Alaimo (Gambler), Milt Tarver (Scientist), Michael Hungerford (Roughneck)

• • • •

Data's head is discovered in a cave on earth, which prompts the Enterprise to lead an investigation into earth's past where they discover aliens abducting humans from the 19th century to the future. Additionally, they discover Guinan!

••••

"We didn't intend to do a cliffhanger this year," explains Michael Piller, "but once *Deep Space Nine* was announced, there were rumors that *Next Generation* was being canceled, that it was being downgraded in importance. There were letters of protest saying pay attention to the show that matters. Rick and I started talking and we both agreed this was not the time to not do a cliffhanger after two years. The next season is going to be the best season we've ever had, and I wanted to have the momentum of having a cliffhanger. I wanted people talking.

"We decided it was going to be a time travel story," he elaborates, "and we were trying to do a show all season long about Data trying to pass himself off as human. We had come up with a scenario about going to a humanoid planet that was very awkward and we couldn't figure out why the Enterprise was not coming back. And somebody said the way to do this story was to have Data come back to Hollywood and walk down Melrose Avenue. We started talking in those terms. That would have been okay, and we kept searching for the era. Do we want to do the 50's, well *Back to the Future* did the 50s. The 60's? Well, maybe everyone does the 60's. And then we had a running gag that Data goes back to save JFK and two weeks after the script was done somebody actually submitted a spec script, totally by coincidence, where the Enterprise goes back in time to save JFK. I don't think this year Gene would have been ready to jump on that bandwagon and then we said the 70's, but we said what is there to go back to see? And then they said the 80's, maybe. We even went to the 90's and we didn't like that. Then we said the near future and Rick Berman finally said what about the 19th century? Why don't we do Marc Twain?

"We sat down and started doing that story and it was going to be fine. I brought everybody in on Sunday to do the

break, because it was really late and it came together late in the season. Joe said something about Guinan and I said we need her in the show, I dictated that and Joe said she'd be alive back then and started going on to other things. I said if she was alive, what if that's where she met everybody and what if that's where the relationship with the *Star Trek* group started and she met Picard. Ultimately that's where Picard helped her out of trouble back then and she came back to find him before he met her, knowing she was going to be on the Enterprise to complete the circle. I called up David Livingston and said can we have Guinan for two days; once in the present, once in the past and this became yes, no, yes, no and Joe was writing one story and then another. Finally, when she heard the story idea, she fell in love with it and committed to do both the current show, which she's already done, and the next show in an expanded role."

"We very much wanted to do an episode that dealt with Data time traveling back to contemporary earth and walking down the street where Beaver Cleaver lives," recalls Rick Berman. "As we got into the story, I found something very contrived and overly coincidental about people coming back to our exact time. It's not believable for me, and we started thinking about other decades. Every decade we thought about had been done or wasn't worth doing. Every decade reflected on something else. It didn't make any sense unless it was something that we could take advantage of living in 20th century America. Contemporary was not working, and I think it was me who came up with a story where Data ran into Mark Twain, which put us into turn of the century California, which was not as easy to do. It became a costume piece, it became a piece where we had to seek out locations."

The difficulties in recreating turn of the century America was a production nightmare for David Livingston and production designer Richard James.

"The last episode is the toughest and an expensive one, but it ended up being that way because it has so many different elements," says Livingston. "We went on location for two days in two different places. Both location days were period pieces

involving a lot of extras in period wardrobe. There was a lot of set dressing and the art department worked to create the proper milieu of San Francisco in the 1890's. So those two locations were big. We had to shoot in this Pasadena mansion for this ballroom set and they have time restrictions, so you're limited in the amount of time you can be there. Anytime you shoot on location in Los Angeles, it's tough. But when we start doing period stuff, you can't come in there and shoot it and leave like shooting a cop show in downtown LA. You have to dress it and make it look right."

Shooting the eerie time travel sequences on Stage 16 were equally challenging, he explains. "The time travel portions of this thing where we see these aliens that time travel and we go meet them on Stage 16 was very difficult shooting. The aliens were blue screened in because they glow. In order to photograph them with our people, it's a three-stage process. We shoot our people on the set, we have to shoot plates and then we have to shoot the aliens. Then Rob Legato has to matte all that stuff together, and the process of shooting something sometimes takes two or three times longer to do than it normally would, because there are so many layers to the process. Everything about the show is big and ambitious, but Michael and Rick said this is our cliffhanger and we want a show that's going to give the audience a lot of stuff. So we gave them a lot of stuff in an unbelievable episode, and I think it's been the hardest of all seasons."

"Rick and Mike both love time travel, but most time travel stories just don't work," says Brannon Braga. "They're hokey or push the boundaries of credibility. We've done three this season. I think it's just because most time travel stories are back in history to that pivotal event, or don't change the timeline. That stuff is cliché and we don't want people to try and develop time travel stories, because it needs to be in house. 'A Matter of Time' was a lot of fun. It was different because it was the story of the man who came to dinner, and 'Cause and Effect' is a story Rick loved, because he had never seen it before. 'Time's Arrow' is a period piece which we haven't done."

••••

#90, March/April '93

$2.50-U.S.

STAR TREK
THE OFFICIAL FAN CLUB

SPECIAL ISSUE
THE MAKING OF RELICS
Recreating The Classic Enterprise Bridge

PLUS
STAR TREK:
DEEP SPACE NINE

This issue of the fan club magazine highlights the making of "Relics," which brought James "Scotty" Doohan to The Next Generation.

CHAPTER TWENTY SIX

SEASON SIX:
An Overview

In May 1993 it became official: *The Next Generation* was making the leap to the silver screen. Ending Paramount's promo reel of upcoming product at Las Vegas' *ShoWest* film exhibitor's convention, the studio announced the *Trek* feature for December of 1994 with great fanfare. Although they didn't make the announcement until August of 1993, the seventh season of *TNG* would be its last on the small screen.

The announcement of the first *Next Generation* feature film followed on the heels of one of the show's most successful seasons both in terms of increasing viewership and quality. "I've been delighted with the episodes of *Next Generation* this season," said series executive producer Rick Berman at the time. "I've been very surprised at the ratings. They continue to get better every single year."

A lot of the credit for the creative flowering of the series in its sixth season can be given to co-executive producer Jeri Taylor, who was promoted from supervising producer at the end of fifth season. Taylor, a veteran television writer/producer, ran the writing staff on a day-to-day basis for Michael Piller and Rick Berman while they devoted much of their time to launching the *Trek* spin-off, *Deep Space Nine*. "I think Jeri cannot get enough praise for what she has done," says Berman. "She had a writing staff — Ron [Moore] and Brannon [Braga, Rene [Echevarria] and Naren [Shankar] — who have a great bond with her and they've worked together beautifully, turning out some great episodes of television. I was able to step back to some degree from *The Next Generation* because of my confidence in these people."

Taylor, who ran the writing staff, was not the only one to shape the show in its sixth year. Other promotions included Merri Howard to line producer, assuming many of David Livingston's responsibilities for producing the series when he was elevated to supervising producer of both shows; and J.P. Farrell, one of *Next Generation*'s film editors, who was promoted to the new position of Supervising Editor, fulfilling many of Berman's former responsibilities on the show.

Although Berman and Piller distanced themselves from the day-to-day involvement that had characterized their respective tenures on the show, their presence continued to be felt by all departments. For Taylor, the sixth season was an arduous, but rewarding year — although far more challenging than she ever expected.

"It was a thousand times worse than I could have imagined," says Taylor. "I don't think 'exciting' is the word I would use to characterize it. It simply felt overwhelming. Michael kept coming in and saying, 'You know, this must feel very creative to you,' and I would say, 'No, it doesn't. It feels like a lot of stress and pressure and anxiety.' It was very difficult."

Taylor's job was complicated by a notable lack of producible premises existing in development. "I looked at the script status report and thought, 'How will we ever do 26?'" Taylor muses. "We had four ideas and beyond that was an abyss. I didn't stop feeling that way until 'Descent' was on stage, but I learned to roll with it and realized that the staff really was coming through.

Piller nonetheless remained the last stop before a story for *The Next Generation* reached great bird Rick Berman's desk.

"We take pitches and come up with story ideas and we run them by Jeri," says Rene Echevarria regarding the development process that had existed on the show. "She has us write it up and we send them over to Michael and he decides what stories we put into development. Then Jeri will decide whether to use the writer who pitched the story or which one of us will write the drafts of a document, which will then go to Michael. And he'll ask for some changes and then it will go to Rick. If Rick approves it, we break the story without Michael and he comes in at the end and either approves it or asks for some changes and then it goes to script and he gives notes. Michael hadn't been doing any rewriting on *Next Generation*. That was Jeri's job. She polished everything. Jeri's hand is in all of those sixth season scripts, some much more than others."

For Piller, who was openly critical of the fifth season of *Next Generation*, Taylor's tenure resulted in a creative renewal which he heartily approved of. "There's no question in my mind that the sixth season was far superior to the fifth," reflects Piller. "I believe that we took more risks, we expanded several characters in fundamental ways. We also took care of some long overdue issues that needed to be addressed; a Geordi love story as well as finding some really wonderful things for Data, who we felt we had been cheating a little the last few years. We also felt at the beginning of the season that we had a franchise that had wonderful opportunities for fun and we rarely took them. I think there are some wonderful episodes that don't take themselves so seriously that are nice breaths of fresh air, counterbalanced by episodes that take themselves terribly seriously and are some of the great television shows of the season."

Piller traced the show's revitalization to its previous year. "I fundamentally believe this happened at the end of fifth season," he states. "If you look at shows like 'Inner Light' and 'The Outcast', you will begin to see a restart of serious creativity in the *Next Generation*. I think essentially what you see the result of is the development of *Deep Space Nine*. *DS9* suddenly stoked the creative fires in a very constructive way. I concentrated on communicating that there was not an 'us-and-them' situation; that these were all people working on *Star Trek*, all in the same building, and we should help each other and contribute to the other's show and learn about each other's show and help the universe grow. What did come, however, was an attitude that we have to be on our toes because there is a parallel development going on, and whatever they're doing on that show over there, I have to be doing just as well over here. So it became a very healthy situation as far as I'm concerned.

"I think we had a better mix

sixth season than certainly the fifth season, and I think its comparable to the fourth," adds Piller. "I have enjoyed *The Next Generation* and I enjoyed watching the show sixth season. A measurement of the success of the season is that the Enterprise did not break down once. That's a measure of how creative the storytelling was. As a result, I would bet that there was a 35% reduction in technobabble. The actors would tell you that. They used to call it Piller-filler, which is unfair since I know less about technology than anybody."

Notes actor Brent Spiner, who along with LeVar Burton has probably spoken the largest share of *Trek* mumbo-science, "That was one of my big complaints starting with the third season. Gene [Roddenberry] always said technobabble should be used as a spice and not as the main course, and I think they got back to that."

One of the reasons is that *Star Trek* began avoiding the cliched jeopardy plots in its A/B story plotting, which had typified the fifth season. The A/B story usually was dual plot development comprised of a personal story coupled with a ship in peril plot, that often had nothing to do with each other. In such episodes as "Cost of Living," in which Mrs. Troi comes aboard and plays surrogate mom to Alexander, the ship is also jeopardized by a mysterious oozing organism. Sometimes these plots worked more effectively than others — as in "Silicon Avatar" which blended the story of the hunt for the crystalline entity with a vengeful mother's sorrow over the loss of her son to that destructive force — but most of the time they seemed forced. A priority for sixth season was abandoning such types of storytelling.

"It was a conscious effort to try to break away from a kind of story that seemed to have become formulaic," says Jeri Taylor. "Every week the ship was in jeopardy from this, that, or the other thing. There was a certain staleness that I think was just beginning to creep in. I don't think it was a real problem, but we definitely knew that we wanted to rejuvenate things and take some chances. If you can't take chances in the sixth or seventh season of a show, when can you do it? The show is very solid and very

strong and so it was time to kind of push the edges a little bit. And we did that."

Naren Shankar, who served as the show's science advisor and became a staff writer the sixth year, was often charged with devising much of the menacing sci-fi contrivances. "The reason we got away from that format was because most everybody on the staff didn't feel it worked," he says. "When we went to an A/B story where A was a character line and B was a straight ship jeopardy, the two didn't overlap. They're not interesting. It's just not generally a good way to tell a story. There are exceptions, 'Hollow Pursuits' was a straight A/B storyline and it was still a good episode because the B story was de-emphasized tremendously. What happens is you end up in this awkward position where in Act 5 you're just dashing to the finish. It's like get the ship in jeopardy in Act 4 and solve the character story and the jeopardy in Act 5 and let's do it and get it over with. You want things to go along in a more organic way. It's more interesting and less artificial, and everybody understands that."

As a result, *Star Trek* looked towards new avenues for exploration and the show became more daring and provocative, often breaking its traditional format and dealing with more controversial issues. "It *was* conscious," emphasizes Michael Piller. "From the beginning of sixth season we said let's take more chances. One of the problems in the fifth season was we said, 'Okay, it's not a great story but we need another story for this week so let's keep going', and I think we said let's wake up and see how far out we can go sixth year. We had some episodes that are as far out as any you've ever seen on this show.

"I made some suggestions, I killed a few things that I thought weren't right, I gave notes on scripts and in one particular case I turned a show inside out ['Suspicions'], but most of it has really been in Jeri's office," Piller continues. " She deserves so much of the credit. Ron Moore has turned into a really strong writer/producer who is a leader in that room, has strong opinions and generally knows *Star Trek* and how to make it work. Brannon Braga is one of the great success stories of the last several years

I've been here. This is a guy who came out of the Television Academy's intern program as raw and inexperienced as you'll ever find with anybody, and has grown each year. Now he's turning in some of the most interesting work you'll ever see. I have great respect for his work and I think he will become recognized as one of the very special writers in television. Then we brought in Rene Echevarria, who had done such wonderful work for us on a freelance basis but didn't seem to do too well under pressure in the earlier years. But his work and attitude had matured and we felt he was really a good candidate to be a future staff member, and he's done a fine job. And Naren Shankar, who had been our technical consultant and also been a Writer's Guild intern, was someone else Jeri felt strongly had the potential to make a significant addition. We brought him in mid-season. If I had any credit to take at all, it was helping these people to know what works and what doesn't."

In fact, in many ways sixth season seemed like two completely different seasons. The year began with part two of "Time's Arrow", in which Mark Twain is inadvertently sent into the future and tours the Enterprise. It was followed by several heavy high-concept science-fiction episodes, including "Realm of Fear", in which Barclay encounters creatures in the transporter; "Man of the People", where Troi becomes a receptacle for the negative emotions of a conflict mediator; and "A Fistful Of Datas", in which the holodeck malfunctions and results in a deadly Data gunfighter facing off against Worf in the center of a computer-generated town. With "Chain of Command", a dark and conflict-ridden two-parter, the season appeared to make a dramatic departure in tone and substance.

"It's a very interesting insight, and not one I probably would have made," says Jeri Taylor. "To say there is an overall design which 'Chain of Command' heralded in tone is not inaccurate, but it was not intentional. We did want to go with some sci-fi, high-concept stories, sort of offbeat, bizarre things. And then after that it was a matter of what do we have here?"

"I agree that it was a more ambitious season," notes Brannon Braga.

"The production staff went a little crazy because each show is so different and that's the fun thing about sixth year. Ambitious is the key word. I think we really tried to do some interesting stories. Mid-season seemed to signal that we were getting antsy and the high-concept wasn't enough. I think its serendipitous. Certainly getting to write 'Birthright' was great for me, because after doing a string of high-concept action shows — which is what I like to do — it was really nice to do something with more profound elements. Observations of a shift are true. Why it happened is serendipity. I think Rene is the only one who thinks the beginning of the season really sucked. I think the shows are a nifty, eclectic mix and I have no qualms at all about the beginning of the season. We were all very happy about it."

Offers Brent Spiner, "I do think 'Chain of Command' was sort of a turning point in the season, even though there were some good episodes prior to it. From what I've read and heard from them, the way the season started off, fans thought we were going to have a dud season and something happened about midway through and everything turned around. From that point on almost every episode was top notch. I wish 'A Fistful Of Datas' had come later in the season, because it's sort of attached to the early batch where it seemed the new writers were trying to find their way with it. Once they clicked in, every week was an exciting episode and something worth watching."

Naren Shankar agrees that the shift was more attributable to happenstance than a conscious decision by the staff to tackle bigger issues. "It may simply be we ran out of high-concept and had to dig deeper," he says. "It did change the tone for the rest of the season."

Other concerns revolved around the future of the show as well as rumors running rampant that Patrick Stewart would not be returning for a seventh year.

"There was concern, but I think we all felt they were going to do features and that was a big carrot to get him to commit to another year," says one member of the writing staff. "When we were doing 'Chain of Command', that's when the first inkling that Patrick might not be coming back was heard. Bringing in a new captain in 'Part One,' you could see how that could give the show a really fresh start if you could find somebody good. Frankly, we were more concerned that Brent wasn't going to come back, because Brent is irreplaceable. You don't just bring on another android or cart out a Vulcan or something to fill his role. You have to have a captain and there was, in fact, some enthusiasm about the possibility of getting someone new. We were talking about bringing a woman in."

While shooting the pilot for *Deep Space Nine*, veteran *Trek* director David Carson considered the possibility of Stewart leaving.

"I believe the show is not about a star and not about a Captain Kirk or a Jean Luc Picard," he noted. "I think there will inevitably be some sort of shake-up, as there always is when a captain leaves a ship, and there will be a feeling of the ground. But you may find that you get a different, richer *Next Generation* out of it and you're not simply retreading the same waters with the same people. The regrouping of the cast and the realignment of the actors towards either new people or redistribution of their own strengths, will inevitably make *Next Generation* different."

Points out Jeri Taylor, "As far as I know, that was completely informal. There were for thirty minutes or so some real concerns Patrick wouldn't be back. Most of the people felt in all probability he *would* be back. The negotiations were difficult and had he not come back then the door would have been wide open."

The idea towards focusing more on science-fiction storytelling had been a priority for the staff ever since the end of the previous season. Fifth year's "Violations", in which alien telepaths were accused of mind rape, served as the template for developing new, high-concept science-fiction stories which blended character drama with a "neat sci-fi gag," as the staff often refers to their high-concepts. Ultimately, after a few episodes early in the season, the well ran dry, thus requiring a new approach which was probably for the best.

"To some degree it's a valid assessment," says Michael Piller. "I would say the high-concept science-fiction stories that dominated the beginning of this season were the result of feeling that we had not been doing very good science-fiction fifth season. When I said we want to have more fun with it, I said let's go out there and see what we can do with setting up some challenges for ourselves in the science-fiction area as well."

Despite meeting the challenge, the staff, some of who had been working on the series for as long as four years, felt a degree of sadness over the fact that they were entering what would be their final year toiling on the starship Enterprise.

"I'm a huge fan of *Next Generation*," says Brannon Braga, "although I had not really watched the show before joining the staff. I tried a few episodes the first season and for whatever reason it wasn't engaging. I've never seen the original series but I'm a huge fan of this show at this point, having written on it for so many years. No more was that more painfully evident to me than when a rumor was going around that there wouldn't be a seventh season. We were all in the dark and I was really depressed. I really felt this show deserved a seventh season. At that time I felt we were just breaking it open in writing terms. As a writer, I felt the show is extremely ambitious and was growing. It could go on for ten years. Why cut it off at six? I was very depressed at the prospect of losing *Next Generation*."

Word ultimately came down that there would indeed be a seventh and final season. "In terms of the seventh season, it was a mixture of melancholy, apprehension and excitement. I was sad that it would be the last season and I was apprehensive because we had twenty-six shows to fill. None of us knew what the season would be like. I think one goal we all had was to push the limits of the show once again and make it the best season yet."

• • • •

253

The Readers of Starlog recently chose the 25 best episodes of Next Generation, among them sixth season's "Relics" and "A Fistful of Datas" (Cover copyright © 1993 Starlog Communications International).

• • • •

CHAPTER TWENTY SEVEN
SEASON SIX

Episode Guide

"Time's Arrow, Part II"

"Realm of Fear"

"Man of the People"

"Relics"

Schisms"

"True Q"

"Rascals"

"A Fistful of Datas"

"The Quality of Life"

"Chain of Command, Part I"

"Chain of Command, Part II"

"Ship in a Bottle"

"Aquiel"

"Face of the Enemy"

"Tapestry"

"Birthright, Part I"

"Birthright, Part II"

"Starship Mine"

"Lessons"

"The Chase"

"Frame of Mind"

"Suspicions"

"Rightful Heir"

"Second Chances"

"Timescape"

"Descent, Part I"

• • • •

Jeri Taylor took over the creative reigns of The Next Generation *during the sixth season, replacing Michael Piller as executive producer as Piller moved over to* Deep Space.

Episode #127
"Times Arrow, Part II"
Original Airdate: 9/21/92
Teleplay by Jeri Taylor
Story by Joe Menosky
Directed by Les Landau
Guest Starring: Whoopi Goldberg (Guinan), Jerry Hardin (Samuel Clemens), Alexander Enberg (Young Reporter), Van Epperson (Morgue Attendant), Pamela Kosh (Mrs. Carmichael), Michael Aron (Jack the Bellboy), James Gleason (Dr. Appollinaire), Bill Cho Lee (Male Patient), William Boyett (Policeman), Mary Stein (Alien Nurse)

The Away Team enters the temporal distortion on Devida Two and finds itself in the 19th century, hoping to rescue Data and put an end to the murders on Earth by strange alien life forms who have been traveling back in time to feed on human neural energy. While the Away Team attempts to return to the 24th century, Samuel Clemens (Jerry Hardin) is inadvertently transported to the future, where he is brought aboard the Enterprise, while Picard remains trapped back in time with Guinan and Data's head.

• • • •

"There is still a whole middle part of their relationship that's missing and may forever be missing," says Jeri Taylor of Guinan and Picard's enigmatic friendship. "This is not a series where we feel we have to explain everything about everybody. Jack Crusher's death was never explained. What happened to Picard and Guinan when they met again may never be either, but the idea that they had met in the past, three hundred years ago, just seemed too provocative an idea to ignore."

Taylor's only sole teleplay credit of the season avoided much of the heavy science-fiction elements set forth in the fifth season cliffhanger.

"I felt the first episode got mired in technobabble," she says. "We wanted to try to stay away from that. I think that in a sense, we might have gone too far, because I'm not sure that a lot of it was ever explained. I think it might still be mystifying to people — just what were those aliens up to and why they were doing it? Every time we started to get into all this long stuff again, we decided we'd just go with the fun.

"Once again," Taylor notes, "we had developed the first part of the cliffhanger without a clue as to what would happen in the second part, which can be an exciting way to work. You paint yourself into a corner and you're forced to be very creative in order to get yourself out. This one was a nightmare. It was just awful to try to get the story going. Even when we finally went to script, we kept changing the story so it was a matter of going back and wrenching out sections and restructuring and plugging in other things and then taking all that away again. It was probably the most troubled episode of the year."

Laughs Brannon Braga of the show's impenetrable time travel scenario, "Breaking 'Time's Arrow II' was a fascinating and almost impossible process. Jeri Taylor went through hell writing that script because it was so complicated. In 'Part One' not only weren't a lot of people sure what the answers were, a lot of people weren't even sure what the questions were. There was a whole B plot about the aliens and what they were trying to do and who they were, which had

to be dropped because there just wasn't enough room in people's brains to assimilate it."

"I thought some of the science was a little intangible in 'Part One,'" says Ron Moore. "'Part Two' is a little more fun in terms of seeing our actors in those costumes and Riker hitting the policeman. I don't think I was satisfied with the Mark Twain part. I felt that we didn't give him his due. To take that sort of historical figure and put him on the starship for an episode felt like there should be more than just one walk through the corridor with Troi. Unfortunately, there was so much story to tell that the needs of the show forced you into really moving that into a sidebar and just playing a scene here and there."

"That was my first episode on staff and we broke it together and it was very tough," recalls Rene Echevarria. "We basically boxed ourselves into a corner with 'Part One' and it prompted very hilarious arguments about time travel and how it worked. 'That's not how time travel works, you idiot', with huge accusations and people falling back on primary sources like *Bill & Ted's*

Whoopi Goldberg appeared as Guinan in the sixth season premiere episode, "Times Arrow, Part II" (photo copyright ©1995 Albert Ortega).

• • • •

Excellent Adventure. 'That's the way it works, you can go meet yourself!' and all sorts of preposterous stuff."

Scenes of Data in 'Part One' had been shot on soundstages and on location at Pico House in Downtown Los Angeles. The more expansive visualization of the past era became a point of contention when the studio tried to convince the production team to use their new $10 million New York Street instead of shooting turn-of-the century San Francisco at Universal.

"We were all ready to shoot at Universal, and we had a meeting with the studio who was concerned that we were not fairly evaluating the New York Street that they had built," recalls David Livingston. "They wanted to make it clear to us that the New York street was there. I knew it was there, I walk by it every day. I had a twinge of conscience when I left the meeting because I had put a strong case for the fact that we had looked at the New York street, evaluated it and decided that it was not appropriate for the show and that Universal was much better. And as I was leaving the meeting, I said, 'Wait a minute, David, are you being totally fair?' I'm a company man, but I am also interested in putting the most money on the screen and getting the most bang for the buck. I asked myself if we were really making the right decision, going over to another studio and paying for all it costs to go over there, spending a lot of money for renting a facility when we might make better use of our facilities. So, I asked that the production designer and the director reevaluate the lot here, and try and make it work. And they did, and I thought the results were wonderful."

For Marina Sirtis, who was packed into a corset for the episode, the period shoot was playtime. "It was fun," she laughs. "I spent most of my career in period costume in England, but, of course, it's never that hot there so you're never that uncomfortable. It was nice to use the corsets, things that we were so uncomfortable in, since I would imagine someone coming back in time from the 24th century would be. It's always play-time when we have to do those things. Robin Hood ['Q-Pid'] was playtime and those are the real fun episodes where we

just let loose. It's like kindergarten on the set. We had a director in the first season who has refused to come back because we were too rowdy and that was in the first season. We became *much* rowdier, so we definitely didn't see him again."

Episode #128
"Realm of Fear"
Original Airdate: 9/28/92
Written by Brannon Braga
Directed by Cliff Bole
Guest Starring: Dwight Schultz (Reginald Barclay), Colm Meaney (O'Brien), Renata Scott (Admiral Hayes), Thomas Velgrey (Crew Member), Patti Yasutake (Nurse Ogawa), Majel Barrett (Computer Voice)

Resident Enterprise milquetoast Barclay (Dwight Schultz) is attacked by a strange creature while transporting on an Away Team mission to explore the disappearance of the crew aboard the U.S.S. Yosemite. At first, no one believes Barclay until he begins displaying the physical manifestations of his encounter inside the transporter beam.

• • • •

"It should have been called 'Realm of Apprehension,'" laughs Brannon Braga, who envisioned the episode as more horrifying than it eventually was. "The first three acts are fun and then the tech gets in the way. Certainly, it was one of my most personal episodes. People around here say I am Barclay. I hate flying and that's where the idea came from. If I lived in the 24th century, I'd be afraid to transport, so I enjoyed exploring some of the deeper neuroses that Barclay had. But I envisioned a scarier episode where the creatures in the transporter were a little more frightening, but then again what a tall order to the effects guys, 'Make it amorphous, but terrifying.' What does that mean? It's easy to write that, but difficult to visualize. I just wanted you to feel scared with this guy and you never really did."

"I thought it was pretty good," says Michael Piller. "I always like the Barclay shows. I think it's a perfectly valid fear to explore, whether you have a phobia about spiders or about being molecularly taken apart and put back together. As *Star Trek* viewers we have

come to take it for granted, but why shouldn't somebody be afraid to get into a transporter? I had always felt that there were too many similarities to that *Twilight Zone* where Shatner looks out and sees the creature on the wing of the plane ['Nightmare at 20,000 Feet']. I felt very strongly we needed to get the episode away from that, and I think we succeeded."

Offers Jeri Taylor, "This was an episode that a lot of people just didn't respond to and I don't know why. I thought it was a wonderful idea. I thought Brannon wrote a terrific script. It just seemed so perfect, Barclay with a transporter phobia just seemed like a marvelous marriage of something people can relate to today and in the future: technology. I just thought everything worked with the exception of the visual effects. The explanation by the end really got painfully detailed. And it's that fine line you try to draw, if we don't say this, is the audience going to be fairly confused and cheated because they don't understand it? But if we do say it, are they going to be overwhelmed by the words? We went one way in 'Time's Arrow II', and maybe we tried too hard to explain things in 'Realm of Fear,' but it's hard to strike that back."

Episode #129
"Man of the People"
Original Airdate: 10/5/92
Written by Frank Abatemarco
Directed by Winrich Kolbe
Guest Starring: Chip Lucia (Alkar), Susan French (Maylor), Stephanie Erb (Liva), Rick Scarry (Jarth), J.P. Hubbell (Ensign), Lucy Boryer (Ensign Janeway), George D. Wallace (Admiral)

Lumerian ambassador Alkar (Chip Lucia) and a woman he identifies as his mother, Maylor (Susan French), beam aboard the Enterprise to mediate a conflict. After Maylor's mysterious death, Alkar engages in a death ritual with Counselor Troi, using Deanna as the receptacle for his negative emotions while mediating the dispute. As a result, Troi transforms first into a jealous vamp and ultimately into a rapidly aging shrew.

• • • •

"The premise was basically 'The Picture of Dorian Gray'," says Rene

Events of "Man of the People" had devastating effects on Marina Sirtis' Counselor Troi (photo copyright ©1995 Albert Ortega).

Echevarria of the script which was staff-written and rushed to the stage when "Relics'" filming was pushed back. "That was the soundbite. We were kind of stuck and we needed something very quickly. Since this was the only thing we had in the pipeline, we gangbanged it all, writing an act and Frank [Abatemarco] tied those acts together. It was a surprisingly good draft considering five different people wrote it. Some shows always do that. *LA Law* wrote everything as a staff like that and there's something compelling about it because overnight you have a first draft instead of someone pulling their hair out for two weeks."

"I would have done it differently," counters Brannon Braga. "I would have made it darker and much more a story about Troi's dark descent from the psychological point of view. A scene we all wanted to see was Troi giving therapy to a young ensign — but make it twice as long and twice as dark as the one that was filmed, and make it much more of a Hannibal Lecter thing. This was a case where Frank Abatemarco saw a different show. He was focusing in on the show as a Prime Directive issue and looking at the character of the guy who was using

Troi as a receptacle. To me, that was the utterly incorrect instinct. After six years, who cares about Prime Directive issues? It's a *Star Trek* cliché. It should have been all about Troi and he would have been the catalyst in two brief scenes. The first three acts were still fun. It was enjoyable to see Troi acting strange and dressing in skimpy outfits. There was some argument in the structuring sessions. Ultimately, Frank was the writer and he was given the opportunity to do it the way he wanted to do it, and it suffered because he was new to the show."

Science advisor Naren Shankar was also called on to explain how Troi is freed of the mental discharges of this alien ambassador.

"It was a difficult script and there are things in this that changed a number of times. My original idea was that this psychic link had set up some kind of conduit between the two of them, and my idea was to have them do something that wasn't mental, but something that was physical like his basically charging her up. If this was a one-way pathway from this guy to Troi, the idea would be to put so much energy into Troi that she could force it backwards in the direction of the power transfer and overwhelm the guy and get rid of all that energy in her body. Some of that survived. I think it was Ron and Brannon who had the idea of Troi actually dying first, which was kind of a nice touch, to sever the link."

Offers director Winrich Kolbe, "I am very happy with it. There are obviously some problems with the script, but what intrigues me is that I took a script that had problems and came out with a damn good show. Marina was really terrific. She knew it was her show and was prepared for it. I think the only thing that I occasionally did was push her a little bit harder to become more of a vamp."

Says Sirtis of her transformation into a cosmic vixen, "I played it like these were underlying parts of Troi that she controlled or managed to suppress. And just looking in the mirror was all I needed to change. When I look in the mirror and see Troi, it's a very soft and gentle look. In the scene in Ten Forward where my hair was up, I saw Anne Bancroft in the mirror. I saw Mrs.

Robinson and that's what I played. Basically, a lot of the performance is governed by the way that one looks. Some actors say they put the shoes for the characters on first and figure out the walk. I look in the mirror and play whatever I see in the mirror — especially when it's a make-up thing like in 'Man of the People,' where the old person was a witch and that's who was in the mirror, so I played a witch."

Episode #130
"Relics"
Original Airdate: 10/12/92
Written by Ronald D. Moore
Directed by Alexander Singer
Guest Starring: James Doohan (Scotty), Lanei Chapman (Ensign Rager), Erick Weiss (Ensign Kane), Stacie Foster (Engineer Bartel), Ernie Mirich (Waiter), Majel Barrett (Computer Voice)

The Enterprise discovers Montgomery Scott (James Doohan) suspended in a transporter beam aboard a Federation transport ship, and rescues him from a seventy-five-year oblivion. Although at first Scotty is a man out of time, he proves vital in saving the Enterprise, one last time, from destruction inside a Dyson's sphere.

• • • •

Enthuses Michael Piller, "One of the great things about 'Relics' is that it wasn't a Scotty show. It was a concept about an engineer or a captain being caught in a transporter beam that we come upon as we do in the show, and I suggested it be Scotty. I thought we were going to have a problem with Mr. Berman, who generally doesn't like to do that gag. Oddly enough, he was in a good mood that day. When I came onboard you could not mention the old *Star Trek* in an episode, you couldn't make a reference to a character without major problems. When we brought Sarek onto the show, it was like, 'My God, we had to march across the street and pay homage,' but at that point, because we were firmly established, I think everybody felt a lot more comfortable that we have proven ourselves. We don't owe anything to the old *Star Trek*, except like the guys who went to the moon, the Mercury guys had to go up there first and we respect them for that, but we're not depending on them anymore. We don't feel we have to bend over backwards not to mention them."

With the return of Scotty approved, Ron Moore then seized upon the idea of having the former chief engineer recreate the former Enterprise bridge on the holodeck, a moment that is one of the highlights of the episode and perhaps *Next Generation*.

"We had Scotty and then Ron came up with this wonderful idea of recreating the old starship. It was an interesting dilemma because it was a very expensive proposition," says Piller. "It was actually cut out after the first meeting with Rick and the production people. But, that's movie magic and we sort of went around three different ways of doing it wrong and all of us knew maybe we'd get back to the right way. We wondered if we could rent a simulation from a convention or pieces of it. Finally the tech guys came up with a way to do it. I thought that was a magical show that worked not just because Scotty was in it but because it was good idea, well executed, and well written with

great special effects."

Helming his first episode of *Star Trek* was veteran director Alexander Singer, who had the challenge of shooting one of *Trek*'s most expensive and complex episodes. "I was very concerned about the special effects and how they would fit into a television schedule," recalls Singer. "I had never done that many special effects in a whole show riddled with these things, so that was my central question."

Another concern for the director was the condition of his guest star, actor James Doohan. "The next question was that I had never worked with Jimmy Doohan and I felt that potentially the show was a kind of classic and I understood what I had in my hands. I did not know, physically, what shape Doohan was in. There was a lot of dialogue and I don't think he ever did a show in the old *Star Trek* where he had this much drama and this many notes to hit. I had seen the *Star Trek* movies and I think that's still true, I don't think he ever was the center, he was always peripheral and in this episode he was the center. By the

time we came to the scene on the old *Star Trek* deck, he was not only the center but he had to support a very powerful dramatic scene. It's a scene that in reading it, I choked up. Part of me is very hardheaded and realistic and then part of me is very romantic and very sensitive and I was deeply moved by that story.

"It's not simply that I am also an old man retiring or an old man looking at the end of a long career," he adds "It's that the concept is deeply moving. I had great sympathy for him and the things Picard was saying to him, and the evocative quality just reading the script sent chills up and down my spine. I still feel it. My wife, who watches virtually no television and has none of my sympathies and none of my interest in science-fiction, watched me shooting that scene and it made her cry."

Singer had his concerns about Doohan allayed during a meeting between him and the actor prior to shooting. "I wanted to meet him first so we didn't meet on the set. He came in graciously, we talked and his delight in doing it and his manner reassured me

Nearly twenty years before returning to the bridge of the Enterprise in "Relics", James "Scotty" Doohan did so with writer Dorothy Fontana and George "Sulu" Takei at a '70s Star Trek convention.

enormously," says the director. "I think that he wanted me to be comfortable and he wanted me to have a sense that he could indeed carry this load, and he convinced me. And subsequently I think there was only one day, one scene, where he had a very technical page of technobabble and he was utterly exhausted at the end of a very long day, that we had any problems whatsoever. For the rest of it he was a delight to work with and he got all the jokes, so to speak."

Another concern was finding the proper balance in the relationship between Scotty and Geordi, which begins as antagonistic and eventually turns into one of mutual affection. "I think I always had an understanding that it wasn't going to destroy Geordi's character," explains Ron Moore. "In a sense, Geordi was right. Who is this guy to be hanging around my engine room and giving me a hard time? As long as he played him straight and eventually made him sort of see Scotty's point of view and understand and be a little sympathetic, I knew it was going to work."

Alexander Singer was less convinced when he received the script, worrying that Geordi's dismissals of Scotty could backfire among the audience who would be naturally sympathetic towards Doohan's character. "I had not worked with LeVar, so what I did was meet with him to talk to him about it," says Singer. "I don't think he'd done that before. I figured it's a new guy and I'd talk to him. But I think he was a little annoyed because in effect I wanted to be reassured that he understood that balance, and LeVar's feeling was, 'Of course I understand it. If I don't understand this, I don't understand anything.' It turned out that LeVar is like the cast in general, some of the best actors I've ever worked with anywhere, and in the scenes it was possible to fine-tune the performance. Sometimes the guys hit the right level immediately. Sometimes we had to work for it. The combination of hostility turning into affection was very moving to me."

In writing the confrontations between Geordi and Scotty, Ron Moore had some distinct ideas about their aspirations and goals in Starfleet which defined them as two very different char-

acters. "Scotty never wanted to be anything else but an engineer," says Moore. "He was happiest in the engine room. The ship was a living being to him. She was a lady and there was a whole different philosophy. And with Geordi, although I know he loves his job and was having a good time at it, it's not the same thing. Geordi used to be on the bridge. I'm sure he wants to command his own ship some day, like probably most engineers in the fleet do. Scotty was different and he had a different relationship."

"Scotty and Geordi are probably the two most different people you could ever imagine," concurs Naren Shankar, another longtime *Star Trek* fan. "Ron felt very strongly about that. His point, which is arguable, is that Geordi doesn't think of himself as an engineer. Geordi is the kind of guy who when he wants to relax might go to the beach, play some classical guitar music or hang out. Scotty is the kind of guy who will go into his room and read technical manuals. Scotty is an engineer through and through and he likes to break rules and do things in an unorthodox manner. He likes to tinker and Geordi is not that way. As a result, I think it's reasonable that they clashed initially."

Originally, Troi was going to ask Scotty if he wanted to know what happened to his colleagues aboard the Enterprise. "There was a line in a scene that got cut out between Troi and Scotty," says Moore. "She said 'Would you like to know what happened to all your friends and family?' and he said 'No, I'm not ready to hear that.' That was the closest allusion we were going to make. My thought is it would clutter it up a little bit to make direct references since once you bring up Bones and say that Mr. Spock is James Bond now and underground on Romulus, you have to talk about everybody else and we didn't want to say what happened to everybody else because we didn't want to lock ourselves into it."

Moore notes that several different scenarios were contemplated for ending the episode, although none of them were the rumored shuttling of Scotty to *Deep Space Nine*. "We could just have sent him to a Starbase but that felt a little flat and we were never going to send him

to a retirement community. There was one ending where Picard is on the bridge and Scotty is in engineering and Picard gives him the order to engage one more time and Scotty's got to run the engine room. But it felt like it wasn't going to be that dramatic. You press a button and that's it. Ultimately, there was some concern that we can't give our shuttles away either, but there's no money in the 24th century so what difference does it make? It's not like they're going to give him a bill for it, but they made me put in that line that it's a loan anyway."

Ultimately, the biggest challenge the producers faced was in visualizing the recreation of the first Enterprise bridge, which Moore had depicted differently in the story's conceptual stage.

"Originally I wanted to do some sequence on the holodeck with the original series characters in some way and we had talked briefly about an idea of doing it," he recalls. "We were going to go down to the holodeck and have him actually interact with clips like the Diet Pepsi commercial with Bogart stuff. We'd use a clip from the original series and have him look at them and talk to them or something, but that was very expensive and prohibitive and we could see that wasn't the right way to go. So I came up with this idea of the old bridge and there was a pause about that. They weren't sure they wanted to do it because it was going to be very, very expensive. The initial estimates to recreate that bridge were exorbitant, so there was a time there for a few days where it was sort of on the edge of whether we would be able to do it at all. But, you know, I think what happened is that a lot of people wanted to do that scene."

The first piece of the puzzle in recreating the original bridge set was laid by production designer Richard James during an early production meeting. "My initial reaction was what we wound up doing," says James. "I said if they could find a clip of the original where there was an empty bridge of the Enterprise, then we could take that film clip and do blue screen and I could just build a piece of the original to shoot the actors against. When Scotty walks in and sees an empty bridge and so forth, what he sees is a blue screen and then I explained that we could take the actor across the blue screen and pick him up walking into the frame again and he'd be against the real set at that point."

"I said we couldn't build the bridge," recalls supervising producer David Livingston. "I'm sure I did. If I didn't, I should have. But that's when Richard brought up looking at the original show and seeing if we could get 'stock footage' off of it. That was like manna from heaven."

A clip from "This Side Of Paradise" was quickly located in which the spore-infected crew of the Enterprise deserts the ship, leaving Kirk alone on the bridge. "It was Kirk leaving the bridge through a turbo-lift that gave us enough footage of the empty original bridge that we could use as the blue screen plate to actually have our people walking in," says Livingston, who pointed out that the post-production team then repeated the clip over and over until they had enough footage to provide the establishing shot of the bridge. "People are literally walking into a shot that was created twenty-five years ago. That was kind of exciting for all of us. To realize that you can literally tie the two eras together so specifically, that was a kick for everybody."

"I didn't see how they were going to do it," admits director Alexander Singer. "I assumed they had a complete bridge. When I was told they had one third of one part of it, I had to put on my thinking cap. I'd like to feel I'm a filmmaker and that given anything to work with I probably can make it work if it's possible. No challenge has been as peculiar as this one, though. We had a monitor on the set and I worked from the monitor and I kept reliving the old *Star Trek* deck, although I was never on it as a director. It's not memorable to me, but all of the sudden I'm living in a place and I don't even have it in front of me to deal with. So the business of creating it was, to me, an enormous cinematic challenge. I had with me an art director and a visual effects director who in terms of their knowledge and sophistication could pace me very comfortably."

"I told Alex that we could take the actor walking across the blue screen and then pick him up walking into frame again, and he'd be against the real set at

that point," explains Richard James, who constructed a pie-shaped wedge of the set which both Picard and Scotty were shot against in their scenes together. "I told him it becomes very restrictive but it will fill okay because I'll have the console out in the center, which he can walk past over to his station. Then I said, 'For your reverses, I'll switch out the panels and it will be different artwork in there so you can do your reverses against the same set.'"

Literally replacing the artwork in the Enterprise bridge monitors allowed the production crew to move the panels around to the other side of the set to make it appear as though a larger circumference of the bridge set had been constructed when, in fact, it was a very small part of it. "I told him it will look like it's on the other side of the set so it will give the illusion that we literally did the full Enterprise bridge of the original series," says James. "We spent lots of time developing the color and looking at old clips and looking at anything we could get a hold of. There was nothing that existed in the way of drawings and we had to develop sketches from photographs. We developed our measurements by saying, 'This looks like it was that high,' and working from there. We really did look for detail and search for detail because we knew so many fans of the old series would be looking for it and it would mean a great deal to them."

The helm console was obtained by a fan who had once constructed a replica of the original bridge set, and still had many relics from his endeavor. "There's a fan that Michael Okuda found that built the command chair and the helm," says Ron Moore. "Because we couldn't afford to build those, he trucked it down in his van from Stockton. He rented it to us for probably a buck or whatever, and we used it on the set and then when that was done he put it back in his van and drove away with a unique souvenir of *Star Trek*."

"Relics" is a tribute to the love that many of the production team still harbor for the original show. Many of the crew who had hid their manic enthusiasm for *Next Generation*'s progenitor came out of the closest in order to mobilize for the production of the ambitious

bridge sequence. "A lot of people put in a lot of extra effort and didn't get paid for it. They put in extra hours to make that possible and just bit the bullet because they wanted to do the scene," says Moore.

Of course, the bridge wasn't the only complex creation for the episode. Moore's script also postulated a Dyson's Sphere, an entire enclosed solar system which the Enterprise becomes trapped in. Contributing to its construction was miniature-builder Greg Jein, who created the panels which were digitally replicated to visualize the enormous sphere. "We used some left over running ship parts to make the corridor from the interior of the Dyson's Sphere to the exterior, so the justification for hoarding all those things these last twenty odd years finally paid off," laughs Jein.

Ironically, the Dyson's Sphere concept had been kicked around by the writing staff for myriad potential B-stories in years past. "It was something that we were trying to put in for a long time and it became a standing joke," says Moore.

Adds Naren Shankar, "I originally thought the interesting thing would be to make it a partially completed Dyson's Sphere because there's some solar radiation thing that had gone on. It ended up being a complete Dyson's Sphere that was uninhabited. When Ron had written about the Dyson's Sphere in the teaser, he wrote tech and when I came I gave him the numbers for the size of it and he was shocked that it was so big. It was like the equivalent of four million earths; it's huge. If you build something the size of the sun's orbit, you're talking about a sphere with a diameter of two hundred million miles."

Several scenes from the show needed to be cut for length, including a lengthy scene in which Counselor Troi talks to Scotty about his feelings of being a man out of time. "That was purely a matter of how long the episode was and that happens a lot," said Marina Sirtis. "What didn't make sense was why I was kissing him at the end if she never met him. It's because the scene was cut out."

"I think it's the most enjoyment I've had writing an episode and it's the best I've done in a personal sense," offers Ron Moore. "It meant the most to me out of a lot of things I've written, because it resonates with my interest in *Star Trek* from way back in that sense. I'm not sure if in the cold light of day that it's the most brilliant thing I've ever written, but it just had a lot of meaning for me."

Episode #131
"Schisms"
Original Airdate: 10/19/92
Teleplay by Brannon Braga
Story by
Ronald Wilkerson and Jean Matthias
Directed by Robert Wiemer
Guest Starring:
Lanei Chapman (Ensign Rager), Ken Thorley (Mott), Scott T. Trost (Lieutenant Shipley), Angelo McCabe (Crewman), Angelina Fiordellisi (Kaminer), John Nelson (Medical Technician), Majel Barrett (Computer Voice)

Geordi's experiments with a new scanning system result in members of the crew being abducted and experimented on in a distant realm of subspace by a strange alien species. Riker is sent into the rupture in hopes of halting the aliens' incursions aboard the Enterprise.

• • • •

Says scripter Brannon Braga of the poetry reading in which Data delivers an ode to his cat, Spot, "That was a decision to do a cold teaser and the poetry reading was an idea we had been kicking around for quite a while. The thing that's great about the teaser is that it's still advancing the plot with Riker falling asleep, even though you don't think that's going to have anything to do with the story."

"I couldn't believe it because not only did it rhyme but it's technobabble and it also had something to say," notes Brent Spiner, who grappled with the line reading. "It had a really sweet point of view towards the cat."

"It's a case where I wrote the most muddled, complex tech plot of all time," adds Braga. "The entire fifth act had practically no dialogue in it, just tech. The first three acts were eerie, but the fourth act was a tech nightmare. I felt it was creepy and weird and terrifying. I like psychological suspense and terror, and when I had a chance to do that on *Star Trek* I jumped at it. It seemed like a scary mystery to me until you see the

aliens which look like monks. Unfortunately, the trailer also gave everything away, 'Aliens are using the Enterprise crew as human guinea pigs.' They showed everything during the coming attractions the week before, which was really annoying."

"But this story looked full of potential. It had some cliched elements to it; getting kidnapped by aliens is not very fresh. I was more interested in those first four acts, the mystery and the weirdness and seeing our people losing their minds, which is not something you get to see very often. And that holodeck sequence I was looking forward to doing. .I like using the holodeck as a tool to solve a mystery like in 'Identity Crisis.' It just seemed like a fun mystery to me and turned out to be sort of a scary episode."

"['Schisms'] was kind of like *Close Encounters of the Third Kind*," says Richard James of his thoughts during the first production meetings. "I really saw that from some of the descriptions that you hear people talk about in their abduction experiences."

James worked closely with make-up supervisor Michael Westmore and costume designer Robert Blackman to find the appropriate look for the eerie, alien domain described in Brannon Braga's script. "The room sort of just drops off into blackness with bright light and there's no detail," he explains. "Everything was kind of fuzzy and that was the set. I used fiberglass, which I had seen cut on a sawhorse in the plaster shop, and I told them that's what I want my set to look like; furry and fuzzy-like. I wanted to give the feeling that it was maybe an insect kind of civilization and that these might be a hybrid of insects and grasshoppers, and it was all done against a black background."

Offers David Livingston of the complicated shoot, "I love the way that Bob Wiemer shot it with the wide angle lens. He made it look very odd, and he did some very unusual and strange camera moves across Jonathan and that device he was restrained on. I thought it was very bizarre. He doesn't hold anything back. He's got a very strong visual imagination, and I respect his work. A lot of it is the luck of the draw for a director too, but he's gotten some scripts that

have allowed him to be able to do that kind of odd, unusual thing. If you can't do it on *Star Trek*, where can you do it?"

Episode #132
"True Q"
Original Airdate: 10/26/92
Written by Rene Echevarria
Directed by Robert Scheerer
Guest Starring: John DeLancie (Q), Olivia d'Abo (Amanda), John P. Connolly (Lote)

An Enterprise intern named Amanda (*Conan the Destroyer*'s Olivia d'Abo) is revealed as a member of the Q continuum. Q (John DeLancie) himself pays another unwanted visit onboard, where he confides to Picard that Amanda's parents were actually Q. Amanda must choose between joining him among the Q — or death!

• • • •

Bought as a premise from Matt Corey, a North Carolina high school student, Rene Echevarria immediately latched onto the storyline when he found an intern reading the spec script submission. "I thought it was charming when she told me the nugget that a young kid finds out he's a Q. I told Jeri and she thought it was a great idea and immediately bought the premise."

After taking an unintentional hiatus for a season and leaving viewers wondering, "Where's Q?", the omnipotent super being was back with a vengeance in three *Star Trek* stories over the course of that television season, terrorizing the crew of the Enterprise twice as well as paying a visit to the new residents of Deep Space Nine.

John DeLancie, who portrays the miser of mirth and malevolence, admits he shared fan concerns when he failed to wreak havoc fifth season.

"After four years of some sort of continuity, I heard there was a script," says DeLancie. "I talked to Jonathan Frakes one day when I was at the studio, and he said, 'You're going to be the third show from January' and gave me a strong indication I was going to be working. When it didn't happen, I thought it was odd, but in our business what we think should happen and shouldn't happen is of very little consequence to what the people who are really running the show think."

In fact, the people running the show very much wanted to have Q back fifth season, but they were having their own problems trying to lick two difficult script premises — "Q-Olympics" and "Q Makes Two" — neither of which made it to the screen sixth season.

In "Q Makes Two," a story that made the rounds of the writing staff for nearly a year, Q creates a duplicate of the Enterprise and the crew. "What made it so difficult was we doubled the entire crew and I thought the whole concept was flawed," says Brannon Braga. "The way I thought it should have gone was Q doubled them and there was one uniform characteristic that's different about all of the crewmembers; they're all evil, greedy or something. That seems simplistic, but I think it could have worked dramatically in a one hour episode. What we tried to do was give each character several psychological characteristics that were different and none of them were the same. So suddenly you have to delineate twelve characters, none of whom are the original. It was so impossibly complicated that we had to write a little chart on the board while we were breaking to keep it clear visually for us who was who. My suggestion as a joke was we should do a 7-11 tie-in where the audience could go to 7-11 and buy a little chart to keep clear who was who in the episode.

"There was a sense of doom from the moment we started, 'Q Makes Two,'" Braga continues. "I think we broke it three times. Rene wrote two drafts and it was ultimately abandoned. It's an interesting notion that Q comes onboard and Picard's saying people are inherently good and we have managed to get rid of our darker elements in the 24th century and we're better people. Q says, 'So you don't think you have dark components and you think you're better without them, well I'm going to show you a thing or two,' and so he extracts the darker components and puts them into doubles. The clean, good components suffer and so do the darker components and neither functions without the other. We see that dramatically, but for some reason we made it more complex than it needed to be. It's a show that could still work. The image in my mind that we

never really got to was the two Enterprises shooting at each other, that's what you want to see."

"'Q Makes Two' was a debacle and it plunged us into a nightmare of having to get 'Man of the People' ready," notes Jeri Taylor. "When we started in on another Q episode, I was a little apprehensive, to say the least. I thought, why are we going back into this so quickly? But this was a delightful premise which came our way from a young man who wrote a spec script and had had notions of playing the part of the young person himself, but we made it a female and ruined that for him. It was definitely a high concept, wonderful idea. This was, in contrast to the other Q episode; it was one that I knew would work. It just felt right."

Although the premise bears some resemblance to season one's "Hide & Q," in which Riker is offered the power of the Q and ordered by Picard not to use it, writer Rene Echevarria didn't overly concern himself with the similarities. "The premise was similar, but a lot of first season stuff we try not to feel bound by because a lot of it wasn't well executed and this was just a much better story," says the story editor. "Her reaction to it was more believable and it was a deliberate choice not to raise the question of Riker's situation since some of those choices and things he went through were so strange that it was better to just hope a lot of people didn't see it."

Ironically, Q's most malevolent moments in "True Q," in which he threatens to terminate the girl, came about during the actual filming of the episode. Up until that point, the subplot hadn't even existed.

"It gave it a sense of momentum and import," says Echevarria. "Michael came up with the idea that Q had been sent to kill her very late in the process, it was too late to do a major rewrite. Most of Act Four had been filmed, which had to do with her being in love with Riker. Several key scenes had been filmed and could not be changed. That shouldn't happen but in this case it did. It was pretty heinous of him to be willing to kill this girl, but I think in a strange way it worked very nicely to have the audience have that knowledge and in the mean-

time they're seeing a very light, romantic story and are saying, 'Doesn't she realize what's at stake here?' That worked in a strange way very well. I doubt we would have written it that way. Michael found a way, very cleanly, in Act Three where Q is walking down the corridor and a Q shadow appears to give Act Four a much more sinister undertone. If we had more time, Act Four probably would have been very different. We probably wouldn't have done the Riker romance stuff. There would have been other beats we would have played."

Says John DeLancie, "After the one in which I lose my powers, 'Deja Q,' I had said to them, 'This is as far as we should go in this area for a while. Let's make the next one have a little bit of bite to it.' Then came the Robin Hood one and I tried quite a bit actually to bend the words and the story to make it as malevolent as possible, but it had quite a bit of a fantasy quality to it. It really didn't lend itself to that 'mad, bad and dangerous to know' quality, but I tried to make it that. When I came back to do 'True Q' and it was kind of Q babysits, I tried to put malevolence in places there, but that didn't really lend itself again. The thing is that I remember having said somewhere along the line, 'Kill her.' They all said 'My god, no, no, no' and I said, 'Why not?' And they said, 'John, you're just being Q-like' and I said 'Well, yeah, you got it. Come in and kill her, assassin.' It's a hardball nature that I would like to try and find again, but I can't do it within the context of birthday parties and babysitting and stuff like that. It's something you need to have the set-up for. I would have liked to have taken it one step further where she *was* killed."

Episode #133
"Rascals"
Original Airdate: 11/2/92
Teleplay by Allison Hock
Story by Ward Botsford & Diana Dru Botsford and Michael Piller
Directed by Adam Nimoy
Guest Starring: Whoopi Goldberg (Guinan), Brian Bonsall (Alexander), David Tristan Birkin (Young Picard), Isis Jones (Young Guinan), Caroline Junko King (Young Keiko), Mike Gomez (Lurin), Tracey Walter (Berik), Michael

Snyder (Morta), Colm Meaney (O'Brien), Michelle Forbes (Ensign Ro), Megan Parlen (Young Ro), Morgan Nagler (Kid #1), Hana Hatae (Molly), Rosalind Chao (Keiko), Majel Barrett (Computer Voice)

Picard, Guinan (Whoopi Goldberg), Ensign Ro (Michelle Forbes) and Keiko (Rosalind Chao) are transformed into children during a shuttle accident, but nonetheless prove vital in saving the Enterprise from Ferengi mercenaries who attempt to take over the starship.

• • • •

"It was not my favorite assignment and it was a difficult show to write," admits Ron Moore. "I felt that this time I hadn't dodged the bullet fast enough and once I got stuck with it, I put aside my feelings about it and tried to do the best that I could. I made a real attempt to find things within it that would work and to dig a little deeper to find some character moments that I thought would play."

A day that Naren Shankar doesn't remember fondly is when he needed to bring all his scientific and technical knowledge to bear in an attempt to explain one of the show's silliest script premises. "'Rascals' was not a happy day," he says. "Do we have to talk about this?"

Ron Moore, who did the final production rewrite on the show, was put in the unenviable position of having to explain what had created their condition. Being a self-described "liberal arts moron," Moore consulted with Shankar and later the discussions made their way into staff meetings. "We were talking about the show and we started talking about whether there could be this sequence in the genes that shows how big they were when they were kids. I said, 'You know what you're doing, this the old antogeny recapitulates philogeny argument.' There was dead silence and I said, 'Am I the only person here who knows what this means?'"

Explains Shankar, "There's that ancient discredited biological theory that the fetus goes through a development that is parallel to the evolution of development, starting out as a fish and finally becoming a human, going through the whole evolutionary cycle, which is silly. The idea was that we

were saying there was a little homonucleus inside your body that shows how you are at each stage of your life. I was saying we can't be doing this. The problem was that it was virtually impossible to come up with a sensible explanation and so we kind of did a lot of hand waving on this episode."

When asked about the *deus ex machina* in which the crew is returned to normal thanks to their pattern being stored in the transporter's pattern buffers, Shankar replies, "Let's not even talk about it. Let's just forget that ever happened. For Adam, that was a helluva way to make a directorial debut. Directing kids is not easy under any circumstances. I think the boy who played Picard was tough because the biggest problem was the voices were not right and it was difficult to see. It's so hard to cast kids. The young Ro was phenomenal. She was the one person in that cast I thought was terrific. In a lot of ways she reminded me of Christina Ricci [*Addams Family*]. This girl who played the young Ro showed a lot of poise and gravity and she was the one I most believed was the person she was supposed to be. The girl who played Whoopi had played her as a young girl in *Sister Act*."

Episode #134
"A Fistful of Datas"
Original Airdate: 11/9/92
Teleplay by Robert Hewitt Wolfe and Brannon Braga
Story by Robert Hewitt Wolfe
Directed by Patrick Stewart
Guest Starring:
Brian Bonsall (Alexander), John Pyper-Ferguson (Eli Hollander), Joy Garrett (Annie), Jorge Cervera (Bandito), Majel Barrett (Computer Voice)

When the holodeck malfunctions, Worf, Alexander and Troi find themselves facing off against the specter of many gunmen as duplicates of Data take over the computer-generated town, turning what was supposed to be a simple fantasy programmed by Alexander into a most dangerous game indeed. In order to rescue Alexander from Eli, one of Data's evil gunmen, Worf must face him in a shoot-out in the town square.

• • • •

"I've seen very few westerns —

The Searchers, One Eyed Jacks, Unforgiven," says Brannon Braga. "It was ironic that I was handed this, not being familiar with the western genre, and Patrick Stewart, who was even less familiar, was going to direct it. It brought a freshness to it and I think this show was more fun to write than any other. I really enjoyed doing it. The first draft, which was written by Robert Wolfe, didn't have a solid western story and it needed one, so I watched *Rio Bravo* and that's the story I decided to kind of utilize for the holodeck fantasy. They're obviously different. I became a lover of the western genre and watched dozens of them and my favorite was *The Outlaw Josie Wales* and *The Searchers*. What great movies. I must have watched twenty-five westerns and those three were superior."

In the original Wolfe story, Alexander's plan was to bring Troi and Worf together romantically. The subplot was quickly deleted. "It was an intriguing notion," says Jeri Taylor. "It just seemed less interesting than other things that were going on. It seemed like more of a soap opera sort of thing. That's the kind of story that you can see on the air anywhere. Every sitcom has children with separated, divorced parents, and all that kind of thing. It's not an element on *Star Trek* I want to concentrate on. I think we probably just mined out all the stories about Alexander and Worf's problems as a daddy. It was beginning to feel very much like contemporary family drama, and we really made an effort to break Worf out of that and give him back his Klingon-hood, rather than to make him a suburban, single father, which is how a lot of that was feeling."

"I cut the Troi and Alexander story right away because it felt false to me," adds Brannon Braga. "This was a holodeck romp and it should be light and fun. Then I pumped up the Data acting bizarre angle a little bit. It was a lot of fun and satisfying to come up with a good gag for the end. What was going to be special about this gunfight? What was going to make it *Star Trek*? Suddenly, that's where it needed to be *Star Trek* again, when you have Worf defeating the holodeck villain in a special *Star Trek* way. I thought the force field was fun as were the characters' reactions to it. The

• • • •

264

one thing I miss was that in my draft there was a Data as a bandito scene with an Alexander scene that was inspired by 'Ransom of Red Chief', where basically you have the bandito holding Alexander hostage in the cave."

"It was originally called 'Western Story' on my contracts," says writer Robert Hewitt Wolfe. "Then it was called 'The Good, The Bad and The Klingon,' which was its title for a while. At the very last minute I thought of 'A Fistful of Datas.'"

"I had the chance to play five or six characters in a show and Patrick directed, which made it additionally fun," enthuses Brent Spiner. "It's certainly the most fun episode I've ever had to do and I would have liked to have done a show called 'For a Few Datas More.'"

"We hadn't done a holodeck malfunctioning story in three seasons, which is a perfectly good track record," says Naren Shankar. "It was a lighthearted show and it was a nice show. People love 'Shore Leave' and this show reminds me of that in a way. I think it's hilarious that Brannon, who doesn't know anything about westerns, wrote it and Patrick, an Englishman, directed it."

Patrick Stewart recalls the episode fondly. "There is nothing I have done in my career anywhere that could match the amazing thrill of directing a western," he smiles. "There had been rumors around the production offices for some months that there was a western episode coming up, and, of course, every director was eager to get a hold of it because everyone feels they have at least one western in them. I was actually supposed to direct another episode when things were switched and the western landed in my lap. I think there was a lot of gnashing teeth from some of my colleagues and the other directors, but it provided me with a fabulous opportunity to have an enormous amount of fun entering into the western.

"If I were to isolate the five or six best days of my thirty-year career to date, I think the one day, working from long before sunrise until after the sun had set, was at the Warner Brothers western town in the Valley," Stewart continues. "That was one of the most exciting days of my life. I had three cam-

eras rolling almost all the time there, including an action slow-motion camera. I had the biggest crane that you could get in Hollywood. I had some wonderful toys to play with and it was an absolutely fantastic day. It was also one of the hottest days of the year, too, so it was truly a sunbaked western scene. I shall never forget it."

Of a location scouting jaunt to Universal Studios, production designer Richard James recalls, "Patrick and I were standing there together talking about the episode when one of their trams came by. I was laughing because Patrick had his back to the tram but the tour guide was pointing out something and all these people recognized Patrick and started taking pictures. I said to him that he had been recognized and he said, 'You know, Richard, 20 years ago I was one of those people on the tram.'"

"It's scary isn't it?" muses David Livingston of Englishman Stewart directing the western. "What does he know about westerns? He has Robin Hood and stuff like that. Patrick did a wonderful job. He had a great time. He was Sergio Leone out there or Clint Eastwood, and Brent chewed every piece of scenery in sight and there wasn't any left by the time he got done. I think he played more characters in that than he ever played because he was everywhere. We shot that at Warner Bros. Burbank Studios out in the valley. It was great high-concept."

"A couple of times I had to really scream at Brannon to put some gags into it, but they worked out pretty well," says Naren Shankar of the teleplay. "It was a fun script. I was a little surprised that it didn't get as positive a reaction as I would have expected. I loved it, I thought it was a very good show. I think it has one of the single greatest end shots I've ever seen on our show [the Enterprise flying into the sunset]. That's great. Some people get possessive of the show and it sometimes interferes with their enjoyment, I think, when they think it's too light for *Star Trek*. You've got to be able to take a step back and just enjoy it. It's a western fantasy in a holodeck with a kid and there are some genuinely great moments. When he goes in there the first time and the outlaw says, 'What are you going to do, arrest me?' and Worf

Data (Brent Spiner) got to play Clint Eastwood in "A Fistful of Datas" (photo copyright ©1995 Albert Ortega).

knocks him out, Alexander says it's too easy and then Worf gets into the bar fight — that's inspired writing."

Episode #135
"The Quality of Life"
Original Airdate: 11/16/92
Written by Naren Shankar
Directed by Jonathan Frakes
Guest Starring: Ellen Bry (Dr. Farallon), David Windsor (Transporter Chief Kelso), Majel Barrett (Computer Voice)

A scientist, Dr. Farallon (Ellen Bry), who has created a revolutionary method for mining using a solar particle fountain, has invented an even more miraculous tool: the exocomp, whose computerized brain allows it to learn. This leads Data to the conclusion that the mechanical devices are a life form, thus pitting him against Riker who wants to sacrifice the automatons to save Picard and Geordi.

• • • •

"They were originally supposed to be called metacomps which I liked better," says Naren Shankar of what actor/director Jonathan Frakes calls 'the little piggies.' "The idea was it stood for metamorphic computer, which is what they were, but apparently metacomp is a company somewhere so our legal department said we should change it. The problem was coming up with a lifeform that was sufficiently alien so that people wouldn't automatically think that they were alive, but where Data's unique insight into the machine — because he's a machine himself — would give him the edge that he needed to make the realizations he needed to make."

The episode presented many pitfalls for Shankar. "To be quite honest, I personally feel I pulled it off," he says. "The main problem was a story problem. You get to a certain point where you have to step back and say — by the logic of the arguments — is practically anything going to be considered a lifeform? That's where the real pitfall of this episode was. Some of the arguments Data is making just aren't that strong. You can apply very similar ideas to bacteria or unicellular life forms of various kinds. According to his argument, these must be an intelligent life form too, but are they? I don't think so. Who's to say where you draw the line? It's almost like I found myself coming down on a right-to-life argument in certain ways —- and I definitely didn't want to find myself there. It's always good as an exercise to argue the opposite point of something. I'm very strongly pro-choice and writing a show like this is in some ways difficult because I didn't necessarily agree with it all the time, but you still have to make a strong case for it. I think in a lot of ways that was accomplished and in other ways it was not."

Says director Frakes, "The only problem I had with 'Quality of Life' is that it was short and they added the poker scene at the beginning. I was amazed that they refused to resolve it at the end. We should have seen the result of the bet the characters made. Either Gates should have been a brunette or we should have been sitting in the chair about to be shaved. I don't know why they would lay it out as a red herring and not have it pay off in some way — as if no one was watching the show."

After fifth season's complicated time-loop installment, "Cause & Effect," "Quality of Life" was less of a challenge for the director who had grappled with shooting several of the same scenes dif-

ferently for his last assignment. "It was a little heavy on technobabble, but all things considered I think that show came out quite well," says Frakes. "A lot of the credit goes to Brent as usual and LeVar and our guest star, Ellen Bry, who was up to it. Unlike most of the actresses I read, she seemed to be able to handle the language which in other actresses' mouths sounded dull. She somehow had passion about it and was able to deliver the lines with the same kind of alacrity as Brent and LeVar did on a daily basis."

The one concern that everyone had in shooting the episode was making the exocomps credible. As flying mechanical computer tools, the exocomps needed to appear functional and also sympathetic as a life form when Data contends that the automatons are sentient.

"We had a lot of discussions about that," says David Livingston. "The question was how to personify them. How to give it some character to make it so you identify and sympathize with it. We went through a lot of designs. Rick Sternbach went through a lot of concepts until we finally all said, 'Yeah, this thing has some character to it.' Then the question was how to avoid spending eight million dollars on the opticals. We ended up doing some of it on the set by lifting them up and down on a pole and doing a little screen work. I think it was quite successful in that regard. Peter Lauritson wanted to do a shot of it going down the tunnel because he thought that it was really important and I put the kibosh on it. I said, 'No, we can't afford it.' Well, Peter found the money and did the shot and he was right. It paid off. It was really fun to see it zipping down the tunnel."

Episode #136
"Chain of Command, Part I"
Original Airdate: 12/14/92
Teleplay by Ron Moore
Story by Frank Abatemarco
Directed by Robert Scheerer
Guest Starring: David Warner (Gul Madred), Ronny Cox (Captain Jellico), Natalija Nogulich (Admiral Nechayev), John Durbin (Gul Lemec), Lou Wagner (Solok)

When hostilities flare with the Cardassians, Picard is reassigned on a

secret mission with Worf and Dr. Crusher to investigate reports the Cardassians are developing a metagenic weapon on Celtris III. Meanwhile, Captain Edward Jellico (Ronny Cox) of the USS Cairo is assigned to the Enterprise as its new captain, where he makes many enemies — including Commander Riker.

••••

Originally intended to be a single episode, Michael Piller made the suggestion that the show be split into two for a number of reasons. Ironically, the foremost consideration behind the decision was financial and not dramatic — although it manifested itself as one of the most astute decisions of the year, jump-starting the floundering sixth season.

"We needed to save money," says Jeri Taylor. "We were in budget trouble and Michael said, 'You know, I think what we could do is make this a two-parter. Have Picard captured and then make it an episode about his relationship with his torturer that takes place in one room. It's a fascinating two-person play and we'll get another episode out of it that way and we'll save a lot of money that will bring us even with the budget.

"The fundamental pitch the gang came in with was you have Picard on a mission and a new captain comes in and how does the crew react to the new captain," notes Michael Piller of the original premise. "Jeri's idea was to cast Ronny Cox and I thought that worked out very well. They wanted to put Picard in a real rugged adventure story and they talked about this mission and he gets caught by the Cardassians and we rescue him and that's about it. I said this is a really good idea, but I was also looking to save money and I realized this might serve two masters. I knew if we divided it into two parts and made the first part the mission and then Picard gets caught, instead of resolving that in an hour, you put Patrick Stewart in a room with another great actor and you do the torture show. You call up Amnesty International and you get their cooperation, which is very important to Patrick, and you build a relationship between two men; one who is trying to beat the other and the other who is trying to survive."

"Chain of Command's" evolution from what would have been a simple action/adventure show into one of the most significant shows of the season, is a dramatic example of how the perpetual money woes on the show don't necessarily impact on it adversely and can often serve as a source of creative inspiration.

"I think that money and creativity have never really gone hand in hand when it comes to *Star Trek*," opines Rick Berman. "Episodes like 'Measure of A Man' was one of our cheapest episodes and one of our best, but an episode like 'Yesterday's Enterprise' was quite expensive and it was wonderful. 'Chain of Command' was a very inexpensive episode and one of the greats."

Adds Michael Piller, "Ultimately, the victory for Picard is just surviving. We made the decision early on that we couldn't say that Captain Picard was such a great man that he would not break under torture, because that would be doing a great disservice to everybody in the human rights struggle who has broken. Nobody can resist torture. Anybody who wants to get you to speak will get you to talk if they're willing to do the hideous things necessary. There had to be a different kind of victory. I can't imagine a better show than 'Chain of Command, Part II' and it had no tricks or whiz bang stuff and it was one of the least expensive shows of the season. David Warner [as the torturer] was sensational and Patrick Stewart was even better. I don't think there's been a better show in the history of this series, and certainly there was not a better hour of television on that year."

Originally, "Chain of Command" had been considered as the first *Deep Space Nine* crossover, an idea that was vetoed by Rick Berman. "We were going to go to DS9 and that's how we were going to get to this planet in the show," recalls Rene Echevarria. "The Enterprise was going to come to DS9 and get a ship. The scene with the Ferengi was written for Quark and I don't think Ron changed a word except the guy's name. We were going to borrow one of their Runabouts which Jellico was going to ask for, but it just didn't work out. Rick wanted to wait a little longer before doing a crossover. Actually, it was less expensive, because if you go to Deep Space Nine you have to use at least one of their regulars."

Ironically, the scene in which Picard, Worf and Dr. Crusher obtain passage to Celtris III was shot on the *Deep Space Nine* soundstages by doing a small redress on one of the corners of the Promenade. "It was difficult to shoot," says David Livingston, "because if you moved the camera around too much you'd see Quark's bar."

"Chain Of Command, Part I" boasted some of the series' most ambitious stage effects during the sixth season, when Picard, Worf and Dr. Crusher infiltrate a Cardassian outpost by making their way through a maze of caves on the alien planet. Livingston reluctantly gave in to the requests of director Robert Scheerer to keep a scene of the three scaling a large rock face.

"Bob is so prepared and together that he makes it seem effortless," says Livingston. "He pleaded to do the repelling down scene and I kept fighting it because I thought it was too much money. He brought me over to the stage with Richard James, and Merri Howard and I stood there and he explained what he wanted to do. We allowed him to do it, and I'm really glad we did. It paid off. It's exciting stuff, and it's all shot on the sound stage. We built just enough to surround the actors. There was literally a foot above their heads and not much on the sides and the rest was a matte painting."

Explains Richard James of the winding caverns on the Cardassian planet, Celtris Three, "We had to create a maze so that they could reuse corridors over and over and you didn't realize, so you shoot it from one direction and shoot it from another direction to make it look like they have much more set than they really do."

Episode #137
"Chain of Command, Part II"
Original Airdate: 12/21/92
Written by Frank Abatemarco
Directed by Les Landau
Guest Starring: Ronny Cox (Captain Jellico), John Durbin (Gul Lemec), David Warner (Gul Madred), Heather Lauren Olson (Jil Orra)

Picard is brutally tortured by a Cardassian inquisitor, Gul Madred (David Warner), who seeks to obtain the

In "Chain of Command, Part II", Captain Picard (Patrick Stewart) is tortured at the hands of Gul Madred (photo copyright ©1995 Albert Ortega).

Federation's defense strategy against a Cardassian takeover of a disputed quadrant. On the Enterprise, Captain Jellico (Ronny Cox) attempts to stop the invasion by using Riker to mine the hulls of Cardassian warships.

• • • •

A film that proved an important reference point for the episode was *Closet Land*, the little-seen eighty-seven-minute drama with Alan Rickman as a seductively low-key, but gleeful torturer and Madeline Stowe, a writer of children's books which are believed to be subversive, as his political prisoner. The film was written and directed by Radha Bharadwaj and features scenes of psychological and physical abuse, including a moment when Rickman electrocutes Stowe by attaching wires to her genitals. The film is set in an unnamed country and boasts elaborate production and costume design by *Dracula*'s Oscar Award winning costume designer, Eiko Ishioka, in which the interrogation area is a large room dotted by ornate columns.

An even greater influence on "Chain of Command" was *Star Trek* itself. It's genesis is in a story Ro Laren related to Picard in "Ensign Ro," where she revealed that her father was tortured in front of her eyes and killed by Cardassians during the occupation of Bajor. Ron Moore was assigned "Part One," having an instant affinity for the Jellico storyline, while former supervising producer Frank Abatemarco took on "Part Two."

Abatemarco, who had yet to prove he could write *Star Trek*, had his job riding on his teleplay for "Chain of Command" and he received copious notes from Jeri Taylor. Reportedly, Abatemarco was excited about the chance to delve into such a thorny subject and did intensive research, consulting Amnesty International about the torture of political prisoners.

"The show was a wonderful exploration of psychological torture," says Brannon Braga. "Frank did a lot of research. A little research goes a long way. He may have done a little too much and his research was showing. There just comes a point where you have to step in as a writer and use your instincts as a person and a writer to bring to life these situations and step away from the research a little bit. I think that's why the first draft suffered. Obviously, Jeri came in and gave it the psychological depth and punch it needed."

Despite the fact that Taylor did a page one rewrite on the teleplay, she does not receive a screen credit on the show, which has upset many of the staff members and happens all too frequently on television. Says Taylor of the initial Abatemarco draft, "I have been a member of Amnesty International for a number of years and have been supportive of their causes. Frank did tons of research. He worked with a group that are surviving torture victims. He talked with a psychiatrist who specializes in treating torture victims and did reams of reading. He did absolutely the most wonderfully exhaustive kind of research. So I was very comfortable that we were getting the best possible tack on it. Patrick called me after reading the first draft to say he was delighted to know that we were doing this and told me of his involvement with Amnesty International. I said, 'Great. I have to tell you that it's going to be rather substantially rewritten.' Patrick got very concerned because he assumed that meant we were going to back off

from the very strong nature of it. He said, 'I don't want that to happen. I think that this hits it head on. I want to do that. I don't want this to become another talky episode where we simply talk about and around something and don't really tell it the way it is.'"

Stewart's concerns, however were shared by Taylor who just didn't feel the script was working yet. "I said, 'Patrick, please trust me. We won't do that, but I think that we can get more out of the script.' And he was very uncertain and disconcerted. He said, 'Well, I'll wait until I see the rewrite, but....' and then he got the rewrite and called back. He was thrilled because we didn't back off an inch. It was very strong stuff."

Stewart turned in a tour de force performance. In the episode, Picard finds himself unable to prevent being mentally and physically assaulted and, in one scene — during which the set was closed to almost everyone but absolutely essential crewmembers — stripped and cuffed to a rack.

"It's a very gutsy and nude performance," says Brannon Braga of Stewart's acting, which provoked some protest among viewers. Says Jeri Taylor, "They didn't want to see Patrick Stewart or anybody else writhing in pain. They felt that it was excessive, that it went too far and that it was disturbing to children. I can't disagree. It's certainly very intense for children. I wish there had been a disclaimer."

Unfortunately, in the money crunch, the resolution of the Cardassian space opera suffered with most of the action transpiring on the Enterprise's main viewing screen. Comments Ron Moore of the conclusion in which Jellico mines the Cardassians ship, "We just couldn't afford the big opticals of having the Enterprise facing off against the fleet in the Nebula. By that point in the season, we had done a lot of expensive things. That show had to save us some cash. It had to be the money saving episode."

In "Part II," Richard James needed to create an interrogation chamber for David Warner's Gul Madred, but he avoided seeing *Closet Land*. "I wasn't familiar with it and I didn't want to be influenced by that because I was fighting

Silence of the Lambs at that time as well," says James. "I really wanted to try and keep myself open to my own kind of vision of it and as it turned out, the lighting played a very important role in what I was planning to do with it and the starkness of it. I wanted it to feel big as opposed to feeling like they were stuck in a small dungeon-type thing."

Episode #138
"Ship in a Bottle"
Original Airdate: 1/25/93
Written by Rene Echevarria
Directed by Alexander Singer
Guest Starring: Daniel Davis (Moriarty), Dwight Schultz (Barclay), Clement Von Franckenstein (Gentleman), Stephanie Beacham (Countess), Majel Barrett (Computer Voice)

Sherlock Holmes' arch-nemesis, Moriarty, created in second season's "Elementary, Dear Data," is accidentally released from computer stasis while Barclay is performing a holodeck diagnostic. The super-genius threatens to destroy the ship unless Picard finds a way for him and his computer-generated lover, the Countess Regina Bartholomew (*seaQuest*'s former chief medical officer, Stephanie Beacham), to leave the holodeck. In the episode's coda, Picard muses over the possibility of their reality merely being an elaborate simulation running inside yet another device.

••••

"I pitched a story after I sold 'The Offspring' about Riker and Picard going on a mission, and Riker beams him into the holodeck from Starbase and it appears as though Riker is taking over the ship and leading it into enemy territory," says Rene Echevarria. "In fact, what he's doing is setting up a scenario where Picard will be protected. It was a plan to discredit some bad guy and Michael remembered it and said he loved the holodeck gag. When we were all at Jeri's house one Sunday having a story session, somebody mentioned we could do Moriarty again. I told everybody there was a story Michael liked that we could use. In the first draft, we figured out a way to help him escape the holodeck by walking in a transporter beam and it breaks up and he dies — but during the break we came up with the notion of giving him what he wants and never letting him know he's been fooled. It was very sweet, having this 18th century genius thinking he'd outsmarted us and just smugly going on."

"I had a peculiar affinity for the theme since I have worked on the holodeck of the 20th century, virtual reality," says director Alexander Singer. "I worked for MCA/Universal in developing it as a technology and I'm still involved. The most difficult aspect of the show was the casting, because the lady put a strange romantic hue on the whole piece. Her casting was the most difficult because we needed someone who could pull off an English accent and had a regal appearance, but who was also very sexy in Victorian clothes. When I saw Stephanie I said that's it, end of story.

Notes Brannon Braga, "My favorite kind of show, a twisty turny complex mystery. In this case I thought it worked pretty well and certainly the pairing of Moriarty and Barclay was inspired. This was such a good show, you had to do it. It's a great title. I tried to kick things off with 'Realm of Fear', which sounds like an old series. One of my favorites."

Jeri Taylor notes that everyone was surprised that this episode ever made it to film, given the legal hassles Paramount had been faced with whenever Data would portray Sherlock Holmes in the holodeck.

"For years we'd been told, you can't do it," she says. "Paramount said no after *Young Sherlock Holmes* had gotten them into a fight with the Conan Doyle estate. We said, 'Oh, okay. Never again. Too bad, that was a great thing.' I opened this inquiry again, though, and we set something in motion that was the beginning when I called our legal person and she called back and said, 'Oh, that's very easy. It's X number of dollars,' which wasn't very much, 'and you can have Moriarty.' I said, 'You're kidding me.' And she said, 'They've done this for someone else here and they're very happy.' Everyone was astonished and Brent was thrilled and amazed, because he'd been told he could never play Holmes again."

Episode #139
"Aquiel"
Original Airdate: 1/23/93
Written by Brannon Braga & Ron Moore
Story by Jeri Taylor
Directed by Cliff Bole
Guest Starring: Renee Jones (Aquiel), Wayne Grace (Governor Torak), Reg E. Cathey (Morag), Majel Barrett (Computer Voice)

Geordi falls for a presumably murdered woman while studying her journals and deducing that the Klingons were involved in her death. But then the woman turns up alive, becoming the prime suspect in another gruesome killing aboard a subspace relay station.

• • • •

"We were looking for a new spin to put on a love story," says Jeri Taylor of the storyline inspired by Otto Preminger's *Laura* at the suggestion of Michael Piller. "A straight love story didn't seem good enough. Geordi falling in love with someone he thought was dead gave it just a nicer kind of feel. Of course, she seemed like an unobtainable person or non-real, which we had seen before with his character, but it quickly turned around. The thing we all wanted to happen was to keep it open for a continuation of the relationship, since we would like to have one of our characters have an ongoing and committed relationship. After we lost the O'Briens, everybody in the 24th century is single and I think it might be nice to suggest enduring relationships are not going to be gone in the future."

"'Aquiel' was a torturous experience," recalls Brannon Braga. "We wrote it together which was fun, but Piller wasn't happy with the way it was going and he had some good story instincts. I thought it was going to be terrible, but when I sat down and watched it I kind of liked the mystery. I rather enjoyed that the dog did it. Ultimately, I didn't think the romance part worked but I liked the feel of the episode, which had a rather tragic, mysterious feel to it. Ultimately disappointing because the romance didn't work. 'Aquiel' was a very fun and compelling process to break in the structure session. It was Jeri, Ron and I spending two days doing it. What we started out with and ended up with at

Geordi LaForge (LeVar Burton) falls in love with a woman who was presumed murdered in "Aquiel" (photo copyright ©1995 Albert Ortega).

the end of the break session was such a rich and interesting show. As a writer, sometimes because you're privy to all the development, you appreciate the show more. You appreciate the process. Whereas a viewer just has the show. It's interesting how the perceptions can be so different. I think the romantic relationship suffered. I never felt any chemistry between the two of them, something wasn't happening, maybe it was the writing. It's always a little contrived to get the actors together like this. All in all, I was more satisfied with the mystery and less satisfied with the romance. The Klingon story is the red herring and that's fun. The subspace relay station looked very cool. It was not classic *Trek*, and a lot of people hated it."

"I thought it was a nice little runner," says Ron Moore of the subplot in which some disagreeable Klingons are accused of the murder at the Federation subspace relay station. "I didn't want to make that any bigger than it was. But in the final product, it was one of the more intriguing things. I never thought it would be, but it was just a cool little C story. Brannon and I wanted to name the show 'Murder, My Pet', but cooler heads prevailed. In our first draft we really tried

• • • •

to get inside Geordi's head and give him all kinds of backstory and family history, but it was so loaded down with it that it didn't work. We had to go back and say, 'What's that love story again?' It's just when you combine a murder mystery with a love story, you cheat it to some extent."

Episode #140
"Face of the Enemy"
Original Airdate: 2/8/93
Written by Naren Shankar
Story by Rene Echevarria
Directed by Gabrielle Beaumont
Guest Starring: Scott MacDonald (N'Vek), Carolyn Seymour (Toreth), Barry Lynch (DeSeve), Robertson Dean (Pilot), Dennis Cockrum (Alien Captain), Pamela Winslow (Ensign McKnight), Majel Barrett (Computer Voice)

Counselor Troi awakens aboard a Romulan warbird and finds she has been transformed into a Romulan officer, Major Rakal, a member of the feared Tal Shiar. She learns she is on a secret mission to assist in the defection of several important Romulan dignitaries to the Federation, bringing her into conflict with the captain of the Romulan ship, Toreth (Carolyn Seymour) — and the Enterprise.

• • • •

Naren Shankar's second writing assignment for the show was "Face of the Enemy," in which Troi finds herself playing 007 aboard a Romulan warbird. "I wrote the first draft of the script in six days because we were really under a time crunch. I was assigned it as a freelancer and halfway through I was brought on staff. The rewrite helped smooth out a lot of things and we had to change the ending a couple of times. The action in Act Five didn't work initially. It was harrowing but it came out well. I think Marina Sirtis is a fine actress and when given the roles and characters to play, she does a terrific job and I was very happy with what she did. I would have been more than delighted to write other stuff for her. I go out of my way to look for stuff for Troi to do because I feel the character is underused."

Enthuses Ron Moore, "Troi kicks some serious butt, which was nice."

"The show worked out very well," muses Michael Piller. "There was trouble in getting The Enemy Below dynamic going at the end of the show and it suddenly just sort of fizzled out, but I thought it was a very successful episode. Marina is one of the great talents and nobody really knew it when this whole thing started. The more we give her to do, the more she seems capable of doing. You do 'Man of the People' where one scene she's a sexpot and the next scene she's a crazy killer. In this show, she's fundamentally forced into being a secret agent. She has an extraordinary range."

Co-executive producer Jeri Taylor's desire to make Star Trek's sixth season the "year of the woman" was reflected as well in "Face of the Enemy."

"I thought it was a great role for Marina," says Taylor. "I thought it was well written for her. I loved Carolyn Seymour as the Romulan Commander, she was outstanding in it. When those two women tee off against each other, it's great because we don't have that much conflict among our people, but between those two it's just spit and vinegar and they were dynamic. I enjoyed seeing those two powerful women get a chance to sort of rise to the occasion and take off on each other."

"Carolyn was great," agrees Sirtis. "We became firm friends. I've seen that episode twice and I wasn't completely happy with my performance in it, But she was a great Romulan commander."

Naren Shankar remembers, "We were sitting around talking about this show and about who this important person would be that's defecting and Michael got this look on his face and said, 'We probably can't do this, but what if the person is Spock? They're getting out and at the end they open it up and it's not Spock. The person we take out is defrosted and we ask him what happened to Spock and he says, 'Spock didn't make it.' I look at Michael like he's crazy and he goes, 'Nah!'"

Shankar, a longtime Trek fan, even suggested casting Joanne Linville as the Romulan Commander as she starred in the original Trek's third season episode, "The Enterprise Incident." Lack of availability precluded this option. "The name Tal Shiar came from the episode

'Journey to Babel,'" says Shankar. "I'm embarrassing myself by showing my Trek roots, but in that episode one of the Tellurite ambassadors is killed by a Vulcan execution method called Tal Shiar and I corrupted that and made that the name of the Romulan secret service. We have talked about bringing back Commander Toreth. She had enough ambiguity to keep it interesting. There are moments when she comes off sympathetic, but doesn't really care that the spaceship was blown up, only that it wasn't her order to fire. She's more than happy to kill people."

Shankar reflects, "We talked a lot about whether the character of the Romulan commander would be a man or a woman. We finally decided on a woman, but we had also talked about there being a little bit of a feel of Hunt for Red October in the show. When I was writing it I just had this strong image of Sean Connery, so all the dialogue I wrote for the show was with Sean Connery's voice in my mind, and then I just changed the name. The interesting thing is there's a line 'The Federation is neither stupid nor foolish,' and I was going off like that. And then to see the same words — with not even a punctuation mark changed — played by a woman was a very interesting thing. It was the same exact words with a different delivery and a different attitude and it worked really well. It was the ultimate gender-blind writing."

Richard James was responsible for showing us the interior of the ship along with its quarters and command area. "We played off of Romulan having a motif represented by certain colors," he says. "We do that for identification so that certainly the Romulans would not have everything that would look just like Earth society. For us to graphically sell the idea of it being Romulan, we need to do it well with the sets, make-up and costumes which are Romulan colors. It helps to reinforce the idea that this is Romulan territory and it was not that much of a challenge because we played off of what's been established for Romulan ships."

In addition to the bridge, viewers saw for the first time a Romulan commissary, which couldn't be easily

• • • •

stocked. "We had rooms that we'd never been into before for the Romulans and we said what would the Romulan plates and silverware look like?" muses James. "You get into all of that — and even simple things like chairs, which you had to design. It's not as though you could go out to the rental store. All these factors come into play."

Not everyone was necessarily pleased with the final result, including "Face of the Enemy" scripter Naren Shankar who had a different idea for what the warbird interiors would look like.

"What we ended up with was Romulan Pizza Kitchen," says Shankar. "If you read my first draft, I was very specific about what the Romulan bridge should look like. I thought we were going to build an entirely new set. And the bridge I described was in an elongated room much like the nose of the Romulan ship. I wanted it to look alien and have the Commander standing at a rail in the back of the room. She always stands, there's no seat for her and the room ends with her back at the wall so there's no one behind her. The idea is they're so suspicious that the commander would never let anybody behind her. The entire cabin is forward of the command position and there's just one pilot and stations around that. To me that would have been cooler."

Episode #141
"Tapestry"
Original Airdate: 2/15/93
Written by Ronald D. Moore
Directed by Les Landau
Guest Starring: John DeLancie (Q), Ned Vaughn (Corey), J.C. Brandy (Marta), Clint Carmichael (Nausicaan #1), Rae Norman (Penny), Clive Church (Maurice Picard), Marcus Nash (Young Picard), Majel Barrett (Computer Voice)

It's not such a wonderful life for Picard when Q (John DeLancie) gives him a chance to relive his rambunctious youth. As Picard lies dying in sickbay from a wound sustained on an Away Team mission, he finds himself in heaven with Q, who gives him a chance to stop the fight which led to the captain being fitted with an artificial heart some years earlier.

• • • •

"I'm very proud of 'Tapestry',"

reflects writer Ron Moore. "I liked it a lot. I immediately fastened onto the idea of Picard going into the white light and having a near death experience and there's Q. The problem is then what do you do? It was also my first shot at doing a Q show and I pictured the line, 'You're dead and I'm God,' as the first thing that came to mind as we started doing the episode."

Moore's first draft departed from the final script in many important respects. Entitled "A Q Carol," Q led Picard through pivotal scenes in his life much the way the ghosts of "A Christmas Carol" took Scrooge to the past, present and future. The irony was not lost on Moore who was of course cognizant of Stewart's recent star-turn on Broadway as Scrooge in "A Christmas Carol."

Says Moore, "Q took Picard back to several points in his life. The 'Samaritan Snare' story was one where he is attacked and needs to get an artificial heart. There was a scene in France with him as a kid with his parents and I even considered doing the Stargazer and having Jack Crusher there."

The premise however was not only too expensive but failed to enthrall Michael Piller. "He thought it was pointless," recalls Moore. "Here are some scenes from your life basically. It didn't have the right resonance so I went back and tried to focus in on one incident to make it a little more meaningful."

In the episode, Q gives Picard a chance to relive his youth where he helped a friend, Corey (Ned Vaughn), rig a gambling table to help get even with a Nausicaan who cheated him, and is almost killed in the ensuing fight. This time Q offers Picard the opportunity to avoid the conflict that led to him being stabbed through the heart, but rather than change his life in a positive way, Picard finds himself in the midst of disintegrating friendships, a failed love affair and, ultimately, an unfulfilling career when he is returned to the Enterprise as a junior grade lieutenant.

The story of Picard's uproarious youth and artificial heart was first revealed in "Samaritan Snare" and mentioned again in "Final Mission." In both cases, they involved Picard reluctantly confessing some of his youthful indiscre-

tions to Wesley.

"It was an interesting little story about him," notes Moore. "That story, to me, said a lot about Picard's character - that he was a different guy in those days. Then he changed. Why did he change? What would be the difference in the young womanizing, hard-drinking, hard-fighting Jean-Luc Picard and the guy that we know today?"

Of this story, which may or may not have been a dream for Picard, John DeLancie, who returned to play Q, offers, "I thought it was a terrific script. I thought that script was a pleasure to work on because it had such a straight throughline, you knew the direction you were moving in and you knew it from the beginning. I just thought it was terrific. There was a speech at the end where I talk about what he would have been, which I thought was a tip-top speech. I just thought that show from beginning to end was terrific."

The on-screen spark between Stewart and DeLancie was a highlight for Moore. "I thought Patrick and John both did a great job. It's the best Q episode that they've done together. When Q is in the white limbo set, I thought the way he played that was so interesting because he played it real low key for Q. He was saying the lines but he was so low key about it that it added a lot of weight to it. It seemed very real because he wasn't just being goofy and running around and laughing. There was a sense that this is heavy shit."

That, however, was not the only reason DeLancie was low-key. One of the last scenes to be filmed for the episode was of Q and Picard in the afterlife, and in it Q wore a white robe. Filmed against a lit white background, director of photography Jonathan West and producer Merri Howard were concerned that Q could become lost in the overexposed *Heaven Can Wait* imagery. Both actors were well aware of the difficulties involved in shooting the scene and feared that it might need to be reshot. The dailies were sent out for immediate development to ascertain whether Q would turn out to be nothing more than a floating head.

"Unfortunately, I think we were all a little bit dragged down and out in all those heaven scenes because of that," says DeLancie. "We started shooting it and it was already late and it was just getting later, and I think we all looked pretty tired."

When Picard returns to his Starfleet Academy days, he also encounters an old platonic girlfriend who, this time around, turns out to be less than platonic. Played by actress J.C. Brandy, Marta rebuffs Picard after they've slept together as Picard begins to watch his life unravel despite having the best of intentions. "The morning-after scene was about four pages," says the actress. "I actually like it a lot better the way they cut it. I had this whole speech which I didn't feel was really Marta. It said the same thing that the scene showed in one minute. Picard comes in and the beginning is the same, but I had this whole speech about how when we first met at the Academy and the Admiral said, 'Look to the left, look to the right of you, one of you isn't going to make it through the next four years and I thought that's me, I'm not going to make it and I looked to the right, and there you were with this cocky look on your face which I thought was so great and I knew from that moment I wanted to be your friend.' The thing that bothered me about that line is to say something like 'I thought, "That's me,"' is such a self-pitying thing to say. You have to be very careful while acting not to fall into that trap. No matter how you deliver it, that one sentence changes the character and that's why I was kind of glad they cut it."

However, the show — which many on the staff regard as the finest of the sixth season — was received less warmly by some fans as well as Michael Piller. "I wasn't much a fan of that show," Piller states. "I thought it was a wonderful premise, I loved the pitch of Picard dying and having the white light experience and reaching out to the hand and it's Q. It's your worst nightmare come true. I found that from the beginning my greatest fear was that it would be It's a Wonderful Life. When a series gets tired, they do It's a Wonderful Life. I don't think we ever solved my problems with it in terms of getting a fresh slant. I felt that it was one of those Christmas-type episodes where the direction and

This model served as the initial conception for the compound that housed both Klingons and Romulans in "Birthright".

the performances were sort of flat. Some of the scenes seemed to be very talky to me. It did not have the power and the impact on me that it seems to have had on other people. I'm delighted that it was a meaningful experience for a lot of people and made them think about their own lives because ultimately that's what Star Trek is trying to do. They should accept themselves rather than wish they had done something else."

However, not everyone appreciated that message. "We've gotten some flack about it," acknowledges Rene Echevarria. "People felt it glorified violence and that it basically says Picard tries to go back and not do the violent thing and solve things by reason and it makes him bland and not captain material. We got big, big letters from people saying this is awful and goes against everything Star Trek stands for. I think the point the show made was much more subtle than that, and I think they lost sight of it."

Richard James was called upon to devise a bar which featured an alien game called Danjaq, which proved to be a pivotal element in the show's plot. "There were never any rules established," says James of the game. "It was a combination of a pool table and a pinball machine and I think we just play-acted the game. There was never any logic to it. With the bar on that one, we treated it

like a college hangout and it was dirty. We don't normally do too many dirty things. Our stuff is really pristine most of the time and all our crew doesn't sweat. That was not true of that bar. It was more down and dirty. We tried an institutional approach with the dorm rooms to get a little bit of the same feeling to it that we had with Starfleet Academy, which we felt it would probably be."

Episode #142
"Birthright, Part I"
Original Airdate: 2/22/93
Written by Brannon Braga
Directed by Winrich Kolbe
Guest Starring: Siddig El Fadil (Dr. Julian Bashir), James Cromwell (Shrek), Cristine Rose (Gi'ral), Jennifer Gatti (Ba'el), Richard Herd (L'Kor)

On a visit to Deep Space Nine, Worf learns from an unscrupulous Uridian merchant, Shrek (James Cromwell), that his father may still be alive in a Romulan prison camp. At the same time, aboard the Enterprise, Data undergoes a power surge that causes him to experience a mysterious vision that turns out to be his first dream.

• • • •

"It was a huge story," states Rene Echevarria of "Birthright." "We broke it as a one-part episode and it took two acts of the script to get Worf down to the prison camp. The end of Act Two was what became the end of 'Part I.' There was basically too much story to tell — and to do it justice, Michael said make it a two-parter. He said you've got all this time on the planet surface so you'll be able to build a better compound and more sets and we came up with the Data story for 'Part One.'"

The story hadn't originally been considered for a two-parter, but when Michael Piller suggested it, the staff was more than pleased to oblige. "They had broken down the story on the board and I felt it was a really good one," says Piller. "Because this was season six, the season of taking risks, of not being afraid of doing things *Star Trek* hadn't done before, I said 'Why not do another two-parter? Why wait until the end of the season or wait for a Spock? If a story justifies being bigger than an hour, let's do it.' I had been very happy with the results of 'Chain of Command' and I said to Rick we should do it and he said fine. I also felt, much mistakenly as it turned out to be, that we would be able to save money if we expanded it into two hours by using the sets twice."

"It was one of my favorite shows," says Rick Berman. "I loved every element of it and so did my son, Tommy, who's a very, very bright eleven-year-old, and it was his favorite episode ever. The B story and the A story were of equal importance to me, and it all clicked."

Once Piller had mandated that the episode become a two-parter, the challenge then became finding a B story to fill out the first episode, which turned out to be the most intriguing plot development of the season: Data's dream.

"We were left with a problem: we needed another B story for 'Part I,'" says Brannon Braga, who wrote the episode. "Ron [Moore] started talking about Data having a religious experience and then I had the idea what if he died and had a vision. We developed that idea and that break session was fun and went very smoothly. I really enjoyed writing the episode. I am compelled by dream imagery and surreal images, and this was finally a chance to do it on *Star Trek*."

Explains Rene Echevarria, "Brannon came up with the idea of Data flat-lining and we were very concerned it

was going to be too similar to 'Tapestry.' We started with the idea that it was a religious experience he had, but we quickly realized we would get ourselves into a lot of trouble trying to say anything absolute or true about something so difficult to know. Instead we came up with the idea of Data dreaming, which I think worked really well. It was an unusual episode in that the two stories were very unconnected, but thematically they were."

In the episode, Data explains his vision to Worf and the Klingon urges him to seek out the true meaning of his dream and to find out whatever he can about his father. As he does, it dawns on him that he cannot ignore the possibility that his own father may be alive. Worf chooses to go to the Romulan prison camp where he has been told his father is still alive. "The scene where Worf tells Data about finding out the truth about the vision of his father is very powerful," says Echevarria. "It was one of the finest scenes in the history of *Star Trek*. I thought it was lovely when Worf realized he was talking about himself and it tied the two stories together and sent Worf on his journey."

"The whole Data thing started in desperation, with our just saying, 'What can we do with Data? What haven't we done with Data?'" muses Jeri Taylor of finding another storyline for the episode. "It came from the Klingons sort of having a mystical, mythical, spiritual side and we thought maybe Data can have one. It started originally as Data exploring a metaphysical aspect or spiritual side to himself. Does he have this? That just kept getting turned and turned until almost the last minute where it became the dreaming thing, which Brannon then took and made this magical, wonderful, literally soaring kind of B story that rightly took over the first part. To me, that whole story by itself is one of the best we've ever done."

Sugar seems to serve Brannon Braga well. It was while pouring syrup onto his pancakes one morning that he came up with the ending for last season's "Cause & Effect" and it was while eating birthday cake that he got his own vision for Data's dream.

"I said to Jeri, 'What if he was deactivated and while he was shut down,

he sees something,' and it took off from there," remembers Braga. "It was up to me to come up with the dream imagery and I really tried to delve into Jungian archetypes and dream images that had never really been shown before. At first Michael didn't find the Data dream story very compelling and he had a couple of notions to fix it, namely showing a piece of the dream early on, which I had not done. His suggestions were very good and made it work and in the end he told me he was very happy with the episode."

"As far as the character was concerned, 'Birthright' was the best concept for the character in a long time," says Brent Spiner. "It expanded an idea really nicely. I thought the idea of Data having a dream program was inspired and really excellent writing."

In visualizing Data's dream, where the android encounters Dr. Soong forging a bird's wing on an anvil and the wing turns real when immersed in water and the bird flies away, director Winrich Kolbe was challenged with the task of providing the requisite surreal imagery for the moments of Data's visions.

"I wanted to go all the way," says Kolbe. "I saw nothing but shades of *2001*. But it was decided by the powers that be, that we would not overexpose or underexpose. If we do anything, I was told we underexpose, but this is not what I had in mind. I wanted to actually flare it out to give it that different look, but some people felt that it had been done too often and would not look good. So then I decided I'm not going to talk about my creative input anymore, I'm just going to do what I want to do. I went over to [director of photography] Jonathan West and said, 'Now listen, what are we going to do? What can we do in here with a wide angle lens without going berserk?' And he said, 'A 10 mm is a perfect thing for this.' And so we ordered a 10 mm lens, which is a marvelous lens, and shot the whole dream sequence with that and a Steadicam."

"The bird [in Data's vision] gave a great performance," says Brannon Braga. "It's one of our best guest stars ever. Kolbe executed the dream sequences with finesse. I was very happy that everything came together for me on that episode. The two stories resonated

"Birthright" was a further exploration of Michael Dorn's on-screen alter ego, Worf (photo copyright ©1995 Albert Ortega).

thematically with one another and I don't have a single complaint."

Says Echevarria, "It was a wonderful episode all the way around. Very well directed, the dream was spectacular. I'm only afraid 'Birthright Part II' was a disappointment."

Episode #143
"Birthright, Part II"
Original Airdate: 3/1/93
Written by Rene Echevarria
Directed by Dan Curry
Guest Starring: James Cromwell (Shrek), Richard Herd (L'Kor), Jennifer Gatti (Ba'El), Sterling Macer (Toq), Christine Rose (Gi'Ral), Alan Scarfe (Tokath)

Worf attempts to instill a sense of heritage into the Klingons living in the Romulan prisoner-of-war camp while trying to execute an escape and rendezvous with Shrek (James Cromwell) to return to the Enterprise.

• • • •

Explains Michael Piller, "I was the one who said instead of Worf being the human in the group, we've taken away so much of his Klingon Nature, let's give him back some and make him the gung-ho Klingon who says, 'You're Klingon, be true to who

you are.' In a sense, I had just seen *Malcolm X* and I said Worf is the guy who's saying 'You're black and you should be proud to be black.' That's where I started from with the character standpoint, but when you get into it and you realize that there is something pretty good in this society and that he'll lose this woman he's in love with when he can't shake his own prejudice, it's a price he has to pay for his character and his code. I think that's great stuff. I think it's wonderful when people act in heroic ways that turn back on them."

Michael Dorn, who plays Worf, enjoyed the episodes which provided continuing character development for the Klingon. "I thought it was great," he says. "It also showed that this is like a bottomless well. It will never go dry. The Klingon story will just go on and on. We still don't know if my father is really dead."

Executing the second episode was more difficult, requiring protracted discussions among the writing staff which were laced with philosophical differences and questions about Worf's actions in splintering the harmony of the contented prison camp inhabitants.

"I thought there was a wonderful *Bridge Over the River Kwai*-type story where you had a fundamentally charged relationship between a Romulan camp leader and Worf and this very interesting love affair where Worf had to reexamine his whole attitude towards the Romulans again," says Michael Piller. "It is always interesting to me whenever you can look at prejudice. I think the script turned out pretty well, the show just did not have quite the power I had hoped it would have. I don't really know why."

The episode was directed by visual effects supervisor Dan Curry in his first directorial outing on the show. "I'm glad Dan did it because I've always liked him," says Michael Dorn. "He's a very interesting guy and very patient. We have a rapport and he was just wonderful to work for."

Curry, who had traveled abroad for many years, including in Thailand as a photographer before

returning to America where he oversaw all visual effects work on *The Next Generation*, made good use of his background for the show, utilizing photography from Laos in a matte painting of the compound which boasted a miniature built by the art department. "I invented the spear game using old spear throwing techniques from sword school in that," says Curry. "I'd been doing second unit directing work on *Star Trek* for five seasons and did live theater in graduate school as well as film. The best thing about this experience was the support from the cast and crew, particularly Jonathan West, our director of photography, who was a major collaborator and lifesaver. Everybody was looking out for me and the thing that gratified me the most was I implicitly trusted every member of the crew to do a great job and they did. Michael Dorn was really great. He couldn't have been a better person to work with. He delivered a knockout performance."

The show, which ran twelve minutes long, needed to be cut for time and as a result several aspects of the story went sadly unexplained. The most conspicuous omission was the motivation of the Yridian, Jaglom Shrek (James Cromwell) who claimed that Worf's father, Mogh, was taken to the prison camp by the Romulans after the massacre at Khitomer.

"That idea was cut for time from the script," says Rene Echevarria of Shrek. "One idea was that Worf was going to see he had some sort of tattoo of having been a prisoner and Shrek was going to talk about being a prisoner and that his government let him rot and it took his family to come and risk their lives to free him. He says he knows how governments can be and doesn't trust them. 'You think I do this for money, but I actually do it because I know what it's like,' Shrek tells Worf."

Another complication was that the actor who portrayed Shrek broke his leg between filming of the two episodes, severely curtailing his availability.

• • • •

Episode #144
"Starship Mine"
Original Airdate: 3/29/93
Written by Morgan Gendel
Directed by Cliff Bole
Guest Starring:
Marie Marshall (Kelsey), David Spielberg (Hutchinson), Tim Russ (Davor), Tom Nibley (Neil), Alan Altshuld (Pomet), Tim de Zarn (Satler), Arlee Reed (Waiter), Glenn Morshower (Orton)

During a routine bayron particle elimination sweep of the Enterprise, terrorists attempt to steal trilithium from the ship's engines. Picard, the sole remaining crewmember aboard the starship, attempts to stop them from escaping with the deadly compound by pretending to be the ship's barber, Mr. Mott.

• • • •

"It didn't feel like *Star Trek* to me," says Michael Piller of a show in which Picard grapples with women in Ten Forward, shoots another man with a crossbow and pulls the plug on a container that destroys an entire ship. "I liked the show and thought it was very effective and well directed by Cliff, but I was worried that it was very violent, which troubled me. Picard slugging it out with the two women wasn't silly, and Patrick did his usual fine job, but it was derivative."

"This was a classic example of a bravura role for Picard," counters Rick Berman. "It had a real tone and style to the look of the show and I think Cliff Bole did a nice job directing it. I enjoyed seeing Patrick as an actor being able to get physical."

Patrick Stewart agrees with a smile, "I enjoyed the episode enormously. It's now in my top half a dozen episodes. It was wonderful to be out of uniform for an entire episode and to be on the ship without any of the other boring crew members."

"The hallmark of Michael's tenure on the show has been character, but once we did that, there's also room to do stuff that is just straight run and jump," says uncredited writer Ron Moore. "I think there's a recognition that sometimes it's okay to do an action show and not to have to try and strain the force of a character piece on top of that. It was fun to do a straight action piece and to

just do comedy on the planet. What you rapidly ran into were the money considerations, as is usual with everything else on the show, so I had to pare back the run and jump and then what we had to deal with is: is this too brutal and too much killing? I'm always the one who kills people in scripts left and right, and people are always asking me to pull it back — it's not *Star Trek*, and I'm always, 'Kill more, kill more!'"

"'Starship Mine' went through a major restructuring at the last minute," says director Cliff Bole. "Michael Piller and Rick just didn't like the way it was going and they said page one rewrite. Pages were coming in about ten a day *while* I was shooting."

In addition to dealing with the script changes, director Bole found himself working on familiar sets with new complications. Since the Enterprise was in dock for its bayron particle elimination sweep, most of the vessel's systems were shut down, including the lighting, which led to Bole being forced to eschew the time-saving pre-lighting and work with Jonathan West to create new lighting schemes for every set.

"This was the first time I was able to shoot the starship in a down mode, color-wise, light-wise, and everything else," Bole says. "It wasn't as bright and up as you normally see it, so it was a challenge. That was the first time that the sets have been shot like that. After six years, you can usually come in and say, 'Okay, we're going to key from here and we're going to do this and we'll do that,' especially on the bridge, which is our phone booth, basically. That's where we go in and try to pick up some time to just change the concept of the lighting in the hallways and everything else. You normally come in and you hit the hallway lights and you pretty much have your fill. But when they're not there, you're starting from scratch."

Bole also lost a day of shooting when the schedule was truncated to a seven day shoot. The director feels it suffered as a result. "I had to cook," he says. "When you lose another twelve hours of production, it hurts creatively. The show still stands, but I could have added a lot more and so could the cameraman. At the end, the little thing he pulled out of

the canister in Ten Forward, which was kind of like a grenade pin, you couldn't see. You didn't know what he had in his hands so we just didn't sell it. I should have done a little bit more."

Although many viewers have viewed "Starship Mine" as "Die Hard on a Starship," it's not an analogy that writer Morgan Gendel supports.

"I'm not going to talk about it as *Die Hard*," he says. "That's somebody else's work. It's an idea we've seen countless times: *Under Siege, Passenger 57*. What I liked was the element I had come up with of the captain going down with his ship, which was rejected as a notion in the 24th century. That was a strong line for me — a captain alone with his ship. My theory is that what Picard loved most was the Enterprise. I don't think the staff agreed with me. I think they thought it was too much of a 20th or 18th century concept, or Kirk."

Gendel did several drafts, altering a variety of things within his teleplay mainly for production reasons.

"Once you pull the thread," he notes, "it starts to unravel pretty quickly and there were a lot of changes that had to be made. I had a couple of action bits and in each subsequent draft I had to tone down the action. First time I saw it, I wasn't sure how well it worked. But when I went back to watch it a second time, I really liked it and thought it was true to what it was trying to do."

Episode #145
"Lessons"
Original Airdate: 4/5/93
Written by Ronald Wilkerson & Jean Louise Matthias
Directed by Robert Wiemer
Guest Starring:
Wendy Hughes (Nella Daren)

Picard becomes romantically involved with the new chief of the Stellar Sciences department, Nella Daren (Wendy Hughes), who shares a mutual love of music. The captain confides in Nella his fifth season "Inner Light" experience, and is forced to send his paramour on a deadly mission to evacuate a Federation colony threatened by a menacing firewall.

• • • •

"My feeling from the start of

that episode was you started off with a concept that was flawed," notes Brannon Braga of the Picard romance tagline. "We said let's do a Picard romance and then came up with this story, which to me was somewhat hackneyed. With a show like 'The Host,' we started off with a great science-fiction gag and said this would make an interesting love story. If you had started with 'let's do a Beverly love story,' what is the chance you would have come up with that? It's a good way to start but you're going to do a show like 'Lessons' which does not have a very compelling science-fiction component. Ultimately, Rene did a great job on the script. There's something about Rene's writing that's very touching. He always finds the genuine emotion."

Says Echevarria, "It's very off format. We cast a woman who's closer to Picard's age than the women we've seen him with in the past, like Jennifer Hetrick and Michelle Phillips, and we're all very happy about it. We wanted somebody who had weight as opposed to it being just purely sexual. It has to do with music and she's a musician and there's that initial bond. 'Lessons' also deals with those issues of how difficult it is to go out with someone you work with, especially someone who is your underling."

"We started thinking about this back in fifth season when we were brainstorming ideas and Michael said maybe it would be interesting to do a love story in which Picard is attracted to someone who is serving under his command," recalls Jeri Taylor. "I said, 'Yes,' and just sort of dropped it at that point. As the season wore on, we got to the point where any glimmer of a story that Michael already has an interest in becomes appealing. If you don't have any stories, you say, 'What was that idea about a love story, great idea — looking better all the time.' I gave the idea to some freelance writers, Jean Matthias and Ronald Wilkerson, who had never gotten to write a teleplay, largely because of time constraints, and they wrote the story and I thought this is never going to go anyplace. I gave it to Michael and he said, 'Great, let's proceed.' It seemed sort of ordinary to me

and then they wrote the screenplay which was quite good and Rene took it over and added some very nice things to it. It had an honesty and simplicity to it that was very engaging. Wendy Hughes, who is a wonderful actress, made the whole relationship believable. You believed that Picard would be enchanted with this woman and I was wrong [to have such a] lukewarm response to it at the beginning. It turned into something that was sweet and endearing."

"It's sort of a *Brief Encounter* on the starship Enterprise, and I thought that Wendy Hughes was perfect casting," offers Michael Piller. "You really had to have that magic to make things work. It was a low-key ending, which may not be what you expect, but I thought it worked well rather than the potential hand-wringing."

Episode #146
"The Chase"
Original Airdate: 4/26/93
Teleplay by Joe Menosky
Story by Ronald D. Moore and Joe Menosky
Directed by Jonathan Frakes
Guest Starring:
John Cothran, Jr. (Nu'Daq), Norman Lloyd (Professor Galen), Ken Thorley (Mott), Linda Thorson (Gul Ocett), Salome Jens (Humanoid), Maurice Roeves (Romulan Captain), Majel Barrett (Computer Voice)

When Professor Galen (Norman Lloyd), Picard's mentor, is killed, the captain pursues a trail of DNA fragments which leads the Enterprise to a planet which has already attracted feuding Cardassians, Klingons and Romulans, all in a search for the secret encoded within the DNA fragment.

• • • •

Missing from the final cut is a scene that Ron Moore had written when it originally appeared the episode would run short, in which Mr. Mott (Ken Thorley), the ship's barber, is approached by Dr. Crusher as one of the non-Federation aliens whose DNA may hold clues to the mystery. "I'm sure I've got the answer," he assures her. "What's the question?" Needless to say, Mott is dumbfounded when he finds out he's been of no use and insists that it's

Beverly who's at fault. The scene ended up being cut when the episode ran long.

Says Rick Berman of "The Chase," "It's a story that's been around forever. It was similar to 'Darmok,' which was a story that was around forever also. 'Darmok' never worked for me until Joe [Menosky] came up with the direction that he came up with — and it turned out to be one of my favorite episodes of all time. This story did not. Conceptually, it's very interesting. I always had some problems with dealing with the whole idea of these kind of prehistoric creatures who are the fathers of us all. It's not Roddenberry-esque, it's very sixties Roddenberry-esque."

"It was a very tough concept to wrestle to the ground," says Michael Piller. "The script was a nightmare. Joe wrote a wonderful first twenty pages and then you turn the page and it begins to go into the tech. One of the great talents of Menosky has always been his ability to see places the rest of us wouldn't even go to look and from page 20 to page 60 he was on a different plane, existing somewhere else. I just had to keep feeding back material saying I don't get it."

Co-writer Ron Moore notes, "Michael had a problem with the story early. There wasn't enough character. He felt there wasn't a strong Picard drive for why he would do this, so it really means going and finding something about Picard to carry it through the episode. 'The Chase' was something that Joe and I had been working on for a long time in development. We knew it was going to be expensive and it took a long time to get it to the point where they wanted to do it finally. It's one of the things about television, you can decide how life began with the stroke of the pen."

"It's the most Roddenberry-esque show we have done," agrees Naren Shankar. "I think the original conception of this was a little bit along the lines of its *It's a Mad, Mad, Mad, Mad World*, but it got more serious and I think that helped it. When we intend to do comedy, we tend to do it rather poorly."

Offers Jonathan Frakes, "The speech that Salome Jens makes at the end would make Roddenberry very proud I think. It's a great cast and it's wonderful to have all those villains and aliens in one place. Linda Thorson played the first female Cardassian we have had and she was astounding. John Cothran, Jr., our Klingon out of Chicago, did a great job and was appalled at the idea that Klingons and Romulans and Cardassians could be vaguely related, which is what the last speech suggests. Norman [Lloyd], a wonderful actor and a wonderful man, was terrific and, of course, this guy Maurice Roeves, who's like Tony Hopkins, was sensational, so we were very lucky with that cast.

"I was very disappointed not to get to shoot outside," adds Frakes. "I think it does look like Planet Hell, but that's the way it goes. The money was being spent across the street [at *Deep Space Nine*]. I don't think it's a secret."

Richard James disagrees, noting that it would have been impossible to use a location for the show because of story considerations. "We were actually going to do location and we scouted locations and there was vegetation which we couldn't use. The location needed to be the salt flats where there's absolutely no vegetation, so we were really forced to do it on stage."

Episode #147
"Frame of Mind"
Original Airdate: 5/3/93
Written by Brannon Braga
Directed by James Conway
Guest Starring: Andrew Prine (Administrator), Susanna Thompson (Inmate), Gary Werntz (Mavek), Allan Dean Moore (Wounded Crewmember), David Selburg (Doctor Syrus)

Riker finds himself propelled between life aboard the Enterprise and as an inmate of an alien mental asylum while acting for Dr. Crusher in a play, "Frame of Mind." Unable to discern reality from fantasy, Riker believes he really is insane and that the Enterprise is a figment of his imagination. Eventually it's revealed that he has been captured on an Away Team mission and the mind probe is actually an attempt to extract information from the commander.

• • • •

Says Jonathan Frakes, who gives one of his strongest performances in the show, "'Frame of Mind' was really dark.

It was a terrifying show and was creepy to do. [Director Jim] Conway came back and it was as big a show as I've had to carry. I thought he was very competent at the helm. It was wonderfully dark and I thank Mr. Braga for that."

"I had a notion: What if Riker woke up in an alien insane asylum and had no idea how he got there and was told he was crazy?" recalls Braga. "It was a very difficult show to structure, it took a long time. But ultimately, it became the most intricate structure of the season and Jim Conway did a brilliant job directing. Writing it was a challenge, but it utilizes a great deal of surreal imagery and eerie elements, namely Riker doubting his sanity which appeals to me a lot. It was fun for me to do. One of my favorite films is Roman Polanski's *Repulsion*, and I think the influence will show through. I've always wanted to write something about someone doubting their sense of reality and I think it works."

Adds Naren Shankar, "I think this is the best script Brannon has ever written for the series. It was a phenomenally cool first draft and it's an incredibly great episode. It's a darker season this year which is funny because, in general, we're not a very dark bunch. Dark stories are very attractive, they're interesting and the emotions they bring up are attractive because they're powerful and off-putting. We have had some very intense episodes and gut-wrenching stuff. There's not a lot of light moments in 'Face of the Enemy' and 'Chain of Command.'"

Episode #148
"Suspicions"
Original Airdate: 5/9/93
Written by
Joe Menosky & Naren Shankar
Directed by Cliff Bole
Guest Starring: Whoopi Goldberg (Guinan), Patti Yasutake (Ogawa), Tricia O'Neil (Kurak), Peter Slutsker (Dr. Reyga), James Horan (Jo'Bril), John S. Ragin (Dr. Christopher), Joan Stuart Morris (T'Pan)

Beverly is relieved of duty after investigating what she believes is the murder of a Ferengi scientist who has created a metaphasic shield designed to take a shuttle through a star's corona.

Actor Jonathan Frakes at a Hollywood premiere (photo copyright ©1995 Albert Ortega).

Relaying the story in flashback to Guinan, Dr. Crusher is intent on solving the murder and salvaging her career.

• • • •

Notes Rick Berman, "My biggest problem with this was it broke rules more than anything else sixth season. The teaser and the first three acts of this are done in flashback and narrated by Beverly. It took me a while to sign off on that. But everybody was very big on it and I think it worked out okay. *Star Trek* is a narrated show in that it uses the concept of the log, but I think it's dangerous to take that and expand upon it. We make it very clear to the writers that the captain's logs cannot be narration. They are basically a narrative tool that we can use to get from A to B but we don't use them to narrate the action that is presently going on. We're very careful in constructing logs and you never have a situation where Picard is in a sense telling us what we're seeing. He's usually telling us what has happened prior to what we're seeing. There's a big difference. I think the logs are quite unique to *Star Trek* and it's a great way to have Picard's voiceover be effective. Having a Tom Selleck-like narration [as in *Magnum p.i.*] is something we try to stay away from."

• • • •

By following her heart rather than Starfleet regulations, Dr. Crusher is nearly relieved of duty in "Suspicions." Seen here are Gates McFadden and Patrick Stewart (photo copyright ©1995 Albert Ortega).

"I had a Ferengi in there that I had to reshoot because I let him get out of character," remembers Cliff Bole. "He was a scientist, so I said that means he's got a little more compassion, maybe he's not as oily as the rest of them. I think I went too far and the guys asked me to reshoot a couple of scenes. Rick Berman said, 'Don't forget, they're still Ferengis.'"

"What I really wanted was a vehicle for Beverly," offers Jeri Taylor. "I felt we had given Troi some really nice things to do, Beverly has had more to do within a number of episodes but she did not have one that was all hers. We wanted to give her something atypical and not a female role. The idea of her playing a Private Eye or Quincy was very appealing. I don't know how successful it is. We had one whole story on it done and Michael felt, rightly, that it was a nicely crafted mystery, but so what? We tried to find an angle that would give it a nice little spin. Who's the last person you would suspect? The person who was killed first. She takes on the world and gets in deeper and deeper because, of all things, she felt compassion for a Ferengi. She bucks the stream and goes up against Picard and disobeys

an order. We had an unusual stylistic flavor that's offbeat."

Episode #149
"Rightful Heir"
Original Airdate: 5/16/93
Story by James E. Brooks
Teleplay by Ronald D. Moore
Directed by Winrich Kolbe
Guest Starring: Alan Oppenheimer (Koroth), Robert O'Reilly (Gowron), Norman Snow (Torin), Charles Esten (Divok), Kevin Conway (Kahless)

While undergoing a spiritual crisis, Worf visits a Klingon monastery on Boreth, where the image of the legendary Klingon warrior, Kahless (Kevin Conway), appears to him. It is Kahless' intention to reclaim his position as leader of the Klingon Empire. Gowron (Robert O'Reilly), leader of the High Council, doubts the veracity of the resurrected prophet/messiah and challenges him in battle, leading Worf to the conclusion that Kahless is a clone.

• • • •

Interestingly, although much of the lore of Kahless is taken from dialogue that was cut from "Birthright II," Kahless actually first appeared in the original *Star Trek's* third season episode, "The Savage Curtain." Played by actor Robert Herron, Kahless was considerably less friendly, representing one of the most evil people in galactic history.

"['Rightful Heir'] was a difficult show to do," says director Winrich Kolbe. "It started out rather conventionally, but once we got on Stage 16, we spent three days there. It was totally smoked in, in order to get that haze...I'm still coughing. The special effects people kept telling us it's non-poisonous and just a slight irritant. Well, I had a very heavy allergy which I think was caused by the smoke, but the show just looks terrific. It looks like a movie."

Of Michael Dorn's strong performance in the episode, Kolbe comments, "Michael and I have an interesting relationship. I try to push him and sometimes I push too hard and then he will fight back. Michael has matured since I met him four or five years ago. He has become a lot more secure and has become a lot better. That obviously helped on this particular show. He knew

it was his show and we went in there from the beginning saying that we're going to make this the best show of the season."

Adds Michael Dorn, "It was a well written script. Usually you get ten different colors or changes, but in 'Rightful Heir' maybe there were two miniscule changes. Rick [Kolbe] and I had mini-discussions about where the character should be. He's wonderful and I trust him — so if he says, 'Michael, try it like this,' you go, 'Okay' and you trust him. There are only one or two times where I said, 'I don't agree, I think it should be another way.' What he does then is he says, 'Let's try it both ways and we'll decide.'"

"It's a show which has some powerful metaphors for modern day religious beliefs. *Star Trek* has never tackled religion with such vigor as in this episode," says Brannon Braga. "The man playing Kahless as the Jesus Christ of the Klingon Empire was great and Michael Dorn's performance is powerful. It has the potential to be a very controversial episode that will take Worf's character in some interesting new directions."

Says writer Ron Moore of the episode, "This is a show I wanted to do. I thought it was a real nifty idea and I thought it was an opportunity to do a show unlike others we've done. The subject wasn't something that we tackled, so I was eager to do it. I wanted to do something interesting. I'm very proud of the script. It deals with faith and belief that we don't normally deal with on *Star Trek*."

Counters Rick Berman, "I had a lot of fights with Ron about this. The character of Kahless and the backstory and the dialogue of Kahless were all a little bit too on the nose Christ-like for me. We had a lot of long debates and eventually it was modified by Ron in a way that I think made it much better. I think he not only solved my problems but made the movie better. Kevin Conway's performance is great and it's a wonderful episode."

For "Rightful Heir," Richard James constructed a Klingon temple where Worf begins his spiritual quest for K'helest. "He did some great coverage on that set," says James of director Winrich Kolbe. "There's one long lens shot that makes the shot look like it goes on forever. It looks wonderful."

• • • •

Episode #150
"Second Chances"
Original Airdate: 5/24/93
Story by Michael A. Medlock
Teleplay by Rene Echevarria
Directed by LeVar Burton
Guest Starring:
Dr. Mae Jemison (Ensign Palmer)

LeVar Burton's freshman directorial outing features Jonathan Frakes in two roles, that of Commander Riker and Lieutenant Riker, a duplicate created in a freak transporter accident eight years earlier. Still in love with Troi, Lieutenant Riker hopes to rekindle their relationship, while a fuming Commander Riker finds himself coming into conflict with his eager and abrasive doppelganger.

• • • •

One idea of the staff's was to kill Commander Riker in "Second Chances" and allow Lieutenant Riker to remain on the Enterprise. "Our Lieutenant Riker didn't make it," says Jeri Taylor. "Maybe we were trying to rock the boat a little too drastically. My original idea, which we thought was very bold and surprising and would energize the seventh season, was to kill our Commander Riker and let Lieutenant Riker come onto the ship as a rejuvenated, energetic, driven, ambitious Lieutenant. He wouldn't be Number One, he would be at ops and have to prove himself and build his career and get into conflict with the others because he had these rough edges from having lived that arduous experience. It gave it a wonderful life that would energize the seventh season with everyone in different places and a new character, and yet our same character was there. I was very, very taken with that. It was just too bold."

"That was one I basically said no to," explains Rick Berman. "But it gave me a lot of pause. My initial knee-jerk reaction was no and then I became a little bit more willing to say yes, but there were other problems it created. Once I started leaning towards yes, we started looking at what that would do and how it would fit into the movies and how it would fit into a lot of the different relationships. Basically, you're putting a character on the ship who has not experienced anything of the last six years and doesn't know any of the characters. How would it affect the movie and other

variables? I ended up feeling rather strongly that I didn't want to kill off Riker and I didn't get any major arguments about it from Michael or Jeri."

"It's a fascinating premise," says Michael Piller. "The most interesting part of it is Older Riker vs. Younger Riker and that changed along the way since they were the same age. I had two very strong feelings about this story. The premise of this was that this was going to be the season cliffhanger and that the new Riker would come onboard and during the course of the episode the Riker we've come to know and love would be killed and the young Riker would take his place as a Lieutenant on the ship next season. Rick and I both did not like this idea, Rick even less than I. Riker has always been a difficult character for writers to write and they said `Let's get some conflict, let's get some excitement and energy,' but the fact is he's a pretty darn good character. A character that I relate to a great deal. When I came into the room and I read the story, I said everything about this story suggests that the new Riker comes onboard and he's everything that the old Riker's lost. I resent that as somebody who wrote [of Riker] in the 'Best of Both Worlds' that he's come to a place in his life where he appreciates what he has and comfortable with his friends and has achieved a great inner peace. I don't believe that the guy who is a loose-end six years ago is necessarily the good part of the man. I fought very hard to protect the Riker that we had on the ship. I think the scenes between Riker and Troi are wonderful and answers a call from the fans that has existed for a long time to put those two back together again and, of course, I came up with the final twist at the end which is that instead of Riker dying, as was originally written, we keep him alive and send him off to who knows where because what other show could ever do that? Everybody in the audience is going to expect him to die."

"It was just a delight for me to write," Rene Echevarria enthuses. "It was full of pitfalls but the first draft I turned in got the best reaction of anything I've ever done on the show. I made a lot of choices about how and why Troi and Riker broke up and people seemed to swallow

them. It's another big Troi show and it's very romantic. We finally see Jonathan and Marina together kissing and it's just a wonderful romance."

"The most-often-asked convention question is what's happening to Troi and Riker," points out Marina Sirtis. "We've never done a convention where that hasn't been asked in the first few minutes, and it's very difficult to tell them. 'Second Chances' I think shows where the relationship is now as far as the two people in it are concerned. Obviously Troi would resume it immediately if Riker opened that little door a chink — and Riker appears to have definitely closed the door on that relationship. That was an interesting kind of development. Because of the second Riker, we managed to actually see that Troi really does still love Will. Jonathan and I have this little running gag that they made a mistake and did the wrong spin-off with *Deep Space Nine*. The spinoff should have been 'The Rikers in Space,' and now that we've met Lieutenant Riker there is a possibility that we will have the Rikers in space."

Says Brannon Braga of the episode, "I really like Riker and I enjoyed breaking this with Jeri and Rene. I was very moved, as is common with Rene's scripts. My theory is a TV show is in trouble when they do an evil twin episode and one could construe this as an evil twin if they hadn't already done it with 'Allegiance.' But this is not an evil twin, it's a tortured twin and it's a twin story I can buy. The main thing I contributed to Rene's brilliant script was the notion of the treasure hunt where Riker takes Troi on a romantic little treasure hunt of notes and gifts — which is a gag I have used in the past in my own romantic relationships to great effect. When all else fails, try the treasure hunt. It worked with Troi."

Reflecting the riskier nature of sixth season was that serious consideration was given to killing off Commander Riker at the end of the episode and allowing his duplicate, Lieutenant Riker, to come aboard as a new officer, completely reshuffling the Enterprise command hierarchy. It was a controversial consideration, ultimately rejected.

• • • •

Episode #151
"Timescape"
Original Airdate: 6/14/93
Written by Brannon Braga
Directed by Adam Nimoy
Guest Starring:
Michael Bofshever (Romulan/Alien)

Returning to the Enterprise via Runabout, Picard, Geordi, Troi and Data find the Enterprise apparently trapped in time in mid-battle with a Romulan warbird due to a strange temporal distortion. Leading an investigation aboard the ships in stasis, Picard realizes they must reverse time if they have any hope of saving the Enterprise and Dr. Crusher, who has been wounded by a phaser blast.

• • • •

Adam Nimoy returned to helm his second episode with "Timescape," a show which made "Rascals" pale in comparison in terms of technical complexity. While "Rascals'" physical challenges were easily apparent, "Timescape" presented a whole new range of problems for the director.

"It was absolutely bizarre," says Jeri Taylor. "It's full of opticals and complicated sequences. Do you do split screen? Do you do blue screen? Do you do anthromorphic lenses? It's endlessly complicated and here's Adam Nimoy back who got 'Rascals' first and now walks into this complicated directorial mess, and was very much on top of it. He's tremendously bright."

Says Rick Berman of Nimoy, "My feeling was that nobody should be asked to be judged on a work that was so unusual in terms of having to come in and direct these kids [in 'Rascals.']. I basically said I would like to give him another shot to work with adults."

In Brannon Braga's script, they have to figure out how to repair the fabric of time while also avoiding death and destruction for the Enterprise. "I think this is the longest optical memo we have ever had," says David Livingston of the sheet delineating all of the show's complicated visual effects. "It's over six pages long. Adam was very specific about what he wanted and I knew he was going to do great on it. He's got good genes."

"It was very different," says Nimoy of the visual effects intensive episode which required several additional days of blue-screen work after wrapping principal photography to depict the Enterprise and Romulan ship's personnel frozen in time. "I relied a lot on the special effects guys in an attempt to keep what I thought was the drama of the scene and deal with the restrictions that special effects put on you in terms of what you can do with the actors while also using those effects to maximum dramatic capacity to make it work with the scene. It's a whole different mindset. I'm learning a lot from these guys. I've known these special effects guys from fifth season as well because they were there and I was there asking them questions just like with everyone else. They know that I am inquisitive, interested and fascinated by what they do and that I really want to come out with a product that is satisfying. It's not a question of me going and sitting in a closed room and blocking all this stuff out and then meeting with them on the set and saying, 'Can I do this?' I want to know now what the parameters are so that I'm very well prepared, as well prepared as I can be, by the time we get there, and that we're in sync. We had a lot of optical meetings in an attempt to work out exactly how the logistics would work to make scenes pay off."

"This is 'Cause & Effect' times ten," says Brannon Braga, referring to his fifth season teleplay involving the Enterprise's destruction while trapped in a temporal loop. "Time is not only looping, it's moving backwards, accelerating and stopping and moving slowly. The premise is that time/space has been shattered like a windshield and caught in the middle of the shatter effect is the Enterprise and a Romulan warbird in mid-battle. Picard, Data, Troi and Geordi have to figure out what happened and they walk around a scene of time being frozen. We have to figure out what happened by looking at pictures of still scenes and things that are actually moving very slowly. I knew the show was impossible to produce. As I was writing it, I was thinking there's no way. There's a great shot where Beverly's been phasered and you see the blast coming out through her back and we have to save her. It was very complex. There's a lot of tech but hopefully I made it clear. Visually, I think it's one of the most interesting shows. I'm fascinated by doing time travel shows that aren't the typical time travel shows. What's most interesting about time manipulation is the way we perceive time and time travel in small increments, matter of minutes or hours. The big time travel shows are fascinating too but so little has been done with other time travel stories which have much more potential."

Episode #152
"Descent, Part I"
Original Airdate: 6/21/93
Teleplay by Ron Moore
Story by Jeri Taylor
Directed by Alexander Singer
Guest Starring: John Neville (Isaac Newton), Jim Norton (Albert Einstein), Natalija Nogulich (Admiral Nechayev), Brian J. Cousins (Crosis), Professor Stephen Hawking (Himself)

The Borg return to menace the Federation as vicious, individualistic killing machines. During this battle, Data experiences his first emotion: anger and subsequently pleasure after killing one of the metamorphosed automatons. After Data flees the ship with one of the captured Borg warriors, the Enterprise pursues his shuttlepod to an unexplored planet where the Away Team finds Data paired up with his evil brother, Lore, as the leader of the once mass-totality.

• • • •

"Descent" boasts a delightful teaser in which Stephen Hawking guest stars along with *Barron Munchausen's* John Neville in an irascible star turn as Sir Isaac Newton. Hawking, 51, who is author of the bestselling book *A Brief History Of Time*, is the Lucasian Professor of Mathematics at Cambridge University, a chair once held by Isaac Newton. His theories on black holes cast doubt on whether the big bang theory was correct and his research has addressed such subjects as the origin of the universe and the unified theory of space and time. Hawking, who was diagnosed with a motor neuron disorder, better known as Lou Gehrig's disease, is confined to a wheelchair and has lost the ability to speak. He uses a finger to communicate by punching commands into a voice synthesizer.

Visiting Stage 8 while at Paramount to promote the video release of

• • • •

Errol Morris' film *A Brief History Of Time*, which chronicles Hawking's life and work, the world-renowned physicist startled people when he made a very unorthodox request through his touch-keypad.

Recalls Rick Berman, "I got a phone call that Stephen Hawking was outside Stage 8 and wanted to come in and see the *Star Trek* sets and was it okay? Of course, I immediately said yes and headed down to the soundstage. I was introduced and asked him if he'd like to see some more of the sets and he, with his computerized voice synthesizer, said he would. When we got to the bridge of the Enterprise, he started punching in something that he was going to say to us. He just moves one thumb and with it he has a computerized monitor that has a dictionary of various word groups so that he can construct sentences and then they eventually come out as a synthesized voice from the computer. After about sixty seconds of punching this little button, out of the computer came a sentence that I will never forget, and it was, 'Would you lift me out of my chair and put me into the Captain's seat?' It was a pretty amazing sight to have perhaps the greatest mind of the latter half of the 20th Century in applied mathematics and theoretical physics wanting more than anything else at that moment to sit in Picard's chair."

Even more surprising to Berman was the call he received the next day from his friend, Leonard Nimoy, who had been at the Hawking video premiere party the evening before. He told Berman that the professor had expressed a desire to be on *Star Trek*. "The next day I called his people and it turned out that he was interested and with the help of Ron Moore, we came up with an idea for a scene where Data goes to the Holodeck to play a little poker and he conjures up images of Sir Isaac Newton, Albert Einstein and Hawking," says Berman. "We told Hawking that we wanted him to give us some notes on the script and he did and he said that he loved it and agreed to do it."

For the season cliffhanger, *Next Generation* once again ventured off the lot to shoot. "We were looking for a building in which eventually the Borg will appear and we found a location that worked for us," says Berman. "I have to get used to the fact Richard has done this

for years and has very strong ideas and very clearly stated ideas and he'll try to get me anything I want. All that I really require is that he's on a level of understanding as quickly as I am and will convert it into film and that he thinks of himself as a filmmaker and he does."

One day of the eight day shoot took place in Simi Valley at the Brandeis Institute where *Star Trek VI* had shot it's climatic Khitomer Conference scenes. "We [designed a hall] that the Borg took over," notes Richard James. "It's a civilization that they have taken over and the architecture is not really representative of the Borg. They've added their own touches which include the floor design and some banners that we hung up. There were a couple of instances where location would have been nice. It opens up the scope of the show. Sixth season didn't seem to have that."

Surprisingly, Rick Berman is not as keen on the Borg as many of the fans who have extolled them as *Trek*'s best villain ever. Says Berman, "I find them very two-dimensional in a way. They are faceless characters without personality and without specific character traits. They're sort of a one-beat group of bad guys to me. In 'Best of Both Worlds' they represented a threat as opposed to characters, and that was a great episode. In 'I, Borg' you had the antithesis of that fact, which was a Borg pulled away from the collective and made human. It turned into a character and was given a personality and something to be sympathetic towards. My only interest in the Borg is when they're used off-center in other than the way they were originally conceived."

"We were toying with the idea of the Enterprise being called to be reassigned as a flagship, kind of Queen Mary type of thing and everyone was going to be dispersed to different postings," recalls Brannon Braga of one of the original ideas for the cliffhanger. "It would have basically been the dismantling of the Enterprise, but people weren't responding to that so we came up with the Borg show. I think it's so good and dark and sinister. This is Data's descent into violent tendencies and anger and hostility and the Borg and Lore's return. It's very dark. Frequently we will allude to classic films to get started and it always

evolves in a new direction. In this case, *Heart of Darkness* was an idea we had. The most compelling thing to me about this episode, aside from the fact that Data is exploring his dark side, is that the first emotion he thinks he feels is anger and that Lore has become this maniac. He's come to a point where he does not want any part of his biological past, he feels the machine life form is the perfect life form and, of course, Lore holds tremendous appeal to the Borg. He's out to eradicate all organic life forms and the superior life form must prevail. It's an interesting genocidal metaphor. Lore is Hitler and the Borg are the Nazis. He's changed them — and now he's found a way to get Data back by tapping into his ethical program. It's a great idea."

"It's pretty freaking dark," agrees Ron Moore. "They're just killers now and they don't care about your technology. Now they don't want to assimilate you, they just want to kill you. That's their whole drive. That is just so horrible. There was a lot of nice stuff in 'Best of Both Worlds' and it's the big act to follow. People expect a lot out of Borg shows. They've changed and they haven't changed for the better. After you go up the river, there's real heavy shit at the end of the cliffhanger."

The *Heart of Darkness* allusion was not lost on anyone, including Jeri Taylor who points to Lore as a Kurtz-ian type of character in the piece. "In a very loose way, we sort of kept calling it 'Up the River' and we talked about the idea that there was this mysterious figure behind the Borg. We did not want to bring the Borg back just to do another one, and nothing came along for quite a while. One of the early incarnations of the season ender involved a new race of villains, since we figured we needed some fresh blood. But Ron Moore mentioned the Borg and the idea that they've changed, and somehow it all fell together with Lore and opened up. If you leave things alone, at the right moment they rise up of their own accord and jump in your lap. It's Lore's ethnic cleansing, if you will, which is the tack we were taking on it. That is the villainous aspect of it and, ultimately, the brothers having to deal with each other in that sort of mythic slaying of the evil brother."

Captains courageous:
Patrick Stewart and
Avery Brooks, heroes
of the final frontier

Cinefantastique *looks at both* The Next Generation *and* Deep Space Nine.

••••

CHAPTER TWENTY EIGHT
SEASON SEVEN:
An Overview

Star Trek's final season on the air presented the show's staff with some of its greatest challenges. It also proved one of the most difficult seasons for its writers, who were charged with creating another twenty-six hours of engaging television viewing while its producers continued to expand the franchise in new directions.

"I'm not sure how everything got done," says executive producer Jeri Taylor, who supervised the writing staff of producers Ronald D. Moore, Brannon Braga, executive story editor Rene Echevarria and story editor Naren Shankar, during the show's final season. "Rick Berman not only took on developing a new series, *Voyager*, but also continued the development of a feature film. I think we were all being kind of pushed to our limits and there were several things that made the season uniquely difficult."

Among the biggest challenges were that the show's senior writers, Moore and Braga, had been hired to write the first *Next Generation* feature film (*Generations*), precluding their full-time involvement early in the season. By the end of the year, Taylor herself was immersed in work on *Voyager*, which she would co-create with Berman and Piller, who himself was attempting to streamline the second season of *Deep Space Nine*.

Says Rene Echevarria, "I did a lot of writing seventh season. I went from one teleplay to another. By the end of the season, I literally went from finishing an episode to doing a rewrite of another episode in five days, to starting an episode that was due five days later. I wrote three episodes in the time you ordinarily have to write one. I was writing ten pages a day to get it done."

The stress of the season also took it's toll on the actors, as evidenced

by the rash of bad press they received during the weeks preceding the airing of the final episode. "The poor cast was exhausted," says Taylor. "Patrick, who directed `Preemptive Strike' just before the finale, was in every scene of this final episode and was really going on adrenaline. I think everybody was stretched thin, but nobody slacked off."

Despite myriad complications, few would argue that the seventh season did boast several standout episodes. However, one wouldn't have forseen the quality of some of its later episodes based on the less than auspicious beginning of the season.

"I think that everybody pretty much would agree that the seventh season got off to a bit of a rocky start," offers Naren Shankar. "I think a lot of it had to do with the fact that we went out of the sixth season on a real roll and it was creatively very exhausting and, unfortunately, we never really got a break between seasons. Rene managed to get away for a couple of weeks but I had less than a week of vacation to get back. Ron and Brannon went to Hawaii, wrote the feature and came back immediately, and we just jumped right in. As a result, I think the beginning of the season shows a little bit of exhaustion and it's unfortunate. You never sit down and say you want this season to suck."

Among the concerns of the staff seventh season was that a longtime prohibition against using the crutch of characters' relatives was frequently being broken. "I complained about that trend all year," says Brannon Braga who notes that such episodes as "Interface," "Inheritance" and "Bloodlines" all involved relatives of the crew. "The one thing I was very disappointed about is that in almost every other show we were introducing a new family member. I found that to be embarrassing. I thought shows like 'Homeward' could have been done without a family member involved. It was somewhat arbitrary."

Echoes Shankar, "Ron Moore started calling it the season of lost souls. You don't set out at the beginning of the season to say we're going to do many relatives this season. It just happened. We even almost had Geordi's sister in `Force Of Nature.' It's almost amusing in an

embarrassing sort of way."

In fact, if it could be said that "Chain of Command" [the episode in which Picard is captured and tortured by the Cardassians] signaled a departure for the series sixth year in graduating from high concept storytelling — like the holodeck western "Fistful of Datas" and the transporter twilight zone of "Realm of Fear" — to compelling character drama, it was "Force of Nature," a show in which the crew discovers that warp drive is destroying the fabric of the universe, that had a profound effect on the writers during the seventh year — however, in a far less positive way.

"`Force of Nature' was something I fought for early on and went to the wall for," says Ron Moore. "We had a big meeting with Rick and Mike and Jeri and we all got on our high horses and we went in there and said we felt strongly about the episode saying, `We want to do this, we want to make a statement, and we want to change the *Star Trek* universe forever. This is important and this is right and we should do it!' Now, I'm just going, `What was I thinking?' because now we have this warp speed limit and in every third episode we have to get permission to go fast. It was such a great idea in concept. We always said that dealing with the environment on this show is incredibly difficult. It's hard to do a show about the ozone, because the ozone is huge and non-personal, and hard to make dramatic. We thought we had found a way to personalize it and make it our problem and it became `Force of Nature'."

Comments Michael Piller, "The truth is I spent so much time on *Deep Space Nine*, particularly at the beginning of the year, that my involvement with *The Next Generation* was that of a Monday morning quarterback. It made me feel uncomfortable at times, sort of being an absentee landlord coming to collect the rent. I would come in to check the stories and read the scripts and give notes, but I felt seventh season my influence was beginning to lessen. It was almost two years since I had been in the room with the guys breaking stories, and these are very good people who deserved to be able to try the things that they always wanted to do."

••••

However, Piller also realized early into the season that the show was not heading in a direction he was pleased with. "'Force Of Nature' certainly inspired us to have several long meetings on where the season was going," he recalls. "I felt we were letting it slip away."

As a result, Piller became adamant that the writers begin to re-dedicate themselves to the show and begin to address long-festering character issues. This ultimately led to shows like "Journey's End," in which Wesley chooses to leave Starfleet Academy, and "Bloodlines," in which Ferengi Daimon Bok returns to confront Picard.

"The problem was that we didn't have a lot of ideas," says Piller. "We had to go with the best ones we could come up with and then within each one of those execute it as best as we could. I was unhappy with the first third of the season, but then I thought we really hit our stride. I was mostly inspired by the emotional impact on myself and others of the Beverly/Jean-Luc 'Attached' episode. That episode did not work in a couple of ways, but the way it did work was to fundamentally go to the heart of the series and force two characters, who had had a subtext of a relationship burning for some seasons, to finally confront those feelings. I found the emotional resonance so affecting and meaningful, that I said to Jeri, 'Let's spend what little time we have left really working on tying up some loose ends.' I think that really inspired much of the last half of the season."

"There were about five episodes in the middle of seventh season that were as strong a group of episodes as I have ever been a part of, going from 'Parallels' to 'Pegasus' to 'Lower Decks,' which was really one of the wonderful shows of the year," he continues. "I also thought that the Beverly Crusher romance with the ghost ['Sub Rosa'] was a very well executed show. It was a terrific group of episodes. I thought we were doing as good as we possibly could. But the appetite of the season begins to gnaw at you and finally you have to say we have to do a show next week — what are we going to do?"

Jeri Taylor admits that each year it gets harder and harder to find

things that haven't been dealt with before. "I talked to Patrick [Stewart] and Brent [Spiner] at one point and asked if there was any facet of their characters that they thought we hadn't explored yet, and both of them turned to me and said, 'Nope,'" she smiles. "They couldn't come up with anything."

Piller admits that the fact that the writers stopped taking pitches — in which prospective writers try to sell ideas to the show — for several weeks during the season was a mistake and helped contribute to the dearth of workable story premises.

The lack of story ideas, coupled with Piller's newfound willingness to allow the writers to develop concepts which would have previously not been approved, resulted in some pushing of the traditional *Trek* boundaries both in terms of interpersonal conflict and storytelling. Says Ron Moore, "I think the final year we thought the magic formula was just to break the rules, based on the success of the sixth season, and then we started hunting for something to do differently, like introducing warp drive limitations and stuff like that, but then we started realizing, so what?"

Among the more radical ideas incorporated into the narrative tapestry of the seventh season was the Worf/Troi romance, which first blossoms in "Parallels," Brannon Braga's story of an alternate timeline in which the two officers are married.

"This was something we had been talking about for quite a while," says Taylor. "'Fistful of Datas,' for instance, was an effort to gradually bring Worf and Troi a little closer together. Their romance just sort of erupted into bloom at the end of this season and I think has given us some very nice moments. It was unexpected and not what the fans predicted, and I think that that's good. I've probably gotten more antagonistic mail on this than anything."

The emerging romance between Troi and Worf precluded the Troi/Riker relationship from moving to the forefront — although several of the writers were anxious to provide that storyline with a sense of closure.

Offers Echevarria, "We were talking about how we wanted to marry

Riker and Troi and we thought the fans would love that. Michael and Rick didn't care for that idea. Michael wanted to explore the Worf-Troi relationship. The actors were not happy about it. Marina has always maintained that Riker is her Imzadi."

Laughs Michael Dorn, who portrays the now-lovestruck Klingon, "I think it was a coincidence because I did lobby for it for a long time at conventions. I would talk to the fans and they would love the idea. They really are a cute couple. They are beauty and the beast. It's an interesting triangle because Worf is interested in Troi because of the way she handled his son. He's grown to admire and respect her and, of course, respect is a big thing with Klingons. The thing [rivalry] between Riker and Worf is interesting because they have a great relationship and my line at conventions was that Worf would come up to Commander Riker and say, 'Excuse me, but are you through with Counselor Troi?' After all, you know how guys are."

Frakes, however, has his own designs on the comely Counselor. "Naturally I would like to see it go further," he says. "I'm selfishly interested in their relationship, which I don't think has been explored as completely as it might have been."

Rene Echevarria is more blunt. "I thought if the series is ending, we don't need to have Riker and Troi free to screw space bimbos. So why not have her marry Lieutenant Riker? One of the biggest regrets I have is the impression we've given that time and time again none of the characters is capable of having a genuine relationship. It is something that the fans are aware of and are disappointed by. I think it would have been the right thing to at least bring one of those relationships all the way home."

Despite the continuing series of *Star Trek* feature films and their new responsibilities on the *Trek* spin-offs, most of the creative team that created *TNG* week after week can't help but wax nostalgically over the completion of filming on the series.

"I'll miss the laughter," says Michael Dorn. "I kept telling everyone I'll miss the laughter and the fun we had more than anything else. I never had this much fun on any of the sets that I worked on. But it's not an ending, we'll still have the conventions and the films."

Muses Jonathan Frakes, "I think it was one of the best shows on television. When it was good, it was a great show. When it was bad, it was still good."

"It was good television which is a rare animal in itself," says Brent Spiner. "I think we satisfied the entertainment angle and, to a large extent, we made allusions to the world we live in. I think we could have been more hard-hitting. I think we waffled on a few issues because there were so many rules that were attached to the world of *Star Trek* and it would have been nice to break some of those rules and stretch the envelope and go beyond what we did do with this wonderful format."

Recalls Michael Piller, who visited Stage 16 during the final evening of shooting "All Good Things," involving Patrick Stewart and John DeLancie, "The day I went down to say goodbye to Patrick on the stage, I felt a loss. It's the loss I felt from missing a character that I've really become attached to. I think Picard is a remarkable character and Patrick Stewart made him that way. I'm singling out Patrick because he is a special talent. It's been five years of surprises and delights and you can't imagine how rare it is in television to have the pleasure of working with talents like these people. So I really felt sad the last day when they were shooting the last shot, because it was really the perfect teaming of writers and performers where we were able to say something through television in an entertaining fashion."

For others, the significance of the end of *The Next Generation* television era came when they received their invitations to the show's wrap party. A letter which ended with a stark picture of an empty bridge reading 1987 to 1994.

"It was like a funeral notice," says Ron Moore. "You just kind of go, `Oh man, it's really ending.' And that was the first time it really hit me. Even writing the final episode, it was just a project that we had to get done."

Even former creative consultant Tracy Torme, who predicted when he left the show after the second season that the popularity of *TNG* would never exceed that of the original, has reassessed his feelings about the future of the show. "I think *The Next Generation* will probably be what everyone thinks of when people think of *Star Trek*," he says. "I think given the direction the world is headed in, you're going to see a lot more of *The Next Generation* and a lot less of the old show. It's an unqualified smash success. It's going to live on."

"I think the show is going to endure strongly," says Naren Shankar. "It has a fundamental appeal. It gets knocked by a lot of people as being too squeaky clean or optimistic or too unrealistic. I think what many people fail to recognize while taking shots at *Star Trek* is that it is precisely those characteristics that give *Star Trek* its appeal. It is a fundamentally optimistic view of the future that says we can get past our petty foibles and baser instincts and make a better place for ourselves while we're more tolerant, a little more understanding; where violence isn't the only recourse toward solving a problem. Maybe on a subconscious level people respond to that. Maybe that's a large part of the popularity of the show. And there is a lot of stuff on television you can watch. Some of it's meaningful, some of it less so. If I never work in this industry again, I can look to the years I spent on this show with a certain level of pride and say at least that I was part of it. And that it had a positive effect on people. Hey, if you can say that about your job, then I think you're doing okay."

NO. 221 • MAY 6, 1994

Entertainment WEEKLY

'TREK'
INSIDE THE TENSE FINAL DAYS

$2.50 (CAN. $2.95)

18

10210

This extended cover of Entertainment Weekly *prepared to say goodbye to* Star Trek: The Next Generation *(photo copyright ©1995 Time Warner).*

• • • •

286

THE 'NEXT GENERATION' CAST:
PATRICK STEWART, GATES McFADDEN,
BRENT SPINER, LEVAR BURTON,
JONATHAN FRAKES, MICHAEL DORN,
AND MARINA SIRTIS

• • • •

CHAPTER TWENTY NINE
SEASON SEVEN

Episode Guide

"Descent, Part II"

"Liaisons"

"Interface"

"Gambit, Part I"

"Gambit, Part II"

"Phantasms"

"Dark Page"

"Attached"

"Force of Nature"

"Inheritance"

"Parallels"

"The Pegasus"

"Homeward"

"Sub Rosa"

"Lower Decks"

"Thine Own Self"

"Masks"

"Eye of the Beholder"

"Genesis"

"Journey's End"

"Firstborn"

"Bloodlines"

"Emergence"

"Preemptive Strike"

"All Good Things"

• • • •

Episode #153
"Descent, Part II"
Original Airdate: 9/20/93
Written by Rene Echevarria
Directed by Alexander Singer
Guest Starring: Jonathan Del Arco (Hugh), Alex Datcher (Taitt), James Horan (Barnaby), Brian Cousins (Crosis)

As the story continues, Hugh is enraged at the Enterprise crew for their introduction of emotions into him and, in turn, the Borg collective consciousness. This action is what led the way for Lore to become their leader. Despite his anger, he works with Picard to help remove Lore from power, which also serves the purpose of freeing Data from his brother's maniacal grip. Meanwhile, in space, Crusher is in command of the Enterprise as it engages a Borg warship.

• • • •

"I don't think it was as good as it could have been," says Brent Spiner, who played both Data and Lore in the episode which was partially filmed on location in Simi Valley at the same synagogue where the Khitomer Conference interiors were filmed for *Star Trek VI.* "There was a real nice potential there, but it was too mammoth an undertaking in the seven days we're allotted to do shows. There was a nice subtext. Lore wasn't really just villainous, he believed in what he was doing."

Explains *TNG* Executive Producer Jeri Taylor of the troubled production, "I think that what we found out was that we had too much story to tell. It was such an embarrassment of riches that a lot of things had to get short shrift. The Lore/Data thing took over, forcing us to almost ignore Hugh, who became a very minor kind of character. We were trying to deal with the themes of cults and how a charismatic leader can lure and beguile people. But we had so many themes. Maybe it was just too ambitious, because we were not able to do justice to any one of the themes. We spread ourselves so thin and that was our mistake."

"It was like many two-part episodes, there were many balls in the air and late in the process, new balls were added," says Rene Echevarria, who wrote the show. "After the first draft was written, Michael [Piller] became intrigued with the David Koresh angle on Lore, so

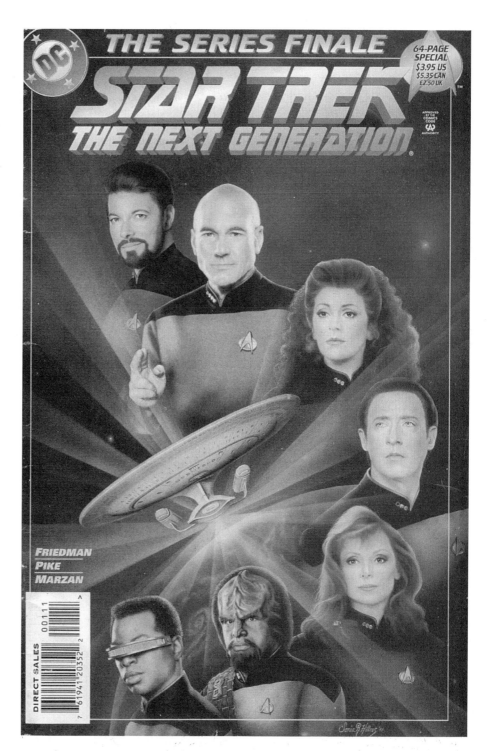

DC Comics adapted the final episode of ST: TNG , "All Good Things"

that needed to be developed. We would have loved to stay on that planet for the entire episode and done Lore, Data and Geordi and our people and all those relationships, but it was unproduceable. We didn't have the sets to keep it from becoming claustrophobic."

Says Brannon Braga of the episode which addressed Data confronting dark emotions brought on by his

Cinefantastique *concludes its yearly visit to the set of* Star Trek: The Next Generation.

evil brother, "I think 'Part II' was less successful than 'Part I' in that not enough time was devoted to the relationship between Geordi and Data and Data's experience with these strange, warped, addicting, dark emotions. That was the most interesting part of it. Unfortunately, you had all these disparate elements like Hugh and Riker, and Worf dealing with Hugh, and Beverly as the commander of the ship which was action and tech. We thought that would sustain the excitement when, in fact, in my opinion, it just served to take away from the more interesting elements. I thought that 'Part I' was better in terms of Data, and his emotional arc, which was all but lost by comparison in 'Part II'. Nevertheless, it was action-packed and successful on that level."

As for the future of the malevolent automatons who have made such a mark on the new *Star Trek* series, Braga offers, "The Borg are endlessly fascinating. I have no doubt we'll see them again. In what guise, I don't know."

Episode #154
"Liaisons"
Original Airdate: 9/28/93
Story by
Roger Eschabacher & Jaq Greenspon
Teleplay by
Jeanne Carrigan Fauci & Lisa Rich
Directed by Cliff Bole

Guest Starring: Barbara Williams (Anna), Eric Pierpoint (Voval), Paul Eiding (Loquel), Michael Harris (Byleth)

Troi, Worf and Picard find themselves manipulated by Lyaaran ambassadors when they agree to partake in a cultural exchange program. Troi's partner, Loquel, is seeking out the more pleasurable aspects of the starship, particularly its food and drinks. Worf's companion, Byleth, continually provokes the Klingon until he explodes in fury, which actually seems to please the Lyaaran. Picard, having agreed to beam down to the Lyaaran home world, is accidentally stranded on a planet which seems to have one other inhabitant, Anna, who claims to be in love with him while at the same time attempting to hold him captive. Ultimately, it all comes down to the fact that these three aliens have been sent by their people to experience the human emotions of aggression, pleasure, and intimacy.

• • • •

"I was never very excited about this story," admits Brannon Braga, who was saddled with the show's rewrite after the original draft was submitted involving Picard's relationship with an obsessive woman. "When I was in Hawaii writing the movie, I just somehow knew that I was going to get this rewrite. I was dreading it, because I was not a fan of this story. Lisa and Jean's first draft had some very nice things in it, but the relationship wasn't working between Picard and the woman. The woman was a Starfleet woman who was very together and they had a very normal relationship and really did kind of start to be interested in each other. When it turns out that she's actually an alien trying to figure out what love's all about, I had asked the question, 'Well, she did such a good job emulating the human female falling in love, why would they need to learn anything?' What I did was make it a darker story and made the relationship much more sinister and disturbing."

Adds Rene Echevarria, "It was actually pitched very slyly by the writers, who pitched it as kind of a take on *Star Trek*-obsessed fans and that's what made me smile and at least pass it on. What if we did *Misery* with Captain Picard and a big fan of his, and that fell by the wayside. That was just too on the nose and it

became something very different."

Jeri Taylor was immediately struck by the pitch when Echevarria passed the premise on to her, "I fell in love with this from the first pitch because it lent itself to something that we had seen work so beautifully in 'Chain of Command II', which is a two-person play with Patrick Stewart. And the idea of a woman who is his captor on a sort of emotional and psychological level seemed, to me, to be fraught with the same kind of dramatic material that we got from 'Chain of Command.' I think it certainly fulfilled that."

In the early drafts of the script, the show's B story involved Troi's promotion to Commander, a plotline used later in the season for "Thine Own Self."

"The B-line of Troi getting pips was written into the script by Lisa and Jean, who did the first draft and it was a very uneasy marriage," says Taylor. "The stories were not comfortable with each other. We felt that there needed to be something that was more organically linked to the Picard story, and that's when Brannon came up with having the other diplomats from the same race of people. I thought he did an absolutely marvelous job of drawing some very droll, delightful characters who were experiencing our way of life for the first time."

Says Braga, "Troi's commander's test was just working against it from the beginning, so what I did was make it a much darker story and put a twist on it. The relationship became much more sinister and disturbing. We did more of a *Fatal Attraction* thing, which would also more believably dramatize the ambassador's struggle. It suddenly made sense. What you think is a fatal, twisted obsession at first is really just someone trying to 'get it,' which I thought was kind of interesting. Once I got rid of the Troi-Commander arc, I wrote a much more humorous arc with the ambassadors on the ship. Why not use a premise which seemed like something disconnected, but was in fact connected to the main story? Was I happy with the script? Yeah. Was I happy with the episode? I don't know.

"I had a lot of fun writing it, and a lot of it was cut for time, mostly the more fun moments," he adds. "Whether or not they actually ended up being funny is another story. It's a matter of opinion. At the end, I give Picard a speech about people who take things to extremes to experience them, and that's what these people do. I thought that was very interesting. In order to understand the culture, you must immerse yourself in that culture. It's still a little scattered, though. In the end, even though it seemed redolent of *Misery* and *Fatal Attraction*, the *Star Trek* twist was, it wasn't at all."

Episode #155
"Interface"
Original Airdate: 10/4/93
Written by Joe Menosky
Directed by Robert Wiemer
Guest Starring:
Madge Sinclair (Captain Silva La Forge), Warren Munson (Admiral Holt), Ben Vereen (Doctor La Forge)

Geordi is hooked up to a new virtual reality probe, and while investigating the wreckage of a doomed ship, he discovers his mother onboard after word that she has disappeared arrives from his father. La Forge fails to heed words of warning from Captain Picard and persists in the experiments in the hopes of saving his mother from death, ultimately learning that the vision is not his mother at all.

• • • •

Offers Ron Moore of the technobabble-ridden episode written by former *Trek* staffer Joe Menosky, "There's one scene which was a high point of tech for the series, where Joe was trying to explain how the mother was on this ship and it's like Geordi's not really on the ship because he's a probe, but then there's this mother on the ship, but she's not there either, but she might have been in a warp funnel from beaming down to a planet, which is sending a projection to the probe which is going to look like Geordi's hand. It was this insane world of tech that Joe understood and no one else did. He sits up in the Alps somewhere and just sends this stuff to us."

Adds Naren Shankar, "This show was something that had been around for a while. We had talked about the possibility of doing a show where Riker's father had just passed

away and Riker's in this virtual reality program where he goes down to the planet and starts seeing images of Alaska. That's what this became eventually. When we realized that it would probably be better to do a story like this with Geordi rather than Riker, we sent it off to Joe immediately and this is what he came back with. To me, it's not real interesting from a gee-whiz standpoint of technology, because we weren't looking at technology four hundred years in the future. I think it's more like forty years into the future. It's almost an overdone type of theme these days. The technology seems out of proportion to the other technologies that we use on the Enterprise."

"It wasn't so much that we hadn't wanted to do it before, we had never quite found a way for the story to work," says Jeri Taylor of the show's virtual reality premise. "It had been pitched two years before as a Riker story and by the time we got around to sort of working it out, we were at the end of the sixth season and we suddenly had a bunch of Riker stories, so it didn't seem appropriate. We decided to hold it until this year when we realized that its subject matter was very similar to `Frame of Mind' involving Riker and an alternate reality. We had planned the death of Riker's father as something that would have an emotional kind of impact on him, but it just seemed too close to things we had done before. When we came up with the idea of using it for Geordi, everything sort of just broke free and it worked much better."

"We've had the family of everybody else on board," says Taylor. "Every other character has had their family dealt with except Geordi and probably the main reason for doing it was there was an order to finally flesh out his character more than it had been, and to show that he didn't spring isolated from Zeus' forehead."

Another reason for finally depicting Geordi's family was that a long simmering story idea in which it would be established that the ship's chief engineer was the child of aliens had been dropped.

Robin Curtis, who portrayed Lt. Saavik in the third and fourth Star Trek features, returned as a Romulan named Tallera in "Gambit" (photo copyright ©1995 Karen Witkowski).

Episode #156
"Gambit, Part I"
Original Airdate: 10/11/93
Teleplay by Naren Shankar
Story by
Chris Hatton and Naren Shankar
Directed by Peter Lauritson
Guest Starring:
Richard Lynch (Baran), Robin Curtis (Tallera), Caitlin Brown (Vekor), Cameron Thor (Narik), Alan Altshuld (Yranac), Bruce Gray (Admiral Chekote).

Riker is abducted by mercenaries who he believes are responsible for killing Captain Picard. Once onboard the alien pirate ship, Riker learns Picard is still alive and passing himself off as Gaylen, one of the smugglers, who are searching for a rare artifact. Meanwhile, Riker tries to convince the smugglers he has turned his back on Starfleet and is going to join them.

• • • •

The show is referred to jokingly on staff as the "yo ho, ho, pirate show," a concept that had long been considered anathema on *TNG*. "I read the script and I was not particularly taken with it when Michael [Piller] gave it to me last season," recalls Jeri Taylor. "And then I put the script aside and four months later I wrote Michael a memo which said something like, `Although I wasn't fond of this story, rather like a hen who sits on her eggs for a long time, I've become attached to it and the more I thought about it I could just sort of say, maybe this could work.' It ended up sort of working so well that we made two parts out of it and, yes, it's a pirate story. But I think that it was a romp."

Writer Naren Shankar's original idea for the xenophobic Vulcan isolationist movement featured in the story was that they were literally planning to phase the planet out of our universe to avoid cultural contamination from alien species. "Everyone was afraid it was going to be like a *Space: 1999* episode," says Shankar. "The notion was to dimensionally shift the planet so you couldn't get to them. In that sense, it would be pure isolation. I still think that's a cool idea. Nobody else does, however."

"I was never very enthused about 'Gambit,'" says Brannon Braga. "When the story was purchased, I was not attracted to the campy, swashbuckling elements and was afraid it would just look very corny. I don't think we do campiness very well — especially, in the way we tried to do it with 'Gambit.' It came off like *Buck Rogers: The Series* and why do that? Is that good? We try many different mediums. I was curious as to why we were involving ourselves in a medium that is not usually a respected one."

Star Trek III's Robin Curtis plays a Vulcan isolationist in the episode, the villainous Tallera.

Episode #157
"Gambit, Part II"
Original Airdate: 10/18/94
Teleplay by Ronald D. Moore
Story by Naren Shankar
Directed by Alexander Singer
Guest Starring:
Richard Lynch (Baran), Robin Curtis (Tallera), Caitlin Brown (Vekor), Cameron Thor (Narik), James Worthy (Koral), Sabrina LeBeauf (Ensign Giusti)

Picard learns that the pirates are seeking a psionic resonator, a mystical device of unspeakable power from Vulcan history. Once they have obtained the location of the resonator, Picard

learns that Tallera is actually a Vulcan operative, but an isolationist who is determined to prevent alien intrusions on the planet Vulcan.

• • • •

"I felt we ran out of story in 'Part II,'" says writer Ron Moore. "There were places where I was treading water. We had to find the lost ark and I didn't know what the lost ark was. Instead, we had a device from ancient Vulcan myth that had mythic properties that you explain are telepathic focusing properties. I was trying really hard to make this thing work and in the end, I just said, 'All right, maybe we should just go for it and make this a classic Gene [Roddenberry] kind of message and go for "think happy thoughts" and make it something which tied into the backstory of Vulcan and of Surak and peace.' I thought it would fit in nicely. I'm not sure if it did. It might have just fallen in on its own gooeyness."

Starring in the episode as the show's villain was Richard Lynch playing Baran. Of course, playing a genre baddie is nothing new for Lynch; he's a familiar staple of sci-fi TV, having appeared in episodes of *Battlestar Galactica*, *Buck Rogers* and countless low-budget horror films. "Richard was simply the best person who read for the part," says Jeri Taylor. "[Producer] Peter Lauritson, who directed the first episode, knew his work, liked him, and really wanted him. It's always a problem to find worthy adversaries for Picard. You need an actor who has the power, stature, and presence to go toe to toe with him and if you don't have that, you don't have an episode. Richard brought all of this and for his campiness and the sort of stereotypical things that he has done, he has that undeniable power and I thought that it was a good trade."

Another casting coup for the episode was a guest appearance by Los Angeles Laker James Worthy as an imposing, foul Klingon warrior. The famous Laker basketball star underwent a prosthetic transformation into the tallest Klingon in the galaxy for "Gambit, Part II" as a mercenary whose craft is intercepted by the Enterprise.

"He called Rick and said he wanted to do *Star Trek* and they had lunch and Rick let me know that he was

interested in doing the show," says Jeri Taylor. "So when we did `Gambit' we developed this part and I told Rick who said `Wait a minute, I didn't say give him a part. He's a basketball player. I don't know if he can act.' But I thought Worthy did a terrific job. He understood this person. He had presence and he had an arrogance. He just stepped right into the part and did an excellent job."

Episode #158
"Phantasms"
Original Airdate: 10/25/93
Written by Brannon Braga
Directed by Patrick Stewart
Guest Starring: Gina Ravarra (Ensign Tyler), Bernard Kates (Sigmund Freud), Clyde Kusatsu (Admiral Nakamura), David L. Crowley (Workman)

When Data begins experiencing some frightening nightmares, including one in which he is disassembled by miners, he realizes that his nightmare images may hold the clue to a parasitic invasion of the ship which could result in the death of the crew.

• • • •

One of this episode's most effective images is Data's vision of Troi transformed into a cake in Ten Forward. "Troi as a cake got the most fevered response from the art department of anything that we have ever done in the four years that I have been here," laughs Jeri Taylor. "They were so disturbed and concerned about this that the entire department stayed after the production of it to implore us not to do this. Brannon and I were somewhat mystified by this because we didn't see it as that big a problem. Brannon had shot a student film in which he had done something very similar and for $1.98 he had managed to bring it off. Then he found a rock video that had a similar kind of thing and we were just sure that it could work. The only problem was that Patrick [Stewart], who directed it, shot one angle that we had expressly told him not to shoot and it made it very clear that it was someone's neck coming out of a cake."

Offers Producer David Livingston, "The writers can write this stuff, but sometimes when we do it in production, it's really hard to pull off. What we lack is R&D time and it always astounds me how the crafts people on this show are able to pull these gags off. I thought that 'Phantasms' did it really well and Patrick did a terrific job on the episode."

Where do these surreal dream images come from? Braga speculates, "I could say something clever like I've always wanted to see somebody eat Counselor Troi, but the truth is those kinds of images perhaps are all most attractive to me because I don't understand where they come from. I see the value in darker imagery, more bizarre imagery and what was especially fun about putting them in the *Star Trek* universe is they're such an incongruous juxtaposition to what people expect from *The Next Generation,* which is a somewhat sterile, reality-based universe. So, when suddenly you got these kind of completely disarming and disturbing images, it works."

The idea of portraying Data's nightmares was not new. Braga had first conceived the premise when he gave Data dreams in sixth season's "Birthright" two-parter. "It wasn't until I came up with the idea of creatures that only Data could subliminally perceive, because of his positronic brain, that I got the story. It was a blast to do and it was a pure pleasure to write."

Braga even created a scene in which Data seeks counseling from Sigmund Freud himself, the groundbreaking psychoanalyst who has proven a source of great fascination for Braga over the years. "I've wanted to dig my claws in for a long time and really undermine the Freudian concepts that have pervaded the American cultural mainstream and are so much a part of therapy and self-help therapy," he says. "The basic Freudian concepts of the subconscious ego and all the other terms have become a given in the way people think about the way the mind works in America. But why? How do we know that's how it works? How do we know any of that stuff is true? It's probably not, and you're seeing a huge backlash starting with Freud. I'm happy to have been one of the first to comment on it.

"Don't get me wrong," he elaborates. "Freud is the most fun of all the psychologists. I'm a huge fan. Do I think

his theory is incredible? Who am I to say? I certainly would like to think there's a subconscious. I don't know. I'm more a fan of Jung when it comes to what's really going on, but who's to say? The interesting thing is when you look at the episode, it is completely Freudian. The premise of the show is Freudian, Data's subconscious mind....the way in which images manifest themselves in his dreams. It's all Freudian mechanisms so at the same time that I was discrediting Freud in the episode, I was using all of his concepts to explain everything. To be honest, it's something I definitely think about because it's not helping people break out of their mindsets about Freudian concepts in this culture when they're seeing them portrayed in the 24th Century as a given. It's not until shows start showing different ways in which the mind works that you are going to get people breaking free of their Freudian concepts — so there's a tremendous contradiction in the episode in that regard."

Episode #159
"Dark Page"
Original Airdate: 11/1/93
Written by Hilary J. Bader
Directed by Les Landau
Guest Starring: Majel Barrett (Lwaxana Troi), Norman Large (Maques), Kirsten Dunst (Hedril), Amick Byram (Mr. Troi)

Troi is forced to enter her mother Lwaxanna's metaconscious mind to discover the hidden trauma which is killing Mrs. Troi. With the help of an alien delegate, Maques, who forments the bonding, Troi begins to explore inside her mother's mind. At the same time, Lwaxana is trying to prevent her daughter from learning that her youngest daughter, who Deanna never knew, drowned when she was very young.

• • • •

"There was a great reluctance to do this episode and 'Phantasms' back to back, but it was one of those predicaments where we didn't have anything else ready to go," says Jeri Taylor. "'Dark Page' had been around a long, long time and it had undergone many permutations. Hillary Bader had pitched this story and it just never seemed to work. It started as a Dr. Crusher story and went through every possible combination of

people on the Enterprise. It wasn't until we hit upon Troi and Mrs. Troi that it really seemed to work, and then it was a long time before we could figure out what the secret was that is hurting Mrs. Troi. Ultimately, I think it worked really well and was an emotional episode. It provided a depth to Mrs. Troi's character that we had not seen before."

Brannon Braga, who was writing "Phantasms" at the same time the writers were breaking "Dark Page," was less enthused about the show. "I was dying to write 'Dark Page' and I couldn't for timing reasons," he says. "I thought it was just a great premise that Bader gave us to dip into with the counselor exploring the psyche of her mother and finding out that it's a dark and scary place. It's is a great idea. But, I was thinking, 'You can't do this one. I want to do this in "Phantasms." You guys are killing me.'"

"I think Rene, who did the production re-write on the episode, did a magnificent job on the show," says Naren Shankar. "It's sort of like *The Joy Luck Club.* It was better than I expected. It was quite touching in many ways."

Episode #160
"Attached"
Original Airdate: 11/8/93
Written by Nicholas Sagan
Directed by Jonathan Frakes
Guest Starring: Robin Gammell (Mauric), Lenore Kasdorf (Lorin)

Picard and Dr. Crusher are kidnapped, and through a telepathic link discover their true feelings for each other while two feuding races, so distrustful of each other and the Federation, have their dispute mediated by a befuddled Commander Riker.

• • • •

Nicholas Sagan, a television and interactive game writer, admits that many of his early pitches for the show were off-base. "I was a little naive," he laughs. "I was trying to do things they wouldn't have wanted me to do. I did one story involving Charlie X from the original *Star Trek* and another which brought back Armis from 'Skin of Evil.'"

Ultimately it was a pitch that Sagan made involving a physical link a la *The Defiant Ones* between Picard and Dr. Crusher that intrigued the writing staff, but a long simmering resistance to explore their relationship had to be overcome before the story was given the go-ahead.

"I believe the actors wanted it, the fans wanted it, the writing staff wanted it, but it was just the very top guys who felt that everything should be done with looks and suggestions and let the audience assume what they wanted from that," says Sagan.

Offers Ron Moore of the blossoming of the Picard/Crusher romance, "There was a real hesitancy of whether we should say any of the stuff up front or whether it should be all subtext. I thought, let's just do it and stop toying around with this non-existent relationship. I wanted to do something that explained how he felt and why he never acted on it."

In the story break for the episode, Picard and Crusher kiss when they find themselves as fugitives on the alien planet. Everyone knew selling the plot point to producer Michael Piller would be the challenge. Mapping the story out on the familiar dry erase board, Sagan bowed out to veteran producer Ron Moore who began outlining the episode for Piller. "I didn't need to be up there and Ron's very good at going through the board," says Sagan. "He explained, 'We have this planet and they're talking and then they kiss.' Michael, who had been sort of quiet but into the story, paused and looked at us and said, 'Absolutely not.' Instead, it became this very touching scene that's in there now where Picard's keeping her warm and it's the most poignant and memorable moment in the entire episode."

Agrees Jonathan Frakes, who directed the episode, "We finally saw Picard and Crusher together and I thought it was great. I particularly liked the long scene of them together by the campfire where they really explored their relationship and their attraction to each other."

"We didn't consciously want to wrap up arcs or bring things to neat conclusions because, of course, the feature film series will continue so we didn't want that sense that we had sewn things nicely into a box," says Jeri Taylor. "We simply wanted to tell good, provocative, interesting stories about

our people. Nick Sagan had pitched the premise originally about Beverly and Picard being linked together physically and I thought that that gave us great dramatic possibility. Michael was not so sure and then we got another pitch of them being linked telepathically and it was the combination of the two that kind of put it over the edge. So we had to sort of overcome that hurdle first. Then it's the question of how far do you go? How much do you push this? What do you say? What do you not say? Where do you leave it? It was a tightrope act every step of the way. I think the fans universally liked this episode up until the last scene and then many, many of them felt very cheated. There's a very vocal group out there that wants this to be explored even more and have them get married. To us, that's not been the right way to go. Patrick doesn't feel that Jean Luc Picard would move in that direction. I think all of us in the decision-making ranks feel that that's not the thing to do and so it was fine to tell a delicate story of unspoken feelings, but to have taken it any further than that would have been wrong."

Sagan notes that the final scene — in which Beverly rebuffs Picard, entreating him that they should just remain close friends — was one of the most important scenes of the show. "I wanted to make the ending as heartbreaking as possible," he says. "I heard criticism of the episode from fans who said what was the point of the episode if they didn't actually get together, and I think that's really missing the point. It's really about people who make choices that prevent them from getting together...or at least from getting married. I think there's something kind of touching about the inability of that to happen."

"I think Picard was shocked and very dismayed," comments Patrick Stewart. "I think it took a long time for him to get to the point where he could make that proposal, and I think with customary male vanity he was a little surprised."

"That was really terrific," Gates McFadden says. "I think Jeri Taylor has always been in agreement that we should do something with Dr. Crusher and Picard and pick up that thread again, which all the fans who write Patrick and

me want to see. We've got so many letters asking what happened to their relationship. I thought the episode was terrific because it doesn't close the door at all."

Episode #161
"Force of Nature"
Original Airdate: 11/15/93
Written by Naren Shankar
Directed by Robert Lederman
Guest Starring:
Michael Corbett (Rabal), Margaret Reed (Serova), Lee Arenberg (Prak)

A pair of alien scientists attempt to warn the Enterprise crew about the dangers of warp drive to the fabric of subspace in their sector, while the Enterprise is engaged in the rescue of a missing Federation vessel. Ultimately, the Enterprise crew discovers that the use of warp drive is having a detrimental effect on space and warp limits are imposed on all Federation starships on non-emergency business.

• • • •

"I think this is the worst show that I collaborated on this season," says Michael Piller. "It certainly inspired us to have several meetings on where the season was going because I felt we were letting it slip away."

"There were preposterous moments in that show," says Brannon Braga. "On the other hand, we knew the risks, but we felt it was real important to at least try to do an environmental show. We struggled with making it a personal story and in the end it just didn't work as well as we wanted it to. We couldn't find a personal angle. When you limit warp drive, the rug is being pulled out from under *Star Trek*. I wish more time had been spent with that, and less time with Spot and Cat."

The genesis of the show, once known as 'Limits,' was in a story idea devised by Joe Menosky who was attempting to craft an allegory for contemporary environmental problems. Yet when Braga told Menosky that the staff was going ahead with the story, Braga relates, "He said, 'Are you crazy? Are you out of your minds?' The reason we'd been avoiding it was because we were afraid it would get preachy and techy and, unfortunately, it was both."

Explains Naren Shankar of the

tenuous link between the show's A story and a B story involving Data training his cat, Spot, "The slightest dramatic connection between those two is the notion that you can't control a force of nature like a cat."

"This was a troubled episode from the first," says Jeri Taylor. "It was a wonderful environmental premise that something we take for granted is doing damage to the space around us. It was the metaphor which most closely evoked our present situation. We had tried it in many guises and it never worked. At the beginning of the seventh year, I sent Naren and Brannon to a big breakfast meeting of an environmental watchdog group that we have here in Hollywood and they came back inspired. Naren was so galvanized. He said, 'I want to take a crack at "Limits." I want to do this. This is important.' I agreed. It was a story I really wanted to do and I think it does make an important statement, but dramatizing a huge issue like that is always the trouble. We started down many roads. At first, we had Geordi's sister come on board to help him adjust to the death of his mother [in 'Interface'], but that seemed to muddle everything completely. We then started the whole little thread of Geordi in competition with the engineer from another ship so that we could show Geordi's deeply felt belief in technology and the benefits of technology, so that he would be at war with himself when realizing that it was contributing to something disastrous.

"When the script was written," she adds, "it turned out to be very, very short and we then started adding scenes about Data's cat. By luck, or by bad luck, all of those scenes turned out to be at the beginning of the show, so you had an episode that started very fitfully and seemed to be about Data's cat and then it took a turn and seemed to be about Geordi and his rivalry with this other guy. Then it went back to the cat and then, finally, in about the third act, the real story began and, by that point, I think people were hopelessly lost. It sort of never got back on track, but it's still an important idea and our intentions were good."

Episode #162
"Inheritance"
Original Airdate: 11/22/93
Teleplay by
Dan Koeppel and Rene Echevarria
Story by Dan Koeppel
Directed by Robert Scheerer
Guest Starring: Fionnula Flanagan (Juliana), William Lithgow (Pran)

Data is surprised to encounter a scientist exploring seismic activity on Atrea who claims to be his "mother," the wife of the late Doctor Noonian Soong. Data is reluctant to believe her, his instinct proving correct when an accident reveals to him that this woman, Juliana, is actually an android constructed by Soong before him. Ultimately he chooses to keep the fact that she's an android from her so that she can continue to live a normal life.

• • • •

"'Inheritance' came to us as a pitch the previous season and Michael's comment at the time was that it doesn't seem like there's enough here to make a story," says Jeri Taylor. "It's an example of a situation in which he was more trusting of us to be able to take a somewhat slender premise and develop it. We went for the emotional part of it, which was Data and his relationship with his mother."

Adds Rene Echevarria, "I loved the pitch when I heard it. I really wanted to write it. I loved Fionnula Flanagan. She just did a wonderful job and was magic. I really poured myself into it and much to my disappointment, I watched it with my wife thinking that she would love it, but she's just not a Data fan and she just couldn't invest herself in it."

"I liked the idea," says Brannon Braga. "I thought it was, for those who weren't party to the story, a shock when you find out she's an android. I just thought it was very well written. I liked their relationship and, ultimately, I just was kind of very intrigued by the moral dilemmas involved. I thought Data's solution was very surprising and thought it turned out great."

Actress Fionnula Flanagan, who plays Juliana, had already appeared in an episode of *Deep Space Nine* the same season, which made her casting problematic. "She came in and read and just

knocked everybody out with her reading," says Jeri Taylor. "But there was some fear that she would be recognizable [from *DS9*] and that we're sort of shattering the curtain of disbelief if you see the same person in a couple of episodes playing a different role. It calls attention to the fact that it's an actor, not a character. However, we looked at her film from *Deep Space Nine* and she was an alien and was very different, so we felt the two roles would be far enough apart and I'm glad it worked out that way, because now it's hard to imagine anyone else having done it."

Episode #163
"Parallels"
Original Airdate: 11/29/93
Written by Brannon Braga
Directed by Robert Wiemer
Guest Starring: Wil Wheaton (Wesley Crusher), Patti Yasutake (Ogawa), Mark Bramhall (Gul Nador)

Returning home from a bat'telh tournament, Worf finds himself experiencing several alternate realities aboard the Enterprise, including one in which he is married to Counselor Troi. After Data learns that a flaw in Geordi's visor has expanded a rift in realities, an attempt is made to return Worf to his own reality. En route he is led to an infinite number of converging universes, including one in which the Federation is losing a war with the Borg.

• • • •

"It began as a Picard story," says Brannon Braga, who notes that it had originally been planned that Tasha Yar would exist in the alternate realities Worf experienced, but it was decided that that would make the episode appear to be too similar to "Yesterday's Enterprise." As a result, Wesley was substituted instead. "What we also realized when we were breaking it was that there's just not a lot of personal stuff that you could do with Picard that would be different in alternate realties, so we decided to make it the Worf story and go through the Worf/Troi romance. It's fascinating. I don't think most people expected it. Viewers who watched closely will see that we've been building their relationship for the past couple of years. Wesley could have been explored in more depth, but I thought it would just be more interesting if he were just there. There was a temptation to do something, but again, I wanted to throw more attention to the Troi/Worf story and have Troi realize that there were realities where Worf never loved her, which is something we all think about. The 'what if's' in our relationships."

Says Jeri Taylor, "I remember when Brannon wrote me the memo in which he sort of outlined this premise. I thought, 'This could be great but it could be very confusing.' I gave the memo to Michael and he wrote back and said, 'Okay. Good luck on the break.' [It was] clearly a potentially very confusing, elaborate premise that we turned into a cohesive story that worked like gangbusters. It was not the intention when we started breaking it that the story would be Worf and Troi. That was a curious little sideline in one of the realities. Later, as the season developed, we began to develop the notion a little more strongly that Worf had been thinking about her ever since his experience in 'Parallels.'"

In fact, the Worf/Troi romance was a subplot that had been brewing since fifth season's "Ethics," in which Worf is paralyzed after an accident in the cargo bay. "In 'Fistful of Datas' there was an effort to gradually bring Worf and Troi a little closer," says Taylor. "It would have happened through Alexander, that she began giving Worf advice about him and functioned as a surrogate mother. That kind of thing is without conscious design. It just sort of erupted into bloom at the end of the last season and I think has given us some very nice moments."

In writing the episode, Brannon Braga needed to avoid playing many of the same beats as in the previous season's "Frame of Mind," in which Riker confronts a reality that is apparently breaking down before him.

"If you watch this episode you'll see that people are wondering, and Worf himself is wondering, whether he's losing his mind, because of a head injury," says Braga. "That's an element I had to be aware to play down because then you would be stepping in 'Frame of Mind' territory, 'Am I going crazy?'"

Episode #164
"The Pegasus"
Original Airdate: 1/10/94
Written by Ronald D. Moore
Directed by LeVar Burton
Guest Starring:
Nancy Vawter (Admiral Blackwell), Terry O' Quinn (Admiral Pressman)

The Enterprise goes in search of a missing starship that vanished twelve years earlier while conducting a mysterious experiment. The ship had been captained by Admiral Pressman, with Riker as a member of his bridge crew.

Riker's loyalties are tested when he must violate Pressman's admonitions and reveal to Picard that they are looking for an illegally tested phasing cloaking device, which the Enterprise eventually uses to escape from being trapped inside an asteroid when the Romulans try to sabotage their salvage efforts.

• • • •

"It started with my notion of doing *Raise The Titanic*," says Ron Moore of the Clive Cussler book in which the Titanic is covertly salvaged for its secret cargo. "I wanted to do a story about a mystery ship from a long time ago that holds a secret within. It's a classic sort of tale and right from the get-go I thought maybe Riker could have been on that ship. What is he protecting?"

Terry O'Quinn, who gives a commanding performance as Admiral Pressman, earns universal kudos from the staff and Michael Piller suggests he could be resurrected for a future episode of *Deep Space Nine*. "It was a gift that we got him," says Jeri Taylor. "He was in town heading home to Baltimore and we hurried over to read him an hour before he was supposed to catch his plane. We lucked out in that this is one of Ron's finest pieces of writing. It's action adventure but with a moral tale at the core, and that's what made this episode one of the best of the season, I think. The story of Riker's moral dilemma was explored beautifully and it was just one of those *Star Trek*'s that's everything *Star Trek* should be."

"I am proud to say that I've written another insane Admiral," laughs Ron Moore. "They must put something in the water at Federation Headquarters. The episode also started with one of my

most insane ideas. It began with Data, Troi and Riker rehearsing *Pygmalion* and I was using Data's learning about acting as some kind of metaphor for improvising, and it later became a way of talking to Riker. Everybody read the scene and said 'I really like the script, but what is this *Pygmalion* stuff?'"

Episode #165
"Homeward"
Original Airdate: 1/17/94
Teleplay by Naren Shankar
Story by Spike Steingasser
Directed by Alexander Singer
Guest Starring: Penny Johnson (Dobara), Brian Markinson (Vorin), Edward Penn (Kateras), Paul Sorvino (Nikolai)

Worf's foster brother, Nikolai, violates the Prime Directive in attempting to save remnants of a dying race, prompting a heated discussion of Prime Directive issues among the senior staff. Rebuffing Picard's orders, Nikolai attempts to recreate the village of the dying race in the holodeck in order to transport the survivors to a new world without them discovering what has happened.

• • • •

"I thought it was a pretty good show," says Michael Piller. "Paul Sorvino gave a very good performance and I think the only thing for me is that I felt a little shortchanged between Worf and his brother. Somehow their relationship never quite had a depth to it, it seemed by the numbers to me."

The show uneasily combines two separate premises and featured good fella Paul Sorvino as Worf's brother. "We constantly get rumors of feature actors and stars who want to do *Star Trek*. We have spent days following up on these rumors only to find that usually they're not true or even if they're true, the people aren't available," says Jeri Taylor. "It's been an exercise in futility. Paul Sorvino called, asked for an appointment with me, came to my office, sat down and said 'I love this series, I want to do something on it. I'm serious. Please believe me. I will be available to you.' So when the story about Worf's brother came along, I thought well, let's see if this man is going to back that up. We called him and he was on board in an instant. I was really thrilled because I thought he brought a great, great presence to the story."

The series in its last few years has eschewed prime directive stories such as second year's "Pen Pals", but in "Homeward" the Federation non-intervention prohibition plays a key role in preventing Picard from helping the doomed Boraalans. "I have problems with the prime directive as it stands," affirms Ron Moore. "I'm sort of the anti-prime directive staff writer which is just the same as a heretic. I was rooting for Worf's brother the whole time. I thought this guy was right and our people are just letting these guys fry. I always thought the prime directive was a little more flexible than the way it gets portrayed on the show."

"It was a pairing of premises," says Taylor. "Rene [Echevarria] came to me one day and said that he had gotten a pitch about the idea of transporting people from a dying world onto the holodeck and fooling them into thinking they were still there. I said, 'Rene, are you crazy? That's not even credible. Get out of here.' So about a month later he came back and said, `I've been thinking about that tribe on the holodeck' and I said, 'Why are you bringing that up? I don't want to hear that. Go away.' So he just kind of kept hanging in there with it and I could never see it and never see it and then about that time we got the pitch about Worf's human brother, who we had never heard anything about. Rene said, 'I was thinking that might be a good way to tell the story of the tribe on the holodeck.' So I finally started thinking about it and thought, 'Well all right. Maybe I overreacted. Maybe it could work. So I memoed Michael and he approved it. It turned out to be a really strong idea."

One point driven home to actor Michael Dorn regarding this episode is the idea of Worf being a central catalyst for conflict on the series. He rejects those who believe The Next Generation is devoid of interpersonal angst.

"Basically that's what my character brings to it," Dorn explains. "He makes you realize that everything isn't wonderful. It isn't so together and so cool. I think it kind of snuck up on the producers, too. They expected Worf to be this enigma and he surprised them and they found a whole wealth of stories

about this guy. It's not the same old love story. We can sit here and debate and air our grievances about what the show is and the movies are, but basically it's one of the most successful shows in television history. How can you say it should be this or that?"

Episode #166
"Sub Rosa"
Original Airdate: 1/31/94
Written by Brannon Braga
Directed by Jonathan Frakes
Guest Starring: Michael Keenan (Maturin), Shay Duffin (Ned Quint), Duncan Regehr (Ronin)

While attending the funeral of her grandmother on a planet which was terraformed to resemble Glasgow, Scotland, Dr. Crusher experiences visions of the ghost (named Ronin) she learns has haunted her family for generations. Meanwhile, Geordi and Data attempt to repair the planet's weather control grid while Picard tries to convince Dr. Crusher to remain with Starfleet when she abruptly hands in her resignation to join Ronin back on the planet. It is only when Picard reveals that he is an apparition metaphasic energy that Ronin's spell is broken and Crusher phasers him out of existence.

• • • •

There are few episodes on which viewers' opinions are more divided than "Sub Rosa." Those who enjoyed the show and those who despised Trek's first foray into the genre of gothic horror can be separated largely across gender lines. In other words, men hated it, women loved it.

"I can still reduce Brannon to shudders when I go into his office and say, 'I can travel on the power transfer beam,'" laughs Rene Echevarria, who was initially wary of doing the episode. "But the cast loved it. Every woman on the lot who read it was coming up to Brannon and patting him. Ultimately I think it was worth doing because it was campy fun and the production values were wonderful. The sets look great and everybody threw themselves into it. Gates did a wonderful job. It just got bigger and bigger and broader and broader and to the point of grandmother leaping out of the grave. Just having Beverly basi-

cally writhing around having an orgasm at 6 o'clock on family TV was great. For that alone it was worth doing. We got away with murder."

"It came as a pitch from a freelance writer," says Jeri Taylor. "The original spec script was that there have been aliens throughout history on Earth who had possessed people and they were responsible for much of what we called supernatural paranormal events. That writer had the idea of the Scottish kind of origins of Beverly. Rick and Michael were very distrustful of this story. They considered it a romance novel in space and felt the possibility for embarrassment was monumental, but I just knew it would work. It's a different kind of story for Star Trek to tell. It is a romance but we do have women in our audience and women do traditionally respond to romantic stories. One of Brannon and my favorite movies is The Innocents, which comes from Henry James' Turn of the Screw. We saw this episode as an homage, and we packed in every sort of gothic ghost story trick that one could imagine."

Says Brannon Braga, "I always loved the idea of a ghost that hangs around the grounds, having sex with the mortals. 'Sub Rosa' was a blast to do. It was exciting to take the gothic horror genre and somehow make it Star Trek, and I thought that was a lot of fun."

Not everyone agreed. Naren Shankar recalls being one of the story's early opponents. "It's a gothic ghost story," he says. "Either you buy it or you don't buy it at all, and I was sort of in the latter category."

Despite some early reluctance on the part of the staff, the show went forward and proved one of the best vehicles for Gates McFadden of the series' seven-year run. "It was the best performance I've ever seen," says Braga. "I just thought she did a wonderful job. Picard catches Beverly masturbating, for crying out loud! What a tough role to play. When I was writing the words, 'She writhes around in the bed having invisible sex,' I just thought, 'Oh, man, we're asking for trouble. Are they gonna be able to pull this off?' Thanks to [director] Jonathan Frakes and Gates, it was not hokey. It was very good.

"Look, I scripted the first orgasm in 'The Game,'" he adds. "This was mild by comparison. Sure, it was racy. Even Rick Berman had said, 'I can't believe we're doing this.' I think they trimmed quite a bit out of the writhing sequences."

Offers Frakes, who embraced directing this offbeat *Trek* installment, "I drew a good straw because it wasn't a *Star Trek*. It was more like *Tales from the Crypt*. Gates and I have worked well together and she was never better than in 'Sub Rosa' and never looked more beautiful. She looked like a movie star."

The title itself is inspired by the Greek myth about a god who was trying to hide a love affair from Cupid. "Sub Rosa" is Latin for "under the rose," and refers to a secret love affair, that is exactly what Beverly Crusher was having in this episode.

Episode #166
"Lower Decks"
Original Airdate: 2/7/94
Teleplay by Rene Echevarria
Story by Ronald Wilkerson and Jean-Louise Matthias
Directed by Gabrielle Beaumont

An episode that focuses on life aboard the Enterprise for several young officers who become involved with a secret mission to return a Cardassian spy across enemy lines.

• • • •

"I tried to keep our people in it," says Rene Echevarria. "I wanted to pair each one of the young officers with one of our characters, so there was some kind of relationship going on with all of them. The idea was to see our people, and a mission, through the eyes of these younger people. To me, this episode was the most joy to write. Basically, I turned in the first draft and with the exception of the fifth act, everything was filmed as I wrote it, which was very satisfying."

As a result of the show running short, additional dialogue was added between Nurse Ogawa and Dr. Crusher. "I thought the show was one of the best ideas we've had in quite awhile," says Ron Moore. "It was a really unique concept. There was a debate early on about how much it was going to be their show and how much it was going to be our

show. Ultimately, Michael said this is their show, which I thought was a good decision — especially since he usually says it has to be about our characters — which is what made the show so good."

Many viewers thought the episode was a backdoor pilot for *Voyager*, a mistaken impression, to say the least. "I don't know how that rumor got started," says Taylor. "It was just a rampant rumor that would not die. I am just mystified as to why people thought that three middle-aged people — Rick, Michael and myself — would ever create a series that had nothing but a bunch of young *90210* people on it. It was just absolutely out of the question. The episode was a wonderful premise from Ron Wilkerson and Jean Matthias, who have given us other wonderful premises and a beautiful script with 'Lessons.' Unfortunately, we were in a time bind. I had to have a staff member do it, so Rene took it over and wrote a wildly off-concept show, but that's what made it work. It was: How does the Enterprise look to those little junior officers who don't get to go into the observation lounge and who don't know what's going on? It was just a really fresh, original idea and, I think as it turned out, one of the best episodes of the season."

One of the show's most appealing characters was that of Ensign Sito, played by Sharon Fill, reprising her role from fifth season's "The First Duty."

"In the early drafts of the script, we left her death somewhat ambiguous because we thought we might pull her back in to help us out in some stories that were happening further on down the road," says Taylor. "When I mentioned that to Michael, he said, 'Absolutely not, she's dead. She stays dead. That would undermine the whole episode.' So I said, 'Fine.' The morning after Michael saw the episode, he came in and said, 'We can't let her stay dead. We've got to bring her back. She was wonderful.' He was really bowled over by the episode."

Before you could say "only Vulcans have a katra," Piller already had a *Deep Space Nine* story in development for the character. When asked about *Trek*'s penchant for reviving its dead,

"Sarek didn't come back," Piller retorts. "We received very insightful, intelligent letters that said, '*Star Trek* is about hope and optimism and you broke all of our hearts,' which is exactly what I wanted to hear on one level. But I also listen to that. I think that the character was so good, and Jeri in her wisdom allowed there to be a loophole, and we got some very good ideas of why it will be successful to bring her back."

Episode #168
"Thine Own Self"
Original Airdate: 2/14/94
Teleplay by Ronald D. Moore
Story by Christopher Hatton
Directed by Winrich Kolbe
Guest Starring: Ronnie Clare Edwards (Talur), Kimberly Callum (Gia), Andy Kossin (Apprentice), Richard Miro (Rainer), Michael G. Hagerty (Kural), Michael Rothhar (Donnell)

An amnesiac Data is stranded on an alien world after his shuttlecraft crashes while carrying dangerously radioactive material, which is adversely affecting the residents of a village. Back on the Enterprise, Troi studies to take her Commander's test under the tutelage of a less-than-understanding Riker.

• • • •

"The story came as a pitch from Christopher Hatton, who had written the spec script from which 'Gambit' came," says Jeri Taylor. "He was a young college student in Iowa and as soon as he had sold his premise to 'Gambit,' he came out here and said, 'I want to be a writer. I want to pitch you some more ideas.' And my heart kind of sank because he didn't realize how difficult it is to pitch stories and that lightning wasn't going to strike twice. But sure enough, he came in to pitch with the idea of Data as Frankenstein, which was just irresistible."

Of course, having the show take place on a planet required that a shipboard B story be written to balance the elaborate production requirements necessitated by building an alien civilization. "It puts extraordinary demands on us in terms of production when a story must happen on a planet or off the Enterprise," says Taylor. "We needed to have a substantial story on the

Enterprise, which would take the pressure off of those sets [for the alien world] and would be as interesting as what was going on in that planet. So we thought 'Well, you know, we never used that story about Troi,' and Ron was able to make that very believable. I thought it was really strong, although we have taken some criticism from people who said, 'How could you promote her over Data and Geordi?' But it would not have been a very interesting story to see Geordi or Data getting their rank. The obstacles she had to overcome were formidable and where you get interesting drama is out of conflict."

"I thought that was a neat idea and was a good move for the character," says Ron Moore of Troi's promotion. "The whole notion was something I wanted to do ever since I read Jeri Taylor's novelization of 'Unification,' where there is a line about Troi reflecting on her experiences in the episode 'Disaster,' where she got command temporarily. Jeri had a line in there about tasting blood and wanting to again, and that stuck with me. I thought that was an interesting direction to take Troi."

As for the episode as a whole, Moore notes, "I have mixed feelings about it. As a writer, I never figured out what it was about. I didn't know what I was trying to say with the episode. It was probably the most difficult writing experience I had on the show because I was very frustrated. It was a bad time in the season. I was tired and I was not having fun, and I think it showed in the writing. When I got this episode, I felt like I didn't have anything to say. What I enjoyed writing was Data as Mr. Wizard on the planet of people who aren't very smart. That was kind of funny. I got a kick out of Data being the guy in the back of the class raising his hand, inventing quantum mechanics with stone knives and bear skins."

Adds Brannon Braga, "It was great to see an episode as fundamental as Data being forced to confront his inner nature. The cool factor was also very high. Seeing Data impaled by a metal rod was just great. I enjoyed the episode. A couple of the performances of townsfolk were a little groggy for my taste, but Data as Frankenstein — what a neat idea. I

thought, all in all, it was a very nice job. In fact, I thought it was probably one of the best ones of this season."

Offers director Winrich Kolbe, "It was interesting because I had done 'Pen Pals,' a show that didn't quite find the right direction. Data seems to have a predilection for little girls, not in a bad way. Here we wind up again with a little girl. There seems to be something about Data that gives writers the idea for the relationship. He has a vulnerability or an innocence, especially at the beginning. It's Brent at his best. I liked the episode. We got some good actors and it was almost like a period piece. It was like going back to the Renaissance."

Episode #169
"Masks"
Original Airdate: 2/21/94
Written by Joe Menosky
Directed by Robert Wiemer

The Enterprise encounters an alien probe which hooks into Data, endowing him with varying personalities from the probe's civilization while it begins transforming the Enterprise into an ancient city. Only by assuming the persona of one of the mythological characters in the alien lore, can Picard prevent the total reconfiguration of the Enterprise.

• • • •

Actor Brent Spiner, who had just completed shooting "Thine Own Self," was admittedly unhappy to be given such little prep time to prepare for "Masks," an episode which required that he portray a number of personas who have taken over his android body.

"I had some good stuff seventh season," says Spiner. "I just wish they had been scheduled differently. I got the script for 'Masks' on the night before we shot it and I was finishing 'Thine Own Self' the midnight before, so I didn't have the time to even absorb the script and digest it and figure out who these people were that I was playing. You could look at it as an opportunity and I would.... under normal circumstances.

"I think I said to Jeri at the time, 'Give me six months and I think I could give all the characters their due,' but as it was, I didn't know who these

people were and so I was doing instant acting and just coming up with whatever I was coming up with because we had to put it on film."

"Brent was very nervous about doing all of those parts," confirms Taylor. "He said Dustin Hoffman had a year to figure out how to do Tootsie and portray a woman. I said, 'You don't have to portray a woman, just portray a leader.' He ended up carving up four unique, distinct personalities which are very, very tough on an actor, especially given the time constraints."

"I remember seeing the initial story and saying, `Jesus, what is this?'" recalls Ron Moore of the original treatment by overseas *Trek* scribe Menosky. "It was pretty out there and then the script came in and we all sort of scratched our heads and looked at each other and wondered what he's smoking out there in the Alps? But when we started to examine it and get into it a little more, we saw what he was doing. He has some real interesting ideas and he approaches things from a fresh angle. It was a fascinating episode. It was just full of wild concepts and from that angle alone it was worth doing. Sometimes you have to take those risks and really go out someplace and do something bizarre."

"Joe is one of those writers who has a unique vision that no one else understands," says Brannon Braga. "Shows need to be nurtured by him and it's very tough to come in on one of his scripts and start rewriting it. He needed to be here and it's unfortunate that it suffered as a result. The first draft had some very confusing elements that needed work. On the whole, it was a very good script, but the last act was unsatisfying and I feel that was because it needed to be simplified, but Joe wasn't here to do it and the staff struggled a little bit. Joe's one of those writers who has a vision and it's tough to second guess it. The best thing about the show is watching the Enterprise being mutated into this weird ancient civilization. The art direction, effects, and the opticals were among our best."

• • • •

Episode #170
"Eye of the Beholder"
Original Airdate: 2/28/94
Teleplay by Rene Echevarria
Story by Brannon Braga
Directed by Cliff Bole
Guest Starring: Mark Rolston (Walter Pierce), Nancy Harewood (Lt. Nara), Tim Lounibos (Lt. Kwan), Johanna McCloy (Calloway)

During an investigation into an officer's supposed suicide, Troi is overwhelmed with psychic images dating back to the ship's construction eight years prior. Before you can say "psychic residual trace, hyperkeritosis in the plasma injectors," Troi finds herself in a tempestuous affair with Worf, jealously eyeing his interest in a younger Ensign, in what turns out to be a dream. Ultimately, Troi's visions hold the key to the man who was responsible for the officer's murder.

• • • •

"The story was actually at one point rejected," says Brannon Braga. "We had heavy scrutiny coming on every episode that we tried to get passed, but there came a point where we hit a real rough dry spot in the season where we had to have stories. We resurrected this because we thought it was worthwhile and the producers took a second look with a different viewpoint and ended up saying go ahead and give it a try."

Says Jeri Taylor, "Brannon had this story idea around for a while. It wasn't a murder mystery but had to deal with a haunted room on the Enterprise and it sort of evolved into a murder mystery. By this point of the season, we were getting down to the very tough crunch in which Ron and Brannon were writing the final episode and I was running out of writers. Brannon, of course, wanted to do his own teleplay but was already on to the final episode, so Rene took it over and did a very nice job with it.

"It was confusing," she adds. "We were hindered by our production restraints. You can do a story in which someone has a hallucination or a dream and make that real clear to the audience if you do it in a location that you never visit at any time except when that hallucination begins or ends. We didn't have that luxury. We had one set, so unfortu-

nately it was utterly perplexing as to exactly when the hallucination started. I can only say I realize that and I'm sorry for it. I hope that the episode had enough sheer mystery to draw one along. I think it did. You never knew quite what was going on there. And, of course, this was where we reprised the second part of our Worf/Troi romance. But, again, it wasn't real. There was nothing substantive in it in either time frame."

Adds Braga, "The Worf/Troi element was not there in my original story and didn't come about until the break session in the same way that it evolved in 'Parallels.' Personally, I found the Worf/Troi angle the least satisfying part of the show in the end, because it was a shaggy dog story. It's a unique couple. They have had a romantic interlude in an alternate reality, in a hallucination and, in the final episode, in an alternate timeline. They have yet to get together. It's bizarre, really, and in that regard I found it sort of unsatisfying because after 'Parallels,' I think audience expectations were so high, people were eager to see them get together and when it ended and it was a hallucination, it was disappointing. On the whole, I thought it was a good mystery. It was fun to watch. I thought Rene did a nice job with the Data scene where Data is talking about having thought about killing himself. That was rather surprising. Perhaps that's what the episode should have been about dramatically, instead of a shaggy dog romance.

"The idea that what Troi experiences happens in the blink of an eye came about in the break session, and we were all very concerned about whether that was going to work," Braga continues. "In the end, it was a little confusing. Rene came up with an idea that it was really happening and in the end she starts to see through someone's eyes on the ship and realizes she's seeing through the killer's eyes. It's kind of *The Eyes of Laura Mars* routine. The finale was going to be Troi being stalked from her own point of view."

"I think it is one of our better murder mysteries," says Ron Moore. "I think it sustains the illusion that you are really on the Enterprise for quite some time until you finally start to get wise and realize something is up."

Episode #171
"Genesis"
Original Airdate: 3/21/94
Written by Brannon Braga
Directed by Gates McFadden
Guest Starring: Patti Yasutake (Ogawa), Dwight Schultz (Barclay)

When Barclay gets the flu, Dr. Crusher inadvertently triggers a genetic virus in an attempt to cure him, which begins to slowly transform the crew into primitive creatures by altering their genetic make-up. Riker is ultimately turned into an ape Barclay into an arachnid, and Troi into an amphibian-like creature.

Returning to the ship, Picard and Data must engineer a cure for the virus before Picard is affected and the Enterprise becomes a "starship of the apes."

• • • •

In Braga's original draft, Data's anti-virus injection was going to turn the entire crew into Barclay. "They discover that the mutated T-cell which came from Barclay isn't just turning people into proto-creatures, but is then going to end up turning everyone into Barclay and restructuring the genetic sequences, which I thought would have been a lot of fun. Mike Piller thought it was one step too far and in the end, when I sat down to write it, I felt he was probably right."

"I think 'Genesis' is classic *Star Trek*," enthuses Ron Moore. "It is right in the spirit of the original series to have everybody in the ship start to become animals. It is very high-concept *Trek* and it could have only been written by Brannon."

"Genesis" marked actress Gates McFadden's directorial debut. "It was very unlike normal *Star Trek*," she observes. "It was very spooky and it starts off with a lot of comedy and all of a sudden it turns out very dark. Many of my favorite shots were cut out and they were only seen in the directors cut. When the shuttle craft first comes back, I had a fabulous thing where I had choreographed some steadicam shots and everything was incredibly dark. They cut all that out and put in this part that was at the very tail end that I never intended to use, that showed the whole shuttle bay and it was very well lit. We also didn't see the excrement of the proto-creatures. There was a line where Picard says `What's that smell?' and Data says the technical term for excrement. It was very funny, there were piles of shit all over the floor."

"Gates is very well-versed in dance and movement, so she really coached the actors in how to move with animal-like movements rather than Starfleet-like people in a mask," adds Jeri Taylor. "The opportunity to direct had been given to a number of other male actors on the show and the feeling was that she deserved the chance. She studied very hard. She worked as an observer for days on other episodes and came to production meetings and really plunged herself into it. It was a very committed endeavor on her part."

Braga notes the origin of the story idea, reflecting his desire to "do something with latent genes in altered states, but I knew that I wanted to do something that was even more believable and wild, hence all of the creatures that evolved along the evolutionary chain. People liked the idea and it was fun to write." In the case of one of Braga's creations, Lt. Barclay as an arachnid, the choice seemed natural. "I just thought it would be fun to make Barclay a spider because I can't imagine anything more awful to become. It just seemed natural since he's a kind of nervous and wiry guy, that maybe he would have had more arachnid ancestors than the other ones, but who knows why we are the way we are today? Maybe latent genetic structures help shape the personalities we have."

Some of the episode's content, which is one of the series' more violent episodes, almost seems like *Alien*-lite, particularly when Worf spews an acid-like substance on to Dr. Crusher. "It was violent and it was in a way more shocking because it's a beloved character," says Braga. "It's weird to see our beloved Beverly screaming in agony and writhing on the floor. This may sound lofty, but I think the difference is that our show has higher aims than say a show with no moral or thematic underpinnings. Our show strives to give more depth — whether it's thematic or ethical issues — so in that way it differs from a show that's just T&A and violence. I think we can get away with a little more and the

violence we convey has more impact. You don't see people shot to pieces every week on our show, and yet our show was rated one of the fifth most violent shows on the air by some independent survey company. I don't know why. In the case of 'Genesis,' in some strange way venom spewing was okay because it was almost like watching a nature show. If it had been, say, Worf grabbing a vile of acid and throwing it in Beverly's face, I bet you that wouldn't have been acceptable. When it's an act of nature vs. an act of intellectual violence, that's an important distinction."

Charged with metamorphosizing the crew of the Enterprise into proto-creatures was the show's make-up supervisor, Michael Westmore. "Most of our time was spent with Michael Westmore," says Jeri Taylor. "We knew that this episode would rise or fall on the basis of the make-up. Our fear was that if it were hokey and over the top, then it would seem just buffoonish and Michael did his usual superb job of making things seem a natural outgrowth of the people. You bought it all. Marina's willingness to look as bizarre as she did in this and to go completely away from glamour to this gilled, gasping creature was remarkably bold for an actor."

Critiques Ron Moore, "Just watching Dwight Schultz do his impersonation of a spider running through the ops lounge was worth the price of admission, and watching Riker getting progressively stupider was just delightful stuff."

Episode #172
"Journey's End"
Original Airdate: 3/28/94
Written by Ronald D. Moore
Directed by Corey Allen
Guest Starring: Wil Wheaton (Wesley Crusher), Tom Jackson (Lakanta), Natalija Nogulich (Admiral Necheyev), Ned Romero (Anthwara), George Aguilar (Wakasa), Richard Poe (Gul Evek), Eric Menyuk (Traveller), Doug Wert (Jack Crusher)

Wesley Crusher returns to the Enterprise struggling with whether or not to remain in Starfleet, when Admiral Necheyev orders Picard into the newly created demilitarized zone to lead the evacuation of a tribe of Native

Wil Wheaton brings the arc for his character Wesley Crusher to a close in "Journey's End" (photo copyright ©1995 Karen Witkowski).

American Indians from Cardassian territory. When they refuse to vacate the planet, Wesley joins with them to prevent them from being forcibly moved. Later, one of the Native Americans, who has brought about Wesley's spiritual awakening, is revealed as the Traveller, who then helps the young ensign transcend this plane of existence and join him in exploring the cosmos.

• • • •

"We started out by saying we were doing two things at once," says Michael Piller. "My son had come in and pitched with his friend an episode about a Native American Indian colony and the problems of them trying to move out of the neutral zone. He had tied it to Riker and the story of his father dying. I didn't want to do another story of a family member dying. At the same time, Ron and Jeri were struggling with the Wesley story and Ron had very much wanted to tie the Wesley story into the Maquis introduction, but it was never a very comfortable marriage. As an episode, I was quite pleased with it and it turned out better in a number of ways than I expected it might. The Wesley story was something I was less than satisfied with but I think it could have worked. The resolution didn't seem to come out of the story. It seemed to have come from the need to resolve it and that always bothers me when that occurs."

Ron Moore had begun to develop a very unique arc for the character of Wesley Crusher in fifth season's "The First Duty," in which he took the interesting and unexpected approach of including Wesley in a conspiracy to hide the fact that he and several fellow cadets were responsible for the death of a peer at Starfleet Academy.

"I thought `First Duty' was a genuine turn for the character of Wesley and I thought it really moved him to a different place and level. I wanted to keep going with that," says Ron Moore. "I also identified with him more strongly in that episode than in a lot of the shows. It's a very personal show for me because I went through a lot of the same things. I had a lot of the same background. My father was a military officer, I grew up with that. I thought I wanted that for myself, but there were all of these other little things in my life as far as writing and the arts that I was doing. I had initially wanted Wesley to just leave the Academy and say he was going to work at the Daystrom Institute or go off and discover himself or something like that. That ran into resistance and the story went up and down all season long. I finally got Michael onboard who said, 'If he is going to leave the Academy, I think Wesley has to go on to something greater instead of just being another scientist.' If you bring back the Traveller, then you have him take Wesley to some cosmic journey, that I can accept.'"

Interestingly, Moore had initially toyed with making the Traveller Boothby, the Starfleet Academy groundskeeper Picard first talked about in second season's "Samaritan Snare." The idea was rejected by Michael Piller. However, one idea that did prove important in the episode was the inclusion of the Maquis, the first *Star Trek* installment to set up the backstory for the new *Voyager* series.

"We felt that this would provide a background for *Voyager* by setting up this Native American culture that had left earth 200 years ago to preserve a way of life and so that in *Voyager* we have our character, Chakotay, who comes from that background with one foot in the 21st century and one in an

earlier era," says Jeri Taylor. "We realized in producing 'Journey's End' that this may be fraught with peril. Native Americans have become a highly politicized voice who are articulate and emphatic and demanding in the way that they have been depicted in the past and the way they want to be depicted now. We hired a Native American as a consultant to help us avoid some of these pitfalls, but what we learned was that there seems to be very little agreement, even among Native American nations. You are probably going to offend somebody at some point no matter what you do. We intended to treat the Native American culture with the utmost respect and show the value of some of their metaphysical ways of approaching life, that it is positive and valuable but even in the depiction of that, we ran into trouble with some groups who don't want that depicted at all."

"It was an added element," says Ron Moore of the inclusion of the Maquis and the Native American aspect of the script. "We had talked about setting up the Maquis in that episode first, and then using the Native American culture came along the same way. I was just so desperate to do the story that any A story they were going to let me do, I grabbed onto because I wanted to do a Wesley show. I said, 'Oh yeah, the Maquis, okay great, oh yeah the American Indians, great. Whatever you are going to let me do with this, I will marry an A story to it.' It was fun to do and it was a very serpentine process to get to the final episode as far as the Indian culture that was there. We started off and we said, 'Okay, we will do the Hopi Indians, make them all Hopi Indians.' Then we found out that might cause certain problems. Maybe the Hopis don't want to be represented on television, they get very sensitive about that. So we [wondered], should we go with another tribe or should we just try to make it a mythical tribe or should we just not say who they are? This is a sensitive issue for a lot of people and these people have the right to be sensitive considering their history. They're understandably careful about what they like said about them and who says what. So there was a lot of internal back and forth about what

would be best. We knew we were not going to be able to please everybody, but it was done with the best of intentions and I hope it was well received."

Says Jeri Taylor of sending Wesley on his cosmic journey with the Traveller, "I'm delighted when we ruffle the audience. I believe that good drama makes people feel something. It should not make them feel content and passive and comfortable. It should shake them up and make them feel stronger kinds of emotions. If people are moved to write because they don't like something, that to me is an indication that we've done our job. This story was lying around a long time. It was a story that Ron Moore has wanted to tell for two or three years because it's a story that is very close to him. He saw parallels with Wesley making the decision to leave Starfleet. Ron too was a young man who lived up to everybody's expectations and was headed for the career that people expected him to be headed for and he ultimately changed his mind and said, 'I want to do what I want to do rather than what I'm expected to do.' And he took the perilous step of deciding to become a writer. As a parent, I can only sympathize with what his parents must have gone through at that point. Wesley too was sort of geared toward going to Starfleet from 'Farpoint' on. He was Gene Roddenberry's alter ego and was following in his father's — and his surrogate father's — footsteps, and he was on the track that everybody expected. It seemed like an important statement for today's young people to take stock of themselves, to look into their hearts and to make the choices which they feel are right for them — even if it means flying in the face of everybody else's wishes."

"The story was a battle between Ron, myself, Michael and Rick with everybody having different positions at different points, with Michael particularly feeling that to have Wesley leave Starfleet was in a sense a slap in Gene Roddenberry's face and that it would be very unsatisfying and disappointing to the audience to see him turn his back on everything that he was working for. Ron and I were the champions of wanting to give him the ability to determine his own fate. Rick was on different sides at different points. Ultimately, it was Michael's idea to turn his leaving Starfleet into a positive and unexpected thing and have him go off with the Traveller to begin a study of something that we can't even articulate because we don't know what it means. It's another plane of existence. Wesley was intended for something even greater than Starfleet, so he's going to go onto something more positive, more elevated rather than simply turning his back on something that is very positive and going off to be a shoe salesman."

Episode #173
"Firstborn"
Original Airdate: 4/25/94
Teleplay by Rene Echevarria
Story by Brian Kalbfeld
Directed by Jonathan West
Guest Starring:
Brian Bonsall (Alexander), Barbara March (Lursa), Gwynith Walsh (B'Etor), Joel Swetow (Yog), Colin Mitchell (Gorta), Rickey D'Shon Collins (Eric), John Shull (Molor), James Sloyan (K'Mtar), Armin Shimerman (Quark)

An adult Alexander comes back in time as K'Mtar, to try and prevent Worf's death. After an assassination attempt is made, apparently on Worf's life, at a Klingon celebration, the Enterprise begins an investigation which leads to Lursa and B'Etor, who claim to have been uninvolved with the murder attempt. It is only when K'Mtar attempts to kill Alexander that Worf learns the truth from his son.

• • • •

"This story came to us as a pitch from a freelance writer and had nothing to do Alexander," says Jeri Taylor. "It had to do with the Romulans and a ship from the future which turned out not even to be a ship from the future, but a ploy by the Romulans. We had bought that story and he wrote it, but it just seemed a little ordinary so we started messing around with it during one of our brainstorming sessions and then we just hit on the idea that Alexander comes back from the future to kill his young self. That seemed wonderful but for a long time that's all we had. We didn't know why he did this. Michael had thought that it had the scope, perhaps at

one point, to be a two-parter. We tried that. It didn't seem there was enough to make it a two-parter. We finally decided to make it one episode and hammered it out. I think it's really one of the most original sci-fi premises."

Says Michael Piller, "There was a big fight all year long about an episode that they desperately wanted to do that I would not let them do, about Alexander getting kidnapped and coming back as a twenty-five-year-old. He's totally lost his youth and is dealing with the consequences of this and I just thought it was a nasty thing that we were basically taking the kid's entire childhood away. I just wouldn't go for it. However, I fell in love with the idea of `First Born' in which we address the psychological implications of a man who feels a failure, who comes back to his own youth to destroy himself at a young age, in order to avoid the pain that he has caused and suffered. There is a tremendous science-fiction premise in that. And if you have been in on any of my therapy, you know that I've dealt with this on a number of different levels."

Interestingly, it had originally been planned that K'ehlyr, Worf's Klingon mate played by Suzi Plakson, would return as well. "It was originally intended that there would be a third mystery character, who was K'ehlyr coming back to intervene between this man's quest to kill himself as a child, and that only changed because the actor was not interested in coming back. I know Rick breathed a sigh of relief because he did not like the idea in the first place. But for better or worse, that might have helped the episode."

The episode was written by Rene Echevarria who assumed the mantle of Klingon scribe from Ron Moore, who had helped craft some of the best of the many Klingon episodes. "I was out of the Klingons, but Rene has a good feel for them," says Ron Moore. "He brings a different cultural flavor to the Klingons than I did. The stuff he did sixth season in 'Birthright' and then what he did with them here is very interesting. Worf and Alexander celebrate at a Klingon outpost and they have this sort of mock opera singing, heroic fights and re-enactments of things in the streets and banners and this was a whole different cultural flavor

to these guys that I hadn't thought of. My take on the Klingons was sort of more Shakespearean with the House of Mogh and that kind of stuff, and the rise and fall of political players. Rene brings in a much different element which I think serves them well."

Casting James Sloyan as Alexander's adult self was fraught with its own difficulties, since Sloyan had recently shot a Deep Space Nine playing Dr. Pol, Odo's Bajoran caretaker, in "The Alternate."

"This was the second time in which we found ourselves with the perfect actor," recalls Jeri Taylor. "When he came in, he just nailed it and we were then told we couldn't use him because he had been on Deep Space Nine and Michael and Rick were afraid that he'd be recognizable. I looked at the Deep Space Nine footage and said, 'No, no, no. He was a Bajoran, now he's going to be a Klingon. You'd never recognize anybody in Klingon make-up.' They felt that his voice would be recognizable and so we kept looking and looking. We must have read 35 to 40 people and there was just no one like James Sloyan. I went back to them and asked them to reconsider. I said, 'This can be a really strong episode or this can be a so-so episode. It will depend on whoever plays that part,' and they relented. We got James Sloyan and I will defy anybody to know the two roles were played by the same person."

Comments Michael Dorn, who Taylor now describes as the "Mr. Mom" of Klingons, "We don't really know what happens now. Just that the future is uncertain. It's just like real life, but Worf is still a terrible father. He hasn't got a clue."

Episode #174
"Bloodlines"
Original Airdate: 5/2/94
Written by Nicholas Sagan
Directed by Les Landau

DaiMon Bok (from first season's "The Battle") returns to get revenge against Picard for the death of his son, by genetically engineering Jason Vigo to appear to be Picard's illegitimate child. By creating a son for Picard and convincing him of his veracity, Bok then plans to

The Ferengi Daimon Bok once again tries to extract revenge upon Patrick Stewart's Picard (photo copyright ©1995 Karen Witkowski).

kill Vigo and finally get his long simmering vengeance against the captain. It is only when the deception is revealed by Beverly Crusher and Bok's fellow Ferengi learn that there is no profit in vengeance, that Bok is once again stopped before he can cause any further harm.

• • • •

"This episode came about because I was on the set of 'Masks' and I was standing with Brent and Patrick and said, 'Are there any aspects of your character we haven't explored?'" recalls Jeri Taylor of the genesis of DaiMon Bok's return. "Patrick said, `It's always fascinated me that there is this creature running around the universe even now who despises me,' and that seemed interesting. I talked to Michael about it and Michael was very open to the idea. Nick Sagan came up with the idea of this son who was cloned so that Bok could kill Picard's son as Picard had killed his own. It wasn't until we were really into it that we realized that this was, in a sense, ground that we had covered in a funny way not just with 'Suddenly Human,' but with Wesley since Picard was a surrogate father to him. Fortunately, Patrick gives probably the most vulnerable performance of his career. He opened him-

self to this young man in a way that I have not seen him do. He was absolutely raw and open and hurting. I think by the power of his performance he brings this to another level of emotional intensity that takes it away from any of those other episodes."

Not everyone was as interested in whatever happened to DaiMon Bok, including some of the show's writers. "I wondered if the world knew or cared if DaiMon Bok came back again," laughs Ron Moore. "I wasn't a big fan of that or 'The Battle' and I didn't see the point of repeating 'Suddenly Human' where we really nailed an interesting arc with Picard having a sort of father/son relationship."

Nick Sagan, who was saddled with the premise, explains, "Jeri said we are trying to do a bottle show because of budget and she told me that she had talked to Patrick Stewart who wanted to see the return of DaiMon Bok from 'The Battle.' I remembered him and I liked the kind of twisted, nasty villain he was and remembered thinking it was one of the few cool episodes first season. She said Patrick was interested in doing something with that character coming back seeking revenge, and to come up with something on that. I said sure and tried to think what it was that he would do. I figured Bok would try and get revenge against Picard's son and who would that be? Is Picard's son the ship? No, Kirk's son is the Enterprise. I decided to make it a genetically engineered pseudo son. Originally, it was a much darker episode.

"Originally called "Fugue," the idea was that Bok had genetically engineered this kid from birth and advanced his growth and had been giving him memories of Picard abandoning him on the Stargazer. Then Bok was using one of the mind balls to give Picard these vague flashes of false memories, making him think that it was possible he had this sort of fugue-like experience where he basically abandoned his son on the Stargazer and blocked it out of his mind.

"I don't know if it would have ever worked or not," adds Sagan, "but it was kind of a really interesting, dark aspect and it gave you a sense of abandonment and trying to recapture this sense of a son that he never had. Then it

turns out that it's not that at all."

At the time, Sagan didn't realize one of the reasons the producers rejected his early story concept was that writers Braga and Moore had already used the theme of Picard as the last of his family line in their script for the first *Star Trek* feature film, and wished to avoid treading on that ground in the episode.

Episode #175
"Emergence"
Original Airdate: 5/9/94
Written by
Brannon Braga & Joe Menosky
Directed by Cliff Bole
Guest Starring: Thomas Kopache (Engineer), David Huddleston (Conductor), Arlee Reed (Hayseed), Vinny Argiro (Dixon Hill)

A mysterious holodeck malfunction, which sends a steam locomotive through Data's performance of *The Tempest*, leads the crew to investigate puzzling anomalies on the holodeck which are creating a series of bizarre images. The passengers aboard the locomotive, the Orient Express, are on their way to "New Veriform City," which we later learn is a sector of space where the Enterprise helps give birth to a new alien lifeform.

• • • •

"I felt if we were going to do another holodeck show, we should do one like we've never seen before," says Braga. "It's a bizarre amalgam of all the holodeck shows we've ever seen. I had in my mind this image of Dixon Hill crossed with King Arthur's Court crossed with the Old West crossed with Modern Day New York - all thrown together and our people trapped in this adventure. I thought that would be neat and ended up coming up with the concept of the ship developing a psyche. These subconscious elements of that psyche would manifest themselves on the holodeck and we have to go in and interpret the symbolism and communicate to the ship through the adventures that it's portraying."

Adds Ron Moore, "I think that holodeck stuff is a riot. The re-creation of the Orient Express alone is worth the price of admission."

"I had one complaint about

the seventh season," points out Michael Dorn, "which is I wish they had taken the last six episodes or even the last four episodes and made it more about us. Troi and Worf is something they didn't deal with in the movie, so it's kind of wasted and now we'll never know what happened to them. I would have liked the last four episodes to tie up loose ends."

Episode #176
"Preemptive Strike"
Original Airdate: 5/16/94
Teleplay by Rene Echevarria
Story by Naren Shankar
Directed by Patrick Stewart
Guest Starring: Michelle Forbes (Ro Laren), John Franklyn-Robbins (Macias), Natalija Nogulich (Admiral Nechayev), William Thomas, Jr. (Santos), Shannon Cochran (Kalita), Richard Poe (Gul Evek)

Ensign Ro Laren returns and is recruited by Starfleet and Captain Picard to infiltrate the Maquis, a rebel band of Federation citizens within the demilitarized zone between the Federation and Cardassian territory. Her objective is to prevent a secret attack on a Cardassian installation. During her time undercover, Ro finds herself becoming attached to those among the Maquis resistance, ultimately deciding — however reluctantly — to betray Picard and join with them to protect their home against the Cardassians.

• • • •

"We were in a real bind for a story and we were racking our brains to come up with things," says Naren Shankar. "Ron and I were kicking around some ideas, we talked about doing a *Next Generation/DS9* crossover. We started to put one together, but it didn't quite work. It was about someone seeking asylum on DS9. We were talking about this and we thought, 'Wouldn't it be funny if that person seeking asylum was Ensign Ro?' Michael thought that was interesting, so we started going on about getting Ensign Ro into the story, testing her loyalties, having her relationship with Picard go somewhere and seeing some resolution to that character."

Notes Jeri Taylor of recruiting Michelle Forbes back to the *Trek* fold,

"We contacted Michelle's people and the word came back to me that it was possible she would do it, but it would depend on a phone conversation I would have with her to see if this was a story she wanted to do. Well, this was the next to the last episode and we didn't have a story. We had days before we had to write a script. We couldn't take the time to develop a story if we didn't know that she was going to be doing it. So I got on the phone with her and did a tap dance. I was concocting things out of thin air. Ro does this and she does that and this is an intense story of a woman's personal, moral dilemma. It sounded very intense and emotional and apparently it worked because within minutes after I had gotten off the phone with her, the word came back that she had called and would do the episode. Then we had to write the story and make it something like what I had spun out.

"I think it's a great coup to get her," Taylor continues. "She's an outstanding actress and it's a character that everybody hated to see go. She does a wonderful job in it."

"Preemptive Strike" was originally titled "The Good Fight." Like "Journey's End," the episode would pave the way for *Voyager* by reinforcing the concept of the Maquis. "The Maquis really existed," says Jeri Taylor. "That was the name of the French resistance fighters in World War II. My husband ironically wrote a teleplay about the real Maquis about thirty years or so ago. [The Maquis in the series] call themselves freedom fighters, the Federation calls them outlaws. They are the people who have taken up arms to defend themselves against Cardassian strikes in the newly created Cardassian de-militarized zone. It's a situation not unlike that of the west bank in Israel where people have been displaced and have to move from homes they've had for a while because of diplomatic decisions. Lines are drawn in space and people get upset by that. And the people who are in that zone have very volatile emotions and beliefs and start throwing rocks at each other. The Cardassians are being supplied secretly by their government because they have a

vested interest in keeping the region unstable and trying to drive out the Federation citizens. The citizens take matters into their own hands and start doing more than defending themselves by making preemptive strikes. It's a situation that will quickly get out of hand. Starfleet fears them, so they must control it. These are renegades. They are outlaws. They must be stopped. The Maquis, of course, are equally convinced that the Federation has let them down, that they have the right to defend themselves and their families. They have no intention of stopping."

Admits Patrick Stewart, "I was, at times, anxious as to whether or not I would get through the end of the season. I'm not being melodramatic. The producers had, once again, been very generous in allowing me to go off and do my *Christmas Carol* one-man show. This time I had done it in London, so my entire Christmas holiday, which is the one substantial break we get in ten months, I was on stage doing a solo show. I flew straight back and went right back into production. Of course, they had saved a lot of heavy episodes for me. I still had one show to direct and I wasn't sure that I was going to be able to stay upright long enough to direct it.

"They found one for me, which was 'Preemptive Strike,'" he adds, "and it turned out to be a show that I was very [performance] heavy in, which had never happened before. This was immediately followed by the final show. In the final two-hour, I was in every single scene of the episode and shifting between time periods so I was being a Picard who was eight years younger, and a Picard who was twenty-five years older. It was a difficult time for me. Towards the end, I got so tired that things got a little rough and raw for me. I know that there were all kinds of rumors circulating — all of them, for the most part, exaggerated — about my bad behavior on the set. It was entirely due to the fact that I was trying to do the best job that I could and, at the same time, there were a lot of people with other needs and demands. I found it all a bit distracting."

• • • •

Episodes #177 & 178
"All Good Things"
Original Airdate: 5/23/94
Written by
Ronald D. Moore and Brannon Braga
Directed by Winrich Kolbe
Guest Starring: John DeLancie (Q),
Denise Crosby (Tasha Yar)

Seven years of starship voyages come to an end as Picard confronts a juxtaposition of time periods in an attempt to solve a puzzling galactic mystery which Q threatens will lead to the destruction of humanity. Propelled through three timelines — the past, present and future — Picard joins with the crew of the Enterprise in each time period to prevent humankind's annihilation.

• • • •

Says finale co-writer Ron Moore, "The toughest thing was getting approval on the story because everyone wanted the story to be really, really special. There was a good week where we kept trying to get the story approved. Time was running out and it was just really frustrating. It was made more difficult by the fact that the final episode, ironically, was going to go into prep before the second to last episode, so there was even less time than there normally would be for the season finale which drove everybody crazy; the director, set designers, everybody on the whole production. The staff really had to go for it on this one."

Next to Richard Kimble finally capturing the One-Armed Man in the classic *Fugitive* series, it would be hard to find an episode of television that was more eagerly anticipated than the finale of *Star Trek: The Next Generation*.

In the show's projected alternative future, the crew is reunited on Picard's farm and Dr. Crusher now commands a medical ship, having been married to and divorced from Captain Picard. "I thought maybe I should have his fish in my ready room, skewered," laughs Gates McFadden of the unexpected twist on the Crusher/Picard relationship. "At the very least, I could have his Shakespeare text ripped in half on my desk."

"We knew since the beginning of the season that that episode was coming at us and would have to be done, and it was intimidating," recalls Jeri Taylor.

"Any final episode of a series is unique and important and for a series like *Star Trek*, which has cut such a niche in the American consciousness, the expectations are really very high.

"Brannon originally came up with the notion of time slipping, which he pitched as an episode idea," adds Taylor. "Michael seized on the idea as having the scope and epic qualities that a final episode should have. When we started breaking the story, we were really flying by the seat of our pants. It seems that some of our best work gets done under pressure, because the adrenaline starts running and we just started brainstorming."

"Michael Piller had some ideas we talked about early on," recalls Ronald D. Moore, who co-wrote the finale with Brannon Braga. "I had originally mentioned that Q should be in the final episode in a different context and Michael liked that idea and hung onto it. He said, `I think you should have Q and I think it should focus on Picard and I think it should have some time travel elements in it,' and then it was just a matter of trying to bring those ideas together."

Says Braga, "Once we had the initial concept of Q's involvement and time shifting, which I had suggested earlier in the season, it became a great struggle again for us because there was great scrutiny by everybody since it was the last episode. It just took a lot of work. The main problem is we didn't have a lot of time left to do it, so we were rewriting stories in one day and that was kind of tough."

Initially, the storyline which involves Picard time-shifting between the Enterprise's first mission to Farpoint, the present, and the far future, in which many of the crew have become estranged, originally was going to include a fourth time period, the Borg attack in "Best of Both Worlds."

"There were going be two paths we were going to play out, including part of the plotline in 'Best of Both Worlds' in which Hugh is aboard to save Picard. It would have been great to see that episode start to play out differently, but they felt it was just too much story and we'd better have only three time periods."

Even with the deletion of the Borg story arc, "All Good Things" was still an immensely complicated show both from the perspective of story and production logistics.

"We had to make the three time periods distinct from each other so the audience wouldn't get lost," says Moore.

Adds Taylor of *The Christmas Carol*-like awakening Picard undergoes, "We wanted to tell a story in which we realized that all the parts of a person's life contribute to making them what they are. Their past informs the present, the present informs the future and determines what they will be. That was the underlying kind of thematic material that we addressed in the context of an epic action/adventure which was still laden with a rich character story that we thought would leave no one disappointed. I think that Ron and Brannon did their finest work on the show. It has scope, it has action, it has humor, it has mystery and it's all packed into two romping hours. It's the quintessential final episode."

"We knew we wanted it to be special," says Braga, "and the culmination of everything that makes *Star Trek* special. It's really a combination of two premises. Ron had a premise floating around for the final episode where Q comes back to put us on trial again and I had an idea about jumping through time. It actually began as an Alexander story. I had this idea where Alexander would experience a time slip and trade places with his future self twenty-five years in the future. The future self would have come back to the past and we would do a story that intercuts between the past and future. It was just a Worf/Alexander story, but Michael Piller liked it so much he said, `If you combine this with the Q idea, I think we may have two more episodes.' And what eventually happened was it became a story about Picard time-slipping through the past, present, and future and Q's involvement in that and the destruction of humanity. I'm just thrilled with the episode. I think it really is a culmination of so many elements of this show that make it memorable. There are Romulan threats, Klingon adventures, space battles and time travel in the way you've never seen

Commander Riker can't believe the series is over, and neither can anyone else in this cover of Sci-Fi Universe.

it before. Structurally, it is the most ambitious episode we've ever done. Telling a story that takes place in three different time periods and trying to tell a unique storyline in each with unique characters in each and showing how the characters change in each, yet having the stories, ultimately, all have to relate with each other was a tremendous challenge."

The challenge of dealing with such an ambitious premise led to several long, hard, break sessions."We broke and rebroke that show and ended up having very little time to write it and then very little time to rewrite it," says Braga. "The most anxious time was when we had to do a page one rewrite on the first draft in one week, but somehow it was appropriate that this happened on the final episode." "Ron and Brannon didn't start writing the two hour episode until nine days before the prep date," says Jeri Taylor of the initial production meeting where the various creative teams meet to discuss what needs to be created to bring a script to the screen. "Those poor production people were behind right from the get-go because, of course, they could not finish writing the two hours in that time. We had a production meeting on the first hour and then we had a production meeting on the second hour, and then Michael and Rick Berman felt that the story wasn't working in the second hour so we had to go back and re-break the entire story all over again. The production people were magnificent in terms of being flexible, good natured and understanding. We were sort of all in this together and somehow we all pulled together and made it happen."

Among the biggest challenges from a production standpoint was re-creating the look of the original two-hour premiere, "Encounter At Farpoint," one of the time periods evoked in the finale. "They began combing the prop department for some of the things we had seven years ago, including the reclining chairs on the bridge that we had. There are many things that had already been tossed out and we had no way of getting them back, so we had to re-create the same feeling as the pilot."

In producing the episode, David Livingston and Merri Howard's production team were challenged by the fact that they were only given the first hour of the script while Moore and Braga rushed to complete work on the second hour.

"The courtroom set was a very complicated and time-consuming set originally in the pilot, but we simplified it and worked out some of the kinks that existed previously in terms of working off the crane," says Livingston of rebuilding the post-atomic court in which Q tried humanity. "I think [director] Rick Kolbe solved the problems quite cleverly and made it look very interesting. The different timelines; past, present, and future were tough because we had to come up with make-up and wardrobe that were appropriate to those periods and determine how much we wanted to re-create the original pilot or not. For instance, Michael Dorn's make-up has changed considerably over the years and one of the questions we asked was whether or not we wanted to go back and re-create exactly what he had looked like in the past. We decided it wouldn't be appropriate because his facial structure has changed."

"It was fun to talk about the different visual elements that we wanted to change in the sets like the Enterprise and the wardrobe and the communicators to try and key to the audience that each individual time period had a unique and different look," he continues. "I think we were pretty successful in doing that."

Complicating production on the final episode was a last-minute rewrite mandated by executive producer Michael Piller. "The script was in continual rewrites and we had a major rewrite right before going into production," says Livingston. "It put all the pressure on the director and Kolbe is a director who does immaculate preparation, which he was not permitted to do because of the time constraints. He was always having to spend an extraordinary amount of time just keeping current with what was going on as well as contending with the schedule, which was an extraordinarily difficult schedule. But he is a man who exists with grace under pressure. He was a point man in Vietnam, so I guess after that nothing's gonna rattle him too much."

Which is not to say that the production schedule didn't bother him.

While "All Good Things" was an emotional show, Kolbe emphasizes that it was a memorable experience production-wise.

"The show changed quite a bit from the original script to the final shooting script," Kolbe explains. "Unfortunately, for most of us it changed too late. I think out of the fourteen days of preparation I had, I sat around for nine days and the last five days were just a frantic struggle to get it all together. The show basically was rewritten. The general idea was there, but scenes were completely rewritten. The problem for me was that these scenes had to be tied together very carefully. There were transitions in there that were given in the script and I was expected to continue these transitions so that if Picard made a particular head move in the past, the moment we switched over that head move would pop up in the present or future. All of these things had to be choreographed."

Kolbe states that his approach is to prep from "the inside out." He reads the script so that he understands what the scenes are about, where they're coming from, where they're going, what are the objectives and what are the dramatic points. From there, he begins staging.

"I think every good director works that way," he muses. "Unfortunately, without a script that's kind of hard to do. When I finally got the script, I said to myself, 'Do I want to spend my time on the set trying to figure out how I'm going to shoot everything? Or do I start prepping from the outside and eliminate some of the logistics, eliminate some of the staging; try to figure out what is happening in a scene and hope that I'm right? If I don't really understand what's going on, I've got Patrick, I've got Jonathan. I've got everybody else who's been doing this for years. They'll help me.' Well, it almost worked out that way. But, unfortunately, tensions were rather taut on that episode."

For one thing, he says, "it was the last episode. Even though there was going to be a feature film, mortality was rearing its ugly head," and the actors were trying to reconcile themselves to the fact that the next job they would go to would probably be one they would have to read for.

"Even though they might say they're glad it's over, I'm sure they all have an ambiguous feeling," he offers. "That's what created the tension. Yes, we want it to end because we have done it and we're bored with it. On the other hand, it's security, it's safety, we don't have to sell shoes. Unfortunately, the movie was there and everybody, especially Patrick, was involved in the movie making, the script conferences. There were all these problems and those problems took away from attention being given to this particular show. So the best laid plans of mice and men began to crumble rather early in the shooting and we had to struggle. There was a lot of tension. There was a lot of fun as well.

"It's a show that I would never want to do again and would love to do again," Kolbe smiles. "I think that's the feeling we all had. I'm very proud of what we did. It's a good-looking show, we gave it a dignified ending, but, boy, what a pain in the ass it was to shoot."

The rewrites on the show were not lost on the cast, who were concerned by the changes being ordered by Piller.

"I got more involved in this than I have on any show on *The Next Generation* for two years," says Piller. "I actually went into the room with the guys and we rewrote the story because it wasn't working. This became controversial because for the first time in four years, Patrick Stewart called me up after seeing the first and later drafts and said, 'I'm terribly unhappy with the changes made in the script.' The problem with the first draft was that the guys were trying to bring as much character interplay into two hours as they possibly could, but there was no plot as far as I was concerned. They were on their way to something until Act 9 in a ten-act structure. I knew in my gut that Act 9 had to be moved to Act 6. Instead of it being a romp with very schticky things that people loved, I wanted it to end with an adventure and a mystery."

Not everyone agreed. Brent Spiner was another of the actors disappointed by the rewrites on the finale, "The first draft that Ron and Brannon wrote was extraordinary," Spiner says. "I think it would have easily been thought of as the greatest *Star Trek* episode of all time. Michael came in and added a few thousand words of technobabble to it and took out some of the character scenes, which he is not keen on. There were moments when I read the first draft that my heart jumped into my throat because I was so excited. There were some wonderful moments between Picard, Geordi, and Data. Nonetheless, it's still a very good episode."

One of the sequences which was lost in the rewrite involved Picard, Data, and Geordi stealing the Enterprise so that they could travel to investigate the temporal anomaly in the future. "They go to the Starfleet Museum where the Enterprise is with a bunch of other ships and they get a guided tour," reveals Braga. "The tour guide doesn't even know who they are and they have to commandeer the Enterprise to go on this crazy mission Picard wants to go on. Just as they're about to go, Admiral Riker comes in with a bunch of security people. They end up going anyway, of course, but to me that was a lot of fun. There was a lot of good character work that was lost. Did we need Geordi's visor to hold the key to the mystery? We've seen that about twenty-five times in the show. Do we really need his eyes to be getting younger? Would it have been better to have more character at the risk of meandering a little bit? Yes, I think so. But that's just my opinion. Michael Pillar's opinion is probably just as valid and I believe the show works either way. I'll tell you it was a lot more fun to write the scene of the crew stealing the Enterprise than it was to write tech about people getting younger and I believe what's more fun to write is more fun to watch."

Comments Ron Moore, "There were some things we just couldn't physically do which we talked about in production meetings. They promised they would do everything they could to re-create the Farpoint look on the Enterprise, but there are certain built-in limitations because some of those things just don't exist anymore. The way the viewscreen looked around the edges is a little different and the cost was just too much to make a whole new viewscreen. We re-carpeted the Enterprise, but who cares about that? Also, in the old days, the ops lounge and the sickbay were physically the same set which was just re-dressed. Now, they're different, so there were certain things we just said we'd shine. Do the best you can. Do the things that are going to be what your eye will visually go to, like the costumes, putting the gold ships back on the wall in ops."

One facet of the production that couldn't be changed was the fact that the cast had aged seven years since the pilot. "We talked about it," says Moore, "but there wasn't much we could do about that so we figured it was only seven years. It wasn't like asking the original series' actors to portray themselves in the sixties. I thought the audience would basically accept it and we were fortunate in that the Farpoint story happens to take Riker out of the picture because we weren't going to make Jonathan shave his beard and make him look younger. Fortunately, we found a clip of him to use with him on the monitor talking to Picard."

In addition to re-creating the past, creating the future was equally daunting, involving complex prosthetics for most of the cast. "The make-up for the future was very difficult. It took time to put it on and we lost hours because of that," says Jeri Taylor. "Gates' skin, for instance, is very fragile and so the prosthetic that is added to her tends to kind of slip. Halfway through each day of shooting we had to completely redo her make-up from scratch."

David Livingston, the show's producer responsible for overseeing physical production on the series, comments, "The last show was an incredibly ambitious one in terms of scope and in terms of recapturing the pilot. I was directing an episode of *DS9* when [director Winrich] Kolbe started shooting, so I didn't have a lot of advice to offer based on my experience working on 'Farpoint,' but I did tell him the courtroom set was a very complicated and time-consuming set originally, in the pilot, and we simplified it and we worked out some of the kinks that existed before in terms of working off the crane. I think Rick Kolbe solved the problems quite cleverly and made it look very interesting."

For the writers, however, the fun was in postulating a future very different than what most viewers would expect. "We thought, 'In what ways can they have become different?'" muses Moore. "Some people should be estranged, we wanted somebody to be dead, we wanted Data to have become very human in the future. We wanted a lot of them to have left Starfleet. The notion that Beverly would be the captain of her own ship seemed like an outgrowth of some things we had started in the series, yet no one would really expect it. We really liked the idea that Geordi, the ultimate tech man, would become a novelist. It was fun coming up with their futureselves. Ultimately, it is an ambitious show and we took some major risks with the characters and that is good. I think it is a bold way to go out. But there was a lot of danger involved in trying to find the right balance of how much of a sci-fi mystery should it be? How much should it be a valentine to the characters? How funny should it be? How much action? What will the Q part of it be? It was certainly the first time that we have dealt with a two-hour piece of the series where we didn't feel like we had to pad at some point. Usually at some point those two hours feel like we don't have quite enough story to keep going. This one had so much story going on that trying to keep it all together within two hours was a bigger challenge."

As for the show's concluding moments in which Picard joins the senior staff at the poker table, Moore offers, "The poker game has become the signature of the series. It was a great idea that brought the crew together in a social situation. It's something we've always played through the years and it seems like them at their best, sitting around, off the bridge, just interacting with each other. Rick Berman's big note on the script was that he wanted the end of the series to have a sweet, nostalgic feel and he wanted everybody to walk away with a warm, fuzzy feeling. That was his dictum to us."

Rick Kolbe remembers directing that particular poker game quite clearly. "That was a very simple climax to the show," he says. "Very well done. I think we shot that on the Friday before we finished. The next two days were basically

the courtroom scenes between John DeLancie and Patrick Stewart. But the poker game was the last time that everybody from the regular crew was together. What you didn't see were the two hundred people around us, wanting to be there for this historic moment."

Inevitable comparisons cropped up in many cast and crew interviews between the two-hour finale, which boasted an epic scope, and the feature film, *Generations*. Says Moore, "I think it is inevitable that people will compare it. We just know that this could never have been the feature. It is such an inside show, you have to know the series a little bit and understand the characters and the relationships to appreciate it."

Adds Brannon Braga, "The final episode is too internal. It relies on knowledge of the show that is too much for a mainstream movie audience to have to know. Its structure is very radical. If the final episode were a movie, I'm convinced it would only play to an art house circuit. It makes *Slaughterhouse Five* look like *Sesame Street*."

Ultimately, most people would agree that "All Good Things" was a remarkable success in bringing to a close the logbooks of the Enterprise-D. With or without its moments of deeper character exploration, the show offered several insights of great relevance to today's world. "I think the episode is a true *Star Trek* adventure that works on a metaphorical level. It deals with the human condition and talks about all the issues that I think *Star Trek* really speaks to," comments Michael Piller. "There are some wonderful performances and Kolbe's direction was terrific. I think that the goal of the episode is not just to speculate about how families change, but also talk about how it takes a lifetime — or many lifetimes — for a man or mankind to create the problems that he has to deal with in this existence, and it also takes a lifetime for him to solve and address the issues and problems that he has created."

TV Guide *bids adieu to* Star Trek: The Next Generation.

•••••

CHAPTER THIRTY

STAR TREK: GENERATIONS
Launching The Next Generation On Film

If the characters of *Star Trek: The Next Generation* were the last of Gene Roddenberry's "children," then those children have grown up in the form of *Generations*, the first motion picture based on the syndicated TV series.

Paramount Pictures decided that they had gone as far as they could with a film franchise featuring the original cast. The time had come for *The Next Generation* to make the leap to the big screen. After all, removing the show from the airwaves while still so popular would virtually guarantee box office success. Besides, reruns of the series would undoubtedly air for decades to come and there were two spin-offs to take its place, *Star Trek: Deep Space Nine* and *Star Trek: Voyager*.

Patrick Stewart, for one, was pleased that the show ended when it did, particularly as he was one of the few holdouts who hadn't necessarily committed to season eight. Rumors have it that his resistance to fighting on for another year was one of the main reasons the studio canceled the series.

"I am flattered by those remarks, that people should think that I have that much power," he smiles. "In fact, Paramount and I had an open arrangement for an eighth season and this time the option was on both sides, which is a little unusual. As it happened, the studio pulled the show. I was never consulted, but I felt their timing was perfect. I liked the idea that we would end the series when we were on top. The very final episode that we did was one of the best that we had done in the whole show. But everyone was pretty much ready to move on. I started to fear that I as an actor might start repeating myself. Days were not as interesting and as exciting as they had been and I was looking for fresh fields and pastures new. I wish we had not had to go into the movie

Captains James T. Kirk (William Shatner) and Jean Luc Picard (Patrick Stewart) meet their maker, the late Gene Roddenberry (photo copyriht ©1995 Albert Ortega).

quite so quickly as we did. I had four days off between wrapping the series and stepping on board the Lady Washington in Santa Monica Bay. Luckily I did not have to do too much character research before we went."

Like Stewart, Brent Spiner was reluctant to come back for an eighth season, and probably wouldn't have appeared had the series continued. "We had done 178 hours," he points out. "One hundred and seventy-eight hours of anything is just about enough, I think, and it was a brutal sort of seven years of work. I was glad not to have to get up at 5:00 in the morning anymore. I think we were really almost all ready to stop doing it. Maybe a couple of people would have been interested in doing an eighth, season, but not many of us really. I think we felt, 'Yeah, we have done this now for seven years and with luck, we will get to come back and do it every couple of years.' I'd like to do more movies for the reason that I get to come back together with my friends and have some fun again. It would be like going to summer camp every couple of years."

Generations began when Paramount Pictures approached series executive producer Rick Berman. "I was asked to do the movie in February of 1993," says Berman. "The plan was I would write two stories with two separate writers and that I would be involved with selecting which one was the best.

One writer for the film was Maurice Hurley, who worked with us before, and the other was the team of Brannon Braga and Ron Moore. We spent the early spring of '93 writing both stories and, by late spring, the studio and I agreed that we wanted to pursue the one with Brannon and Ron. The studio embraced the story very quickly."

One similarity between both scripts is that they featured, in some shape or form, members of the original *Star Trek* cast which was not, surprisingly, an edict of the studio.

"When I was first asked to do this, I was not asked to do anything with the original characters," emphasizes Berman. "They wanted a *Next Generation* movie. I went to them and said, 'I would like to integrate the characters from the original series, do you have any problem with it?' Sherry Lansing and John Goldwyn, the people I was dealing with in the motion picture division, said great. They said contact Bill and Leonard and see if they have a problem with it and they did not. Then in the script that Ron and Brannon wrote, we developed a story that had all of the characters, originally focusing mostly on the character of Kirk."

Warping To The Big Screen

When writing their screenplay, Ron Moore and Brannon Braga, who

•••••

Time *heralds the theatrical release of* Star Trek: Generations *by featuring William Shatner and Patrick Stewart on the cover of its November 28, 1994 issue (photo copyright ©1994 Time Warner).*

• • • •

have subsequently joined the respective staffs of *DS9* and *Voyager*, most definitely had a game plan, beginning with screenings of the first six films in the series.

"We sat down and watched the first six several times," says Moore. "We watched *IV* closely. We watched *The Wrath of Khan* several times because it's my favorite of the six films and I think the best as far as the story level and execution. We just sort of looked for how they handled some things. We didn't really say let's make them like the other ones, but we wanted to get a feel for how *Star Trek* translated to the big screen and what the action sequences were like. For instance, we got very, very used to writing tightly controlled space battles on the series where there are only two exterior shots when a phaser hits and you shake the camera a lot. To break ourselves out of that, we watched the Reliant attack on the Enterprise and how they really milk it."

Adds Braga, "Undoubtedly the two best films are *Wrath of Khan* and *The Voyage Home*. *Voyage Home* was laughs. It's the most fun, it's the best movie, I think. But *II* was wonderful because it had a very serious undercurrent, and Khan was a great villain. If we've done our job, we've captured the best of both worlds. Ron and I both feel that we have captured just the right mix of humor, action and character."

One point that Moore makes clear is that writing the film had a different set of requirements than the series did.

"It has to appeal to a different audience, in a sense," he notes. "The studio tells us that we can't assume that everyone going to this movie is familiar with the television show. It couldn't be a story that depended on the TV series and was mired in our backstories. We also didn't want something incredibly technical. We wanted something that was broader and had more action and adventure. We also wanted something with a lot more humor than we normally do on the series. We had a lot more money so we wanted to do things that you couldn't do on the series and yet we wanted to be able to do things that were big and fun and not like, 'Oh gee, they got loose in the candy store and they really just gorged themselves and it became stupid.' It was a fine line. We had to maintain

what the show is about and be true to the series that we worked on for seven years and what it had become — and we had to translate that into a different format and into a different structure."

Braga concurs, "It was very important to us that this film not be so self-referential to this franchise that the people who aren't familiar with *Star Trek* would be confused. There are embellishments throughout the movie — Farpoint is referred to passingly, as is the Borg, but you've got to be careful on the big screen. This movie's got to have a broader appeal."

Coming up with the actual scenario for the film was not, Braga emphasizes, difficult. "It's tough coming up with stories week to week on the series," he says. "The movie was not so tough because we had some spectacular story elements in place at the get-go. We knew Kirk was going to be in it and that some of the other original series' characters were going to be in it. We knew that Guinan would be there. We knew what we wanted to do with Data. We had some *major* stuff we wanted to accomplish, so we had great story elements in place. Coming up with the actual space-time Nexus and what the villain is doing was not a struggle. It was a lot of fun. Because it's a movie, you can take big risks with the characters and do more event kind of plotting techniques, because you're not obligated to do an episode the following week. I think what we ended up with was a very funny film with a lot of humor, but a dark film as well. Its theme does deal with death. Picard suffers a terrible personal tragedy, Kirk is facing profound regret in his life. There are some somber moments and ultimately there are some very dark things that happen. I think there are some surprisingly somber sections."

According to Moore, one of the earliest concerns was exactly how the two crews would be brought together, and to what extent.

"The image that Brannon and I were most in love with was the idea of a movie poster for the film showing the Enterprise-D and the Enterprise-A locked in combat, shooting at each other. If you could have a situation where you had the two ships coming to blows, that would

be really cool. But it quickly became apparent that finding the motivation for the two to be at such odds and then keeping them both sympathetic and heroic was going to be a real tough sell. It was going to be too much trouble to get to this one cool scene at the end of the film. We knew we didn't want to do a time travel story and we didn't want the original crew to all be ancient like McCoy was in the 24th century, so Rick came up with the idea of a mystery that started in the 23rd century, then picked up seventy-eight years later in the 24th century. We knew that everyone was going to want the two captains to meet, since they had never met, and that led to a discussion of having them meet somewhere other than the 23rd or 24th centuries, in a place where time had no meaning. That led us to the Nexus."

For Berman, who had been the final arbiter of all things *Trek* since the death of Gene Roddenberry, the idea of having other voices involved in lording over this particular universe was an alien notion.

"The development stages of writing the film and being involved with Ron and Brannon's script was the most delightful part of making the film," says Berman. "It was a very creative time. On the production part of it there were a lot of budgetary battles that had to be fought in the early stages and a lot of people whom I was not used to working with. We also had tremendous problems negotiating with the actors. All the actors wanted to do the movie, but here was a 130-page script with characters they were playing which put them in a very good negotiating position, so the negotiations, which I was never personally involved with, were very traumatic in terms of the pressure that went on between the actors and the studio."

Directing The Generations Gap

While Moore and Braga wrote their script, Berman and the studio turned their collective sights toward the director's chair. Initially there had been some talk of hiring a so-called "big screen" director to helm this voyage of the Enterprise, but that plan was abandoned.

The point had apparently been driven home by *Star Trek: The Motion Picture*, directed by the highly esteemed Robert Wise, that Academy Awards don't make up for a lack of *Trek* knowledge.

In the case of *Star Trek: Generations*, Berman initially approached actor / director Leonard Nimoy, but he declined the offer to helm the project and play a cameo role as Spock. "We had a difference of opinion about the script," offers Nimoy diplomatically. "It didn't work for me."

Next, Berman wisely looked to his own, choosing director David Carson. To his credit, Carson had helmed some of the best episodes of *The Next Generation* (including "Yesterday's Enterprise") as well as the twelve million dollar premiere episode of *Deep Space Nine*, which one would assume served as an appropriate "sample reel" for someone tapped to direct a $26 million feature.

"I think everybody at Paramount was pleased with the pilot of *Deep Space Nine*," offers the English-born Carson, whose other episodic credits include *L.A. Law* and *Alien Nation*, and who had scored as director of many Jeremy Brett Sherlock Holmes dramas in England. "When it was decided that Rick was going to produce the movie, I think everybody thought it would be a good idea if I directed it, keeping up the partnership with him, as it were. It also has to be said that I'm going to be cheaper, which I know had nothing to do with Paramount's decision."

The choice of Carson was an exciting one for many members of the cast.

"David is one of those rare breed who is an actor's director *and* a technical director," enthuses Marina Sirtis. "*Star Trek* needs someone like that. We had directors on the series who were very good with the actors and bringing out the motivations, but when it came time to make the show look interesting, they fell flat on their face. Or we had the opposite, where they were moving the camera around and had these great action shots, but when it came time to say, 'Why should I be here?' the answer was, 'The camera's there, that's why.' So he's the rare combination of the two. A real joy."

Concurs William Shatner, who hadn't worked with Carson before, "He's an actor's director. He brought an entertainer's intellect to the film; a man who's always looking for the entertainment qualities of the scene."

Brent Spiner notes that Carson's approach on a feature film wasn't very different than their collaborations on the small screen, with the exception that they had the luxury of more time and, of course more money.

"Generally on the series we were shooting between eight and ten pages a day," he says. "On the feature we were doing between two and three pages a day. That afforded both David and the cast the opportunity to try more and to actually get it right as opposed to just get it. But as a director in general — and I was more aware of it on the film because in the episodes David has directed, I never had that much to do — I found him really, really bright, prepared and whenever I would be at a loss of where to take something, he had a real clear vision on where it should go. I found him enormously helpful and I admired his sort of digging his heels in because as always happens, I think there are time and monetary constraints that the studio has to be concerned about. But David made his primary concern, I think, to make a good picture and just basically refused to be budged on that notion. He would basically just dig his heels in and say, 'I don't want to just make a movie, I would like to make a very good movie if possible,' and he stuck to that all the way through the final day of shooting."

The choice of Carson also belies the fear that the attitude on *Generations* — as it had been on *Star Trek: The Motion Picture* — would be one of making changes for the sake of change simply because the show is being adapted for film.

"Frankly, I don't think there's a lot of difference between television and film," offers Carson. "There's all this big noise about how amazing it is and how different movies and TV are, but I think that it's a lot of nonsense. Everyone who's been involved in the series has been doing it for seven years. For example, the guys making the costumes and doing the make-up have been doing it for seven years. How stupid it would be to say, 'Oh, this is a movie, let's get some movie costume and make-up people in here.' I don't think this is a case where one needs to change everything, because everything's working very well. You don't need to say, 'This is a movie, we better do this and change it all so nobody recognizes the Enterprise.' You can make modifications to some small things that will delight everybody, but I just think it's a waste of time, money, and everything else to make changes for no reason."

He points out, however, when you're operating at the speed necessary for television, it's a medium that's far more forgiving than the big screen.

"Things that we do on television, like laser things and beam-ins and beam-outs, have to be treated differently on the large screen because you can see it all so clearly. You can't get away with as much as you can on the little screen. Similarly, in terms of color schemes, you can't light the bidge flatly, which is what it basically is on television. It's just a flat, even lighting which the people live in. When you put it up on the big screen, I think you're going to need more contrasts, more light and shades. At the same time, it's much better, it seems to me, to have the people who have been doing the TV series mold themselves to a new concept rather than necessarily bringing in a whole new team. So I think all the prejudice against TV people making features is silly. On the other hand, bringing in feature people to help us to make this look wonderful is probably wise of us."

One assumed difference between working on *Generations* and the TV series was the relationship between Carson and Rick Berman, given the fact that motion pictures are much more a director's medium than a producer's. Carson denies that this was ever a problem.

"When you work on television," says Carson, "you are a guest of the production, the producers, the writers and the actors, and you try to serve the production the best that you can within the parameters and guidelines of what everyone is doing on a regular basis. When you do two-hour movies or pilots, then the same team structure applies except that you are in on the ground floor and

Scotty (James Doohan) teams up with Captain Kirk one last time in Star Trek: Generations *(photo copyright ©1995 Albert Ortega).*

you can work more or less on an even footing with the producers and the writers. Then again, you have to be aware that if you're doing a pilot, as I was with *Deep Space Nine*, all of these people are planning for seven years of work. You're doing two hours of material, but after those two hours it's 'Thank you very much. Good-bye.' Therefore they have to make decisions which affect your two-hour show because they are making their decisions for the future of the series.

"When you come to a movie," he elaborates, "everyone starts with their delineated roles. In Rick's and my relationship, we had worked closely and happily together on episodes of the series and the pilot of *Deep Space Nine*, but with the parameters that I described. Therefore, when we came to do the film, our roles did not change automatically. What happened was that Rick gave me the space that a film director is normally accorded, which was extremely generous of him because he was working with the same people he had worked on the series with. And he, as producer, is accustomed to having the last word. But he handed me the baton, as it were, to conduct the orchestra and I conducted it. In return for that courtesy, I always

worked closely with him in the creation of the whole thing."

Several problems faced the duo before shooting even began. Initially, when the first draft script was handed in, it featured an opening sequence that starred the entire original cast. Unfortunately, with the exception of Shatner, James Doohan and Walter Koenig, no one else wanted to be involved, feeling that they had said a more meaningful farewell in the last film, *The Undiscovered Country*.

"*Generations* would have been wonderful if it had been a genuine passing of the torch," says George Takei, whose Mr. Sulu became captain of the Excelsior in *Star Trek VI*. "As it turns out, it's a little prologue, a brief cameo at the beginning. That was not as attractive as I had originally envisioned. For me, *Star Trek VI* was such a glorious experience, that I didn't want to dilute that wonderful after-taste."

Patrick Stewart explains, "It had been an argument of mine that the film should include as many of the original *Star Trek* members as we could get. For the most part, I was alone in this feeling. Most of my colleagues didn't share this point-of-view and felt, since this would be a transitional movie, we should just cut the original cast off. I felt having members of the original cast would provide the opportunity to present something really intense and dramatic. I was thrilled and relieved when offers did go out to the original cast and it saddened me when only three of them were in it. I was particularly saddened that Leonard and De were not in it. I felt they would have made a marvelous contribution. But critical to all this was to have Bill. I felt that having the two captains share screen space was something audiences would enjoy seeing."

Rick Berman elaborates on this, noting that the way the story evolved, the only integral character from the original series was Kirk.

"This has nothing to do with Leonard Nimoy," he says pointedly. "The other [characters] all had relatively minor roles. And in the case of Leonard and De Kelley, they both felt that they had made appropriate good-byes in *Star Trek VI* and there was no reason to bring the

characters back for — I wouldn't call them cameos, but they were only in the first fifteen minutes and that was it. In the case of Bill, it was a whole different story. His part has a great deal more depth to it."

David Carson understands the implications of bringing together these two pop-culture legends. "I'm well aware that Kirk and his crew are American icons who have achieved a certain mythology in American folk art, if you like. They have a very specific place beyond simply being characters in a TV show. And I am aware of the responsibility of having Kirk and Picard together. It's very tantalizing to have them in the same place, interacting."

Similar problems arose from within, when several members of the ensemble voiced reservations about the screenplay and their relatively minor roles in it. Most notable among the dissenters were Michael Dorn and Marina Sirtis.

"In hindsight, I think it was my own inexperience in filmmaking in Hollywood that messed me up," Sirtis admits sheepishly. "In England it's very different. There you get a script and you shoot a script. In America, that isn't the way it works. Rewriting is happening up until the day you shoot it. When we were approached about doing the movie, we were reading the first draft. The first draft bore no relation to the final draft. When we finally wrapped the movie, we were

Walter Koenigs final appearance as Chekov in the early sequences of Generations *(photo copyright ©1995 Albert Ortega).*

• • • •

all very excited about how good it was. I'm very happy with it."

Concurs Jonathan Frakes, "It changed so much and we were really cut out of the other part of the story. Worf and I have the 'B' story now and, originally, we were tied in a little bit to the Nexus story. Now we no longer are. It's like a big Picard episode, with the B story being those on the Away Team. That's what it all comes down to, but, hey, it's a great job. Maybe I'll have more to do in the next movie. I'm not one to complain."

Brannon Braga points out that through the course of a season there were twenty-six hours to explore the various characters, whereas *Generations* would have, at the most, two hours to tell its story.

"We had to choose who this movie was about," says Braga. "The movie's about Picard and Data. To an extent, it's about Kirk. The other characters all have great moments, Dr. Crusher the least of which. But this is just the reality of our time situation. It's not to say if there's another film we won't focus on other characters. We just felt it had to be about Picard because he's our captain and our primary focus. And Data has to be the second most popular character, and we had to tell a story about him. But everyone has a role to play."

Marina Sirtis doesn't see the ensemble falling into the so-called "gang of four" syndrome of original series cast members, due primarily to the fact that the *Next Generation* cast usually had much more to do than their predecessors.

"I think *Generations* is a transitional movie," she offers, "and consequently had William Shatner and members of the original cast. However, we as a cast always got much more to do on the show than the original gang of four did. They were really supporting actors. On our show, Patrick and Brent were the main characters, but Worf got a hell of a lot, and I got four or five scripts a season based on my character, Gates got storylines, LeVar had much more to do than Jimmy Doohan did as chief engineer. So I don't think we were excluded as much as they were."

Rick Berman was very much aware of the fact that there would be some unhappiness on the part of certain cast members concerning their seemingly diminished roles.

"This was a movie that had fifteen roles in it that had already been cast before we wrote the movie," he explains, "so you are not dealing with actors who read for a role and get it and are happy just to get it. You have actors who have the role already, who feel they know more about the character than you do, and who undoubtedly feel underpaid and underused. That is something you've got to deal with very sensitively. We have seven characters from *The Next Generation*, Whoopi is eight, three characters from the original series. That is eleven, and a couple of others. You've got fifteen characters, but you can't have fifteen stars in the movie. As this story evolved, we ended up with Kirk and Picard and Data having the three major arcs in this film, and Soran, our guest villain.

"What you try to do is create minor storylines or scenes that the other actors will have that will showcase them to some degree," he adds. "It is frustrating for the actors and sometimes those things will be minimized in the cutting room, not because that is the way it was planned, but because when you are pasting the movie in the cutting room and you've got to lose things and shorten things, you end up bringing things down. LeVar had a wonderful scene that was cut dramatically short, not because of LeVar but because of the pacing of the movie. I think if you look at the original *Star Trek* movies, you will see numerous films where a number of the actors had small parts. It is part of the game. When you have an ensemble in any one given movie, it is going to just feature certain people. There were hurt feelings, but I worked diligently with every one of our actors on their parts, because these people know these characters very well. They played them for over seven years and we worked with them and everybody had notes — especially with Patrick, Brent and Bill — and we made a lot of changes and accommodations. They helped make it better."

NCC 1701-B

The final draft of *Generations* begins with Kirk continuing his battle with mortality and trying to cope with the aging process. He no longer feels that he's making a difference. In an opening sequence that was cut from the film, he takes a mid-life crisis to new extremes when he space-dives — for want of a better word — from Earth's atmosphere to a designated area, where he ebulliently greets a waiting duo — the unlikely Scotty and Chekov, rather than Spock and McCoy.

"It *was* a bit of a reach," laughs Shatner, who felt strange shooting a *Star Trek* adventure without Nimoy and DeForest Kelley. "It was very odd. I felt very lonely without my two buddies and I told them that several times."

David Carson explains that the scene was cut for a very specific reason, all tied in to the nuances of the film he was attempting to create.

"Bill was parachuting out of orbital skydiving into a hayfield and landing undignified," recalls Carson, "and Scotty ran along behind him: 'What are you doing? You are too old to be doing this sort of thing,' which is very much like how some of the old movies started. It started with a joke and all of that. I said to Bill, 'The point about this movie is not that you are going off to do deeds of daring for two hours or so, therefore it will be good to have a scene where you are shown as a human being and it is funny and it is sort of interesting. In this movie, the first time you see Captain Kirk, he *is* Captain Kirk. He is a hero.'"

As evidenced on screen, those early sequences have Kirk, Scotty and Chekov proceed to the christening of the Enterprise-B (an Excelsior class vessel), where a quick press demonstration will have the starship head out to Pluto and back again. Unfortunately, the vessel intercepts a distress call from the transport ship Lakul, one of two transporting El-Aurian refugees to Earth, which is caught in an energy distortion. Enterprise proceeds to the coordinates, where they see the ships ensnared by tendrils of energy. One vessel explodes, taking the lives of 265 people with it. Forty-seven out of the 150 people — including Dr. Tolian Soran (Malcolm McDowell) and Guinan (Whoopi Goldberg) — being transported on the Lakul are saved before that ship is destroyed as well.

The Enterprise itself is then caught by one of the tendrils. To free the ship, Kirk proceeds to deck fifteen and the deflector relays so that he can "simulate a torpedo blast using a resonance burst from the main deflector dish" (it's called technobabble, ladies and gentlemen). His efforts are a success and the starship is set free, but not before one final energy blast rips open part of the Enterprise, including deck fifteen. Captain James T. Kirk is gone.

These scenes represent the first time that David Carson had had the opportunity to work with Shatner, and he found himself amazed at the actor's commitment to the character and the character's place in our pop-culture lexicon. "He absolutely gets into shape for it, physically and mentally," says Carson. "He slims down to get ready for the role, he puts on that uniform and he *is* Captain Kirk."

Carson wasn't the only one impressed with Shatner; indeed, some of the actors playing Enterprise-B crewmembers were overwhelmed by his presence, as Carson was to discover.

"All of the supporting players are very good, very professional actors," the director notes. "I spent some intensive auditions with them to get the right mix. And yet on the first day, some of [their performances] were quite a bit under where they had been in the auditions. With one in particular, I began to wonder if I had made a mistake, so I called him and said, 'Look, do you have a problem? Are you okay?' He said, 'I'm sorry about today. It was just the situation.' I asked, 'Situation? What are you talking about?' And he said, 'You're English, so you probably don't understand what it means to a twenty-nine-year-old American actor to be on the bridge of the Enterprise with Captain Kirk. It is a mind-blowing experience. Even though I'm an actor in a scene, I'm also on a legendary ship with a legendary captain. It's extraordinary. We all felt it.' It really is amazing. They're all twenty-nine-to-mid-thirties, very experienced actors and not ones who normally feel that kind of stage fright."

Such opening-day jitters helped Carson recognize Kirk's role as a symbol of both progress and the future for millions of people. "I think you have to take great care of the legend and treat it with respect and deference. I think in something like *Star Trek* you can't ignore its roots. You have to assimilate its history and then take it further, improving it by doing it better than it's been done before."

For production designer Herman Zimmerman, the Enterprise-B sequences were a pleasure in that they gave him the opportunity to enhance what had come before.

"Enterprise-B," he explains, "is a further improvement on the Enterprise bridge that you saw in *Star Trek V* and *Star Trek VI*. When I did *Star Trek V*, the bridge from the features, which had been used in all the features, was falling apart and needed serious refurbishing. At that point I rebuilt the bridge and made it a little less Buck Rogers. I felt the original design from *Star Trek: The Motion Picture* was a little further away from science fiction as I felt the seriousness of the property itself warranted. So I took the opportunity to make calculated changes, and essentially that's the bridge you see in the feature.

"It's always nice to have the opportunity to work on something like the bridge over a period of time so that you get the opportunity to investigate the things you might have thought were mistakes and make them right. Certainly because the studio does give you a limit on what you can spend, there are things I didn't do on *V* that I did do on *VI*, and there are things I did on *Star Trek: Generations* that I didn't do on either of those. It's all the same scenery, but used in a fresh way, I hope. I like the Enterprise-B. I think we've made some interesting changes to the Excelsior model that made it a new ship. And we saw the deflector room, which we'd never seen on any of the other ships. All of it really starts the picture off with a bang."

Carson definitely viewed life on the two Enterprises as being very different from each other. "We tried to treat the Enterprise-B and the people in it as if we were dealing with a period piece," he notes. "We were consciously doing a film that was one hundred years older

Alan Ruck, who appeared as Captain John Harriman during the Enterprise-B sequences of Generations *(photo copyright ©1995 Albert Ortega).*

than the other one, and we tried to light it differently and use our camera slightly differently. It seems to have worked because people have commented to me that it was slightly more old-fashioned than the Enterprise-D."

Sea Trek

As initially conceived, the first sequence of *Generations* featuring the *Next Generation* crew would have taken place on the Amargosa Observatory prior to a Romulan attack.

"We opened with two ensigns sitting by a big window," says Ron Moore. "They're sitting there and they're bored, just staring out at the stupid stars they've been studying for a year and they're saying, 'Yeah, join Starfleet. Meet interesting people. Explore the galaxy — and we're here. Nothing ever happens.' Suddenly there's a trembling and the station starts to shake. They look right out the window and there's a Romulan warbird decloaking. The Romulans beam in and start shooting. There's a big shoot-em-up action sequence and one of the ensigns gets thrown against the bulkhead. One Romulan says, 'Where is the trilithium?' and the ensign replies, 'I don't know what you're talking about,' and then he looks over and reacts. The

Romulan turns and looks out the window and coming out of the sun is the Enterprise to the rescue. They beam aboard and Worf kicks the shit out of the Romulans, and our introduction of the *Next Generation* crew is as they fight off the Romulan attack."

The scene fell by the wayside after comments offered by *Next Generation* and *Voyager* producer Jeri Taylor dampened the writers' enthusiasm for the sequence. "She said, 'You've just left a big action sequence in the prologue with running and jumping and ships exploding and Kirk getting pulled away. Then there's a fade-to-black and then another action sequence.' It just felt wrong structurally. And it didn't seem like the best way to introduce the *Next Generation* cast."

Instead, we're on the holodeck of the Enterprise-D, where Picard's crew has re-created a 19th century three-mast sailing vessel traveling the ocean. On board, everyone — dressed in full naval uniform — is participating in the promotion of Worf to lieutenant commander, the result of which is his having to walk the plank (apparently when Troi was promoted, she was fed to the lions in ancient Rome). Everyone laughs, with the exception of Data who, attempting to join in while not understanding why, shoves Dr. Crusher overboard. She does *not* appreciate it.

The holodeck program comes to an end when Picard receives a shocking personal communiqué and Riker is informed that the Amargosa observatory is under attack.

Besides using a nautical analogy to *Star Trek*, these sequences represented certain problems.

"It was a week of hell," sighs Marina Sirtis. "It looks cute, but it's not fun if you get seasick, which I do. It did convince me that I'm never going to shoot a movie on a boat again."

Counters Jonathan Frakes, "That was a ball. We were at sea — two miles off the coast of Santa Monica — outside in the sun, and most of what we were doing was action, so there weren't any heavy dialogue things to concern your brain with. I found it wonderful because I like to be on boats. A couple of people in the cast were not thrilled with the heav-

ing of the sea....that's probably the wrong choice of words."

Then there were the usual budget constraints, with Paramount initially reluctant to finance such an expenditure.

"You come to them and say, 'I really want to make this great'," explains David Carson, "and they say, 'You don't have the money, just cut the script.' That scene was a primary candidate to be cut. But I feel that when you're doing a film that's on space ships all the time, you need as much breath as you can get, so we hung on to it in the face of the opposition that said we should reduce the budget. Basically this was indicative of the fact that we had a script that was too big and complex to shoot in fifty days. I think it was only because of the skill of the people involved that we got through it."

Which is not to say that those sequences didn't fall behind schedule. "Boats rock," says Carson matter-of-factly, "they sway, they don't hold still when you want them to. The sun was constantly moving so you had to constantly turn the ship to get the light right. The ship was also very small so you couldn't have everybody on board all the time. You had to take them off and put them on other boats and then bring the boats up and try and get them together without dropping the actors in the water between. It's quite good fun."

For Herman Zimmerman, it was exciting to use the Enterprise's holodeck in a way that truly represented what that area of the ship was capable of delivering. Also exciting was finding the real ship where those sequences would be shot on.

"It's the Lady Washington out of Seattle, a ship used as a promotion vessel for the city of Seattle," he says. "It has a really fine captain and a lot of very energetic young people. We almost didn't get the ship. Very coincidentally it came sailing in to Dana Point Harbor when we were down there looking at another vessel. When we saw this one, we ran right over and said, 'What will it take for us to use your ship?' It turned out to be a very happy accident."

Like Carson, Zimmerman bristled at Paramount's suggestion that the sequence be cut for fiscal reasons. "Nobody wanted to do that because of

the obvious tie-ins to Gene's original basing of Starfleet Command on the 19th century English Maritime tradition. It was indeed fortunate we were able to find a ship we could use and schedule it in such a way that we could keep our budgetary constraints in line and include that wonderful production value. Everybody who knew anything about *Star Trek* was delighted to have the opportunity to do this because it was so right on to the way that the *Star Trek* military structure was created. It's a beautiful ship and well photographed. It's not easy to shoot anything on the deck of a rolling ship, and it's pretty exciting stuff. It is the second opening of the movie. It's like we have a long cold opening, then the *real* opening is here on the holodeck."

This type of fiscal confrontation plagued much of the production, and it was a particular sticking-point between Carson and executive producer Bernie Williams. The director, for his part, wanted to make the best film he possibly could, while Williams essentially represented the studio's interests.

"David would always look at the producer as 'he's taking away from me,'" says Williams. "But I never took anything from him. What David felt he deserved more of was shooting time. The whole point of giving a television director a break was that when you make these [television] shows in eight or ten days, fifty days should be enough to make this movie. So, we gave him fifty days and he struggled through it, but it was fine. He turned in a very good movie. I've worked with Kubrick, David Lean and Fred Zinnemann, and if David has a problem, that's *his* problem. I don't give a shit. I'm very experienced and I can't cowtow to the whims of a director who wants, wants, wants. I have a responsibility to the movie, to the studio and 30 million dollars for this movie was enough."

Carson remained philosophical about the situation throughout production, handling these conflicts so stoically he would do a Vulcan proud. "Fifty days is extraordinary for a huge epic movie," says Carson. "People trim things down and you have to pull your horns in a bit. I immediately think of the next creative solution. One can't afford to sit around and think, I lost all this money, what can

I do about it?' I just turn around and go, 'Right, I'm not going to win that fight, so let's approach it like this.' That actually resulted in some happy accidents, like being able to turn long steps into a vertical twenty-five-foot shaft which made for a very exciting scene in the deflector room of the Enterprise-B."

For Brannon Braga, the scene taking place on the open ocean is dramatically important in that it serves as the impetus for the android Data to install a computer chip that will enable him to experience the full gamut of human emotions.

"When he pushes Crusher into the water, it's an awful moment," says Braga. "No one thinks it's funny and Data realizes he can't even grasp such a basic concept as humor, something so fundamental. Imagine what it's like not being able to laugh with everyone else. It must feel awful. He's the only guy in the room day after day after day who just doesn't get it. Yes, there are more formidable and important emotions to consider in life, but what could be sweeter than laughing? That seemed like a very poignant incident to make him suddenly decide to try it. It's a nice motivating factor."

According to Brent Spiner, the opportunity to play a new and different kind of Data was like "dying and going to heaven."

"I had been sort of euphemistically painting on a very narrow palette for a long time with kind of muted colors," Spiner explains, "so it was a real opportunity to cut loose. When I first read the script, I was a little concerned about it just because it was so different from the character, even though it represented an evolution. In thinking about it, I finally came to the conclusion that in worst-case scenario, they would love me in France."

Dr. Soran, I Presume?

When the Enterprise reaches the Amargosa solar observatory, they see signs of a recent battle and only five of nineteen life forms are being detected. An Away Team beams over to the observatory where among the survivors is Dr. Soran — seemingly unaged from when he was first seen aboard the Enterprise-B.

Everyone beams back to the starship, where Riker fills Picard in, though the captain still seems distant.

"The Amargosa station is a fragile, older station," explains Herman Zimmerman. "It's probably sixty years old when we see it and it's more in line with the original series in terms of design. It's like doing the history of the future. For instance, in the original series they used plastic buttons and cubes of clear acrylic that were just glued on to painted surfaces — which we now use keypads for — as controls for various computer elements, and we went back to that inside the observatory. We were trying to pay homage to the original series because we had an excuse to do so."

As the story for *Generations* unfolds, the audience learns that Soran is attempting to make his way back to an alternate dimensional plane known as the Nexus; a place where time has no meaning and you can be anywhere with anyone that you choose. Like Guinan, Soran had been on board the Lakul which had entered the Nexus when they were transported away by the Enterprise-B. Now, Soran is working with the Klingon renegades Lursa and B'Etor to put his plan into action.

At the same time, Data has an extremely difficult time dealing with the flood of emotions that are overwhelming him, while Picard must cope with that communiqué from Earth which stated his brother and nephew have burned to death in a fire. The captain reveals to Counselor Troi that his relationship with his nephew was the closest he's ever come to having a child of his own. But, now, there is no one left to carry on the Picard name.

"During the months prior to filming, my attention shifted to the character of Picard and in creating a storyline for the captain which had something more than just the narrative sequences in it," explains Patrick Stewart. "One of the things I was happy with was that, through meetings with the writers and producers, we developed a B story for Picard that is very private, personal, and a very intense emotional story that runs parallel to the main action story. For me, that was the most satisfying element of the pre-production on the movie."

Malcolm McDowell is Dr. Tolian Soran, the man who killed Kirk (photo copyright ©1995 Albert Ortega).

Originally, Picard's brother, Robert, died of a heart attack in his vineyard, and there was a moment when Picard says, "I wear this uniform and there are risks that go along with being a starship captain, which I accept, but Robert walked out to his vineyard one morning and died of a heart attack and his only enemy was time."

"That brought home a certain realization that, 'I can fight Klingons and I can do this and do that, but there is one enemy out there waiting for me that's going to get me eventually. It gets everybody, no matter what kind of job they have.' So that, we liked," says Ron Moore. "But Patrick felt that he was missing the element of continuation of the family line, the tradition, and that those mean a lot to some people. Patrick felt that he wanted more of that sense of family and that it's something very important for Picard. Once we heard that, we realized that could give us some interesting beats to play in the Nexus. At the end, Patrick was the one who said, 'And it should be a tragic, horrible death. If the captain is going to react in a way he's never reacted before, this one better really hit him between the eyes. You know, burn him to death.'"

Although one may argue that

it's an extreme dramatic development to rip apart Picard's family, David Carson felt that it fit very nicely into the film's theme of mortality, which began with Kirk's experiences in the past.

"One of the strands of the theme of mortality is, of course, your immortality through your progeny or family," he offers. "You don't have many movies about mortality or death. It's one of the great things that *Star Trek* is able to do; it's able to take an enormously grand theme and play variations on it. Kirk's variation was different, Picard's was different. Soran's is different. But they are all variations on that theme. Everything has to do with death and rebirth, some way or another."

One of the things that David Carson wanted to do to elevate *Generations* above the television series that inspired it, was to enhance the presentation of the Klingons, who played an integral role in Soran's plan.

"These are Klingon scenes like you ain't ever seen them before," he laughs. "As a group, they're much more animalistic and a more potentially violent bunch of people than they've been before — as you see them as a group running this ship, clustering around, and behaving *not* like Enterprise officers. They very much have an animalistic quality to them. They're not subtle, which is why I like them. If you make them all like Worf, you've flattened them out. I always felt that Worf represented a civilized Klingon, but when you get down to the level of a renegade Klingon, they're a pretty rough bunch of people, grunting and snorting and pushing and shoving. Lower depth Klingons."

For Malcolm McDowell, veteran of such genre fare as *A Clockwork Orange, Time After Time, Blue Thunder* and *Tank Girl*, this approach to the Klingons provided him with some enjoyable acting opportunities.

"Soran is fun because he can't stand these filthy pigs, the Klingons," he smiles. "I play it like he's got utter contempt for these barbarians. It's not there overtly, but it's like, 'My God, they stink. When was the last time they cleaned their teeth?' They threw me for a loop and I could barely get my lines out because there was so much hissing,

spitting, and groin-rubbing going on. But the Klingons are fun and their make-up is incredible."

McDowell was pleased with the character, particularly the background — despite it being underplayed — in which Soran's wife, children, and most of the El-Aurian race was wiped out by the Borg. Soran's motivation was an important aspect in the character's creation.

"We tried to craft a more multi-dimensional villain and a formidable nemesis for Picard that, in a way, had never been done in the series," says Brannon Braga. "In movies you seem to need a bigger villain. Soran is obsessed with time and time running out and time as a predator stalking him. He's desperate to get back to the Nexus and cheat death. Yet he's a villain who's suffered a personal tragedy as well. The Borg killed not only his family, but his entire world. Hopefully there's a sympathetic element to him. Hopefully people will relate to him, perhaps more than anybody. At the same time, you're appalled at what he's doing to get back there, while you can totally understand why he wants to get back to the Nexus. I don't think he's your typical cardboard cut-out bad guy."

Which is precisely what drew Malcolm McDowell to the character. "He's obviously a very strange man and there's a bit of a poet in him as well. Of course he does have his dark side, but I never play villains as if they are villains," says the actor. "I play them as quite normal people doing quite nasty things, although there's a reason for everything. Nobody is just black or white; there's always those gray-shaded areas and those are the most fascinating things to play.

"I read the script," he adds, "and I didn't really understand a word of it with all that Nexus stuff. I didn't know what the hell they were talking about, but I thought there was a glimmer of a part there. A glimmer of something that could be fun. So they asked for a meeting and I went into a meeting with them, and they asked me to read for it. I said, 'No, I won't.' It was ridiculous. What do they think it is, Shakespeare? So I wouldn't read it, but I had a very good meeting with Rick Berman and David Carson and I got the part."

David Carson considers

McDowell a key to the movie, believing that if the villain isn't satisfactorily frightening and powerful in a *Star Trek* vehicle, the story quickly flattens out. "I think McDowell's wonderful — we were very lucky to get him," he says. "Like all the *Star Trek* villains, he has to go up against everybody, so he carries half the movie. He sits at the same level as Picard and Kirk, and he does very well. Malcolm McDowell is especially equipped to be a *Star Trek* villain because he is such an incredibly talented performer, an instinctive actor who can also handle words, which people on *Star Trek* need to be able to do."

Beyond Soran, Carson was intrigued by the basic idea of the Nexus, likening it to a temptation or drug. "It's something that affects you like a drug, therefore it's something that is desirable, not unlike a hallucinogen into which you can sink and be happy, within the confines of it. You really need to be able to find the strength to deny it. So for us it has a sort of addictive feel to it. From the craving that the addiction can breed comes the behavior of someone like Soran, who is trying desperately to get his fix, no matter what the cost and how many lives it takes."

"*That's* what I played," interjects McDowell. "I enjoyed finding the character, because it really wasn't on the page of the script. I really — in my mind — have this idea that this man was like a drug addict who had to get a fix and wouldn't let anything divert him from that. He was a very concentrated man. I really liked Soran as a character."

To get back to the Nexus, Soran utilizes a trilithium device that has the power to literally collapse a star, the result of which — beyond wiping out all the planets in a particular system — is to alter gravitational waves, thus changing the path of the energy ribbon that serves as a dimensional entrance way. As all ships that have approached the ribbon have been destroyed, Soran's goal is to bring the ribbon to him on a world called Veridian Three. The problem is that when he destroys the Veridian star, he will also decimate Veridian Four, which has a population of 230 million.

• • • •

Destroying The Enterprise... Again

Discovering Soran's plan, the Enterprise proceeds to Veridian Three, where the starship engages the Bird of Prey in battle while Picard beams down to reason with Soran. In space, the Federation ship, under Riker's command, manages to destroy the Klingon vessel, but not before there's a warp core coolant leak. In five minutes there will be a full breach, so Riker orders everyone to evacuate into the saucer section, which will then be separated from the ship.

Separation is complete with only ten seconds to spare, but before the saucer section can move to a safe distance the Enterprise explodes, the force of the explosion knocking the saucer section into the planet's atmosphere. From there it plows its way through a dense rain forest, tearing up the jungle as it travels. When it finally comes to a stop, the saucer section is split open.

Needless to say, the destruction of the Enterprise raised the ire of more than a few Trekkers, as did the original Enterprise's demise in *Star Trek III: The Search for Spock*.

"But look at that crash sequence," proclaims Brannon Braga. "It's great. It's something we always wanted to do on the series, but didn't because saucer separation was very expensive and elaborate. But we always wanted to crash that sucker! Come on, we've been with that same starship for seven years. Let's get a new one!"

Ron Moore adds that the genesis of the Enterprise's destruction began in a story called "All Good Things," which had nothing to do with the series finale of the same name. "It was a story that was going to be the cliffhanger for the sixth season," he said. "Brannon and I had come up with a story where Starfleet recalls the Enterprise home and is going to split the crew up. The Enterprise was going to become the Queen Mary, basically, and on the way home, the characters all decide what they're going to do with their lives, and in the course of returning home there is a big battle and the saucer separates from the battle section, which explodes and the saucer crashes on the planet's sur-

face. The producers hated that story for the cliffhanger and we tossed it aside, but when we were doing the movie, this crash of the saucer was one of the first things Brannon and I came to Rick with. It's a statement that we're going in a different direction with the features and that we're going to take risks and be bold. It's not just going to be another episode thrown up on the big screen."

David Carson stands completely behind the decision to destroy the Enterprise, particularly in this manner.

"I think it's interesting that you have a battle where you have a winner and a loser, but as a by-product of winning, you find that your ship is in trouble. So, no sooner do you have a chance to celebrate your victory than your ship hits the rocks, as it were. You generally believe, I think, like all the good guys, that the Enterprise is going to make it. Well, we have a small problem in the warp core, we evacuate the ship, do the separation sequence and the damn thing blows up, and off we go back on the rollercoaster again.

"The action sequences inside the ship are very, very exciting," he continues. "You have battle scenes and suddenly you've got a disaster movie like *The Towering Inferno*, with all these people being moved out of the ship and scurrying into different areas. It's sort of like getting ready for an earthquake. You know it's going to happen and everyone's preparing for it. And everything's getting worse and then the crash happens and it just goes on and on. It should, I hope, be a very frightening and terrifying sequence that takes you just beyond the battle and puts everybody into a *major* jeopardy situation. I think that will be real exciting."

On the planet, Picard fails to stop Soran, whose probe destroys the Veridian star, resulting in the two men being swept into the Nexus. There, Picard finds himself in a living room at Christmas time with a wife and children — his children — clamoring for his attention. Picard suddenly has everything he has ever wanted: a family he could call his own. He's removed from this euphoria when he looks at an ornament that features a star which blinks out, its light expanding outward in its glass sphere.

MAD *presents the meeting of the two captains that many people wanted to see (photo copyright Time Warner)*

Although it's the way the ornament is designed, it reminds Picard of exactly why he's there.

He's stunned to suddenly find Guinan standing next to him. She explains that she is on the Enterprise but also here, and that he should consider this Guinan an "echo" of the one he left behind. Since time has no meaning in the Nexus, Picard wants to go back to the mountaintop on Veridian Three to stop Soran before he can destroy the star. He'll need help, but Guinan can't go with him. She suggests someone who can.

"It happened in a cabin near Mount Whitney in a town called Lone Pine, California," says Rick Berman of the following scene, "and it was terrific. Everybody had chills going up and down their backs."

Picard meets Captain James T. Kirk, who is living out the life he has always wanted. He's residing in a rustic home, his dog Butler is with him, and he's living with a woman, Antonia — the one he let get away many years ago.

Picard tries to convince him to leave the Nexus, but Kirk refuses, determined to make things "different this time." Moments later he's riding a horse on his uncle's farm, spurring the animal on and making a dangerous leap over a ravine. This jump, however, has a disturbing effect and he realizes why: the numerous times he made that leap in the past, it was scary as hell. But this time it wasn't. "Because....it's not real," muses Kirk.

At that moment, he's back to being the Kirk we've always known, telling Picard to not let them ever promote or transfer him. "Don't let anything take you off the bridge of that ship," he says, "because while you're there, you can *make a difference.*"

Of this scene, David Carson enthuses, "Each character discovers why it is they are where they are as they go through their scenes, more specifically Kirk, who discovers what's happening. Which actually makes the themes interesting from the audience's point of view because it pulls you along a storyline that the character is discovering within himself. You see what the temptation is and why he doesn't want to go anywhere. So it's quite an interesting and seductive thing to do to an audience at that stage of the movie."

Patrick Stewart gleefully recalls one particular exchange between Picard and Kirk in which Picard states, "You are a Starfleet officer. You have a duty!"

Laughs Stewart, "I'm told that the cinema audiences cheer when Kirk says, 'Don't you talk to me like that. I was out saving the galaxy when you're grandfather was still in diapers.' It's a funny line and, of course, it reverberates in a multitude of different ways, too, because it's not only Kirk speaking to Picard but it is the actor Bill Shatner speaking to Patrick Stewart. I thought that was charming."

Using the unique properties of the Nexus, Picard and Kirk are deposited on the Veridian Three mountaintop, working together to stop Soran from achieving his goal, and they're only able to do so after Kirk makes the ultimate sacrifice, plummeting to his death after doing all that he can to save the two hundred and thirty million inhabitants of Veridian Four.

You're Dead, Jim

For William Shatner, those closing sequences of his involvement in *Star Trek* bring a variety of emotions to mind. On the one hand there was the interaction between him, Stewart, and McDowell ("I've always admired Malcolm," says Shatner. "To have the opportunity to play opposite him and Patrick Stewart was to take on part of the Royal Academy class.") as well as the fact that he has played a character through nearly every stage of its adult life.

"I don't know whether it's ever been done," he notes. "There was definitely a conscious effort along the way to take the aging into consideration as well as the changes in psychology. While it's extraordinary to play a character over 30 years, it hasn't been thirty years for me. It's been intermittent. After three years of making the series ten years go by and then there was a movie we shot for a couple of months, and then it disappears for another two or three years. It is very intermittent, although the *Star Trek* comet trails the people in it. But to have people think of the character as an entity and to mourn the death as though it was a real person, that's a wonderful feeling."

Then, of course, there was the character's death scene, which probably required more preparation for Shatner than any other piece of film he has ever shot.

"You can only play, you can only perform, you can only read the lines as a result of your own experiences," Shatner explains. "I can't read a laugh line or a line of love the way you would because I don't have your experience of it, I only have my own. So, my coloring of a line is based on my experience. As a result, playing the death scene required me to look at what I would feel like if I were to die, and we all avoid looking at our own death. We all wear rose-colored glasses, not on life so much but on the absolute certainty that you are going to die. For all intents and purposes, your life is meaningless because you have lived and died and who remembers? So, all those thoughts that we avoid completely and only in the most stressful moments do we think of, and then avoid thinking about them again until the next stressful moment, I had to think about because I wanted to play the death of the character as honestly as I could. I required myself to look at what I would feel like if I was to die and how I would like to die and what it was like to die. That's what I played.

"It was odd and it grew to be more and more odd and stranger as the time to shoot it approached," he adds. "But I believe you die the way you live. Captain Kirk lived pretty much the way I wanted him to live. He was a distillation of all that I would like to be: heroic and romantic, forceful in battle and gentle in love, wise and profound. The ideal soldier/philosopher."

For Brannon Braga, it was a very "strange" moment when he and Ron Moore wrote the words "Kirk dies."

"I know it sounds corny and pretentious," he reflects, "but when we wrote that line, sitting in a condo in Mauii, we kind of sat there for a moment, a little shell-shocked. Ron especially, because he had been a big Kirk fan most of his life. So it was weird. We knew this was imaginary, yet this moment would be meaningful to a lot of people."

Adds Moore, "When we got to *the* scene, I was walking, pacing the room, talking, and Bran was at the computer. We were discussing it, on a roll, and then I said the line, 'Kirk dies.' It just sort of hit me. I had to sit down for a minute. There were tears in my eyes. 'Wow, I just killed a childhood hero.' I'll always remember that moment."

Those final moments of battle were exciting to Malcolm McDowell, who also thought it was funny to be watching what was going on from the inside. "There was this actor who had been performing this part for 30 years, there was the usurper of the crown and there's the guy, me, in the middle who's about to kill him," laughs McDowell. "It was kind of weird. Of course, he refused to die. It took him days and days and days to die. He didn't want to go. The scene seemed to go on forever and I can understand why after thirty years.

"For his book [*Star Trek Movie Memories*], Shatner interviewed me and asked, 'What's it like to kill Captain Kirk?' I said, 'Well, I think half the country is going to applaud me and the other half is going to want to kill me.' And he said, 'Which half is going to applaud you?' and I said, 'That's the half that's so sick of you after thirty years that they want to strangle you.' He took it in good sport."

When Leonard Nimoy killed Spock in *Star Trek II*, his death was a slow, emotionally drawn out one. Kirk, on the other hand, parts with the words to Picard, "It's been fun."

"I think it's really simple and doesn't get maudlin or too meaningful," says David Carson. "He's been meaningful about how important it is to make a difference and the bad boy in him, the naughty schoolboy, is twinkling because the odds are against them, it sounds like fun. It sort of has an irony to it. An enjoyment of life that's important for the Kirk character, and rather than quoting Shakespeare, Peter Pan, or something pretentious, like the other movies have given him to do, I think to make it very simple and moving is the best way to approach it."

At the film's conclusion, Picard, having buried Kirk, is picked up by a shuttlecraft and brought back to the remains of the Enterprise, where survivors are being transported aboard the recently arrived USS Farragut.

As Picard arrives at the crash site, Data and Troi are searching through rubble, seeking a life form picked up by Troi's tricorder. From within the debris, Data removes his cat, Spot, and actually begins to cry. He believes his emotion program is malfunctioning again, but Troi responds that it's working perfectly.

Searching through what's left of the ready room, Picard and Riker find the captain's family photo album. Riker looks around, disappointed that the ship is gone, having hoped to one day sit in its center seat. "Somehow," says Picard, "I doubt this will be the last ship to carry the name Enterprise."

The final moment with Data crying, was significant to Brannon Braga because it signified the fact that the Data storyline had become more prominent and meaningful than either he or Ron Moore had anticipated.

"I think a lot of people relate to Data's arc in a very basic way," he says, "though it supplies more than anything the comic relief in the movie. It's also a very poignant storyline, a very touching one, and having seen it on film, it turned out even better than we could have hoped. I think the Data story will perhaps be more popular than the rest of the movie, which wasn't exactly what we expected."

Brent Spiner saw the character's

arc in Generations as merely the beginning of a new path for Data to follow. "If I had my way about it," he muses, "which I hardly ever have, to me it seems that the character went from being child-like and naive in the series to being a different kind of child in this one because of the newness of the emotions and the inability to control them and know exactly how to handle them. He was a child with emotion and I think the obvious place to take the character is into gradual maturity, an emotional maturity, and that can only mean romance, can't it? What I would hope would happen would be a deepening of emotion — the subtleties of emotion — and how to deal with them."

In terms of Picard's rather laid back response to the ruined Enterprise, David Carson felt that it was an appropriate one.

"Picard, you have to remember, has died once [on the series], gone to heaven and come back," points out Carson. "He's now the Picard that you've known. To see Picard moved as he is by the deaths of his brother and nephew is a totally new thing for everybody. We won't have seen Patrick act like that before. I think he should be restored to understanding at the end of the movie, and I don't think we should wander around the ship with Patrick as he says, 'Oh my God, what happened?' He is more philosophical about it. His thing at that point is to deal with mortality, not only on his own level but from the point of view of the ship as well. That's why the last line is so important. He goes on, continues, and evolves."

Considering the entire film, Brannon Braga attempts to sum up his and Ron Moore's dramatic intention.

"We wanted to explore mortality," says Braga. "We didn't want to be religious the way Star Trek V was. It didn't really hit us until late in the process that it might be similar. In that film, Kirk met God. One could construe that Soran is searching for paradise/God. I really don't like to think of it that way, because that's not the kind of science fiction we do. The Nexus is a space-time phenomenon that has, certainly, very mysterious properties to it, but we wanted to keep it grounded in believability.

"What this film is absolutely

William Shatner says farewell to his most famous role, Captain James T. Kirk in Star Trek: Generations (photo copyright ©1995 Albert Ortega).

about is time," he continues. "It's about Picard, a man obsessed with what the future holds and his impending death and the death of his family line; a man obsessed with the past, Kirk. What he did or didn't accomplish in his life and was it right? And a Nexus in space-time that gives both men the ability to cheat death and live in any time that they want forever. Ultimately they realize that it's not real. Why would you *want* to cheat death? It's a part of life. Cheating death in a sense is like cheating life. It's not real. Picard has a line in the movie where he says, 'What we leave behind is not as important as how we lived.' So it's really about how these different characters come to terms with their particular personal dilemmas."

Trek Rumors

Throughout its production, Star Trek: Generations was plagued by a variety of rumors which gradually had the effect of creating a negative buzz of intergalactic proportions.

"We lived with rumors for years with the television show because Star Trek is so popular and it means so much to so many people," says Rick Berman. "They are so passionate about it, yet you get gossip and you get rumors. But it wasn't until we made a movie that the rumors were getting printed in national magazines. There were stories printed about the test screenings that we had that were totally false — just made up by somebody. Not even somebody misinterpreting something." The majority of those rumors had to do with the film supposedly being a disaster, which Berman finds difficult to fathom. "I was just envisioning sixteen-year-old disgruntled kids who for some reason didn't get an autograph or something like that," he muses, "sitting down on the Internet at 3:00 in the morning and typing out some kind of a story. And the next day it is in a national newspaper."

While the tabloids focused on a supposed feud between Patrick Stewart and William Shatner (categorically denied by both actors), the greatest amount of attention was probably aimed at the reshooting of the film's climax. A variety of publications, most notably *Entertainment Weekly*, indicated that a screening of the film on September 13, 1994 went disastrously; that the audience hated it. Executive producer Rick Berman countered this by stating to *EW*, "It's a tiny little piece of the film that we're going to fix."

Berman was obviously downplaying the mega-hype of the mainstream press. His "tiny little piece of the film" was actually the entire ending sequence when Picard and Kirk use the Nexus to go back in time to stop Soran. To achieve this, and to enhance some of the film's special effects, Paramount okayed an additional $4 million to the budget.

The reason for all this is simple: the audience apparently enjoyed the movie but felt that it was anti-climactic, given all that had come before.

"The press doesn't know what they're talking about," proclaims Malcolm McDowell. "The screening went extremely well, but, in fact, even when we were shooting the end of the film we always felt it was rather anticlimactic, which is what the audience intimated. They were rather silent and quiet. People *should* have wanted to cheer when I got killed and they didn't. Remember in *Blue Thunder* when I got killed? Everyone cheered. Kirk's death happened too quickly."

Rick Berman disagrees, noting,

"I don't think that we knew it was anticlimactic. We knew that we had less time to shoot the ending than we wanted. This was at the very end of the shoot and we were running out of time — that's what the movie's about, right? And we didn't have the time to do it properly. When we came back and screened the film for a test audience, we had a wonderful reception to the movie, but the test audience — and more importantly, all of us — saw the six-and-a-half minutes involving Picard, Kirk and Soran, and felt that it was not as exciting as it could be and we were blessed in that Paramount said to us, 'If you want to go back an redo it, go back and redo it.' So, there was a part of us that kept moaning about the fact that we would have to go back to that dreadful mountain in Nevada, but we did. We went back and reshot that six-and-a-half minutes and made it better."

David Carson explains that the interesting thing about the film's two endings was that the same basic ideas used in the first version are in the second version as well.

"In other words," he says, "that Captain Kirk gives his life for 230 million people; that he dies trying to save the universe and dies with Captain Picard. He uses his strength and his ability to leap into battle with a smile on his lips and all that sort of thing to physically attack and deal with Soran who, as we have seen already in the film, Picard can't deal with — he's head-butted down a ravine. So when [Picard] comes back, he needs Kirk's physical skills and his ability to deal with things physically while Picard goes and deals with the launcher, and that is basically the first ending.

"When we put it together," Carson points out, "we discovered that the huge climax of the Enterprise crashing has people thrown around inside the ship. We developed that into an enormous climax and we developed the Klingon battle into this huge, noisy battle and we found also that we had to go with the moodiness at the end of the scene. We have this extraordinary scene where Picard discovers that his family is burned to death and he cries. We had moving scenes of highs and lows coming up, so the simplicity of this ending was also governed by the fifty-day schedule that

we had to deal with. So we had to make some simplicity work on our side, but to make a long story short, when we got to the end and discovered that we had these huge calamities in our ending, which were satisfactory and good and true and simple, it wasn't satisfying enough. It didn't go that whole way to satisfy.

"So, we went as the filmmakers to Sherry Lansing and said, 'We are very anxious about the ending. We would like to do some more.' We know from *Casablanca* that endings have been reshot, so it is nothing new. I thought that perhaps with a bit of luck they would let me have the actors and bits of metal and we could get on a building on top of Paramount somewhere and do it, and I would get a day to shoot it if I was lucky. I thought I could change it enough to make it more powerful and stronger, but when Sherry saw the film, she said, 'This is a wonderful film. Let's go for the ending. Let's go and expand it and get the guys together more.' So, what we did was instead of having Kirk nose-to-nose constantly with Soran, which is how the first one was, we put him in a different sort of physical danger, which was the bridge and the danger created by Soran. We just expanded the ending, but we didn't throw one ending away and rewrite it."

William Shatner explains that when he was told that a reshoot would be necessary, his reaction mirrored Stewart's and McDowell's: "Was it my performance?"

"Somehow," Shatner shrugs, "everybody lost sight of the fact that I was being shot in the back and the whole ending kind of slipped away. They wanted more and they were going to change the shot in the back, but the dialogue remained the same. So, yes, I had to go back and die again, but by that time I had worked out the performance, so I didn't need to look at it with the clarity of what's it like to die and what am I going to be like when I die and how frightened I am of dying and what would Captain Kirk do when he crosses the threshold? I had already done that, so the second time I knew the performance."

David Carson didn't find the shooting of Kirk's death scene — either one of them — to be particularly difficult.

"The challenging thing about it is not that he dies, but *how* he dies, and the expectations of everybody who has been with him in his various mythical exploits over the last thirty years. The hero dies and he has to die correctly. That was the most challenging thing to work out. I think, for example, part of the mythology has been when Kirk dies, he dies alone. Now, because our story is about the handing of the torch, obviously when he dies he passes the torch in many ways. His mortality, which is what the film is about, comes into the new generation, the next generation. So, he had to die with Picard and one of the differences we made between the ending that we created to start with and then the change that was made, was that I tried to create this barrier around Kirk so that Picard could not get at him and he couldn't touch him. He was under all this incredible amount of metal which was tangled. So, I started in a way where you see Picard coming down and you see him see this thing in a distance, and then you see him for a long time looking through the metal and see what the damage is and he doesn't see Kirk. And we reveal Kirk right at the end when Picard comes to look at him and you see the distance between them; the two men are incredibly well separated. So, we tried to be truthful to those things and yet looked at our own needs. I think the performance that Bill gave, and that we worked on for that week, was a very delicate and moving one."

"The new ending," Herman Zimmerman adds to the scenario, "has much more interaction between Kirk and Picard. You see that they like each other, they're friends, and when Kirk does make a heroic gesture that ends in his death, it's that much more poignant that these two friends, having barely gotten to know and respect each other, have parted so soon."

Patrick Stewart was also pleased that the ending was being reshot in order to enhance the film. "At the moment when Bill says, 'It sounds like fun' and we gallop out of the Nexus and arrive at the planet, basically I said, 'Okay, Captain, you go this way and I'll go that way,' and we split up. Whereas that's not what everyone wanted to see. The fans wanted to see the two captains shoulder-to-shoulder. That was the whole purpose

of bringing them together and that's not how it was. So the reshoot was a very sensible action. I think it could have been even more of that buddy quality in the last part of the movie."

Paramount, which would have cut their losses by simply dropping the film into release if they thought that its chances were slim (i.e. *Star Trek V: The Final Frontier*), decided to invest more for a greater return. It's exactly the same scenario that surrounded the studio's *Fatal Attraction*, the revised ending of which is often credited for the film's worldwide box office success.

Being given the opportunity to do the reshoot was rather surprising to the filmmakers, but indicative of the studio's shifting attitude throughout production.

"Even though I complain about the size of the budget and the length of the shooting schedule, we have managed to go to town in a grand way in much of it," David Carson says. "The studio sort of started out saying, 'Well, it's *only Star Trek*,' and we didn't subscribe to that. We thought we would push the envelope and try to get as much as we could. When they [Paramount] started to see what we were doing, they started saying, 'Wow, we have a great action movie coming out. Not only a great action movie, but it's got emotion, humor and it's going to be a great movie. Get ready, everybody,' and they started turning attention our way." Which ultimately led to the financing of the reshoot.

Generations: The Aftermath

Star Trek: Generations opened in America on November 18th, 1994 to generally mixed reviews.

On the negative side, *USA Today* awarded the film two-and-a-half stars out of four. Wrote reviewer Susan Wloszczyna, "Bottom line: The highly awaited time-travel teaming of Picard and Kirk....isn't quite the clash of the follicle-impaired titans that it's meant to be....[There's] too much technochat about plasma cores. Not enough plot core. "The New York *Daily News* stated, "'Generations' is full of wizardly special effects — including a stunning but ultra-long crash sequence that gets repeated for good measure — but quickly becomes

uninvolving. The screenplay could use one of those emotion chips from Data's skull." Michael Medved of *Sneak Previews* savaged the film more than most, noting, "This bloated bomb turns 'Star Trek' into 'Star Drek.' It's the seventh motion picture in this profitable series and by far the worst — even less satisfying than 'Star Trek V: The Final Frontier,' the previous runt of the litter....Unfortunately, the lavish sets and dazzling explosions only provide distractions in the midst of the plodding plot, which culminates in an old-fashioned fist-fight involving three superannuated actors (Shatner, Stewart, and McDowell) whose stodgily choreographed fisticuffs resemble the bare-knuckle brawls in Grade B westerns of sixty years ago."

On a positive note, *Newsweek* reviewed, "This time out the Powers That Beam have found solid footing with *Star Trek: Generations*....The film serves up lots of familiar faces and shtick, big-bang special effects, new hardware and character development and an ageless theme. For Trek devotees, it's a supernova of unpredictable sci-fi thrills." *Time*, which made the film its November 28th cover story, enthused, "The new film [is] a smashingly entertaining mix of outer-space adventure and spaced-out metaphysics." *Newsday*, which gave the film three out of four stars, stated, "As bombastic and self-involved as any 'Star Trek' movie, this may be the best by virtue of balance: thoughtful storyline, grandiose special effects and Patrick Stewart. Add a star if you've already been beamed aboard."

As far as the appeal of *Star Trek: Generations* for the moviegoing audience, the film's production designer, Herman Zimmerman notes, "This script is an examination of all our lives. It's an examination of our situation as human beings. That's why I think Gene Roddenberry would like this movie. It's an examination of us facing our mortality. No other animal except the human species understands that he's a finite creature and is going to die some day."

The same, apparently, can't be said of this franchise, which keeps trekking along, growing stronger as it does so. As they said fifteen years ago, and as they are undoubtedly saying now as the Enterprise-D continues to boldly go, the human adventure is just beginning.

Entertainment WEEKLY

'TREK' WARS

CAN 'DEEP SPACE NINE' REPEL 'BABYLON 5' AND TV'S SLEW OF NEW SCI-FI CHALLENGERS?

$2.50 (CAN. $2.95)

02

10210

0 724464 3

Major Kira, Comdr. Benjamin Sisko, and Quark of 'Star Trek: Deep Space Nine'

Entertainment Weekly *covers the sci-fi wars on TV, including* Star Trek: Deep Space Nine *(photo copyright Time Warner).*

• • • •

••••

CHAPTER THIRTY ONE
SECRETS OF DEEP SPACE NINE

"I think one of the things they're striving for is to look at the people in the 24th century who are not as much at peace with themselves as the crew of the Enterprise was in *Star Trek: The Next Generation*," explains director David Carson, who helmed the two-hour premiere episode of the second *Trek* spin-off, *Deep Space Nine*. "In *The Next Generation*, it's always been a big thing when a character goes through an emotional or personal crisis. The stories usually end at peace with hope, not only hope in society but hope in the behavior of people, who most of the time behave in an exemplary manner.

"I have a feeling that the darker, grittier tone is one of the reasons they wanted me to direct the pilot," continues Carson, who has helmed such *Next Gen* episodes as "The Enemy," "Yesterday's Enterprise," and "Redemption" and the first *TNG* feature film, *Generations*. "They wanted my experience with grit in *Star Trek*. It is true that this is a much grittier environment than the Enterprise, which is part of the attraction. And it's my feeling that that part of the grittiness of *Deep Space Nine* is not only the setting, but the attempt to access the slightly weaker side of human nature, while still telling extremely powerful and insightful stories. Perhaps the most striking thing about *Deep Space Nine* is the immense strength of the two-hour movie's storyline, which had a universality that was quite striking."

Star Trek: Deep Space Nine, created by *Next Gen*'s executive producers Rick Berman and Michael Piller, debuted in January 1993 with a two-hour premiere and was followed by eighteen one-hour episodes in its first season. The big question in the beginning, of course, was would it fly or would it prove to live up to any of the disparaging monikers with which it had been labeled, such as

"Deep Space Nine From Outer Space", "Deep Space:1999" or what Jonathan Frakes jokingly referred to as "Deep Throat Nine"?

Boasting that their new series carried the same substantial budget as *Star Trek: The Next Generation* and state-of-the-art special effects, Berman and Piller have attempted to give *Deep Space Nine* its own distinct identity, in much the same way *Next Generation* consciously steered clear of comparisons with *Trek Classic*. It remains to be seen if *Star Trek* will work as well as a brand name as it has a phenomenon, though after three years on the air, it appears the results are mixed. While *Deep Space Nine* has clearly earned the devotion of many of its most ardent fans, many rabid *TNG* followers are still reluctant to embrace the new show.

"I believe that because *Deep Space Nine* is a show that is grounded in a space station, there are fundamental elements to the show that are going to be less attractive than a show like *The Next Generation* or *Voyager*, that takes place on a starship," says Rick Berman. "*Star Trek* has always been a show about people going forth and exploring the stars, so the minute you're locked down on a space station and a single spot, it isn't the same thing."

As a result, Berman notes that the perception that *DS9* has strayed from a strict definition of what *Star Trek* is about may be accurate. "I think it's some great television but I believe to a lot of people it's not exactly what *Star Trek* is. It wasn't like we said, 'Hey, I've got an idea, Michael. Let's not create a show that has to do with being on a spaceship.' *Next Generation* was already out there on the Enterprise and these two shows were supposed to run concurrently, so there was no question that we needed to come up with something different — which we did. This show is definitely a little darker and there's a lot more conflict."

For co-executive producer Ira Steven Behr, such questions are much ado about nothing. To him, what's important is the work and the quality of the episodes being broadcast. "We just do the best job putting it out there that we can and then whatever happens after that is almost beside the point. Will it be

Rick Berman and Michael Piller, creators of Deep Space Nine (photo copyright ©1995 Albert Ortega).

embraced with the love that *The Next Generation* has been embraced with? I don't know. We're obviously a grittier show and we don't quite have the rosey outlook [of *TNG*], although I think we're a very positive show in our own way."

Michael Piller draws an interesting analogy between *Deep Space Nine* and its predecessor in the syndicated TV universe by comparing them to two popular comic book superheroes. "*Next Generation* is like Superman and *Deep Space Nine* is like Batman. Clearly, the complications and the psychological underpinnings and the quality of the storytelling and the angst is greater in Batman, but they both exist in the same DC comic universe and they occasionally meet. The point is, if you think of all the pale imitations of Superman, they have all gone right out the window but Batman has endured because it touches people in a certain, specific way. It is a more adult comic book and somehow we have managed to do that with *Deep Space Nine*. Batman was never as popular as Superman was, but it has its own special audience. I think we've got that on *Deep Space Nine* — at least I hope so."

The genesis for a new *Star Trek* series can be traced to a lunchtime con-

••••

The cast of **Deep Space Nine** *with their creators, Michael Piller and Rick Berman (photo copyright ©1995 Albert Ortega).*

versation between Piller and Berman several years ago.

"Michael and I started talking about the possibility of doing another series, a spin-off, a sequel, another show set within the *Star Trek* universe, and we spent a number of lunches tossing it around," recalls Berman. "We had a number of ideas which were both *Star Trek* in nature and those that were non-*Star Trek* in nature. Michael and I discussed it with Gene when we were still in the early stages, but never anything conceptual. Then I got a call from Brandon Tartikoff, who was the new chairman of Paramount Pictures [subsequently replaced by Sherry Lansing]. He asked me to come in and talk to him. He wanted us to do another series. Not necessarily another *Star Trek* series, but another dramatic series. A series that could be brought to you 'from the people who give you *Star Trek: The Next Generation*.' I told him the best way to do that was to couch it in the structure of another series set within the umbrella of *Star Trek*."

One person not involved with the show was the late Gene Roddenberry, who was already very ill by the time Berman and Piller had completed their brainstorming about the series.

"We never got a chance to discuss it with Gene," says Berman. "By the time we had it to the point that it was discussable, he was in pretty bad shape and not really in the kind of condition that it would have been wise to discuss it with him. On two specific occasions I was with him at his house and we tried to bring it up, but it wasn't really appropriate."

Roddenberry had said on several occasions that only he could successfully create and cast a *Star Trek* series, which was the argument he used to defeat Harve Bennett's *Starfleet Academy* film prequel idea. Berman rejects the notion that he and Piller are attempting to co-opt the mythos.

"I'm not concerned about it," he says. "Before Gene died we worked together for close to five years and within the first of those five years I had his total confidence. I learned his language and his religion and his outlook. It's not necessarily my religion, my language, and my outlook, but I learned it and I have been obsessively true to it through the second season, the third, the fourth, the fifth, and so on. Gene's involvement in *The Next Generation* had been minimal since the first year of the show and this series—and any other *Star Trek* venture that I am involved with—will be absolutely true to that vision for the simple reason, that's what this show is.

"This show has been very successful because it's a show that rests on Gene's idea of the future," adds Berman. "That will not change and I'm totally confident I can maintain Gene's ideals for the television series in terms of philosophy, in terms of attitude, in terms of his feelings regarding fiction versus science fiction, fact versus fantasy, believability. Things that were very important to Gene have been important to me for enough years that it's very easy for me to continue what I have been doing."

Piller believes that *Deep Space Nine* continues to carry forth the same *Star Trek* philosophy that *Next Generation* rigidly adhered to over its seven-year run.

"The philosophy of Gene Roddenberry guides us. He didn't have any exposure to the specifics of this series, but he's with us in anything having to do with *Star Trek*," says Piller. "We have learned from him and from experience that stories that combine science fiction with a philosophy with optimism with a comment on social issues and an exploration of human values, are the stories that work for *Star Trek*. Those are the stories that work for us."

Like the creation of *The Next Generation*, determining what the next *Star Trek* series would be was an important consideration during the conceptual stages.

"We realized that if we were going to do another Star Trek series that was going to overlap *Next Generation* by a couple of years, it would be foolish to bring another Enterprise or the like into it," says Berman. "We had an opportunity to have five years of experience on *The Next Generation*. (For me five, Michael three) And when you do a television show for that period of time there's all sorts of things you wish for that you don't have. An analogy that I've used is if you build a house and it's one of your first houses and you start living in it, you find yourselves saying: We should have moved the kitchen door over here. It would have been more practical if we had made the steps one step higher. We could have gotten that in there if we had put the family room off the kitchen instead of off the living room.' We were in that wonderful position of being able to build that second house and taking advantage of all the wish-we-could-ofs."

The series premiere was written by Michael Piller and was based on a story by Berman and Piller. During the years that Piller was on *TNG*, Berman and he cultivated a growing friendship and mutual respect.

"Michael and I are pretty much on the same wavelength," says Berman.

"We have our own little fights and squabbles like any people trying to create something, but philosophically and creatively we're remarkably in sync. There's never been any argument in terms of the direction the series will go or the direction any of the characters will go. It's something we've been in sync about since we started talking about it."

Says Michael Piller, "This was something that I was looking forward to for a long time and something Rick and I have been talking about for years. We asked the studio to allow us to develop something a couple of years ago and we had Gene's blessing and the studio said, 'No, we're never going to do a *Star Trek* spin-off,' and Brandon Tartikoff came and a month later there was a call saying we're going to do a *Star Trek* spin-off."

Piller agrees that finding new avenues for conflict was an important priority in fashioning the new series.

"We learned that the most difficult part of writing *Star Trek: The Next Generation* is when you're dealing with the kind of characters we have who love each other, who are good people, and all top-of-the-line Starfleet officers. It's hard to have conflict between those people," says Piller. "We have to find ways of getting new conflicts, which has been a wonderful challenge. I think as a writer I've grown because I haven't been able to rely on traditional tricks that writers would like to be able to use to find conflict between characters. In the development of this new series we felt we had the opportunity to create an environment that by its very nature brought people into conflict again.

"Instead of the state-of-the-art Enterprise, which is the most comfortable spaceship in the imagination, you have a bunch of Starfleet officers onboard an alien space station that doesn't work all that well, that isn't built up to Federation or Starfleet specs, and is the most uncomfortable environment. We put them next to the planet Bajor, which is where Ensign Ro originated from, which we have created as an extraordinary, spiritual, mystic planet which could not be more different than the humanist 24th century man that we have evolved into in *Star Trek*. These are friends and they think that things

that occur in the universe are divine intervention. We're dealing with logic and this is another source of conflict. We are not on a Starfleet facility, we're sort of the Federation administration on this Bajoran space station which is called Deep Space Nine. And on this station you have aliens of all shapes and sizes who are coming through for various reasons, all with their own agendas, and we have to deal with that."

Director David Carson never saw this potentially static setting to be a problem. "I think the space station has been designed in such a way that is completely different from the ship, so it does have a different feeling to it. It's sort of like a town, I suppose, in a funny kind of way. A town in terms of its social set-up. I suppose a good analogy would be on the Enterprise we very rarely leave the officers or people who are driving the ship and that side of things, but there are hundreds of other people on board the Enterprise doing whatever it is they do. I think one of the things *Deep Space Nine* does is expand its frame of reference from not just the officers that deal with the space station, but [to] the other people who we rarely see. That's what I mean by a town-like setting."

Adds director Winrich Kolbe, "*Deep Space Nine* is Gunsmoke. It's the town that everybody comes to. Get the characters in there. That's actually the selling point and because of its setting, it will become more of a character show. We get the people in there who represent the different opinions. We don't have to schlep through some deserted canyon in order to get there, they have to come to us."

The New Cast And Characters

Star Trek: Deep Space Nine introduces a new ensemble of characters and actors who, like those of previous *Treks*, is anchored by a leader along the lines of Captains James T. Kirk and Jean Luc Picard. In this case his name is Commander Benjamin Sisko, and he brings with him quite a package of emotional quandaries to be conquered.

"Our commander is somebody who's lived a life of tragedy," explains Michael Piller, "in essence because when

Picard was with the Borg and led the Borg on their attack, he was a commander on one of the ships destroyed. Sisko lost his wife and now he's raising his son by himself and he hasn't really been able to go on with his life since he lost her. One of the arcs of the first story is some conflicts with Picard and how he gets by some of those things."

Adds David Carson, "I think when you have somebody like that, who leads the story, he has to come to terms with what has happened to him, otherwise he spends his entire time in a bitter rage, which he doesn't. This is a buried part of his psyche, but it's nevertheless there."

Nonetheless, believes director Winrich Kolbe, this aspect of Sisko's character paves the way for something emotionally explosive down the line.

"Anybody who saw the pilot has to be aware of the fact that we had an unwilling leader of the group in Sisko," he points out. "Now *that* is intriguing. If he was unwilling once, even though at the end he said he's going to fulfill his obligations, there is a time bomb in that character. He's not the character anymore who says, 'I'm loyalty above all and I'm going down with the ship.' There is a possibility that he might do something totally different, totally unexpected."

The role is played by Avery Brooks, a black actor perhaps best known as Hawk in the television series *Spenser: For Hire* and *A Man Called Hawk*. The casting of Brooks as Sisko was heralded in *Newsweek* as a "revolutionary" move.

"We decided that the role could be played either by a white man or a black man, or as in the case of Picard by an American or Englishman, or Belgian or German," Carson, who was deeply involved in the casting of the series, details. "In fact, we did interview a Belgian actor and a German actor who came over from England. What race or creed he was *was* very important, but it was never a question of whether or not there were opportunities for everyone, every type of person to play the role. In the end, even though you would expect us to say this, I think all of us can quite truthfully say that we were able to come down to what we considered to be the

• • • •

Avery Brooks as Commander Benjamin Sisko (photo copyright ©1995 Albert Ortega).

best actor for the job. I think that Avery Brooks is a phenomenal actor. I've rarely come across an actor with a combination of his incredible depth of ability to portray emotions and feelings, but also his extraordinary technical skill in front of the camera and an amazing strength of performing with the lens. He's a real joy to work with. And the way he senses out a character.....He has developed his character beyond 'Emissary' into a very subtle blend of types of feeling with which he handles himself in different situations. He's extraordinarily deft and constantly interesting, and I think the character gives him much more ability to have these differences in his psychological make-up than Picard, who's a much more straightforward character you can probably predict will react in a certain way in different situations. It's very difficult to do with Sisko, and Avery plays with delight those opportunities."

For Brooks, finding himself confined within three soundstages on the Paramount lot is a far cry from the location shooting in Boston and Washington, D.C. he had done on *Spenser* and *Hawk*, respectively. "Of course when you're moving around and on location you work fourteen to sixteen hours a day,"

says Brooks. "It's a different kind of rhythm. Working inside requires that you not lose your energy and your focus and your concentration, because it's easy after twelve or thirteen hours to realize you've been working that long and your body says, 'I want to go home.' This pilot was particularly difficult. Of course, now I can't blame my performance on the weather."

When Stewart and Shatner were cast, both, despite an impressive array of supporting credits, were not as well known as Avery Brooks. Brooks had created a very recognizable visual icon during his three years playing Hawk, slowly but malevolently enunciating, "S-p-e-n-c-e-r" to Robert Urich week after week. Executive Producer Rick Berman didn't feel his lack of anonymity was a liability in casting him as Sisko.

"He played the second role on a show and it did not last a long time," says Berman. "There are actors I tend to stay away from because I feel they have overly familiar faces. But to me a good actor is somebody you don't think about how familiar they are. If they're right, they're right."

Brooks was chosen just days before the beginning of principal photography on the pilot. Interestingly, Brooks played his best known role bald and the question remained, in light of Patrick Stewart's well-noted baldness, would Brooks continue the tradition?

"We think he looks best with hair," says producer David Livingston. "In fact, we looked at several variations of hair and we felt the one we chose was the most appealing and the way he looked best. It was simply a cosmetic decision and had no bearing on Patrick Stewart."

"It happened very quickly for me," recalls Brooks on his casting. "I was in the Caribbean and I talked to my agent and he asked me if I was a fan of *Star Trek*. I said, 'Well, I watch it, of course.' He said, 'I have a script you might want to read.' I read it and I was thrilled. The writing was extraordinary, the story very compelling. And so I pursued it. And then, I was on my way to lay down something on tape in New York and my car started to slip out of gear. I called my wife and said, 'I don't

think I can make it.' I called the people frantically and said, 'I don't think I can make it in.' They said, 'We need you to come to California now,' so I flew out from Atlanta and it happened very, very fast and I'm thrilled."

Like Stewart, Brooks commands an instant respect on the set from his fellow actors and will no doubt prove to be not only a role model for people of all races, but write a new chapter for the advancement and depiction of blacks on television. "I think you can see that quality when you meet him," states Michael Piller. "When we walked into the room, we knew we had found our Sisko. We had been looking for a quality that continued the heroic leadership potential, but we knew that very big boots had to be filled. We had two great stars in the leadership role of captains and commanders in the past, and it was very difficult to find someone who really impressed everybody in the room with the same presence of command that Avery had."

Adds Rick Berman, "I think the key word is presence. We needed someone who could match, or hopefully exceed, the sense of presence that Patrick Stewart exudes on a pretty regular basis as Captain Picard. We didn't want to go backwards, we wanted to go forwards. We were looking for a good actor, but more than anything we were looking for someone with that sense of commanding presence, which this guy seems to give us."

For Brooks, *Deep Space*'s allegorical approach to addressing contemporary issues is a refreshing change from the mundane fare offered on network television. This is reflected in the fact that he portrays a single parent, which he feels illustrates the show's topicality in addressing nineties concerns within the framework of future society.

"We're dealing with a single parent and single parenting," says Brooks. "In the last twenty years there's a very different notion in our society and, indeed, our world about what that means, so of course in an allegorical way this show is very nineties. We're on the verge of the 21st century and then it will be very teens. Teens in the 21st century."

Although new to *Star Trek*, Brooks admits to an instant affinity for the material. Says Brooks, "Of course, I was familiar with it because I grew up watching television, but I am definitely a fan now. Science fiction appeals to the child in all adults and when you tease the mind as well, the people are going to come in flocks."

However, some have complained the character of Sisko has been a bit of a cypher to the audience. In addition, there has been some nagging criticism of Avery Brooks' performance from some viewers as well. Piller, writer/producer Ira Behr, and the writing staff dismiss those contentions, but at the same time admit to the need to continue to define Sisko's role in the future.

"I think that Avery is an amazingly interesting and talented actor," says Behr. "We went to see him in his one-man show and it blew us away. He was charismatic, funny, talented, he sang, he danced, he told jokes, he made you cry. He did everything. We were dumbfounded at just how powerful he was as a presence and some of that's not coming through in the show. I think some of it is us and some of it is that the pilot seemed to cover the character so well that after the pilot was over we didn't know what else to do with him. We've been talking about it a lot and we're going to be working on that a lot. You're going to learn more about Sisko than just the fact he loves baseball."

Morgan Gendel, a frequent *TNG* contributor and the writer of *DS9*'s "The Passenger" and "Armageddon Game," comments, "I think Sisko is a good character. To me, he's like Mary Tyler Moore, who's the center and you have all these other characters squirelling around her, but you couldn't do the show without her."

Offers Michael Piller, "We believe it's time that Sisko no longer lives in the past, but in the present and that we see what his agenda is; what he, as a hero, wants to accomplish here in this sector and in the Gamma Quadrant."

Shifting Allegiances

A key factor in the success of the original *Star Trek* bridge crew was the inclusion of Mr. Spock, an alien who could provide a unique perspective on

humanity. That same function was fulfilled on *Next Generation* by Data and, now, on *Deep Space Nine* by station security chief Odo.

Explains Michael Piller, "He was the security chief assigned to the space station when the Cardassians were there. We inherit him because he's very savvy about the goings-on of this Promenade. But he's a guy who has his own way of doing things and he'll take the law into his own hands to make things the way he wants to. He also happens to be a shape-shifter and he has a very interesting backstory."

Director Winrich Kolbe finds the character of Odo an intriguing one. "I did a show where Odo is trying to discover where he came from, but he unfortunately winds up with somebody he doesn't believe," says Kolbe. "He doesn't believe anybody to begin with, but this guy he *really* doesn't believe. When this guy suddenly begins to tune in on Odo's shape-shifting capability, he says, 'Maybe I know something that might be intriguing to you.' And then Odo's character says, 'Forget it, you're a liar and a thief and I can't trust you,' but then follows him anyway. It's intriguing because here is a person who's very, very distrustful, which makes the perfect sheriff. He pushes the envelope of what the police should be. The police should be trusting nobody, and Odo's philosophy of arrest first, ask questions later is an intriguing aspect of his profession, which obviously puts him into conflict with Sisko. We're talking about issues about society. We're talking about death penalty, the Napoleonic code versus the Anglo-Saxon code. Are we guilty until proven innocent or innocent until proven guilty? That is something intriguing, and Rene Auberjonois is such a fascinating actor."

Although viewers may best remember Rene Auberjonois as Clayton Endicott III on the hit ABC series *Benson*, it would be difficult to recognize him underneath the prosthetic that Michael Westmore has designed to transform the Emmy and Tony Award winning actor into Odo.

David Carson points out, "Like Avery Brooks, Rene has this extraordinary classical background. He, like Avery, is a classically trained stage actor.

Rene Auberjonois as the shape-shifting Odo (photo copyright ©1995 Albert Ortega).

Both of them have come out of this tradition of performance. So to have the luxury of someone like Rene Auberjonois playing a shape-shifter is quite extraordinary, because he isn't really first and foremost a TV actor who comes out of *Benson*. He has turned this character into somebody absolutely fascinating. And the fact that he is classically trained makes him particularly able to work with the mask-like thing that's on his face. He's an actor who's learned how to work with and through a mask because he's trained with masks and, I think, trained other people to act with masks. You get much more richness and depth out of somebody like him than somebody who doesn't have that depth of experience."

"Odo, in terms of the kind of person he is and his incredible dignity and sense of justice, is very appealing to me," says Auberjonois. "He's sort of a curmudgeon and he's a very rigid man. He's uptight but he's also got a wonderful deadpan kind of humor."

As a shape-shifter who metamorphosizes into numerous shapes and sizes every episode, the actor is the focus of many of the series' state-of-the-art visual effects. Since the work is often done in post-production, it requires a

Siddig El Fadil as Dr. Julian Bashir (photo copyright ©1995 Albert Ortega).

special discipline to imagine a world of creatures and illusions that doesn't exist until the visual effects team's fertile imagination gets to incorporate them.

"It's the nature of being an actor," Auberjonois explains. "For people who are not professional actors, the easiest thing to do is just to remember what it's like to play house. I remember as a kid there was a place in the attic where my brother and I used to go to pretend to be scientists. It's just this willing suspension of disbelief. There's something wonderful about Odo because I turn into all these different things. We shoot things where I just sort of stand there and I know that I've just turned back from being a rat and it's magical for me to see that."

Portraying Odo is not Auberjonois' first foray into the *Star Trek* universe. The actor played the nefarious Colonel West at the request of personal friend and director Nicholas Meyer, in a sub-plot that had been cut from *Star Trek VI*'s theatrical release, but restored for its subsequent video edition. In these scenes, the Colonel plots with Klingon conspirators and the Romulan ambassador Nanclus to prevent a peace treaty from being signed between the Klingons and the Federation. Ultimately, Colonel West is revealed as the man under the Klingon make-up attempting to assassinate the Federation president at the Khitomer Peace Conference.

"I wasn't in *Star Trek VI* because the character was cut out," says Auberjonois, who admits to often being cast as a villain. "I have not seen it. I did it because Nick Meyer is a personal friend and asked me to. I was in Scotland hiking with my wife and rushed back to get the make-up all done. I've played a lot of different kinds of parts and I usually play villains and I love them. I remember when my son was much younger and I was doing *Richard III* at the same time I was doing *Benson*. He asked, 'Why do you always play the bad guy?' and I said, 'It's because they're usually the best parts to play.'"

However, Auberjonois' Odo is certainly a hero of the series and he's thrilled to be probing the limits of the final frontier, both literally and figuratively. Odo was the focus of one of the series' earliest episodes, directed by Paul Lynch, "A Man Alone," which addresses prejudice and discrimination. It reflects an evolution for the character that pleases Auberjonois as does the discovery of his origin and people in "The Search," the third season premiere. "It's evolving and there are certain things that I know about him that are clear from the scripts that we've done so far and the bible," points out the actor. "The writers know a lot more about where it's going than I do. I like not knowing and opening the script each week and seeing a new facet of the character for me to consider. I like that challenge each week and it keeps it fresh for me, which is very important when you're doing a week-in and week-out schedule and watching the character develop like this. When you're doing a series, the characters always develop to a degree, but I think in this kind of situation, more than a sit-com (where the characters really are cast and you know what's going to happen), there's a certain wisdom revealed in the character. He has an incredible intelligence and there's a weakness in his character that's revealed, a rigidity he has to work through, a human quality which is very interesting."

Auberjonois hopes that Odo is as well-accepted as Spock and Data, and is pleased to have been cast in the role. "It's certainly a good gig, there's no question about that," he says. "I guess it would be less than candid for me to say that when I first approached it that it was in a very mercenary sense that I'm an actor with two kids in college and I wanted to get this job and it was a good part. My main intention was to go out as an actor and be practicing my craft and get the job. I was never a big Trekker. I've seen my share of *Star Trek* and *The Next Generation* and always admired them and thought it was something I felt would be appropriate for me to do. I have a lot of classical training and my background is in the theater, so all of those things motivated me to think it's a good job to get involved with. As I've been absorbed into this world and read all the bibles and backstories and done my homework, I have been more and more impressed by the depth of the subjects that it deals with in a general sense. On a personal level, my character, Odo, is wonderful."

Also pleasing to the actor are the interrelationships developing with the other characters on the show. "There's something specific with every other character," he notes. "My relationship with Nana Visitor who plays Major Kira Nerys is a very interesting one, because she is above me in rank and yet she comes to me for a certain kind of wisdom. I'm very interested in seeing how that develops."

In fact, in season two's "The Collaborator," Auberjonois began to take the Odo/Kira relationship in a fascinating new direction when, with just a look, he conveys that the changeling may be in love with Kira, a subplot that continues to be developed on the show.

Following in the steps of Dr. Leonard "Dammit Jim" McCoy and Dr. Beverly Crusher is no easy task, but that's exactly what Julian Bashir is attempting as chief medical officer of Deep Space Nine. Notes Michael Piller wryly, "Julian Bashir is a young, ambitious, wet behind the ears, thinks-he-knows-it-all young man who just graduated from Starfleet Medical, and came out here because this is where heroes are made and this is where the adventure is and this is the wilderness. He's got a lot to learn."

• • • •

Cast in the role of Bashir was then twenty-six-year-old Londoner, Siddig El Fadil, who has starred on stage in productions of *Brother Eichmann* and *Sinbad, the Sailor*. He probably made his greatest impression as King Feisal in the PBS prequel to *Lawrence of Arabia, A Dangerous Man*. That was the role that caught the interest of *Deep Space Nine* executive producer Rick Berman.

"The one casting credit I feel I can take and am very proud of is Siddig," says Berman. "I had seen Siddig on public television and I sought him out and had the Paramount people in London find him. He read for us in London and he's someone no one would have ever considered. He is, as time will tell, an extraordinary actor."

Enthuses director David Carson, "What a wonderful actor he is, freshly minted from British drama school. A very wonderful candor and openness of feeling about him. And for such a young actor, very experienced with the lens. Very good at turning his hand to all the tricks of the emotions the writers have asked of him so far. He's a wonderful addition to the team."

It's a testament to *Star Trek*'s ability to transcend ethnic and racial boundaries that an actor like Siddig could be cast in a role patterned in such a distinctly Michael J. Fox vein (the character was originally named Julian Ambrose). "I read in London with about thirty people," recalls Siddig. "I think they auditioned all over Europe. And then I did one for the big cheeses here. It was bizarre, one day I did the test in London and two days later they asked me to fly to Hollywood where I had never been and, on the same day, they gave me the job, which was great."

Siddig found he didn't need to do much preparation for the role. "I read through the whole medical encyclopedia," he laughs. "No, actually I didn't do a thing because I'm incredibly lazy. What's state-of-the-art medical now is completely irrelevant in the future. It's nice to know about genealogy or genetics or whatever, which I can pick up from my education, which I just finished recently, but I haven't gone into it because the words have their own life regardless of what's written in the manu-

als. I just want to sound like I know what I'm doing. When they mention a word in the scripts that I don't know, you sometimes have to look it up because the only way it will make sense is if you know what it actually means. You just stick that funny-looking thing [a hypo device] in someone's neck and pray to God that it's the right place."

Unfortunately, as the doctor onboard Deep Space Nine, El Fadil has found himself wrestling with the longtime *Trek* dilemma of technobabble, the mystical *Trek* jmbo mumbo science that passes for scientific accuracy in depicting a 24th century civilization.

"They have a sadistic love of it," laughs El Fadil. "But I actually quite enjoy it. It's the nearest thing to Shakespeare. Stretching the mind to get your tongue around it and make sense of it when you talk. I actually quite enjoy trying to see if I can make something of it without making it sound flat. That's part of the lie of trying to make it sound like I'm actually a doctor or a science officer. Data on *The Next Generation* is an unbelievable android because he does it flawlessly."

The actor quickly points out that he's not fearful of comparisons with the previous *Star Trek* doctors since his character is so dramatically different than either of the roles which have preceded him. "I've seen the other shows, but they're such different people than I am," he says. "They've gone for someone younger and he's more naive and not burdened with anything except for the novelty of everything he sees and how best to negotiate it. It completely mirrors my experience — jumping around and being overly enthusiastic comes very naturally to me."

"The most difficult role to cast is always a beautiful girl," claims Rick Berman. "Beautiful women are few and far between and to find one who can act and who doesn't want to bypass television to go into the movies is very difficult since there are very few of them. Fortunately, we finally found Terry."

Finally is the operative word for Berman, since the role of Science Officer Dax was the last one to be cast several weeks after production began on the pilot, complicating an already arduous

Terry Farrell as science officer Dax (photo copyright ©1995 Albert Ortega).

casting process. The search for Dax makes casting Vivien Leigh in *Gone With the Wind* — or Captain Janeway in *Voyager* — look like child's play.

"It's so overwhelming," says Terry Farrell. "I'm so glad it's over. It's so incredible getting *Star Trek* anyway because it's such a legend. When I first got it, it was like a rollercoaster ride that I couldn't get off of, and you don't know what's going to happen."

Rick Berman admits that part of the difficulty of casting the role was the problems they had in explaining the part to those auditioning. "It was very difficult to say you're a beautiful woman and a 400-year-old androgynous character at the same time."

Recalls Michael Piller, "We were already in production when we cast Terry and part of the reason that it's so difficult to cast is because it's a character that's a little harder to define. I could write a book about Trills now, but what does that mean in the day-to-day existence of these people? How do we make it different from Terry Farrell? How do you make it something alien and yet accessible? It's a very interesting mix of qualities that I think the studio wanted. Rick and I felt that we wanted a woman

Cirroc Lofton as Jake Sisko (photo copyright ©1995 Albert Ortega).

who was attractive and yet a superior actress. We saw a lot of very talented young women, but they just didn't get it. Some would change their voices, to make it sound like a man's voice coming out of a woman. It was hard. The casting people will tell you that the roles of people twenty-five to thirty-five, attractive and brainy are the hardest roles to cast in television. It's hard to find the next Meryl Streep. It's hard to find the next Glenn Close."

Fortunately, Terry Farrell, who had recently finished work on the Tony Hickox film *Hellraiser III*, was called in by casting director Junie Lowry-Johnson to audition. "Terry came in the last day or two of casting for this show and we had her back a couple of times," says Piller. "We had two or three others that we were very interested in, but truth is Terry was the only actress who came in to read where Rick and I looked at each other and agreed that she had hit the scenes that she was reading. We had finally gotten to the place where we had to cast somebody and Terry did not have the experience of some of the others, and we knew, and she knows that there's a great challenge of acting and performance ahead of her. So far, it's amazing

to watch her because you can see a much stronger performance. She's starting to grow more and find this role."

Farrell agrees and says the key to her audition was playing the role with an amused detachment as opposed to attempting to personify a woman with a "short, fat snake inside."

"I think she has fun with people," says Farrell. "In the scene I had to audition in, I said I used to be an old man and Avery expects to see him in that context. He had never seen me before as a woman so how else do you play that other than to have fun with somebody? It would be fun if you dressed up in make-up and the other person doesn't know you're fooling them and they're trying to believe you're who they say you are, but you don't look anything like you did last week. Just having fun with it was the key for me."

Recalls David Carson, "Most of the time with Terry was struggling to see what in fact a Trill should look like. Together with the fact that she was cast very late, we had all these problems of what should be stuck on her face. There were countless tests and some people didn't like this, some people didn't like that, until eventually she came out with spots. I don't know if you know this, but Trills have an established look which is a sort of lumpy prosthetic look on their faces. As you'll notice, she in fact doesn't have any. When we first started shooting her, she had these old prosthetic lumps on her face. But frankly they did not add to her undeniable attractiveness, so everybody decided that her face should be left alone and spots should be added which went under the collar of her costume, thereby being suggestive of where else the spots might be. Not that anybody will ever know."

Farrell didn't prepare for the role by boning up on her science. "In biology I did really well, I got straight A's, but this is different," she explains. "I'm not the doctor! You just open the writer's guide, and I call and ask them and ask Michael Piller—who's really nice if you have a question—about the technical jargon. Sometimes they write a question mark where the 'tech' should be and you wonder what's going to be the word there. Cough it up! I know

they're going to freak me out and then I end up getting something like 'The ionic L-band emission patterns don't match.' I'm supposed to know this by heart? Tech with a question mark? I'm getting more used to it now. That's what really upset me during the pilot because I didn't even know where to start. What am I talking about? I'd try to relate it to a car and it wasn't working."

As for the future, Farrell admits she does have some concerns about the inevitable stardom that comes from being a part of the *Star Trek* mythos — although typecasting isn't one of them.

"I get real worried about it and become private and inwards," says Farrell. "I don't know if I'm ready for Spago's. On my way to work at four in the morning, I worry about it. You forget when you're doing an interview like this when I'm saying it to you it doesn't feel like I'm saying it to nine million people. You don't realize the impact of it. When I did *Paper Dolls* I got a lot of attention and I had the Andy Warhol fifteen minutes of fame and I couldn't go to the mall anymore. Then I stopped for awhile and I could go back to the mall again. Now if I can't...it's okay, because I don't like the mall anyway."

Cirroc Lofton makes his television debut as Jake, the son of commander Benjamin Sisko. Having lived on four different starships and been stationed on two planets, Jake yearns to return to earth rather than be forced to live aboard Deep Space Nine.

Unlike the usually venal reaction engendered by children on most science-fiction series, the character of Jake Sisko is dissimilar to the infamous Boxey of *Battlestar: Galactica* or Wesley Crusher, who earned the derision of fans of *The Next Generation* for saving the ship. Jake is simply a young teenager who has been forced by his father's job to pick up roots and move yet again. It's a dilemma that many members of the audience can relate to and a role that Michael Piller hopes will explore the real issues facing single fathers and their offspring. "This has nothing to do with the Wil Wheaton character which was a super genius who seemed to save the ship every week," says Piller. "This is a kid who is growing up in his life with his dad. The two of them struggle as fathers and sons do everyday in our lives. This kid does not have any great technical skills, he's not going to save the ship. He's a kid. The bottom line is that this hero, this leader, our star, had to be different. He couldn't be Picard, he couldn't be Kirk. He had to be Sisko. And to me, and to Rick, we felt giving him a son as an added burden enriched his character and the opportunities to see him on a personal level that we rarely got to see Kirk and Picard on."

Equally important to the creators of the series was addressing the contemporary issue of single fatherhood. Avery Brooks' Sisko is very much a man of the nineties in the way that Picard has been representative of the eighties and Kirk, the sixties.

"Frankly, I think that anything you could do to provide a role model for kids and parents is a good thing," says Piller of Jake's relationship with his father. "Family values has become a curse word this year, but I think it's important that we, as writers and creators, continue to provide strong role models on television for parents and for television."

Of Lofton, David Carson opines, "A very, very talented young man. He had minimal drama training, according to his mother, and for a boy who's had so little training, he's really quite good. He was way and above the best actor that we saw for the role, and we saw many, many actors. I think he has a refinement of manner and a refinement of feature as well, which makes him just that little bit set apart, which I think is very good for Sisko's son. His family comes from Ethiopia and I suppose his background has had some effect on him, his bearing, and how he looks. I think he's very bright and has a big future."

Perhaps if one is looking for a deeper subtext to the show, it appears to be that only through inclusion and the creation of an extended family of characters is the re-building of Deep Space Nine achieved. Ultimately, *Trek* is about a family, an ensemble of characters that work together for the common good bringing together people of different races, ethnic persuasions and even species. If *Star Trek* is indeed preaching, if only maybe to the converted, it tells us that only by becoming a global family, an extension of Sisko's immediate family through which he has undergone catharsis, can we aspire to achieve even greater good and the utopian ethos of Roddenberry's universe that humankind strives to attain.

Colm Meaney has served aboard the Enterprise since its first encounter at Farpoint, although most fans won't remember it since he was a nameless face on the battle bridge. Since then, through sheer charisma, the actor has elevated himself from an anonymous transporter chief to the only married recurring character on *The Next Generation* and now as a co-star aboard *Deep Space Nine*.

"My favorite on *Star Trek* since the beginning has been Colm Meaney," says Rick Berman of the actor who personifies Miles O'Brien, a name which was finally revealed during the series' fourth year. "I adore Colm's work."

Sharing Berman's enthusiasm is director David Carson. "I've worked with him before on *Next Generation*, and he's tremendous. Very wonderful, warm, interesting varied actor, and I think it's an interesting choice to have him come over from *Next Generation*. He wasn't particularly prominent over there and to suddenly reveal him is a good way of linking the two series without doing it heavy-handedly. I think that's a really good choice."

"I was in New York for a year with *Breaking the Code* and that was the year of the writer's strike, so *Star Trek* didn't get going again until September or October," recalls Meaney of his return to *Next Generation* after having shot the pilot. "When I came back, they brought me on as Chief O'Brien. For the first five or six shows that I did, he just kept cropping up and I was Transporter Chief. Then, a script arrived and suddenly he had a name."

Meaney has kept busy on the silver screen as well as the small screen, starring for Alan Parker in *The Commitments*; in *The Snapper* as a reverent fan of Elvis; and in Ron Howard's *Far*

Colm Meaney as Chief O'Brien (photo copyright ©1995 Albert Ortega).

and Away. During his treks away from the decks of the Enterprise, the actor has also appeared as the ill-fated captain of a 747 in *Die Hard II: Die Harder*, a cop in *Dick Tracy*, Dennis Quaid's brother in Alan Parker's *Come See the Paradise* and, most recently, as the malevolent terrorist who menaces Steven Seagal in *Under Siege*. Given his busy film schedule it was surprising that Meaney agreed to join the cast of *Deep Space Nine* when he was approached by producers Rick Berman and Michael Piller.

"We knew we wanted to do something with O'Brien, who we brought over to the show," says writer/producer Ira Behr. "Colm is a really fine actor and he's had limited chances on *The Next Generation*. Now he's a lead and we're trying to find different and new things to do with him. One of those things is to team him up with Bashir in a certain way. Bashir sees O'Brien as kind of the old pro from Dover, the guy who's done it all. The way I see O'Brien is as the working man's hero and so does Bashir. Bashir wants to be like him and wants to know him and emulate him. O'Brien looks at this young kid from the Academy with that English, upper class accent and it's like, 'Go away kid, you bother me.' It

• • • •

Armin Shimerman as Ferengi barkeep, Quark (photo copyright ©1995 Albert Ortega).

could be fun because you don't usually see that. We shot a scene where Bashir is talking, talking, talking and he turns to O'Brien and says something to him and O'Brien just gives Bashir a look, with not one line of dialogue, that's like 'Get the hell away from me kid.' It's funny, it's good, and it's character."

Meaney agrees that O'Brien has sort of become the everyman of *Star Trek*. "O'Brien is somebody who is more human," says Meaney. "He obviously likes his job, but he also has other aspects to his personality. He doesn't have the element of being a fearless superhuman. There are situations they get into which, because of their Starfleet training, they react to as if it's normal, with steely nerves and all that, but I think O'Brien doesn't like that stuff too much."

Armin Shimerman is no stranger to Ferengi. Having pioneered the weasley role of a Ferengi in the first season *Next Generation* episode introducing the race, "The Last Outpost," Shimerman was a natural choice for the role of Quark, the barkeep of Deep Space Nine.

A veteran of such series as *Brooklyn Bridge*, *Beauty and the Beast*, and *Alien Nation*, Shimerman has also

appeared in the films *Blind Date, Like Father, Like Son* and *Death Warrant*. The actor is quick to contrast his character of Quark with previous Ferengi incarnations, which many fans dismissed as an inept attempt by *Trek* to find a new adversary for the Federation during its early evolution. "The Ferengi have always seemed to be very broad and on the verge of slapstick," says Shimerman. "I don't know what was in their heads about the comic values of myself, but what I think they found in the early episodes is the great comic potential between Odo and Quark. There's this sort of Mutt and Jeff relationship that both Rene and I are savoring a great deal. I think that's where a lot of the humor is going to come from. Quark is still libidinous, Quark is still avaricious, he's still ambitious and he's still short...but I think the humor will come from all those things and his relationships with the humans and the shape-shifter."

Ira Behr shares Shimerman's enthusiasm for the developing relationship between Quark and Odo. "I think Michael and Rick both realized that this is a learning process of finding out together who these people are. Then, of course, you cast the goddamn thing and the actors make it who they are and you sit back and say, 'Okay, maybe that's not what I had in mind exactly,' but it works and so all the best-laid plans of all these things go out the window the second the cameras roll. What I found interesting and fun about this show is not so much each individual character but how the characters began to interact on the show. Making Odo and Quark this kind of twosome is just going to have juice for ages because Odo is this kind of repressed, haunted figure. Rene's really playing the make-up to a certain extent, which is that he's a man alone, which you don't see a lot in the 24th century, and Quark is a Ferengi. He's not your typical cringing Ferengi, he's a Ferengi with a little edge to him too."

Shimerman attributes his casting to his previous outings as a Ferengi on the series and felt he could best personify the new Ferengi character they had created for *Deep Space Nine*.

"They remembered me from five years ago as one of the first Ferengi,"

says Shimerman. "I think what Rick said to me was they remembered how strong a Ferengi I was because they wanted that for Quark. He also has to be able to play chess with Sisko. They wanted that quality. I did not have to audition as many times for a series regular as I would if they had not seen my work. The first time that I had a callback, and usually there are a number of actors sitting there, it was only me and Max Grodenchik. He's played a Ferengi before because we had done the most Ferengi [episodes]. At the final audition it was just me and they gave me the impression after I was cast that they had indeed written the part with me in mind."

Grodenchik, who played a Ferengi in "Captain's Holiday" and "The Perfect Mate," was eventually cast as Rom, Quark's bumbling brother, and has made an equally indelible impression on viewers as the Fredo of Ferengi.

"I got to know Armin a bit during the audition process," enthuses Grodenchik. "He had so much more history with the show. I'd be lying if I didn't say I was disappointed that I didn't get the role of Quark, but it made me feel better knowing that Armin landed the role. I thought it was fair and I also felt he was a better foil for Sisko since I watched some of his old episodes and thought he could play very strong emotions very well. When they asked me to do Rom, I was thrilled. I had no idea that it would turn into such a recurring role, so I don't think things could have worked out better even if I had gotten Quark because I depend on Armin a lot. I ask him everything. Sometimes, he even answers me."

As originally conceived, first officer of Deep Space Nine would have been *Next Generation*'s Ensign Ro, but those plans were scrapped when actress Michelle Forbes decided that she would rather pursue a film career than get tied down to a series for five years or more.

"Michelle Forbes is a wonderful actress and her character of Ensign Ro created the entire canvas for this new series," says Michael Piller. "It had always been assumed that she would be one of the people spun off and moved over to the new series. [But] she wants to

• • • •

be a feature actress."

Fortunately, Forbes' departure from these plans came at the same time Piller was working on a rewrite of the pilot to strengthen the first act, which meant changing the character of Ro to another Bajoran with a new and different backstory. This, he soon discovered, proved an advantage rather than a disadvantage for the new series.

"I found there was a great deal more conflict in having the Bajoran not be Starfleet," explains Piller. "Immediately you have different priorities and agendas, and the two people immediately have a conflict with each other the moment they step onto the station. The one between Sisko and Ro would have been a much different one because ultimately she's Starfleet and has to do what the boss says. Kira can do things which are not appropriate Starfleet behavior. We created this character and it was really a matter of rewriting two or three scenes that defined where she was from and a couple of speeches in other scenes which were mostly action-type scenes."

One of the moments that episode director Winrich Kolbe remembers upon viewing the pilot is a confrontation between Sisko and Major Kira Nerys, Ro's replacement , in which Sisko warns her that if she ever goes over his head again, he'll serve it on a silver platter.

"I love that," smiles Kolbe. "That, to me, is more human, it is more contemporary. Sometimes we have to work together with people with whom we occasionally disagree and have differences of opinion with, yet — despite that — they are capable of fulfilling their job. In the pilot, I think Sisko said, 'I want you because you're Bajoran.' He could have had any one of a million Bajorans, somebody who would say, 'Yes, sir, whatever you want.' He wanted somebody who comes from the background of Kira, who was in the underground against the Cardassians. A nationalist, so to speak. It intrigues me because I feel that, yes, we are changing, but we are not necessarily becoming more advanced. There's nationalism two thousand years from now and it will always be there because it's something genetically inside us. Like racism, which is something that's always coming out. We only seemingly live in a

better social society if we are able to combat it, but the moment we let our guard down, bingo, there's the conflict. I like that in *DS9*, when it comes down to the Kira/Sisko conflict. It's politics, but it's the politics of Starfleet, of the larger unit which says, 'We want to expand our influence,' and the small unit, which is the planet Bajor, which says, 'Hey, it's all very nice but you're taking over. We don't want you either.' "

David Carson admits that the casting of Kira was difficult. "Though no more so than when you're setting up something completely new, because on these television things everything is done by committee. So you're juggling three million opinions at the same time. It's sort of a different world from the one that I'm used to in that sense. You feel as though you're walking through a minefield as you struggle towards the final choice in television, it seems to me, because there are a whole mixture of opinions to be taken into account, some informed, and some uninformed. Sometimes, as we all know, terrible mistakes happen in casting. I think, though, we were extremely lucky this time and everybody had the necessary patience to not say yes because we had to start shooting. In fact, some of the roles weren't cast until we were three weeks into it. We had to change the schedule around to accommodate it. With a show like this, getting a good cast is really so important."

Nana Visitor, a veteran of a number of television shows including the short-lived *Working Girl*, based on the hit motion picture, was cast as the former Bajoran terrorist and second-in-command of Deep Space Nine. She confesses to not being an avid *Star Trek* fan when she joined the new series. "I watched *Star Trek* when it was in re-runs," she says. "I think I know them all from cooking dinner in my brownstone in New York. I was a fan of the quality of the show, but I was not a Trekkie."

Ironically, Visitor didn't even realize *Deep Space Nine* was a *Star Trek* spin-off when she read for the role. "I didn't get it and I didn't understand that this was *Star Trek* when I auditioned," says Visitor. "I did not understand what I was getting into. I didn't even know I

Nana Visitor as Major Kira Nerys (photo copyright ©1995 Albert Ortega).

was wearing a nose and I talked to Rick Berman and he said, 'At least the prosthetic is one of the least we have,' and I said, 'What prosthetic?' And he said, 'It's nothing, it's just a small elephant nose that you wear.' And he had me going for five seconds. But I didn't know, I had no idea. I just knew I wanted to play this woman very badly."

"The cast and company is so lucky to have her," says David Carson. "She's one of these rare chameleon kind of actors who is able to assimilate herself into a character and transform it into something you don't expect. She's also very beautiful and she obviously delights in playing this role. I was very pleased when she walked into the room and I think that once she did, she was the only Kira that we thought could play the role. Of course we weren't going to tell anybody that until we'd signed a deal with her. She was and is extraordinary. She's also delightful to work with and she's able to tune her emotions to the camera. She also has this specific, tangible relationship with the lens, which is delightful for a director to work with."

For Visitor, *Deep Space* is a region of the universe she hopes to be exploring for a long time. "*Star Trek* has

Avery Brooks, Nana Visitor and Majel Barrett at the premiere of Star Trek: Generations *(photo copyright ©1995 Albert Ortega).*

got so much strength and age behind it and it's cutting edge television," she notes. "We're doing things I've never done or seen on television, and there's this kind of care and the kind of scripts I've never seen. Once in a while I'll have someone I haven't heard from in a year say, 'Wow, I hear you're on *Deep Space Nine*, I'm such a Trekkie,' and then I'll say, 'Gee, this is new and different.' I feel that in those very faraway moments on the telephone but in the day-to-day it doesn't mean a thing."

No Sophomore Slump

Although *Star Trek: Deep Space Nine* was a ratings success throughout its first season, executive producer Michael Piller knew there were several problems he was intent on redressing. "I came out feeling that we still have a lot to prove to people who kept telling me, 'Well, you can't fly anywhere.' I was determined to say to these people, 'We can do everything that makes good television. We can have spaceships, we can fly into this station, we can have space battles, we can meet aliens. We can have anything you want on *Deep Space Nine*.' I thought we had done that first season, but as I went back and watched many of the episodes,

I realized some episodes had credibility lapses in performance, in direction, in scripting, in the sets, and the difference between having a credible hour of futuristic television and having an hour of unconvincing futuristic television is so slight. One wrong performance, one bad costume can blow the whole thing."

He adds, "We had a show in the first season that I thought was a terrific script and was not a terrific show called 'Battle Lines.' I thought it was a terrific concept, but the nature of the direction and the performances in that show made it feel operatic. You have people with funny costumes, in alien make-up, flying around in spaceships, and if you act at the top of your lungs it's going to seem like grand opera and that's the danger. That's what Patrick Stewart taught me very early on in the game. You take it and bring it down to the most human levels and you underplay it so that what you find is a truth in the human performance that makes the credibility of everything else work.

"In the first year, there always seemed to be just enough credibility lacking in certain moments so that you'd never believe that you were in a futuristic space station," continues Piller. "I felt like we'd have to prove that in the sec-

ond season and we worked on the sets, but I think most of all we worked on the scripts. The first three-parter was a commitment to say, 'Hey, look at us. Look at what we can do.' It was, in a sense, supposed to do for us what 'Best of Both Worlds' had done for *Next Generation*. I think that we succeeded. Those three shows really did show the breadth of ambition of storytelling that we were able to do and the special effects were terrific, the guest stars were great, and the credibility was there."

In fact, Piller believes that the beginning of *DS9*'s second season was consistently strong, producing some of its finest episodes. "I think we started out with a terrific momentum," he says. "The first eight shows of *Deep Space Nine* were as strong a series of shows as I have been involved with."

One of the aspects of *Star Trek* that has often been cited as intrinsic to its nearly universal appeal is the family feeling of its crews. Some have criticized *Deep Space* for lacking a warm family-like ensemble, a notion disputed by its producers.

"We get the same old stuff," says Ira Behr. "It's not a family. Well, it is a family — sometimes a dysfunctional family, but we have much more of a family like the original series than *TNG*. Spock and Bones may not get along, but they love each other. These characters care about one another; Odo and Quark, Bashir and Garak, Kira and Dax, Dax and Sisko, Odo and Kira. I can't believe that it's such a hard concept to grasp. There are no unlikable people. I see that men are threatened by Kira and they say they don't like her because she's too strong, but that's because we live in a screwed-up society, not because she's a bad character."

"*Deep Space Nine* has got a pretty big following for as young a show as it is," says Marc Alaimo who portrays Gul Dukat, the former Cardassian commander of the station. "And it deals with conflicts we have as human beings that we can't really deal with human-to-human. The show can deal with prejudice and greed and hate and all that stuff in more interesting ways than human-to-human."

And that may be the very ele-

Sci-Fi Universe *features an unflinching look at the making of* Star Trek: Deep Space Nine.

• • • •

ment that has caused some of the vast *Star Trek* audience to drop in and tune out. The heavily politicized nature of the show, which weaves its intricate stories of political intrigue and Shakespearean theatrics on a tapestry encompassing the recently freed Bajoran world and the Federation's place in helping to maintain a stable political landscape while also fending off Cardassian aggression, isn't quite as simple as the Enterprise's mandate to "boldly go."

"I think we do politics awfully well," comments Michael Piller. "The problem with that is there may be something to the fact that people would rather watch space monsters, enigmas, and anomalies than politics. But one of the things I was proudest of with *Deep Space Nine* is that I began to realize that it takes a great deal more courage to stay and deal with the consequences of your actions and to deal with problems that don't get solved than it is to go in, meet somebody, change their lives or have them teach us something and then zoom out to the next person."

Adds Ira Behr, "I think [Story Editor] Robert Wolfe explains it best. [*DS9*] unlike *TNG* and the original series, where you go out into the great void and explore and map and meet people and have adventures and then you leave. We know every move that Sisko makes, every thought he has, every action he takes, has repercussions that we can go back to and work on and play with. That's why we have the best supporting characters on television. From Dukat to Garak and Rom and Winn and all these wonderful people that we can continue to explore because they don't go away. We can leave as much as we want but we always come back and the station is still there.

"And that's what I think Sisko's job is ultimately," says Behr. "What we were trying to show without really articulating it while we were doing it was to demonstrate that Sisko's job is in a way more important, or certainly more complicated, than Picard's or Kirk's because they're explorers and he's a builder. What he has to do is basically build an alliance and build a relationship. It's a different thing than they get to do. They get to have fun. He gets to have fun too

but he has to make sure that his fun doesn't come and bite him on the ass three episodes down the line. That's what we realized last season and I think it worked. There's a whole bubbling cauldron that just seemed to take on some new heat, at least for the writers. And we really realized we were on a unique show with its own identity."

Interestingly, Sisko makes an impassioned speech in the second season episode "The Maquis" which could prove defining for the young show. In it, he points out how earth may be a paradise in the 24th century but the rest of the galaxy is not, positioning the show within the Roddenberry universe in a unique way. "We were able to give a speech about how it's easy to be safe in paradise," says Ira Behr who wrote the episode. "The whole Roddenberry thing was a believable thing when you're living back on earth. We thought it was a fundamental thing to state. We're not pissing on *Star Trek*, it's a great view of the future, but we are on the frontier. It's not as simple as everyone behaving themselves. It's a difficult place to be."

With Piller's attention largely being focused on the launch of *Voyager* as well as the launch of a new series, *Legend*, for the United-Paramount Network, Behr assumed the role of show runner, overseeing the development of scripts and working with both Berman and Piller on casting and other production issues third season. "It is a difficult position to be in because I do the day-to-day running of the show."

Among the most dramatic changes occurring on-screen third season were the introduction of the Defiant, a prototype ship built to fight the Borg, which has now been co-opted by Sisko for jaunts into the Gamma Quadrant and conflicts with the Dominion, the series' new adversary set up at the end of the show's second season. "For two years we were dying to somehow find a way to get the show to be a little less stationary and the feeling was that if we could come up with a ship that was slightly bigger than a Runabout it would give us a little more freedom," notes Rick Berman. "On the other hand, it still is not the same thing as being on a starship. If you get on the Nina or the Pinto or the Santa Maria and

go to find the new world, you're an explorer. If you do it in such a way that you have to come back to Barcelona every weekend, it's not the same thing."

In addition, a new ops lounge set was built for crew conferences. "We never really had a place for our crew to sit and shmooze," says Berman. "They never had a place for them to be a family together and the feeling was that it would be worthwhile to develop a set that would be similar to the observation lounge in *Next Generation*."

By the beginning of third season, *DS9* took the bold step of revealing Odo's heritage, depicting his race of shape-shifters as the Founders of the Dominion. Among other episodes, "Equilibrium" attempted to focus on the characters revealing that Dax had a symbiont wiped from her memory, "House of Quark" was a comedic yarn in which Quark becomes involved with a bar fight and takes credit for killing a Klingon warrior, and "Past Tense" was an ambitious two-part installment which addressed the homeless issue by sending Sisko, Bashir, and Dax back to 21st century earth in a storyline reminiscent of *Trek Classic*'s "City on the Edge of Forever."

"There are going to be people who are not going to like what we do and they're going to say we're screwing it up and it's a mistake, but you can't please everyone," says Ira Behr philosophically. "At least to us, we're doing the right thing, I think we're doing the bold thing. We're taking a series and expanding it. It's a different *Star Trek*. You cannot just keep exploring the galaxy, coming and going, saying 'Hi and goodbye.' You've got to make it a rich place and we have all the elements and characters that are just full of possibilities. No one will ever say that we did not attempt to explore as many of those possibilities as we could. What more can you ask for?"

What more, indeed.

Siddig El Fadil and Colm Meaney appear at the Museum of Broadcasting.

• • • •

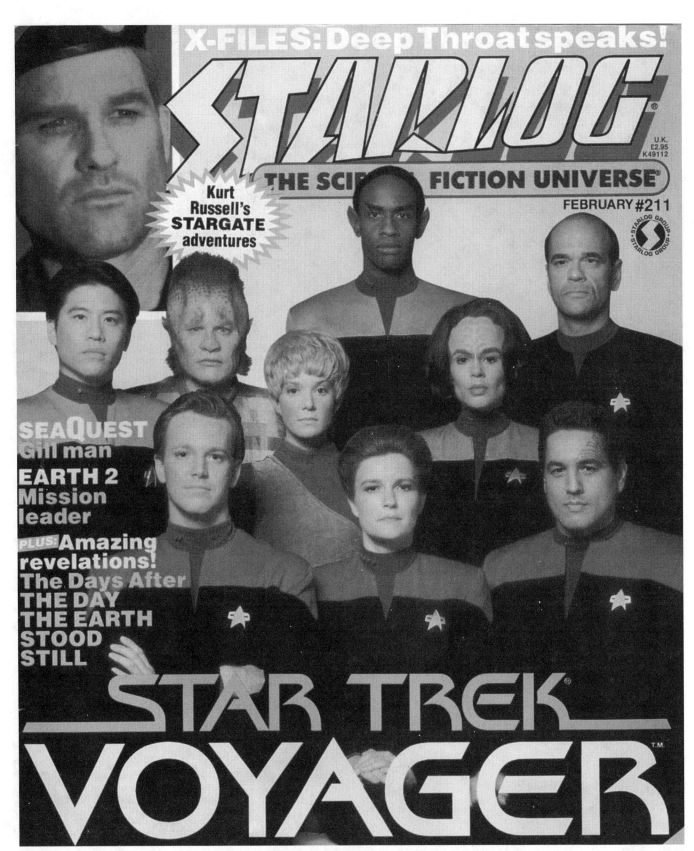

Starlog magazine introduces the cast of the latest incarnation of Gene Roddenberry's creation, Star Trek: Voyager.

••••

CHAPTER THIRTY TWO
NOW, VOYAGER
The Star Trek Team's Latest Enterprise

Stranded on the distant fringes of the galaxy, the starship Voyager has begun its trek homeward.

In contrast to what was done on the original *Star Trek*, *Next Generation* and *Deep Space Nine*, the creative team behind *Voyager* — executive producers Rick Berman, Michael Piller and Jeri Taylor — have taken the bold step of creating a series which is inherently unable to take advantage of the voluminous *Star Trek* backstory, which is intrinsically part of the more familiar regions of the *Trek* universe.

According to Rick Berman, the defining criteria of any *Star Trek* spin-off is that it be different from its predecessors, so that the writers remain creatively invigorated and the audience stays interested.

"We wanted *Voyager* to be different, so we made it different, primarily, in three ways," Berman explains. "First of all, Gene Roddenberry didn't want conflict amongst his characters. That's great, but it doesn't help when you're writing drama because conflict is what drives drama. Without breaking Gene's rules we're always trying to find ways of creating conflict. This show features the inherent conflict between Captain Janeway's crew and that of the Maquis vessel. The Maquis become provisional Starfleet officers, but there will always be conflict between them, and that gave us something new and unique.

"Second," he adds, "we have our people seventy years away from home. They're not necessarily spending the rest of their lives getting home, but they are looking, while at the same time exploring space. The most unique thing about that is that it enables us to no longer be in contact with Starfleet. It's not like we can call home all the time for instructions. We're on our own. The final

The cast of Voyager *make a public appearance (photo copyright ©1995 Albert Ortega).*

thing is we put a woman at the helm, which is something we felt it was time to do and it gave us a new direction to travel in."

Jeri Taylor concurs, noting that the challenge of staying fresh and original is "the main reason that we took the very risky move of throwing our people to the opposite end of the galaxy and cutting ties with everything that's familiar. No Starfleet, no Klingons, no Ferengi — all of those things that have been very comfortable for the audience. It was a universe that they knew well and that they loved exploring, and we turned our backs on that. It was very scary but we felt that we would force ourselves into having a fresh slant on things and fresh storytelling. It was tough to make that decision."

Adds Michael Piller of devising *Voyager's* new *Star Trek* premise, "We needed to do something that was unique and hadn't been done before but at the same time create the kind of environment that a spaceship provides. It was the same process of decision making that we did on *Deep Space Nine*, 'What can you do in a spaceship that is not the same as the *Next Generation*?' One of us said, 'You know those shows where Q sends

the Enterprise off to some strange quadrant and we meet the Borg, but we solve everything in an hour and get back home? Well, what if we don't? What if we get stuck there in space and it is completely unknown to us and this is the story of that journey and of our trying to find our way back?'"

The producing troika immediately gravitated to the idea, particularly when they realized some of the allegorical underpinnings to the premise. "When we hooked on this idea we realized, in a sense, we were talking about a journey that is very much like the journey that all of us in this country are embarking on today," says Michael Piller. "We were sort of in the afterglow of the last presidential election and it seemed clear the kind of problems that this country is facing are not problems that are going to be easily solved in our lifetime. We have to begin on solutions that may take more than one generation to see the final result of. In fact, our children might be the ones who get to see the results of our hard work if we start now. In a sense, the ship franchise of *Voyager* is that kind of journey, because we are on a ship of men and women who are beginning a journey that conceivably we may not see the end

••••

Rick Berman, Kate Mulgrew, Michael Piller and Jeri Taylor present a special award to astronaut Sally Ride (photo copyright ©1995 Albert Ortega).

of — and we are working in the best interests of everybody on board to try to solve our problem and to make the best life we can for ourselves on this ship; to find the way back home.

"But in the end," he adds, "we realize we may have lost what we really love forever and that the journey back is seventy years, even at our best speed. The bottom line is that we felt that this was a very contemporary kind of message to be dealing with. We said to ourselves this is what Roddenberry had to deal with back in the original days when he was trying to figure out what *Star Trek* was going to be. The original Enterprise really was about being alone out there. It was about being in a ship in space, facing unknown aliens. If you look at the years since, it's gotten very crowded in our part of the galaxy. We know all the political scenarios there are in *Star Trek*, we know the Bajorans and we know the Klingons, we know the Vulcans and we know the Cardassians. When we sent this ship out to the Delta quadrant alone, the canvas is clear and the same things Roddenberry had to do are the things we're going to have to do. It's really back to basics and that's a huge creative challenge and should produce creative rewards."

In "Caretaker," the two-hour premiere of *Voyager*, the Federation starship Voyager pursues a rebel Maquis ship into a galactic phenomenon that transports them to an unknown region of space so distant that it would take them decades at maximum warp to return to known territory. The Maquis ship is destroyed during this adventure, though its crew is rescued by the Voyager. Facing an unenviable future in oblivion, both crews form an uneasy alliance in their search for a way home.

"They want to go home," emphasizes "Caretaker" director Rick Kolbe, who has helmed numerous episodes of the first two *Star Trek* spin-offs. "Isn't that basically what all of us are trying to do in some sense or another? That gives us a different point of view and a different objective when you have to make a decision. Do you want to get involved in an altercation that happens on planet 'x,' or do you want to go home? If you want to go home, sometimes you have to go two steps back to go one step forward. I think it's going to be interesting, particularly if you're forced to ask if the Prime Directive applies, or if your primary directive is to go home. But what happens if on the way home there are obstacles that will have to be negotiated in those terms? I

guess that's where the decision-making process will come in."

Kolbe compares the pervasive conflict between the rebel and Federation crews to the premise of *The Defiant Ones*. In the Academy Award-winning 1958 film, two dissimilar and distrustful convicts escape from prison while shackled together, forcing them to cooperate with one another.

"It's an old plot," he concedes, "but it worked in *The Defiant Ones* and it'll work for us. We have two groups that at any moment could have serious personality conflicts. The Maquis could suddenly say, 'Wait a minute, that's not the way we're going to do it,' and there's the conflict. I like that there are great possibilities for conflict on the ship itself, which is something that was missing in *TNG*. It just wasn't there, which could be a problem dramatically. There will always be conflict between human beings; we need those conflicts to grow and survive."

Which is not to say, he emphasizes, that this series disposes of Roddenberry's overall philosophy.

"Rick Berman and Michael Piller may create new series," he notes, "but they never forget who started this

Avery Brooks and Tim Russ (photo copyright ©1995 Albert Ortega).

whole thing. Ultimately, as long as it's *Star Trek*, it will be Gene Roddenberry's. It's all a matter of where you start from. I started in Germany, I still have a German accent. I can't deny it. I'm now living longer here than I did in Germany, but the origins are still there and they will always be there."

If *Deep Space Nine*'s premiere could be likened to the cerebral original Trek pilot, "The Cage," then "Caretaker" could be considered more akin to the action/adventure of "Where No Man Has Gone Before," *Star Trek*'s second pilot. "I think what we have concocted is a wonderful action/adventure romp," says Taylor. "It's very different in character from 'All Good Things.' It's very different from the movie [*Generations*] and very different from the premiere episode of *Deep Space Nine*, which was sort of heavily metaphysical and philosophical and intensely devoted to one character [Sisko]. This is a romp and it's a true action/adventure."

Notes Piller, "We thought that the best thing that we could do right now was to have a pilot and a show that really concentrated on adventure. *Deep Space Nine* was a show that went straight to character. It's a much more internal, psychological show — and for some viewers it's been too taxing. I think what the audience is asking for is a slam-bang adventure show, and that's what *Voyager* is. Having said that, you know from my contributions to *Star Trek* that we will never lose site of character."

Once the premise was established for the series, the creative team had the equally daunting task of creating the characters that would inhabit this new universe. "There was just a wide array of combinations of both males and females, human and alien, that had already been used," says Taylor. "Every time we said 'What about A?,' we'd realize that we were re-creating Data or re-creating Odo. It seemed like all the good people and good species were used up. It took weeks and weeks, if not months, to create a tapestry of people."

That tapestry blends both Federation officers and Maquis renegades, including Vulcan security/tactical chief Tuvok (Tim Russ), Maquis first officer Chakotay (Robert Beltran), holo-

Star Trek aliens unite: Ethan Phillips (Neelix), Rene Auberjonois (Odo) and Armin Shimerman (Quark) (photo copyright ©1995 Albert Ortega).

graphic chief medical officer Doc Zimmerman (named after *DS9* production designer Herman Zimmerman, and played by Robert Picardo), Klingon-human hybrid B'Elanna Torres (Roxann Biggs-Dawson), who is a Maquis member serving as Voyager chief engineer; ops and communications officer Harry Kim (Garrett Wang), helmsman Tom Paris (Robert Duncan McNeil) and the aliens Neelix (Ethan Phillips) and Kes (Jennifer Lien). Then there's Captain Kathryn Janeway (Kate Mulgrew), the casting of which monopolized all of the early press coverage of the show.

The casting of Janeway was an arduous process, with a wide variety of possible names being bandied about, including Lindsay Wagner (*The Bionic Woman*), Linda Hamilton (*Beauty and the Beast, T2*) and Joanna Cassidy (*Roger Rabbit*). The situation was made even more difficult by a reported struggle between executive producer Rick Berman and Paramount Pictures as to the gender of the captain. The studio supposedly wanted a male, while Berman insisted that a female would continue *Star Trek*'s forward-thinking ideals.

"We had made attempts to look at male actors for the part when time was running out and it seemed that we might have a problem," Rick Kolbe admits, "but

it was never the studio's position, 'Hey, guys, knock it off, you've gotta get a guy in there.' I can assure you that every time a male read the same pages that were written for Janeway, I couldn't quite get my head into it. There *is* a difference. She does take care of business differently. Her relationship with people is different. It's a very subtle affair, but a woman in this particular case will not look at things the way a man does.

"I had the feeling and hope that we could end up with someone that could propel the story forward," he adds. "We had two good candidates, one male and one female and we picked the female. The male was [Englishman] Nigel Havers. He was excellent, and to be very honest, one could almost say that he would have been it, but he wasn't here. He wasn't with us, we couldn't see him. We had tried to get him over here but there were some problems on the other side, so he couldn't make it. By the time he came in, someone said, 'Genevieve Bujold,' and we jumped."

Perhaps they shouldn't have. In a much publicized arrival and departure, Ms. Bujold, whose credits include *Coma* and *Dead Ringers*, quit the series less than a week into production. In the ensuing weeks, rumors ran rampant as to exactly why she left the show, with the

actress complaining about a "cartoon" character and Berman noting that she wasn't prepared for the long hours required by television.

"She had a different concept about the show," Kolbe explains. "At this particular point, I do not understand why she took the show in the first place. It seems to me she was not prepared for what happened. Yet the day before she said yes, Rick Berman called her and told her, step by step, what was expected. He told her television is a brutal schedule, it goes on day after day after day for long hours. Directors will change, scripts will come in at the last minute, that it was not easy. She called back the next day and said, 'I thought about it. I've seen *Star Trek*, I want to do it.' Whether that was based on truth, I don't know. But it turned out that her concept of the captain was not being a captain, but being a scientist. She wanted to be Genevieve Bujold, not Captain Janeway.

"She didn't want to run the ship," he elaborates. "We shot for a day and a half and we did *a lot* of things and she was pretty much involved in everything we did. I tried to get her to give us the authority that I wanted from the character, and that never came through. We had a chat about it and I said, 'Why can't you give it to me?' She said to me, 'I don't want to be Janeway, I want to be Genevieve Bujold.' Genevieve Bujold is a very fragile human being on the outside — with a strong inside, I cannot say. I

didn't work with her long enough to find that out. That fragile human being, to me, could not take over command of the ship. I'm not saying she's a bad actress. She's a very good actress. But she was *not* right for the part."

Kolbe remembers meeting her for the first time in Rick Berman's office. Rather than delivering a reading of the script, she was merely chatting with the producer. It was at that moment that the director was struck by her fragility.

"On that same day," he smiles wryly, "I told Rick, 'There are two things going through my mind right now. One is total disaster and the other is total triumph.' At that point I didn't know which it was going to be. There *was* something in her that *could* have blown everybody away, but that never came through. It might have never been there. It's a real fine line. At that particular moment, I guess there was a little panic to get somebody so we could get going. Some of us were very high on Genevieve, so we hired her."

At that time, production began with about four days' worth of sequences being shot.

Kolbe continues, "We started shooting her on Monday and on Thursday afternoon we were just about ready to break for lunch, when she said, 'It's just not working out too well. I don't think I'm right for the part.' To which I said, probably a little bit on the angry side, 'Don't ever say that!' Not because I wanted to lecture her, but why is she saying this in front of the crew? It creates a psychological problem. The captain of the ship is supposed to be the captain of the ship, and the captain of the ship is supposed to be the captain of our crew, of us. The star of a show is not just an actor or an actress. He or she defines how a unit works. Patrick Stewart did it in his way, Avery Brooks does it in his way. When the star of the show says, 'I don't think I'm right for the part,' you can hear the reaction from the entire crew. At that moment I got together with her, we had a chat about the situation. I called the producers and about a half an hour later it was decided to cancel her relationship with the show. It wasn't Paramount or anyone that fired her, she just decided to pull out."

Driving later on that day, Kolbe had the sensation of leaving combat in Vietnam. "You have the feeling of not being in the real world," he notes, "whether you're alive or dead, you haven't figured out yet. Even though you have the crackle of bullets whizzing around your ears, your adrenaline is very high for survival. Then comes the moment when you lose all feeling, and that's what happened at that particular moment."

Adds Jeri Taylor, "The captain is the person that gets the white hot glare of publicity as the first female ever to head one of the *Star Trek* series and she had to be just right. We considered, auditioned, looked at tape of what seemed like every actress between the ages of probably thirty and fifty-five in Los Angeles, New York, Chicago, Canada, London and Europe. We had several people we were happy with. Some of the studio executives didn't necessarily share our feelings. Finally, with days to go, we were made aware that Genevieve Bujold was interested and we were ecstatic. So, we went ahead with that and thought 'Wow, we've got it' and, of course, when that didn't work out it was distressing for everybody. I am deeply grateful to her that she did this when she did instead of after six weeks or two months, because that would have destroyed us. She did what she knew in her heart was right, which is the way she functions as a person and as an actress."

The entire shooting schedule was rearranged for the following week so that sequences could be shot around the Janeway character. In essence, this provided one final week for the role to be cast. Revisiting many of their previous candidates, they agreed to look, for a third time, at Kate Mulgrew, who had been sidelined by a cold on a previous audition. "The third time she absolutely nailed the part," says Taylor. "She was so right and, in all of her work, she has continued to validate that choice."

"I was shooting when Kate Mulgrew was mentioned," says Kolbe. "Then Kate Mulgrew was hired and I had a meeting with her in the make-up trailer. When she came on the set, I was very impressed with her already. She was informed about what she had to do, she

NO. 258 • JANUARY 20, 1995

Entertainment
WEEKLY

STAR TREK
VOYAGER
BOLDLY GOING WHERE ONLY
MEN HAVE GONE BEFORE

KATE
MULGREW,
CAPTAIN
OF THE
STARSHIP

$2.50 (CAN. $2.95)

03

10210

0 724464 3

Entertainment Weekly *presents Kate Mulgrew as Captain Kathryn Janeway, the commander of Star Trek: Voyager (photo copyright Time Warner)*

• • • •

Kate Mulgrew served on a silver platter (photo copyright ©1995 Albert Ortega).

watched a lot of episodes and a lot of my episodes, and I felt so good about her that I brought her to the set on stage nine and said, 'Ladies and gentlemen, the captain!' And everyone applauded. It was very nice and I suddenly felt that we were taking off. We were taxiing up until that point.

"It seems to me she's going to do a hell of a lot for women on television," he says confidently. "She is definitely a woman but she can handle any situation in her own particular way. I would follow her. The way she moves, the way she thinks, the way she looks is wonderful. We have to find a way of not writing her as a man but writing her as a woman, which might be a difficult thing to do because there are not that many female writers on *Star Trek*, though hopefully we'll do something about that in order to get that perspective. That will make the difference."

Taylor admits that the most pressing concern about a female captain was whether or not a woman in command would be universally embraced. "Will they accept that a whole crew would follow her, report to her, trust her in battle?" muses Taylor. "This is the most important selling point in a woman. Kate Mulgrew has that without even

working at it. As a person, as a human being, she is everything that we envisioned Janeway being. She has power coming out of her genetic code and the moment she walked out on that bridge the first day, she owned it."

Adds Taylor, "I have always said during this whole process that surely by the 21st century women can assume roles of leadership without acting like men. We have created and will continue to explore the softer, nurturing side of her. She can be a caring and compassionate person. We are going to see that she interacts much more easily on a social level with the crew in a way that Picard never did."

In comparing Janeway to previous *Trek* commanders, Kolbe points out that Sisko is a somewhat distant character, while Picard began distant but eventually grew closer with his crew. Janeway, he feels, will be the next step.

"There are moments where you get a sense of the difference," he explains. "There is more concern for what is going on inside. There is more concern with feelings. Even so, it will never affect her capabilities. If she has to send someone into a life threatening situation on a planet, she will do that. But she can also agonize openly about the fate of the crewmember. That's something a woman might talk about, but a man never would really bring it up. He would be staring into space and it would be implied, but he never would talk about it. I think the story approach from a character point of view has a much broader band to work on than if it was a male captain. We've had a lot of women leaders, but they've all suffered from the hidden penis syndrome."

Kate Mulgrew, seemingly overwhelmed by all the attention her being cast has brought, notes with a smile, "I am allegedly a woman, and that lends itself to maternity, to compassion, to warmth, to a lot of qualities which our culture has encouraged in women. Men, of course, enjoy them and reveal them as we do. But I think that women are *encouraged* to reveal them and express them. This will take the character of Janeway into greater dimensions, I think, emotionally as a woman than perhaps a male captain would feel free to do."

Although it may have been forgotten in the whole Bujold situation, there are other characters on board the Voyager as well. First up is Starfleet Lieutenant Tom Paris, latest in a long line of Starfleet officers who, while in the academy, disgraced the family name and has been given a second chance by Janeway.

Offers Kolbe, "My problem with the character, originally, was that he was too much an on-the-nose rebel. A little too clichéd. Other than that, I don't forsee a major problem with it. We have established that he has come out of a Federation penal system and that he is not a hardened criminal who is out to slice your throat unless you work with him. He's not as on-the-nose as I thought he was at the beginning.

"He was probably the easiest character to cast," continues Kolbe. "He was basically white, middle class. All we needed was someone who had a sense of being a little bit overbearing, a little bit snotty at times. A character with something in the closet, somebody who's willing to take unusual steps in order to progress themselves. What was important to me was that his father had such high expectations of him, thinking he would

Robert Duncan McNeill who portrays Lieutenant Tom Paris on Voyager *(photo copyright ©1995 Albert Ortega).*

• • • •

be the thirty-sixth and ongoing in a military family, and then he decided, 'The hell with that, I'm not going to play that game. I want to do something else.'"

Actor Robert Duncan McNeill, who portrays Paris, is intrigued by the character's less than illustrious background. "One thing that I think is interesting about *Voyager* is that every character has a great backstory," he says, "and I don't think that they've all been explored completely. That's what makes it interesting. Everybody's got sort of a dark side — an edge — which is different than the other *Star Trek* shows."

Chakotay is the American Indian captain of the Maquis vessel, who ends up serving as first officer aboard the Voyager under Janeway's command — a fact certain to create conflict. The character is portrayed by Robert Beltran, formerly of *Models, Inc.* This was a difficult role to cast due to the relatively small number of Native American actors available through SAG.

"You're probably talking about two handfuls of actors," Kolbe points out, "who are well known enough to ask to be considered. We had another actor in mind, but there were pros and cons. Opinions were flying because that particular actor was older. The question was, without talking about age discrimination,

Robert Beltran who co-stars on the series as first officer Chakotay (photo copyright ©1995 Albert Ortega).

which this wasn't, would he provide a balance? We had nine actors and we had to mix them. The question now is who do we want as a possible executive officer on the ship? Going with the assumption that usually it was Jonathan Frakes as Riker who led the Away Team, we needed somebody who was physically believable and fit enough to do that.

"Ultimately it came down to two actors, one of which was Robert Beltran. I think he was called in two or three times. He was extremely soft-spoken in the beginning, and I think that was in part due to the script, where he was described as a calm, stoic Indian. I don't know where we got that from. It's some kind of myth that's still hanging around today, that you can throw a spear through an Indian and he won't even flinch. I'm not an expert on Indians, but I'm a human being and I know Indians are human beings and they will probably react as violently as anybody else. They might deal with it differently, but pain is pain and concentration is concentration. Living in a Maquis ship and fighting a life and death battle with the Cardassians, no one is going to sit around there and calmly say, 'Okay, there, give me full forward power and let's get the hell out of here.' It's not going to happen. There's got to be that tension there. Robert, I think, developed better and better as he came in."

Serving as security chief of the Voyager is Tuvok, a full-blooded Vulcan portrayed by Tim Russ (*Mr. Saturday Night*). Kolbe finds Tuvok an interesting character, and is particularly pleased with the casting of Russ.

"Originally Tuvok was supposed to be 160-years-old," he notes. "Again we had a problem. When we were looking for an established, older actor to play the part of Tuvok, we had some damn good actors come in and read for us, but physically they weren't right. So we kept scaling down. We went from the sixties to the fifties to the forties to the thirties, and it just went down. A little longer, I'm sure we would have to have a tutor on the set. Also playing into this was who was going to be the captain? Obviously the relationship between Tuvok and the male captain would have

Tim Russ (Tuvok) strikes a decidedly Vulcan pose (photo copyright ©1995 Albert Ortega).

to be rewritten, as well as Chakotay. That opened up a whole other can of peas. There was some concern that Tuvok should be older, or the show might be too yuppie, too young, too *Melrose Place* or *Beverly Hills 90210*. On the other hand, we couldn't find the right actor for the part. I'm not talking about acting capability. I'm talking about the character, the presence, the look. If we reject somebody, if we say we couldn't find a black older actor, that doesn't mean there aren't any good black older actors. That's not the point. The point is that we all have a certain image of that particular character in mind and we're trying to cast toward that particular image. If we don't find him or her, there might be some problem and we have to readdress.

"The nice thing about Tim," he comments, "is that he came in and gave us a wonderful reading. You have to understand another thing: these stoic parts like Chakotay and Tuvok are very difficult to act. What you're telling those guys is, 'I want you to withdraw. I want you to be distant, but I want you to have character. I want you to be a Vulcan, logical, but I don't want you to be boring. I don't want you to be a nerd who pontificates.' That is very difficult to do and Tim

Garrett Wang who portrays Ensign Harry Kim, fresh out of the Academy and lost in space with the Voyager (photo copyright ©1995 Albert Ortega).

is one of the very few actors we saw who could nail it. He had an intensity and a sense of humor when it came time to dealing with Neelix, *without* losing his capacity to be a stoic Vulcan."

Similarly, the Spock/McCoy relationship on the original series worked so well due to Spock's subtle sense of humor regarding the doctor.

"Exactly," says Kolbe. "Leonard Nimoy obviously set the tone for this whole thing. There was nothing boring or nerdy or bland about Spock. On the contrary. There was always something happening, and that's very similar to what Tim Russ is going to give us."

Of the entire *Voyager* cast, it is Tim Russ who is the biggest Trekker, and his being cast as Tuvok is a dream come true.

"There was a very big victory for me in getting this," admits russ. "I have been interested in working on the show ever since the original *Next Generation* was created, and I read for Mr. Berman back then. I did not know at the time that LeVar Burton was also going to be considered for the role [of Geordi La Forge]. So it was in retrospect that I realized that, and Mr. Berman has been in my corner ever since. In getting the role of Tuvok, I

believe that the writers are going to assist me in seeking out different aspects and areas of Tuvok's character. He will be similiar to his predecessor [Mr. Spock] in that he has to maintain a certain consistency with the Vulcan principles and philosophy that we will uphold. But there will also be exploration of my character as an individual in terms of the intricacies of his personality and what his intentions may be."

Harry Kim (portrayed by *Angry Cafe*'s Garrett Wang) is fresh out of Starfleet Academy, and serves as Voyager's ops and communications officer.

"Probably the most inexperienced, naive character of them all," offers Kolbe. "And he's probably the character who will have to fight hardest to stay in the forefront. When we were casting, we said we wanted a young Asian male, and that's another SAG minority. There are not that many Japanese or Asian actors. It was a very hard role to cast, but we finally wound up with two actors who we liked and we chose Garrett.

"Actually," he adds, "Harry Kim is close to [*DS9*'s Dr.] Bashir in his naiveté, but Siddig El Fadil was able to develop that character and has much straighter responsibility. On *DS9* we're talking about six actors, here we're talking nine. What is he going to do? What do we have on him? With Paris we know there is a certain element in the closet there. Same with Chakotay. We have Tuvok, who can be developed and obviously we have Janeway. With Kim, I don't know what the writers have in store for him. We'll see."

Going the alien-human hybrid route on *Voyager* is B'Elanna Torres (Roxann Biggs-Dawson), the half Klingon Chief Engineer who, like Spock on the original series, wages an inner war with the intertwining blood of two species. In this case, her Klingon side is disturbing to her, so she tries to suppress it.

Recalls Kolbe, "Roxann might have been the actress that came in on day one and we cast her. Not that we didn't keep looking, but she was pretty well set from the first day. I think she along with Kim are going to be the two

characters who are going to fight for airtime. One thing she has going for her is a volatile temper, which could go off at any time when things don't work. She's the only one who challenges Captain Janeway's final decision in the pilot. B'Elanna Torres is a land-mine — a hand grenade with the pin pulled out. She is also the chief engineer, so we'll see how that develops. I do think in this particular case, and I might be wrong, that she will be on the bridge a lot more than Geordi was on *TNG*."

Although she is of Latino descent, a true pleasure of the show is that Biggs-Dawson's heritage has never been an issue.

"It hasn't been brought up in any way because it really doesn't make a difference," she points out. "I love that the attention is being brought to the fact that it's half human and half Klingon. I love that the conversations regarding Tuvok center around the fact that he is Vulcan, and that we don't discuss that he's a black Vulcan. And I love the fact that nobody on the crew, except for one little moment, discusses that it's a big deal that we have a female captain. What matters is character, how we're coming across and who we are as people."

Roxann Biggs-Dawson is the human/Klingon hybrid, chief engineer B'Elanna Torres (photo copyright ©1995 Albert Ortega).

Robert Picardo, Coach Cutlip on The Wonder Years, is Doc Zimmerman (photo copyright ©1995 Albert Ortega).

One of the most offbeat characters is Doc Zimmerman (Robert Picardo of *The Wonder Years*), an Experimental Medical Program (E.M.P.). Essentially he is a holographic medical officer taking care of the crew's needs.

"We had a lot of different actors come in once we decided we were going to go with a comedian," explains Kolbe. "Nobody else seemed to get it. They all played it too holographic and computer-like. We wanted somebody who really came out charging and gave us the comic relief we needed. In some ways, Zimmerman is similar to Data. Maybe not quite as complex, but that could develop. Data at the beginning was not really what he was at the end of 'All Good Things.' There was a character (and Zimmerman might move along the same lines) who pushed himself further and further up the ladder and became more and more essential to the ship. In the beginning Data was just a preposterous wind-up toy. Then things began to develop. There was, 'I want to be human. What about my emotions? What is death?' and so on. He's a guy who, due to his capacity to memorize things — particularly the whole human conundrum — was able to develop. The same

might be true of Zimmerman, although the one disadvantage he has is that he's restricted to sickbay. However, all you have to do is reroute one computer chip and the guy might be all over the ship.

"Robert Picardo has that almost insane-at-times look that we desperately wanted," he adds with a laugh. "There is a certain sardonic twist to that man, and this whole element of desertion when everybody leaves him alone in sickbay. That's going to be an interesting character to follow. I would put money on the idea that that character is going to take off. He's a very capable doctor with the lousiest bedside manner in the universe."

Two aliens joining the crew are Neelix, described as part scavenger, trader, con man, procurer and sage, and Kes, Neelix's Ocampa lover. For his part, Kolbe believes that Neelix will give Robert Picardo a run for his money in the humor department.

"Neelix is a very funny character and also a hustler," Kolbe emphasizes. "In a way he's also, if you go to Joseph Campbell's mythology, the guide. He's the only one who knows that particular area. Nobody else knows where we are really. Nobody knows who the

Although you wont recognize it from this photo, Jennifer Lien portrays the alien Kes (photo copyright ©1995 Albert Ortega).

Ethan Phillips, sans make-up, who portrays Neelix (photo copyright ©1995 Albert Ortega).

Ocampa are and what's going on there. He does. He will be a very important part of it because he is the sage; he's the guide. And Kes is his alter ego in a way. Plus it gives us a certain romance that we might want to explore, because you don't want to have it be strictly business. Neelix and Kes provide romance and a certain amount of comedy on the ship.

"Neelix was rather easy to cast," he elaborates. "We narrowed it down to three actors, and Ethan Phillips was the one pulled out. He was an inspired choice, and he's the life of the party on the set. Kes was the usual problem you have when you try to cast twenty-something actresses or younger. There are a lot of beautiful women around, especially in Hollywood, but not a lot of them can act. We went through quite a procession of beautiful girls, not bad as actresses but not good enough. You didn't want a ball buster, you didn't want to have tank-like women saying, 'Follow me!' We wanted somebody who could be fragile, but with a steely will underneath. Jennifer Lien gives us that."

Of Neelix, Ethan Philips says, "I think he's a pretty lovable guy. It's an amazing role because there are so many wonderful colors to the man, and it may

From left to right: Ethan Phillips, Roxann Biggs-Dawson, Tim Russ and Jennifer Lien (photo copyright ©1995 Albert Ortega).

be one of the best roles I've ever had an opportunity to play. There's something deep and heightened about him, and playing him is an incredible challenge."

It's a challenge that the entire cast seems to be rising to, as noted during a post-screening reception of the pilot. Executive producer Rick Berman proclaimed, "It only gets better from here," adding that the chemistry among the latest *Star Trek* ensemble was "clicking like a fourth season show."

That sentiment is shared by the cast members, who have already achieved a warm, amiability amongst themselves.

"It was a short, grueling pilot schedule, but it was fun," says Robert Beltran, cast as *Voyager* first officer, Chakotay. "The cast came together like magic. I don't know if they could have chosen a better ensemble as far as camaraderie and support goes. It's fun to come to work."

Adds Ethan "Neelix" Phillips, "The cast has gotten along fantastic. It feels like we've been working together for years. They really took their time with the pilot and treated it like a feature. There was never a sense that you were rushing. I guess this show has a reputation for having very, very long hours. I'm seeing that in more of the episodes now. They'll keep you there forever until they get it right."

Considering the show's heavy demands on an actor, it's probably a good thing that the cast has already achieved that easy rapport.

"It's been just non-stop work," says Garrett Wang, who plays ops/communications officer Harry Kim. "People on the crew told me, 'You're going to make a lot of money, but you're going to have no time to spend it.' And they're right. I get home at two in the morning and I'm out like a rock for the whole weekend to rev up for Monday. But I have no complaints."

In fact, Wang couldn't be more happy with the reception his already beloved character has received. "Overall," he says, "I think Harry Kim is well-liked. There are conflicts between Chakotay and Paris and Janeway and B'Elanna, but everyone loves Kim, which is a good thing."

Robert McNeill, a veteran from *The Next Generation* fifth season episode "The First Duty," shares Wang's enthusiasm for *Voyager*. "A great thing about this show," he says, "is that, as an actor, sometimes you do work and then it's forgotten. Or you do a play and fifty people see it. One thing that's great about this is that for the rest of our lives, people will know this part of our work and it's great to have that sort of longevity."

Overall, director Winrich Kolbe is pleased with the mixture of actors and characters, believing, at least for the moment, that they're a more interesting

mix than the ones that populated *The Next Generation*. "I do have to point out that that might not be a fair assessment because the *Voyager* people are all new," he clarifies. "It's exciting. It's different. Right now I'm very high on *Voyager*. I think we have an excellent opportunity to just take off and break new ground. We're pushing the envelope here. Let's keep on pushing."

Which is exactly what *Voyager*'s staff is attempting to do, and will undoubtedly continue to do for several years to come, working amongst themselves as well as with freelance writers.

"I feel very sorry for the writers who are trying to pitch," says Jeri Taylor. "We are still struggling with who are these people? What are the voices? Where do we want to take them? We don't have clear guidelines ourselves in a lot of instances. We're feeling our way through it. The writers on the outside aren't even part of that process so it's extremely difficult for them. In many instances, people go for the obvious. Everyone is pitching a Chakotay 'Visionquest' and everyone else is pitching 'we think we got home, but we didn't.' We have to populate this universe and so we will get stories out of that and we've come up with what we think are some intriguing new aliens that will give us stories, but it's a continuing struggle and it will continue to be a struggle for as long as these series are on the air."

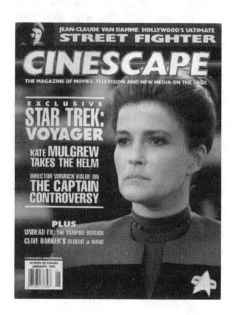

INDEX